Nietzsche

VOLUMES I AND II

The Will to Power as Art

The Eternal Recurrence of the Same

HarperCollins Editions of
MARTIN HEIDEGGER

MARTIN HEIDEGGER

Nietzsche

Volume I: The Will to Power as Art

Volume II: The Eternal Recurrence of the Same

Translated from the German by

DAVID FARRELL KRELL

HarperSanFrancisco

A Division of HarperCollins*Publishers*

Volume One of Martin Heidegger's text was originally published in *Nietzsche,* Erster Band, © Verlag Günther Neske, Pfullingen, 1961.

NIETZSCHE. *Volume I: The Will to Power as Art.* Copyright © 1979 by Harper & Row, Publishers, Inc. Appendix and Analysis copyright © 1979 by David Farrell Krell. Introduction to the Paperback Edition, copyright © 1991 by David Farrell Krell.

Volume Two was originally published in *Nietzsche,* Erster Band, © Verlag Günther Neske, Pfullingen, 1961, and in *Vorträge und Aufsätze,* copyright © 1954 by Verlag Günther Neske, Pfullingen.

NIETZSCHE. *Volume II: The Eternal Recurrence of the Same.* Copyright © 1984 by Harper & Row, Publishers, Inc. Analysis copyright © 1984 by David Farrell Krell.

Manufactured in the United Kingdom by HarperCollins Publishers Ltd.

FIRST HARPERCOLLINS PAPERBACK EDITION PUBLISHED IN 1991.

Designed by Jim Mennick

Library of Congress Cataloging-in-Publication Data

Heidegger, Martin, 1889–1976.
   [Nietzsche. English]
   Nietzsche / Martin Heidegger ; edited by David Farrell Krell. — 1st HarperCollins pbk. ed.
     p.   cm.
   Translation of: Nietzsche.
   Reprint. Originally published: San Francisco : Harper & Row, 1979–1987.
   Includes bibliographical references.
   Contents: v. 1–2. The will to power as art ; The eternal recurrence of the same — v. 3–4. The will to power as knowledge and as metaphysics ; Nihilism.
   ISBN 0–06–063841–9 (v. 1–2). — ISBN 0–06–063794–3 (v. 3–4)
   1.Nietzsche, Friedrich Wilhelm. 1844–1900.   I. Krell, David Farrell.
II. Title.
B3279.H48N5413   1991
193—dc20   90–49074
                                                     CIP

92 93 94 95 96 HCMG 12 11 10 9 8 7 6 5 4 3 2

MARTIN HEIDEGGER

Nietzsche

Volume I:
The Will to Power as Art

Translated from the German, with Notes and an Analysis, by

DAVID FARRELL KRELL

With a Facsimile Page from the Original Manuscript

Contents

Volume II begins following page 263.

Introduction to the Paperback Edition

Heidegger Nietzsche Nazism

By David Farrell Krell

Take the thinker of the "blond beast." Add another who is a card-carrying member of the Nazi Party. The result bodes ill for the matter of *thinking* that is Heidegger's *Nietzsche*. Even after Walter Kaufmann's labors to defend Nietzsche against the charge of being the prototypical ideologue of National Socialism—a charge brought by virtually all the Postwar literature on nazism and fascism—Nietzsche's virulence continues to eat away at today's reader. And now the "second wave" of the "Heidegger scandal" (the first came immediately after World War II, carried out in part in *Les temps modernes*) leaves in its wake the conviction that Heidegger the man and the thinker was embroiled in National Socialism to a far greater extent than we hitherto believed. Nevertheless, Heidegger himself insisted that it was precisely in his *Nietzsche,* in these volumes the reader now has in hand, that his *resistance* to National Socialism can most readily be seen. In the *Spiegel* interview of 1966, first published after his death on May 26, 1976, Heidegger asserts: "Everyone who had ears to hear was able to hear in these lectures [that is, the series of lectures on Nietzsche given from 1936 to 1940] a confrontation with National Socialism."[1]

---

[1] "*Nur noch ein Gott kann uns retten* [Only a God Can Save Us Now]," *Der Spiegel,* vol. 30, no. 23 (May 31, 1976), p. 204; trans. by Maria P. Alter and John C. Caputo in *Philosophy Today,* vol. 20, no. 4 (Winter 1976), p. 274.

Let us set aside the "Nietzsche case" for the moment, and, without attempting a thorough evaluation of Heidegger's claims concerning his *Nietzsche* as resistance, try to gain some perspective on two questions. First, what was the nature of Heidegger's involvement in National Socialism? Second, what does Heidegger's *Nietzsche* tell us about that engagement?

HEIDEGGER'S INVOLVEMENT

The only detailed and reliable accounts of Heidegger's involvement in National Socialism are those by the Freiburg historians Hugo Ott and Bernd Martin.[2] Their research indicates that Heidegger's engagement in the university politics of National Socialism was far more intense, and his statements on his own behalf after the War far more unreliable and self-serving, than anyone has suspected. His role as Party member and rector of the University of Freiburg in 1933–1934 was not merely that of a reluctant fellow traveler caught up in a fleeting episode of political enthusiasm. Heidegger was not a dupe, not a victim of his own political naiveté. The problem is not that Heidegger lacked a political theory and a political praxis but that at least for a time he had them. He devoted his rectorship to devising and carrying out plans for the full synchronization or consolidation (*Gleichschal-*

---

[2] Hugo Ott, *Martin Heidegger: Unterwegs zu seiner Biographie* (Frankfurt and New York: Campus Verlag, 1988), esp. pp. 131–246; and Bernd Martin, ed., *Freiburger Universitätsblätter*, Heft 92, "Martin Heidegger: Ein Philosoph und die Politik" (June 1986), esp. pp. 49–69; now reprinted in Bernd Martin, ed., *Martin Heidegger und das dritte Reich* (Darmstadt: Wissenschaftliche Buchgesellschaft, 1989). Among the philosophical responses, see the excellent brief statement by Robert Bernasconi in *Bulletin of the German Historical Institute*, London, vol. 12, no. 1 (1990). For an extended, thought-provoking response, see Jacques Derrida, *De l'esprit: Heidegger et la question* (Paris: Galilée, 1987), translated as *Of Spirit: Heidegger and the Question*, by Geoffrey Bennington and Rachel Bowlby (Chicago: University of Chicago Press, 1989); see also my "Spiriting Heidegger," in *Research in Phenomenology*, vol. XVIII (1988), 205–30, for a brief discussion of Derrida's demanding text. Finally, see Otto Pöggeler, *Der Denkweg Martin Heideggers*, 2nd ed. (Pfullingen: Neske, 1983), pp. 319–55; translated as *Martin Heidegger's Path of Thinking*, by Daniel Magurshak and Sigmund Barber (Atlantic Highlands, NJ: Humanities, 1987).

tung) of the German university with the Third Reich. To this end he worked closely with the National-Socialist culture ministries in Karlsruhe and Berlin, that is to say, at both the state and national levels. His active support and leadership of the "reformed" (that is, Party-dominated) student government, his proselytizing on behalf of Hitler and National Socialism in those crucial early years, and, above all, his plan to cripple the university senate and to arrogate to himself as rector full administrative power, to serve as the *Führer-Rektor* of the university and as the spiritual-intellectual guide of the Party as a whole, are the most damning consequences of that involvement.[3] Even more sinister are his denunciations of university students and colleagues who were recalcitrant to the "Movement," or who could be made to seem so.[4] Finally, Heidegger's efforts in his own defense after the War are, to say the least, less than candid. Both his statement to the denazification committee in 1945 and the *Spiegel* interview of 1966 distort the record on several important matters, including Heidegger's nomination to and resignation from the rectorship.[5]

Yet what Heidegger *said* after the War pales in comparison with what he left *unsaid*. Whether for reasons of shame or feelings of help-lessness and hopelessness; whether in proud refusal of public apology or in avoidance of the almost universal sycophancy of those days, dur-ing which countless ex-nazis claimed to have seen, heard, said, done, and been nothing, nowhere, at no time whatsoever; or whether simply out of an incapacity to face the brutal facts, facts beyond wickedness and imagination—whatever the reasons, Heidegger never uttered a

---

[3] See Krell, "Heidegger's Rectification of the German University," in Richard Rand, ed., *Our Academic Contract: "Mochlos" in America* (Lincoln: University of Nebraska, 1990), forthcoming.

[4] See Hugo Ott on the Baumgarten and Staudinger cases, pp. 183–84, 201–13, 232–33, and 315–17.

[5] See Ott, throughout, but esp. pp. 138–39 and 224–25. See also Franz Vonessen's review in the *Badische Zeitung* for May 5, 1983 (no. 103, p. 6) of Hermann Heidegger's edition of the rectoral address and the 1945 statement, Martin Heidegger, *Die Selbstbe-hauptung der deutschen Universität; Das Rektorat, 1933/34, Tatsachen und Gedan-ken* (Frankfurt: Klostermann, 1983); Karsten Harries has translated both documents in *The Review of Metaphysics*, vol. 38, no. 3 (March 1985), 467–502.

public word on the extermination of the Jews in the death camps of the Third Reich. While always ready to commiserate with the German soldiers and refugees in eastern Europe, and while always prepared to bemoan the plight of a divided Postwar Germany, Heidegger consigned the horrors of the Holocaust to total silence. A silence intensified by his acknowledgment of the sufferings of his countrymen and his fatherland, a silence framed and set off by what he did lament. A silence, in short, that betrays and belittles the matter of his *thinking,* which he claimed to be his sole concern.

For certain issues in his thinking cry for an end to the silence. His meditations on the technological reduction of human beings to mere stockpiles, on the upsurgence of evil and malignancy in the wake of the departed gods, and on the limitations of contemporary ethical and political thinking remain fundamentally incomplete if they fail to confront the Extermination. The death camps cry for painstaking thinking and writing, though not overhasty speech. And Heidegger's silence is more deafening than all the noise of his rectorship.

HEIDEGGER'S *NIETZSCHE*

Precisely because of that silence, the words of Heidegger's *Nietzsche,* first published in 1961, are terribly important. They reveal a thinker who is repelled by the racism and biologism of his Party, yet one whose nationalism almost always gets the better of him. It is not yet a chauvinism, not yet a xenophobia, but a nationalism that conforms to the nation of thinkers and poets, a nationalism of the German academic aristocracy of which Heidegger yearned to be a part. Nationalism and a certain militancy and even militarism, or at least an admiration of things military, of World War I heroes, of striving and struggle, reticence and resoluteness, "the hard and the heavy."

Let me now, by way of introduction, indicate some of those places in the four volumes reprinted in this two-volume paperback edition of *Nietzsche* where Heidegger's involvement in or resistance to National Socialism comes to the fore. It seems to me that there are four recurrent themes in these volumes that are particularly relevant to the question of Nietzsche, Heidegger, and National Socialism: Heidegger's *nationalism,* his call for decision, what we might call his *decisionism,* his protracted and difficult discussion of *nihilism,* and his ambivalent position vis-à-vis Nietzsche's alleged *biologism.*

1. **Nationalism.** Heidegger's nationalism is not of the flag-waving variety. It is a nationalism of high cultural expectations and intellectual demands, shaped by Hölderlin's and Nietzsche's challenges to the German people. In Heidegger's view, the matter of thinking as such has to do principally with ancient Greece and contemporary Germany, along something like an Athens-Freiburg Axis. Hölderlin's and Nietzsche's responses to early Greek thinking and poetry compel nothing less than a historic decision that the German people must confront. There are moments when a crasser form of nationalism obtrudes, as when Heidegger refers to the British destruction of the French fleet at Oran, Algeria, on July 3, 1940 (IV, 144–45); or a more critical form, as when de decries the situation of scientific research in the mobilized and subservient German university that he helped to create (II, 102–4). However, the issue of nationalism is usually far more subtle, as when Heidegger criticizes Nietzsche by suggesting that his primary motivation in metaphysical matters was Latin, Roman, or Italianate, rather than pristinely Greek (IV, 165). Every bit as subtle, yet far more worrying, is Heidegger's suppression of Nietzsche's acerbic anti-Germanism and his positive pan-Europeanism. The latter does emerge occasionally in Heidegger's account, as in the passage we are about to cite, but Heidegger's more persistent attitude is betrayed in a note jotted down in 1939: he calls Nietzsche *undeutsch*—taking that to be a criticism! More troubling still is the pervasive tendency of his lectures and essays to take nihilism and the collapse of values as a matter of the *Volk,* a matter that calls for bold deeds and interminable struggle:

> There is no longer any goal in and through which all the forces of the historical existence of peoples can cohere and in the direction of which they can develop; no goal of such a kind, which means at the same time and above all else no goal of such power that it can by virtue of its power conduct Dasein to its realm in a unified way and bring it to creative evolution. . . . To ground the goal means to awaken and liberate those powers

which lend the newly established goal its surpassing and pervasive energy to inspire commitment. . . . Here, finally, and that means primordially, belongs the growth of forces . . . which induce it to undertake bold deeds. (I, 157–58)

Heidegger emphasizes that such bold deeds cannot be the property of "individual groups, classes, and sects," nor even "individual states and nations," that such deeds must be "European at least." Yet *European* is to be taken, not "internationally," but nationally, as though someone were dreaming of reducing all Europe to a single national or imperial power:

> That does not mean to say that it should be "international." For implied in the essence of a creative establishment of goals . . . is that it comes to exist and swings into action, as historical, only in the unity of the fully historical Dasein of men in the form of particular nations. That means neither isolation from other nations nor hegemony over them. Establishment of goals is in itself confrontation, the initiation of struggle [*Kampf*]. *But the genuine struggle is the one in which those who struggle excel, first the one then the other, and in which the power for such excelling unfolds within them.* (I, 158)

Nietzsche's "grand politics," according to Heidegger, rejects the "exploitative power politics of imperialism." Yet Heidegger's own grand politics retains sufficient emphasis on struggle and boldness to trouble us: the *agon* between historical peoples, who for reasons Heidegger neglects to provide can swing into action only as *nations*, will allow no alternation of excellence.

2. Decisionism. Heidegger's view of the will and willing is far from straightforward, and it appears to undergo development during the years 1936–1940. That view becomes far more critical, betraying a waxing anxiety in the face of will and power. Yet the call for decision, *Entscheidung,* is a constant in Heidegger's writings of the 1930s and 1940s. If his is not a voluntarism of the usual sort, it is decidedly a decisionism.

We find examples in all four volumes. In the first lecture course,

"The Will to Power as Art," decision derives from a transcendent will to power and is equated with self-assertion, *Selbstbehauptung*. Heidegger declares that *"self-assertion is original assertion of essence"* (I, 61). The word and entire rhetoric of self-assertion are reminiscent of Heidegger's inaugural address as rector of Freiburg University in 1933, "The Self-Assertion of the German University," in which the language of academic freedom cloaks Heidegger's own plans for synchronization. Yet decision need not always be a matter of overt political or institutional action. Decision has to do preeminently with thinking: "... in a time of decline, a time when all is counterfeit and pointless activity, *thinking in the grand style* is genuine *action*, indeed, action in its most powerful—though most *silent*—form" (II, 10–11). Thus decision straddles the threshold of the Nietzschean gateway called "Moment" or "Flash of an Eye," *Augenblick*. All depends on whether one spectates from the sidelines or stands in the gateway of the two eternities, which is the gateway of time: "That which is to come is precisely a matter for decision, since the ring is not closed in some remote infinity but possesses its unbroken closure in the Moment, as the center of the striving; what recurs—if it is to recur—is decided by the Moment ..." (II, 57). Crucial in Heidegger's view is whether or not the thought of return convinces us that decision is useless, always already too late, so that it "deprives us of the ballast and steadying weight of decision and action" (II, 132). Thus the entire eighteenth section of the second lecture course, "The Eternal Recurrence of the Same," takes up "the thought of return—and freedom."

Heidegger argues that eternal recurrence is neither a scientific hypothesis to be tested nor a religious belief to be professed and propounded. Rather, it is a possibility of thought and decision. The latter, *Entscheidung,* involves "an authentic appropriation of the self" but also implies "the *propriative event* [Ereignis] for historical mankind as a whole." Decision is therefore a bridge between Heidegger's thinking of the ecstatic temporality of Dasein and the historical unfolding of being as such; a bridge, in other words, connecting Heidegger's project of a fundamental ontology of human existence with his later preoccupation with the truth and history of being as such. We should therefore pause a moment in order to examine those "supreme and ultimate decisions" (II, 133) that Heidegger sees as the proper horizon of eternal recurrence. For just as the supreme and ultimate decision to condemn Heidegger as a nazi is suspect, so is Heidegger's own passion for apocalyptic decision suspect, decision as "the proper truth of the thought" (II, 133). It cannot be a matter of our reaffirming the sort of moral freedom that Kant is thought to have secured in his Critical project, inasmuch as Heidegger (together with Nietzsche) is confronting that project quite explicitly in these lectures (II, 134). Nor would it be a matter of hoping to find in some post-Kantian thinker—such as Schelling, for example—a justification of freedom that Heidegger might simply have "overlooked." It would rather be a matter of analyzing more carefully Heidegger's hope that we can "shape something supreme out of the next moment, as out of every moment" (II, 136); his hope, in other words, that a decisive thinking can shape something *momentous.* "It will be decided on the basis of what you will of yourself, what you are *able* to will of yourself" (II, 136).

Is it such statements as these that Heidegger will rue later in his critique of the will-to-will? And does even that critique go to the heart of Heidegger's own decisionism?

Perhaps the best critical tool we have at our disposal to counter such willfulness is Heidegger's and Nietzsche's discussion of the desire to "settle accounts" by means of "infinite calculation" (II, 137). Just as we mistrust the endeavor to "settle accounts" once and for all with Heidegger, Nietzsche, and nazism, so too we must suspect the decisionism that forgets the finitude of time. (Heidegger reminds us here of Aristotle's treatise on time in his *Physics* IV, chapters 10–14.) We would have to ask whether Heidegger himself forgets the finitude of time when he tells his students that "the *decisive* condition is you *yourself,* that is to say, the manner in which you achieve your self by becoming your own master . . . " (II, 138).

Self? Mastery? What if, as Pierre Klossowski argues, the thinking of eternal recurrence as the finitude of time makes precisely such self-mastery impossible? What if the thinking of eternal return is catapulted outside and beyond every concept of self?[6] Mastery is the absorption of oneself into the will, says Heidegger: " . . . by seeing to it that when you engage your will essentially you take yourself up into that will and so attain freedom" (II, 138). Can what sounds like the most traditional of freedoms be so free? "We are free only when we become free, and we become free only by virtue of our wills" (II, 138). Does not Heidegger's decisionism at times seem a massive voluntarism? However, when it comes to decisions about matters of thought, we would be hard-pressed to find better advice than the following—from the very section (no. 18) we have been reading: "Yet so much is clear: the doctrine of return should never be contorted in such a way that it fits into the readily available 'antinomy' of freedom and necessity. At the same time, this reminds us once again of our sole task—to think this most difficult thought as it demands to be thought, on its own terms, leaving aside all supports and makeshifts" (II, 139).

That said, it remains troubling that Nietzsche's thought of eternal recurrence of the same is persistently thought in the direction of "a *historical decision—a crisis*" (II, 154). It is as though Heidegger were seeking in history and in the life of the *Volk* that "final, total scission" of which Schelling dreamt. Heidegger resists the "politics" to which Alfred Baeumler would bend Nietzsche's thoughts (II, 164), yet himself seeks the *domain* of Nietzsche's thought of return in the history of *nihilism*—more precisely, in the *countermovement* of that history. He condemns the automatic association of nihilism with Bolshevism (common in the Germany of his day, as in the America of ours) as "not merely superficial thinking but unconscionable demagogy" (II, 173).

However, when Heidegger's and Nietzsche's own ways of thinking nihilism are condemned as protofascist and totalitarian, are the superficiality and demagogy any less conspicuous? How are we to think in

---

[6] See the references to Klossowski's *Cercle vicieux* and the discussion of its thesis in my Analysis in vol. II, pp. 278–81; for further discussion, see chap. seven of Krell, *Of Memory, Reminiscence, and Writing: On the Verge* (Bloomington: Indiana University Press, 1990), pp. 278–83.

a way that is serious and not simply journalistic the problematic character of Nietzsche's and Heidegger's desire to "confront" and "forthwith overcome" the history of nihilism (II, 182)? For this very desire is what we most have to ponder. The desire to *overcome* nihilism exhibits a craving for *results* in history, a craving that itself has a history, a history that is none other than the history of nihilism.[7]

3. Nihilism. The entire fourth volume in this series focuses on the issue of nihilism, so that there is no way I can do justice to it here. Not only that. Each of the remaining volumes touches on this complex matter: will to power as art is proclaimed the countermovement to nihilism, a nihilism Nietzsche sees at work already in Platonism (I, 151); the thought of eternal return has as its *domain* the historical arena where nihilism is overcome (II, 170); in short, nihilism is an essential rubric of Nietzsche's metaphysics (III, 201–8); and as the fourth volume emphasizes throughout, *nihilism* is the name of our essential history, the history in which being comes to nothing.

If an introduction to all these facets of nihilism is virtually impossible, let me at least try to state in a general way Heidegger's thesis concerning nihilism, and then move on to the question of the political context of that thesis. Heidegger is concerned to show that all the sundry diagnoses and proffered therapies of nihilism are bound to fail; no, not only bound to fail, but also likely to aggravate our situation by dangling hopes of facile solutions before our eyes. For Heidegger, nihilism results from our persistent failure to *think the nothing,* to confront in our thought the power of the *nihil* in human existence, which is mortal existence, and in history, which is the history of the oblivion *of* being and the abandonment *by* being. Such thinking requires a protracted confrontation with the history of Western thought since Plato—which is what Heidegger's *Nietzsche* is all about—and unflinching meditation on human mortality and the finitude of time,

---

[7] See Krell, *Intimations of Mortality: Time, Truth, and Finitude in Heidegger's Thinking of Being* (University Park, PA: Pennsylvania State University Press, 1986), chap. 9, esp. pp. 138–40.

being, and propriation. If dogged thought on human mortality seems unduly pessimistic, and if thought on the history of philosophy seems onerous, Heidegger replies that our optimism always underestimates the challenge of mortal thinking and that our reluctance to take the onus of history seriously reflects nothing if not the historical impact of nihilism itself.

No matter how brief my own analyses of the political "context" of nihilism in Heidegger's *Nietzsche* may be, I nevertheless want to direct readers of this new edition of *Nietzsche* to them (see III, 263–74, and IV, 262–76). The Analyses focus on two matters. First, Heidegger's indebtedness to Ernst Jünger's books, *Total Mobilization* (1930) and *The Worker* (1932). Jünger's influence on Heidegger's thought concerning planetary technology is profound. Technology constitutes the major political dilemma of our time, according to both Jünger and Heidegger, a dilemma that no known political system is capable of discering, much less solving. Yet Heidegger resists Jünger's "cultic" and "numinous" celebration of technology. He resists Jünger's technophiliac "symbols," spurns his language. Heidegger's opposition to Jünger's notions of will and power translates eventually into a resistance—quite strong by 1939—to Nietzsche's notion of will to power. Will to power is will-to-will, and such redoubled willing is machination. Second, in both Analyses much is said about Heidegger's contemporary, Alfred Baeumler, who became professor of philosophy in Berlin from 1933 to 1945 after Heidegger elected to "stay in the provinces." Baeumler's influential monograph, *Nietzsche the Philosopher and Politician* (1931) is important both for what Heidegger accepts from it and what he rejects. What he rejects is Baeumler's "politics."

No doubt much remains to be said about the importance for Heidegger of both Jünger and Baeumler, as of Carl Schmitt, the jurist who supported National Socialism in both theory and practice. Yet no matter how much my remarks need fleshing out, I can largely affirm today what they say. Yet I would formulate differently the "withering" of the attraction of National Socialism for Heidegger after 1934: the fact is that Heidegger's resignation from the rectorship was a symptom of his failed bid for Party leadership in the university, the state, and the country. His withdrawal from political life and internal emigration cannot be interpreted in terms of genuine resistance as easily as we once thought. Finally, I would alter altogether my account of Heidegger's accession to the rectorship (IV, 268–69), in order to bring that account into line with current research.[8]

4. **Biologism.** For an audience that was receiving uninterrupted instruction in its racial superiority, indeed, its racial supremacy, the issue of Nietzsche's alleged biologism must have been of signal importance. Here Heidegger's resistance to Party doctrine is most visible, especially in his sardonic remarks on poetry, digestion, and a healthy people in the Hölderlin lectures (IV, 269). Yet Heidegger's sarcasm does not resolve all the problems or banish all our suspicions.

His account of Nietzsche's physiology of artistic rapture (I, 126–31) suggests that Nietzsche himself overcomes both the physiological-biological and the aesthetic positions. Whether the Party's racist and biologistic dogmas cause Heidegger to overreact to the point where he is unable or unwilling to elaborate the "new interpretation of sensuousness," is an arresting question: readers of the first lecture course would do well to keep it in mind. Although Heidegger does stress that the human body is essential to existence, inasmuch as Dasein is some body who is alive (Heidegger plays with the words *leben* and *leiben,* living and "bodying forth"), his reluctance to confront the biological body is everywhere in evidence. Much of the third lecture course, "The Will to Power as Knowledge," takes up the question of Nietzsche's putative biologism (III, 39–47; 101–10). To be sure, Nietzsche's thinking seems to be biologistic, and to that extent Heidegger is highly critical of it. Yet the accusation of biologism in fact "presents the *main obstacle* to our penetrating to his fundamental thought" (III, 41). For even when Nietzsche invokes "life," he does so *metaphysically,* not biologically (III, 46). Even when Nietzsche discusses the law of noncontradiction in terms of biology, the discussion remains at an ontological level (III, 103–4; 115–22). Heidegger empha-

---

[8] Again, see my "Rectification of the German University," esp. Part II.

sizes by way of conclusion: *"Nietzsche thinks the 'biological,' the essence of what is alive, in the direction of commanding and poetizing, of the perspectival and horizonal: in the direction of freedom"* (III, 122). A conclusion that would take us back to the question of freedom—and Heidegger's decisionism.

In the 1940 lectures on "European Nihilism" (IV, 147–49), Heidegger betrays how sensitive an issue biologism is for him. Here he contraposes Nietzsche's metaphysics to that of Hegel: if Hegel's is a metaphysics of reason and spirit, as the culmination of Cartesian subjectivism, Nietzsche's is one of animality, yet still within that same Cartesian tradition. "The absolute essence of subjectivity necessarily develops as the *brutalitas* of *bestialitas*. At the end of metaphysics stands the statement *Homo est brutum bestiale*" (IV, 148). The end of metaphysics, one might say by way of pun or typo, is the beginning of meatphysics. Heidegger now claims that Nietzsche's avowal of the "blond beast" is "not a casual exaggeration, but the password and countersign" of Nietzsche's historical entanglements. How odd that Heidegger should cite (critically) the phrase with which this Introduction began—the phrase that delineates in a straight line, without punctuation or deviation, the triad from which Heidegger would want to extricate himself: Heidegger Nietzsche Nazism. In "Nietzsche's Metaphysics" (III, 218), Heidegger argues that Nietzsche's "nihilistic negation of reason" does not so much exclude reason as place it in the service of animality. Or, more precisely, it subjects both spirit and body to a metaphysics of the will to power as command, calculative thought, and the positing of values (III, 224). Yet even in his censure of Nietzschean overman, or perhaps of a caricature of the *Übermensch,* with the overman as a product of technological mechanization and machination, Heidegger avoids leveling the charge of biologism:

> The breeding of human beings is not a taming in the sense of a suppression and hobbling of sensuality; rather, breeding is the accumulation and purification of energies in the univocity of the strictly controllable "automatism" of every activity. Only where the absolute subjectivity of will to power comes to be the truth of beings as a whole is the *principle* of

a program of racial breeding possible; possible, that is, not merely on the basis of naturally evolving races, but in terms of the self-conscious *thought* of race. That is to say, the principle is metaphysically necessary. Just as Nietzsche's thought of will to power was ontological rather than biological, even more was his racial thought metaphysical rather than biological in meaning. (III, 230–31)

Enough of meatphysics, then: neither Nietzsche nor Heidegger would be guilty of it. Yet is Heidegger writing here in his own voice, or is he trying, whether successfully or not, merely to report on Nietzsche's thought? No matter how we decide, and such decisions are always excruciating if not impossible to make, the thoughts expressed here give us pause. To this *ontological* or *metaphysical* elevation of the thought of race, Jacques Derrida has posed the inevitable and painful question: When Heidegger or Nietzsche or Heidegger/Nietzsche appeals to a *principle* of a programmed racial breeding; when he subordinates biology to a metaphysics of will to power; when he abjures the contingency of "naturally evolving races" and adopts instead—as though suddenly ventriloquizing Hegel, speaking through the spiritual mouth of Hegelian spirit—"the self-conscious *thought* of race"; when he does all these things, does he alleviate or aggravate the thought of race and racism, the *Rassengedanke?* Does metaphysics dissolve or confirm the rule of racism? "A metaphysics of race—is this more grave or less grave than a naturalism or a biologism of race?"[9]

By leaving the question in suspense, Derrida does not mean that we should suspend thought about it. Anything but that. The apparently academic question of "biologism" is an issue that every reader of these volumes will have to confront, finding his or her own way between Nietzsche, Heidegger, and the worst violence of the night.

HEIDEGGER'S *CONTRIBUTIONS*

The very issues we have been raising in an introductory fashion—nationalism, decisionism, nihilism, and biologism—are by no means

---

[9] Derrida, *De l'esprit,* pp. 118–19; Engl. trans., p. 74.

reserved to the *Nietzsche* volumes. They might well lead us to Heidegger's second major work of the 1930s, his *Contributions to Philosophy (Of Propriation)*, written between 1936 and 1938, that is to say, simultaneously with the first two parts of the *Nietzsche,* but published only recently.[10]

Here Heidegger's nationalism and decisionism remain profoundly disconcerting. No matter how reassuring his polemics against "racism" and the "distorted animality" of technologized man may be, his scorn of "liberalism" and his fears of "Bolshevism" undermine the reader's confidence (see *65,* 19, 25, 28, 53–54, 163, and elsewhere). He shares that scorn and those fears with every "young conservative" intellectual of the Weimar era. No matter how reassuring his mockery of the Stefan George Circle, with their adulation of Nietzsche and antiquity (*65,* 73), Heidegger himself equates philosophy with "the philosophy of a people," and the only two peoples he mentions are the ancient Greeks and contemporary Germans (*65,* 42, 319, 390, 399, 414). He shares the fascinations of the George-Kreis. No matter what justice there may be in his claim that ecclesiastical Christendom and the Third Reich both subscribe to the "totalizing worldview" (*65,* 40–41, 140), his desire to "grant historical mankind a goal once again" (*65,* 16) seems to be every bit as totalizing. And whatever "justice" there may be in such "judgments," the question of *justice* as the culmination of the history of truth as the correctness of propositions will have to be raised more perspicuously than Heidegger has raised it in the *Nietzsche* volumes (see III, 137–49 and 235–51; cf. IV, 139–46). His call for apocalyptic or at least eschatological "decision" (*65,* 87–103) is as unnerving in the *Contributions* as in the *Nietzsche.* His need to enkindle the "hearth fires" of philosophy and the nation is not exactly heart-warming, his willingness to bandy about the shib-

---

[10] Martin Heidegger, *Beiträge zur Philosophie (Vom Ereignis),* vol. 65 of the Martin Heidegger Gesamtausgabe (Frankfurt am Main: Klostermann, 1989). Throughout these *Nietzsche* volumes, the Gesamtausgabe volumes are cited as MHG, or simply by volume (in *italic*) and page, e.g., *65,* 54. See my Analysis to vol. II, pp. 269–81, which of course could only anticipate the contents of the *Beiträge.* And see the chapter entitled "Contributions to Life" in my forthcoming book, *Daimon Life: Heidegger and "Lebensphilosophie."*

boleths of his day—no matter what the "tendency" of his remarks, no matter how resistant to the slogans of National Socialism—is frightening:

> ... the final form of Marxism, which has essentially nothing to do with Jewry or even with the Russians; if an undeveloped spirituality slumbers anywhere today, then it is in the Russian people; Bolshevism is originally a Western, European possibility: the upsurgence of the masses, industry, technology, the withering of Christianity; yet insofar as the dominion of reason in the equality of all is merely a consequence of Christianity, which, at bottom, is of Jewish origin (cf. Nietzsche's thought on the slave-rebellion of morality), Bolshevism is indeed Jewish; but then Christianity is, at bottom, also Bolshevik! And what sorts of decisions would be necessary on this basis? ... (65, 54; cf. 163)

One shudders at the sorts of decisions that might be made on such a basis, on the basis of those big words that make us so unhappy. Unless, of course, all this is a desperate attempt on Heidegger's part to caricature and to resist the very decisionism that he finds so tempting.

Finally, Heidegger's observation that it is not an essential index of nihilism "whether or not churches and monasteries [*Kirchen und Klöster*] are destroyed and human beings slaughtered [*und Menschen hingemordet*]" (65, 139) is not so much callous as it is out of touch. If the year is 1936 or after, and the place is Germany, then the churches and cloisters are relatively secure, and murder is occurring at other sites.

CONCLUSIONS

To summarize now, and to come to a close. No, not a close, but an opening—the reader's opening of Heidegger's *Nietzsche*. Heidegger's resistance to the crude biologism, racism, and anti-Semitism of the Nazi Party cannot, I believe, be doubted. Yet his ardent nationalism and anti-liberalism, his intransigent conservatism in matters economic, social, and political, along with his passion for historic decisions at the national level, made him an easy prey to hopes of resurgence.

Was Heidegger a nazi? Yes, if carrying the membership card and paying the dues is our standard. No, not if we stress the most horrifying aspect of National Socialism, its vulgar racism and virulent anti-Semitism. Yes, if we stress the importance of Hitler himself and of his cult of nationalism, militarism, and anti-parliamentarian elitism. Indeed, when Heidegger conjoins liberalism and the dominant National Socialism, which has declined his spiritual leadership, there is reason to observe that if Heidegger was not a nazi it was only because the Party was too liberal for him. At the same time, we have to remember the Party's rejection of Heidegger's "private" version of National Socialism already in 1934 and the waxing intensity of the polemics against him by Party ideologues in the mid-1930s. Furthermore, Heidegger's disaffection from the Party in the course of the 1930s has direct relevance for his work on Nietzsche: when Party censorship of the Nietzsche edition that Heidegger was helping to prepare intensified in 1938, he stopped working with the Commission that was charged with the edition. Thus the year 1938 assumes symbolic importance for our theme: as the Party insists on sanitizing the Nietzsche edition, purging from it Nietzsche's anti-anti-Semitism and anti-Germanism, Heidegger opts for Nietzsche, and the triad of terms in our title falls apart. In a word, and to answer a complex question peremptorily: if we stress Heidegger's active and inventive support of the regime in 1933–34, the answer is a resounding, catastrophic *yes;* as the 1930s come to a close, opening onto an even more disastrous era, the answer is *no.* As for Heidegger's silence after the war, it responds to our own need to know why with—silence.

Is Heidegger's relation to National Socialism the sole important aspect of his lectures and essays on Nietzsche? Not at all. His reading of eternal recurrence of the same as mortal transition and downgoing; of the will to power as artistic creativity and the pursuit of knowledge "in the grand style"; of the Nietzschean revaluation of all values as a remnant of metaphysical and calculative valuative thinking; and of nihilism as the history of being from Plato through Nietzsche—these issues await the reader and will challenge her or him to the full. No peremptory discussion can resolve them.

Perhaps what is most disturbing about the "Heidegger scandal" today is the avidity with which Heidegger's involvement in National Socialism has been taken up, a fervor that cannot be explained by reference to the usual dependable pleasures of righteous indignation. Academics and philosophers today seem to hope that if they can shift attention to a Heidegger-exposed-at-last they will be able to forget the vacuity and aimlessness of their own projects. That if their kind of philosophy has run out of problems, then the only way to keep the conversation going endlessly is to churn out endless scandals. The hope blossoms that a social-critical, emancipatory discourse will suddenly make sense again if adherents can divert everyone's attention to another time and place, newsflash 1933, expatiating on a foreign yet ostensibly familiar situation, excoriating the same old set of villains. Villains safely past. Museum pieces of wickedness or credulity. Or, finally, that the American mind—modest generalization though it may be—will suddenly burst into bloom once again if only its captors (Heidegger, Nietzsche, and the rest of the French) can be expunged from the curriculum. With a sterilized Socrates or antiseptic Aristotle mounted in their place. How much more satisfying it is to scan accounts of scandals in the Sunday supplements than to wrestle with *Sophist* or *Metaphysics* or *Being and Time*. How much more satisfying to settle once and for all questions of crime and punishment, to banish a thinker and renounce all his works, to burn all those difficult books.

Heidegger's *Nietzsche* is the easiest of those difficult books, the least painful to read. No doubt, these volumes need to be read closely *and* critically. For even more disturbing than the avidity of the Heidegger bashers is the business-as-usual attitude of the Heidegger acolytes. The crippling conservatism and militancy, the longing for mettle and metal, *Härte und Schwere,* the perfervid anti-Communism, and the endless fascination with and confidence in the German *Volk*—none of these traits can be forgotten or relegated to some safely "nonphilosophical" realm. In Heidegger himself these traits remain profoundly troubling; in Heidegger's *followers,* in his circles and societies, they are an abomination, if also a farce.

Heidegger's *Nietzsche* is one of those ventures and adventures that compels the reader again and again to scribble into the margins *No! No!* The *yeses* come slowly and painfully. When they do come, after all the necessary caution and resistance, the reader will discover that he or she does not need a book of matches for this book of powerfully formulated yet altogether tentative thoughts.

No doubt, other significant readings of Nietzsche will come along, or have already arrived on the scene, with Bataille, Deleuze, Klossowski, and Derrida. Yet none of these writers can readily separate the names Nietzsche/Heidegger. None can pry apart this laminate. As though one of the crucial confrontations for thinkers today were what one might call heidegger's nietzsche, nietzsche's heidegger.

Editor's Preface

From 1936 to 1940 Martin Heidegger offered four lecture courses at the University of Freiburg-im-Breisgau on selected topics in Nietzsche's philosophy. During the decade 1936–1946 he composed a number of individual lectures and essays on that thinker. After lecturing again on Nietzsche during the early 1950s Heidegger determined to publish these and the earlier materials; in 1961 the Neske Verlag of Pfullingen released two large volumes of Heidegger's early lectures and essays on Nietzsche. A four-volume English version of Heidegger's two-volume *Nietzsche* (cited throughout these volumes as NI, NII, with page number) appeared during the years 1979–1987.

The four hardbound volumes of Heidegger's *Nietzsche* are here reproduced in two paperback volumes, the first containing volumes I and II of the first English edition, the second uniting volumes III and IV. In order to keep the cost of the paperback edition as low as possible, the volumes have been reprinted with a minimum of changes. Errors that came to my attention over the years have been corrected and a new Introduction added. The order of the essays in the hardbound edition has been retained: it deviates from that of the hardbound Neske edition, following the order of Neske's paperback version of *Nihilismus*, which is also the order Heidegger approved for the English translation.

In the intervening years, the Martin Heidegger Gesamtausgabe (cited throughout as MHG, with volume number in *italic*) has produced a number of volumes relevant to the *Nietzsche*. Division I of the Gesamtausgabe reproduces the 1961 Neske volumes as volumes 6.1 and 6.2. These contain the lectures and essays in the form that Heidegger himself gave them in 1960 and 1961, reworking and condensing the material. The Gesamtausgabe editors have also produced a second set of versions of the lectures, based on the holographs plus student notes and transcriptions. These appear in Division II of the edition as volumes 43 (*Nietzsche: Der Wille zur Macht als Kunst,* winter semester 1936–1937), 44 (*Nietzsches metaphysische Grundstellung im abendländischen Denken: Die ewige Wiederkehr des Gleichen,* summer semester 1937), 47 (*Nietzsches Lehre vom Willen zur Macht als Erkenntnis,* summer semester 1939), and 48 (*Nietzsche: Der europäische Nihilismus,* second trimester 1940). Two further volumes are in preparation: 46 (*Nietzsches II. Unzeitgemäße Betrachtung,* winter semester 1938–1939), and 50 (*Nietzsches Metaphysik,* announced for the winter semester of 1941–1942 but not given). These versions of the lectures differ in several significant ways from the 1961 Neske edition on which the translation was based: first, they include a number of "repetitions" or "summaries and transitions" that Heidegger customarily presented at the beginning of each lecture hour, materials that Heidegger himself eliminated when he edited the *Nietzsche* for publication; second, they also include a number of passages that he decided to strike, apparently because he felt they were too polemical, too repetitious, or of dubious relevance; third, they include a number of notes found on unattached sheets in the handwritten lectures.

Let a single example of such deleted material suffice, of the second type: when Heidegger edited the first lecture course he cut two paragraphs of material on Jaspers' treatment of Nietzschean eternal recurrence of the same, paragraphs that "put quite sharply" why it is that philosophy is "altogether impossible" for Jaspers. (See NI, 31 and cf. MHG *43,* 26.) The substance of the critique remains in these pages (see, in this paperback edition, I, 23), but the remarks on Jaspers' "moralizing psychology" and his inability to ask genuinely philosophical questions are deleted.

It therefore has to be said that scholars who feel the need to focus sharply on a particular passage in Heidegger's *Nietzsche* should refer to the corresponding volumes in MHG Division II. Yet we can be confident that with the Neske edition, prepared by Heidegger himself, we have the core of his confrontation with Nietzsche. It would not have been possible for me to "work into" this translation materials from the lectures as they appear in MHG Division II, precisely for the reasons that it was impossible for the German editors to work them into the MHG reprint of the Neske edition. If only for reasons of bulk: the word count for the first three courses is 192,500 in Neske, 270,000 in MHG.

The Neske edition too ultimately derives from Heidegger's handwritten lectures. Heidegger collated these notes with the help of a number of assistants and approved the final typescript in spring of 1961. Since access to the original notes is restricted, and because the notes themselves are fascinating documents, I have prepared a description of one complete page of the notes and a comparison of it to the relevant pages of the Neske edition as an Appendix to the present volume. (See also a photographic facsimile of that page following p. 223.) There is one serious error on this page as transcribed in the Neske edition, volume one, page 51, line 22. An examination of the holograph page (listed in the Marbach Archive as no. A 33/14) shows that line 22 ends one of Heidegger's long emendations designed for insertion into the body of the text. The line is difficult to read with certainty; it is easy to see how the error in the published text occurred. But the sense of the holograph page is clear, and with the aid of the only extant *Abschrift* or typescript (Archive no. II 19/27) an accurate reconstruction is possible. After having examined MHG *43*, 48, 11. 5–6 f.b., I propose the following reading:

> *strike line 22 of NI, 51, and insert:* Streben auf. Wille dagegen, [als] Entschlossenheit zu sich, ist immer über sich *etc.*

I have adopted this reading for the translation, p. 41, lines 13–14. A more detailed discussion appears in the Appendix.

The only other serious error in the Neske edition of which I am aware is the duplication of the word *nicht* at NI, 189, line 5 from the bottom (cf. MHG *43*, 199, 1. 11 f.b.), which ought to read:

> Sinnlichen, als ein Nichtseiendes und Nicht-sein-sol- *etc.*

Occasional typographical errors in the Neske edition and minor inaccuracies in the quotations I have corrected without drawing attention to them.

I have translated all passages from Nietzsche's works in Heidegger's text, as well as the quotations from Hegel, Wagner, Dilthey, and others. But I am grateful to have had the translation of *The Will to Power* by Walter Kaufmann and R. J. Hollingdale (New York: Random House, 1967) for reference and comparision.

Heidegger's many references to *Der Wille zur Macht* are cited in these English volumes as WM, followed by aphorism—not page—number, e.g.: (WM, 794). His references to all other Nietzschean texts are to the *Grossoktavausgabe* (Leipzig, 1905 ff.); in the body of the text they are cited simply by volume and page, e.g.: (XIV, 413–67); in my own explanatory footnotes I cite the *Grossoktavausgabe* as GOA. In these notes the letters CM refer to the new *Kritische Gesamtausgabe* of Nietzsche's works and letters, edited by Giorgio Colli and Mazzino Montinari (Berlin: Walter de Gruyter, 1967 ff.). I have checked as many of Heidegger's references to the GOA in CM as time, the incompleteness of CM, and its one-way concordances allowed. Where no major discrepancies emerged I let the GOA text stand. However, readers who wish to focus on a specific reference by Heidegger to the GOA should themselves check CM carefully before proceeding.

Heidegger's text contains no footnotes; all notes in the present volume are my own. I have tried to keep them to a minimum, since it is hard to know when such notes are helpful and when they are a nuisance. I hope that readers who have difficulties with the editorial matter or any aspect of the translation will write me about them in care of the publisher. As for the translation itself, its apologist is Jerome, whose *Preface to Eusebius' Chronicle* William Arrowsmith has rendered (in *Arion*, New Series, 2/3, 1975, p. 359):

Jerome to Vincentius and Gallienus: Greetings
    . . . It is difficult, when you are following in another man's footsteps, to keep from going astray somewhere. And it is extremely difficult to preserve in translation the particular verbal felicities of a foreign language. The original meaning, for instance, may be conveyed in a single word—a word which has no single Latin equivalent. If the translator tries to catch the full meaning, he must resort to lengthy paraphrase. To these difficulties must be added the problems of word-order, differences in case and rhetorical figures, and finally, the *native* genius of the language itself. If I

translate word for word, the result is ludicrous; if I am forced to change the words or rearrange them, it will look as though I had failed in my duty as a translator.

So, my dear Vincentius and Gallienus, I beg of you, if you find signs of haste and confusion, to read this work rather as friends than critics.

I owe thanks to many generous people for help with this project over the past fifteen years: Jochen Barkhausen, Robert Bernasconi, Friederike Born, Helm Breinig, Frank Capuzzi, Chris Fynsk, Sherry Gray Martin, Ulrich Halfmann, Elfride Heidegger, Hermann Heidegger, F.-W. von Herrmann, Elisabeth Hoffmann, Eunice Farrell Krell, Marta Krell, Will McNeill, Sabine Mödersheim, Thomas Müller, Ashraf Noor, Bruce Pye, John Sallis, Jupp Schöpp, John Shopp, Joan Stambaugh, and Joachim W. Storck. And special debts of gratitude to Martin Heidegger and J. Glenn Gray.

Chicago   D.F.K.

Plan of the English Edition

3. "Nietzsche's Metaphysics," a typescript dated August–December 1940, apparently derived from an unscheduled and heretofore unlisted course on Nietzsche's philosophy [NII, 257–333].*

Volume IV: Nihilism

1. "European Nihilism," a lecture course delivered at the University of Freiburg during the first trimester of 1940 [NII, 31–256].
2. "Nihilism as Determined by the History of Being," an essay composed during the years 1944–46 but not published until 1961 [NII, 335–398].

The three remaining essays in volume two of the Neske edition, "Metaphysics as History of Being" [NII, 399–457], "Sketches for a History of Being as Metaphysics" [NII, 458–80], and "Recollection of Metaphysics" [NII, 481–90], all from the year 1941, appear in English

---

*"Nietzsche's Metaphysics" appears as the title of a lecture course for the winter semester of 1941–42 in all published lists of Heidegger's courses. The earliest prospectuses of the Klostermann firm cited such a lecture course as volume 52 of the Heidegger "Complete Edition" (*Gesamtausgabe*). But the Heidegger Archive of the Schiller-Nationalmuseum in Marbach contains no manuscript for such a course. It does contain the sixty-four-page typescript in question, with many handwritten alternations, composed in August 1940 and revised during the months of September, October, and December of that year. One of the typescript's several title pages refers to the winter semester of 1938–39, in all probability not to any lecture or seminar in the published lists but to an unlisted *Übung* [exercise] entitled "Toward an Interpretation of Nietzsche's Second 'Untimely Meditation,' *On the Advantage and Disadvantage of History for Life*." On September 29, 1975, I asked Heidegger about the discrepancy of the dates for "Nietzsche's Metaphysics" in the Neske edition (1940) and in the published lists and catalogues of his courses (winter semester 1941–42). (At the time of our conversation on this matter the above information, supplied by the archive, was unknown to me.) Heidegger reaffirmed the date 1940 as the time of composition. He explained that the material had been prepared during a seminar, title and date not specified, and conceded that he might have employed the same material for the WS 1941–42 lecture course. The more recent prospectuses of the *Gesamtausgabe* list both the 1938–39 course ("Nietzsche's Second 'Untimely Meditation' ") and the essay "Nietzsche's Metaphysics" as volumes 46 and 50, respectively. "Nietzsche's Metaphysics" is said to have been "announced, but not taught, in the winter semester of 1941–42." In volume 50 it is coupled (for no apparent reason) with the 1944–45 course, "Thinking and Poetizing."

The problem awaits the more patient scrutiny of the archive's curators. But this may suffice to explain why Heidegger cites 1940 (and not 1942, as the catalogues would lead us to expect) as the closing date for his early lectures on Nietzsche.

translation in Martin Heidegger, *The End of Philosophy,* trans. Joan Stambaugh (New York: Harper & Row, 1973). *The End of Philosophy* also contains the essay "Overcoming Metaphysics" (1936–46), related thematically and chronologically to the *Nietzsche* material and originally published in *Vorträge und Aufsätze,* pp. 71–99. The lecture in which Heidegger summarizes much of the material in volume II of *Nietzsche,* "The Word of Nietzsche: 'God is Dead'" (1943), appears in English translation in Martin Heidegger, *The Question Concerning Technology and Other Essays,* trans. William Lovitt (New York: Harper & Row, 1977). Other references to Nietzsche in Heidegger's works are listed in the second, revised edition of Hildegard Feick, *Index zu Heideggers "Sein und Zeit"* (Tübingen: M. Niemeyer, 1968), p. 120.

Author's Foreword to All Volumes

Nietzsche himself identifies the experience that determines his thinking:

"Life ... more mysterious since the day the great liberator came over me—the thought that life should be an experiment of knowers."

The Gay Science 1882
(Book IV, no. 324)

"Nietzsche"—the name of the thinker stands as the title for *the matter* of his thinking.

The matter, the point in question, is in itself a confrontation. To let our thinking enter into the matter, to prepare our thinking for it— these goals determine the contents of the present publication.

It consists of *lecture courses* held at the University of Freiburg-im-Breisgau during the years 1936 to 1940. Adjoined to them are *treatises* which originated in the years 1940 to 1946. The treatises further extend the way by which the lecture courses—still at that time under way— paved the way for the confrontation.

The text of the lectures is divided according to content, not hours of presentation. Nevertheless, the lecture character has been retained, this necessitating an unavoidable breadth of presentation and a certain amount of repetition.

It is intentional that often the same text from Nietzsche's writings is discussed more than once, though each time in a different context. Much material has been presented that may be familiar and even well known to many readers, since in everything well known something worthy of thought still lurks. The repetitions are intended to provide occasions for thinking through, in ever renewed fashion, those several thoughts that determine the whole. Whether, and in what sense, with what sort of range, the thoughts remain worthy of thought becomes clear and is decided through the confrontation. In the text of the lectures unnecessary words and phrases have been deleted, involuted sentences simplified, obscure passages clarified, and oversights corrected.

For all that, the written and printed text lacks the advantages of oral presentation.

Considered as a whole, the publication aims to provide a view of the path of thought I followed from 1930 to the "Letter on Humanism" (1947). The two small lectures published just prior to the "Letter," "Plato's Doctrine of Truth" (1942) and "On the Essence of Truth" (1943), originated back in the years 1930–31. The book *Commentaries on Hölderlin's Poetry* (1951), which contains one essay and several lectures from the years between 1936 and 1943, sheds only indirect light on that path.

Whence the confrontation with the "Nietzsche matter" comes and whither it goes may become manifest to the reader when he himself sets off along the way the following texts have taken.

M. H.

Freiburg-im-Breisgau
May, 1961

Nietzsche

VOLUME I

The Will to Power as Art

"Well-nigh two thousand years and not a single new god!"

The Antichrist 1888
(VIII, 235–36)

1. Nietzsche as Metaphysical Thinker

In *The Will to Power,* the "work" to be treated in this lecture course, Nietzsche says the following about philosophy (WM, 420):

> I do not wish to persuade anyone to philosophy: it is inevitable and perhaps also desirable that the philosopher should be a *rare* plant. I find nothing more repugnant than didactic praise of philosophy as one finds it in Seneca, or worse, Cicero. Philosophy has little to do with virtue. Permit me to say also that the man of knowledge is fundamentally different from the philosopher. —What I desire is that the genuine concept of the philosopher not perish utterly in Germany. . . .

At the age of twenty-eight, as a professor in Basel, Nietzsche writes (X, 112):

> There are times of great danger in which philosophers appear—times when the wheel rolls ever faster—when philosophers and artists assume the place of the dwindling *mythos.* They are far ahead of their time, however, for the attention of contemporaries is only quite slowly drawn to them. A people which becomes aware of its dangers produces the genius.

The Will to Power—the expression plays a dual role in Nietzsche's thinking. First, it serves as the title of Nietzsche's chief philosophical work, planned and prepared over many years but never written. Second, it names what constitutes the basic character of all beings. "Will to power is the ultimate *factum* to which we come" (XVI, 415).

It is easy to see how both applications of the expression "will to power" belong together: only because the expression plays the second role can and must it also adopt the first. As the name for the basic character of all beings, the expression "will to power" provides an answer to the question "What is being?" Since antiquity that question has been *the* question of philosophy. The name "will to power" must therefore come to stand in the title of the chief philosophical work of a thinker who says that all being ultimately is will to power. If for Nietzsche the work of that title is to be the philosophical "main structure," for which *Zarathustra* is but the "vestibule," the implication is that Nietzsche's thinking proceeds within the vast orbit of the ancient guiding question of philosophy, "What is being?"

Is Nietzsche then not at all so modern as the hubbub that has surrounded him makes it seem? Is Nietzsche not nearly so subversive as he himself was wont to pose? Dispelling such fears is not really necessary; we need not bother to do that. On the contrary, the reference to the fact that Nietzsche moves in the orbit of the question of Western philosophy only serves to make clear that Nietzsche knew what philosophy is. Such knowledge is rare. Only great thinkers possess it. The greatest possess it most purely in the form of a persistent question. The genuinely grounding question, as the question of the essence of Being, does not unfold in the history of philosophy as such; Nietzsche too persists in the guiding question.

The task of our lecture course is to elucidate the fundamental position within which Nietzsche unfolds the guiding question of Western thought and responds to it. Such elucidation is needed in order to prepare a confrontation with Nietzsche. If in Nietzsche's thinking the prior tradition of Western thought is gathered and completed in a decisive respect, then the confrontation with Nietzsche becomes one with all Western thought hitherto.

The confrontation with Nietzsche has not yet begun, nor have the prerequisites for it been established. For a long time Nietzsche has been either celebrated and imitated or reviled and exploited. Nietzsche's thought and speech are still too contemporary for us. He and we have not yet been sufficiently separated in history; we lack the distance necessary for a sound appreciation of the thinker's strength.

Confrontation is genuine criticism. It is the supreme way, the only way, to a true estimation of a thinker. In confrontation we undertake to reflect on his thinking and to trace it in its effective force, not in its weaknesses. To what purpose? In order that through the confrontation we ourselves may become free for the supreme exertion of thinking.

But for a long time it has been declaimed from chairs of philosophy in Germany that Nietzsche is not a rigorous thinker but a "poet-philosopher." Nietzsche does not belong among the philosophers, who think only about abstract, shadowy affairs, far removed from life. If he is to be called a philosopher at all then he must be regarded as a "philosopher of life." That rubric, a perennial favorite, serves at the same time to nourish the suspicion that any other kind of philosophy is something for the dead, and is therefore at bottom dispensable. Such a view wholly coincides with the opinion of those who welcome in Nietzsche the "philosopher of life" who has at long last quashed abstract thought. These common judgments about Nietzsche are in error. The error will be recognized only when a confrontation with him is at the same time conjoined to a confrontation in the realm of the grounding question of philosophy. At the outset, however, we ought to introduce some words of Nietzsche's that stem from the time of his work on "will to power": "For many, abstract thinking is toil; for me, on good days, it is feast and frenzy" (XIV, 24).

Abstract thinking a feast? The highest form of human existence? Indeed. But at the same time we must observe how Nietzsche views the essence of the feast, in such a way that he can think of it only on the basis of his fundamental conception of all being, will to power. "The feast implies: pride, exuberance, frivolity; mockery of all earnestness and respectability; a divine affirmation of oneself, out of animal plenitude and perfection—all obvious states to which the Christian may not honestly say Yes. *The feast is paganism par excellence*" (WM, 916). For that reason, we might add, the feast of thinking never takes place in Christianity. That is to say, there is no Christian philosophy. There is no true philosophy that could be determined anywhere else than from within itself. For the same reason there is no pagan philosophy, inasmuch as anything "pagan" is always still something Christian —the counter-Christian. The Greek poets and thinkers can hardly be designated as "pagan."

Feasts require long and painstaking preparation. This semester we want to prepare ourselves for the feast, even if we do not make it as far as the celebration, even if we only catch a glimpse of the preliminary festivities at the feast of thinking—experiencing what meditative thought is and what it means to be at home in genuine questioning.

2. The Book, *The Will to Power*

The question as to what being is seeks the Being of beings. All Being is for Nietzsche a Becoming. Such Becoming, however, has the character of action and the activity of willing. But in its essence will is will to power. That expression names what Nietzsche thinks when he asks the guiding question of philosophy. And for that reason the name obtrudes as the title for his planned *magnum opus,* which, as we know, was not brought to fruition. What lies before us today as a book with the title *The Will to Power* contains preliminary drafts and fragmentary elaborations for that work. The outlined plan according to which these fragments are ordered, the division into four books, and the titles of those books also stem from Nietzsche himself.

At the outset we should mention briefly the most important aspects of Nietzsche's life, the origins of the plans and preliminary drafts, and the later publication of these materials after Nietzsche's death.

In a Protestant pastor's house in the year 1844 Nietzsche was born. As a student of classical philology in Leipzig in 1865 he came to know Schopenhauer's major work, *The World as Will and Representation.* During his last semester in Leipzig (1868–69), in November, he came into personal contact with Richard Wagner. Apart from the world of the Greeks, which remained decisive for the whole of Nietzsche's life, although in the last years of his wakeful thinking it had to yield some ground to the world of Rome, Schopenhauer and Wagner were the earliest intellectually determinative forces. In the spring of 1869, Nietzsche, not yet twenty-five years of age and not yet finished with his doctoral studies, received an appointment at Basel as associate professor of classical philology. There he came into amicable contact with Jacob

Burckhardt and with the Church historian Franz Overbeck. The question as to whether or not a real friendship evolved between Nietzsche and Burckhardt has a significance that exceeds the merely biographical sphere, but discussion of it does not belong here. He also met Bachofen,* but their dealings with one another never went beyond reserved collegiality. Ten years later, in 1879, Nietzsche resigned his professorship. Another ten years later, in January, 1889, he suffered a total mental collapse, and on August 25, 1900, he died.

During the Basel years Nietzsche's inner disengagement from Schopenhauer and Wagner came to completion. But only in the years 1880 to 1883 did Nietzsche find himself, that is to say, find himself as a thinker: he found his fundamental position within the whole of beings, and thereby the determinative source of his thought. Between 1882 and 1885 the figure of "Zarathustra" swept over him like a storm. In those same years the plan for his main philosophical work originated. During the preparation of the planned work the preliminary sketches, plans, divisions, and the architectonic vision changed several times. No decision was made in favor of any single alternative; nor did an image of the whole emerge that might project a definitive profile. In the last year before his collapse (1888) the initial plans were finally abandoned. A peculiar restlessness now possessed Nietzsche. He could no longer wait for the long gestation of a broadly conceived work which would be able to speak for itself, on its own, as a work. Nietzsche himself had to speak, he himself had to come forth and announce his basic position vis-à-vis the world, drawing the boundaries which were to prevent anyone's confusing that basic position with any other. Thus the smaller works originated: *The Wagner Case, Nietzsche contra Wagner, Twilight of the Idols, Ecce Homo,* and *The Antichrist*—which first appeared in 1890.

But Nietzsche's philosophy proper, the fundamental position on the basis of which he speaks in these and in all the writings he himself

---

*J. J. Bachofen (1815–1887), Swiss historian of law and religion, interested in myths and symbols in primitive folklore, today best known as the author of the classic work on matriarchy, *Das Mutterrecht,* published in 1861.

published, did not assume a final form and was not itself published in
any book, neither in the decade between 1879 and 1889 nor during the
years preceding. What Nietzsche himself published during his creative
life was always foreground. That is also true of his first treatise, *The
Birth of Tragedy from the Spirit of Music* (1872). His philosophy
proper was left behind as posthumous, unpublished work.

In 1901, a year after Nietzsche's death, the first collection of his
preliminary drafts for a *magnum opus* appeared. It was based on
Nietzsche's plan dated March 17, 1887; in addition, the collection
referred to notes in which Nietzsche himself arranged particular fragments into groups.

In the first and in later editions the particular fragments selected
from the handwritten *Nachlass* were numbered sequentially. The first
edition of *The Will to Power* included 483 selections.

It soon became clear that this edition was quite incomplete when
compared to the available handwritten material. In 1906 a new and
significantly expanded edition appeared, retaining the same plan. It
included 1,067 selections, more than double the number in the first
edition. The second edition appeared in 1911 as volumes XV and XVI
of the *Grossoktav* edition of Nietzsche's works. But even these volumes
did not contain the amassed material; whatever was not subsumed
under the plan appeared as two *Nachlass* volumes, numbered XIII and
XIV in the *Collected Works.*

Not long ago the Nietzsche Archive in Weimar undertook to publish
a historical-critical complete edition of Nietzsche's works and letters in
chronological order. It should become the ultimate, definitive edition.*
It no longer separates the writings Nietzsche himself published and the
Nachlass, as the earlier complete editions do, but collates for each
period both published and unpublished materials. The extensive

---

*The *Historisch-kritische Gesamtausgabe der Werke und Briefe* (Munich: C. H.
Beck, 1933–42), edited by a group of scholars including H. J. Mette, W. Hoppe, and
K. Schlechta, under the direction of Carl August Emge, published fewer than a dozen
of the many volumes of works and letters planned. For an account of the "principles"
of the edition—with which Heidegger takes issue below—see the Foreword to the
Nietzsche *Gesamtausgabe,* I, x–xv.

collection of letters, which thanks to new and rich finds is growing steadily, is also to be published in chronological sequence. The historical-critical complete edition, which has now begun, remains in its foundations ambiguous. First of all, as a historical-critical "complete edition" which brings out every single thing it can find, guided by the fundamental principle of completeness, it belongs among the undertakings of nineteenth-century publication. Second, by the manner of its biographical, psychological commentary and its similarly thorough research of all "data" on Nietzsche's "life," and of the views of his contemporaries as well, it is a product of the psychological-biological addiction of our times.

Only in the actual presentation of the authentic "Works" (1881–89) will this edition have an impact on the future, granted the editors succeed in their task. That task and its fulfillment are not a part of what we have just criticized; moreover, the task can be carried out without all that. But we can never succeed in arriving at Nietzsche's philosophy proper if we have not in our questioning conceived of Nietzsche as the end of Western metaphysics and proceeded to the entirely different question of the truth of Being.

The text recommended for this course is the edition of *The Will to Power* prepared by A. Baeumler for the Kröner pocket edition series. It is a faithful reprint of volumes XV and XVI of the *Grossoktavausgabe,* with a sensible Afterword and a good, brief outline of Nietzsche's life history. In addition, Baeumler has edited for the same series a volume entitled *Nietzsche in His Letters and in Reports by Contemporaries.* For a first introduction the book is useful. For a knowledge of Nietzsche's biography the presentation by his sister, Elisabeth Förster-Nietzsche, *The Life of Friedrich Nietzsche* (published between 1895 and 1904), remains important. As with all biographical works, however, use of this publication requires great caution.

We will refrain from further suggestions and from discussion of the enormous and varied secondary literature surrounding Nietzsche, since none of it can aid the endeavor of this lecture course. Whoever does not have the courage and perseverance of thought required to become involved in Nietzsche's own writings need not read anything *about* him either.

Citation of passages from Nietzsche's works will be by volume and page number of the *Grossoktav* edition. Passages from *The Will to Power* employed in the lecture course will not be cited by the page number of any particular edition but by the fragment number which is standard in all editions. These passages are for the most part not simple, incomplete fragments and fleeting observations; rather, they are carefully worked out "aphorisms," as Nietzsche's individual notations are customarily called. But not every brief notation is automatically an aphorism, that is, an expression or saying which absolutely closes its borders to everything inessential and admits only what is essential. Nietzsche observes somewhere that it is his ambition to say in a brief aphorism what others in an entire book . . . do *not* say.

3. Plans and Preliminary Drafts of the "Main Structure"

Before we characterize more minutely the plan on which the presently available edition of *The Will to Power* is based, and before we indicate those passages with which our inquiry shall begin, let us introduce testimony from several of Nietzsche's letters. Such testimony sheds light on the origin of the preliminary drafts for the planned chief work and suggests the fundamental mood from which the work derives.

On April 7, 1884, Nietzsche writes to his friend Overbeck in Basel:

> For the past few months I've been preoccupied with "world history," enchanted by it, in spite of many hair-raising results. Did I ever show you Jacob Burckhardt's letter, the one which led me by the nose to "world history"? If I get to Sils Maria this summer I want to undertake a revision of my *metaphysica* and my epistemological views. Now I must work through a whole series of disciplines step by step, for I am resolved to devote the next five years to the construction of my "philosophy," for which I have in my *Zarathustra* constructed a vestibule.

We should take this opportunity to observe that the common assumption that Nietzsche's *Thus Spoke Zarathustra* was to present his philosophy in poetic form, and that, since *Zarathustra* did not achieve this goal, Nietzsche wanted to transcribe his philosophy into prose for purposes of greater intelligibility, is an error. The planned major work, *The Will to Power,* is in truth as much a poetic work as *Zarathustra* is a work of thought. The relationship between the two works remains one of vestibule and main structure. Nevertheless, between 1882 and 1888 several essential steps were taken which remain wholly concealed in prior collections of the *Nachlass* fragments, such concealment preventing a glimpse into the essential structure of Nietzsche's metaphysics.

In mid-June, 1884, Nietzsche writes to his sister:

> So, the scaffolding for the main structure ought to be erected this summer; or, to put it differently, during the next few months I want to draw up the schema for my philosophy and my plan for the next six years. May my health hold out for this purpose!*

From Sils Maria on September 2, 1884, to his friend and assistant Peter Gast:

> In addition, I have completely *finished* the major task I set myself for this summer—the next six years belong to the elaboration of a schema in which I have outlined my "philosophy." The prospects for this look good and promising. Meanwhile, *Zarathustra* retains only its entirely personal meaning, being my "book of edification and consolation"—otherwise, for Everyman, it is obscure and riddlesome and ridiculous.

To Overbeck, July 2, 1885:

> I have dictated for two or three hours practically every day, but my "philosophy"—if I have the right to call it by the name of something that has maltreated me down to the very roots of my being—is *no longer* communicable, at least not in print.

Here doubts about the possibility of a presentation of his philosophy

---

*According to Karl Schlechta's "Philologischer Nachbericht," in *Friedrich Nietzsche Werke in drei Bänden* (Munich: C. Hanser, 6th ed., 1969), III, 1411, 1417, and 1420–22, this letter, number 379 in the edition by Frau Förster-Nietzsche, is a forgery. More specifically, it appears that Nietzsche's sister altered the addressee (the letter was sent not to her but to Malwida von Meysenbug) and enlarged upon the original contents of the letter. Because she managed to destroy all but a fragment of the original, it is virtually impossible to determine whether or not the words Heidegger cites are Nietzsche's. Nevertheless, the fragment does contain the following lines, relevant to the present issue: ". . . nachdem ich mir diese Vorhalle meiner Philosophie gebaut habe, muss ich die Hand wieder anlegen und nicht müde werden, bis auch der Haupt-Bau fertig vor mir steht." In translation: ". . . now that I have built this vestibule for my philosophy, I must get busy once again and not grow weary until the main structure too stands finished before me."

in book form are already stirring. But a year later Nietzsche is again confident.

To his mother and sister, September 2, 1886:

> For the next four years the creation of a four-volume *magnum opus* is proposed. The very title is fearsome: "*The Will to Power:* Attempt at a Revaluation of All Values." For it I have *everything* that is necessary, health, solitude, good mood, and maybe a wife.*

With this mention of his major work Nietzsche refers to the fact that on the cover of the book that had appeared during that year, *Beyond Good and Evil,* a work with the above-mentioned title was cited as the volume to appear next. In addition, Nietzsche writes in his *Toward a Genealogy of Morals,* which appeared in 1887 (See Division Three, no. 27):

> ... with respect to which [i.e., the question of the meaning of the ascetic ideal] I refer to a work I am now preparing: **The Will to Power,** *Attempt at a Revaluation of All Values.*

Nietzsche himself emphasized the title of his planned work by means of special, heavy print.

To Peter Gast, September 15, 1887:

> I vacillated, to be honest, between Venice and—Leipzig: the latter for learned purposes, since in reference to the major *pensum* of my life, which is presently to be resolved, I still have much to learn, to question, and to read. But for that I would need, not an "autumn," but an *entire winter* in Germany: and, all things considered, my health forcefully discourages such a dangerous experiment for *this* year. Therefore it has turned out to be a matter of Venice and Nice: —and also, as you yourself may judge to be true, I now need the profound isolation which in my case is even more compelling than further study and exploration into five thousand particular problems.

To Carl von Gersdorff, December 20, 1887:

> In a significant sense my life stands right now at *high noon:* one door is closing, another opening. All I have done in the last few years has been a

---

*Schlechta (ibid.) does *not* cite this letter as a forgery.

settling of accounts, a conclusion of negotiations, an adding up of things past; by now I have finished with men and things and have drawn a line under it all. *Who* and *what* remain for me, whither I must now go, toward the really most important matter of my existence (a transition to which I have *been condemned*), are now capital questions. For, between you and me, the tension in which I live, the pressure of a great task and passion, is now too great for me to allow still more people to approach me. The desert that surrounds me is vast indeed. I really can bear only complete strangers or passers-by, or, on the other hand, people who have been a part of me for a long time, even from childhood. Everyone else has drifted away or has been *repulsed* (there was much violence and much pain in that—).

Here it is no longer simply the matter of a *magnum opus.* Here already are early signs of the last year of his thinking, the year in which everything about him radiates an excessive brilliance and in which therefore at the same time a terrible boundlessness advances out of the distance. In that year, 1888, the plan of the work changes altogether. When madness overwhelms Nietzsche in the first days of January, 1889, he writes to the composer Peter Gast, as a final word to his friend and helper, a postcard dated January 4 with the following contents:

> *To my maëstro Pietro. Sing me a new song: the world is transfigured and all the heavens rejoice. The Crucified.*

Although Nietzsche expresses in them what is most interior, these few pieces of evidence can for us at first be only an extrinsic indication of the fundamental mood in which the planning of the work and its preliminary casting moved. But at the same time we need to refer to the plans themselves and to their transformation; and even that can occur at first only from the outside. The plans and proposals are published in volume XVI, pages 413–67.

Three fundamental positions can be distinguished in the sequence of proposals: the first extends chronologically from 1882 to 1883 (*Thus Spoke Zarathustra*); the second from 1885 to 1887 (*Beyond Good and Evil, Toward a Genealogy of Morals*); the third embraces the years 1887 and 1888 (*Twilight of the Idols, Ecce Homo, The Antichrist*). But these are not stages of development. Neither can the three fundamental positions be distinguished according to their scope: each is concerned with the whole of philosophy and in each one the other two are implied, although in each case the inner configuration and the location of the center which determines the form vary. And it was nothing else than the question of the center that genuinely "maltreated" Nietzsche. Of course, it was not the extrinsic question of finding a suitable connection or link among the handwritten materials available; it was, without Nietzsche's coming to know of it or stumbling across it, the question of philosophy's self-grounding. It concerns the fact that, whatever philosophy is, and however it may exist at any given time, it defines itself solely on its own terms; but also that such self-determination is possible only inasmuch as philosophy always has already grounded itself. Its proper essence turns ever toward itself, and the more original a philosophy is, the more purely it soars in turning about itself, and therefore the farther the circumference of its circle presses outward to the brink of nothingness.

Now, when closely examined, each of the three fundamental positions may be identified by a predominant title. It is no accident that the two titles displaced in each case by the main title recur under that title.

The first fundamental position derives its character from the main title, "Philosophy of Eternal Return," with the subtitle "An Attempt at the Revaluation of All Values" (XVI, 415). A plan pertaining to this title (p. 414) contains as its crowning, concluding chapter (the fifth) "The doctrine of eternal return as *hammer* in the hand of the most powerful man." Thus we see that the thought of power, which always means will to power, extends through the whole simultaneously from top to bottom.

The second fundamental position is marked by the title "The Will to Power," with the subtitle "Attempt at a Revaluation of All Values." A plan pertaining to this title (p. 424, number 7) contains as the fourth part of the work "The Eternal Return."

The third fundamental position transposes what was only the subtitle of the two previous positions to the main title (p. 435), "Revaluation of All Values." The plans pertaining to this title contain as their fourth part the "Philosophy of Eternal Return," and they propose another part, concerning the "yes-sayers," whose place within the whole was not fixed. Eternal Recurrence, Will to Power, Revaluation: these are the three guiding phrases under which the totality of the planned major work stands, the configuration in each case differing.*

Now, if we do not thoughtfully formulate our inquiry in such a way that it is capable of grasping in a unified way the doctrines of the eternal return of the same and will to power, and these two doctrines in their most intrinsic coherence as revaluation, and if we do not go on to comprehend this fundamental formulation as one which is also necessary in the course of Western metaphysics, then we will never grasp Nietzsche's philosophy. And we will comprehend nothing of the twentieth century and of the centuries to come, nothing of our own metaphysical task.

---

*An examination of CM VIII, 1, 2, and 3 reveals that the selection of plans provided as an appendix to the GOA, the edition Heidegger employed, oversimplified the matter of the organization of the *Nachlass*. Yet Heidegger's analysis of the changing stratification of eternal recurrence, will to power, and revaluation in Nietzsche's plans still seems tenable.

4. The Unity of Will to Power, Eternal Recurrence, and Revaluation

The doctrine of the eternal return of the same coheres in the most intimate way with that of will to power. The unity of these teachings may be seen historically as the revaluation of all values hitherto.

But to what extent do the doctrines of the eternal return of the same and will to power belong essentially together? This question must animate us more thoroughly, indeed as the decisive one. For the present, therefore, we offer a merely provisional answer.

The expression "will to power" designates the basic character of beings; any being which is, insofar as it is, is will to power. The expression stipulates the character that beings have as beings. But that is not at all an answer to the first question of philosophy, its proper question; rather, it answers only the final preliminary question. For anyone who at the end of Western philosophy can and must still question philosophically, the decisive question is no longer merely "What basic character do beings manifest?" or "How may the Being of beings be characterized?" but "What is this 'Being' itself?" The decisive question is that of "the meaning of Being," not merely that of the Being of beings. "Meaning" is thereby clearly delineated conceptually as that from which and on the grounds of which Being in general can become manifest as such and can come into truth. What is proffered today as ontology has nothing to do with the question of Being proper; it is a very learned and very astute analysis of transmitted concepts which plays them off, one against the other.

What is will to power itself, and how is it? Answer: the eternal recurrence of the same.

Is it an accident that the latter teaching recurs continually in decisive passages throughout all plans for the philosophical main work? What can it mean when in one plan, which bears the unadorned title "Eternal Return" (XVI, 414), Nietzsche lists the first part under the title "The most difficult thought"? To be sure, the question of Being is the most difficult thought of philosophy, because it is simultaneously its innermost and uttermost thought, the one with which it stands and falls.

We heard that the fundamental character of beings is will to power, willing, and thus Becoming. Nevertheless, Nietzsche does not cling to such a position—although that is usually what we are thinking when we associate him with Heraclitus. Much to the contrary, in a passage purposely and expressly formulated to provide an encompassing overview (WM, 617), Nietzsche says the following: "*Recapitulation:* To *stamp* Becoming with the character of Being—that is the supreme *will to power.*" This suggests that Becoming only *is* if it is grounded in Being as Being: "That *everything recurs* is the closest *approximation of a world of Becoming to one of Being: peak of the meditation.*"* With his doctrine of eternal return Nietzsche in his way thinks nothing else than the thought that pervades the whole of Western philosophy, a thought that remains concealed but is its genuine driving force. Nietzsche thinks the thought in such a way that in his metaphysics he reverts to the beginnings of Western philosophy. More precisely, he reverts to that beginning which Western philosophy became accustomed to seeing in the course of its history. Nietzsche shared in

---

* Heidegger often cites the "Recapitulation" aphorism during the *Nietzsche* lectures and essays. See, for example, NI, 466 and 656; NII, 288, 327, and 339. He employs it also for instance in "The Anaximander Fragment," the first chapter of Martin Heidegger, *Early Greek Thinking,* tr. D. F. Krell and F. A. Capuzzi (New York: Harper & Row, 1975), p. 22. Yet it was not Nietzsche but Peter Gast (Heinrich Köselitz) who supplied the title of the aphorism: see Walter Kaufmann's note in his edition of *The Will to Power,* p. 330, and cf. CM VIII, l, p. 320, which does not print the title. Furthermore, WM, 617 is a note the *entire* context and contents of which must be carefully examined. The problem will be discussed in the Analysis of volume III in the present series.

such habituation in spite of his otherwise original grasp of pre-Socratic philosophy.

In the popular view, and according to the common notion, Nietzsche is the revolutionary figure who negated, destroyed, and prophesied. To be sure, all that belongs to the image we have of him. Nor is it merely a role that he played, but an innermost necessity of his time. But what is essential in the revolutionary is not that he overturns as such; it is rather that in overturning he brings to light what is decisive and essential. In philosophy that happens always when those few momentous questions are raised. When he thinks "the most difficult thought" at the "peak of the meditation," Nietzsche thinks and meditates on Being, that is, on will to power as eternal recurrence. What does that mean, taken quite broadly and essentially? Eternity, not as a static "now," nor as a sequence of "nows" rolling off into the infinite, but as the "now" that bends back into itself: what is that if not the concealed essence of Time? Thinking Being, will to power, as eternal return, thinking the most difficult thought of philosophy, means thinking Being as Time. Nietzsche thinks that thought but does not think it as the *question* of Being and Time. Plato and Aristotle also think that thought when they conceive Being as *ousia* (presence), but just as little as Nietzsche do they think it as a question.

If we do ask the question, we do not mean to suggest that we are cleverer than both Nietzsche and Western philosophy, which Nietzsche "only" thinks to its end. We know that the most difficult thought of philosophy has only become more difficult, that the peak of the meditation has not yet been conquered and perhaps not yet even discovered at all.

If we bring Nietzsche's "will to power," that is, his question concerning the Being of beings, into the perspective of the question concerning "Being and Time," that does not at all mean that Nietzsche's work is to be related to a book entitled *Being and Time* and that it is to be measured and interpreted according to the contents of that book. *Being and Time* can be evaluated only by the extent to which it is equal or unequal to the question it raises. There is no standard other than the question itself; only the question, not the book, is essential. Furthermore, the book merely leads us to the threshold of the question, not yet into the question itself.

Whoever neglects to think the thought of eternal recurrence together with will to power, as what is to be thought genuinely and philosophically, cannot adequately grasp the metaphysical content of the doctrine of will to power in its full scope. Nevertheless, the connection between eternal recurrence as the supreme determination of Being and will to power as the basic character of all beings does not lie in the palm of our hand. For that reason Nietzsche speaks of the "most difficult thought" and the "peak of the meditation." It is nonetheless true that the current interpretation of Nietzsche does away with the properly philosophical significance of the doctrine of eternal recurrence and thus irremediably precludes a fertile conception of Nietzsche's metaphysics. We will introduce two examples, each quite independent of the other, of such a treatment of the doctrine of eternal return in Nietzsche's philosophy: Alfred Baeumler, *Nietzsche: Philosopher and Politician* (1931), and Karl Jaspers, *Nietzsche: Introduction to an Understanding of His Philosophizing* (1936).* The negative position taken by each author with respect to the doctrine of eternal recurrence—and for us that means the misinterpretation by each—varies in kind and has different grounds.

Baeumler portrays what Nietzsche calls the most difficult thought and the peak of the meditation as an entirely personal, "religious" conviction of Nietzsche's. He says, "Only one can be valid: either the doctrine of eternal return or the doctrine of will to power" (p. 80). He tries to ground this either-or by the following argument: will to power is Becoming; Being is grasped as Becoming; that is the ancient doctrine of Heraclitus on the flux of things and it is also Nietzsche's genuine teaching. His thought of eternal recurrence has to deny the unlimited flux of Becoming. The thought introduces a contradiction into

---

*Alfred Baeumler, *Nietzsche der Philosoph und Politiker* (Leipzig: P. Reclam, 1931), and Karl Jaspers, *Nietzsche. Einführung in das Verständnis seines Philosophierens* (Berlin and Leipzig: Walter de Gruyter, 1936). Both books are discussed in the Analysis (section II) at the end of this volume. The analyses to the later volumes of the present series will treat Baeumler more thoroughly.

Nietzsche's metaphysics. Therefore, either the doctrine of will to power or that of eternal recurrence, only one of them, can define Nietzsche's philosophy. Baeumler writes, "In truth, seen from the point of view of Nietzsche's *system*, this thought is without importance." And on page 82 he opines, "Now, Nietzsche, who is a founder of religion, also accomplishes an Egyptification of the Heraclitean world." According to Baeumler's account, the doctrine of eternal recurrence implies bringing Becoming to a standstill. With his either-or, Baeumler presupposes that Heraclitus teaches the eternal flux of things, in the sense of the ever-ongoing. For some time now we have known that this conception of Heraclitus' doctrine is utterly foreign to the Greek. Just as questionable as the interpretation of Heraclitus, however, is whether Nietzsche's will to power should automatically be taken as Becoming in the sense of the onward-flowing. In the end, such a concept of Becoming is so superficial that we had better not be too quick to ascribe it to Nietzsche. The immediate result of our considerations so far is that there is not necessarily a contradiction between the two statements "Being is Becoming" and "Becoming is Being." Precisely that is Heraclitus' teaching. But assuming that there is a contradiction between the doctrines of will to power and eternal recurrence, we have known since Hegel's day that a contradiction is not necessarily proof against the truth of a metaphysical statement, but may be proof for it. If therefore eternal recurrence and will to power contradict one another, perhaps the contradiction is precisely the demand to *think* this most difficult thought, instead of fleeing into the "religious." But even if we concede that here we have a contradiction which cannot be transcended and which compels us to decide in favor of either will to power or eternal recurrence, why does Baeumler then decide *against* Nietzsche's most difficult thought, the peak of his meditation, and *for* will to power? The answer is simple: Baeumler's reflections on the relationship between the two doctrines do not press toward the realm of actual inquiry from either side. Rather, the doctrine of eternal recurrence, where he fears "Egypticism," militates against his conception of will to power, which, in spite of the talk about metaphysics, Baeumler does not grasp metaphysically but interprets politically.

Nietzsche's doctrine of eternal recurrence conflicts with Baeumler's conception of politics. It is therefore "without importance" for Nietzsche's system. This interpretation of Nietzsche is all the more remarkable since Baeumler belongs among those few commentators who reject Klages' psychological-biologistic interpretation of Nietzsche.*

The second conception of Nietzsche's doctrine of eternal return is that of Karl Jaspers. True, Jaspers discusses Nietzsche's teaching in greater detail and discerns that here we are in the presence of one of Nietzsche's decisive thoughts. In spite of the talk about Being, however, Jaspers does not bring the thought into the realm of the grounding question of Western philosophy and thereby also into actual connection with the doctrine of will to power. For Baeumler the doctrine of eternal recurrence cannot be united with the political interpretation of Nietzsche; for Jaspers it is not possible to take it as a question of great import, because, according to Jaspers, there is no conceptual truth or conceptual knowledge in philosophy.

But if in contrast to all this the doctrine of eternal recurrence is seen to coincide with the very center of Nietzsche's metaphysical thinking, is it not misleading, or at least one-sided, to collate all the preliminary sketches for a philosophical *magnum opus* under the plan that takes as its definitive title "Will to Power"?

That the editors selected the middle one of the three basic positions in the plans testifies to their considerable understanding. For Nietzsche himself first of all had to make a decisive effort to visualize the basic character of will to power throughout beings as a whole. Yet this was never for him the ultimate step. Rather, if Nietzsche was the thinker we are convinced he was, then the demonstration of will to power would always have to revolve about the thought of the Being of beings, which for Nietzsche meant the eternal recurrence of the same.

---

*Ludwig Klages (1872–1956) developed as his life's work a "biocentric metaphysics" which was to clarify once and for all the problem of the body-soul-mind relationship. His major work is the three-volume *Der Geist als Widersacher der Seele* (1929–32); the work Heidegger refers to here is *Die psychologischen Errungenschaften Nietzsches* (1926). Cf. section 17, below, and section II of the Analysis. For a critical edition of Klages' writings see Ludwig Klages, *Sämtliche Werke* (Bonn: Bouvier, 1964 ff.).

But even if we grant the fact that this edition of the preliminary sketches for the major work, dominated by the theme of will to power, is the best edition possible, the book that lies before us is still something supplementary. Nobody knows what would have become of these preliminary sketches had Nietzsche himself been able to transform them into the main work he was planning. Nevertheless, what is available to us today is so essential and rich, and even from Nietzsche's point of view so definitive, that the prerequisites are granted for what alone is important: actually to think Nietzsche's genuine philosophical thought. We are all the more liable to succeed in this endeavor the less we restrict ourselves to the sequence of particular fragments as they lie before us, collected and subsumed into book form. For such ordering of particular fragments and aphorisms within the schema of divisions, a schema which does stem from Nietzsche himself, is arbitrary and inessential. What we must do is think through particular fragments, guided by the movement of thought which occurs when we ask the genuine questions. Therefore, measured against the order established by the text before us, we will jump about within various particular divisions. Here too an arbitrariness, within certain limits, is unavoidable. Still, in all this what remains decisive is to hear Nietzsche himself; to inquire with him and through him *and therefore at the same time against him,* but *for* the one single innermost matter that is common to Western philosophy. We can undertake such a task only if we limit its scope. But the important thing is to know where these limits are to be set. Such limitation does not preclude but expects and demands that in time, with the help of the book *The Will to Power,* you will work through whatever is not explicitly treated in the lectures, in the spirit and manner of our procedure here.

5. The Structure of the "Major Work." Nietzsche's Manner of Thinking as Reversal

Nietzsche's basic metaphysical position may be defined by two statements. First, the basic character of beings as such is "will to power." Second, Being is "eternal recurrence of the same." When we think through Nietzsche's philosophy in a questioning way, along the guidelines of those two statements, we advance beyond the basic positions of Nietzsche and of philosophy prior to him. But such advance only allows us to come back to Nietzsche. The return is to occur by means of an interpretation of *"The Will to Power."*

The plan upon which the published edition is based, a plan Nietzsche himself sketched and even dated (March 17, 1887), takes the following form (XVI, 421):

THE WILL TO POWER

Attempt at a Revaluation of All Values

Book I: *European Nihilism.*
Book II: *Critique of the Highest Values.*
Book III: *Principle of a New Valuation.*
Book IV: *Discipline and Breeding.*

Our inquiry proceeds immediately to the third book and restricts itself to that one. The very title, "Principle of a New Valuation," suggests that here a laying of grounds and an erection of structures are to be brought to language.

Accordingly, in Nietzsche's view, philosophy is a matter of valuation, that is, establishment of the uppermost value in terms of which and according to which all beings are to be. The uppermost value is the one that must be fundamental for all beings insofar as they are beings. A "new" valuation would therefore posit another value, in opposition to the old, decrepit one, which should be determinative for the future. For that reason a critique of the highest values hitherto is advanced beforehand, in Book II. The values in question are religion, specifically, the Christian religion, morality, and philosophy. Nietzsche's manner of speaking and writing here is often imprecise and misleading: religion, morality, and philosophy are not themselves the supreme values, but basic ways of establishing and imposing such values. Only for that reason can they themselves, mediately, be posited and taken as "highest values."

The critique of the highest values hitherto does not simply refute them or declare them invalid. It is rather a matter of displaying their origins as impositions which must affirm precisely what ought to be negated by the values established. Critique of the highest values hitherto therefore properly means illumination of the dubious origins of the valuations that yield them, and thereby demonstration of the questionableness of these values themselves. Prior to this critique, which is offered in Book II, the first book advances an account of European nihilism. Thus the work is to begin with a comprehensive presentation of the basic development of Western history, which Nietzsche recognizes in its range and intensity here for the first time: the development of nihilism. In Nietzsche's view nihilism is not a *Weltanschauung* that occurs at some time and place or another; it is rather the basic character of what happens in Occidental history. Nihilism is at work even—and especially—there where it is not advocated as doctrine or demand, there where ostensibly its opposite prevails. Nihilism means that the uppermost values devalue themselves. This means that whatever realities and laws set the standard in Christendom, in morality since Hellenistic times, and in philosophy since Plato, lose their binding force, and for Nietzsche that always means creative force. In his view nihilism is never merely a development of his own times; nor does it pertain only to the nineteenth century. Nihilism begins in the pre-

Christian era and it does not cease with the twentieth century. As a historical process it will occupy the centuries immediately ahead of us, even and especially when countermeasures are introduced. But neither is nihilism for Nietzsche mere collapse, valuelessness, and destruction. Rather, it is a basic mode of historical movement that does not exclude, but even requires and furthers, for long stretches of time, a certain creative upswing. "Corruption," "physiological degeneration," and such are not causes of nihilism but effects. Nihilism therefore cannot be overcome by the extirpation of those conditions. On the contrary, an overcoming of nihilism would merely be delayed by countermeasures directed toward alleviation of its harmful side effects. In order to grasp what Nietzsche designates in the word "nihilism" we need profound insight and even more profound seriousness.

Because of its necessary involvement in the movement of Western history, and on account of the unavoidable critique of prior valuations, the *new* valuation is necessarily a *re*valuation of all values. Hence the subtitle, which in the final phase of Nietzsche's philosophy becomes the main title, designates the general character of the countermovement to nihilism *within* nihilism. No historical movement can leap outside of history and start from scratch. It becomes all the more historical, which is to say, it grounds history all the more originally, as it overcomes radically what has gone before by creating a new order in that realm where we have our roots. Now, the overwhelming experience derived from the history of nihilism is that all valuations remain without force if the corresponding basic attitude of valuing and the corresponding manner of thinking do not accompany them.

Every valuation in the essential sense must not only bring its possibilities to bear in order to be "understood" at all, it must at the same time develop a breed of men who can bring a new attitude to the new valuation, in order that they may bear it into the future. New requirements and prerequisites must be bred. And this process consumes, as it were, most of the time that is allotted to nations as their history. Great ages, because they are great, are in terms of frequency quite rare and of endurance very brief, just as the most momentous times for individual men often consist of a single moment. A new valuation itself implies the creation and inculcation of requirements and demands that conform to the new values. For that reason the work is to find its conclusion in the fourth book, "Discipline and Breeding."

At the same time, however, it is a basic experience gained from the history of valuations that even the positing of the uppermost values does not take place at a single stroke, that eternal truth never blazes in the heavens overnight, and that no people in history has had its truth fall into its lap. Those who posit the uppermost values, the creators, the new philosophers at the forefront, must according to Nietzsche be experimenters; they must tread paths and break trails in the knowledge that they do not have *the* truth. But from such knowledge it does not at all follow that they have to view their concepts as mere betting chips that can be exchanged at any time for any currency. What does follow is just the opposite: the solidity and binding quality of thought must undergo a grounding in the things themselves in a way that prior philosophy does not know. Only in this way is it possible for a basic position to assert itself over against others, so that the resultant strife will be actual strife and thus the actual origin of truth.* The new thinkers must attempt and tempt. That means they must put beings themselves to the test, tempt them with questions concerning their Being and truth. So, when Nietzsche writes in the subtitle to his work, "attempt" at a revaluation of all values, the turn of phrase is not meant to express modesty and to suggest that what follows is still incomplete; it does not mean an "essay" in the literary sense; rather, in an utterly clearminded way, it means the basic attitude of the new inquiry that grows out of the countermovement against nihilism. "—We are conducting an experiment with truth! Perhaps mankind will perish because of it! Fine!" (XII, 410).

---

*The reference to strife and to the origin of truth is to "Der Ursprung des Kunstwerkes" ["The Origin of the Work of Art"]. See Martin Heidegger, *Holzwege* (Frankfurt/Main: V. Klostermann, 1950), pp. 37–38 ff.; cf. the revised edition (Stuttgart: P. Reclam, 1960), pp. 51–52 ff. Heidegger first reworked this essay during the autumn of 1936, which is to say, while the first Nietzsche course was in session. We will hardly be surprised therefore to hear echoes of each in the other. For an English translation of the essay, see Martin Heidegger, *Poetry, Language, Thought,* tr. Albert Hofstadter (New York: Harper & Row, 1971), pp. 17–87.

We new philosophers, however, not only do we begin by presenting the actual gradations in rank and variations in value among men, but we also desire the very opposite of an assimilation, an equalizing: we teach estrangement in every sense, we tear open gaps such as never were, we want man to become more wicked than he ever was. Meanwhile, we ourselves live as strangers to one another, concealed from one another. It is necessary for many reasons that we be recluses and that we don masks—consequently, we shall do poorly in searching out our comrades. We shall live alone and probably come to know the torments of all seven solitudes. If perchance our paths should cross, you may wager that we will mistake one another or betray one another (WM, 988).

Nietzsche's procedure, his manner of thinking in the execution of the new valuation, is perpetual reversal. We will find opportunity enough to think through these reversals in a more detailed way. In order to clarify matters now we will bring forward only two examples. Schopenhauer interprets the essence of art as a "sedative for life," something that ameliorates the miseries and sufferings of life, that puts the will—whose compulsiveness makes existence miserable—out of commission. Nietzsche reverses this and says that art is the *stimulans* of life, something that excites and enhances life, "what eternally *compels* us to life, to eternal life" (XIV, 370). *Stimulans* is obviously the reverse of sedative.

A second example. To the question "What is truth?" Nietzsche answers, "*Truth is the kind of error* without which a certain kind of living being could not live. The value for *life* ultimately decides" (WM, 493). " 'Truth': this, according to my way of thinking, does not necessarily denote the antithesis of error, but in the most fundamental cases only the position of various errors in relation to one another" (WM, 535). It would of course be utterly superficial to explain such statements in the following way: Nietzsche takes everything that is an error to be true. Nietzsche's statement—truth is error, error truth—can be grasped only in terms of his fundamental position in opposition to all Western philosophy since Plato. If we have grasped this fact, then the statement already sounds less alien. Nietzsche's procedure of reversal at times becomes a conscious mania, if not indeed a breach of good taste. With reference to the expression "Whoever laughs last, laughs best," he says, by way of reversal, "And today whoever laughs best also laughs last" (VIII, 67). In contrast to "Blessed are they who do not see and still believe," he speaks of "seeing and still not believing." This he calls "the primary virtue of knowers," whose "greatest tempter" is whatever is "clear to the eyes" (XII, 241).

One need not penetrate too far into Nietzsche's thought in order to determine without difficulty that his procedure everywhere is one of reversal. On the basis of that determination a basic objection to Nietzsche's procedure and to his entire philosophy has been raised: reversal is merely denial—in setting aside the previous order of values no new values yet arise. With objections of this kind it is always advisable to suppose at least provisionally that the philosopher under consideration was after all alert enough to experience such doubts himself. Nietzsche not only avers that by means of reversal a new order of values should originate; he says explicitly that in this way an order should originate *"of itself."* Nietzsche says, "If the tyranny of previous values has thus been shattered, if we have abolished the 'true world,' then a *new order of values* must follow of itself."* Merely by doing away with the old, something new should eventuate of itself! Are we to ascribe such an opinion to Nietzsche, or do such "abolition" and "reversal" signify something other than what we usually represent to ourselves with the help of everyday concepts?

What is the principle of the new valuation? At the outset it is important to clarify in general the meaning of the title of the third book, to which we are limiting ourselves. "Principle," comes from *principium,* beginning. The concept corresponds to what the Greeks call *archē,* that on the basis of which something is determined to be what it is and how it is. Principle: the ground on which something stands, pervading it, guiding it in its whole structure and essence. We also conceive of principles as fundamental propositions. But these are

---

*Heidegger cites no source, but the passage probably derives from WM, 461. If so, Heidegger misreads the phrase ". . . *Ordnung der Werte"* as "Ordnung der Welt." I have restored Nietzsche's text in the translation.

"principles" only in a derived sense and only because and insofar as they posit something as the fundament of something else within a statement. A statement as such can never be a principle. The principle of a new valuation is that in which valuing as such has its supporting and guiding ground. The principle of a new valuation is that kind of ground which inaugurates a valuing that is new in contrast to previous kinds. The valuing is to be new: not only what is posited as a value but above all else the manner in which values are posited in general. If one objects that Nietzsche was basically uncreative and did not really establish any new values, such an objection first needs to be tested carefully. But however it turns out, the objection itself does not touch what Nietzsche actually wanted to do above all else, namely, to ground anew the manner in which values are posited, to lay a new ground for this purpose. Therefore, if we want to grasp what is thought here, we must read the title of Book III, "Principle of the New Valuation,"* as having the following sense: the new ground from which in the future the manner and kind of valuing will spring and upon which it will rest. How are we to conceive that ground?

If the work as a whole involves will to power, and if the third book is to exhibit the ground-laying and structuring principle of the new valuation, then the principle can only be will to power. How are we to understand this? We said by way of anticipation that will to power is a name for the basic character of all beings. It means precisely *what* properly constitutes the being in beings. Nietzsche's decisive consideration runs as follows: if we are to establish what properly should be, and what must come to be in consequence of that, it can be determined only if truth and clarity already surround whatever *is* and whatever constitutes *Being*. How else could we determine what is to be?

In the sense of this most universal consideration, whose ultimate tenability we must still leave open, Nietzsche says, "Task: to *see* things *as they are!*" (XII, 13). "My philosophy—to draw men away from *semblance,* no matter *what* the danger! And no fear that life will perish!" (XII, 18). Finally: "Because you lie concerning what is, the

---

*Heidegger changes here the indefinite article, *einer,* to the definite, *der,* Cf. p. 25.

thirst for what should come to be does not grow in you" (XII, 279).

Demonstration of will to power as the basic character of beings is supposed to expunge the lies in our experience of beings and in our interpretation of them. But not only that. It is also supposed to ground the principle, and establish the ground, from which the valuation is to spring and in which it must remain rooted. For "will to power" is already in itself an estimating and valuing. If beings are grasped as will to power, the "should" which is supposed to hang suspended over them, against which they might be measured, becomes superfluous. If life itself is will to power, it is itself the ground, *principium,* of valuation. Then a "should" does not determine Being; Being determines a "should." "When we talk of values we are speaking under the inspiration or optics of life: life itself compels us to set up values; life itself values through us *whenever* we posit values. . . ." (VIII, 89).*

To exhibit the principle of the new valuation therefore first of all means to display will to power as the basic character of beings throughout all groups and regions of beings. With a view to that task the editors of *The Will to Power* divided the third book into four divisions:

    I. Will to Power as Knowledge.
    II. Will to Power in Nature.
    III. Will to Power as Society and Individual.
    IV. Will to Power as Art.

Several of Nietzsche's sets of instructions could have been used for such a division, for example, Plan I, 7, dated 1885 (XVI, 415): "Will to Power. Attempt at an interpretation of all occurrence. Foreword on the 'meaninglessness' that threatens. Problem of pessimism." Then comes a list of topics arranged vertically: "Logic. Physics. Morals, Art. Politics." These are the customary disciplines of philosophy; the only one that is missing, and not by accident, is speculative theology. For

---

*To this analysis of the "should" compare that in Heidegger's lecture course during the summer semester of 1935, published as *Einführung in die Metaphysik* (Tübingen: M. Niemeyer, 1953), pp. 149–52; in the English translation, Martin Heidegger, *An Introduction to Metaphysics,* tr. Ralph Manheim (Garden City, N.Y.: Doubleday-Anchor, 1961), pp. 164–67.

the decisive stance vis-à-vis Nietzsche's interpretation of beings as will to power it is important to know that from the very start he saw beings as a whole in the perspectives of traditional disciplines of academic philosophy.

As a further aid in apportioning the aphorisms which appear in the handwritten notebooks into the chapters mentioned, the editors employed an index in which Nietzsche himself numbered 372 aphorisms and divided them into particular books cited in a plan which, it is true, originates at a later date (Plan III, 6; XVI, 424). The index is printed in volume XVI, 454–67; it stems from the year 1888.*

The disposition of the third book of *The Will to Power,* as it lies before us today, is accordingly as well grounded as it could be on the basis of the extant handwritten materials.

However, we shall begin the interpretation of Book III not with the first chapter, "Will to Power as Knowledge," but with the fourth and final one, "Will to Power as Art."

This chapter consists of aphorisms 794 to 853. Why we are beginning with the fourth chapter will soon become clear on the basis of that chapter's contents. Our immediate task must be to ask in what way Nietzsche perceives and defines the essence of art. As the very title of the chapter suggests, art is a configuration of will to power. If art is a configuration of will to power, and if within the whole of Being art is accessible in a distinctive way for us, then we should most likely be able to grasp what will to power means from the Nietzschean conception of art. But lest the expression "will to power" remain an empty term any longer, let us delineate our interpretation of the fourth chapter by means of a preliminary observation. This we will do by asking, first, what does Nietzsche mean by the expression "will to power"; and second, why should it not surprise us that the basic character of beings is here defined as *will?*

---

*Karl Schlechta indicates that the list of 372 aphorisms could apply to a number of plans other than that dated March 17, 1887. See Schlechta, *Der Fall Nietzsche* (Munich: C. Hanser, 2nd ed., 1959), pp. 74 ff. and 88 ff.

6. The Being of beings as Will in Traditional Metaphysics

We shall begin with the second question. The conception of the Being of all beings as will is very much in line with the best and greatest tradition of German philosophy. When we look back from Nietzsche our glance falls immediately upon Schopenhauer. His main work, which at first impels Nietzsche toward philosophy but then later repels him, bears the title *The World as Will and Representation*. But what Nietzsche himself understands by "will" is something altogether different. Nor is it adequate to grasp Nietzsche's notion of will as the reversal of the Schopenhauerian.

Schopenhauer's major work appeared in the year 1818. It was profoundly indebted to the main works of Schelling and Hegel, which had already appeared by that time. The best proof of this debt consists in the excessive and tasteless rebukes Schopenhauer hurled at Hegel and Schelling his life long. Schopenhauer called Schelling a "windbag," Hegel a "bumbling charlatan." Such abuse, directed repeatedly against philosophy in the years following Schopenhauer, does not even have the dubious distinction of being particularly "novel."

In one of Schelling's most profound works, the treatise *On the Essence of Human Freedom*, published in 1809, that philosopher writes: "In the final and ultimate instance there is no other Being at all than Willing. Willing is Primal Being" (I, VII, 350).* And in his

---

*During the previous semester (summer 1936) Heidegger had lectured on Schelling. See Martin Heidegger, *Schellings Abhandlung über das Wesen der menschlichen Freiheit (1809)*, ed. Hildegard Feick (Tübingen: M. Niemeyer, 1971). Especially useful in

Phenomenology of Spirit (1807) Hegel grasps the essence of Being as knowing, but grasps knowing as essentially identical to willing.

Schelling and Hegel were certain that with the interpretation of Being as will they were merely thinking the essential thought of another great German thinker—the concept of Being in Leibniz. Leibniz defined the essence of Being as the original unity of *perceptio* and *appetitus,* representation and will. Not accidentally, Nietzsche himself referred to Leibniz in two decisive passages of *The Will to Power:* "German philosophy as a whole—Leibniz, Kant, Hegel, Schopenhauer, to name the great ones—is the most thoroughgoing kind of *romanticism* and homesickness that has ever existed: the longing for the best there ever was" (WM, 419). And: "Händel, Leibniz, Goethe, Bismarck —characteristic of the *strong German type*" (WM, 884).

Now, to be sure, one should not assert that Nietzsche's doctrine of will to power is dependent upon Leibniz or Hegel or Schelling, in order by such a pronouncement to cancel all further consideration. "Dependence" is not a concept by which we can understand relationships among the greats. But the small are always dependent on the great; they are "small" precisely because they think they are independent. The great thinker is one who can hear what is greatest in the work of other "greats" and who can transform it in an original manner.

Reference to Nietzsche's predecessors with regard to the doctrine of Being as will is not meant to calculate some sort of dependence; it is rather to suggest that such a doctrine within Western metaphysics is not arbitrary but perhaps even necessary. Every true thinking lets itself be determined by what is to be thought. In philosophy the Being of beings is to be thought. For philosophy's thinking and questioning there is no loftier and stricter commitment. In contrast, all the sciences think always only of *one* being among others, *one* particular region of beings. They are committed by this region of beings only in an indirect manner, never straightforwardly so. Because in philosophical thought

---

the context of Heidegger's reading of Nietzsche are the notes sketched five years later for a seminar on that same treatise. The notes appear in an appendix to Heidegger's *Schelling.* See esp. pp. 224–25.

the highest possible commitment prevails, all great thinkers think the same. Yet this "same" is so essential and so rich that no single thinker exhausts it; each commits all the others to it all the more strictly. To conceive of beings according to their basic character as will is not a view held by particular thinkers; it is a necessity in the history of the Dasein which those thinkers ground.

7. Will as Will to Power

But now, to anticipate the decisive issue, what does Nietzsche himself understand by the phrase "will to power"? What does "will" mean? What does "will to power" mean? For Nietzsche these two questions are but one. For in his view will is nothing else than will to power, and power nothing else than the essence of will. Hence, will to power is will to will, which is to say, willing is self-willing. But that requires elucidation.

With our attempt, as with all conceptual definitions elaborated in a similar fashion which claim to grasp the Being of beings, we must keep two things in mind. First, a precise conceptual definition that ticks off the various characteristics of what is to be defined remains vacuous and false, so long as we do not really come to know in an intimate way what is being talked about and bring it before our mind's eye. Second, in order to grasp the Nietzschean concept of will, the following is especially important: if according to Nietzsche will as will to power is the basic character of all beings, then in defining the essence of will we cannot appeal to a particular being or special mode of Being which would serve to explain the essence of will.

Hence, will as the pervasive character of all beings does not yield any immediate sort of directive from which its concept, as a concept of Being, might be derived. Of course, Nietzsche never explicated this state of affairs systematically and with attention to principles; but he knew quite clearly that here he was pursuing an unusual question.

Two examples may illustrate what is involved. According to the usual view, will is taken to be a faculty of the soul. What will is may be determined from the essence of the psyche. The latter is dealt with in psychology. The psyche is a particular being, distinct from body and mind. Now, if in Nietzsche's view will determines the Being of every sort of being, then it does not pertain to the psyche; rather, the psyche somehow pertains to the will. But body and mind too are will, inasmuch as such things "are." Furthermore, if will is taken to be a faculty, then it is viewed as something that can do something, is in a position to do it, possessing the requisite power and might. Whatever is intrinsically power, and for Nietzsche that is what will is, thus cannot be further characterized by defining it as a faculty or power. For the essence of a faculty is grounded in the essence of will as power.

A second example. Will is taken to be a kind of cause. We say that a man does something not so much by means of his intellect as by sheer willpower. Will brings something about, effects some consequence. But to be a cause is a particular mode of Being; Being as such cannot be grasped by means of causation. Will is not an effecting. What we usually take to be a thing that effects something else, the power of causation, is itself grounded in will (cf. VIII, 80).

If will to power characterizes Being itself, there is nothing *else* that will can be defined *as*. Will is will—but that formally correct definition does not say anything. It is in fact quite deceptive if we take it to mean that things are as simple as the simple phrase suggests.

For that reason Nietzsche can declare, "Today we know that it [i.e., the will] is merely a word" (*Twilight of the Idols,* 1888; VIII, 80). Corresponding to this is an earlier assertion from the period of *Zara-thustra:* "I laugh at your free will and your unfree one too: what you call will is to me an illusion; there is no will" (XII, 267). It is remarkable that the thinker for whom the basic character of all beings is will should say such a thing: "There is no will." But Nietzsche means that there is no *such* will as the one previously known and designated as "a faculty of the soul" and as "striving in general."

Whatever the case, Nietzsche must constantly repeat what will is. He says, for example, that will is an "affect," a "passion," a "feeling," and a "command." But do not such characterizations of will as "affect," "passion," and so on speak within the domain of the psyche and of states of the soul? Are not affect, passion, feeling, and command each something different? Must not whatever is introduced in order to illuminate the essence of will itself be adequately clear at the outset? But what is more obscure than the essence of affect and passion, and the distinction between the two? How can will be all those things simultaneously? We can hardly surmount these questions and doubts concerning Nietzsche's interpretation of the essence of will. And yet, perhaps, they do not touch on the decisive issue. Nietzsche himself emphasizes, "Above all else, willing seems to me something *complicated,* something that is a unity only as a word; and precisely in this one word a popular prejudice lurks which has prevailed over the always meager caution of philosophers" (*Beyond Good and Evil;* VII, 28). Nietzsche here speaks primarily against Schopenhauer, in whose opinion will is the simplest and best-known thing in the world.

But because for Nietzsche will as will to power designates the essence of Being, it remains forever the actual object of his search, the thing to be determined. What matters—once such an essence is discovered— is to locate it thoroughly, so that it can never be lost again. Whether Nietzsche's procedure is the sole possible one, whether the singularity of the *inquiry concerning Being* became sufficiently clear to him at all, and whether he thought through in a fundamental manner the ways that are necessary and possible in this regard, we leave open for now. This much is certain: for Nietzsche there was at the time no other alternative—given the ambiguity of the concepts of will and the multiplicity of prevailing conceptual definitions—than to clarify what he meant with the help of what was familiar and to reject what he did not mean. (Cf. the general observation concerning philosophical concepts in *Beyond Good and Evil;* VII, 31 ff.)

If we try to grasp willing by that peculiarity which, as it were, first forces itself upon us, we might say that willing is a heading toward . . . , a going after . . . ; willing is a kind of behavior directed toward something. But when we look at something immediately at hand, or observantly follow the course of some process, we behave in a way that can be described in the same terms: we are directed toward the thing by way of representation—where willing plays no role. In the mere observation of things we do not want to do anything "with" them and do not expect anything "from" them; we let things be just as they are. To be directed toward something is not yet a willing, and yet such directedness is implied in willing. . . .

But we can also "want" [i.e., will-to-have] some thing, e.g., a book or a motorbike. A boy "wills" to have a thing, that is, he would like to have it. This "would like to have" is no mere representation, but a kind of striving after something, and has the special characteristic of wishing. But to wish is not yet to will. Whoever only wishes, in the strict sense of the word, does not will; rather, he hopes that his wish will come true without his having to do anything about it. Is willing then a wishing to which we add our own initiative? No, willing is not wishing at all. It is the submission of ourselves to our own command, and the resoluteness of such self-command, which already implies our carrying out the command. But with this account of willing we have suddenly introduced a whole series of definitions that were not given in what we first discussed, namely, directing oneself toward something.

Yet it seems as though the essence of will would be grasped most purely if this "directing oneself toward," as pure willing, were canceled abruptly in favor of a directing oneself toward something in the sense of sheer desire, wishing, striving, or mere representing. Will would thus be posited as the pure relation of a simple heading toward or going after something. But this approach is misconceived. Nietzsche is convinced that Schopenhauer's fundamental error is his belief that there is such a thing as pure willing, a willing that becomes purer as what is willed is left more and more indeterminate and the one who wills left more and more decisively out of the picture. Much to the contrary, it is proper to the essence of willing that what is willed and the one who wills be brought into the willing, although not in the extrinsic sense in which we can say that to every striving belongs something that strives and something that is striven for.

The *decisive question* is this: how, and on what grounds, do the willed and the one who wills belong to the willing to will? Answer: on the grounds of willing and by means of willing. Willing wills the one who wills, as such a one; and willing posits the willed as such. Willing is resoluteness toward oneself, but as the one who wills what is posited in the willing as willed. In each case will itself furnishes thoroughgoing determinateness to its willing. Someone who does not know what he wants does not want anything and cannot will at all. There is no willing-in-general. "For the will, as an affect of command, is the decisive distinguishing mark of self-mastery and force" (*The Gay Science*, Bk. V, 1886; V, 282). In contrast, striving can be indeterminate, both with respect to what is actually striven for and in relation to the very one who strives. In striving and in compulsion we are caught up in movement toward something without knowing what is at stake. In mere striving after something we are not properly brought before ourselves. For that reason it is not possible for us to strive beyond ourselves; rather, we merely strive, and get wholly absorbed in such striving. By way of contrast, will, as resolute openness to oneself, is always a willing out beyond oneself. If Nietzsche more than once emphasizes the character of will as command, he does not mean to provide a prescription or set of directions for the execution of an act; nor does he mean to characterize an act of will in the sense of resolve. Rather, he means resoluteness—that by which willing can come to grips with what is willed and the one who wills; he means coming to grips as a founded and abiding decisiveness. Only he can truly command—and commanding has nothing to do with mere ordering about —who is always ready and able to place himself under command. By means of such readiness he has placed himself within the scope of the command as first to obey, the paragon of obedience. In such decisiveness of willing, which reaches out beyond itself, lies mastery over . . . , having power over what is revealed in the willing and in what is held fast in the grips of resoluteness.

Willing itself is mastery over . . . , which reaches out beyond itself; will is intrinsically power. And power is willing that is constant in itself. Will is power; power is will. Does the expression "will to power" then have no meaning? Indeed it has none, when we think of will in the sense of Nietzsche's conception. But Nietzsche employs this expression anyhow, in express rejection of the usual understanding of will, and especially in order to emphasize his resistance to the Schopenhauerian notion.

Nietzsche's expression "will to power" means to suggest that will as we usually understand it is actually and only will to power. But a possible misunderstanding lurks even in this explanation. The expression "will to power" does not mean that, in accord with the usual view, will is a kind of desiring that has power as its goal rather than happiness and pleasure. True, in many passages Nietzsche speaks in that fashion, in order to make himself provisionally understood; but when he makes will's goal power instead of happiness, pleasure, or the unhinging of the will, he changes not only the goal of will but the essential definition of will itself. In the strict sense of the Nietzschean conception of will, power can never be pre-established as will's goal, as though power were something that could first be posited outside the will. Because will is resolute openness toward itself, as mastery out beyond itself, because will is a willing beyond itself, it is the strength that is able to bring itself to power.

The expression "to power" therefore never means some sort of appendage to will. Rather, it comprises an elucidation of the essence of will itself. Only when we have clarified Nietzsche's concept of will in these respects can we understand those designations Nietzsche often chooses in order to exhibit the complicated nature of what that simple word "will" says to him. He calls will—therefore will to power—an "affect." He even says, "My theory would be that *will to power* is the primitive form of affect, that all other affects are but its configurations" (WM, 688).* Nietzsche calls will a "passion" as well, or a "feeling." If we understand such descriptions from the point of view of our common psychology—something that always seems to happen—then we might easily be tempted to say that Nietzsche abandons the essence of will to the "emotional," or that he rescues it from the rationalistic misinterpretations perpetrated by Idealism.

Here we must ask two things. First, what does Nietzsche mean when

---

*Walter Kaufmann notes that the phrase "My theory would be" stems from the editors, not from Nietzsche himself. See his edition of *The Will to Power*, p. 366, n. 73.

he emphasizes the character of will as affect, passion, and feeling? Second, when we believe we have found that the idealistic conception of will has nothing to do with Nietzsche's, how are we understanding "Idealism"?

8. Will as Affect, Passion, and Feeling

In the passage last cited Nietzsche says that all affects are "configurations" of will to power. If we ask what will to power is, Nietzsche answers that it is the original affect. Affects are forms of will; will is affect. That is called a circular definition. Common sense feels itself superior when it discovers such "errors of logic" even in a philosopher. Affect is will and will is affect. Now, we already know—at least roughly —that the question of will to power involves the question concerning the *Being of beings;* Being itself can no longer be determined by any given beings, since it is what determines them. Therefore, if any designation of Being is brought forward at all, and if it is supposed to say the same as Being, yet not in a merely empty way, then the determination brought to bear must of necessity be drawn from beings—and the circle is complete. Nevertheless, the matter is not all that simple. In the case at hand Nietzsche says with good grounds that will to power is the original form of affect; he does not say that it is simply one affect, although we often find such turns of phrase in his hastily composed argumentative presentations.

To what extent is will to power the original form of affect, i.e., that which constitutes the Being of an affect in general? What is an affect? To this, Nietzsche provides no clear and precise answer. Just as little does he answer the questions as to what a passion or a feeling may be. The answer ("configurations" of will power) does not immediately conduct us any farther. Rather, it assigns us the task of divining what it is in what we know as affect, passion, and feeling that signifies the essence of will to power. In that way we could derive particular characteristics which are suitable for making clearer and richer the previous attempts to define the essential concept of will. This work we must do ourselves. Yet the questions (what are affect, passion, and feeling?) remain unanswered. Nietzsche himself often equates the three; he follows the usual ways of representing them, ways still accepted today. With these three words, each an arbitrary substitute for the others, we depict the so-called irrational side of psychic life. For customary representational thought that may suffice, but not for true knowledge, and certainly not if our task is to determine by such knowledge the Being of beings. Nor is it enough to revamp the current "psychological" explanations of affects, passions, and feelings. We must above all see that here it is not a matter for psychology, nor even for a psychology undergirded by physiology and biology. It is a matter of the basic modes that constitute Dasein, a matter of the ways man confronts the *Da,* the openness and concealment of beings, in which he stands.

We cannot deny that the things physiology grapples with—particular states of the body, changes in internal secretions, muscle flexions, occurrences in the nervous system—are also proper to affects, passions, and feelings. But we have to ask whether all these bodily states and the body itself are grasped in a metaphysically adequate way, so that one may without further ado borrow material from physiology and biology, as Nietzsche, to his own detriment, so often did. The one fundamental point to realize here is that no result of any science can ever be applied *immediately* to philosophy.

How are we to conceive of the essence of affect, passion, and feeling, indeed in such a way that in each case it will be fruitful for an interpretation of the essence of will in Nietzsche's sense? Here we can conduct our examination only as far as illumination of Nietzsche's characterization of will to power requires.

Anger, for instance, is an affect. In contrast, by "hate" we mean something quite different. Hate is not simply another affect, it is not an affect at all. It is a passion. But we call both of them "feelings." We speak of the feeling of hatred and of an angry feeling. We cannot plan or decide to be angry. Anger comes over us, seizes us, "affects" us. Such a seizure is sudden and turbulent. Our being is moved by a kind of excitement, something stirs us up, lifts us beyond ourselves, but in such a way that, seized by our excitement, we are no longer masters of ourselves. We say, "He acted on impulse," that is to say, under the influence of an affect. Popular speech proves to be keensighted when it says of someone who is stirred up and acts in an excited manner, "He isn't altogether himself." When we are seized by excitement, our being "altogether there" vanishes; it is transformed into a kind of "falling apart." We say, "He's beside himself with joy."

Nietzsche is obviously thinking of that essential moment in the affect when he tries to characterize will in its terms. Such being lifted beyond ourselves in anger, the seizure of our whole being, so that we are not our own master, such a "not" does not at all mean to deny that in anger we are carried beyond ourselves; such "not being master" in the affect, in anger, distinguishes the affect from mastery in the sense of will, for in the affect our being master of ourselves is transformed into a manner of being beyond ourselves where something is lost. Whatever is contrary we call "counter." We call anger a counter-will that subsists beyond us, in such a way that in anger we do not remain together with ourselves as we do when willing, but, as it were, lose ourselves. Here will is a counter-will. Nietzsche turns the state of affairs around: the formal essence of the affect is will, but now will is visualized merely as a state of excitement, of being beyond oneself.

Because Nietzsche says that to will is to will out beyond oneself, he can say that, in view of such being beyond oneself in the affect, will to power is the original form of affect. Yet he clearly wants to add the other moment of the affect for the sake of the essential characterization of will, that moment of seizure in the affect by which something comes over us. That too, and precisely that, in a manifold and Protean sense of course, is proper to the will. That we can be beyond or outside ourselves in this or that way, and that we are in fact constantly so, is possible only because will itself—seen in relation to the essence of man—is seizure pure and simple.

Will itself cannot be willed. We can never resolve to have a will, in the sense that we would arrogate to ourselves a will; for such resoluteness is itself a willing. When we say, "He wants to have his will carried out in this or that matter," it means as much as, he really wants to stand firm in his willing, to get hold of himself in his entire being, to be master over his being. But that very possibility indicates that we are always within the scope of will, even when we are unwilling. That genuine willing which surges forward in resoluteness, that "yes," is what instigates the seizure of our entire being, of the very essence within us.

Nietzsche designates will as passion just as often as affect. We should not automatically conclude that he identifies affect and passion, even if he does not arrive at an explicit and comprehensive clarification of the essential distinction and connection between these two. We may surmise that Nietzsche knows the difference between affect and passion. Around the year 1882 he says regarding his times, "Our age is an agitated one, and precisely for that reason, not an age of passion; it heats itself up continuously, because it feels that it is not warm— basically it is freezing. I do not believe in the greatness of all these 'great events' of which you speak" (XII, 343). "The age of the greatest events will, in spite of all that, be the age of the most meager effects if men are made of rubber and are all too elastic." "In our time it is merely by means of an echo that events acquire their 'greatness'—the echo of the newspapers" (XII, 344).

Usually Nietzsche employs the word "passion" interchangeably with "affect." But if anger and hate, for example, or joy and love, not only are different as one affect is from another, but are distinct as affects and passions respectively, then here too we need a more exact definition. Hate too cannot be produced by a decision; it too seems to overtake us—in a way similar to that when we are seized by anger. Nevertheless, the manner in which it comes over us is essentially different. Hate can explode suddenly in an action or exclamation, but only because it has already overtaken us, only because it has been growing within us for a long time, and, as we say, has been nurtured in us. But something can be nurtured only if it is already there and is alive. In contrast, we do not say and never believe that anger is nurtured. Because hate lurks much more deeply in the origins of our being it has a cohesive power; like love, hate brings an original cohesion and perdurance to our essential being. But anger, which seizes us, can also release us again—it "blows over," as we say. Hate does not "blow over." Once it germinates it grows and solidifies, eating its way inward and consuming our very being. But the permanent cohesion that comes to human existence through hate does not close it off and blind it. Rather, it grants vision and premeditation. The angry man loses the power of reflection. He who hates intensifies reflection and rumination to the point of "hardboiled" malice. Hate is never blind; it is perspicuous. Only anger is blind. Love is never blind: it is perspicuous. Only infatuation is blind, fickle, and susceptible—an affect, not a passion. To passion belongs a reaching out and opening up of oneself. Such reaching out occurs even in hate, since the hated one is pursued everywhere relentlessly. But such reaching out in passion does not simply lift us up and away beyond ourselves. It gathers our essential being to its proper ground, it exposes our ground for the first time in so gathering, so that the passion is that through which and in which we take hold of ourselves and achieve lucid mastery over the beings around us and within us.

Passion understood in this way casts light on what Nietzsche calls will to power. Will as mastery of oneself is never encapsulation of the ego from its surroundings. Will is, in our terms, resolute openness, in which he who wills stations himself abroad among beings in order to keep them firmly within his field of action.* Now the characteristic traits are not seizure and agitation, but the lucid grip which simultaneously gathers that passionate being.

Affect: the seizure that blindly agitates us. Passion: the lucidly gathering grip on beings. We talk and understand only extrinsically when we say that anger flares and then dissipates, lasting but a short time,

---

*Perhaps a word is needed concerning the traditional translation of *Entschlossenheit*, "resoluteness." Heidegger now hyphenates the German word to emphasize that *Ent-schlossenheit*, far from being a sealing-off or closing-up of the will in decision, means unclosedness, hence a "resolute openness." The word thus retains its essential ties to *Erschlossenheit*, the disclosure of Being in Dasein. On *Entschlossenheit* see Martin Heidegger, *Sein und Zeit*, 12th ed. (Tübingen: M. Niemeyer, 1972), esp. p. 297; "Vom Wesen der Wahrheit," in *Wegmarken* (Frankfurt/Main: V. Klostermann, 1967), p. 90; and *Gelassenheit* (Pfullingen: G. Neske, 1959), p. 59. Cf. *Martin Heidegger: Basic Writings*, ed. D. F. Krell (New York: Harper & Row, 1977), p. 133 n.

while hate lasts longer. No, hate and love not only last longer, they bring perdurance and permanence for the first time to our existence. An affect, in contrast, cannot do that. Because passion restores our essential being, because it loosens and liberates in its very grounds, and because passion at the same time reaches out into the expanse of beings, for these reasons passion—and we mean great passion—possesses extravagance and resourcefulness, not only the ability but the necessity to submit, without bothering about what its extravagance entails. It displays that self-composed superiority characteristic of great will.

Passion has nothing to do with sheer desire. It is not a matter of the nerves, of ebullition and dissipation. All of that, no matter how excited its gestures, Nietzsche reckons as attrition of the will. Will is what it is only as willing out beyond itself, willing more. Great will shares with great passion that serenity of unhurried animation that is slow to answer and react, not out of insecurity and ponderousness, but out of the broadly expansive security and inner buoyancy of what is superior.

Instead of "affect" and "passion" we also say "feeling," if not "sensation." Or, where affects and passions are distinguished, the two are conjoined in the genus "feeling." Today if we apply the term "feeling" to a passion, it is understood as a kind of reduction. For we believe that a passion is not a mere feeling. Nevertheless, the simple fact that we refrain from calling passions feelings does not prove that we possess a more highly developed concept of the essence of passion; it may only be a sign that we have employed too paltry a concept of the essence of feeling. So it is in fact. But it may seem that here we are merely inquiring into word meanings and their appropriate applications. Yet the *matter* that is here in question is, first, whether what we have now indicated as being the essence of affect and of passion exhibits an original, essential connection between these two, and second, whether this original connection can truly be understood if only we grasp the essence of what we call "feeling."

Nietzsche himself does not shy from conceiving willing simply as feeling: "Willing: a compelling feeling, quite pleasant! It is the epiphenomenon of all *discharge of energy*" (XIII, 159). To will—a feeling of pleasure? "Pleasure is only a symptom of the feeling of power attained, a consciousness of difference (—it [a living creature] does not strive for pleasure: rather, pleasure enters on the scene when it achieves what it is striving for: pleasure accompanies, it does not motivate—)" (WM, 688). Is will accordingly but an "epiphenomenon" of energy discharge, an accompanying feeling of pleasure? How does that jibe with what was said about the essence of will in general, and in particular with respect to the comparison with affect and passion? There will appeared as what properly sustains and dominates, being synonymous with mastery itself. Is it now to be reduced to a feeling of pleasure that merely accompanies something else?

From such passages we see clearly how unconcerned Nietzsche is about a unified, solidly grounded presentation of his teaching. We realize that he is only getting under way, that he is resolutely open. His task is not a matter of indifference to him; neither is it of only supplemental interest. He knows, as only a creator can, that what from the outside looks like a summary presentation is actually the configuration of the real issue, where things collide against one another in such a way that they expose their proper essence. Nevertheless, Nietzsche remains under way, and the immediate casting of what he wants to say always forces itself upon him. In such a position he speaks directly the language of his times and of the contemporary "science." When he does so he does not shy from conscious exaggeration and one-sided formulations of his thoughts, believing that in this way he can most clearly set in relief what in his vision and in his inquiry is different from the run-of-the-mill. Yet when he proceeds in such a manner he is always able to keep his eye on the whole; he can make do, as it were, with one-sidedness. The results are fatal when others, his readers, latch onto such statements in a superficial way and, depending on what Nietzsche just then is offering them, either declare it his sole opinion on the matter or, on the grounds of any given particular utterances, all too facilely refute him.

If it is true that will to power constitutes the basic character of all beings, and if Nietzsche now defines will as an accompanying feeling of pleasure, these two conceptions of will are not automatically compatible. Nor will one ascribe to Nietzsche the view that Being simply accompanies something else as a feeling of pleasure—that "something else" being yet another entity whose Being would have to be determined. The only way out is to assume that the definition of will as an accompanying feeling of pleasure, which is at first so foreign to what was presented earlier, is neither *the* essential definition of will nor one such definition among others. It is much more the case that it refers to something altogether proper to the full essence of will. But if this is the case, and if in our earlier remarks we have sketched an outline of the essential structure of will, then the definition just mentioned must somehow fit into the general pattern we have presented.

"Willing: a compelling feeling, quite pleasant!" A feeling is the way we find ourselves in relationship to beings, and thereby at the same time to ourselves. It is the way we find ourselves particularly attuned to beings which we are not and to the being we ourselves are. In feeling, a state opens up, and stays open, in which we stand related to things, to ourselves, and to the people around us, always simultaneously. Feeling is the very state, open to itself, in which our Dasein hovers. Man is not a rational creature who also wills, and in addition to thinking and willing is equipped with feelings, whether these make him admirable or despicable; rather, the state of feeling is original, although in such a way that thinking and willing belong together with it. Now the only important matter that remains for us to see is that feeling has the character of opening up and keeping open, and therefore also, depending on the kind of feeling it is, the character of closing off.

But if will is willing out beyond itself, the "out beyond" does not imply that will simply wanders away from itself; rather, will gathers itself together in willing. That the one who wills, wills himself into his will, means that such willing itself, and in unity with it he who wills and what is willed, become manifest in the willing. In the essence of will, in resolute openness, will discloses itself to itself, not merely by means of some further act appended to it, some sort of observation of the willing process and reflection on it; on the contrary, it is will itself that has the character of opening up and keeping open. No self-observation or self-analysis which we might undertake, no matter how penetrating, brings to light our self, and how it is with our self. In contrast, in willing and, correspondingly, in not willing, we bring ourselves to light; it is a light kindled only by willing. Willing always brings the self to itself; it thereby finds itself out beyond itself. It maintains itself within the thrust away from one thing toward something else. Will therefore has the character of feeling, of keeping open our very state of being, a state that in the case of will—being out beyond itself—is a pulsion. Will can thus be grasped as a "compelling feeling." It is not only a feeling of something that prods us, but is itself a prodding, indeed of a sort that is "quite pleasant." What opens up in the will—willing itself as resolute openness—is agreeable to the one for whom it is so opened, the one who wills. In willing we come toward ourselves, as the ones we properly are. Only in will do we capture ourselves in our most proper essential being. He who wills is, as such, one who wills out beyond himself; in willing we know ourselves as out beyond ourselves; we sense a mastery over . . . , somehow achieved; a thrill of pleasure announces to us the power attained, a power that enhances itself. For that reason Nietzsche speaks of a "consciousness of difference."

If feeling and will are grasped here as "consciousness" or "knowledge," it is to exhibit most clearly that moment of the opening up of something in will itself. But such opening is not an observing; it is feeling. This suggests that willing is itself a kind of state, that it is open in and to itself. Willing is feeling (state of attunement). Now since the will possesses that manifold character of willing out beyond itself, as we have suggested, and since all this becomes manifest as a whole, we can conclude that a multiplicity of feelings haunts our willing. Thus in *Beyond Good and Evil* (VII, 28–29) Nietzsche says:

> . . . in every willing there is in the first place a multiplicity of feelings, namely, the feeling of the state *away from* which, the feeling of the state *toward* which, the feeling of this very "away" and "toward"; then there is also an accompanying feeling in the musculature that comes into play by force of habit as soon as we "will," even if we do not set "arms and legs" in motion.

That Nietzsche designates will now as affect, now as passion, now as feeling should suggest that he sees something more-unified, more original, and even more fertile behind that single rude word, "will." If he calls will an affect, it is not a mere equation, but a designation of will with regard to what distinguishes the affect as such. The same is true for the concepts of passion and feeling. We have to go even further and reverse the state of affairs. What we otherwise recognize as affect, passion, and feeling, Nietzsche recognizes in its essential roots as will to power. Thus he grasps "joy" (normally an affect) as a "feeling-stronger," as a feeling of being out beyond oneself and of being capable of being so (WM, 917):

> To feel stronger—or, to express it differently, joy—always presupposes comparison (but *not* necessarily with others; rather, with oneself, within a state of growth, and without first knowing to what extent one is comparing—).

This is a reference to that "consciousness of difference" which is not knowledge in the sense of mere representation and cognition.

Joy does not simply presuppose an unwitting comparison. It is rather something that brings us to ourselves, not by way of knowledge but by way of feeling, by way of an away-beyond-us. Comparison is not presupposed. Rather, the disparity implied in being out beyond ourselves is first opened up and given form by joy.

If we examine all this from the outside rather than the inside, if we judge it by the standards of customary theories of knowledge and consciousness, whether idealistic or realistic, we proceed to declare that Nietzsche's concept of will is an emotional one, conceived in terms of our emotional lives, our feelings, and that it is therefore ultimately a biological notion. All well and good. But such explanations pigeonhole Nietzsche in that representational docket which he would like to escape. That is also true of the interpretation that tries to distinguish Nietzsche's "emotional" concept of will from the "idealistic" one.

9. The Idealistic Interpretation of Nietzsche's Doctrine of Will

We have now arrived at the second of the questions posed above [p. 43], which asks: if we believe we have found that the idealistic concept of will has nothing to do with Nietzsche's, how are we understanding "Idealism"?

Generally we can call "idealistic" that mode of observation which looks to ideas. Here "idea" means as much as representation. To represent means to envisage in the widest sense: *idein*. To what extent can an elucidation of the essence of will see in will a trait of representation?

Willing is a kind of desiring and striving. The Greeks call it *orexis*. In the Middle Ages and in modern times it is called *appetitus* and *inclinatio*. Hunger, for example, is sheer compulsion and striving, a compulsion toward food for the sake of nourishment. In the case of animals the compulsion itself as such does not have explicitly in view what it is being compelled toward; animals do not represent food as such and do not strive for it as nourishment. Such striving does not know what it will have, since it does not will at all; yet it goes after what is striven for, though never going after it *as* such. But will, as striving, is not blind compulsion. What is desired and striven for is represented as such along with the compulsion; it too is taken up into view and co-apprehended.

To bring something forward and to contemplate it is called in Greek *noein*. What is striven for, *orekton*, in the willing is at the same time something represented, *noēton*. But that does not at all mean that willing is actually representation of such a kind that a striving tags along after what is represented. The reverse is the case. We shall offer as unequivocal proof a passage from Aristotle's treatise *Peri psychēs,* "On the Soul."

When we translate the Greek *psychē* as "soul" we dare not think of it in the sense of "life experiences," nor may we think of what we know in the consciousness of our *ego cogito,* nor finally may we think of the "unconscious." For Aristotle *psychē* means the principle of living creatures as such, whatever it is that makes living things to be alive, what pervades their very essence. The treatise just mentioned discusses the essence of life and the hierarchy of living creatures.

The treatise contains no psychology, and no biology either. It is a metaphysics of living creatures, among which man too belongs. What lives moves itself by itself. Movement here means not only change of place but every mode of behavior and self-alteration. Man is the highest form of living creature. The basic type of self-movement for him is action, *praxis.* So the question arises: what is the determining ground, the *archē,* of action, i.e., of proceeding in a considered fashion and establishing something? What is determinative here, the represented as such or what is sought? Is the representing-striving determined by representation or desire? To ask it another way: is will a representing, and is it therefore determined by ideas, or not? If what is taught is that will is in essence a representing, then such a doctrine of will is "idealistic."

What does Aristotle teach concerning will? The tenth chapter of Book III deals with *orexis,* desiring. Here Aristotle says (433a 15 ff.):

Kai hē orexis heneka tou pasa · hou gar hē orexis, hautē archē tou praktikou nou · to d' eschaton archē tēs praxeōs. Hoste eulogōs dyo tauta phainetai ta kinounta, orexis kai dianoia praktikē · to orekton gar kinei, kai dia touto hē dianoia kinei, hoti archē autēs esti to orekton.

And every desire has that on account of which it is desire [what the desire aims at]; it is that on the basis of which the *considering* intellect *as such determines itself;* the terminal point is that by which the action is determined. Therefore these two, desiring and the considering intellect, show themselves with good grounds to be what moves; for what is desired in the desiring moves, and the intellect, representation, moves only because it represents to itself what is desired in the desiring.

Aristotle's conception of the will becomes definitive for all Western thought; it is still today the common conception. In the Middle Ages *voluntas* is interpreted as *appetitus intellectualis,* i.e., *orexis dianoētikē,* the desiring which is proper to intellectual representation. For Leibniz *agere,* doing, is *perceptio* and *appetitus* in one; *perceptio* is *idea,* representation. For Kant the will is that faculty of desire which works *according to* concepts, which is to say, in such a way that what is willed, as something represented in general, is itself determinative of action. Although representation sets in relief the will as a faculty of desire over against sheer blind striving, it does not serve as the proper moving and willing force in will. Only a conception of will that would ascribe to representation or the *idea* such an unjustified preeminence could be classified as idealistic in the strict sense. Indeed we do find such conceptions. In the Middle Ages, Thomas Aquinas inclines toward such an interpretation of the will, although even with him the question is not decided so unequivocally. Viewed as a whole, the great thinkers have never assigned to representation the highest rank in their conceptions of the will.

If by an "idealistic interpretation of the will" we understand every conception that in any way emphasizes representation, thought, knowledge, and concept as essential components of will, then Aristotle's interpretation of will is undoubtedly idealistic. So in the same way are those of Leibniz and Kant; but then so too is that of Nietzsche. Proof for this assertion is quite easy to come by: we need only read a bit farther into that passage where Nietzsche says that will consists of a multiplicity of feelings.

Therefore, just as we must acknowledge feeling, and indeed many types of feelings, as ingredients of the will, so must we also in the second place acknowledge thinking: in every act of the will there is a commandeering thought; —and one should not think that he can sever this thought from the "willing," as though will would be what were left over! (VII, 29).

That is spoken clearly enough, not only against Schopenhauer, but against all those who want to appeal to Nietzsche when they defy thinking and the power of the concept.

In the light of these clear statements by Nietzsche, an outright rejection of the idealistic interpretation of his doctrine of will seems futile. But perhaps one might argue that Nietzsche's conception of will differs from that of German Idealism. There too, however, the Kantian and Aristotelian concept of will is adopted. For Hegel, knowing and willing are the same, which is to say, true knowledge is also already action and action is only in knowledge. Schelling even says that what actually wills in the will is the intellect. Is that not unclouded Idealism, if one understands by that a tracing of will back to representation? But by his extravagant turn of phrase Schelling wants to emphasize nothing else than what Nietzsche singles out in the will when he says that will is command. For when Schelling says "intellect," and when German Idealism speaks of knowing, they do not mean a faculty of representation as the discipline of psychology would think it; they do not mean the kind of behavior that merely accompanies and observes the other processes of psychic life. Knowing means opening upon Being, which is a willing—in Nietzsche's language, an "affect." Nietzsche himself says, "*To will is to command:* but commanding is a particular *affect* (this affect is a sudden explosion of energy)—intent, clear, having one thing exclusively in view, innermost conviction of its superiority, certain that it will be obeyed—" (XIII, 264). To have one thing clearly, intently, exclusively in view: what else is that than, in the strict sense of the word, holding one thing before oneself, presenting it before oneself? But *intellect,* Kant says, is the faculty of representation.

No designation of will is more common in Nietzsche than the one just cited: to will is to command; in the will lies a commandeering thought. But at the same time no other conception of will emphasizes more decisively than this one the essential role of knowledge and representation, the role of intellect, in the will.

Hence, if we want to get as close as we can to Nietzsche's conception of the will, and stay close to it, then we are well advised to hold all the usual terminology at a distance. Whether we call his conception idealistic or nonidealistic, emotional or biological, rational or irrational—in each case it is a falsification.

10. Will and Power. The Essence of Power

Now we can—indeed it seems we must—gather together the series of determinations of the essence of will which we have elaborated and conjoin them in a single definition: will as mastery over something, reaching out beyond itself; will as affect (the agitating seizure); will as passion (the expansive plunge into the breadth of beings); will as feeling (being the state of having a stance-toward-oneself); and will as command. With some effort we certainly could produce a formally proper "definition" bristling with all these attributes. All the same, we will forego that. Not as though we laid no value on strict and univocal concepts—on the contrary, we are searching for them. But a notion is not a concept, not in philosophy at any rate, if it is not founded and grounded in such a way as to allow what it is grasping to become its standard and the pathway of its interrogation, instead of camouflaging it under the net of a mere formula. But what the concept "will," as the basic character of beings, is to grasp, i.e., Being, is not yet in our vicinity; better, *we* are not close enough to *it*. To be cognizant, to know, is not mere familiarity with concepts. Rather, it is to grasp what the concept itself catches hold of. To grasp Being means to remain knowingly exposed to its sudden advance, its presencing. If we consider what the word "will" is to name, the essence of beings themselves, then we shall comprehend how powerless such a solitary word must remain, even when a definition is appended to it. Hence Nietzsche can say, "Will: that is a supposition which clarifies nothing else for me. For those who know, there is no willing" (XII, 303). From such statements we should not conclude that the whole effort to capture the essence of will is without prospect, nothing worth, and that therefore it is a matter of indifference and arbitrariness what words or concepts we use when speaking of "will." On the contrary, we have to question, right from the start and continually, on the basis of the matter itself. Only in that way do we arrive at the concept and at the proper use of the word.

Now, in order from the outset to avoid the vacuity of the word "will," Nietzsche says "will to power." Every willing is a willing to be more. Power itself only *is* inasmuch as, and so long as, it remains a willing to be more power. As soon as such will disappears, power is no longer power, even if it still holds in subjection what it has overmastered. In will, as willing to be more, as will to power, enhancement and heightening are essentially implied. For only by means of perpetual heightening can what is elevated be held aloft. Only a more powerful heightening can counter the tendency to sink back; simply holding onto the position already attained will not do, because the inevitable consequence is ultimate exhaustion. In *The Will to Power* Nietzsche says (WM, 702):

> —what man wants, what every smallest part of a living organism wants, is an *increase of power*.... Let us take the simplest case, that of primitive nourishment: the protoplasm stretches its pseudopodia in order to search for something that resists it—not from hunger but from will to power. It then attempts to overcome this thing, to appropriate it, to incorporate it. What we call "nourishment" is merely a derivative appearance, a practical application of that original will to become *stronger*.*

To will is to want to become stronger. Here too Nietzsche speaks by way of reversal and at the same time by way of defense against a contemporary trend, namely, Darwinism. Let us clarify this matter briefly. Life not only exhibits the drive to maintain itself, as Darwin

---

*Walter Kaufmann notes that all editions omit a sentence from this note. It should be inserted after the phrase "not from hunger but from will to power." In translation it reads: "Duality as the consequence of too weak a unity." See Kaufmann's edition of *The Will to Power*, p. 373, n. 80.

thinks, but also is self-assertion. The will to maintain merely clings to what is already at hand, stubbornly insists upon it, loses itself in it, and so becomes blind to its proper essence. Self-assertion, which wants to be ahead of things, to stay on top of things, is always a going back into its essence, into the origin. *Self-assertion is original assertion of essence.*

Will to power is never the willing of a particular actual entity. It involves the Being and essence of beings; it is this itself. Therefore we can say that will to power is always essential will. Although Nietzsche does not formulate it expressly in this way, at bottom that is what he means. Otherwise we could not understand what he always refers to in connection with his emphasis on the character of enhancement in will, of the "increase of power," namely, the fact that will to power is something creative. That designation too remains deceptive; it often seems to suggest that in and through will to power something is to be produced. What is decisive is not production in the sense of manufacturing but taking up and transforming, making something other than. . . , other in an essential way. For that reason the need to destroy belongs essentially to creation. In destruction, the contrary, the ugly, and the evil are posited; they are of necessity proper to creation, i.e., will to power, and thus to Being itself. To the essence of Being nullity belongs, not as sheer vacuous nothingness, but as the empowering "no."

We know that German Idealism thought Being as will. That philosophy also dared to think the negative as proper to Being. It suffices to refer to a passage in the Preface to Hegel's *Phenomenology of Spirit.* Here Hegel avers that the "monstrous power of the negative" is the "energy of thinking, of the pure ego." He continues:

> Death, if we want to name that unreality so, is the most frightful thing, and to hold fast to what is dead requires the greatest force. Beauty without force hates the intellect because intellect demands of her something of which she is incapable. But the life of Spirit is not one that shies from death and merely preserves itself from corruption; it is rather the life that endures death and maintains itself in death. Spirit achieves its truth only inasmuch as it finds itself in absolute abscission. It is not this power as something positive that

averts its glance from everything negative, as when we say of something that it is nothing, or false, and that now we are done with it and can leave it behind and go on to something else; rather, it is this power only insofar as it looks the negative in the eye and lingers with it.*

Thus German Idealism *too* dares to think evil as proper to the essence of Being. The greatest attempt in this direction we possess in Schelling's treatise *On the Essence of Human Freedom.* Nietzsche had a much too original and mature relation to the history of German metaphysics to have overlooked the might of thoughtful will in German Idealism. Hence at one point he writes (WM, 416):

> The significance of German philosophy (Hegel): to elaborate a pantheism in which evil, error, and suffering are *not* felt to be arguments against divinity. *This grandiose initiative* has been misused by the existing powers (the state, etc.), as though it sanctioned the rationality of those who happened to be ruling.
>
> In contrast, Schopenhauer appears as the stubborn moral-man who in order to retain his moral estimation finally becomes a *world-denier,* ultimately a "mystic."

This passage also reveals clearly that Nietzsche was by no means willing to join in the belittling, denegrating, and berating of German Idealism which became common with Schopenhauer and others in the middle of the nineteenth century. Schopenhauer's philosophy, which had been available in its finished form since 1818, began to reach a broader public by mid-century. Richard Wagner and the young Nietzsche were also caught up in the movement. We obtain a vivid picture of the enthusiasm for Schopenhauer which moved young people at that time from the letters of the youthful Baron Carl von Gersdorff to Nietzsche. They were friends since their high school days at Schulpforta. Especially important are the letters Gersdorff wrote to Nietzsche while at the front in 1870–71. (See *Die Briefe des Freiherrn Carl von Gersdorff an Friedrich Nietzsche,* edited by Karl Schlechta, first part: 1864–71, Weimar, 1934; second part: 1871–74, Weimar, 1935.)

---

*G. W. F. Hegel, *Phänomenologie des Geistes* (Hamburg: F. Meiner, 1952), pp. 29–30.

Schopenhauer interpreted the state of affairs—that he was suddenly now being read by the educated classes—as a philosophical victory over German Idealism. But Schopenhauer advanced to the forefront of philosophy at that time not because his philosophy conquered German Idealism philosophically, but because the Germans lay prostrate before German Idealism and were no longer equal to its heights. Its decline made Schopenhauer a great man. The consequence was that the philosophy of German Idealism, seen from the point of view of Schopenhauer's commonplaces, became something foreign, an oddity. It fell into oblivion. Only by detours and byways do we find our way back into that era of the German spirit; we are far removed from a truly historical relation to our history. Nietzsche sensed that here a "grandiose initiative" of metaphysical thought was at work. Yet for him it remained, had to remain, a mere glimmer. For the one decade of creative labor on his major work did not grant him the time and tranquillity to linger in the vast halls of Hegel's and Schelling's works.

Will is in itself simultaneously creative and destructive. Being master out beyond oneself is always also annihilation. All the designated moments of will—the out-beyond-itself, enhancement, the character of command, creation, self-assertion—speak clearly enough for us to know that will in itself is already will to power. Power says nothing else than the actuality of will.

Prior to our general description of Nietzsche's concept of will we made brief reference to the metaphysical tradition, in order to suggest that the conception of Being as will is not in itself peculiar. But the same is true also of the designation of Being as power. No matter how decisively the interpretation of Being as will to power remains Nietzsche's own, and no matter how little Nietzsche explicitly knew in what historical context the very concept of power as a determination of Being stood, it is certain that with this interpretation of the Being of beings Nietzsche advances into the innermost yet broadest circle of Western thought.

Ignoring for a moment the fact that for Nietzsche power means the same as will, we note that the essence of power is just as intricate as the essence of will. We could clarify the state of affairs by proceeding as we did when we listed the particular definitions of will that Nietzsche gives. But we will now emphasize only two moments within the essence of power.

Nietzsche often identifies power with force, without defining the latter more closely. Force, the capacity to be gathered in itself and prepared to work effects, to be in a position to do something, is what the Greeks (above all, Aristotle) denoted as *dynamis*. But power is every bit as much a being empowered, in the sense of the process of dominance, the being-at-work of force, in Greek, *energeia*. Power is will as willing out beyond itself, precisely in that way to come to itself, to find and assert itself in the circumscribed simplicity of its essence, in Greek, *entelecheia*. For Nietzsche power means all this at once: *dynamis, energeia, entelecheia.*

In the collection of treatises by Aristotle which we know under the title *Metaphysics* there is one, Book Theta (IX), that deals with *dynamis, energeia,* and *entelecheia,* as the highest determinations of Being.*

What Aristotle, still on the pathway of an original philosophy, but also already at its end, here thinks, i.e., asks, about Being, later is transformed into the doctrine of *potentia* and *actus* in Scholastic philosophy. Since the beginning of modern times philosophy entrenches itself in the effort to grasp Being by means of thinking. In that way the determinations of Being, *potentia* and *actus,* slip into the vicinity of the basic forms of thought or judgment. Possibility, actuality, and necessity along with them become modalities of Being and of thinking. Since then the doctrine of modalities becomes a component part of every doctrine of categories.

What contemporary academic philosophy makes of all this is a matter of scholarship and an exercise in intellectual acuity. What we find

---

* Heidegger had lectured in the summer of 1931 on Aristotle, *Metaphysics IX.* (The text of that course appeared in 1981 as vol. 33 of the *Gesamtausgabe.*) On the question of *alētheia* and Being in chapter 10 of *Metaphysics IX,* see Martin Heidegger, *Logik: Die Frage nach der Wahrheit* (Frankfurt/Main: V. Klostermann, 1976), pp. 170–82, the text of his 1925–26 lecture course. Cf. the review of this volume in *Research in Phenomenology,* VI (1976), 151–66.

in Aristotle, as knowledge of *dynamis, energeia, entelecheia,* is still philosophy; that is to say, the book of Aristotle's *Metaphysics* which we have referred to is the most worthy of question of all the books in the entire Aristotelian corpus. Although Nietzsche does not appreciate the concealed and vital connection between his concept of power, as a concept of Being, and Aristotle's doctrine, and although that connection remains apparently quite loose and undetermined, we may say that the Aristotelian doctrine has more to do with Nietzsche's doctrine of will to power than with any doctrine of categories and modalities in academic philosophy. But the Aristotelian doctrine itself devolves from a tradition that determines its direction; it is a first denouement of the first beginnings of Western philosophy in Anaximander, Heraclitus, and Parmenides.

However, we should not understand the reference to the inner relation of Nietzsche's will to power to *dynamis, energeia,* and *entelecheia* in Aristotle as asserting that Nietzsche's doctrine of Being can be interpreted immediately with the help of the Aristotelian teaching. Both must be conjoined in a more original context of questions. That is especially true of Aristotle's doctrine. It is no exaggeration to say that we today simply no longer understand or appreciate anything about Aristotle's teaching. The reason is simple: we interpret his doctrine right from the start with the help of corresponding doctrines from the Middle Ages and modern times, which on their part are only a transformation of and a decline from Aristotelian doctrine, and which therefore are hardly suited to provide a basis for our understanding.

Thus when we examine various aspects of the essence of will to power as powerfulness of will, we recognize how that interpretation of beings stands within the basic movement of Western thought. We discern how solely for that reason it is able to bring an essential thrust to the task of thinking in the twentieth century.

But of course we will never comprehend the innermost historicity of Nietzschean thought, by virtue of which it spans the breadth of centuries, if we only hunt for reminiscences, borrowings, and divergences in an extrinsic manner. We must grasp what it was that Nietzsche properly wanted to think. It would be no great trick—better, it would be precisely that, a mere trick—if, armed with a readymade conceptual apparatus, we proceeded to flush out particular disagreements, contradictions, oversights, and overhasty and often superficial and contingent remarks in Nietzsche's presentations. *As opposed to that, we are searching for the realm of his genuine questioning.*

In the final year of his creative life Nietzsche was wont to designate his manner of thinking as "philosophizing with the hammer." The expression has more than one meaning, in accordance with Nietzsche's own viewpoint. Least of all does it mean to go in swinging, wrecking everything. It means to hammer out a content and an essence, to sculpt a figure out of stone. Above all it means to tap all things with the hammer to hear whether or not they yield that familiar hollow sound, to ask whether there is still solidity and weight in things or whether every possible center of gravity has vanished from them. That is what Nietzsche's thought wants to achieve: it wants to give things weight and importance again.

Even if in the execution much remained unaccomplished and only projected, we should not conclude from the manner of Nietzsche's speech that the rigor and truth of the concept, the relentless effort to ground things by inquiring into them, was of secondary importance for his philosophical exertions. Whatever is a need in Nietzsche, and therefore a right, does not apply to anyone else; for Nietzsche is who he is, and he is unique. Yet such singularity takes on definition and first becomes fruitful when seen within the basic movement of Western thought.

11. The Grounding Question and the Guiding Question of Philosophy

We provided a general characterization of the will as will to power in order to illuminate to some extent the region we must now investigate.

We will begin the interpretation of Book III, "Principle of a New Valuation," with the fourth and final chapter, "Will to Power as Art." As we make clear in rough outline how Nietzsche grasps art and how he approaches the question of art, it will become clear at the same time *why an interpretation of the nucleus of will to power must begin precisely here, with art.*

Of course, it is decisive that the basic philosophical intention of the interpretation be held fast. Let us try to sharpen that intention further. The inquiry goes in the direction of asking what the being is. This traditional "chief question" of Western philosophy we call the guiding question. But it is only the *penultimate* question. The *ultimate,* i.e., *first* question is: what is Being itself? This question, the one which above all is to be unfolded and grounded, we call the grounding question of philosophy, because in it philosophy first inquires into the ground of beings *as ground,* inquiring at the same time into its own ground and in that way grounding itself. Before the question is posed explicitly, philosophy must, if it wants to ground itself, get a firm foothold on the path of an epistemology or doctrine of consciousness; but in so doing it remains forever on a path that leads only to the anteroom of philosophy, as it were, and does not penetrate to the very center of philosophy. The grounding question remains as foreign to Nietzsche as it does to the history of thought prior to him.

But when the guiding question (What is the being?) and the grounding question (What is Being?) are asked, we are asking: What is . . . ? The opening up of beings as a whole and of Being is the target for thought. Beings are to be brought into the open region of Being itself, and Being is to be conducted into the open region of its essence. The openness of beings we call unconcealment—*alētheia,* truth. The guiding and the grounding questions of philosophy ask what beings and Being in truth are. With the question of the essence of Being we are inquiring in such a way that nothing remains outside the question, not even nothingness. Therefore the question of what Being in truth is must at the same time ask what the truth in which Being is to be illumined itself is. Truth stands with Being in the realm of the grounding question, not because the possibility of truth is cast in doubt epistemologically, but because it already belongs to the essence of the grounding question in a distinctive sense, as its "space." In the grounding and guiding questions concerning Being and beings, we are also asking simultaneously and inherently about the essence of truth. "Also" about truth, we say, speaking altogether extrinsically. For truth cannot be what "also" comes forward somewhere in proximity to Being. Rather, the questions will arise as to how both are united in essence and yet are foreign to one another, and "where," in what domain, they somehow come together, and what that domain itself "is." Those are indeed questions that inquire beyond Nietzsche. But they alone provide the guarantee that we will bring his thought out into the open and make it fruitful, and also that we will come to experience and know the essential borders between us, recognizing what is different in him.

But if will to power determines beings as such, which is to say, in their truth, then the question concerning truth, i.e., the question of the essence of truth, must always be inserted into the interpretation of beings as will to power. And if for Nietzsche *art* attains an exceptional position within the task of a general interpretation of all occurrence, which is understood as will to power, then the question of *truth* must play a leading role precisely here.

12. Five Statements on Art

We shall now attempt a first characterization of Nietzsche's total conception of the essence of art. We will do this by exhibiting a sequence of five statements on art which provide weighty evidence.

Why is art of decisive importance for the task of grounding the principle of the new valuation? The immediate answer is found in number 797 of *The Will to Power,* which really ought to stand in the position of number 794* : "The phenomenon 'artist' is still the most *perspicuous*—." At first we will read no further, but consider only this statement. "The most perspicuous," that is, what for us is most accessible in its essence, is the phenomenon "artist"—the being of an artist. With this being, the artist, Being lights up for us most immediately and brightly. Why? Nietzsche does not explicitly say why; yet we can easily discover the reason. To be an artist is to be able to bring something forth. But to bring forth means to establish in Being something that does not yet exist. It is as though in bringing-forth we dwelled upon the coming to be of beings and could see there with utter clarity their essence. Because it is a matter of illuminating will to power as the basic character of beings, the task must begin where what is in question shows itself most brightly. For all clarifying must proceed from what is clear to what is obscure, not the other way round.

Being an artist is a way of *life*. What does Nietzsche say about life in general? He calls life "the form of Being most familiar to us" (WM, 689). For him "Being" itself serves only "as a generalization of the

---

*I.e., as the *first* of all the aphorisms and notes gathered under the title "Will to Power as Art."

concept 'life' (breathing), 'being besouled,' 'willing, effecting,' 'becoming' " (WM, 581). " 'Being'—we have no other way to represent it than as *'living.'* How then can something dead 'be'?" (WM, 582). "If the innermost essence of Being is will to power . . ." (WM, 693).

With these somewhat formula-like references we have already taken measure of the framework within which the "artist phenomenon" is to be conceived, the framework that is to be maintained throughout the coming considerations. We repeat: the being of an artist is the most perspicuous mode of life. Life is for us the most familiar form of Being. The innermost essence of Being is will to power. In the being of the artist we encounter the most perspicuous and most familiar mode of will to power. Since it is a matter of illuminating the Being of beings, meditation on art has in this regard decisive priority.

However, here Nietzsche speaks only of the "artist phenomenon," not about art. Although it is difficult to say what art "as such" is, and how it is, still it is clear that works of art too belong to the reality of art, and furthermore so do those who, as we say, "experience" such works. The artist is but one of those things that together make up the actuality of art as a whole. Certainly, but this is precisely what is decisive in Nietzsche's conception of art, that he sees it in its essential entirety in terms of the *artist;* this he does consciously and in explicit opposition to that conception of art which represents it in terms of those who "enjoy" and "experience" it.

That is a guiding principle of Nietzsche's teaching on art: art must be grasped in terms of creators and producers, not recipients. Nietzsche expresses it unequivocally in the following words (WM, 811): "Our aesthetics heretofore has been a woman's aesthetics, inasmuch as only the recipients of art have formulated their experiences of 'what is beautiful.' In all philosophy to date the artist is missing. . . ." Philosophy of art means "aesthetics" for Nietzsche too—but masculine aesthetics, not feminine aesthetics. The question of art is the question of the artist as the productive, creative one; *his* experiences of what is beautiful must provide the standard.

We now go back to number 797: "The phenomenon 'artist' is still the most *perspicuous*—." If we take the assertion in the guiding context of the question of will to power, with a view to the essence of art, then we derive at once two essential statements about art:

1. Art is the most perspicuous and familiar configuration of will to power;
2. Art must be grasped in terms of the artist.

And now let us read further (WM, 797): ". . . from that position to scan the *basic instincts of power,* of nature, etc.! Also of religion and morals!" Here Nietzsche says explicitly that with a view toward the essence of the artist the other configurations of will to power also— nature, religion, morals, and we might add, society and individual, knowledge, science, and philosophy—are to be observed. These kinds of beings hence correspond in a certain way to the being of the artist, to artistic creativity, and to being created. The remaining beings, which the artist does not expressly bring forth, have the mode of Being that corresponds to what the artist creates, the work of art. Evidence for such a thought we find in the aphorism immediately preceding (WM, 796): "The work of art, where it appears *without* artist, e.g., as body, as organization (the Prussian officer corps, the Jesuit order). To what extent the artist is only a preliminary stage. The world as a work of art that gives birth to itself—." Here the concept of art and of the work of art is obviously extended to every ability to bring forth and to everything that is essentially brought forth. To a certain extent that also corresponds to a usage that was common until the outset of the nineteenth century. Up to that time art meant every kind of ability to bring forth. Craftsmen, statesmen, and educators, as men who brought something forth, were artists. Nature too was an artist, a female artist. At that time art did not mean the current, narrow concept, as applied to "fine art," which brings forth something beautiful in its work.

However, Nietzsche now interprets that earlier, extended usage of art, in which fine art is only one type among others, in such a way that all bringing-forth is conceived as corresponding to fine art and to the artist devoted to it. "The artist is only a preliminary stage" means the artist in the narrower sense, one who brings forth works of fine art. On that basis we can exhibit a third statement about art:

3. According to the expanded concept of artist, art is the basic occurrence of all beings; to the extent that they are, beings are self-creating, created.

But we know that will to power is essentially a creating and destroying. That the basic occurrence of beings is "art" suggests nothing else than that it is will to power.

Long before Nietzsche grasps the essence of art explicitly as a configuration of will to power, in his very first writing, *The Birth of Tragedy from the Spirit of Music,* he sees art as the basic character of beings. Thus we can understand why during the time of his work on *The Will to Power* Nietzsche returns to the position he maintained on art in *The Birth of Tragedy.* An observation that is pertinent here is taken up into *The Will to Power* (WM, 853, Section IV). The final paragraph of the section reads: "Already in the Foreword [i.e., to the book *The Birth of Tragedy*], where Richard Wagner is invited, as it were, to a dialogue, this confession of faith, this artists' gospel, appears: 'art as the proper task of life, art as its *metaphysical* activity. . . .' " "Life" is not only meant in the narrow sense of human life but is identified with "world" in the Schopenhauerian sense. The statement is reminiscent of Schopenhauer, but it is already speaking against him.

Art, thought in the broadest sense as the creative, constitutes the basic character of beings. Accordingly, art in the narrower sense is that activity in which creation emerges for itself and becomes most perspicuous; it is not merely one configuration of will to power among others but the *supreme* configuration. Will to power becomes genuinely visible in terms of art and as art. But will to power is the ground upon which all valuation in the future is to stand. It is the principle of the new valuation, as opposed to the prior one which was dominated by religion, morality, and philosophy. If will to power therefore finds its supreme configuration in art, the positing of the new relation of will to power must proceed from art. Since the new valuation is a revaluation of the prior one, however, opposition and upheaval arise from art. That is averred in *The Will to Power,* no. 794:

Our religion, morality, and philosophy are *decadence*-forms of humanity.
—The *countermovement: art.*

According to Nietzsche's interpretation the very first principle of morality, of Christian religion, and of the philosophy determined by Plato reads as follows: This world is worth nothing; there must be a "better" world than this one, enmeshed as it is in sensuality; there must be a "true world" beyond, a supersensuous world; the world of the senses is but a world of appearances.

In such manner this world and this life are at bottom negated. If a "yes" apparently is uttered to the world, it is ultimately only in order to deny the world all the more decisively. But Nietzsche says that the "true world" of morality is a world of lies, that the true, the supersensuous, is an error. The sensuous world—which in Platonism means the world of semblance and errancy, the realm of error—is the true world. But the sensuous, the sense-semblant, is the very element of art. So it is that art affirms what the supposition of the ostensibly true world denies. Nietzsche therefore says (WM, 853, section II): "Art as the single superior counterforce against all will to negation of life, art as the anti-Christian, anti-Buddhist, anti-Nihilist *par excellence.*" With that we attain a fourth statement about the essence of art:

4. Art is the distinctive countermovement to nihilism.

The artistic creates and gives form. If the artistic constitutes metaphysical activity pure and simple, then every deed, especially the highest deed and thus the thinking of philosophy too, must be determined by it. The concept of philosophy may no longer be defined according to the pattern of the teacher of morality who posits another higher world in opposition to this presumably worthless one. Against the nihilistic philosopher of morality (Schopenhauer hovers before Nietzsche as the most recent example of this type) must be deployed the philosopher who goes counter, who emerges from a countermovement, the "artist-philosopher." Such a philosopher is an artist in that he gives form to beings as a whole, beginning there where they reveal themselves, i.e., in man. It is with this thought in mind that we are to read number 795 of *The Will to Power:*

The *artist*-philosopher. Higher concept of *art.* Whether a man can remove himself far enough from other men, in order to *give them form?* (—Preliminary exercises: 1. the one who gives himself form, the hermit; 2. the artist *hitherto,* as the insignificant perfecter of a piece of raw material.)

Art, particularly in the narrow sense, is yes-saying to the sensuous, to semblance, to what is not "the true world," or as Nietzsche says succinctly, to what is not "the truth."

In art a decision is made about what truth is, and for Nietzsche that always means true beings, i.e., beings proper. This corresponds to the necessary connection between the guiding question and the grounding question of philosophy, on the one hand, and to the question of what truth is, on the other. Art is the will to semblance as the sensuous. But concerning such will Nietzsche says (XIV, 369): "The will to *semblance,* to illusion, to deception, to Becoming and change is deeper, more 'metaphysical,' than the will to *truth,* to reality, to Being." The true is meant here in Plato's sense, as being in itself, the Ideas, the supersensuous. The will to the sensuous world and to its richness is for Nietzsche, on the contrary, the will to what "metaphysics" seeks. Hence the will to the sensuous is metaphysical. That metaphysical will is actual in art.

Nietzsche says (XIV, 368):

> Very early in my life I took the question of the relation of *art* to *truth* seriously: even now I stand in holy dread in the face of this discordance. My first book was devoted to it. *The Birth of Tragedy* believes in art on the background of another belief—that it *is not possible to live with truth,* that the "will to truth" is already a symptom of degeneration.

The statement sounds perverse. But it loses its foreignness, though not its importance, as soon as we read it in the right way. "Will to truth" here (and with Nietzsche always) means the will to the "true world" in the sense of Plato and Christianity, the will to supersensuousness, to being in itself. The will to such "true beings" is in truth a no-saying to our present world, precisely the one in which art is at home. Because this world is the genuinely real and only true world, Nietzsche can declare with respect to the relation of art and truth that "art is *worth more* than truth" (WM, 853, section IV). That is to say, the sensuous stands in a higher place and *is* more genuinely than the supersensuous.

In that regard Nietzsche says, "We have *art* in order *not to perish from the truth*" (WM, 822). Again "truth" means the "true world" of the supersensuous, which conceals in itself the danger that life may perish, "life" in Nietzsche's sense always meaning "life which is on the ascent." The supersensuous lures life away from invigorating sensuality, drains life's forces, weakens it. When we aim at the supersensuous, submission, capitulation, pity, mortification, and abasement become positive "virtues." "The simpletons of this world," the abject, the wretched, become "children of God." They are the true beings. It is the lowly ones who belong "up above" and who are to say what is "lofty," that is, what reaches their own height. For them all creative heightening and all pride in self-subsistent life amount to rebellion, delusion, and sin. But we have art so that we do not perish from such supersensuous "truth," so that the supersensuous does not vitiate life to the point of general debility and ultimate collapse. With regard to the essential relation of art and truth yet another statement about art, the final one in our series, results:

5. Art is worth more than "the truth."

Let us review the preceding statements:

1. Art is the most perspicuous and familiar configuration of will to power;
2. Art must be grasped in terms of the artist;
3. According to the expanded concept of artist, art is the basic occurrence of all beings; to the extent that they are, beings are self-creating, created;
4. Art is the distinctive countermovement to nihilism.

At the instigation of the five statements on art, we should now recall an utterance of Nietzsche's on the same subject cited earlier: ". . . we find it to be the greatest *stimulans* of life—" (WM, 808). Earlier the statement served only as an example of Nietzsche's procedure of reversal (in this case the reversal of Schopenhauer's sedative). Now we must grasp the statement in terms of its most proper content. On the basis of all the intervening material we can easily see that this definition of

art as the stimulant of life means nothing else than that art is a configuration of will to power. For a "stimulant" is what propels and advances,
what lifts a thing beyond itself; it is increase of power and thus power
pure and simple, which is to say, will to power. Hence we cannot merely
append to the five previous statements the one about art as the greatest
stimulant of life. On the contrary, it is Nietzsche's *major statement on
art*. Those five statements enlarge upon it.

On the cursory view, we are already at the end of our task. We were
to indicate art as a configuration of will to power. Such is Nietzsche's
intention. But with a view to Nietzsche we are searching for something
else. We are asking, first, what does this conception of art achieve for
the essential definition of will to power and thereby for that of beings
as a whole? We can come to know that only if beforehand we ask,
second, what is the significance of this interpretation for our knowledge
of art and for our position with respect to it?

13. Six Basic Developments in the History of Aesthetics

We shall begin with the second question. In order to come to terms with it we must characterize Nietzsche's procedure for defining the essence of art with greater penetration and must place it in the context of previous efforts to gain knowledge of art.

With the five statements on art that we brought forward the essential aspects of Nietzsche's interrogation of art have been established. From them one thing is clear: Nietzsche does not inquire into art in order to describe it as a cultural phenomenon or as a monument to civilization. Rather, by means of art and a characterization of the essence of art, he wants to show what will to power is. Nevertheless, Nietzsche's meditation on art keeps to the traditional path. The path is defined in its peculiarity by the term "aesthetics." True, Nietzsche speaks against feminine aesthetics. But in so doing he speaks for masculine aesthetics, hence for aesthetics. In that way Nietzsche's interrogation of art is aesthetics driven to the extreme, an aesthetics, so to speak, that somersaults beyond itself. But what else should inquiry into art and knowledge of it be than "aesthetics"? What does "aesthetics" mean?

The term "aesthetics" is formed in the same manner as "logic" and "ethics." The word *epistēmē,* knowledge, must always complete these terms. Logic: *logikē epistēmē:* knowledge of *logos,* that is, the doctrine of assertion or judgment as the basic form of thought. Logic is knowledge of thinking, of the forms and rules of thought. Ethics: *ēthikē epistēmē:* knowledge of *ēthos,* of the inner character of man and of the way it determines his behavior. Logic and ethics both refer to human behavior and its lawfulness.

The word "aesthetics" is formed in the corresponding way: *aisthētikē epistēmē:* knowledge of human behavior with regard to sense, sensation, and feeling, and knowledge of how these are determined.

What determines thinking, hence logic, and what thinking comports itself toward, is the true. What determines the character and behavior of man, hence ethics, and what human character and behavior comport themselves toward, is the good. What determines man's feeling, hence aesthetics, and what feeling comports itself toward, is the beautiful. The true, the good, and the beautiful are the objects of logic, ethics, and aesthetics.

Accordingly, aesthetics is consideration of man's state of feeling in its relation to the beautiful; it is consideration of the beautiful to the extent that it stands in relation to man's state of feeling. The beautiful itself is nothing other than what in its self-showing brings forth that state. But the beautiful can pertain to either nature or art. Because art in its way brings forth the beautiful, inasmuch as it is "fine" art, meditation on art becomes aesthetics. With relation to knowledge of art and inquiry into it, therefore, aesthetics is that kind of meditation on art in which man's affinity to the beautiful represented in art sets the standard for all definitions and explanations, man's state of feeling remaining the point of departure and the goal of the meditation. The relation of feeling toward art and its bringing-forth can be one of production or of reception and enjoyment.

Now, since in the aesthetic consideration of art the artwork is defined as the beautiful which has been brought forth in art, the work is represented as the bearer and provoker of the beautiful with relation to our state of feeling. The artwork is posited as the "object" for a "subject"; definitive for aesthetic consideration is the subject-object relation, indeed as a relation of feeling. The work becomes an object in terms of that surface which is accessible to "lived experience."

Just as we say that a judgment that satisfies the laws of thought promulgated in logic is "logical," so do we apply the designation "aesthetic," which really only means a kind of observation and investigation with regard to a relation of feeling, to this sort of behavior itself. We speak of aesthetic feeling and an aesthetic state. Strictly speaking, a state of feeling is not "aesthetic." It is rather something that can become the object of aesthetic consideration. Such consideration is called "aesthetic" because it observes from the outset the state of feeling aroused by the beautiful, relates everything to that state, and defines all else in terms of it.

The name "aesthetics," meaning meditation on art and the beautiful, is recent. It arises in the eighteenth century. But the matter which the word so aptly names, the manner of inquiry into art and the beautiful on the basis of the state of feeling in enjoyers and producers, is old, as old as meditation on art and the beautiful in Western thought. Philosophical meditation on the essence of art and the beautiful even *begins* as aesthetics.

In recent decades we have often heard the complaint that the innumerable aesthetic considerations of and investigations into art and the beautiful have achieved nothing, that they have not helped anyone to gain access to art, that they have contributed virtually nothing to artistic creativity and to a sound appreciation of art. That is certainly true, especially with regard to the kind of thing bandied about today under the name "aesthetics." But we dare not derive our standards for judging aesthetics and its relation to art from such contemporary work. For, in truth, the fact whether and how an era is committed to an aesthetics, whether and how it adopts a stance toward art of an aesthetic character, is decisive for the way art shapes the history of that era—or remains irrelevant for it.

Because what stands in question for us is art as a configuration of will to power, which is to say, as a configuration of Being in general, indeed the distinctive one, the question of aesthetics as the basic sort of meditation on art and the knowledge of it can be treated only with respect to fundamentals. Only with the help of a reflection on the essence of aesthetics developed in this way can we get to the point where we can grasp Nietzsche's interpretation of the essence of art; only with the help of such a reflection can we at the same time take a position with regard to Nietzsche's interpretation, so that on this basis a *confrontation* can flourish.

In order to characterize the essence of aesthetics, its role in Western thought, and its relation to the history of Western art, we shall introduce six basic developments for consideration. Such consideration, of course, can only be by way of brief reference.

1. The magnificent art of Greece remains without a corresponding cognitive-conceptual meditation on it, such meditation not having to be identical with aesthetics. The lack of such a simultaneous reflection or meditation on great art does not imply that Greek art was only "lived," that the Greeks wallowed in a murky brew of "experiences" braced by neither concepts nor knowledge. It was their good fortune that the Greeks had no "lived experiences." On the contrary, they had such an originally mature and luminous knowledge, such a passion for knowledge, that in their luminous state of knowing they had no need of "aesthetics."

2. Aesthetics begins with the Greeks only at that moment when their great art and also the great philosophy that flourished along with it comes to an end. At that time, during the age of Plato and Aristotle, in connection with the organization of philosophy as a whole, those basic concepts are formed which mark off the boundaries for all future inquiry into art. One of those basic notions is the conceptual pair *hylē-morphē, materia-forma,* matter-form. The distinction has its origin in the conception of beings founded by Plato, the conception of beings with regard to their outer appearance: *eidos, idea.* Where beings are apprehended as beings, and distinguished from other beings, in view of their outer appearance, the demarcation and arrangement of beings in terms of outer and inner limits enters on the scene. But what limits is form, what is limited is matter. Whatever comes into view as soon as the work of art is experienced as a self-showing according to its *eidos,* as *phainesthai,* is now subsumed under these definitions. The *ekphanestaton,* what properly shows itself and is most radiant of all, is the beautiful. By way of the *idea,* the work of art comes to appear in the designation of the beautiful as *ekphanestaton.*

With the distinction of *hylē-morphē,* which pertains to beings as such, a second concept is coupled which comes to guide all inquiry into art: art is *technē.* We have long known that the Greeks name art as well as handicraft with the same word, *technē,* and name correspondingly both the craftsman and the artist *technitēs*. In accordance with the later "technical" use of the word *technē*, where it designates (in a way utterly foreign to the Greeks) a mode of production, we seek even in the original and genuine significance of the word such later content: we aver that *technē* means hand manufacture. But because what we call fine art is also designated by the Greeks as *technē*, we believe that this implies a glorification of handicraft, or else that the exercise of art is degraded to the level of a handicraft.

However illuminating the common belief may be, it is not adequate to the actual state of affairs; that is to say, it does not penetrate to the basic position from which the Greeks define art and the work of art. But this will become clear when we examine the fundamental word *technē*. In order to catch hold of its true significance, it is advisable to establish the concept that properly counters it. The latter is named in the word *physis*. We translate it with "nature," and think little enough about it. For the Greeks, *physis* is the first and the essential name for beings themselves and as a whole. For them the being is what flourishes on its own, in no way compelled, what rises and comes forward, and what goes back into itself and passes away. It is the rule that rises and resides in itself.

If man tries to win a foothold and establish himself among the beings (*physis*) to which he is exposed, if he proceeds to master beings in this or that way, then his advance against beings is borne and guided by a knowledge of them. Such *knowledge* is called *technē*. From the very outset the word is not, and never is, the designation of a "making" and a producing; rather, it designates that knowledge which supports and conducts every human irruption into the midst of beings. For that reason *technē* is often the word for human knowledge without qualification. The kind of knowledge that guides and grounds confrontation with and mastery over beings, in which new and other beings are expressly produced and generated in addition to and on the basis of the beings that have already come to be (*physis*), in other words, the kind of knowledge that produces utensils and works of art, is then specially designated by the word *technē*. But even here, *technē* never means making or manufacturing as such; it always means knowledge, the disclosing of beings as such, in the manner of a knowing guidance of bringing-forth. Now, since the manufacture of utensils and the creation of artworks each in its way inheres in the immediacy of everyday existence, the knowledge that guides such procedures and modes of bringing-forth is called *technē* in an exceptional sense. The artist is a *technitēs*, not because he too is a handworker, but because the bringing-forth of artworks as well as utensils is an irruption by the man who knows and who goes forward in the midst of *physis* and upon its basis. Nevertheless, such "going forward," thought in Greek fashion, is no kind of attack: it lets what is already coming to presence arrive.

With the emergence of the distinction between matter and form, the essence of *technē* undergoes an interpretation in a particular direction; it loses the force of its original, broad significance. In Aristotle *technē* is still a mode of knowing, if only one among others (see the *Nicomachean Ethics*, Bk. VI). If we understand the word "art" quite generally to mean every sort of human capacity to bring forth, and if in addition we grasp the capacity and ability more originally as a knowing, then the word "art" corresponds to the Greek concept of *technē* also in its broad significance. But to the extent that *technē* is then brought expressly into relation with the production of beautiful things, or their representation, meditation on art is diverted by way of the beautiful into the realm of aesthetics. What in truth is decided in the apparently extrinsic and, according to the usual view, even misguided designation of art as *technē* never comes to light, neither with the Greeks nor in later times.

But here we cannot show how the conceptual pair "matter and form" came to be the really principal schema for all inquiry into art and all further definition of the work of art. Nor can we show how the distinction of "form and content" ultimately came to be a concept applicable to everything under the sun, a concept under which anything and everything was to be subsumed. It suffices to know that the distinction of "matter and form" sprang from the area of manufacture of tools or utensils, that it was not originally acquired in the realm of art in the narrower sense, i.e., fine art and works of art, but that it was merely transferred and applied to this realm. Which is reason enough to be dominated by a deep and abiding doubt concerning the trenchancy of these concepts when it comes to discussions about art and works of art.

3. The third basic development for the history of knowledge about art, and that now means the origin and formation of aesthetics, is once again a happenstance that does not flow immediately from art or from meditation on it. On the contrary, it is an occurrence that involves our entire history. It is the beginning of the modern age. Man and his unconstrained knowledge of himself, as of his position among beings, become the arena where the decision falls as to how beings are to be experienced, defined, and shaped. Falling back upon the state and condition of man, upon the way man stands before himself and before things, implies that now the very way man freely takes a position toward things, the way he finds and feels them to be, in short, his "taste," becomes the court of judicature over beings. In metaphysics that becomes manifest in the way in which certitude of all Being and all truth is grounded in the self-consciousness of the individual ego: *ego cogito ergo sum*. Such finding ourselves before ourselves in our own state and condition, the *cogito me cogitare*, also provides the first "object" which is secured in its Being. I myself, and my states, are the primary and genuine beings. Everything else that may be said to be is measured against the standard of this quite certain being. My having various states—the ways I find myself to be with something—participates essentially in defining how I find the things themselves and everything I encounter to be.

Meditation on the beautiful in art now slips markedly, even exclusively, into the relationship of man's state of feeling, *aisthēsis*. No wonder that in recent centuries aesthetics as such has been grounded and conscientiously pursued. That also explains why the name only now comes into use as a mode of observation for which the way had long been paved: "aesthetics" is to be in the field of sensuousness and feeling precisely what logic is in the area of thinking—which is why it is also called "logic of sensuousness."

Parallel to the formation of aesthetics and to the effort to clarify and ground the aesthetic state, another decisive process unfolds within the history of art. Great art and its works are great in their historical emergence and Being because in man's historical existence they accomplish a decisive task: they make manifest, in the way appropriate to works, what beings as a whole are, preserving such manifestation in the work. Art and its works are necessary only as an itinerary and sojourn for man in which the truth of beings as a whole, i.e., the unconditioned, the absolute, opens itself up to him. What makes art great is not only and not in the first place the high quality of what is created. Rather, art is great because it is an "absolute need." Because it is that, and to the extent it is that, it also can and must be great in rank. For only on the basis of the magnitude of its essential character does it also create a dimension of magnitude for the rank and stature of what is brought forth.

Concurrent with the formation of a dominant aesthetics and of the aesthetic relation to art in modern times is the decline of great art, great in the designated sense. Such decline does not result from the fact that the "quality" is poorer and the style less imposing; it is rather that art forfeits its essence, loses its immediate relation to the basic task of representing the absolute, i.e., of establishing the absolute definitively as such in the realm of historical man. From this vantage point we can grasp the fourth basic development.

4. At the historical moment when aesthetics achieves its greatest possible height, breadth, and rigor of form, great art comes to an end. The achievement of aesthetics derives its greatness from the fact that it recognizes and gives utterance to the end of great art as such. The final and greatest aesthetics in the Western tradition is that of Hegel. It is recorded in his *Lectures on Aesthetics*, held for the last time at the University of Berlin in 1828–29 (see Hegel's *Works*, vol. X, parts 1, 2 and 3). Here the following statements appear:

> ... yet in this regard there is at least no absolute need at hand for it [the matter] to be brought to representation by *art* (X, 2, p. 233).

> In all these relations art is and remains for us, with regard to its highest determination, something past (X, 1, p. 16).

> The magnificent days of Greek art, like the golden era of the later Middle Ages, are gone (X, 1, pp. 15–16).

One cannot refute these statements and overcome all the history and happenings that stand behind them by objecting against Hegel that since 1830 we have had many considerable works of art which we might point to. Hegel never wished to deny the possibility that also in the future individual works of art would originate and be esteemed. The fact of such individual works, which exist as works only for the enjoyment of a few sectors of the population, does not speak against Hegel but for him. It is proof that art has lost its power to be the absolute, has lost its absolute power. On the basis of such loss the position of art and the kind of knowledge concerning it are defined for the nineteenth century. This we can demonstrate briefly in a fifth point.

5. Catching a glimpse of the decline of art from its essence, the nineteenth century once more dares to attempt the "collective artwork." That effort is associated with the name Richard Wagner. It is no accident that his effort does not limit itself to the creation of works that might serve such an end. His effort is accompanied and undergirded by reflections on the principles of such works, and by corresponding treatises, the most important of which are *Art and Revolution* (1849), *The Artwork of the Future* (1850), *Opera and Drama* (1851), *German Art and German Politics* (1865). It is not possible here to clarify to any great extent the complicated and confused historical and intellectual milieu of the mid-nineteenth century. In the decade 1850–1860 two streams interpenetrate in a remarkable fashion, the genuine and well-preserved tradition of the great age of the German movement, and the slowly expanding wasteland, the uprooting of human existence, which comes to light fully during the Gilded Age. One can never understand this most ambiguous century by describing the sequence of its periods. It must be demarcated simultaneously from both ends, i.e., from the last third of the eighteenth century and the first third of the twentieth.

Here we have to be satisfied with one indication, delineated by our guiding area of inquiry. With reference to the historical position of art, the effort to produce the "collective artwork" remains essential. The very name is demonstrative. For one thing, it means that the arts should no longer be realized apart from one another, that they should be conjoined in *one* work. But beyond such sheer quantitative unification, the artwork should be a celebration of the national community, it should be *the* religion. In that respect the definitive arts are literary and musical. Theoretically, music is to be a means for achieving effective drama; in reality, however, music in the form of opera becomes the authentic art. Drama possesses its importance and essential character, not in poetic originality, i.e., not in the well-wrought truth of the linguistic work, but in things pertaining to the stage, theatrical arrangements and gala productions. Architecture serves merely for theater construction, painting provides the backdrops, sculpture portrays the gestures of actors. Literary creation and language remain without the essential and decisive shaping force of genuine knowledge. What is wanted is the domination of art as music, and thereby the domination of the pure state of feeling—the tumult and delirium of the senses, tremendous contraction, the felicitous distress that swoons in enjoyment, absorption in "the bottomless sea of harmonies," the plunge into frenzy and the disintegration into sheer feeling as redemptive. The "lived experience" as such becomes decisive. The work is merely what arouses such experience. All portrayal is to work its effects as foreground and superficies, aiming toward the impression, the effect, wanting to work on and arouse the audience: theatrics. Theater and orchestra determine art. Of the orchestra Wagner says:

> The orchestra is, so to speak, the basis of infinite, universally common feeling, from which the individual feeling of the particular artist can blossom to the greatest fullness: it dissolves to a certain extent the static, motionless basis of the scene of reality into a liquid-soft, flexible, impressionable, ethereal surface, the immeasurable ground of which is the sea of feeling itself. (*The Artwork of the Future,* in *Gesammelte Schriften und Dichtungen,* 2nd ed., 1887, p. 157.)

To this we should compare what Nietzsche says in *The Will to Power* (WM, 839) about Wagner's "means of achieving effects":

> Consider the means of achieving effects to which Wagner most likes to turn (and which for the most part he had to invent): to an astonishing extent they resemble the means by which the hypnotist achieves his effect (his selection

of tempi and tonal hues for his orchestra; a repulsive avoidance of the logic and intervals of rhythm; the lingering, soothing, mysterious, hysterical quality of his "endless melody"). And is the state to which the prelude to *Lohengrin* reduces its listeners, especially the lady listeners, essentially different from that of a somnambulistic trance?—I heard an Italian woman who had just listened to that prelude say, flashing those lovely mesmerized eyes that Wagneriennes know how to affect, "Come si *dorme* con questa musica!"

Here the essential character of the conception "collective artwork" comes to unequivocal expression: the dissolution of everything solid into a fluid, flexible, malleable state, into a swimming and floundering; the unmeasured, without laws or borders, clarity or definiteness; the boundless night of sheer submergence. In other words, art is once again to become an absolute need. But now the absolute is experienced as sheer indeterminacy, total dissolution into sheer feeling, a hovering that gradually sinks into nothingness. No wonder Wagner found the metaphysical confirmation and explanation of his art in Schopenhauer's main work, which he studied diligently four different times.

However persistently Wagner's will to the "collective artwork" in its results and influence became the very opposite of great art, the will itself remains singular for his time. It raises Wagner—in spite of his theatricality and recklessness—above the level of other efforts focusing on art and its essential role in existence. In that regard Nietzsche writes (XIV, 150–51):

Without any doubt, Wagner gave the Germans of this era the most considerable indication of what an artist *could* be: reverence for "the artist" suddenly grew to great heights; he awakened on all sides new evaluations, new desires, new hopes; and this perhaps not least of all because of the merely preparatory, incomplete, imperfect nature of his artistic products. Who has not *learned* from him!

That Richard Wagner's attempt had to fail does not result merely from the predominance of music with respect to the other arts in his work. Rather, that the music could assume such preeminence at all has its grounds in the increasingly aesthetic posture taken toward art as a whole—it is the conception and estimation of art in terms of the unalloyed state of feeling and the growing barbarization of the very state to the point where it becomes the sheer bubbling and boiling of feeling abandoned to itself.

And yet such arousal of frenzied feeling and unchaining of "affects" could be taken as a rescue of "life," especially in view of the growing impoverishment and deterioration of existence occasioned by industry, technology, and finance, in connection with the enervation and depletion of the constructive forces of knowledge and tradition, to say nothing of the lack of every establishment of goals for human existence. Rising on swells of feeling would have to substitute for a solidly grounded and articulated position in the midst of beings, the kind of thing that only great poetry and thought can create.

It was the frenzied plunge into the whole of things in Richard Wagner's person and work that captivated the young Nietzsche; yet his captivation was possible only because something correlative came from him, what he then called the Dionysian. But since Wagner sought sheer upsurgence of the Dionysian upon which one might ride, while Nietzsche sought to leash its force and give it form, the breach between the two was already predetermined.

Without getting into the history of the friendship between Wagner and Nietzsche here, we shall indicate briefly the proper root of the conflict that developed early on, slowly, but ever more markedly and decisively. On Wagner's part, the reason for the breach was personal in the widest sense: Wagner did not belong to that group of men for whom their own followers are the greatest source of revulsion. Wagner required Wagnerians and Wagneriennes. So far as the personal aspect is concerned, Nietzsche loved and respected Wagner all his life. His struggle with Wagner was an essential one, involving real issues. Nietzsche waited for many years, hoping for the possibility of a fruitful confrontation with Wagner. His opposition to Wagner involved two things. First, Wagner's neglect of inner feeling and proper style. Nietzsche expressed it once this way: with Wagner it is all "floating and swimming" instead of "striding and dancing," which is to say, it is a floundering devoid of measure and pace. Second, Wagner's deviation into an insincere, moralizing Christianity mixed with delirium and tumult. (See *Nietzsche contra Wagner,* 1888; on the relationship of Wagner and Nietzsche, cf. Kurt Hildebrandt, *Wagner und Nietzsche: ihr Kampf gegen das 19. Jahrhundert,* Breslau, 1924).

We hardly need to note explicitly that in the nineteenth century there were sundry essential works in the various artistic genres besides those of Wagner's and even opposed to his. We know, for example, in what high esteem Nietzsche held such a work as Adalbert Stifter's *Late Summer,* whose world is well-nigh the perfect antithesis to that of Wagner.

But what matters is the question of whether and how art is still known and willed as the definitive formation and preservation of beings as a whole. The question is answered by the reference to the attempt to develop a collective artwork on the basis of music and to its inevitable demise. Corresponding to the growing incapacity for metaphysical knowledge, knowledge of art in the nineteenth century is transformed into discovery and investigation of mere developments in art history. What in the age of Herder and Winckelmann stood in service to a magnificent self-meditation on historical existence is now carried on for its own sake, i.e., as an academic discipline. Research into the history of art as such begins. (Of course, figures like Jacob Burckhardt and Hippolyte Taine, as different from one another as they may be, cannot be measured according to such academic standards.) Examination of literary works now enters the realm of philology; "it developed in its sense for the minuscule, for genuine philology" (Wilhelm Dilthey, *Gesammelte Schriften,* XI, 216). Aesthetics becomes a psychology that proceeds in the manner of the natural sciences: states of feeling are taken to be facts that come forward of themselves and may be subjected to experiments, observation, and measurement. (Here Friedrich Theodor Vischer and Wilhelm Dilthey are also exceptions, supported and guided by the tradition of Hegel and Schiller.) The history of literature and creative art is ostensibly of such a nature that there can be a science of art and literature that brings to light important insights and at the same time keeps alive the cultivation of thought. Pursuit of such science is taken to be the proper actuality of the "spirit." Science itself is, like art, a cultural phenomenon and an area of cultural activity. But wherever the "aesthetic" does not become an object of research but determines the character of man, the aesthetic state becomes one among other possible states, e.g., the political or the scientific. The "aesthetic man" is a nineteenth-century hybrid.

> The aesthetic man seeks to realize balance and harmony of feelings in himself and in others. On the basis of this need he forms his feeling for life and his intuitions of the world. His estimation of reality depends on the extent to which reality guarantees the conditions for such an existence. (Dilthey, in commemoration of the literary historian Julian Schmidt, 1887; *Gesammelte Schriften,* XI, 232.)

But there must be culture, because man must progress—whither, no one knows, and no one is seriously asking anymore. Besides, one still has his "Christianity" at the ready, and his Church; these are already becoming essentially more political than religious institutions.

The world is examined and evaluated on the basis of its capacity to produce the aesthetic state. The aesthetic man believes that he is protected and vindicated by the whole of a culture. In all of that there is still a good bit of ambition and labor, and at times even good taste and genuine challenge. Nevertheless, it remains the mere foreground of that occurrence which Nietzsche is the first to recognize and proclaim with full clarity: nihilism. With that we come to the final development to be mentioned. We already know its contents, but they now require explicit definition.

6. What Hegel asserted concerning art—that it had lost its power to be the definite fashioner and preserver of the absolute—Nietzsche recognized to be the case with the "highest values," religion, morality, and philosophy: the lack of creative force and cohesion in grounding man's historical existence upon beings as a whole.

Whereas for Hegel it was art—in contrast to religion, morality, and philosophy—that fell victim to nihilism and became a thing of the past, something nonactual, for Nietzsche art is to be pursued as the counter-movement. In spite of Nietzsche's essential departure from Wagner, we see in this an outgrowth of the Wagnerian will to the "collective artwork." Whereas for Hegel art as a thing of the past became an object of the highest speculative knowledge, so that Hegel's aesthetics assumed the shape of a metaphysics of spirit, Nietzsche's meditation on art becomes a "physiology of art."

In the brief work *Nietzsche contra Wagner* (1888) Nietzsche says (VIII, 187): "Of course, aesthetics is nothing else than applied physiology." It is therefore no longer even "psychology," as it usually is in the nineteenth century, but investigation of bodily states and processes and their activating causes by methods of natural science.

We must keep the state of affairs quite clearly in view: on the one hand, art in its historical determination as the countermovement to nihilism; on the other, knowledge of art as "physiology"; art is delivered over to explanation in terms of natural science, relegated to an area of the science of facts. Here indeed the aesthetic inquiry into art in its ultimate consequences is thought to an end. The state of feeling is to be traced back to excitations of the nervous system, to bodily conditions.

With that we have defined more closely both Nietzsche's basic position toward art as historical actuality and the way in which he knows and wants to know about art: aesthetics as applied physiology. But at the same time we have assigned places to both in the broad context of the history of art, in terms of the relation of that history to the knowledge of art prevailing at a given time.

14. Rapture as Aesthetic State*

But our genuine intention is to conceive of art as a configuration of will to power, indeed as its distinctive form. This means that on the basis of Nietzsche's conception of art and by means of that very conception we want to grasp will to power itself in its essence, and thereby being as a whole with regard to its basic character. To do that we must now try to grasp Nietzsche's conception of art in a unified way, which is to say, to conjoin in thought things that at first blush seem to run wholly contrary ways. On the one hand, art is to be the countermovement to nihilism, that is, the establishment of the new supreme values; it is to prepare and ground standards and laws for historical, intellectual existence. On the other hand, art is at the same time to be properly grasped by way of physiology and with its means.

Viewed extrinsically, it seems easy to designate Nietzsche's position toward art as senseless, nonsensical, and therefore nihilistic. For if art is just a matter of physiology, then the essence and reality of art dissolve into nervous states, into processes in the nerve cells. Where in such

---

*Der Rausch als ästhetischer Zustand. Rausch is commonly rendered as "frenzy" in translations of Nietzsche's writings, but "rapture," from the past participle of rapere, to seize, seems in some respects a better alternative. No single English word—rapture, frenzy, ecstasy, transport, intoxication, delirium—can capture all the senses of Rausch. Our word "rush" is related to it: something "rushes over" us and sweeps us away. In modern German Rausch most often refers to drunken frenzy or narcotic intoxication, as Heidegger will indicate below; but Nietzsche's sense for the Dionysian is both more variegated and more subtle than that, and I have chosen the word "rapture" because of its complex erotic and religious background. But Rausch is more than a problem of translation. The reader is well advised to examine Nietzsche's analyses of Rausch in the works Heidegger cites in this section, especially Die Geburt der Tragödie and Götzen-Dämmerung.

blind transactions are we to find something that could of itself determine meaning, posit values, and erect standards?

In the realm of natural processes, conceived scientifically, where the only law that prevails is that of the sequence and commensurability (or incommensurability) of cause-effect relations, every result is equally essential and inessential. In this area there is no establishment of rank or positing of standards. Everything is the way it is, and remains what it is, having its right simply in the fact that it is. Physiology knows no arena in which something could be set up for decision and choice. To deliver art over to physiology seems tantamount to reducing art to the functional level of the gastric juices. Then how could art also ground and determine the genuine and decisive valuation? Art as the counter-movement to nihilism and art as the object of physiology—that's like trying to mix fire and water. If a unification is at all possible here, it can only occur in such a way that art, as an object of physiology, is declared the utter apotheosis of nihilism—and not at all the counter-movement to it.

And yet in the innermost will of Nietzsche's thought the situation is altogether different. True, there is a perpetual discordance prevailing in what he achieves, an instability, an oscillation between these opposite poles which, perceived from the outside, can only confuse. In what follows we will confront the discordancy again and again. But above all else we must try to see what it is that is "altogether different" here.

All the same, in so trying we may not close our eyes to what Nietzsche's aesthetics-as-physiology says about art and how it says it. To be sure, a conclusive presentation of that aesthetics is seriously impaired by the fact that Nietzsche left behind only undetailed observations, references, plans, and claims. We do not even possess an intrinsic, carefully projected outline of his aesthetics. True, among the plans for *The Will to Power* we find one of Nietzsche's own sketches with the title "Toward the Physiology of Art" (XVI, 432–34). But it is only a list of seventeen items, not arranged according to any visible guiding thought. We will present in full this collection of headings of investigations that remained to be carried out, because in terms of pure content it offers an immediate overview of what such an aesthetics was to treat.

TOWARD THE PHYSIOLOGY OF ART

1. Rapture as presupposition: causes of rapture.
2. Typical symptoms of rapture.
3. The *feeling* of force and plenitude in rapture: its *idealizing* effect.
4. The factual *increase* of *force:* its factual beautification. (The increase of force, e.g., in the *dance* of the sexes.) The pathological element in rapture: the physiological danger of art—. For consideration: the extent to which our value "beautiful" is completely *anthropocentric:* based on biological presuppositions concerning growth and progress—.
5. The Apollonian, the Dionysian: basic types. In broader terms, compared with our specialized arts.
6. Question: where architecture belongs.
7. The part artistic capacities play in normal life, the tonic effect of their exercise: as opposed to the ugly.
8. The question of epidemic and contagion.
9. Problem of "health" and "hysteria": genius = neurosis.
10. Art as suggestion, as means of communication, as the realm of invention of the *induction psycho-motrice.*
11. The inartistic states: objectivity, the mania to mirror everything, neutrality. The impoverished *will;* loss of capital.
12. The inartistic states: abstractness. The impoverished *senses.*
13. The inartistic states: vitiation, impoverishment, depletion—will to nothingness (Christian, Buddhist, nihilist). The impoverished *body.*
14. The inartistic states: the *moral* idiosyncrasy. The fear that characterizes the weak, the mediocre, before the senses, power, rapture (instinct of those whom life has defeated).
15. How is *tragic* art possible?
16. The romantic type: ambiguous. Its consequence is "naturalism."
17. Problem of the *actor.* The "dishonesty," the typical ability to metamorphose as a *flaw in character*.... Lack of shame, the Hanswurst, the satyr, the buffo, the Gil Blas, the actor who plays the artist....*

---

*The new historical-critical edition of Nietzsche's works (CM VIII, 3, p. 328) lists an eighteenth note, printed in none of the earlier editions.

18. Die Kunst als *Rausch,* medizinisch: Amnestie. tonicum ganze und partielle Impotenz.

The meaning of the passage is anything but obvious; it is easy to understand why previous editors let it fall. An attempt at translation:

18. Art as *rapture,* medically: tonic oblivion, complete and partial impotence.

A multiplicity of different points of inquiry lies before us here, but no blueprint or outline of a structure, not even a preliminary mapping out of the space in which all this is to be joined. Yet at bottom the same is the case with those fragments assembled between numbers 794 and 853 in *The Will to Power,* except that these go beyond mere catchwords and headlines in providing greater detail. The same is also true of the pieces taken up into volume XIV, pp. 131–201, which belong here thematically. We must therefore try all the harder to bring a higher determination and an essential coherence to the materials that lie before us. To that end we will follow a twofold guideline: for one thing, we will try to keep in view the whole of the doctrine of will to power; for another, we will recall the major doctrines of traditional aesthetics.

But on our way we do not want merely to become cognizant of Nietzsche's teachings on aesthetics. Rather, we want to conceive how the apparently antithetical directions of his basic position with respect to art can be reconciled: art as countermovement to nihilism and art as object of physiology. If a unity prevails here, eventuating from the essence of art itself as Nietzsche sees it, and if art is a configuration of will to power, then insight into the possibility of unity between the antithetical determinations should provide us with a higher concept of the essence of will to power. That is the goal of our presentation of the major teachings of Nietzsche's aesthetics.

At the outset we must refer to a general peculiarity of most of the larger fragments: Nietzsche begins his reflections from various points of inquiry within the field of aesthetics, but he manages at once to touch upon the general context. So it is that many fragments treat the same thing, the only difference being in the order of the material and the distribution of weight or importance. In what follows we shall forego discussion of those sections that are easy to comprehend on the basis of ordinary experience.

Nietzsche's inquiry into art is aesthetics. According to the definitions provided earlier, art in aesthetics is experienced and defined by falling back upon the state of feeling in man that corresponds and pertains to the bringing-forth and the enjoyment of the beautiful. Nietzsche himself uses the expression "aesthetic state" (WM, 801) and speaks of "aesthetic doing and observing" (VIII, 122). But this aesthetics is to be "physiology." That suggests that states of feeling, taken to be purely psychical, are to be traced back to the bodily condition proper to them. Seen as a whole, it is precisely the unbroken and indissoluble unity of the corporeal-psychical, the living, that is posited as the realm of the aesthetic state: the living "nature" of man.

When Nietzsche says "physiology" he does mean to emphasize the bodily state; but the latter is in itself always already something psychical, and therefore also a matter for "psychology." The bodily state of an animal and even of man is essentially different from the property of a "natural body," for example, a stone. Every body is also a natural body, but the reverse does not hold. On the other hand, when Nietzsche says "psychology" he always means what also pertains to bodily states (the physiological). Instead of "aesthetic" Nietzsche often speaks more correctly of "artistic" or "inartistic" states. Although he sees art from the point of view of the artist, and demands that it be seen that way, Nietzsche does not mean the expression "artistic" only with reference to the artist. Rather, artistic and inartistic states are those that support and advance—or hamper and preclude—a relation to art of a creative or receptive sort.

The basic question of an aesthetics as physiology of art, and that means of the artist, must above all aim to reveal those special states in the essence of the corporeal-psychical, i.e., living nature of man in which artistic doing and observing occur, as it were, in conformity with and confinement to nature. In defining the basic aesthetic state we shall at first not refer to the text of *The Will to Power* but restrict ourselves to what Nietzsche says in the last writing he himself published (*Twilight of the Idols*, 1888; VIII, 122–23). The passage reads:

> *Toward the psychology of the artist.* — If there is to be art, if there is to be any aesthetic doing and observing, one physiological precondition is indispensable: *rapture*. Rapture must first have augmented the excitability of the entire machine: else it does not come to art. All the variously conditioned forms of rapture have the requisite force: above all, the rapture of sexual arousal, the oldest and most original form of rapture. In addition, the rapture that comes as a consequence of all great desires, all strong affects;

the rapture of the feast, contest, feat of daring, victory; all extreme movement; the rapture of cruelty; rapture in destruction; rapture under certain meteorological influences, for example, the rapture of springtime; or under the influence of narcotics; finally, the rapture of will, of an overfull, teeming will.

We can summarize these remarks with the general statement that rapture is the basic aesthetic state, a rapture which for its part is variously conditioned, released, and increased. The passage cited was not chosen simply because Nietzsche published it but because it achieves the greatest clarity and unity of all the Nietzschean definitions of the aesthetic state. We can readily discern what remains unresolved throughout the final period of Nietzsche's creative life, although in terms of the matter itself it does not deviate essentially from what has gone before, when we compare to this passage number 798 (and the beginning of 799) of *The Will to Power.* Here Nietzsche speaks of "two states in which art itself emerges as a force of nature in man." According to the aphorism's title, the two states meant are the "Apollonian" and the "Dionysian." Nietzsche developed the distinction and opposition in his first writing, *The Birth of Tragedy from the Spirit of Music* (1872). Even here, at the very beginning of his distinguishing between the Apollonian and the Dionysian, the "physiological symptoms" of "dream" and "rapture" were brought into respective relation. We still find this connection in *The Will to Power,* number 798 (from the year 1888!): "Both states are rehearsed in normal life as well, only more weakly: in dreams and in rapture." Here, as earlier, rapture is but one of the two aesthetic states, juxtaposed to the dream. But from the passage in *Twilight of the Idols* we gather that rapture is the basic aesthetic state without qualification. Nonetheless, in terms of the genuine issue the same conception prevails also in *The Will to Power.* The first sentence of the following aphorism (WM, 799) reads: "In Dionysian rapture there is sexuality and voluptuousness: in the Apollonian they are not lacking." According to *The Birth of Tragedy,* to the remarks in *The Will to Power,* number 798, and elsewhere, the Dionysian alone is the rapturous and the Apollonian the dreamlike; now, in *Twilight of the Idols,* the Dionysian and the Apollonian are two kinds of rapture, rapture itself being the basic state. Nietzsche's ultimate doctrine must be grasped according to this apparently insignificant but really quite essential clarification. We must read a second passage from *Twilight of the Idols* in company with the first (VIII, 124): "What is the meaning of the conceptual opposition, which I introduced into aesthetics, of the Apollonian and the Dionysian, both conceived as kinds of rapture?" After such clear testimony it can no longer be a matter simply of unraveling Nietzsche's doctrine of art from the opposition of the Apollonian and the Dionysian, an opposition quite common ever since the time of its first publication, but not very commonly grasped, an opposition which nevertheless still retains its significance.

Before we pursue the opposition within the framework of our own presentation, let us ask what it is that according to Nietzsche's final explanation pervades that opposition. With this intention, let us proceed with a double question. First, what is the general essence of rapture? Second, in what sense is rapture "indispensable if there is to be art"; in what sense is rapture *the* basic aesthetic state?

To the question of the general essence of rapture Nietzsche provides a succinct answer (*Twilight of the Idols;* VIII, 123): "What is essential in rapture is the feeling of enhancement of force and plenitude." (Cf. "Toward the Physiology of Art," above: "The *feeling* of force and plenitude in rapture.") Earlier he called rapture the "physiological precondition" of art; what is now essential about the precondition is feeling. According to what we clarified above, feeling means the way we find ourselves to be with ourselves, and thereby at the same time with things, with beings that we ourselves are not. Rapture is always rapturous feeling. Where is the physiological, or what pertains to bodily states, in this? Ultimately we dare not split up the matter in such a way, as though there were a bodily state housed in the basement with feelings dwelling upstairs. Feeling, as feeling oneself to be, is precisely the way we are corporeally. Bodily being does not mean that the soul is burdened by a hulk we call the body. In feeling oneself to be, the body is already contained in advance in that self, in such a way that the body in its bodily states permeates the self. We do not "have" a body in the way we carry a knife in a sheath. Neither is the body a natural

body that merely accompanies us and which we can establish, expressly
or not, as being also at hand. We do not "have" a body; rather, we "are"
bodily. Feeling, as feeling oneself to be, belongs to the essence of such
Being. Feeling achieves from the outset the inherent internalizing
tendency of the body in our Dasein. But because feeling, as feeling
oneself to be, always just as essentially has a feeling for beings as a
whole, every bodily state involves some way in which the things around
us and the people with us lay a claim on us or do not do so. When our
stomachs are "out of sorts" they can cast a pall over all things. What
would otherwise seem indifferent to us suddenly becomes irritating and
disturbing; what we usually take in stride now impedes us. True, the
will can appeal to ways and means for suppressing the bad mood, but
it cannot directly awaken or create a countermood: for moods are
overcome and transformed always only by moods. Here it is essential
to observe that feeling is not something that runs its course in our
"inner lives." It is rather that basic mode of our Dasein by force of
which and in accordance with which we are always already lifted beyond
ourselves into being as a whole, which in this or that way matters to
us or does not matter to us. Mood is never merely a way of being
determined in our inner being for ourselves. It is above all a way of
being attuned, and letting ourselves be attuned, in this or that way in
mood. Mood is precisely the basic way in which we are *outside* ourselves. But that is the way we are essentially and constantly.

   In all of this the bodily state swings into action. It lifts a man out
beyond himself or it allows him to be enmeshed in himself and to grow
listless. We are not first of all "alive," only then getting an apparatus
to sustain our living which we call "the body," but we are some body
who is alive.* Our being embodied is essentially other than merely
being encumbered with an organism. Most of what we know from the

---

   Wir leben, indem wir leiben, "we live in that we are embodied." Heidegger plays
with the German expression *wie man leibt und lebt,* "the way somebody actually is,"
and I have tried to catch the sense by playing on the intriguing English word "somebody." Heidegger makes this play more than once: see NI, 565 (volume III of this series,
p. 79); see also *Early Greek Thinking,* p. 65.

natural sciences about the body and the way it embodies are specifications based on the established misinterpretation of the body as a mere natural body. Through such means we do find out lots of things, but the essential and determinative aspects always elude our vision and grasp. We mistake the state of affairs even further when we subsequently search for the "psychical" which pertains to the body that has already been misinterpreted as a natural body.

Every feeling is an embodiment attuned in this or that way, a mood that embodies in this or that way. Rapture is a feeling, and it is all the more genuinely a feeling the more essentially a unity of embodying attunement prevails. Of someone who is intoxicated we can only say that he "has" something like rapture. But he *is* not enraptured. The rapture of intoxication is not a state in which a man rises by himself beyond himself. What we are here calling rapture is merely—to use the colloquialism—being "soused," something that deprives us of every possible state of being.

At the outset Nietzsche emphasizes two things about rapture: first, the feeling of enhancement of force; second, the feeling of plenitude. According to what we explained earlier, such enhancement of force must be understood as the capacity to extend beyond oneself, as a relation to beings in which beings themselves are experienced as being more fully in being, richer, more perspicuous, more essential. Enhancement does not mean that an increase, an increment of force, "objectively" comes about. Enhancement is to be understood in terms of mood: to be caught up in elation—and to be borne along by our buoyancy as such. In the same way, the feeling of plenitude does not suggest an inexhaustible stockpile of inner events. It means above all an attunement which is so disposed that nothing is foreign to it, nothing too much for it, which is open to everything and ready to tackle anything— the greatest enthusiasm and the supreme risk hard by one another.

With that we come up against a third aspect of the feeling of rapture: the reciprocal penetration of all enhancements of every ability to do and see, apprehend and address, communicate and achieve release. "—In this way states are ultimately interlaced which perhaps would have reason to remain foreign to one another. For example, the feeling of religious rapture and sexual arousal (—two profound feelings coordinated quite precisely to an all but astonishing degree)" (WM, 800).

What Nietzsche means by the feeling of rapture as the basic aesthetic state may be gauged by the contrary phenomenon, the inartistic states of the sober, weary, exhausted, dry as dust, wretched, timorous, pallid creatures "under whose regard life suffers" (WM, 801, 812). Rapture is a feeling. But from the contrast of the artistic and inartistic states it becomes especially clear that by the word *Rausch* Nietzsche does not mean a fugitive state that rushes over us and then goes up in smoke. Rapture may therefore hardly be taken as an affect, not even if we give the term "affect" the more precise definition gained earlier. Here as in the earlier case it remains difficult, if not impossible, to apply uncritically terms like affect, passion, and feeling as essential definitions. We can employ such concepts of psychology, by which one divides the faculties of the psyche into classes, only as secondary references—presupposing that we are inquiring, from the beginning and throughout, on the basis of the phenomena themselves in each instance. Then perhaps the artistic state of "rapture," if it is more than a fugitive affect, may be grasped as a passion. But then the question immediately arises: to what extent? In *The Will to Power* there is a passage that can give us a pointer. Nietzsche says (WM, 814), "Artists are *not* men of *great* passion, whatever they like to tell us—and themselves as well." Nietzsche adduces two reasons why artists cannot be men of great passion. First, simply because they are artists, i.e., creators, artists must examine themselves; they lack shame before themselves, and above all they lack shame before great passion; as artists they have to exploit passion, hiding in ambush and pouncing on it, transforming it in the artistic process. Artists are too curious merely to *be* magnificent in great passion; for what passion would have confronting it is not curiosity but a sense of shame. Second, artists are also always the victims of the talent they possess, and that denies them the sheer extravagance of great passion. "One does not *get over* a passion by portraying it; rather, the passion *is over when* one portrays it" (WM,

814). The artistic state itself is never *great* passion, but still it is passion. Thus it possesses a steady and extensive reach into beings as a whole, indeed in such a way that this reach can take itself up into its own grasp, keep it in view, and compel it to take form.

From everything that has been said to clarify the general essence of rapture it ought to have become apparent that we cannot succeed in our efforts to understand it by means of a pure "physiology," that Nietzsche's use of the term "physiology of art" rather has an essentially covert meaning.

What Nietzsche designates with the word *Rausch,* which in his final publications he grasps in a unified way as the basic aesthetic state, is bifurcated early in his work into two different states. The natural forms of the artistic state are those of dream and enchantment, as we may say, adopting an earlier usage of Nietzsche's in order to avoid here the word *Rausch* which he otherwise employs. For the state he calls rapture is one in which dream and ecstatic transport first attain their art-producing essence and become the artistic states to which Nietzsche gives the names "Apollonian" and "Dionysian." The Apollonian and the Dionysian are for Nietzsche two "forces of nature and art" (WM, 1050); in their reciprocity all "further development" of art consists. The convergence of the two in the unity of one configuration is the birth of the supreme work of Greek art, tragedy. But if Nietzsche both at the beginning and at the end of his path of thought thinks the essence of art, which is to say, the essence of the metaphysical activity of life, in the selfsame opposition of the Apollonian and the Dionysian, still we must learn to know and to see that his interpretation in the two cases differs. For at the time of *The Birth of Tragedy* the opposition is still thought in the sense of Schopenhauerian metaphysics, although— rather, because—it is part of a confrontation with such metaphyics; by way of contrast, at the time of *The Will to Power* the opposition is thought on the basis of the fundamental position designated in that title. So long as we do not discern the transformation with adequate clarity and so long as we do not grasp the essence of will to power, it would be good for us to put aside for a while this opposition, which all too often becomes a vacuous catchword. The formula of Apollonian and Dionysian opposites has long been the refuge of all confused and confusing talk and writing about art and about Nietzsche. For Nietzsche the opposition remained a constant source of boundless obscurities and novel *questions.*

Nietzsche may well lay claim to the first public presentation and development of the discovery of that opposition in Greek existence to which he gives the names "Apollonian" and "Dionysian." We can surmise from various clues, however, that Jacob Burckhardt in his Basel lectures on Greek culture, part of which Nietzsche heard, was already on the trail of the opposition; otherwise Nietzsche himself would not expressly refer to Burckhardt as he does in *Twilight of the Idols* (VIII, 170–71) when he says, ". . . the most profound expert on their [the Greeks'] culture living today, such as Jacob Burckhardt in Basel." Of course, what Nietzsche could not have realized, even though since his youth he knew more clearly than his contemporaries who Hölderlin was, was the fact that Hölderlin had seen and conceived of the opposition in an even more profound and lofty manner.

Hölderlin's tremendous insight is contained in a letter to his friend Böhlendorff. He wrote it on December 4, 1801, shortly before his departure for France (*Works,* ed. Hellingrath, V, 318 ff.*). Here

---

*Hölderlin's letter to Casimir Ulrich Böhlendorff (1775–1825), a member of Hölderlin's circle of poet-friends in Homburg, contains the following lines (*Hölderlin Werke und Briefe,* Frankfurt/Main: Insel, 1969, II, 940–41):

"My friend! You have attained much by way of precision and skillful articulation and sacrificed nothing by way of warmth; on the contrary, the elasticity of your spirit, like that of a fine steel blade, has but proven mightier as a result of the schooling to which it has been subjected. . . . Nothing is more difficult for us to learn than the free employment of our national gift. And I believe that clarity of presentation is originally as natural to us as the fire of heaven was to the Greeks. On that account the Greeks are to be *surpassed* more in magnificent passion . . . than in the commanding intellect and representational skill which are typical of Homer.

"It sounds paradoxical. But I assert it once again and submit it for your examination and possible employment: what is properly national will come to have less and less priority as one's education progresses. For that reason the Greeks are not really masters of holy pathos, since it is innate in them, while from Homer on they excel in representa-

Hölderlin contrasts "the holy pathos" and "the Occidental *Junonian sobriety* of representational skill" in the essence of the Greeks. The opposition is not to be understood as an indifferent historical finding. Rather, it becomes manifest to direct meditation on the destiny and determination of the German people. Here we must be satisfied with a mere reference, since Hölderlin's way of knowing could receive adequate definition only by means of an interpretation of his work. It is enough if we gather from the reference that the variously named conflict of the Dionysian and the Apollonian, of holy passion and sober representation, is a hidden stylistic law of the historical determination of the German people, and that one day we must find ourselves ready and able to give it shape. The opposition is not a formula with the help of which we should be content to describe "culture." By recognizing this antagonism Hölderlin and Nietzsche early on placed a question mark after the task of the German people to find their essence historically. Will we understand this cipher? One thing is certain: history will wreak vengeance on us if we do not.

We are trying first of all to sketch the outline of Nietzsche's "aesthetics" as a "physiology of art" by limiting ourselves to the general phenomenon of rapture as the basic artistic state. In that regard we

---

tional skill. For that extraordinary man was so profoundly sensitive that he could capture the *Junonian sobriety* of the Western world for his Apollonian realm and adapt himself faithfully to the foreign element. . . .

"But what is one's own must be learned as thoroughly as what is foreign. For that reason the Greeks are indispensable to us. But precisely in what is our own, in what is our national gift, we will not be able to keep apace with them, since, as I said, the *free* employment of *what is one's own* is most difficult."

Hölderlin's letter has occasioned much critical debate. Heidegger discusses it in his contribution to the *Tübinger Gedenkschrift,* "Andenken," reprinted in *Erläuterungen zu Hölderlins Dichtung,* fourth, expanded ed. (Frankfurt/Main: V. Klostermann, 1971), esp. pp. 82 and 87 ff. A critical review of the literature may be found in Peter Szondi, "Hölderlins Brief an Böhlendorff vom 4. Dezember 1801," *Euphorion: Zeitschrift für Literaturgeschichte,* vol. 58 (1964), 260–75. Szondi's article hardly does justice to Heidegger's reading of the letter and in general is too polemical to be very enlightening; but it does indicate the dimensions and sources of the critical discussion in, for example, Wilhelm Michel, Friedrich Beissner, Beda Allemann, Walter Bröcker, and others.

were to answer a second question: in what sense is rapture "indispens-able if there is to be art," if art is to be at all possible, if it is to be realized? What, and how, "is" art? Is art in the creation by the artist, or in the enjoyment of the work, or in the actuality of the work itself, or in all three together? How then is the conglomeration of these different things something actual? How, and where, is art? Is there "art-as-such" at all, or is the word merely a collective noun to which nothing actual corresponds?

But by now, as we inquire into the matter more incisively, everything becomes obscure and ambiguous. And if we want to know how "rap-ture" is indispensable if there is to be art, things become altogether opaque. Is rapture merely a condition of the commencement of art? If so, in what sense? Does rapture merely issue and liberate the aesthetic state? Or is rapture its constant source and support, and if the latter, how does such a state support "art," of which we know neither how nor what it "is"? When we say it is a configuration of will to power, then, given the current state of the question, we are not really saying anything. For what we want to grasp in the first place is what that determination means. Besides, it is questionable whether the essence of art is thereby defined in terms of art, or whether it isn't rather defined as a mode of the Being of beings. So there is only one way open to us by which we can penetrate and advance, and that is to ask further about the general essence of the aesthetic state, which we provisionally characterized as rapture. But how? Obviously, in the direction of a survey of the realm of aesthetics.

Rapture is feeling, an embodying attunement, an embodied being that is contained in attunement, attunement woven into embodiment. But attunement lays open Dasein as an enhancing, conducts it into the plenitude of its capacities, which mutually arouse one another and foster enhancement. But while clarifying rapture as a state of feeling we emphasized more than once that we may not take such a state as something at hand "in" the body and "in" the psyche. Rather, we must take it as a mode of the embodying, attuned stance toward beings as a whole, beings which for their part determine the pitch of the attunement. Hence, if we want to characterize more broadly and fully the essential structure of the basic aesthetic mode, it behooves us to ask: what is determinative in and for this basic mode, such that it may be spoken of as aesthetic?

15. Kant's Doctrine of the Beautiful. Its Misinterpretation by Schopenhauer and Nietzsche

At the outset, we know in a rough sort of way that just as "the true" determines our behavior in thinking and knowing, and just as "the good" determines the ethical attitude, so does "the beautiful" determine the aesthetic state.

What does Nietzsche say about the beautiful and about beauty? For the answer to this question also Nietzsche provides us with only isolated statements—proclamations, as it were—and references. Nowhere do we find a structured and grounded presentation. A comprehensive, solid understanding of Nietzsche's statements about beauty might result from study of Schopenhauer's aesthetic views; for in his definition of the beautiful Nietzsche thinks and judges by way of opposition and therefore of reversal. But such a procedure is always fatal if the chosen opponent does not stand on solid ground but stumbles about aimlessly. Such is the case with Schopenhauer's views on aesthetics, delineated in the third book of his major work, *The World as Will and Representation.* It cannot be called an aesthetics that would be even remotely comparable to that of Hegel. In terms of content, Schopenhauer thrives on the authors he excoriates, namely, Schelling and Hegel. The one he does not excoriate is Kant. Instead, he thoroughly misunderstands him. Schopenhauer plays the leading role in the preparation and genesis of that misunderstanding of Kantian aesthetics to which Nietzsche too fell prey and which is still quite common today. One may say that Kant's *Critique of Judgment,* the work in which he presents his aesthetics, has been influential up to now only on the basis of misunderstandings, a happenstance of no little significance for the history of philosophy. Schiller alone grasped some essentials in relation to Kant's doctrine of the beautiful; but his insight too was buried in the debris of nineteenth-century aesthetic doctrines.

The misunderstanding of Kant's aesthetics involves an assertion by Kant concerning the beautiful. Kant's definition is developed in sections 2–5 of *The Critique of Judgment*. What is "beautiful" is what purely and simply pleases. The beautiful is the object of "sheer" delight. Such delight, in which the beautiful opens itself up to us as beautiful, is in Kant's words "devoid of all interest." He says, "*Taste* is the capacity to judge an object or mode of representation by means of delight or revulsion, *devoid of all interest*. The object of such delight is called *beautiful.*"*

Aesthetic behavior, i.e., our comportment toward the beautiful, is "delight devoid of all interest." According to the common notion, disinterestedness is indifference toward a thing or person: we invest nothing of our will in relation to that thing or person. If the relation to the beautiful, delight, is defined as "disinterested," then, according to Schopenhauer, the aesthetic state is one in which the will is put out of commission and all striving brought to a standstill; it is pure repose, simply wanting nothing more, sheer apathetic drift.

And Nietzsche? He says that the aesthetic state is rapture. That is manifestly the opposite of all "disinterested delight" and is therefore at the same time the keenest opposition to Kant's definition of our comportment toward the beautiful. With that in mind we understand the following observation by Nietzsche (XIV, 132): "Since Kant, all talk of art, beauty, knowledge, and wisdom has been smudged and besmirched by the concept 'devoid of interest.'" Since Kant? If this is thought to mean "through" Kant, then we have to say "No!" But if it is thought to mean since the Schopenhauerian misinterpretation of Kant, then by all means "Yes!" And for that reason Nietzsche's own effort too is misconceived.

_____

*Immanuel Kant, *Kritik der Urteilskraft*, Akademieausgabe, B 16.

But then what does Kant mean by the definition of the beautiful as the object of "disinterested" delight? What does "devoid of all interest" mean? "Interest" comes from the Latin *mihi interest,* something is of importance to me. To take an interest in something suggests wanting to have it for oneself as a possession, to have disposition and control over it. When we take an interest in something we put it in the context of what we intend to do with it and what we want of it. Whatever we take an interest in is always already taken, i.e., represented, with a view to something else.

Kant poses the question of the essence of the beautiful in the following way. He asks by what means our behavior, in the situation where we find something we encounter to be beautiful, must let itself be determined in such a way that we encounter the beautiful *as* beautiful. What is the determining ground for our finding something beautiful?

Before Kant says constructively what the determining ground is, and therefore what the beautiful itself is, he first says by way of refutation what never can and never may propose itself as such a ground, namely, an interest. Whatever exacts of us the judgment "This is beautiful" can never be an interest. That is to say, in order to find something beautiful, we must let what encounters us, purely as it is in itself, come before us in its own stature and worth. We may not take it into account in advance with a view to something else, our goals and intentions, our possible enjoyment and advantage. Comportment toward the beautiful as such, says Kant, is *unconstrained favoring.* We must release what encounters us as such to its way to be; we must allow and grant it what belongs to it and what it brings to us.

But now we ask, is this free granting, this letting the beautiful be what it is, a kind of indifference; does it put the will out of commission? Or is not such unconstrained favoring rather the supreme effort of our essential nature, the liberation of our selves for the release of what has proper worth in itself, only in order that we may have it purely? Is the Kantian "devoid of interest" a "smudging" and even a "besmirching" of aesthetic behavior? Or is it not the magnificent discovery and approbation of it?

The misinterpretation of the Kantian doctrine of "disinterested delight" consists in a double error. First, the definition "devoid of all interest," which Kant offers only in a preparatory and path-breaking way, and which in its very linguistic structure displays its negative character plainly enough, is given out as the single assertion (also held to be a positive assertion) by Kant on the beautiful. To the present day it is proffered as *the* Kantian interpretation of the beautiful. Second, the definition, misinterpreted in what it methodologically tries to achieve, at the same time is not thought in terms of the content that *remains* in aesthetic behavior when interest in the object falls away. The misinterpretation of "interest" leads to the erroneous opinion that with the exclusion of interest every essential relation to the object is suppressed. The opposite is the case. Precisely by means of the "devoid of interest" the essential relation to the object itself comes into play. The misinterpretation fails to see that now for the first time the object comes to the fore as pure object and that such coming forward into appearance is the beautiful. The word "beautiful" means appearing in the radiance of such coming to the fore.*

What emerges as decisive about the double error is the neglect of actual inquiry into what Kant erected upon a firm foundation with respect to the essence of the beautiful and of art. We will bring one example forward which shows how stubbornly the ostensibly self-evident misinterpretation of Kant during the nineteenth century still obtains today. Wilhelm Dilthey, who labored at the history of aesthetics with a passion unequaled by any of his contemporaries, remarked in 1887 (*Gesammelte Schriften* VI, 119) that Kant's statement con-

---

*Das Wort "schön" meint das Erscheinen im Schein solchen Vorscheins. Although the words *schön* and *Schein* vary even in their oldest forms (see Hermann Paul, *Deutsches Wörterbuch,* 6th ed. [Tübingen, M. Niemeyer, 1966], pp. 537b f. and 569b f.), their meanings converge early on in the sense of the English words "shine" and "shining," related to the words "show," "showy." Perhaps the similar relationship between the words "radiate" and "radiant" comes closest to the German *Schein* and *schön*. But it is not simply a matter of alliterative wordplay: the nexus of *schön* and *Schein* is, according to Heidegger, what Plato means by *ekphanestaton* (discussed in section 21, below); and if Nietzsche's task is to overturn Platonism, this issue must be near the very heart of the Heidegger-Nietzsche confrontation. On the relation of *Schein* and *schön* see also Martin Heidegger, "Hegel und die Griechen," in *Wegmarken,* pp. 262, 267, and elsewhere.

cerning disinterested delight "is presented by Schopenhauer with special brilliance." The passage should read, "was fatally misinterpreted by Schopenhauer."

Had Nietzsche inquired of Kant himself, instead of trusting in Schopenhauer's guidance, then he would have had to recognize that Kant alone grasped the essence of what Nietzsche in his own way wanted to comprehend concerning the decisive aspects of the beautiful. Nietzsche could never have continued, in the place cited (XIV, 132), after the impossible remark about Kant, "In *my* view what is beautiful (observed historically) is what is visible in the most honored men of an era, as an expression of what is *most worthy* of honor." For just this—purely to honor what is of worth in its appearance—is for Kant the essence of the beautiful, although unlike Nietzsche he does not expand the meaning directly to all historical significance and greatness.

And when Nietzsche says (WM, 804), "*The* beautiful exists just as little as *the* good, *the* true," that too corresponds to the opinion of Kant.

But the purpose of our reference to Kant, in the context of an account of Nietzsche's conception of beauty, is not to eradicate the firmly rooted misinterpretation of the Kantian doctrine. It is to provide a possibility of grasping what Nietzsche himself says about beauty on the basis of its own original, historical context. That Nietzsche himself did not see the context draws a boundary line that he shares with his era and its relation to Kant and to German Idealism. It would be inexcusable for us to allow the prevailing misinterpretation of Kantian aesthetics to continue; but it would also be wrongheaded to try to trace Nietzsche's conception of beauty and the beautiful back to the Kantian. Rather, what we must now do is to allow Nietzsche's definition of the beautiful to sprout and flourish in its own soil—and in that way to see to what discordance it is transplanted.

Nietzsche too defines the beautiful as what pleases. But everything depends on the operative concept of pleasure and of what pleases as such. What pleases we take to be what corresponds to us, what speaks to us. What pleases someone, what speaks to him, depends on who that someone is to whom it speaks and corresponds. Who such a person is, is defined by what he demands of himself. Hence we call "beautiful" whatever corresponds to what we demand of ourselves. Furthermore, such demanding is measured by what we take ourselves to be, what we trust we are capable of, and what we dare as perhaps the extreme challenge, one we may just barely withstand.

In that way we are to understand Nietzsche's assertion about the beautiful and about the judgment by which we find something to be beautiful (WM, 852): "To pick up the scent of what would nearly finish us off if it were to confront us in the flesh, as danger, problem, temptation—this determines even our aesthetic 'yes.' ('That is beautiful' is an *affirmation*.)" So also with *The Will to Power*, number 819: "The firm, mighty, solid, the life that rests squarely and sovereignly and conceals its strength—that is what '*pleases*,' i.e., that corresponds to what one takes oneself to be."

The beautiful is what we find honorable and worthy, as the image of our essential nature. It is that upon which we bestow "unconstrained favor," as Kant says, and we do so from the very foundations of our essential nature and for its sake. In another place Nietzsche says (XIV, 134), "Such 'getting rid of interest and the ego' is nonsense and imprecise observation: on the contrary, it is the thrill that comes of being in *our* world now, of getting rid of our anxiety in the face of things foreign!" Certainly such "getting rid of interest" in the sense of Schopenhauer's interpretation is nonsense. But what Nietzsche describes as the thrill that comes of being in our world is what Kant means by the "pleasure of reflection." Here also, as with the concept of "interest," the basic Kantian concepts of "pleasure" and "reflection" are to be discussed in terms of the Kantian philosophical effort and its transcendental procedure, not flattened out with the help of everyday notions. Kant analyzes the essence of the "pleasure of reflection," as the basic comportment toward the beautiful, in *The Critique of Judgment*, sections 37 and 39.*

---

*Neske prints §§57 and 59, but this is obviously an error: *die Lust am Schönen*, as *Lust der blossen Reflexion*, is not mentioned in §57 or §59, but *is* discussed indirectly in §37 and explicitly in §39. See especially B 155.

According to the quite "imprecise observation" on the basis of which Nietzsche conceives of the essence of interest, he would have to designate what Kant calls "unconstrained favoring" as an interest of the highest sort. Thus what Nietzsche demands of comportment toward the beautiful would be fulfilled from Kant's side. However, to the extent that Kant grasps more keenly the essence of interest and therefore excludes it from aesthetic behavior, he does not make such behavior indifferent; rather, he makes it possible for such comportment toward the beautiful object to be all the purer and more intimate. Kant's interpretation of aesthetic behavior as "pleasure of reflection" propels us toward a basic state of human being in which man for the first time arrives at the well-grounded fullness of his essence. It is the state that Schiller conceives of as the condition of the possibility of man's existence as historical, as grounding history.

According to the explanations by Nietzsche which we have cited, the beautiful is what determines us, our behavior and our capability, to the extent that we are claimed supremely in our essence, which is to say, to the extent that we ascend beyond ourselves. Such ascent beyond ourselves, to the full of our essential capability, occurs according to Nietzsche in rapture. Thus the beautiful is disclosed in rapture. The beautiful itself is what transports us into the feeling of rapture. From this elucidation of the essence of the beautiful the characterization of rapture, of the basic aesthetic state, acquires enhanced clarity. If the beautiful is what sets the standard for what we trust we are essentially capable of, then the feeling of rapture, as our relation to the beautiful, can be no mere turbulence and ebullition. The mood of rapture is rather an attunement in the sense of the supreme and most measured determinateness. However much Nietzsche's manner of speech and presentation sounds like Wagner's turmoil of feelings and sheer submergence in mere "experiences," it is certain that in this regard he wants to achieve the exact opposite. What is strange and almost incomprehensible is the fact that he tries to make his conception of the aesthetic state accessible to his contemporaries, and tries to convince them of it, by speaking the language of physiology and biology.

In terms of its concept, the beautiful is what is estimable and worthy as such. In connection with that, number 852 of *The Will to Power* says, "It is a question of *strength* (of an individual or a nation), *whether* and *where* the judgment 'beautiful' is made." But such strength is not sheer muscle power, a reservoir of "brachial brutality." What Nietzsche here calls "strength" is the capacity of historical existence to come to grips with and perfect its highest essential determination. Of course, the essence of "strength" does not come to light purely and decisively. Beauty is taken to be a "biological value":

> For consideration: the extent to which our value "beautiful" is completely anthropocentric: based on biological presuppositions concerning growth and progress—. ("Toward the Physiology of Art," no. 4 [cf. p. 94, above].)

> The fundament of all aesthetics [is given in] the general principle that aesthetic values rest on biological values, that aesthetic delights are biological delights (XIV, 165).

That Nietzsche conceives of the beautiful "biologically" is indisputable. Yet the question remains what "biological," *bios*, "life," mean here. In spite of appearances created by the words, they do *not* mean what *biology* understands them to be.

16. Rapture as Form-engendering Force

Now that the aesthetic state too has been clarified by way of an elucidation of the beautiful, we can try to survey more precisely the realm of that state. We can do this by studying the basic modes of behavior that are operative in the aesthetic state: aesthetic doing and aesthetic observing—or creation by the artist and reception by those who examine works of art.

If we ask what the essence of creation is, then on the basis of what has gone before we can answer that it is the rapturous bringing-forth of the beautiful in the work. Only in and through creation is the work realized. But because that is so, the essence of creation for its part remains dependent upon the essence of the work; therefore it can be grasped only from the Being of the work. Creation creates the work. But the essence of the work is the origin of the essence of creation.

If we ask how Nietzsche defines the work, we receive no answer. For Nietzsche's meditation on art—and precisely this meditation, as aesthetics in the extreme—does not inquire into the work as such, at least not in the first place. For that reason we hear little, and nothing essential, about the essence of creation as bringing-forth. On the contrary, only creation as a life-process is discussed, a life-process conditioned by rapture. The creative state is accordingly "an *explosive* state" (WM, 811). That is a chemical description, not a philosophical interpretation. If in the same place Nietzsche refers to vascular changes, alterations in skin tone, temperature, and secretion, his findings involve nothing more than changes in the body grasped in an extrinsic manner, even if he draws into consideration "the automatism of the entire muscular system." Such findings may be correct, but they hold also for

other, pathological, bodily states. Nietzsche says it is not possible to be
an artist and not be ill. And when he says that making music, making
art of any kind, is also a kind of making children, it merely corresponds
to that designation of rapture according to which "sexual rapture is its
oldest and most original form."

But if we were to restrict ourselves to these references by Nietzsche
we would heed only one side of the creative process. The other side,
if it makes sense to speak here of sides at all, we must present by
recalling the essence of rapture and of beauty, namely ascent beyond
oneself. By such ascent we come face to face with that which corresponds to what we take ourselves to be. With that we touch upon the
character of decision in creation, and what has to do with standards and
with hierarchy. Nietzsche enters that sphere when he says (WM, 800),
"Artists should see nothing as it is, but more fully, simply, strongly:
for that, a kind of youth and spring, a kind of habitual rapture, must
be proper to their lives."

Nietzsche also calls the fuller, simpler, stronger vision in creation an
"idealizing." To the essential definition of rapture as a feeling of
enhancement of power and plenitude (*Twilight of the Idols,* VIII, 123)
Nietzsche appends: "From this feeling, one bestows upon things, one
compels them to take from us, one violates them—this process is called
idealization." But to idealize is not, as one might think, merely to omit,
strike, or otherwise discount what is insignificant and ancillary. Idealization is not a defensive action. Its essence consists in a "*sweeping
emphasis* upon the main features." What is decisive therefore is an-
ticipatory discernment of these traits, reaching out toward what we
believe we can but barely overcome, barely survive. It is that attempt
to grasp the beautiful which Rilke's "First Elegy" describes wholly in
Nietzsche's sense:

> ... For the beautiful is nothing
> but the beginning of the terrible, a beginning we but barely endure;
> and it amazes us so, since calmly it disdains
> to destroy us.*

---

*Rainer Maria Rilke, *Werke in drei Bänden* (Frankfurt/Main: Insel, 1966) I, 441,
from lines 4–7 of the first Duino Elegy:

Creation is an emphasizing of major features, a seeing more simply and strongly. It is bare survival before the court of last resort. It commends itself to the highest law and therefore celebrates to the full its survival in the face of such danger.

> For the artist "beauty" is something outside all hierarchical order, since in it opposites are joined—the supreme sign of power, power over things in opposition; furthermore, without tension: —that there is no further need of force, that everything so easily *follows, obeys,* and brings to its obedience the most amiable demeanor—this fascinates the will to power of the artist (WM, 803).

Nietzsche understands the aesthetic state of the observer and recipient on the basis of the state of the creator. Thus the effect of the artwork is nothing else than a reawakening of the creator's state in the one who enjoys the artwork. Observation of art follows in the wake of creation. Nietzsche says (WM, 821), "—the effect of artworks is *arousal of the art-creating state,* rapture." Nietzsche shares this conception with the widely prevalent opinion of aesthetics. On that basis we understand why he demands, logically, that aesthetics conform to the creator, the artist. Observation of works is only a derivative form and offshoot of creation. Therefore what was said of creation corresponds precisely, though derivatively, to observation of art. Enjoyment of the work consists in participation in the creative state of the artist (XIV, 136). But because Nietzsche does not unfold the essence of creation from what is to be created, namely, the work; because he develops it from the state of aesthetic behavior; the bringing-forth of the work does not receive an adequately delineated interpretation which would distinguish it from the bringing-forth of utensils by way of handicraft. Not only that. The behavior of observation is not set in relief against creation, and so it remains undefined. The view that the observation of works somehow follows in the wake of creation is so little true that

---

... Denn das Schöne ist nichts
als des Schrecklichen Anfang, den wir noch grade ertragen,
und wir bewundern es so, weil es gelassen verschmäht,
uns zu zerstören.

not even the relation of the *artist* to the work as something created is one that would be appropriate to the creator. But that could be demonstrated only by way of an inquiry into art that would begin altogether differently, proceeding from the work itself; through the presentation of Nietzsche's aesthetics offered here it ought to have become clear by now how little he treats the work of art.*

And yet, just as a keener conception of the essence of rapture led us to the inner relation to beauty, so here examination of creation and observation enables us to encounter more than mere corporeal-psychical processes. The relation to "major features" emphasized in "idealization," to the simpler and stronger aspects which the artist anticipates in what he meets, once again becomes manifest in the aesthetic state. Aesthetic feeling is neither blind and boundless emotion nor a pleasant contentment, a comfortable drifting that permeates our state of being. Rapture in itself is drawn to major features, that is, to a series of traits, to an articulation. So we must once more turn away from the apparently one-sided consideration of mere states and turn toward *what* this mood defines in our attunement. In connection with the usual conceptual language of aesthetics, which Nietzsche too speaks, we call it "form."

The artist—out of whom, back to whom, and within whom Nietzsche always casts his glance, even when he speaks of form and of the work—has his fundamental character in this: he "ascribes to no thing a value unless it knows how to become form" (WM, 817). Nietzsche explains such becoming-form here in an aside as "giving itself up," "making itself public." Although at first blush these words seem quite strange, they define the essence of form. Without Nietzsche's making explicit mention of it here or elsewhere, the definition corresponds to the original concept of form as it develops with the Greeks. We cannot discuss that origin here in greater detail.

But by way of a commentary on Nietzsche's definition let us say only

---

*The reference to an inquiry that would begin "altogether differently" is to that series of lectures Heidegger was reworking during the winter semester of 1936–37 (which is to say, during the period of these Nietzsche lectures), later published as "The Origin of the Work of Art."

this: form, *forma,* corresponds to the Greek *morphē.* It is the enclosing limit and boundary, what brings and stations a being into that which it is, so that it stands in itself: its configuration. Whatever stands in this way is what the particular being shows itself to be, its outward appearance, *eidos,* through which and in which it emerges, stations itself there as publicly present, scintillates, and achieves pure radiance.

The artist—we may now understand that name as a designation of the aesthetic state—does not comport himself to form as though it were expressive of something else. The artistic relation to form is love of form for its own sake, for what it is. Nietzsche says as much on one occasion (WM, 828), putting it in a negative way with a view to contemporary painters:

> *Not one* of them is simply a painter: they are all archeologists, psychologists, people who devise a scenario for any given recollection or theory. They take their pleasure from our erudition, our philosophy. . . . They do not love a form for what it is; they love it for what it *expresses.* They are the sons of a learned, tormented and reflective generation—a thousand miles removed from the old masters who did not read and whose only thought was to give their eyes a feast.

Form, as what allows that which we encounter to radiate in appearance, first brings the behavior that it determines into the immediacy of a relation to beings. Form displays the relation itself as the state of original comportment toward beings, the festive state in which the being itself in its essence is celebrated and thus for the first time placed in the open. Form defines and demarcates for the first time the realm in which the state of waxing force and plenitude of being comes to fulfillment. Form founds the realm in which rapture as such becomes possible. Wherever form holds sway, as the supreme simplicity of the most resourceful lawfulness, there is rapture.

Rapture does not mean mere chaos that churns and foams, the drunken bravado of sheer riotousness and tumult. When Nietzsche says "rapture" the word has a sound and sense utterly opposed to Wagner's. For Nietzsche rapture means the most glorious victory of form. With respect to the question of form in art, and with a view to

Wagner, Nietzsche says at one point (WM, 835): "An error—that what Wagner has created is a *form:* —it is formlessness. The possibility of *dramatic* structure remains to be discovered.... Whorish instrumentation."

Of course, Nietzsche does not conduct a meditation devoted expressly to the origin and essence of form in relation to art. For that his point of departure would have to have been the work of art. Yet with a bit of extra effort we can still discern, at least approximately, what Nietzsche means by form.

By "form" Nietzsche never understands the merely "formal," that is to say, what stands in need of content, what is only the external border of such content, circumscribing it but not influencing it. Such a border does not give bounds; it is itself the result of sheer cessation. It is only a fringe, not a component, not what lends consistency and pith by pervading the content and fixing it in such a way that its character as "contained" evanesces. Genuine form is the only true content.

> What it takes to be an artist is that one experience what all nonartists call "form" as *content,* as "the matter itself." With that, of course, one is relegated to an *inverted world.* For from now on one takes content to be something merely formal—including one's own life (WM, 818).

When Nietzsche tries to characterize lawfulness of form, however, he does not do so with a view to the essence of the work and the work's form. He cites only that lawfulness of form which is most common and familiar to us, the "logical," "arithmetical," and "geometrical." But logic and mathematics are for him not merely representative names designating the purest sort of lawfulness; rather, Nietzsche suggests that lawfulness of form must be traced back to logical definition, in a way that corresponds to his explanation of thinking and Being. By such tracing back of formal lawfulness, however, Nietzsche does not mean that art is nothing but logic and mathematics.

"Estimates of aesthetic value"—which is to say, our finding something to be beautiful—have as their "ground floor" those feelings that relate to logical, arithmetical, and geometrical lawfulness (XIV, 133).

The basic logical feelings are those of delight "in the ordered, the surveyable, the bounded, and in repetition." The expression "logical feelings" is deceptive. It does not mean that the feelings themselves are logical, that they proceed according to the laws of thought. The expression "logical feelings" means having a feeling for, letting one's mood be determined by, order, boundary, the overview.

Because estimates of aesthetic value are grounded on the logical feelings, they are also "more fundamental than moral estimates." Nietzsche's decisive valuations have as their standard enhancement and securement of "life." But in his view the basic logical feelings, delight in the ordered and bounded, are nothing else than "the pleasurable feelings among all organic creatures in relation to the danger of their situation or to the difficulty of finding nourishment; the familiar does one good, the sight of something that one trusts he can easily *over-power* does one good, etc." (XIV, 133).

The result, to put it quite roughly, is the following articulated structure of pleasurable feelings: underlying all, the biological feelings of pleasure that arise when life asserts itself and survives; above these, but at the same time in service to them, the logical, mathematical feelings; these in turn serve as the basis for aesthetic feelings. Hence we can trace the aesthetic pleasure derived from form back to certain conditions of the life-process as such. Our view, originally turned toward lawfulness of form, is deflected once more and is directed toward sheer states of life.

Our way through Nietzsche's aesthetics has up to now been determined by Nietzsche's basic position toward art: taking rapture, the basic aesthetic state, as our point of departure, we proceeded to consider beauty; from it we went back to the states of creation and reception; from these we advanced to what they are related to, to what determines them, i.e., form; from form we advanced to the pleasure derived from what is ordered, as a fundamental condition of embodying life; with that, we are back where we started, for life is life-enhancement, and ascendant life is rapture. The realm in which the whole process forward and backward itself takes place, the whole within which and as which rapture and beauty, creation and form, form and life have their reciprocal relation, at first remains *undefined*. So does the kind of context for and relationship between rapture and beauty, creation and form. All are proper to art. But then art would only be a collective noun and not the name of an actuality grounded and delineated in itself.

For Nietzsche, however, art is more than a collective noun. *Art is a configuration of will to power.* The indeterminateness we have indicated can be eliminated only through consideration of will to power. The essence of art is grounded in itself, clarified, and articulated in its structure only to the extent that the same is done for will to power. Will to power must originally ground the manner in which all things that are proper to art cohere.

Of course, one might be tempted to dispose of the indeterminateness in a simple way. We have only to call whatever is related to rapture "subjective," and whatever is related to beauty "objective," and in the same fashion understand creation as subjective behavior and form as objective law. The unknown variable would be the relation of the subjective to the objective: the subject-object relation. What could be more familiar than that? And yet what is more questionable than the subject-object relation as the starting point for man as subject and as the definition of the nonsubjective as object? The commonness of the distinction is not yet proof of its clarity; neither is it proof that the distinction is truly grounded.

The illusory clarity and concealed groundlessness of this schema do not help us much. The schema simply casts aside what is worthy of question in Nietzsche's aesthetics, what is worthwhile in the confrontation and therefore to be emphasized. The less we do violence to Nietzsche's "aesthetics" by building it up as an edifice of apparently obvious doctrines; the more we allow his quest and questioning to go its own way; the more surely do we come across those perspectives and basic notions in which the whole for Nietzsche possesses a unity that is fully mature, albeit obscure and amorphous. If we want to grasp the basic metaphysical position of Nietzsche's thought, we ought to clarify these notions. Therefore we must now try to simplify Nietzsche's presentations concerning art to what is essential; yet we may not relinquish the multiplicity of perspectives there, nor impose on his thoughts some dubious schema from the outside.

For our summary, which is to simplify our previous characterization of Nietzsche's conception of art, we can limit ourselves to the two predominant basic determinations, rapture and beauty. They are reciprocally related. Rapture is the basic mood; beauty does the attuning. But just how little the distinction between the subjective and the objective can contribute to our present commentary we can see easily in what follows. Rapture, which does constitute the state of the subject, can every bit as well be conceived as objective, as an actuality for which beauty is merely subjective, since there is no beauty in itself. It is certain that Nietzsche never achieved conceptual clarity here and was never able to ground these matters successfully. Even Kant, who because of his transcendental method possessed a larger number of more highly refined possibilities for interpreting aesthetics, remained trapped within the limits of the modern concept of the subject. In spite of everything, we must try to make more explicit what is essential in Nietzsche as well, going beyond him.

Rapture as a state of feeling explodes the very subjectivity of the subject. By having a feeling for beauty the subject has already come out of himself; he is no longer subjective, no longer a subject. On the other side, beauty is not something at hand like an object of sheer representation. As an attuning, it thoroughly determines the state of man. Beauty breaks through the confinement of the "object" placed at a distance, standing on its own, and brings it into essential and original correlation to the "subject." Beauty is no longer objective, no longer an object. The aesthetic state is neither subjective nor objective. Both basic words of Nietzsche's aesthetics, rapture and beauty, designate with an identical breadth the entire aesthetic state, what is opened up in it and what pervades it.

17. The Grand Style

Nietzsche has in view the whole of artistic actuality whenever he speaks of that in which art comes to its essence. He calls it *the grand style*. Here too we seek in vain when we look for an essential definition and fundamental explanation of the meaning of "style." As is typical for the realm of art, everything named in the word "style" belongs to what is most obscure. Yet the way Nietzsche ever and again invokes the "grand style," even if only in brief references, casts light on everything we have mentioned heretofore about Nietzsche's aesthetics.

> The "masses" have never had a sense for three good things in art, for elegance, logic, and beauty—*pulchrum est paucorum hominum*—; to say nothing of an even better thing, the *grand style*. Farthest removed from the grand style is Wagner: the dissipatory character and heroic swagger of his artistic means are altogether *opposed* to the grand style (XIV, 154).

Three good things are proper to art: elegance, logic, beauty; along with something even better: the grand style. When Nietzsche says that these remain foreign to the "masses," he does not mean the class concept of the "lower strata" of the population. He means "educated" people, in the sense of mediocre cultural Philistines, the kind of people who promoted and sustained the Wagner cult. The farmer and the worker who is really caught up in his machine world remain entirely unmoved by swaggering heroics. These are craved only by the frenetic petit bourgeois. His world—rather, his void—is the genuine obstacle that prevents the expansion and growth of what Nietzsche calls the grand style.

Now, in what does the grand style consist? "The grand style consists in contempt for trivial and brief beauty; it is a sense for what is rare and what lasts long" (XIV, 145).

We recall that the essence of creation is emphasis of major traits. In the grand style occurs

> . . . a triumph over the plenitude of living things; *measure* becomes master, that *tranquillity* which lies at the base of the strong soul, a soul that is slow to be moved and that resists what is all too animated. The general case, the rule, is *revered* and *emphasized;* the exception is on the contrary thrust aside, the nuance obliterated (WM, 819).

We think of beauty as being most worthy of reverence. But what is most worthy of reverence lights up only where the magnificent strength to revere is alive. To revere is not a thing for the petty and lowly, the incapacitated and underdeveloped. It is a matter of tremendous *passion;* only what flows from such passion is in the grand style (cf. WM, 1024).*

What Nietzsche calls the grand style is most closely approximated by the rigorous style, the classical style: "The classical style represents essentially such tranquillity, simplification, abbreviation, concentration —in the classical type the *supreme feeling of power* is concentrated. Slow to react: a tremendous consciousness: no feeling of struggle" (WM, 799). The grand style is the highest feeling of power. From that it is clear that if art is a configuration of will to power, then "art" here is grasped always in its highest essential stature. The word "art" does not designate the concept of a mere eventuality; it is a concept of rank. Art is not just one among a number of items, activities one engages in and enjoys now and then; art places the whole of Dasein in decision and keeps it there. For that reason art itself is subject to altogether singular conditions. In Nietzsche's view the task therefore arises: "To think to the end, without prejudice and faintness of heart, in what soil a classical

---

*Number 1024 of *The Will to Power* reads: "A period in which the old masquerade and the moralistic laundering of the affects arouses revulsion; *naked nature;* where *quanta of power* are simply admitted as being *decisive* (as *determining rank*); where the *grand style* emerges once again as a consequence of *grand passion.*"

taste may grow. To make man hard, natural, strong, more wicked: all these belong together" (WM, 849).

But not only do the grand style and wickedness belong together, emblematic of the unification of flagrant contradictions in Dasein. Two other things belong together which at first seemed incompatible to us: art as countermovement to nihilism and art as object of a physiological aesthetics.

Physiology of art apparently takes its object to be a process of nature that bubbles to the surface in the manner of an eruptive state of rapture. Such a state would evanesce without deciding anything, since nature knows no realm of decision.

But art as countermovement to nihilism is to lay the groundwork for establishment of new standards and values; it is therefore to be rank, distinction, and decision. If art has its proper essence in the grand style, this now means that measure and law are confirmed only in the subjugation and containment of chaos and the rapturous. Such is demanded of the grand style as the condition of its own possibility. Accordingly, the physiological is the basic condition for art's being able to be a creative countermovement. Decision presupposes divergence between opposites; its height increases in proportion to the depths of the conflict.

Art in the grand style is the simple tranquillity resulting from the protective mastery of the supreme plenitude of life. To it belongs the original liberation of life, but one which is restrained; to it belongs the most terrific opposition, but in the unity of the simple; to it belongs fullness of growth, but with the long endurance of rare things. Where art is to be grasped in its supreme form, in terms of the grand style, we must reach back into the most original states of embodying life, into physiology. Art as countermovement to nihilism and art as state of rapture, as object of physiology ("physics" in the broadest sense) and as object of metaphysics—these aspects of art include rather than exclude one another. The unity of such antitheses, grasped in its entire essential fullness, provides an insight into what Nietzsche himself knew —and that means willed—concerning art, its essence and essential determination.

However often and however fatally Nietzsche both in language and in thought was diverted into purely physiological, naturalistic assertions about art, it is an equally fatal misunderstanding on our part when we isolate such physiological thoughts and bandy them about as a "biologistic" aesthetics. It is even worse to confuse them with Wagner. We turn everything inside out when we make a philosophy of orgiastics out of it, as Klages does, thoroughly falsifying matters by proclaiming it Nietzsche's authentic teaching and genuine accomplishment.

In order to draw near to the essential will of Nietzsche's thinking, and remain close to it, our thinking must acquire enormous range, plus the ability to see beyond everything that is fatally contemporary in Nietzsche. His knowledge of art and his struggle on behalf of the possibility of great art are dominated by one thought, which he at one point expresses briefly in the following way: "What alone can regenerate us? Envisionment of what is perfect" (XIV, 171).

But Nietzsche was also aware of the immense difficulty of such a task. For who is to determine what the perfect is? It could only be those who are themselves perfect and who therefore know what it means. Here yawns the abyss of that circularity in which the whole of human Dasein moves. What health is, only the healthy can say. Yet healthfulness is measured according to the essential starting point of health. What truth is, only one who is truthful can discern; but the one who is truthful is determined according to the essential starting point of truth.

When Nietzsche associates art in the grand style with classical taste, he does not fall prey to some sort of classicism. Nietzsche is the first—if we discount for the moment Hölderlin—to release the "classical" from the misinterpretations of classicism and humanism. His position vis-à-vis the age of Winckelmann and Goethe is expressed clearly enough (WM, 849):

> It is an amusing comedy, which we are only now learning to laugh at, which we are now for the first time *seeing,* that the contemporaries of Herder, Winckelmann, Goethe, and Hegel claimed *to have rediscovered the classical ideal* . . . and Shakespeare at the same time! And this same generation had in a rather nasty way declared itself independent of the French classical

school, as if the essential matters could not have been learned there as well as here! But they wanted "nature," "naturalness": oh, stupidity! They believed that the classic was a form of naturalness!

If Nietzsche emphasizes constantly and with conscious exaggeration the physiological aspects of the aesthetic state, it is in reaction to the poverty and lack of antithesis within classicism; he wants to put in relief the original conflict of life and thereby the roots of the necessity for a victory. The "natural" to which Nietzsche's aesthetics refers is not that of classicism: it is not something accessible to and calculable for a human reason which is apparently unruffled and quite sure of itself; it is not something without hazard, comprehensible to itself. On the contrary, Nietzsche means what is bound to nature, which the Greeks of the Golden Age call *deinon* and *deinotaton,* the frightful.*

In contrast to classicism, the classical is nothing that can be immediately divined from a particular past period of art. It is instead a basic structure of Dasein, which itself first creates the conditions for any such period and must first open itself and devote itself to those conditions. But the fundamental condition is an equally original freedom with regard to the extreme opposites, chaos and law; not the mere subjection of chaos to a form, but that mastery which enables the primal wilderness of chaos and the primordiality of law to advance under the same yoke, invariably bound to one another with equal necessity. Such mastery is unconstrained disposition over that yoke, which is as equally removed from the paralysis of form in what is dogmatic and formalistic as from sheer rapturous tumult. Wherever unconstrained disposition over that yoke is an event's self-imposed law, there is the grand style; wherever the grand style prevails, there art in the purity of its essential plenitude is actual. Art may be adjudged only in accordance with what its essential actuality is; only in accordance

---

*During the summer semester of 1935 Heidegger had elaborated the meaning of *deinon, deinotaton* in a course entitled "Introduction to Metaphysics." There he translated the word also as *das Unheimliche,* the uncanny, and *das Gewaltige,* the powerful, in his interpretation of a choral song (verses 332–75) from Sophocles' *Antigone.* See Martin Heidegger, *Einführung in die Metaphysik,* pp. 112 ff.; in the English translation pp. 123 ff.

with its essential actuality should it be conceived as a configuration of beings, that is to say, as will to power.

Whenever Nietzsche deals with art in the essential and definitive sense, he always refers to art in the grand style. Against this backdrop, his innermost antipathy to Wagner comes to light most sharply, above all because his conception of the grand style includes at the same time a fundamental decision, not only about Wagner's music, but about the essence of music as such. [Cf. these remarks from the period of *The Dawn*, 1880–81: "Music has no resonance for the transports of the spirit" (XI, 336); "The poet allows the drive for knowledge *to play;* the musician lets it take a rest" (XI, 337). Especially illuminating is a longer sketch from the year 1888 with the title " 'Music'—and the Grand Style" (WM, 842).]*

Nietzsche's meditation on art is "aesthetics" because it examines the state of creation and enjoyment. It is the "extreme" aesthetics inasmuch as that state is pursued to the farthest perimeter of the bodily state as such, to what is farthest removed from the spirit, from the spirituality of what is created, and from its formalistic lawfulness. However, precisely in that far remove of physiological aesthetics a sudden reversal occurs. For this "physiology" is not something to which everything essential in art can be traced back and on the basis of which it can be explained. While the bodily state as such continues to participate as a condition of the creative process, it is at the same time what in the created thing is to be restrained, overcome, and surpassed. The aesthetic state is the one which places itself under the law of the grand style which is taking root in it. The aesthetic state itself is truly what it is only as the grand style. Hence such aesthetics, within

---

*The brackets appear in Heidegger's text, presumably because the reference is a kind of "footnote"; it is not likely that these remarks were added to the manuscript at the time of publication. The opening lines of *The Will to Power* number 842 are perhaps most relevant here: "The greatness of an artist is not measured by the 'beautiful feelings' he arouses: that is what the little ladies like to believe. Rather, it is measured by gradients of approximation to the grand style, by the extent to which the artist is capable of the grand style. That style has in common with great passion that it disdains to please; that it forgets about persuading; that it commands; that it *wills*. . . . To become master of the chaos that one is; to compel one's chaos to become form: logical, simple, unequivocal; to become mathematics, *law*—that is the grand ambition here.—"

itself, is led beyond itself. The artistic states are those which place themselves under the supreme command of measure and law, taking themselves beyond themselves in their will to advance. Such states are what they essentially are when, willing out beyond themselves, they are more than they are, and when they assert themselves in such mastery.

The artistic states are—and that means art is—nothing else than *will to power*. Now we understand Nietzsche's principal declaration concerning art as the great "stimulant of life." "Stimulant" means what conducts one into the sphere of command of the grand style.

But now we also see more clearly in what sense Nietzsche's statement about art as the great stimulant of life represents a reversal of Schopenhauer's statement which defines art as a "sedative of life." The reversal does not consist merely in the fact that "sedative" is replaced by "stimulant," that the calming agent is exchanged for an excitant. The reversal is a transformation of the essential definition of art. Such thinking about art is philosophical thought, setting the standards through which historical confrontation comes to be, prefiguring what is to come. This is something to consider, if we wish to decide in what sense Nietzsche's question concerning art can still be aesthetics, and to what extent it in any case must be such. What Nietzsche says at first with respect to music and in regard to Wagner applies to art as a whole: ". . . we no longer know how to *ground* the concepts 'model,' 'mastery,' 'perfection'—in the realm of values we grope blindly with the instincts of old love and admiration; we nearly believe that 'what is good is what pleases *us*' " (WM, 838).

In opposition to the "complete dissolution of style" in Wagner, rules and standards, and above all the grounding of such, are here demanded clearly and unequivocally; they are identified as what comes first and is essential, beyond all sheer technique and mere invention and enhancement of "means of expression." "What does all expansion of the means of expression matter when that which expresses, namely art itself, has lost the law that governs it!" Art is not only subject to rules, must not only obey laws, but is in itself legislation. Only as legislation is it truly art. What is inexhaustible, what is to be created, is the law. Art that dissolves style in sheer ebullition of feelings misses the mark, in that its discovery of law is essentially disturbed; such discovery can become actual in art only when the law drapes itself in freedom of form, in order in that way to come openly into play.

Nietzsche's aesthetic inquiry explodes its own position when it advances to its own most far-flung border. But aesthetics is by no means overcome. Such overcoming requires a still more original metamorphosis of our Dasein and our knowledge, which is something that Nietzsche only *indirectly* prepares by means of the whole of his metaphysical thought. *Our sole concern is to know the basic position of Nietzsche's thought.* At first glance, Nietzsche's thinking concerning art is aesthetic; according to its innermost will, it is metaphysical, which means it is a definition of the Being of beings. The historical fact that every true aesthetics—for example, the Kantian—explodes itself is an unmistakable sign that, although the aesthetic inquiry into art does not come about by accident, it is not what is essential.

For Nietzsche art is the essential way in which beings are made to be beings. Because what matters is the creative, legislative, form-grounding aspect of art, we can aim at the essential definition of art by asking what the creative aspect of art at any given time is. The question is not intended as a way of determining the psychological motivations that propel artistic creativity in any given case; it is meant to decide whether, when, and in what way the basic conditions of art in the grand style are there; and whether, when, and in what way they are not. Neither is this question in Nietzsche's view one for art history in the usual sense: it is for art history in the essential sense, as a question that participates in the formation of the future history of Dasein.

The question as to what has become creative in art, and what wants to become creative in it, leads directly to a number of other questions. What is it in the stimulant that properly stimulates? What possibilities are present here? How on the basis of such possibilities is the configuration of art determined? How is art the awakening of beings as beings? To what extent is it will to power?

How and where does Nietzsche think about the question concerning what is properly creative in art? He does it in those reflections that try to grasp in a more original way the distinction and opposition between the classical and romantic, in numbers 843 to 850 of *The Will to Power*. Here we cannot go into the history of the distinction and its role in art criticism, where it both clarifies and confuses. We can only pursue the matters of how Nietzsche by way of an original definition of the distinction delineates more sharply the essence of art in the grand style, and how he provides enhanced clarity for his statement that art is the stimulant of life. Of course, it is precisely these fragments that show how very much all this remains a project for the future. Here also, when clarifying the distinction between the classical and the romantic, Nietzsche has in view as his example, not the period of art around 1800, but the art of Wagner and of Greek tragedy. He thinks always on the basis of the question of the "collective artwork." That is the question of the hierarchy of the arts, the question of the form of the essential art. The terms "romantic" and "classic" are always only foreground and by way of allusion.

"A romantic is an artist whose great dissatisfaction with himself makes him creative—one who averts his glance from himself and his fellows, and looks back" (WM, 844). Here what is properly creative is discontent, the search for something altogether different; it is desire and hunger. With that, its opposite is already foreshadowed. The contrary possibility is that the creative is not a lack but plenitude, not a search but full possession, not a craving but a dispensing, not hunger but superabundance. Creation out of discontent takes "action" only in revulsion toward and withdrawal from something else. It is not active but always reactive, utterly distinct from what flows purely out of itself and its own fullness. With a preliminary glance cast toward these two basic possibilities of what is and has become creative in art, Nietzsche poses the question of "whether or not behind the antithesis of the *classical* and *romantic* that of the active and reactive lies concealed" (WM, 847). Insight into this further and more originally conceived opposition implies, however, that the classical cannot be equated with the active. For the distinction of active and reactive intersects with another, which distinguishes whether "the cause of creativity is longing after immobility, eternity, *'Being,'* or longing after destruction, change, *Becoming*" (WM, 846). The latter distinction thinks the difference between Being and Becoming, a juxtaposition that has remained dominant from the early period of Occidental thought, through its entire history, up to and including Nietzsche.

But such differentiation of longing after Being and longing after Becoming in the creative principle is still ambiguous. The ambiguity can be transformed into a clear distinction by an examination of the distinction between the active and the reactive. The latter "schema" is to be given preference over the former one and must be posited as the basic schema for the determination of the possibilities of the creative principle in art. In *The Will to Power*, number 846, Nietzsche exhibits the twofold significance of longing after Being and longing after Becoming with the help of the schema of the active and the reactive. If we use the term "schema" here, it is not to suggest an extrinsically applied framework for a mere descriptive classification and division of types. "Schema" means the guideline derived from the essence of the matter, previewing the way the decision will take.

Longing after Becoming, alteration, and therefore destruction too, can be—but need not necessarily be—"an expression of superabundant strength, pregnant with the future." Such is Dionysian art. But longing after change and Becoming can also spring from the dissatisfaction of those who hate everything that exists simply because it exists and stands. Operative here is the counterwill typical of the superfluous, the underprivileged, the disadvantaged, for whom every existent superiority constitutes in its very superiority an objection to its right to exist.

Correspondingly, the longing after Being, the will to eternalize, may derive from the possession of plenitude, from thankfulness for what is; or the perduring and binding may be erected as law and compulsion by the tyranny of a willing that wants to be rid of its inmost suffering. It therefore imposes these qualities on all things, in that way taking its revenge on them. Of such kind is the art of Richard Wagner, the art of "romantic pessimism." On the contrary, wherever the untamed and overflowing are ushered into the order of self-created law, there is classical art. But the latter cannot without further ado be conceived as the active: the purely Dionysian is also active. Just as little is the classical merely longing for Being and duration. Of such kind is romantic pessimism also. The classical is a longing for Being that flows from the fullness of gift-giving and yes-saying. With that, once more, an indication of the grand style is given.

Indeed it first seems as though the "classical style" and the "grand style" simply coincide with one another. Nevertheless, we would be thinking too cursorily were we to explain the state of affairs in this customary way. True, the immediate sense of Nietzsche's statements seems to speak for such an equation. By proceeding in that way, however, we do not heed the decisive thought. Precisely because the grand style is a bountiful and affirmative willing toward Being, its essence reveals itself only when a decision is made, indeed by means of the grand style itself, about the meaning of the Being of beings. Only on that basis is the yoke defined by which the antitheses are teamed and harnessed. But the essence of the grand style is initially given in the foreground description of the classical. Nietzsche never expresses himself about it in another way. For every great thinker always *thinks* one jump more originally than he directly *speaks*. Our interpretation must therefore try to say what is unsaid by him.

Therefore, we can demarcate the essence of the grand style only with explicit reservations. We may formulate it in the following way: the grand style prevails wherever abundance restrains itself in simplicity. But in a certain sense that is also true of the rigorous style. And even if we clarify the greatness of the grand style by saying it is that superiority which compels everything strong to be teamed with its strongest antithesis under one yoke, that too applies also to the classical type. Nietzsche himself says so (WM, 848): "In order to be the *classical* type, one must possess *all* strong, apparently contradictory gifts and desires: but in such a way that they go together under one yoke." And again (WM, 845): "Idealization of the *magnificent blasphemer* (the sense for his *greatness*) is Greek; the humiliation, defamation, vilification of the sinner is Judeo-Christian."

But whatever keeps its antithesis merely beneath it or even outside of it, as something to be battled and negated, cannot be great in the sense of the grand style, because it remains dependent upon, and lets itself be led by, what it repudiates. It remains reactive. On the contrary, in the grand style nascent law grows out of original action, which is itself the yoke. (Incidentally, we should note that the image of the "yoke" stems from the Greek mode of thought and speech.) The grand style is the active will to Being, which takes up Becoming into itself.*

But whatever is said about the classical type is said with the intention of making the grand style visible by means of what is most akin to it. Hence only what assimilates its sharpest antithesis, and not what merely holds that antithesis down and suppresses it, is truly great; such transformation does not cause the antithesis to disappear, however, but to come to its essential unfolding. We recall what Nietzsche says about the "grandiose initiative" of German Idealism, which tries to think of evil as proper to the essence of the Absolute. Nevertheless, Nietzsche would not consider Hegel's philosophy to be a philosophy in the grand style. It marks the end of the classical style.

But quite beyond the effort to establish a "definition" of the grand style, we must investigate the more essential matter of the way in which Nietzsche tries to determine what is creative in art. This we can do with the aid of a classification of artistic styles within the framework of the distinctions active-reactive and Being-Becoming. In that regard some basic determinations of Being manifest themselves: the active and reactive are conjoined in the essence of motion (*kinēsis, metabolē*). With a view to these determinations, the Greek definitions of *dynamis* and *energeia* take shape as determinations of Being in the sense of presencing. If the essence of the grand style is determined by these ultimate and primal metaphysical contexts, then they must rise to meet us wherever Nietzsche tries to interpret and grasp the Being of beings.

Nietzsche interprets the Being of beings as will to power. Art he considers the supreme configuration of will to power. The proper

---

Der grosse Stil ist der aktive Wille zum Sein, so zwar, dass dieser das Werden in sich aufhebt. The Hegelian formulation *das Werden in sich aufheben* at first seems to mean that the will to Being cancels and transcends Becoming. But the will to Being would have to be a kind of surpassing that *preserves* Becoming—else it would be, in Hegel's words, the lifeless transcendence of an empty universal, in Nietzsche's, the subterfuge of clever but weary men who must avenge themselves on Time. In the fourth and final section of his *Introduction to Metaphysics* Heidegger suggests how *Sein* and *Werden* may be, must be, thought together as *physis*.

essence of art is exemplified in the grand style. But the latter, because of its own essential unity, points to an original, concrescive unity of the active and reactive, of Being and Becoming. At the same time we must consider what the precedence of the distinction active-reactive, which is expressly emphasized over the distinction of Being and Becoming, suggests about Nietzsche's metaphysics. For formally one could sub-sume the distinction active-reactive under one member of the subordi-nate distinction of Being and Becoming—i.e., under Becoming. The articulation of the active, and of Being and Becoming, into an original unity proper to the grand style must therefore be carried out in will to power, if will to power is thought metaphysically. But will to power *is* as eternal recurrence. In the latter Nietzsche wants his thinking to fuse Being and Becoming, action and reaction, in an original unity. With that we are granted a vista onto the metaphysical horizon upon which we are to think what Nietzsche calls the grand style and art in general.

However, we would like to clear the path to the metaphysical realm first of all by passing through the essence of art. It may now become clearer why our inquiry into Nietzsche's basic metaphysical position takes art as its point of departure, and that our starting point is by no means arbitrary. The grand style is the highest feeling of power. Ro-mantic art, springing from dissatisfaction and deficiency, is a wanting-to-be-away-from-oneself. But according to its proper essence, willing is to-want-oneself. Of course, "oneself" is never meant as what is at hand, existing just as it is; "oneself" means what first of all wants to become what it is. Willing proper does not go away from itself, but goes way beyond itself; in such surpassing itself the will captures the one who wills, absorbing and transforming him into and along with itself. Want-ing-to-be-away-from-oneself is therefore basically a not-willing. In con-trast, wherever superabundance and plenitude, that is, the revelation of essence which unfolds of itself, bring themselves under the law of the simple, willing wills itself in its essence, and *is* will. Such will is will to power. For power is not compulsion or violence. Genuine power does not yet prevail where it must simply hold its position in response to the threat of something that has not yet been neutralized. Power prevails only where the simplicity of calm dominates, by which the antithetical is preserved, i.e., transfigured, in the unity of a yoke that sustains the tension of a bow.

Will to power is properly there where power no longer needs the accoutrements of battle, in the sense of being merely reactive; its superiority binds all things, in that the will releases all things to their essence and their own bounds. When we are able to survey what Nietzsche thinks and demands with regard to the grand style, only then have we arrived at the peak of his "aesthetics," which at that point is no longer aesthetics at all. Now for the first time we can glance back over our own way and try to grasp what up to now has eluded us. Our path toward an understanding of Nietzsche's thought on art advanced as follows.

In order to attain that field of vision in which Nietzsche's inquiry moves, five statements (in addition to his principal statement) on art were listed and discussed along general lines, but not properly grounded. For the grounding can unfold only by way of a return back to the essence of art. But the essence of art is elaborated and determined in Nietzsche's "aesthetics." We tried to portray that aesthetics by bringing together traditional views into a new unity. The unifying center was provided by what Nietzsche calls the grand style. So long as we do not make an effort to establish internal order in Nietzsche's doctrine of art, in spite of the matter's fragmentary character, his utterances remain a tangle of accidental insights into and arbitrary observations about art and the beautiful. For that reason the path must always be held clearly in view.

It advances from rapture, as the basic aesthetic mood, to beauty, as attuning; from beauty, as the standard-giver, back to what takes its measure from beauty, to creation and reception; from these, in turn, over to that in which and as which the attuning is portrayed, to form. Finally, we tried to grasp the unity of the reciprocal relation of rapture and beauty, of creation, reception, and form, as the grand style. In the grand style the essence of art becomes actual.

18. Grounding the Five Statements on Art

How, and to what extent, can we now ground the five statements on art listed earlier?

The *first* statement says: art is for us the most familiar and perspicuous configuration of will to power. To be sure, we may view the statement as grounded only when we are familiar with other forms and stages of will to power, that is to say, only when we have possibilities for comparison. But even now elucidation of the statement is possible, merely on the basis of the clarified essence of art. Art is the configuration most familiar to us, since art is grasped aesthetically as a state; the state in which it comes to presence and from which it springs is a state proper to man, and hence to ourselves. Art belongs to a realm where we find ourselves—we are the very realm. Art does not belong to regions which we ourselves are not, and which therefore remain foreign to us, regions such as nature. But art, as a human production, does not belong simply in a general way to what is well known to us; art is *the most* familiar. The grounds for that lie in Nietzsche's conception of the kind of givenness of that in which, from the aesthetic point of view, art is actual. It is actual in the rapture of embodying life. What does Nietzsche say about the givenness of life? "Belief in the body is more fundamental than belief in the *soul*" (WM, 491). And: "Essential: to proceed from the *body* and use it as the guideline. It is the much richer phenomenon, which admits of more precise observation. Belief in the body is better established than belief in the spirit" (WM, 532).

According to these remarks the body and the physiological are also more familiar; being proper to man, they are what is most familiar to him. But inasmuch as art is grounded in the aesthetic state, which must be grasped physiologically, art is the most familiar configuration of will to power, and at the same time the most perspicuous. The aesthetic state is a doing and perceiving which we ourselves execute. We do not dwell alongside the event as spectators; we ourselves remain within the state. Our Dasein receives from it a luminous relation to beings, the sight in which beings are visible to us. The aesthetic state is the envisionment through which we constantly see, so that everything here is discernible to us. Art is the most visionary configuration of will to power.*

The *second* statement says: art must be grasped in terms of the artist. It has been shown that Nietzsche conceives of art in terms of the creative behavior of the artist; why such a conception should be necessary has not been shown. The grounding of the demand expressed in the statement is so odd that it does not seem to be a serious grounding at all. At the outset, art is posited as a configuration of will to power. But will to power, as self-assertion, is a constant creating. So art is interrogated as to that in it which is creative, superabundance or privation. But creation within art actually occurs in the productive activity of the artist. Thus, initiating the inquiry with the activity of the artist most likely guarantees access to creation in general and thereby to will to power. The statement follows from the basic premise concerning art as a configuration of will to power.

The listing and the grounding of this statement do not mean to suggest that Nietzsche holds up prior aesthetics in front of him, sees that it is inadequate, and notices too that it usually, though not exclusively, takes the man who enjoys works of art as its point of departure. With these facts staring him in the face it occurs to him to try another way for once, the way of the creators. Rather, the first and leading basic experience of art itself remains the experience that it has a significance

---

*"Visionary" is to translate *durchsichtig,* otherwise rendered as "lucid" or "perspicuous." The entire paragraph expands upon Nietzsche's statement concerning art as the most perspicuous form of will to power by interpreting the vision, *die Sicht,* and envisionment, *das Sichtige,* that art opens up for beings.

for the grounding of history, and that its essence consists in such significance. Thus the creator, the artist, must be fixed in view. Nietzsche expresses the historical essence of art early on in the following words: "Culture can proceed only on the basis of the centralizing significance of an art or an artwork" (X, 188).

The *third* statement says: art is the basic occurrence within beings as a whole. On the basis of what has gone before, this statement is the least transparent and least grounded of all, that is, within and on the basis of Nietzsche's metaphysics. Whether, and to what extent, beings are most in being in art can be decided only when we have answered two questions. First, in what does the beingness of beings consist? What is the being itself in truth? Second, to what extent can art, among beings, be more in being than the others?

The second question is not altogether foreign to us, since in the fifth statement something is asserted of art which ascribes to it a peculiar precedence. The fifth statement says: art is worth more than truth. "Truth" here means the true, in the sense of true beings; more precisely, beings that may be considered true being, being-in-itself. Since Plato, being-in-itself has been taken to be the supersensuous, which is removed and rescued from the transiency of the sensuous. In Nietzsche's view the value of a thing is measured by what it contributes to the enhancement of the actuality of beings. That art is of more value than truth means that art, as "sensuous," is more in being than the supersensuous. Granted that supersensuous being served heretofore as what is highest, if art is more in being, then it proves to be the being most in being, the basic occurrence within beings as a whole.

Yet what does "Being" mean, if the sensuous can be said to be more in being? What does "sensuous" mean here? What does it have to do with "truth"? How can it be even higher in value than truth? What does "truth" mean here? How does Nietzsche define its essence? At present all this is obscure. We do not see any way in which the *fifth* statement might be sufficiently grounded; we do not see how the statement *can* be grounded.

Such questionableness radiates over all the other statements, above all, the third, which obviously can be decided and grounded only when the fifth statement has been grounded. But the fifth statement must be presupposed if we are to understand the *fourth* as well, according to which art is the countermovement to nihilism. For nihilism, i.e., Platonism, posits the supersensuous as true being, on the basis of which all remaining beings are demoted to the level of proper nonbeing, demoted, denigrated, and declared nugatory. Thus everything hangs on the explanation and grounding of the *fifth* statement: art is worth more than truth. What is truth? In what does its essence consist?

That question is always already included in the guiding question and the grounding question of philosophy. It runs ahead of them and yet is most intrinsic to these very questions. It is the primal question of philosophy.

19. The Raging Discordance between Truth and Art

That the question concerning art leads us directly to the one that is preliminary to all questions already suggests that in a distinctive sense it conceals in itself essential relations to the grounding and guiding questions of philosophy. Hence our previous clarification of the essence of art will also be brought to a fitting conclusion only in terms of the question of truth.

In order to discern the connection between art and truth right from the outset, the question concerning the essence of truth and the way in which Nietzsche poses and answers the question should be prepared. Such preparation is to occur through a discussion of what it is in the essence of art that calls forth the question concerning truth. To that end we should remember once more Nietzsche's words on the connection between art and truth. He jotted them down in the year 1888 on the occasion of a meditation on his first book: "Very early in my life I took the question of the relation of *art* to *truth* seriously: and even now I stand in holy dread in the face of this discordance" (XIV, 368).

The relation between art and truth is a discordance that arouses dread.* To what extent? How, and in what respects, does art come into relation to truth? In what sense is the relation for Nietzsche a discordance? In order to see to what extent art as such comes into

---

*Ein Entsetzen erregender Zwiespalt. In the title of this section, *Der erregende Zwiespalt zwischen Wahrheit und Kunst,* the phrase *erregende Zwiespalt* is actually a condensation of the statement made here. That is to say, discordance between art and truth "rages" insofar as it *arouses dread.*

relation to truth, we must say more clearly than we have before what Nietzsche understands by "truth." In our previous discussions we gave some hints in this direction. But we have not yet advanced as far as a conceptual definition of Nietzsche's notion of truth. For that we require a preparatory reflection.

A meditation on fundamentals concerning the realm in which we are moving becomes necessary whenever we speak the word "truth" in a way that is not altogether vacuous. For without insight into these contexts we lack all the prerequisites for understanding the point where all the bypaths of Nietzsche's metaphysical thought clearly converge. It is one thing if Nietzsche himself, under the burdens that oppressed him, did not achieve sufficient perspicuity here; it is another if we who follow him renounce the task of penetrating meditation.

Every time we try to achieve clarity with regard to such basic words as truth, beauty, Being, art, knowledge, history, and freedom, we must heed two things.

First, that a clarification is necessary here has its grounds in the concealment of the essence of what is named in such words. Such clarification becomes indispensable from the moment we experience the fact that human Dasein, insofar as it is—insofar as it is itself—is steered directly toward whatever is named in such basic words and is inextricably caught up in relations with them. That becomes manifest whenever human Dasein becomes historical, and that means whenever it comes to confront beings as such, in order to adopt a stance in their midst and to ground the site of that stance definitively. Depending on what knowledge retains essential proximity to what is named in such basic words, or lapses into distance from it, the content of the name, the realm of the word, and the compelling force of the naming power vary.

When we consider this state of affairs in relation to the word "truth" in an extrinsic and desultory manner, we are accustomed to saying that the word has sundry meanings which are not sharply distinguished from one another, meanings that belong together on the basis of a common ground which we are vaguely aware of but which we do not clearly perceive. The most extrinsic form in which we encounter the ambiguity of the word is the "lexical." In the dictionary the meanings are enumerated and exhibited for selection. The life of actual language consists in multiplicity of meaning. To relegate the animated, vigorous word to the immobility of a univocal, mechanically programmed sequence of signs would mean the death of language and the petrifaction and devastation of Dasein.

Why speak of such commonplaces here? Because the "lexical" representation of the multiplicity of meanings for such a basic word easily causes us to overlook the fact that here all the meanings and the differences among them are historical and therefore necessary. Accordingly, it can never be left to caprice, and can never be inconsequential, which of the word meanings we choose in our attempt to grasp the essence named—and thus already illuminated—in the basic word and to classify it as a key word for a given discipline and area of inquiry. Every attempt of this kind is a historical decision. The leading meaning of such a basic word, which speaks to us more or less clearly, is nothing evident, although our being accustomed to it seems to suggest that. *Basic words are historical.* That does not mean simply that they have various meanings for various ages which, because they are past, we can survey historically; it means that they ground history now and in the times to come in accordance with the interpretation of them that comes to prevail. The historicity of the basic words, understood in this fashion, is one of the things that must be heeded in thinking through those basic words.

Second, we must pay attention to the way such basic words vary in meaning. Here there are principal orbits or routes; but within them meanings may oscillate. Such oscillation is not mere laxity in linguistic usage. It is the breath of history. When Goethe or Hegel says the word "education," and when an educated man of the 1890s says it, not only is the formal content of the utterance different, but the kind of world encapsulated in the saying is different, though not unrelated. When Goethe says "nature," and when Hölderlin speaks the same word, different worlds reign. Were language no more than a sequence of communicative signs, then it would remain something just as arbitrary and indifferent as the mere choice and application of such signs.

But because in the very foundations of our being language as resonant signification roots us to our earth and transports and ties us to our world, meditation on language and its historical dominion is always the action that gives shape to Dasein itself. The will to originality, rigor, and measure in words is therefore no mere aesthetic pleasantry; it is the work that goes on in the essential nucleus of our Dasein, which is historical existence.

But in what sense are there what we have called principal orbits or routes for the historical expansion of meanings among the basic words? Our example will be the word "truth." Without insight into these connections, the peculiarity, difficulty, and genuine excitement apropos of the question of truth remain closed to us; so does the possibility of understanding Nietzsche's deepest need with respect to the question of the relation of art and truth.

The assertion "Among Goethe's accomplishments in the field of science the theory of colors also belongs" is true. With the statement we have at our disposal something that is true. We are, as we say, in possession of "a truth." The assertion $2 \times 2 = 4$ is true. With this statement we have another "truth." Thus there are many truths of many kinds: things we determine in our everyday existence, truths of natural science, truths of the historical sciences. To what extent are these truths what their name says they are? To the extent that they satisfy generally and in advance whatever is proper to a "truth." Such is what makes a *true assertion* true. Just as we call the essence of the just "justice," the essence of the cowardly "cowardice," and the essence of the beautiful "beauty," so must we call the essence of the true "truth." But truth, conceived as the essence of the true, is solely one. For the essence of something is that in which everything of that kind—in our case, everything true—dovetails. If truth suggests the essence of the true, then truth is but one: it becomes impossible to talk about "truths."

Thus we already have two meanings for the word "truth," basically different but related to one another. If the word "truth" is meant in the sense which admits of no multiplicity, it names the essence of the true. On the contrary, if we take the word in the sense where a plurality is meant, then the word "truth" means not the essence of the true but any given truth as such. The essence of a matter can be conceived principally or exclusively as what may be attributed to anything that satisfies the essence of the matter. If one restricts himself to this plausible conception of essence, which, however, is neither the sole nor the original conception, as the one which is valid for many, the following may be readily deduced concerning the essential word "truth." Because being true may be asserted of every true statement as such, an abbreviated form of thought and speech can also call what is true itself a "truth." But what is meant here is "something true." Something true now is called simply "truth." The name "truth" is in an essential sense ambiguous. Truth means the one essence and also the many which satisfy the essence. Language itself has a peculiar predilection for that sort of ambiguity. We therefore encounter it early on and constantly. The inner grounds for the ambiguity are these: inasmuch as we speak, and that means comport ourselves to beings through speech, speaking on the basis of beings and with reference back to them, we mean for the most part beings themselves. The being in question is always this or that individual and specific being. At the same time it is a being as such, that is, it is of such a genus and species, such an essence. This house as such is of the essence and species "house."

When we mean something true, we of course understand the essence of truth along with it. We must understand the latter if, whenever we intend something true, we are to know what we have in front of us. Although the essence itself is not expressly and especially named, but always only previewed and implied, the word "truth," which names the essence, is nevertheless used for true things themselves. The name for the essence glides unobtrusively into our naming such things that participate in that essence. Such slippage is aided and abetted by the fact that for the most part we let ourselves be determined by beings themselves and not by their essence as such.

The manner in which we examine the basic words therefore moves along two principal routes: the route of the essence, and that which veers away from the essence and yet is related back to it. But an interpretation which is as old as our traditional Western logic and grammar makes this apparently simple state of affairs even simpler and therefore more ordinary. It is said that the essence—here the essence of the true, which makes everything true be what it is—because it is valid for many true things, is the generally and universally valid. The truth of the essence consists in nothing else than such universal validity. Thus truth, as the essence of the true, is the universal. However, the "truth" which is one of a plurality, "truths," the individual truth, true propositions, are "cases" that fall under the universal. Nothing is clearer than that. But there are various kinds of clarity and transparency, among them a kind that thrives on the fact that what seems to be lucid is really vacuous, that the least possible amount of thought goes into it, the danger of obscurity being thwarted in that way. But so it is when one designates the essence of a thing as the universal concept. That in certain realms—not all—the essence of something holds for many particular items (manifold validity) is a consequence of the essence, but it does not hit upon its essentiality.

The equating of essence with the character of the universal, even as an essential conclusion which has but conditional validity, would of itself not have been so fatal had it not for centuries barred the way to a decisive question. The essence of the true holds for the particular assertions and propositions which, as individuals, differ greatly from one another according to content and structure. The true is in each case something various, but the essence, as the universal which is valid for many, is one. But universal validity, which is valid for many things that belong together, is now made what is universally valid without qualification. "Universally valid" now means not only valid for many particular items that belong together, but also what is always and everywhere valid in itself, immutable and eternal, transcending time.

The result is the proposition of the immutability of essences, including the essence of truth. The proposition is logically correct but metaphysically untrue. Viewed in terms of the particular "cases" of the many true statements, the essence of the true is that in which the many dovetail. The essence in which the many dovetail must be one and the same thing for them. But from that it by no means follows that the essence in itself cannot be changeable. For, supposing that the essence of truth did change, that which changes could always still be a "one" which holds for "many," the transformation not disturbing that relationship. But what is preserved in the metamorphosis is what is unchangeable in the essence, which essentially unfolds in its very transformation. The essentiality of essence, its inexhaustibility, is thereby affirmed, and also its genuine selfhood and selfsameness. The latter stands in sharp contrast to the vapid selfsameness of the monotonous, which is the only way the unity of essence can be thought when it is taken merely as the universal. If one stands by the conception of the selfsameness of the essence of truth which is derived from traditional logic, he will immediately (and from that point of view quite correctly) say: "The notion of a change of essence leads to relativism; there is only one truth and it is the same for everybody; every relativism is disruptive of the general order and leads to sheer caprice and anarchy." But the right to such an objection to the essential transformation of truth stands and falls with the appropriateness of the representation of the "one" and the "same" therein presupposed, which is called the absolute, and with the right to define the essentiality of essence as manifold validity. The objection that essential transformation leads to relativism is possible only on the basis of deception concerning the essence of the absolute and the essentiality of essence.

That digression must suffice for our present effort to unfold what Nietzsche in his discussions of the relation between art and truth understands by "truth." According to what we have shown, we must first ask upon which route of meaning the word "truth" moves for Nietzsche in the context of his discussions of the relationship between art and truth. The answer is that it moves along the route which deviates from the essential route. That means that in the fundamental question which arouses dread Nietzsche nevertheless does not arrive at the proper question of truth, in the sense of a discussion of the essence of the true. That essence is presupposed as evident. For Nietzsche truth is not the essence of the true but the true itself, which satisfies the essence of truth. It is of decisive importance to know that Nietzsche does not pose the question of truth proper, the question concerning the essence of the true and the truth of essence, and with it the question of the ineluctable possibility of its essential transformation. Nor does he ever stake out the domain of the question. This we must know, not only in order to judge Nietzsche's position with regard to the question of the relation of art and truth, but above all in order to estimate and measure in a fundamental way the degree of originality of the inquiry encompassed by Nietzsche's philosophy as a whole. That the question of the essence of truth is missing in Nietzsche's thought is an oversight unlike any other; it cannot be blamed on him alone, or him first of all—if it can be blamed on anyone. The "oversight" pervades the entire history of Occidental philosophy since Plato and Aristotle.

That many thinkers have concerned themselves with the concept of truth; that Descartes interprets truth as certitude; that Kant, not independent of that tendency, distinguishes an empirical and a transcendental truth; that Hegel defines anew the important distinction between abstract and concrete truth, i.e., truth of science and truth of speculation; that Nietzsche says "truth" is error; all these are advances of thoughtful inquiry. And yet! They all leave untouched the essence of truth itself. No matter how far removed Nietzsche is from Descartes and no matter how much he emphasizes the distance between them, in what is essential he still stands close to Descartes. All the same, it would be pedantic to insist that the use of the word "truth" be kept within the strict bounds of particular routes of meaning. For as a basic word it is at the same time a universal word; thus it is entrenched in the laxity of linguistic usage.

We must ask with greater penetration what Nietzsche understands by truth. Above we said that he means the true. Yet what is the true? What is it here that satisfies the essence of truth; in what is that essence itself determined? The true is true being, what is in truth actual. What does "in truth" mean here? Answer: what is in truth known. For our knowing is what can be true or false right from the start. Truth is truth of knowledge. Knowledge is so intrinsically the residence of truth that a knowing which is untrue cannot be considered knowledge. But knowledge is a way of access to beings; the true is what is truly known, the actual. The true is established as something true in, by, and for knowledge alone. Truth is proper to the realm of knowledge. Here decisions are made about the true and the untrue. And depending on the way the essence of knowledge is demarcated, the essential concept of truth is defined.

Our knowing as such is always an approximation to what is to be known, a measuring of itself upon something. As a consequence of the character of measurement, knowing implies a relation to some sort of standard. The standard, and our relation to it, can be interpreted in various ways. In order to clarify the interpretive possibilities with regard to the essence of knowing, we will describe the principal trait of two basically different types. By way of exception, and for the sake of brevity, we will take up two terms which are not to suggest any more than what we will make of them here: the conceptions of knowledge in "Platonism" and "Positivism."

20. Truth in Platonism and Positivism. Nietzsche's Attempt to Overturn Platonism on the Basis of the Fundamental Experience of Nihilism

We say "Platonism," and not Plato, because here we are dealing with the conception of knowledge that corresponds to that term, not by way of an original and detailed examination of Plato's works, but only by setting in rough relief one particular aspect of his work. Knowing is approximation to what is to be known. What is to be known? The being itself. Of what does it consist? Where is its Being determined? On the basis of the Ideas and *as* the *ideai*. They "are" what is apprehended when we look at things to see how they look, to see what they give themselves out to be, to see their what-being (*to ti estin*). What makes a table a table, table-being, can be seen; to be sure, not with the sensory eye of the body, but with the eye of the soul. Such sight is apprehension of what a matter is, its Idea. What is so seen is something nonsensuous. But because it is that in the light of which we first come to know what is sensuous—that thing there, as a table—the nonsensuous at the same time stands above the sensuous. It is the supersensuous and the proper what-being and Being of the being. Therefore, knowledge must measure itself against the supersensuous, the Idea; it must somehow bring forward what is not sensuously visible for a face-to-face encounter: it must put forward or present.* Knowledge is presentative measurement

---

*"To put forward or present" is an attempt to translate the hyphenated word *vor-stellen*, which without the hyphen is usually translated as "to represent."

of self upon the supersensuous. Pure nonsensuous presentation, which unfolds in a mediating relation that derives from what is represented, is called *theōria*. Knowledge is in essence theoretical.

The conception of knowledge as "theoretical" is undergirded by a particular interpretation of Being; such a conception has meaning and is correct only on the basis of metaphysics. To preach the "eternally immutable essence of science" is therefore either to employ an empty turn of phrase that does not take seriously what it says, or to mistake the basic facts concerning the origin of the concept of Western science. The "theoretical" is not merely something distinguished and differentiated from the "practical," but is itself grounded in a particular basic experience of Being. The same is true also of the "practical," which for its part is juxtaposed to the "theoretical." Both of these, and the difference between them, are to be grasped solely from the essence of Being which is relevant in each case, which is to say, they are to be grasped metaphysically. Neither does the practical change on the basis of the theoretical, nor does the theoretical change on the basis of the practical: both change always simultaneously on the basis of their fundamental metaphysical position.

The interpretation of knowledge in positivism differs from that in Platonism. To be sure, knowing here too is a measuring. But the standard which representation must respect, right from the start and constantly, differs: it is what lies before us from the outset, what is constantly placed before us, the *positum*. The latter is what is given in sensation, the sensuous. Here too measurement is an immediate presenting or putting forward ("sensing"), which is defined by a mediating interrelation of what is given by way of sensation, a judging. The essence of judgment in turn can itself be interpreted in various ways—a matter we will not pursue any further here.

Without deciding prematurely that Nietzsche's conception of knowledge takes one of these two basic directions—Platonism or positivism—or is a hybrid of both, we can say that the word "truth" for him means as much as the true, and the true what is known in truth. Knowing is a theoretical-scientific grasp of the actual in the broadest sense.

That suggests in a general way that Nietzsche's conception of the essence of truth keeps to the realm of the long tradition of Western thought, no matter how much Nietzsche's particular interpretations of that conception deviate from earlier ones. But also in relation to our particular question concerning the relation of art and truth, we have just now taken a decisive step. According to our clarification of the guiding conception of truth, what are here brought into relation are, putting it more strictly, on the one hand, art, and on the other, theoretical-scientific knowledge. Art, grasped in Nietzsche's sense in terms of the artist, is creation; creation is related to beauty. Correspondingly, truth is the object related to knowledge. Thus the relation of art and truth that is here in question, the one which arouses dread, must be conceived as the relation of art and scientific knowledge, and correlatively the relation of beauty and truth.

But to what extent is the relation for Nietzsche a discordance? To what extent do art and knowledge, beauty and truth at all enter into noteworthy relation? Surely not on the basis of the wholly extrinsic grounds, definitive for the usual philosophies and sciences of culture, that art exists and that science is right there beside it; the fact that both belong to a culture; and the fact that if one wants to erect a system of culture, one must also provide information about the interrelations of these cultural phenomena. Were Nietzsche's point of inquiry merely that of the philosophy of culture, intending to erect a tidy system of cultural phenomena and cultural values, then the relation of art and truth could surely never become for it a discordance, much less one that arouses dread.

In order to see how for Nietzsche art and truth can and must in some way come into noteworthy relation, let us proceed with a renewed clarification of his concept of truth, since we have already treated sufficiently the other member of the relation, art. In order to characterize more precisely Nietzsche's concept of truth, we must ask in what way he conceives of knowledge and what standard he applies to it. How does Nietzsche's conception of knowledge stand in relation to the two basic tendencies of epistemological interpretation described above, Platonism and positivism? Nietzsche once says, in a brief observation found among the early sketches (1870–71) for his first treatise, "My philosophy an *inverted Platonism:* the farther removed from true being, the purer, the finer, the better it is. Living in semblance as goal" (IX, 190). That is an astonishing preview in the thinker of his entire later philosophical position. For during the last years of his creative life he labors at nothing else than the overturning of Platonism. Of course, we may not overlook the fact that the "inverted Platonism" of his early period is enormously different from the position finally attained in *Twilight of the Idols.* Nevertheless, on the basis of Nietzsche's own words we can now define with greater trenchancy his conception of truth, which is to say, his conception of the true.

For Platonism, the Idea, the supersensuous, is the true, true being. In contrast, the sensuous is *mē on.* The latter suggests, not nonbeing pure and simple, *ouk on,* but *mē*—what may not be addressed as being even though it is not simply nothing. Insofar as, and to the extent that, it may be called being, the sensuous must be measured upon the supersensuous; nonbeing possesses the shadow and the residues of Being which fall from true being.

To overturn Platonism thus means to reverse the standard relation: what languishes below in Platonism, as it were, and would be measured against the supersensuous, must now be put on top; by way of reversal, the supersensuous must now be placed in its service. When the inversion is fully executed, the sensuous becomes being proper, i.e., the true, i.e., truth. The true is the sensuous. That is what "positivism" teaches. Nevertheless, it would be premature to interpret Nietzsche's conception of knowledge and of the kind of truth pertaining to it as "positivistic," although that is what usually happens. It is indisputable that prior to the time of his work on the planned magnum opus, *The Will to Power,* Nietzsche went through a period of extreme positivism; these were the years 1879–81, the years of his decisive development toward maturity. Such positivism, though of course transformed, became a part of his later fundamental position also. But what matters is precisely the transformation, especially in relation to the overturning of Platonism as a whole. In that inversion Nietzsche's philosophical thought proper comes to completion. For Nietzsche the compelling task from early on was to think through the philosophy of Plato, indeed from two different sides. His original profession as a classical philologist brought him to Plato, partly through his teaching duties, but above all through a philosophical inclination to Plato. During the Basel years he held lectures on Plato several times: "Introduction to the Study of the Platonic Dialogues" in 1871–72 and 1873–74, and "Plato's Life and Teachings" in 1876 (see XIX, 235 ff.).

But here again one discerns clearly the philosophical influence of Schopenhauer. Schopenhauer himself grounds his entire philosophy, indeed consciously and expressly, on Plato and Kant. Thus in the Preface to his major work, *The World as Will and Representation* (1818), he writes:

> Hence *Kant's* is the sole philosophy a basic familiarity with which is all but presupposed by what will be presented here. —If, however, the reader has in addition lingered awhile in the school of the divine Plato, he will be all the more receptive and all the better prepared to hear me.

As a third inspiration Schopenhauer then names the Indian Vedas. We know how much Schopenhauer misinterprets and vulgarizes the Kantian philosophy. The same happens with regard to Plato's philosophy. In the face of Schopenhauer's coarsening of the Platonic philosophy, Nietzsche, as a classical philologist and a considerable expert in that area, is not so defenseless as he is with respect to Schopenhauer's Kant-interpretation. Even in his early years (through the Basel lectures) Nietzsche achieves a remarkable autonomy and thereby a higher truth in his Plato interpretation than Schopenhauer does in his. Above all he rejects Schopenhauer's interpretation of the apprehension of the Ideas as simple "intuition." He emphasizes that apprehension of the Ideas is "dialectical." Schopenhauer's opinion concerning such apprehension, that it is intuition, stems from a misunderstanding of Schelling's teaching concerning "intellectual intuition" as the basic act of metaphysical knowledge.

However, the interpretation of Plato and of Platonism which tends to follow the direction of philology and the history of philosophy, although it is an aid, is not the decisive path for Nietzsche's philosophical advance toward the Platonic doctrine and confrontation with it. It is not the decisive path of his experiencing an insight into the necessity of overturning Platonism. Nietzsche's fundamental experience is his growing insight into the basic development of our history. In his view it is nihilism. Nietzsche expresses incessantly and passionately the fundamental experience of his existence as a thinker. To the blind, to those who cannot see and above all do not want to see, his words easily sound overwrought, as though he were raving. And yet when we plumb the depths of his insight and consider how very closely the basic historical development of nihilism crowds and oppresses him, then we may be inclined to call his manner of speech almost placid. One of the essential formulations that designate the event of nihilism says, "God is dead." (Cf. now *Holzwege*, 1950, pp. 193–247.)* The phrase "God is dead" is not an atheistic proclamation: it is a formula for the fundamental experience of an event in Occidental history.

Only in the light of that basic experience does Nietzsche's utterance, "My philosophy is inverted Platonism," receive its proper range and intensity. In the same broad scope of significance, therefore, Nietzsche's interpretation and conception of the essence of truth must be conceived. For that reason we ought to remember what Nietzsche understands by nihilism and in what sense alone that word may be used as a term for the history of philosophy.

By nihilism Nietzsche means the historical development, i.e., event, that the uppermost values devalue themselves, that all goals are an-

---

*See the English translation, "The Word of Nietzsche: 'God is Dead,' " in Martin Heidegger, *The Question Concerning Technology and Other Essays,* translated by William Lovitt (New York: Harper & Row, 1978). Heidegger's reference, placed in parentheses, apparently was added in 1961. Note that the "event" of nihilism, cited four times in this and the following paragraphs, occasions one of the earliest "terminological" uses of the word *Ereignis* in Heidegger's published writings. (Cf. the use of the word *Geschehnis* in the *Holzwege* article, p. 195, and in *Einführung in die Metaphysik,* p. 4.) The word's appearance in the context of Nietzsche's account of nihilism assumes even more importance when we recall a parenthetical remark in the "Protocol" to the Todt-nauberg Seminar on "Zeit und Sein" (*Zur Sache des Denkens* [Tübingen: M. Niemeyer, 1969], p. 46): "The relationships and contexts which constitute the essential structure of *Ereignis* were worked out between 1936 and 1938," which is to say, precisely at the time of the first two Nietzsche lecture courses.

nihilated, and that all estimates of value collide against one another. Such collision Nietzsche describes at one point in the following way:

> . . . we call good someone who does his heart's bidding, but also the one who only tends to his duty;
>
> we call good the meek and the reconciled, but also the courageous, unbending, severe;
>
> we call good somone who employs no force against himself, but also the heroes of self-overcoming;
>
> we call good the utterly loyal friend of the true, but also the man of piety, one who transfigures things;
>
> we call good those who are obedient to themselves, but also the pious;
>
> we call good those who are noble and exalted, but also those who do not despise and condescend;
>
> we call good those of joyful spirit, the peaceable, but also those desirous of battle and victory;
>
> we call good those who always want to be first, but also those who do not want to take precedence over anyone in any respect.
>
> (From unpublished material composed during the period of *The Gay Science,* 1881–82; see XII, 81.)

There is no longer any goal in and through which all the forces of the historical existence of peoples can cohere and in the direction of which they can develop; no goal of such a kind, which means at the same time and above all else no goal of such power that it can by virtue of its power conduct Dasein to its realm in a unified way and bring it to creative evolution. By establishment of the goal Nietzsche understands the metaphysical task of ordering beings as a whole, not merely the announcement of a provisional whither and wherefore. But a genuine establishment of the goal must at the same time ground its goal. Such grounding cannot be exhaustive if, in its "theoretical" exhibition of the reasons which justify the goal to be established, it asseverates that such a move is "logically" necessary. To ground the goal means to awaken and liberate those powers which lend the newly established goal its surpassing and pervasive energy to inspire commitment. Only in that way can historical Dasein take root and flourish in the realm opened and identified by the goal. Here, finally, and that means primordially, belongs the growth of forces which sustain and propel preparation of the new realm, the advance into it, and the cultivation of what unfolds within it, forces which induce it to undertake bold deeds.

Nietzsche has all this in view when he speaks of nihilism, goals, and establishment of goals. But he also sees the necessary range of such establishment, a range determined by the incipient dissolution of all kinds of order all over the earth. It cannot apply to individual groups, classes, and sects, nor even to individual states and nations. It must be European at least. That does not mean to say that it should be "international." For implied in the essence of a creative establishment of goals and the preparation for such establishment is that it comes to exist and swings into action, as historical, only in the unity of the fully historical Dasein of men in the form of particular nations. That means neither isolation from other nations nor hegemony over them. Establishment of goals is in itself confrontation, the initiation of struggle. *But the genuine struggle is the one in which those who struggle excel, first the one then the other, and in which the power for such excelling unfolds within them.*

Meditation of such kind on the historical event of nihilism and on the condition for overcoming it utterly—meditation on the basic metaphysical position needed to that end, thinking through the ways and means of awakening and outfitting such conditions—Nietzsche sometimes calls "grand politics."* That sounds like the "grand style." If we *think* both as belonging originally together, we secure ourselves against misinterpretations of their essential sense. Neither does the "grand style" want an "aesthetic culture," nor does the "grand politics" want the exploitative power politics of imperialism. The grand style can be created only by means of the grand politics, and the latter has the most

---

*Nietzsche uses the phrase *die grosse Politik* during the period of the preparation of *Beyond Good and Evil;* cf. WM, 463 and 978, both notes from the year 1885. The source for Heidegger's entire discussion of *Zielsetzung* seems to be section 208 of *Beyond Good and Evil.* Cf. also the entire eighth part of that work, "Nations and Fatherlands." We should also note that *die grosse Politik* occupied the very center of interest in Nietzsche in Germany after World War I: not only the Stefan George circle and Alfred Baeumler, but even Karl Jaspers (see his *Nietzsche,* Bk. II, chap. 4), emphasized it.

intrinsic law of its will in the grand style. What does Nietzsche say of the grand style? "What makes the *grand style:* to become master of one's *happiness,* as of one's *unhappiness:* —" (from plans and ideas for an independent sequel to *Zarathustra,* during the year 1885; see XII, 415). To be master over one's happiness! That is the hardest thing. To be master over unhappiness: that can be done, if it has to be. But to be master of one's happiness. . . .

In the decade between 1880 and 1890 Nietzsche thinks and questions by means of the standards of the "grand style" and in the field of vision of "grand politics." We must keep these standards and the scope of the inquiry in view if we are to understand what is taken up into Book One and Book Two of *The Will to Power,* which present the insight that the basic force of Dasein, the self-assuredness and power of such force to establish a goal, is lacking. Why is the basic force that is needed in order to attain a creative stance in the midst of beings missing? Answer: because it has been in a state of advanced atrophy for a long time, and because it has been perverted into its opposite. The major debility of the basic force of Dasein consists in the calumniation and denegration of the fundamental orienting force of "life" itself. Such defamation of creative life, however, has its grounds in the fact that things are posited *above* life which make negation of it desirable. The desirable, the ideal, is the supersensuous, interpreted as genuine being. This interpretation of being is accomplished in the Platonic philosophy. The theory of Ideas founds the ideal, and that means the definitive preeminence of the supersensuous, in determining and dominating the sensuous.

Here a new interpretation of Platonism emerges. It flows from a fundamental experience of the development of nihilism. It sees in Platonism the primordial and determining grounds of the possibility of nihilism's upsurgence and of the rise of life-negation. Christianity is in Nietzsche's eyes nothing other than "Platonism for the people." As Platonism, however, it is nihilism. But with the reference to Nietzsche's opposition to the nihilistic tendency of Christianity, his position as a whole with respect to the historical phenomenon of Christianity is not delineated exhaustively. Nietzsche is far too perspicacious and too sovereignly intelligent not to know and acknowledge that an essential presupposition for his own behavior, the probity and discipline of his inquiry, is a consequence of the *Christian* education that has prevailed for centuries. To present two pieces of evidence from among the many available:

> *Probity* as a *consequence* of long moral training: the *self-critique of morality* is at the same time a *moral* phenomenon, an event of morality (XIII, 121).

> We are no longer Christians: we have grown out of Christianity, not because we dwelled too far from it, but because we dwelled too near it, even more, because we have grown *from* it—it is our more rigorous and fastidious piety itself that *forbids* us today to be Christians (XIII, 318).

Within the field of vision maintained by meditation on nihilism, "inversion" of Platonism takes on another meaning. It is not the simple, almost mechanical exchange of one epistemological standpoint for another, that of positivism. Overturning Platonism means, first, shattering the preeminence of the supersensuous as the ideal. Beings, being what they are, may not be despised on the basis of what should and ought to be. But at the same time, in opposition to the philosophy of the ideal and to the installation of what ought to be and of the "should," the inversion sanctions the investigation and determination of that which is—it summons the question "What is being itself?" If the "should" is the supersensuous, then being itself, that which is, conceived as liberated from the "should," can only be the sensuous. But with that the essence of the sensuous is not given; its definition is given up. In contrast, the realm of true being, of the true, and thereby the essence of truth, is demarcated; as before, however, already in Platonism, the true is to be attained on the path of knowledge.

In such inversion of Platonism, invoked and guided by the will to overcome nihilism, the conviction shared with Platonism and held to be evident is that truth, i.e., true being, must be secured on the path of knowledge. Since, according to the inversion, the sensuous is now the true, and since the sensuous, as being, is now to provide the basis for the new foundation of Dasein, the question concerning the sensuous and with it the determination of the true and of truth receive enhanced significance.

The interpretation of truth or true being as the sensuous is of course, considered formally, an overturning of Platonism, inasmuch as Platonism asserts that genuine being is supersensuous. Yet such inversion, and along with it the interpretation of the true as what is given in the senses, must be understood in terms of the overcoming of nihilism. But the definitive interpretation of art, if it is posited as the countermovement to nihilism, operates within the same perspective.

Against Platonism, the question "What is true being?" must be posed, and the answer to it must be, "The true is the sensuous." Against nihilism, the creative life, preeminently in art, must be set to work. But art creates out of the sensuous.

Now for the first time it becomes clear to what extent art and truth, whose relationship in Nietzsche's view is a discordance that arouses dread, can and must come into relation at all, a relation that is more than simply comparative, which is the kind of interpretation of both art and truth offered by philosophies of culture. Art and truth, creating and knowing, meet one another in the single guiding perspective of the rescue and configuration of the sensuous.

With a view to the conquest of nihilism, that is, to the foundation of the new valuation, art and truth, along with meditation on the essence of both, attain equal importance. According to their essence, intrinsically, art and truth come together in the realm of a new historical existence.

What sort of relationship do they have?

21. The Scope and Context of Plato's Meditation on the Relationship of Art and Truth

According to Nietzsche's teaching concerning the artist, and seen in terms of the one who creates, art has its actuality in the rapture of embodying life. Artistic configuration and portrayal are grounded essentially in the realm of the sensuous. Art is affirmation of the sensuous. According to the doctrine of Platonism, however, the supersensuous is affirmed as genuine being. Platonism, and Plato, would therefore logically have to condemn art, the affirmation of the sensuous, as a form of nonbeing and as what ought not to be, as a form of *mē on*. In Platonism, for which truth is supersensuous, the relationship to art apparently becomes one of exclusion, opposition, and antithesis; hence, one of discordance. If, however, Nietzsche's philosophy is reversal of Platonism, and if the true is thereby affirmation of the sensuous, then truth is the same as what art affirms, i.e., the sensuous. For inverted Platonism, the relationship of truth and art can only be one of univocity and concord. If in any case a discordance should exist in Plato (which is something we must still ask about, since not every distancing can be conceived as discordance), then it would have to disappear in the reversal of Platonism, which is to say, in the cancellation of such philosophy.

Nevertheless, Nietzsche says that the relationship is a discordance, indeed, one which arouses dread. He speaks of the discordance that arouses dread, not in the period *prior to* his own overturning of Platonism, but precisely during the period in which the inversion is decided for him. In 1888 Nietzsche writes in *Twilight of the Idols,* "On the contrary, the grounds upon which 'this' world [i.e., the sensuous] was designated as the world of appearances ground the reality of this world —*any other* kind of reality is absolutely indemonstrable" (VIII, 81). During the same period when Nietzsche says that the sole true reality, i.e., the true, is the sensuous world, he writes concerning the relationship of art and truth, ". . . and even now [i.e., in the autumn of 1888] I stand in holy dread in the face of this discordance."

Where is the path that will take us to the hidden, underlying sense of this remarkable phrase concerning the relationship of art and truth? We have to get there. For only from that vantage point will we be able to see Nietzsche's basic metaphysical position in its own light. It would be a good idea to take as our point of departure that basic philosophical position in which a discordance between art and truth at least seems to be possible, i.e., Platonism.

The question as to whether in Platonism a conflict between truth (or true being) and art (or what is portrayed in art) necessarily and therefore actually exists can be decided only on the basis of Plato's work itself. If a conflict exists here, it must come to the fore in statements which, comparing art and truth, say the opposite of what Nietzsche decides in evaluating their relationship.

Nietzsche says that art is worth more than truth. It must be that Plato decides that art is worth less than truth, that is, less than knowledge of true being as philosophy. Hence, in the Platonic philosophy, which we like to display as the very blossom of Greek thought, the result must be a depreciation of art. This among the Greeks—of all people—who affirmed and founded art as no other Occidental nation did! That is a disturbing matter of fact; nevertheless, it is indisputable. Therefore we must show at the outset, even if quite briefly, how the depreciation of art in favor of truth appears in Plato, and see to what extent it proves to be necessary.

But the intention of the following digression is by no means merely one of informing ourselves about Plato's opinion concerning art in this respect. On the basis of our consideration of Plato, for whom a sundering of art and truth comes to pass, we want to gain an indication of where and how we can find traces of discordance in Nietzsche's inversion of Platonism. At the same time, on our way we should provide a richer and better defined significance for the catchword "Platonism."

We pose two questions. First, what is the scope of those determinations which in Plato's view apply to what we call "art"? Second, in what context is the question of the relationship of art and truth discussed?

Let us turn to the first question. We customarily appeal to the word *techne* as the Greek designation of what we call "art." What *techne* means we suggested earlier (cf. p. 80). But we must be clear about the fact that the Greeks have no word at all that corresponds to what we mean by the word "art" in the narrower sense. The word "art" has for us a multiplicity of meanings, and not by accident. As masters of thought and speech, the Greeks deposited such multiple meanings in the majority of their sundry univocal words. If by "art" we mean primarily an ability in the sense of being well versed in something, of a thoroughgoing and therefore masterful *know-how,* then this for the Greeks is *techne.* Included in such know-how, although never as the essential aspect of it, is knowledge of the rules and procedures for a course of action.

In contrast, if by "art" we mean an ability in the sense of an acquired capacity to carry something out which, as it were, has become second nature and basic to Dasein, ability as behavior that accomplishes something, then the Greek says *melete, epimeleia,* carefulness of concern (see Plato's *Republic,* 374).* Such carefulness is more than practiced diligence; it is the mastery of a composed resolute openness to beings; it is "care." We must conceive of the innermost essence of *techne* too as such care, in order to preserve it from the sheer "technical"

---

*Cf. especially *Republic* 374e 2: the task of the guardians requires the greatest amount of *technes te kai epimeleias.* Socrates has been arguing that a man can perform only one *techne* well, be he shoemaker, weaver, or warrior. Here *techne* seems to mean "skill" or "professional task." In contrast, *meletaino* means to "take thought or care for," "to attend to, study, or pursue," "to exercise and train." *He melete* is "care," "sustained attention to action." *Epimeleia* means "care bestowed upon a thing, attention paid to it." Schleiermacher translates *epimeleia* as *Sorgfalt,* meticulousness or diligence. Such is perhaps what every *techne* presupposes. *Epimeleia* would be a welcome addition to the discussion of *cura, Sorge,* in *Being and Time,* section 42.

interpretation of later times. The unity of *melete* and *techne* thus characterizes the basic posture of the forward-reaching disclosure of Dasein, which seeks to ground beings on their own terms.

Finally, if by "art" we mean *what is brought forward in a process of bringing-forth,* what is produced in production, and the producing itself, then the Greek speaks of *poiein and poiesis.* That the word *poiesis* in the emphatic sense comes to be reserved for designation of the production of something in words, that *poiesis* as "poesy" becomes the special name for the art of the word, poetic creation, testifies to the primacy of such art within Greek art as a whole. Therefore it is not accidental that when Plato brings to speech and to decision the relationship of art and truth he deals primarily and predominantly with poetic creation and the poet.

Turning to the second question, we must now consider where and in what context Plato poses the question concerning the relationship of art and truth. For the way he poses and pursues that question determines the form of the interpretation for the whole of Plato's multifaceted meditation on art. Plato poses the question in the "dialogue" which bears the title *Politeia* [*Republic*], his magnificent discussion on the "state" as the basic form of man's communal life. Consequently, it has been supposed that Plato asks about art in a "political" fashion, and that such a "political" formulation would have to be opposed to, or distinguished essentially from, the "aesthetic" and thereby in the broadest sense "theoretical" point of view. We can call Plato's inquiry into art political to the extent that it arises in connection with *politeia;* but we have to know, and then say, what "political" is supposed to mean. If we are to grasp Plato's teaching concerning art as "political," we should understand that word solely in accordance with the concept of the essence of the *polis* that emerges from the dialogue itself. That is all the more necessary as this tremendous dialogue in its entire structure and movement aims to show that the sustaining ground and determining essense of all political Being consists in nothing less than the "theoretical," that is, in essential knowledge of *dike* and *dikaiosyne*. This Greek word is translated as "justice," but that misses the proper sense, inasmuch as justice is transposed straightaway into the moral or even the merely "legal" realm. But *dikē* is a metaphysical concept, not originally one of morality. It names Being with reference to the essentially appropriate articulation of all beings.* To be sure, *dikē* slips into the twilight zone of morality precisely on account of the Platonic philosophy. But that makes it all the more necessary to hold onto its metaphysical sense, because otherwise the Greek backgrounds of the dialogue on the state do not become visible. Knowledge of *dikē*, of the articulating laws of the Being of beings, is philosophy. Therefore the decisive insight of the entire dialogue on the state says, *dei tous philosophous basileuein* (*archein*): it is essentially necessary that philosophers be the rulers (see *Republic*, Bk. V, 473). The statement does not mean that philosophy professors should conduct the affairs of state. It means that the basic modes of behavior that sustain and define the community must be grounded in essential knowledge, assuming of course that the community, as an order of being, grounds itself on its own basis, and that it does not wish to adopt standards from any other order. The unconstrained self-grounding of historical Dasein places itself under the jurisdiction of knowledge, and not of faith, inasmuch as the latter is understood as the proclamation of truth sanctioned by divine revelation. All knowledge is at bottom commitment to beings that come to light under their own power. Being becomes visible, according to Plato, in the "Ideas." They constitute the Being of beings, and therefore are themselves the true beings, the true.

Hence, if one still wants to say that Plato is here inquiring politically into art, it can only mean that he evaluates art, with reference to its position in the state, upon the essence and sustaining grounds of the state, upon knowledge of "truth." Such inquiry into art is "theoretical" in the highest degree. The distinction between political and theoretical inquiry no longer makes any sense at all.

---

*Cf. Martin Heidegger, *An Introduction to Metaphysics,* pp. 134–35 and 139–40. (N.B.: in the Anchor Books edition, p. 139, line 11, the words *technē* and dikē are misplaced: *dikē* is the overpowering order, *technē* the violence of knowledge). On *dikē*, cf. also "The Anaximander Fragment" (1936) in Martin Heidegger, *Early Greek Thinking,* pp. 41–47.

That Plato's question concerning art marks the beginning of "aesthetics" does not have its grounds in the fact that it is generally theoretical, which is to say, that it springs from an interpretation of Being; it results from the fact that the "theoretical," as a grasp of the Being of beings, is based on a *particular* interpretation of Being. The *idea*, the envisioned outward appearance, characterizes Being precisely for that kind of vision which recognizes in the visible as such pure presence. "Being" stands in essential relation to, and in a certain way means as much as, self-showing and appearing, the *phainesthai* of what is *ekphanes*.* One's grasp of the Ideas, with regard to the possible accomplishment of that grasp, though not to its established goal, is grounded upon *erōs*, which in Nietzsche's aesthetics corresponds to rapture. What is most loved and longed for in *erōs*, and therefore the Idea that is brought into fundamental relation, is what at the same time appears and radiates most brilliantly. The *erasmiōtaton*, which at the same time is *ekphanestaton*, proves to be the *idea tou kalou*, the Idea of the beautiful, beauty.

Plato deals with the beautiful and with Eros primarily in the *Symposium*. The questions posed in the *Republic* and *Symposium* are conjoined and brought to an original and basic position with a view to the fundamental questions of philosophy in the dialogue *Phaedrus*. Here Plato offers his most profound and extensive inquiry into art and the beautiful in the most rigorous and circumscribed form. We refer to these other dialogues so that we do not forget, at this very early stage, that the discussions of art in the *Republic*—for the moment the sole important ones for us—do not constitute the whole of Plato's meditation in that regard.

But in the context of the dialogue's guiding question concerning the state, how does the question of art come up? Plato asks about the structure of communal life, what must guide it as a whole and in totality, and what component parts belong to it as what is to be guided. He does not describe the form of any state at hand, nor does he

---

*On the meaning of *phainesthai* see section 7A of *Being and Time*; in *Basic Writings*, pp. 74–79.

elaborate a utopian model for some future state. Rather, the inner order of communal life is projected on the basis of Being and man's fundamental relation to Being. The standards and principles of education for correct participation in communal life and for active existence are established. In the pursuit of such inquiry, the following question emerges, among others: does art too, especially the art of poetry, belong to communal life; and, if so, how? In Book Three (1–18)* that question becomes the object of the discussion. Here Plato shows in a preliminary way that what art conveys and provides is always a portrayal of beings; although it is not inactive, its producing and making, *poiein,* remain *mimēsis,* imitation, copying and transforming, poetizing in the sense of inventing. Thus art in itself is exposed to the danger of continual deception and falsehood. In accord with the essence of its activity, art has no direct, definitive relation to the true and to true being. That fact suffices to produce one irremediable result: in and for the hierarchy of modes of behavior and forms of achievement within the community, art cannot assume the highest rank. If art is admitted into the community at all, then it is only with the proviso that its role be strictly demarcated and its activities subject to certain demands and directives that derive from the guiding laws of the Being of states.

At this point we can see that a decision may be reached concerning the essence of art and its necessarily limited role in the state only in terms of an original and proper relation to the beings that set the standard, only in terms of a relationship that appreciates *dikē,* the matter of order and disorder with respect to Being. For that reason, after the preliminary conversations about art and other forms of achievement in the state, we arrive at the question concerning our basic relation to Being, advancing to the question concerning true comportment toward beings, and hence to the question of truth. On our way through these conversations, we encounter at the beginning of the seventh book the discussion of the essence of truth, based on the Allegory of the Cave. Only after traversing this long and broad path

---

*I.e., topics 1–18 in Schleiermacher's arrangement; in the traditional Stephanus numbering, 386a–412b.

to the point where philosophy is defined as masterful knowledge of the Being of beings do we turn back, in order to ground those statements which were made earlier in a merely provisional manner, among them the statements concerning art. Such a return transpires in the tenth and final book.

Here Plato shows first of all what it means to say that art is *mimēsis,* and then why, granting that characteristic, art can only occupy a subordinate position. Here a decision is made about the metaphysical relation of art and truth (but only in a certain respect). We shall now pursue briefly the chief matter of Book Ten, without going into particulars concerning the movement of the dialogue, and also without referring to the transformation and refinement of what is handled there in Plato's later dialogues.

One presupposition remains unchallenged: all art is *mimēsis.* We translate that word as "imitation." At the outset of Book Ten the question arises as to what *mimēsis* is. Quite likely we are inclined to assume that here we are encountering a "primitivistic" notion of art, or a one-sided view of it, in the sense of a particular artistic style called "naturalism," which copies things that are at hand. We should resist both preconceptions from the start. But even more misleading is the opinion that when art is grasped as *mimēsis* the result is an arbitrary presupposition. For the clarification of the essence of *mimēsis* which is carried out in Book Ten not only defines the word more precisely but also traces the matter designated in the word back to its inner possibility and to the grounds that sustain such possibility. Those grounds are nothing other than basic representations the Greeks entertained concerning beings as such, their understanding of Being. Since the question of truth is sister to that of Being, the Greek concept of truth serves as the basis of the interpretation of art as *mimēsis.* Only on that basis does *mimēsis* possess sense and significance—but also necessity. Such remarks are needed in order that we fix our eyes on the correct point of the horizon for the following discussion. What we will consider there, after two thousand years of tradition and habituation of thought and representation, consists almost entirely of commonplaces. But seen from the point of view of Plato's age, it is all first discovery and definitive utterance. In order to correspond to the mood of this dialogue, we would do well to put aside for the moment our seemingly greater sagacity and our superior air of "knowing all about it already." Of course, here we have to forgo recapitulation of the entire sequence of individual steps in the dialogue.

22. Plato's *Republic:* The Distance of Art (*Mimēsis*) from Truth (*Idea*)

Let us formulate our question once again. How does art relate to truth? Where does art stand in the relationship? Art is *mimēsis*. Its relation to truth must be ascertainable in terms of the essence of *mimēsis*. What is *mimēsis*? Socrates says to Glaucon (at 595 c): *Mimēsin holōs echois an moi eipein hoti pot' estin; oude gar toi autos pany ti synnoō ti bouletai einai.* "Imitation, viewed as a whole: can you tell me at all what that is? For I myself as well am totally unable to discern what it may be."

Thus the two of them begin their conversation, *episkopountes*, "keeping firmly in view the matter itself named in the word." This they do *ek tēs eiōthuias methodou,* "in the manner to which they are accustomed to proceeding, being in pursuit of the matter," since that is what the Greek word "method" means. That customary way of proceeding is the kind of inquiry Plato practiced concerning beings as such. He expressed himself about it continually in his dialogues. Method, the manner of inquiry, was never for him a fixed technique; rather, it developed in cadence with the advance toward Being. If therefore at our present position method is formulated in an essential statement, such a designation by Platonic thought concerning the Ideas corresponds to that stage of the Platonic philosophy which is reached when Plato composes the dialogue on the state. But that stage is by no means the ultimate one. In the context of our present inquiry this account of method is of special significance.

Socrates (i.e., Plato) says in that regard (at 596 a): *eidos gar pou ti hen hekaston eiōthamen tithesthai peri hekasta ta polla, hois tauton onoma epipheromen.* "We are accustomed to posing to ourselves (letting lie before us) one *eidos,* only one of such kind for each case, in relation to the cluster (*peri*) of those many things to which we ascribe the same name." Here *eidos* does not mean "concept" but the outward appearance of something. In its outward appearance this or that thing does not become present, come into presence, in its particularity; it becomes present as that which it is. To come into presence means Being; Being is therefore apprehended in discernment of the outward appearance. How does that proceed? In each case one outward appearance is posed. How is that meant? We may be tempted to have done with the statement, which in summary fashion is to describe the method, by saying that for a multiplicity of individual things, for example, particular houses, the Idea (house) is posited. But with this common presentation of the kind of thought Plato developed concerning the Ideas, we do not grasp the heart of the method. It is not merely a matter of positing the Idea, but of finding that approach by which what we encounter in its manifold particularity is brought together with the unity of the *eidos,* and by which the latter is joined to the former, both being established in relationship to one another. What is established, i.e., brought to the proper approach, i.e., located and presented for the inquiring glance, is not only the Idea but also the manifold of particular items that can be related to the oneness of its unified outward appearance. The procedure is therefore a mutual accommodation between the many particular things and the appropriate oneness of the "Idea," in order to get both in view and to define their reciprocal relation.

The essential directive in the procedure is granted by language, through which man comports himself toward beings in general. In the word, indeed in what is immediately uttered, both points of view intersect: on the one hand, that concerning what in each case is immediately addressed, this house, this table, this bedframe; and on the other hand, that concerning what this particular item in the word is addressed *as*—this thing *as* house, with a view to its outward appearance. Only when we read the statement on method in terms of such an interpretation do we hit upon the full Platonic sense. We have long been accustomed to looking at the many-sided individual thing simultaneously with a view to its universal. But here the many-sided individual appears as such in the scope of its outward appearance as such, and in that consists the Platonic discovery. Only when we elaborate upon that discovery does the statement cited concerning "method" provide us with the correct directive for the procedure now to be followed in pursuit of *mimēsis*.

Mimēsis means copying, that is, presenting and producing something in a manner which is typical of something else. Copying is done in the realm of production, taking it in a very broad sense. Thus the first thing that occurs is that a manifold of produced items somehow comes into view, not as the dizzying confusion of an arbitrary multiplicity, but as the many-sided individual item which we name with *one* name. Such a manifold of produced things may be found, for example, in *ta skeuē*, "utensils" or "implements" which we find commonly in use in many homes. *Pollai pou eisi klinai kai trapedzai* (596 b): ". . . many, which is to say, many according to number and also according to the immediate view, are the bedframes and tables there." What matters is not that there are many bedframes and tables at hand, instead of a few; the only thing we must see is what is co-posited already in such a determination, namely, that there are many bedframes, many tables, yet just *one* Idea "bedframe" and *one* Idea "table." In each case, the one of outward appearance is not only one according to number but above all is one and the same; it is the one that continues to exist in spite of all changes in the apparatus, the one that maintains its consistency. In the outward appearance, whatever it is that something which encounters us "is," shows itself. To Being, therefore, seen Platonically, permanence belongs. All that becomes and suffers alteration, as impermanent, has no Being. Therefore, in the view of Platonism, "Being" stands always in exclusive opposition to "Becoming" and change. We today, on the contrary, are used to addressing also what changes and occurs, and precisely that, as "real" and as genuine being. In opposition to that, whenever Nietzsche says "Being" he always means it Platonically—even after the reversal of Platonism. That is to say, he means it in antithesis to "Becoming."

Alla ideai ge pou peri tauta ta skeuē dyō, mia men klinēs, mia de trapedzēs. "But, of course, the Ideas for the clusters of these implements are two: one in which 'bedframe' becomes manifest, and one in which 'table' shows itself." Here Plato clearly refers to the fact that the permanence and selfsameness of the "Ideas" is always *peri ta polla,* "*for* the cluster of the many and *as* embracing the many." Hence it is not some arbitrary, undefined permanence. But the philosophic search does not thereby come to an end. It merely attains the vantage point from which it may ask: how is it with those many produced items, those implements, in relation to the "Idea" that is applicable in each case? We pose the question in order to come to know something about *mimēsis.* We must therefore cast about, within the realm of our vision, with greater penetration, still taking as our point of departure the many implements. They are not simply at hand, but are at our disposal for use, or are already in use. They "are" with that end in view. As produced items, they are made for the general use of those who dwell together and are with one another. Those who dwell with one another constitute the *dēmos,* the "people," in the sense of public being-with-one-another, those who are mutually known to and involved with one another. For them the implements are made. Whoever produces such implements is therefore called a *dēmiourgos,* a worker, manufacturer, and maker of something for the sake of the *dēmos.* In our language we still have a word for such a person, although, it is true, we seldom use it and its meaning is restricted to a particular realm: *der Stellmacher,* one who constructs frames, meaning wagon chassis (hence the name *Wagner*).* That implements and frames are made by a framemaker—that is no astonishing piece of wisdom! Certainly not.

All the same, we ought to think through the simplest things in the

---

Der Stellmacher is a wheelwright, maker of wheeled vehicles; but he makes the frames (*Gestelle*) for his wagons as well. Heidegger chooses the word because of its kinship with *herstellen,* to produce. He employs the word *Ge-stell* in his essay on "The Origin of the Work of Art" (in the Reclam edition, p. 72). Much later, in the 1950s, Heidegger employs it as the name for the essence of technology; cf. *Vorträge und Aufsätze* (Pfullingen: G. Neske, 1954), p. 27 ff., and *Ursprung des Kunstwerkes,* "Zusatz" (1956), Reclam edition, pp. 97–98.

simplest clarity of their relationships. In this regard, the everyday state
of affairs by which the framemaker frames and produces frames gave
a thinker like Plato something to think about—for one thing, this: in
the production of tables the tablemaker proceeds *pros tēn idean blepōn
poiei,* making this or that table "while at the same time looking to the
Idea." He keeps an "eye" on the outward appearance of tables in
general. And the outward appearance of such a thing as a table? How
is it with that, seen from the point of view of production? Does the
tablemaker produce the outward appearance as well? No. *Ou gar pou
tēn ge idean autēn dēmiourgei oudeis tōn dēmiourgōn.* "For in no case
does the craftsman produce the Idea itself." How should he, with axe,
saw, and plane be able to manufacture an Idea? Here an end (or
boundary) becomes manifest, which for all "practice" is insurmounta-
ble, indeed an end or boundary *precisely with respect to what "practice" itself needs* in order to be "practical." For it is an essential matter
of fact that the tablemaker cannot manufacture the Idea with his tools;
and it is every bit as essential that he look to the Idea in order to be
who he is, the producer of tables. In that way the realm of a workshop
extends far beyond the four walls that contain the craftsman's tools and
produced items. The workshop possesses a vantage point from which
we can see the outward appearance or Idea of what is immediately on
hand and in use. The framemaker is a maker who in his making must
be on the lookout for something he himself cannot make. The Idea is
prescribed to him and he must *subscribe* to it. Thus, as a maker, he
is already somehow one who copies or imitates. Hence there is nothing
at all like a *pure* "practitioner," since the practitioner himself necessarily and from the outset is always already *more* than that. Such is the
basic insight that Plato strives to attain.

But there is something else we have to emphasize in the fact that
craftsmen manufacture implements. For the Greeks themselves it was
clearly granted, but for us it has become rather hazy, precisely because
of its obviousness. And that is the fact that what is manufactured or
produced, which formerly was not in being, now "is." It "is." We
understand this "is." We do not think very much about it. For the
Greeks the "Being" of manufactured things was defined, but different-

ly than it is for us. Something produced "is" because the Idea lets it
be seen as such, lets it come to presence in its outward appearance, lets
it "be." Only to that extent can what is itself produced be said "to be."
Making and manufacturing therefore mean to bring the outward appearance to show itself in something else, namely, in what is manufactured, to "pro-duce" the outward appearance, not in the sense of
manufacturing it but of letting it radiantly appear. What is manufactured "is" only to the extent that in it the outward appearance, Being,
radiates. To say that something manufactured "is" means that in it the
presence of its outward appearance shows itself. A worker is one who
fetches the outward appearance of something into the presence of
sensuous visibility. That seems to delineate sufficiently what, and how,
it is that the craftsman properly makes, and what he cannot make.
Every one of these pro-ducers of serviceable and useful implements and
items keeps to the realm of the one "Idea" that guides him: the
tablemaker looks to the Idea of table, the shoemaker to that of shoe.
Each is proficient to the extent that he limits himself purely to his own
field. Else he botches the job.

But how would it be if there were a man, *hos panta poiei, hosaper
heis hekastos tōn cheirotechnōn* (596 c), "who pro-duced everything
that every single other craftsman" is able to make? That would be a
man of enormous powers, uncanny and astonishing. In fact there is
such a man: *hapanta ergadzetai,* "he produces anything and everything." He can produce not only implements, *alla kai ta ek tēs gēs
phuomena hapanta poiei kai zōia panta ergadzetai,* "but also what
comes forth from the earth, producing plants and animals and everything else"; *kai heauton,* "indeed, himself too," and besides that, earth
and sky, *kai theous,* "even the gods," and everything in the heavens and
in the underworld. But such a producer, standing above all beings and
even above the gods, would be a sheer wonderworker! Yet there is such
a *dēmiourgos,* and he is nothing unusual; each of us is capable of
achieving such production. It is all a matter of observing *tini tropōi
poiei,* "in what way he produces."

While meditating on what is produced, and on production, we must
pay heed to the *tropos.* We are accustomed to translating that Greek

word, correctly but inadequately, as "way" and "manner." *Tropos* means how one is turned, in what direction he turns, in what he maintains himself, to what he applies himself, where he turns to and remains tied, and with what intention he does so. What does that suggest for the realm of pro-duction? One may say that the way the shoemaker proceeds is different from that in which the tablemaker goes to work. Certainly, but the difference here is defined by what in each case is to be produced, by the requisite materials, and by the kind of refinements or operations such materials demand. Nevertheless, the same *tropos* prevails in all these ways of producing. How so? This query is to be answered by that part of the discussion we shall now follow.

Kai tis ho tropos houtos; "And what *tropos* is that," which makes possible a production that is capable of producing *hapanta,* "anything and everything," to the extent designated, which is in no way limited? Such a *tropos* presents no difficulties: by means of it one can go ahead and produce things everywhere and without delay. *Tachista de pou, ei 'theleis labōn katoptron peripherein pantachēi* (596 d), "but you can do it quickest if you just take a mirror and point it around in all directions."

Tachy men hēlion poiēseis kai ta en tōi ouranōi, tachy de gēn, tachy de sauton te kai talla zōia kai skeuē kai phyta kai panta hosa nyndē elegeto. "That way you will quickly produce the sun and what is in the heavens; quickly too the earth; and quickly also you yourself and all other living creatures and implements and plants and everything else we mentioned just now."

With this turn of the conversation we see how essential it is to think of *poiein*—"making"—as *pro-ducing* in the Greek sense. A mirror accomplishes such production of outward appearance; it allows all beings to become present just as they outwardly appear.

But at the same time, this is the very place to elaborate an important distinction in the *tropos* of production. It will enable us for the first time to attain a clearer concept of the *dēmiourgos* and thereby also of *mimēsis,* "copying." Were we to understand *poiein*—"making"—in some indefinite sense of manufacturing, then the example of the mirror would have no effect, since the mirror does not manufacture the sun.

But if we understand pro-duction in a Greek manner, in the sense of bringing forth the Idea (bringing the outward appearance of something into something else, no matter in what way), then the mirror *does* in this particular sense *pro-duce* the sun.

With regard to "pointing the mirror in all directions," and to its mirroring, Glaucon must therefore agree immediately: *Nai,* "Certainly," that is a producing of "beings"; but he adds, *phainomena, ou mentoi onta ge pou tēi alētheiai.* But what shows itself in the mirror "only looks like, but all the same is not, something present in uncon-cealment," which is to say, undistorted by the "merely outwardly appearing as," i.e., undistorted by semblance. Socrates supports him: *kalōs, . . . kai eis deon erchēi tōi logōi.* "Fine, and by saying that you go to the heart of what is proper (to the matter)." Mirroring does produce beings, indeed as self-showing, but not as beings in un-con-cealment or nondistortion. Juxtaposed to one another here are *on phainomenon* and *on tēi alētheiai,* being as self-showing and being as undistorted; by no means *phainomenon* as "semblance" and "the merely apparent," on the one hand, and *on tēi alētheiai* as "Being," on the other; in each case it is a matter of *on*—"what is present"—but in different ways of presencing. But is that not the same, the self-showing and the undistorted? Yes and no. Same with respect to *what* becomes present (house), same to the extent that in each case it is a presencing; but in each case the *tropos* differs. In one case the "house" becomes present by showing itself and appearing in, and by means of, the glittering surface of the mirror; in the other the "house" is present by showing itself in stone and wood. The more firmly we hold on to the selfsameness, the more significant the distinction must become. Plato here is wrestling with the conception of the varying *tropos,* that is, at the same time and above all, with the determination of that "way" in which *on* itself shows itself most purely, so that it does not portray itself by means of something else but presents itself in such a way that its outward appearance, *eidos,* constitutes its Being. Such self-showing is the *eidos* as *idea.*

Two kinds of presence result: the house (i.e., the *idea*) shows itself in the mirror or in the "house" itself at hand. Consequently, two kinds of production and producers must be differentiated and clarified. If we call every pro-ducer a *dēmiourgos,* then one who mirrors is a particular type of *dēmiourgos.* Therefore Socrates continues: *tōn toioutōn gar oimai dēmiourgōn kai ho zōgraphos estin.* "For I believe that the painter too belongs to that kind of pro-ducing," which is to say the mirroring kind. The artist lets beings become present, but as *phainomena,* "showing themselves by appearing through something else." *Ouk alēthē . . . poiein ha poiei,* "he does not bring forward what he produces as unconcealed." He does not produce the *eidos. Kaitoi tropōi ge tini kai ho zōgraphos klinēn poiei.* "All the same, the painter too produces [a] bedframe"—*tropōi tini,* "in a certain way." *Tropos* here means the kind of presence of the *on* (the *idea*); hence it means that in which and through which *on* as *idea* produces itself and brings itself into presence. The *tropos* is in one case the mirror, in another the painted surface, in another the wood, in all of which the table comes to presence.

We are quick on the uptake, so we say that some of them produce "apparent" things, others "real" things. But the question is: what does "real" in this case mean? And is the table manufactured by the carpenter the "real" table according to the Greeks; is it in being? To ask it another way: when the carpenter manufactures this or that table, any given table, does he thereby produce the table that is in being; or is manufacturing a kind of bringing forward that will never be able to produce the table "itself"? But we have already heard that there is also something which he does *not* pro-duce, something which he, as framemaker, with the means available to him, cannot pro-duce: *ou to eidos* (*tēn idean*) *poiei,* "but he does not produce the pure outward appearance (of something like a bedframe) in itself." He presupposes it as already granted to him and thereby brought forth unto and produced for him.

Now, what is the *eidos* itself? What is it in relation to the individual bedframe that the framemaker produces? *To eidos . . . ho dē phamen einai ho esti klinē,* "the outward appearance, of which we say that it is what the bedframe is," and thereby *what* it is *as such:* the *ho esti, quid est, quidditas,* whatness. It is obviously that which is essential in

beings, by means of which they "first and last are," *teleōs on* (597 a).
But if the craftsman does not pro-duce precisely this *eidos* in itself, but
in each case merely looks to it as something already brought to him;
and if *eidos* is what is properly in being among beings; then the
craftsman does not produce the Being of beings either. Rather, he
always produces this or that being—*ouk . . . ho esti klinē, alla klinēn
tina,* "not the what-being of the bedframe, but some bedframe or
other."

So it is that the craftsman, who grapples with a reality you can hold
in your hands, is not in touch with beings themselves, *on tēi alētheiai.*
Therefore, Socrates says, *mēden ara thaumadzōmen ei kai touto (to
ergon tou dēmiourgou) amydron ti tynchanei on pros alētheian.* "In
no way would it astonish us, therefore, if even this (what is manufactured by the craftsman) proves to be something obscure and hazy in
relation to unconcealment." The wood of the bedframe, the amassed
stone of the house, in each case bring the *idea* forth into appearance;
yet such pro-duction dulls and darkens the original luster of the *idea.*
Hence the house which we call "real" is in a certain way reduced to
the level of an image of the house in a mirror or painting. The Greek
word *amydron* is difficult to translate: for one thing it means the
darkening and distorting of what comes to presence. But then such
darkening, over against what is undistorted, is something lusterless and
feeble; it does not command the inner power of the presencing of
beings themselves.

Only now do the speakers attain the position from which Socrates
may demand that they try to illuminate the essence of *mimēsis* on the
basis of what they have so far discussed. To that end he summarizes
and describes in a more pointed way what they have already ascertained.

The approach to their considerations established that there are, for
example, many individual bedframes set up in houses. Such a "many"
is easy to see, even when we look around us in a lackadaisical sort of
way. Therefore, Socrates (Plato) says at the beginning of the discussion,
with a very profound, ironic reference to what is to follow and which
we are now on the verge of reaching (596 a), *polla toi oxyteron blepon-
tōn amblyteron horōntes proteroi eidon.* "A variety and multiplicity is

what those who look with dull eyes see, rather than those who examine things more keenly." Those who examine things more keenly see fewer things, but for that reason they see what is essential and simple. They do not lose themselves in a sheer variety that has no essence. Dull eyes see an incalculable multiplicity of sundry particular bedframes. Keen eyes see something else, even—and especially—when they linger upon one single bedframe at hand. For dull eyes the many always amounts to "a whole bunch," understood as "quite a lot," hence as abundance. In contrast, for keen eyes the simple is simplified. In such simplification, essential plurality originates. That means: the first (one), produced by the god, (the pure) one-and-the-same outward appearance, the Idea; the second, what is manufactured by the carpenter; the third, what the painter conjures in images. What is simple is named in the word *klinē.* But *trittai tines klinai hautai gignontai* (597 b). We must translate: "In a certain way, a first, a second, and a third bedframe have resulted here." *Mia men hē en tēi physei ousa,* "for what is being in nature is *one.*" We notice that the translation does not succeed. What is *physis,* "nature," supposed to mean here? No bedframes appear in nature; they do not grow as trees and bushes do. Surely *physis* still means emergence for Plato, as it does primarily for the first beginnings of Greek philosophy, emergence in the way a rose emerges, unfolding itself and showing itself out of itself. But what we call "nature," the countryside, nature out-of-doors, is only a specially delineated sector of nature or *physis* in the essential sense: that which of itself unfolds itself in presencing. *Physis* is the primordial Greek grounding word for Being itself, in the sense of the presence that emerges of itself and so holds sway.

Hē en tēi physei ousa, the bedframe "which is in nature," means that what is essential in pure Being, as present of itself, in other words, what emerges by itself, stands in opposition to what is pro-duced only by something else. *Hē physei klinē:* what pro-duces itself as such, without mediation, by itself, in its pure outward appearance. What presences in this way is the purely, straightforwardly envisioned *eidos,* which is not seen by virtue of any medium, hence the *idea.* That such a thing lights up, emerges, *phyei,* no man can bring about. Man cannot produce the *idea;* he can only be stationed before it. For that reason, of the *physei klinē* Socrates says: *hēn phaimen an, hōs egōimai, theon ergasasthai,* "of which we may well say, as I believe, that a god produced it and brought it forth."

Mia de ge hēn ho tektōn. "But it is a different bedframe which the craftsman manufactures." *Mia de hēn ho zōgraphos.* "And again another which the painter brings about."

The threefold character of the one bedframe, and so naturally of every particular being that is at hand, is captured in the following statement (597 b): *Zōgraphos dē, klinopoios, theos, treis houtoi epistatai trisin eidesi klinōn.* "Thus the painter, the framemaker, the god—these three are *epistatai,* those who dedicate themselves to, or preside over, three types of outward appearance of the bedframe." Each presides over a distinct type of self-showing, which each sees to in his own way; he is the overseer for that type, watching over and mastering the self-showing. If we translate *eidos* here simply as "type," three types of bedframes, we obfuscate what is decisive. For Plato's thought is here moving in the direction of visualizing how the selfsame shows itself in various ways: three ways of self-showing; hence, of presence; hence, three metamorphoses of Being itself. What matters is the unity of the basic character that prevails throughout self-showing in spite of all difference: appearing in this or that fashion and becoming present in outward appearance.

Let us also observe something else that accompanied us everywhere in our previous considerations: whenever we mentioned genuine being we also spoke of *on tēi alētheiai,* being "in truth." Grasped in a Greek manner, however, "truth" means nondistortion, openness, namely for the self-showing itself.

The interpretation of Being as eidos, *presencing in outward appearance, presupposes the interpretation of truth as* alētheia, *nondistortion.* We must heed that if we wish to grasp the relation of art (*mimēsis*) and truth in Plato's conception correctly, which is to say, in a Greek manner. Only in such a realm do Plato's questions unfold. From it they derive the possibility of receiving answers. Here at the peak of the Platonic interpretation of the Being of beings as *idea,* the question arises as to why the god allowed only one *idea* to go forth for each realm of individual things, for example, bedframes. *Eite ouk ebouleto, eite tis anankē epēn mē pleon ē mian en tēi physei apergasas-thai auton klinēn* (597 c). "Either he desired, or a certain necessity compelled him, not to permit more than one bedframe to emerge in outward appearance." *Dyo de toiautai ē pleious oute ephuteuthēsan hypo tou theou oute mē phyōsin.* "Two or more such Ideas neither were brought forward by the god, nor will they ever come forth." What is the reason for that? Why is there always only one Idea for one thing?

Let us illustrate briefly Plato's answer, with a glance back to the essence of the true, which we discussed earlier, the true in its singularity and immutability.

What would happen if the god were to allow several Ideas to emerge for one thing and its manifold nature—"house" and houses, "tree" and trees, "animal" and animals? The answer: *ei dyo monas poiēseien, palin an mia anaphaneiē hēs ekeinai an au amphoterai to eidos echoien, kai eiē an ho estin klinē ekeinē all' oukh hai dyo.* "If instead of the single 'Idea' house he were to allow more to emerge, even if only two, then one of them would have to appear with an outward appearance that both would have to have as their own; and the what-being of the bedframe or the house would be that one, whereas both could not be." Hence unity and singularity are proper to the essence of the *idea.* Now, according to Plato, where does the ground for the singularity of each of the Ideas (essences) lie? It does not rest in the fact that when two Ideas are posited the one allows the other to proceed to a higher level; it rests in the fact that the god, who knew of the ascent of representation from a manifold to a unity, *boulomenos einai ontōs klinēs poiētēs ontōs ousēs, alla mē klinēs tinos mēde klinopoios tis, mian physei autēn ephysen* (597 d), "wanted to be the essential producer of the essential thing, not of any given particular thing, and not like some sort of framemaker." Because the god wanted to be such a god, he allowed such things—for example, bedframes—"to come forth in the unity and singularity of their essence." In what, then, is the essence of the Idea, and thereby of Being, ultimately grounded for Plato? In the initiating action of a creator whose essentiality appears to be saved only when what he creates is in each case something singular, a one; and also there where allowance is made in the representation of a manifold for an ascent to the representation of its one.

The grounding of this interpretation of Being goes back to the initiating action of a creator and to the presupposition of a one which in each case unifies a manifold. For us a question lies concealed here. How does Being, as presencing and letting come to presence, cohere with the one, as unifying? Does the reversion to a creator contain an answer to the question, or does the question remain unasked, since Being as presencing is not thought through, and the unifying of the one not defined with reference to Being as presencing?

Every single being, which we today take to be the particular item which is "properly real," manifests itself in three modes of outward appearance. Accordingly, it can be traced back to three ways of self-showing or being pro-duced. Hence there are three kinds of producers.

First, the god who lets the essence emerge—*physin phyei*. He is therefore called *phytourgos,* the one who takes care of and holds in readiness the emergence of pure outward appearance, so that man can discern it.*

Second, the craftsman who is the *dēmiourgos klinēs*. He produces a bed according to its essence, but lets it appear in wood, that is, in the kind of thing where the bedframe stands as this particular item at our disposal for everyday use.

Third, the painter who brings the bedframe to show itself in his picture. May he therefore be called a *dēmiourgos?* Does he work for the *dēmos,* participating in the public uses of things and in communal life? No! For neither does he have disposition over the pure essence, as the god does (he rather darkens it in the stuff of colors and surfaces), nor does he have disposition over and use of what he brings about with respect to what it is. The painter is not *dēmiourgos* but *mimētēs hou ekeinoi dēmiourgoi,* "a copier of the things of which those others are

---

*Schleiermacher translates *phytourgos* (*Republic,* 597 d 5) as *Wesensbildner,* "shaper of essences"; the word literally means gardener, "worker with plants." Aeschylus' suppliant maidens use the word as an epithet of Zeus the Father (*Supp.* 592).

the producers for the public." What, consequently, is the *mimētēs?* The copier is *ho tou tritou gennēmatos apo tēs physeōs* (597 e); he is *epistatēs;* "he presides and rules over" one way in which Being, the *idea,* is brought to outward appearance, *eidos.* What he manufactures —the painting—is *to triton gennēma,* "the third kind of bringing-forth," third *apo tēs physeōs,* "reckoned in terms of the pure emergence of the *idea,* which is first." In the pictured table, "table" is somehow manifest in general, showing its *idea* in some way; and the table in the picture also manifests a particular wooden frame, and thus is somehow what the craftsman properly makes: but the pictured table shows both of them in something else, in shades of color, in some third thing. Neither can a usable table come forward in such a medium, nor can the outward appearance show itself purely as such. The way the painter pro-duces a "table" into visibility is even farther removed from the Idea, the Being of the being, than the way the carpenter produces it.

The distance from Being and its pure visibility is definitive for the definition of the essence of the *mimētēs.* What is decisive for the Greek-Platonic concept of *mimēsis* or imitation is not reproduction or portraiture, not the fact that the painter provides us with the same thing once again; what is decisive is that this is precisely what he cannot do, that he is even less capable than the craftsman of duplicating the same thing. It is therefore wrongheaded to apply to *mimēsis* notions of "naturalistic" or "primitivistic" copying and reproducing. Imitation is subordinate pro-duction. The *mimētēs* is defined in essence by his position of distance; such distance results from the hierarchy established with regard to ways of production and in the light of pure outward appearance, Being.

But the subordinate position of the *mimētēs* and of *mimēsis* has not yet been sufficiently delineated. We need to clarify in what way the painter is subordinate to the carpenter as well. A particular "real" table offers different aspects when viewed from different sides. But when the table is in use such aspects are indifferent; what matters is the particular table, which is one and the same. *Mē ti diapherei autē heautēs* (598 a), "it is distinguished (in spite of its various aspects) in no way from itself." Such a single, particular, and selfsame thing the carpenter can manufacture. In contrast, the painter can bring the table into view only from one particular angle. What he pro-duces is consequently but *one* aspect, *one* way in which the table appears. If he depicts the table from the front, he cannot paint the rear of it. He produces the table always in only one view or *phantasma* (598 b). What defines the character of the painter as *mimētēs* is not only that he cannot at all produce any particular usable table, but also that he cannot even bring that one particular table fully to the fore.

But *mimēsis* is the essence of all art. Hence a position of distance with respect to Being, to immediate and undistorted outward appearance, to the *idea,* is proper to art. In regard to the opening up of Being, that is, to the display of Being in the unconcealed, *alētheia,* art is subordinate.

Where, then, according to Plato, does art stand in relation to truth (*alētheia*)? The answer (598 b): *Porrō ara pou tou alēthous hē mimētikē estin.* "So, then, art stands far removed from truth." What art produces is not the *eidos* as *idea* (*physis,*) but *touto eidōlon,* which is but the semblance of pure outward appearance. *Eidōlon* means a little *eidos,* but not just in the sense of stature. In the way it shows and appears, the *eidōlon* is something slight. It is a mere residue of the genuine self-showing of beings, and even then in an alien domain, for example, color or some other material of portraiture. Such diminution of the way of pro-ducing is a darkening and distorting. *Tout' ara estai kai ho tragōidopoios, eiper mimētēs esti, tritos tis apo basileōs kai tēs alētheias pephykōs, kai pantes hoi alloi mimētai* (597 e). "Now, the tragedian will also be of such kind, if he is an 'artist,' removed three times, as it were, from the master who rules over the emergence of pure Being; according to his essence he will be reduced to third place with regard to truth (and to the grasp of it in pure discernment); and of such kind are the other 'artists' as well."

A statement by Erasmus which has been handed down to us · is supposed to characterize the art of the painter Albrecht Dürer. The statement expresses a thought that obviously grew out of a personal conversation which that learned man had with the artist. The statement runs: *ex situ rei unius, non unam speciem sese oculis offerentem ex-primit:* by showing a particular thing from any given angle, he, Dürer the painter, brings to the fore not only one single isolated view which offers itself to the eye. Rather—we may complete the thought in the following way—by showing any given individual thing as this particular thing, in its singularity, he makes Being itself visible: in a particular hare, the Being of the hare; in a particular animal, the animality. It is clear that Erasmus here is speaking against Plato. We may presume that the humanist Erasmus knew the dialogue we have been discussing and its passages on art. That Erasmus and Dürer could speak in such a fashion presupposes that a transformation of the understanding of Being was taking place.*

In the sequence of sundry ways taken by the presence of beings, hence by the Being of beings, art stands far below truth in Plato's metaphysics. We encounter here a distance. Yet distance is not discordance, especially not if art—as Plato would have it—is placed under the guidance of philosophy as knowledge of the essence of beings. To pursue Plato's thoughts in that direction, and so to examine the further contents of Book Ten, is not germane to our present effort.

---

*Compare to the above Heidegger's reference to Albrecht Dürer in *Der Ursprung des Kunstwerkes,* Reclam edition, p. 80; "The Origin of the Work of Art," in *Poetry, Language, Thought,* p. 70.

23. Plato's *Phaedrus*: Beauty and Truth in Felicitous Discordance

Our point of departure was the question as to the nature of the discordance between art and truth in Nietzsche's view. The discordance must loom before him on the basis of the way he grasps art and truth philosophically. According to his own words, Nietzsche's philosophy is inverted Platonism. If we grant that there is in Platonism a discordance between art and truth, it follows that such discordance would in Nietzsche's view have to vanish as a result of the cancellation which overturns Platonism. But we have just seen that there is no discordance in Platonism, merely a distance. Of course, the distance is not simply a quantitative one, but a distance of order and rank. The result is the following proposition, which would apply to Plato, although couched in Nietzsche's manner of speech: truth is worth more than art. Nietzsche says, on the contrary: art is worth more than truth. Obviously, the discordance lies hidden in these propositions. But if in distinction to Plato the relation of art and truth is reversed within the hierarchy; and if for Nietzsche that relation is a discordance, then it only follows that for Plato too the relation is a discordance, but of a reverse sort. Even though Nietzsche's philosophy may be understood as the reversal of Platonism, that does not mean that through such reversal the discordance between art and truth must vanish. We can only say that if there is a discordance between art and truth in Plato's teaching, and if Nietzsche's philosophy represents a reversal of Platonism, then such discordance must come to the fore in Nietzsche's philosophy in the reverse form. Hence Platonism can be for us a directive for the discov-

ery and location of the discordance in Nietzsche's thought, a directive
that would indicate by way of reversal. In that way Nietzsche's knowledge of art and truth would finally be brought to its sustaining ground.

What does discordance mean? Discordance is the opening of a gap
between two things that are severed. Of course, a mere gap does not
yet constitute a discordance. We do speak of a "split" in relation to the
gap that separates two soaring cliffs; yet the cliffs are not in discordance
and never could be; to be so would require that they, of themselves,
relate to each other. Only two things that are related to one another
can be opposed to each other. But such opposition is not yet discordance. For it is surely the case that their being opposed to one another
presupposes a being drawn toward and related to each other, which is
to say, their converging upon and agreeing with one another in one
respect. Genuine political opposition—not mere dispute—can arise
only where the selfsame political order is willed; only here can ways and
goals and basic principles diverge. In every opposition, agreement prevails in one respect, whereas in other respects there is variance. But
whatever diverges in the same respect in which it agrees slips into
discordance. Here the opposition springs from the divergence of what
once converged, indeed in such a way that precisely by being apart they
enter into the supreme way of belonging together. But from that we
also conclude that severance is something different from opposition,
that it does not need to be discordance, but may be a concordance.
Concordance too requires the twofold character implied in severance.

Thus "discordance" is ambiguous. It may mean, first, a severance
which at bottom can be a concordance; second, one which must be a
discordance (abscission). For the present we purposely allow the word
"discordance" to remain in such ambiguity. For if a discordance prevails in Nietzsche's inverted Platonism, and if that is possible only to
the extent that there is discordance already in Platonism; and if the
discordance is in Nietzsche's view a dreadful one; then for Plato it must
be the reverse, that is to say, it must be a severance which nevertheless
is concordant. In any case, any two things that are supposed to be able
to enter into discordance must be balanced against one another, be of
the same immediate origin, of the same necessity and rank. There can

be an "above" and "below" in cases of mere distance and opposition, but never in the case of discordance, for the former do not share an equivalent standard of measure. The "above" and "below" are fundamentally different; in the essential respect they do not agree.

Therefore, so long as art in the *Republic* remains in third position when measured in terms of truth, a distance and a subordination obtain between art and truth—but a discordance is not possible. If such discordance between art and truth is to become possible, art must first of all be elevated to equal rank. But is there as a matter of fact a "discordance" between art and truth? Indeed Plato speaks—in the *Republic,* no less (607 b)—in a shadowy and suggestive way of the *palaia men tis diaphora philosophiai te kai poiētikēi,* "of a certain ancient quarrel between philosophy and poetry," which is to say, between knowledge and art, truth and beauty. Yet even if *diaphora* here is to suggest more than a quarrel—and it is—in this dialogue it is not and cannot be a matter of "discordance." For if art must become equal in rank with truth, so as to become "discordant" with it, then it becomes necessary to consider art in yet another respect.

That other respect in which art must be viewed can only be the same one in which Plato discusses truth. Only that one and the same respect grants the presupposition for a severance. We must therefore investigate in what other regard—in contrast to the conversation carried on in the *Republic*—Plato treats the question of art.

If we scrutinize the traditional configuration of Plato's philosophy as a whole we notice that it consists of particular conversations and areas of discussion. Nowhere do we find a "system" in the sense of a unified structure planned and executed with equal compartments for all essential questions and issues. The same is true of Aristotle's philosophy and of Greek philosophy in general. Various questions are posed from various points of approach and on various levels, developed and answered to varying extents. Nevertheless, a certain basic way of proceeding prevails in Plato's thought. Everything is gathered into the guiding question of philosophy—the question as to what beings are.

Although the congelation of philosophical inquiry in the doctrines and handbooks of the Schools is prepared in and by the philosophy of

Plato, we must be chary of thinking about his questions on the guide-lines of particular dogmatic phrases and formulations found in the later philosophical disciplines. Whatever Plato says about truth and knowl-edge, or beauty and art, we may not conceive of it and pigeonhole it according to later epistemology, logic, and aesthetics. Of course that does not preclude our posing the question, in relation to Plato's medita-tion on art, of whether and where the issue of beauty is also treated in his philosophy. Granted that we must allow the whole matter to remain open, we may ask about the nature of the relation between art and beauty—a relation that long ago was accepted as a matter of course.

In his discussions Plato often speaks of "the beautiful" without taking up the question of art. To one of his dialogues the tradition has appended the express subtitle *peri tou kalou,* "On the Beautiful." It is that conversation which Plato called *Phaedrus,* after the youth who serves as the interlocutor in it. But the dialogue has received other subtitles over the centuries: *peri psychēs,* "On the Soul," and *peri tou erōtos,* "On Love." That alone is enough to produce uncertainty con-cerning the contents of the dialogue. All those things—the beautiful, the soul, and love—are discussed, and not merely incidentally. But the dialogue speaks also of *technē,* art, in great detail; also of *logos,* speech and language, with great penetration; of *alētheia,* truth, in a quite essential way, of *mania*—madness, rapture, ecstasy—in a most compel-ling manner; and finally, as always, of the *ideai* and of Being.

Every one of these words could with as much (or as little) right serve as the subtitle. Nevertheless, the content of the dialogue is by no means a jumbled potpourri. Its rich content is shaped so remarkably well that this dialogue must be accounted the most accomplished one in all essential respects. It therefore may not be taken to be the earliest work of Plato, as Schleiermacher believed; just as little does it belong to the final period; it rather belongs to those years which comprise the *akmē* of Plato's creative life.

Because of the inner greatness of this work of Plato's, we cannot hope to make the whole of it visible at once and in brief; that is even less possible here than it was in the case of the *Republic.* Our remarks concerning the title suffice to show that the *Phaedrus* discusses art, truth, speech, rapture, and the beautiful. Now we will pursue only what is said concerning the beautiful in relation to the true. We do this in order to estimate whether, to what extent, and in what way, we can speak of a severance of the two.

Decisive for correct understanding of what is said here about the beautiful is knowledge of the context and the scope in which the beautiful comes to language. To begin with a negative determination: the beautiful is discussed neither in the context of the question of art nor in explicit connection with the question of truth. Rather, the beautiful is discussed with the range of the original question of man's relation to beings as such. But precisely because Plato reflects upon the beautiful within the realm of that question, its connection with truth and art comes to the fore. We can demonstrate that on the basis of the latter half of the dialogue.

We will first of all select several guiding statements, in order to make visible the scope in which the beautiful is discussed. Second, we will comment upon what is said there about the beautiful, while remaining within the limits of our task. Third, and finally, we will ask about the kind of relation between beauty and truth which confronts us there.

Turning to the first matter, we note that the beautiful is discussed with the scope characteristic of man's relation to beings as such. In that regard we must consider the following statement (249 e): *pasa men anthrōpou psychē physei tetheatai ta onta, ē ouk an ēlthen eis tode to zōion.* "Every human soul, rising of itself, has already viewed beings in their Being; otherwise it would never have entered into this form of life." In order for man to be this particular embodying/living man, he must already have viewed Being. Why? What is man, after all? That is not stated in so many words; it remains tacit and presupposed. Man is the essence that comports itself to beings as such. But he could not be such an essence, that is to say, beings could not show themselves to him as beings, if he did not always ahead of time have Being in view by means of "theory." Man's "soul" must have viewed Being, since Being cannot be grasped by the senses. The soul "nourishes itself," *trephetai,* upon Being. Being, the discerning relation to Being, guarantees man his relation to beings.

If we did not know what variation and equality were, we could never encounter various things; we could never encounter things at all. If we did not know what sameness and contrariety were, we could never comport ourselves toward ourselves as selfsame in each case; we would never be with ourselves, would never be our selves at all. Nor could we ever experience something that stands over against us, something other than ourselves. If we did not know what order and law, or symmetry and harmonious arrangement were, we could not arrange and construct anything, could not establish and maintain anything in existence. The form of life called man would simply be impossible if the view upon Being did not prevail in it in a fundamental and paramount way.

But now we must catch a glimpse of man's other essential determination. Because the view upon Being is exiled in the body, Being can never be beheld purely in its unclouded brilliance; it can be seen only under the circumstance of our encountering this or that particular being. Therefore the following is generally true of the view upon Being which is proper to man's soul: *mogis kathorōsa ta onta* (248 a), "it just barely views being [as such], and only with effort." For that reason most people find knowledge of Being quite laborious, and consequently *ateleis tēs tou ontos theas aperchontai* (248 b), "the *thea*, the view upon Being, remains *atelēs* to them, so that it does not achieve its end, does not encompass everything that is proper to Being." Hence their view of things is but half of what it should be: it is as though they looked cockeyed at things. Most people, the cockeyed ones, give it up. They divert themselves from the effort to gain a pure view upon Being, *kai apelthousai trophēi doxastēi chrōntai,* "and in turning away are no longer nourished by Being." Instead, they make use of the *trophē doxastē,* the nourishment that falls to them thanks to *doxa,* i.e., what offers itself in anything they may encounter, some fleeting appearance which things just happen to have.

But the more the majority of men in the everyday world fall prey to mere appearance and to prevailing opinions concerning beings, and the more comfortable they become with them, feeling themselves confirmed in them, the more Being "conceals itself" (*lanthanei*) from man. The consequence for man of the concealment of Being is that he is overcome by *lēthē,* that concealment of Being which gives rise to the illusion that there is no such thing as Being. We translate the Greek word *lēthē* as "forgetting," although in such a way that "to forget" is thought in a metaphysical, not a psychological, manner. The majority of men sink into oblivion of Being, although—or precisely because— they constantly have to do solely with the things that are in their vicinity. For such things are not beings; they are only such things *ha nyn einai phamen* (249 c), "of which we now say that they are." Whatever matters to us and makes a claim on us here and now, in this or that way, as this or that thing, is—to the extent that it is at all—only a *homoiōma,* an approximation to Being. It is but a fleeting appearance of Being. But those who lapse into oblivion of Being do not even know of the appearance as an appearance. For otherwise they would at the same time have to know of Being, which comes to the fore even in fleeting appearances, although "just barely." They would then emerge from oblivion of Being. Instead of being slaves to oblivion, they would preserve *mnēmē* in recollective thought on Being. *Oligai dē leipontai hais to tēs mnēmēs hikanōs parestin* (250 a 5): "Only a few remain who have at their disposal the capacity to remember Being." But even these few are not able without further ado to see the appearance of what they encounter in such a way that the Being in it comes to the fore for them. Particular conditions must be fulfilled. Depending on how Being gives itself, the power of self-showing in the *idea* becomes proper to it, and therewith the attracting and binding force.

As soon as man lets himself be bound by Being in his view upon it, he is cast beyond himself, so that he is stretched, as it were, between himself and Being and is outside himself. Such elevation beyond oneself and such being drawn toward Being itself is *erōs.* Only to the extent that Being is able to elicit "erotic" power in its relation to man is man capable of thinking about Being and overcoming oblivion of Being.

The proposition with which we began—that the view upon Being is proper to the essence of man, so that he can be as man—can be understood only if we realize that the view upon Being does not enter on the scene as a mere appurtenance of man. It belongs to him as his most intrinsic possession, one which can be quite easily disturbed and deformed, and which therefore must always be recovered anew. Hence the need for whatever makes possible such recovery, perpetual renewal, and preservation of the view upon Being. That can only be something which in the immediate, fleeting appearances of things encountered also brings Being, which is utterly remote, to the fore most readily. But that, according to Plato, is the beautiful. When we defined the range and scope in which the beautiful comes to language we were basically already saying what the beautiful is, with regard to the possibility and the preservation of the view upon Being.

We proceed now to the second stage, adducing several statements in order to make the matter clearer. These statements are to establish the essential definition of the beautiful and thereby to prepare the way for the third stage, namely, a discussion of the relation of beauty and truth in Plato. From the metaphysical founding of communal life in Plato's dialogue on the state we know that what properly sets the standard is manifested in *dikē* and *dikaiosynē,* that is, in the well-wrought jointure of the order of Being. But viewed from the standpoint of the customary oblivion of Being, the supreme and utterly pure essence of Being is what is most remote. And to the extent that the essential order of Being shows itself in "beings," that is to say, in whatever we call "beings," it is here very difficult to discern. Fleeting appearances are inconspicuous; what is essential scarcely obtrudes. In the *Phaedrus* (250 b) Plato says accordingly: *dikaiosynēs men oun kai sōphrosynēs kai hosa alla timia psychais ouk enesti phengos ouden en tois tēide homoiōmasin.* "In justice and in temperance, and in whatever men ultimately must respect above all else, there dwells no radiance whenever men encounter them as fleeting appearances." Plato continues: *alla di' amydrōn organōn mogis autōn kai oligoi epi tas eikonas iontes theōntai to tou eikasthentos genos.* "On the contrary, we grasp Being with blunt instruments, clumsily, scarcely at all; and few of those who approach the appearances in question catch a glimpse of the original source, i.e., the essential origin, of what offers itself in fleeting appearances." The train of thought continues as Plato interposes a striking antithesis: *kallos de,* "With beauty, however," it is different. *Nun de kallos monon tautēn esche moiran, hōst' ekphanestaton einai* *kai erasmiōtaton* (250 d). "But to beauty alone has the role been allotted [i.e., in the essential order of Being's illumination] to be the most radiant, but also the most enchanting." The beautiful is what advances most directly upon us and captivates us. While encountering us as a being, however, it at the same time liberates us to the view upon Being. The beautiful is an element which is disparate within itself; it grants entry into immediate sensuous appearances and yet at the same time soars toward Being; it is both captivating and liberating.* Hence it is the beautiful that snatches us from oblivion of Being and grants the view upon Being.

The beautiful is called that which is most radiant, that which shines in the realm of immediate, sensuous, fleeting appearances: *kateilēpha-men auto dia tēs enargestatēs aisthēseōs tōn hemeterōn stilbon enarge-stata*. "The beautiful itself is given [to us men, here] by means of the most luminous mode of perception at our disposal, and we possess the beautiful as what most brightly glistens." *Opsis gar hēmin oxytate tōn dia tou sōmatos erchetai aisthēseōn*. "For vision, viewing, is the keenest way we can apprehend things through the body." But we know that *thea*, "viewing," is also the supreme apprehending, the grasping of Being. The look reaches as far as the highest and farthest remoteness of Being; simultaneously, it penetrates the nearest and brightest proximity of fleeting appearances. The more radiantly and brightly fleeting appearances are apprehended as such, the more brightly does that of which they are the appearances come to the fore—Being. According to its most proper essence, the beautiful is what is most radiant and

---

*Heidegger translates *erasmiōtaton* as *das Entrückendste*, modifying it now as *das Berückend-Entrückende*. Although both German words could be rendered by the English words "to entrance, charm, enchant," their literal sense is quite different. *Rücken* suggests sudden change of place; the prefixes (*be-*, *ent-*) both make the verb transitive. But *berücken* suggests causing to move toward, *entrücken* causing to move away. Heidegger thus tries to express the disparate, i.e., genuinely erotic character of the beautiful, which both captivates and liberates us, by choosing two German words that manifest a kind of felicitous discordance. The same formulation appears in *"Wie wenn am Feiertage . . ."* (1939–40) in Martin Heidegger, *Erläuterungen zu Hölderlins Dichtung*, pp. 53–54.

sparkling in the sensuous realm, in a way that, as such brilliance, it lets Being scintillate at the same time. Being is that to which man from the outset remains essentially bound; it is in the direction of Being that man is liberated.

Since the beautiful allows Being to scintillate, and since the beautiful itself is what is most attractive, it draws man through and beyond itself to Being as such. We can scarcely coin an expression that would render what Plato says in such a lucid way about radiance through those two essential words, *ekphanestaton kai erasmiōtaton.*

Even the Latin translation from Renaissance times obscures everything here when it says, *At vero pulchritudo sola habuit sortem, ut maxime omnium et perspicua sit et amabilis* ["But true beauty alone has been destined to be the most transparent of things and the loveliest of all"]. Plato does not mean that the beautiful itself, as an object, is "perspicuous and lovely." It is rather what is most luminous and what thereby most draws us on and liberates us.

From what we have presented, the essence of the beautiful has become clear. It is what makes possible the recovery and preservation of the view upon Being, which devolves from the most immediate fleeting appearances and which can easily vanish in oblivion. Our capacity to understand, *phronēsis,* although it remains related to what is essential, of itself has no corresponding *eidōlon,* no realm of appearances which brings what it has to grant us into immediate proximity and yet at the same time elevates us toward what is properly to be understood.

The third question, inquiring about the relationship between beauty and truth, now answers itself. To be sure, up to now truth has not been treated explicitly. Nevertheless, in order to achieve clarity concerning the relation of beauty and truth, it suffices if we think back to the major introductory statement and read it in the way Plato himself first introduces it. The major statement says that the view upon Being is proper to the essence of man, that by force of it man can comport himself to beings and to what he encounters as merely apparent things. At the place where that thought is first introduced (249 b), Plato says, not that the basic condition for the form of man is that he *tetheatai ta onta,* that he "has beings as such in view ahead of time," but *ou gar hē ge mēpote idousa tēn alētheian eis tode hēxei to schēma,* that "the soul would never have assumed this form if it had not earlier viewed the unconcealment of beings, i.e., beings in their unconcealment."

The view upon Being opens up what is concealed, making it unconcealed; it is the basic relation to the true. That which truth essentially brings about, the unveiling of Being, that and nothing else is what beauty brings about. It does so, scintillating in fleeting appearances, by liberating us to the Being that radiates in such appearances, which is to say, to the openedness of Being, to truth. Truth and beauty are in essence related to the selfsame, to Being; they belong together in one, the one thing that is decisive: to open Being and to keep it open.

Yet in that very medium where they belong together, they must diverge for man, they must separate from one another. For the openedness of Being, truth, can only be nonsensuous illumination, since for Plato Being is nonsensuous. Because Being opens itself only to the view upon Being, and because the latter must always be snatched from oblivion of Being, and because for that reason it needs the most direct radiance of fleeting appearances, the opening up of Being must occur at that site where, estimated in terms of truth, the *mē on (eidōlon),* i.e., nonbeing, occurs. But that is the site of beauty.

When we consider very carefully that art, by bringing forth the beautiful, resides in the sensuous, and that it is therefore far removed from truth, it then becomes clear why truth and beauty, their belonging together in one notwithstanding, still must be two, must separate from one another. But the severance, discordance in the broad sense, is not in Plato's view one which arouses dread; it is a felicitous one. The beautiful elevates us beyond the sensuous and bears us back into the true. Accord prevails in the severance, because the beautiful, as radiant and sensuous, has in advance sheltered its essence in the truth of Being as supersensuous.

Viewed more discerningly, a discordance in the strict sense lies here as well. But it belongs to the essence of Platonism that it efface that discordance by positing Being in such a way that it can do so without the effacement becoming visible as such. But when Platonism is overturned everything that characterizes it must also be overturned; whatever it can cloak and conceal, whatever it can pronounce felicitous, on the contrary, must out, and must arouse dread.

24. Nietzsche's Overturning of Platonism

We conducted an examination of the relation of truth and beauty in Plato in order to sharpen our view of things. For we are attempting to locate the place and context in Nietzsche's conception of art and truth where the severance of the two must occur, and in such a way that it is experienced as a discordance that arouses dread.

Both beauty and truth are related to Being, indeed by way of unveiling the Being of beings. Truth is the immediate way in which Being is revealed in the thought of philosophy; it does not enter into the sensuous, but from the outset is averted from it. Juxtaposed to it is beauty, penetrating the sensuous and then moving beyond it, liberating in the direction of Being. If beauty and truth in Nietzsche's view enter into discordance, they must previously belong together in one. That one can only be Being and the relation to Being.

Nietzsche defines the basic character of beings, hence Being, as will to power. Accordingly, an original conjunction of beauty and truth must result from the essence of will to power, a conjunction which simultaneously must become a discordance. When we try to discern and grasp the discordance we cast a glance toward the unified essence of will to power. Nietzsche's philosophy, according to his own testimony, is inverted Platonism. We ask: in what sense does the relation of beauty and truth which is peculiar to Platonism become a different sort of relation through the overturning?

The question can easily be answered by a simple recalculation, if "overturning" Platonism may be equated with the procedure of standing all of Plato's statements on their heads, as it were. To be sure, Nietzsche himself often expresses the state of affairs in that way, not only in order to make clear what he means in a rough and ready fashion, but also because he himself often thinks that way, although he is aiming at something else.

Only late in his life, shortly before the cessation of his labors in thinking, does the full scope required by such an inversion of Platonism become clear to him. That clarity waxes as Nietzsche grasps the necessity of the overturning, which is demanded by the task of overcoming nihilism. For that reason, when we elucidate the overturning of Platonism we must take the structure of Platonism as our point of departure. For Plato the supersensuous is the true world. It stands over all, as what sets the standard. The sensuous lies below, as the world of appearances. What stands over all is alone and from the start what sets the standard; it is therefore what is desired. After the inversion—that is easy to calculate in a formal way—the sensuous, the world of appearances, stands above; the supersensuous, the true world, lies below. With a glance back to what we have already presented, however, we must keep a firm hold on the realization that the very talk of a "true world" and "world of appearances" no longer speaks the language of Plato.

But what does that mean—the sensuous stands above all? It means that it is the true, it is genuine being. If we take the inversion strictly in this sense, then the vacant niches of the "above and below" are preserved, suffering only a change in occupancy, as it were. But as long as the "above and below" define the formal structure of Platonism, Platonism in its essence perdures. The inversion does not achieve what it must, as an overcoming of nihilism, namely, an overcoming of Platonism in its very foundations. Such overcoming succeeds only when the "above" in general is set aside as such, when the former positing of something true and desirable no longer arises, when the true world—in the sense of the ideal—is expunged. What happens when the true world is expunged? Does the apparent world still remain? No. For the apparent world can be what it is only as a counterpart of the true. If the true world collapses, so must the world of appearances. Only then is Platonism overcome, which is to say, inverted in such a way that philosophical thinking twists free of it. But then where does such thinking wind up?

During the time the overturning of Platonism became for Nietzsche a twisting free of it, madness befell him. Heretofore no one at all has recognized this reversal as Nietzsche's final step; neither has anyone perceived that the step is clearly taken only in his final creative year (1888). Insight into these important connections is quite difficult on the basis of the book *The Will to Power* as it lies before us in its present form, since the textual fragments assembled here have been removed from a great number of manuscripts written during the years 1882 to 1888. An altogether different picture results from the examination of Nietzsche's original manuscripts. But even without reference to these, there is a section of the treatise *Twilight of the Idols,* composed in just a few days during that final year of creative work (in September of 1888, although the book did not appear until 1889), a section which is very striking, because its basic position differs from the one we are already familiar with. The section is entitled "How the 'True World' Finally Became a Fable: the History of an Error" (VIII, 82–83; cf. WM, 567 and 568, from the year 1888.*)

The section encompasses a little more than one page. (Nietzsche's handwritten manuscript, the one sent to the printer, is extant.) It belongs to those pieces the style and structure of which betray the fact that here, in a magnificent moment of vision, the entire realm of Nietzsche's thought is permeated by a new and singular brilliance. The title, "How the 'True World' Finally Became a Fable," says that here a history is to be recounted in the course of which the supersensuous, posited by Plato as true being, not only is reduced from the higher to the lower rank but also collapses into the unreal and nugatory. Nietzsche divides the history into six parts, which can be readily recognized as the most important epochs of Western thought, and which lead directly to the doorstep of Nietzsche's philosophy proper.

---

*In these two complex notes Nietzsche defines the "perspectival relation" of will to power. Whereas in an earlier note (WM, 566) he spoke of the "true world" as "always the apparent world *once again,*" he now (WM, 567) refrains from the opposition of true and apparent worlds as such: "Here there remains not a shadow of a *right* to speak of *Schein* ...," which is to say, of a world of mere appearances.

For the sake of our own inquiry we want to trace that history in all brevity, so that we can see how Nietzsche, in spite of his will to subvert, preserved a luminous knowledge concerning what had occurred prior to him.

The more clearly and simply a decisive inquiry traces the history of Western thought back to its few essential stages, the more that history's power to reach forward, seize, and commit grows. This is especially the case where it is a matter of overcoming such history. Whoever believes that philosophical thought can dispense with its history by means of a simple proclamation will, without his knowing it, be dispensed with by history; he will be struck a blow from which he can never recover, one that will blind him utterly. He will think he is being original when he is merely rehashing what has been transmitted and mixing together traditional interpretations into something ostensibly new. The greater a revolution is to be, the more profoundly must it plunge into its history.

We must measure Nietzsche's brief portrayal of the history of Platonism and its overcoming by this standard. Why do we emphasize here things that are evident? Because the form in which Nietzsche relates the history might easily tempt us to take it all as a mere joke, whereas something very different is at stake here (cf. *Beyond Good and Evil*, no. 213, "What a philosopher is," VII, 164 ff.).

The six divisions of the history of Platonism, culminating in emergence from Platonism, are as follows.

"1. The true world, attainable for the wise, the pious, the virtuous man—he lives in it, *he is it.*"

Here the founding of the doctrine by Plato is established. To all appearances, the true world itself is not handled at all, but only how man adopts a stance toward it and to what extent it is attainable. And the essential definition of the true world consists in the fact that it is attainable here and now for man, although not for any and every man, and not without further ado. It is attainable for the virtuous; it is the supersensuous. The implication is that virtue consists in repudiation of the sensuous, since denial of the world that is closest to us, the sensuous world, is proper to the Being of beings. Here the "true world" is not yet anything "Platonic," that is, not something unattainable, merely desirable, merely "ideal." Plato himself is who he is by virtue of the fact that he unquestioningly and straightforwardly functions on the basis of the world of Ideas as the essence of Being. The supersensuous is the *idea*. What is here envisioned in the eyes of Greek thought and existence is truly seen, and experienced in such simple vision, as what makes possible every being, as that which becomes present to itself (see *Vom Wesen des Grundes,* 1929, part two). Therefore, Nietzsche adds the following commentary in parentheses: "(Oldest form of the idea, relatively sensible, simple, convincing. Circumlocution for the sentence 'I, Plato, *am* the truth.')" The thought of the Ideas and the interpretation of Being posited here are creative in and of themselves. Plato's work is not yet Platonism. The "true world" is not yet the object of a doctrine; it is the power of Dasein; it is what lights up in becoming present; it is pure radiance without cover.

"2. The true world, unattainable for now, but promised for the wise, the pious, the virtuous man ('for the sinner who repents')."

With the positing of the supersensuous as true being, the break with the sensuous is now expressly ordained, although here again not straightaway: the true world is unattainable only in this life, for the duration of earthly existence. In that way earthly existence is denigrated and yet receives its proper tension, since the supersensuous is promised as the "beyond." Earth becomes the "earthly." The essence and existence of man are now fractured, but that makes a certain ambiguity possible. The possibility of "yes and no," of "this world as well as that one," begins; the apparent affirmation of this world, but with a reservation; the ability to go along with what goes on in this world, but keeping that remote back door ajar. In place of the unbroken essence of the Greek, which while unbroken was not without hazard but was passionate, which grounded itself in what was attainable, which drew its definitive boundaries here, which not only bore the intractability of fate but in its affirmation struggled for victory—in place of that essence begins something insidious. In Plato's stead, Platonism now rules. Thus:

"(Progress of the idea: it becomes more subtle, insidious, ungraspable
—*it becomes woman,* it becomes Christian. . . .)" The supersensuous
is no longer present within the scope of human existence, present for
it and for its sensuous nature. Rather, the whole of human existence
becomes this-worldly to the extent that the supersensuous is interpreted as the "beyond." In that way the true world now becomes even
truer, by being displaced ever farther beyond and away from this world;
it grows ever stronger in being, the more it becomes what is promised
and the more zealously it is embraced, i.e., believed in, as what is
promised. If we compare the second part of the history with the first,
we see how Nietzsche in his description of the first part consciously sets
Plato apart from all Platonism, protecting him from it.

   "3. The true world, unattainable, indemonstrable, unpromisable,
but even as thought, a consolation, an obligation, an imperative."

This division designates the form of Platonism that is achieved by
the Kantian philosophy. The supersensuous is now a postulate of practical reason; even outside the scope of all experience and demonstration
it is demanded as what is necessarily existent, in order to salvage adequate grounds for the lawfulness of reason. To be sure, the accessibility
of the supersensuous by way of cognition is subjected to critical doubt,
but only in order to make room for belief in the requisition of reason.
Nothing of the substance and structure of the Christian view of the
world changes by virtue of Kant; it is only that all the light of knowledge is cast on experience, that is, on the mathematical-scientific interpretation of the "world." Whatever lies outside of the knowledge
possessed by the sciences of nature is not denied as to its existence but
is relegated to the indeterminateness of the unknowable. Therefore:
"(The old sun, basically, but seen through haze and skepticism; the idea
rarified, grown pallid, Nordic, Königsbergian.)" A transformed world
—in contrast to the simple clarity by which Plato dwelled in direct
contact with the supersensuous, as discernible Being. Because he sees
through the unmistakable Platonism of Kant, Nietzsche at the same
time perceives the essential difference between Plato and Kant. In that
way he distinguishes himself fundamentally from his contemporaries,

who, not accidentally, equate Kant and Plato—if they don't interpret Plato as a Kantian who didn't quite make it.

"4. The true world—unattainable? In any case, unattained. And as unattained also *unknown*. Consequently, also, not consolatory, redemptive, obligating: to what could something unknown obligate us? . . ."

With the fourth division, the form to which Platonism commits itself as a consequence of the bygone Kantian philosophy is historically attained, although without an originally creative overcoming. It is the age following the dominance of German Idealism, at about the middle of the last century. With the help of its own chief principle, the theoretical unknowability of the supersensuous, the Kantian system is unmasked and exploded. If the supersensuous world is altogether unattainable for cognition, then nothing can be known about it, nothing can be decided for or against it. It becomes manifest that the supersensuous does not come on the scene as a part of the Kantian philosophy on the grounds of basic philosophical principles of knowledge but as a consequence of uneradicated Christian-theological presuppositions.* In that regard Nietzsche on one occasion observes of Leibniz, Kant, Fichte, Schelling, Hegel, and Schopenhauer, "They are all mere Schleiermachers" (XV, 112). The observation has two edges: it means not only that these men are at bottom camouflaged theologians but also that they are what that name suggests—*Schleier-macher,* makers of veils, men who veil things. In opposition to them stands the somewhat halfhearted rejection of the supersensuous as something unknown, to which, after Kant, no cognition can in principle attain. Such rejection is a kind of first glimmer of "probity" of meditation amid the

---

Unerschütterter theologisch-christlicher Voraussetzungen. The formulation is reminiscent of Heidegger's words in *Being and Time,* section 44 C: "The assertion of 'eternal truths' and the confusion of the phenomenally grounded 'ideality' of Dasein with an idealized absolute subject belong to those residues of Christian theology in philosophical problems which have not yet been radically extruded [zu den längst noch nicht radikal ausgetriebenen Resten von christlicher Theologie innerhalb der philosophischen Problematik.]"

captiousness and "counterfeiting" that came to prevail with Platonism. Therefore: "(Gray morning. First yawnings of reason. Cockcrow of positivism.)" Nietzsche descries the rise of a new day. Reason, which here means man's knowing and inquiring, awakens and comes to its senses.

"5. The 'true world'—an idea which is of use for nothing, which is no longer even obligating—an idea become useless, superfluous, *consequently,* a refuted idea: let us abolish it!"

With this division Nietzsche designates the first segment of his own way in philosophy. The "true world" he now sets in quotation marks. It is no longer his own word, the content of which he himself could still affirm. The "true world" is abolished. But notice the reason: because it has become useless, superfluous. In the shimmering twilight a new standard of measure comes to light: whatever does not in any way at any time involve man's Dasein can make no claim to be affirmed. Therefore: "(Bright day; breakfast; return of *bon sens* and of cheerfulness; Plato's embarrassed blush; pandemonium of all free spirits.)" Here Nietzsche thinks back on the years of his own metamorphosis, which is intimated clearly enough in the very titles of the books he wrote during that time: *Human, All Too Human* (1878), *The Wanderer and His Shadow* (1880), *The Dawn* (1881), and *The Gay Science* (1882). Platonism is overcome inasmuch as the supersensuous world, as the true world, is abolished; but by way of compensation the sensuous world remains, and positivism occupies it. What is now required is a confrontation with the latter. For Nietzsche does not wish to tarry in the dawn of morning; neither will he rest content with mere forenoon. In spite of the fact that the supersensuous world as the true world has been cast aside, the vacant niche of the higher world remains, and so does the blueprint of an "above and below," which is to say, so does Platonism. The inquiry must go one step farther.

"6. The true world we abolished: which world was left? the apparent one perhaps? ... But no! *along with the true world we have also abolished the apparent one!*"

That Nietzsche appends a sixth division here shows that, and how, he must advance beyond himself and beyond sheer abolition of the supersensuous. We sense it directly from the animation of the style and manner of composition—how the clarity of this step conducts him for the first time into the brilliance of full daylight, where all shadows dwindle. Therefore: "(Midday; moment of the shortest shadow; end of the longest error; highpoint of humanity; INCIPIT ZARATHUSTRA.)" Thus the onset of the final stage of his own philosophy.

The portrayal of all six divisions of the history of Platonism is so arranged that the "true world," the existence and legitimacy of which is under consideration, is in each division brought into connection with the type of man who comports himself to that world. Consequently, the overturning of Platonism and the ultimate twist out of it imply a metamorphosis of man. At the end of Platonism stands a decision concerning the transformation of man. That is how the phrase "high-point of humanity" is to be understood, as the peak of decision, namely, decision as to whether with the end of Platonism man as he has been hitherto is to come to an end, whether he is to become that kind of man Nietzsche characterized as the "last man," or whether that type of man can be overcome and the "overman" can begin: "Incipit Zara-thustra." By the word "overman" Nietzsche does not mean some miraculous, fabulous being, but the man who surpasses former man. But man as he has been hitherto is the one whose Dasein and relation to Being have been determined by Platonism in one of its forms or by a mixture of several of these. The last man is the necessary consequence of unsubdued nihilism. The great danger Nietzsche sees is that it will all culminate in the last man, that it will peter out in the spread of the increasingly insipid last man. "The opposite of the overman is the *last man:* I created him at the same time I created the former" (XIV, 262).

That suggests that the end first becomes visible as an end on the basis of the new beginning. To put it the other way round, overman's identity first becomes clear when the last man is perceived as such.

Now all we must do is bring into view the extreme counterposition to Plato and Platonism and then ascertain how Nietzsche successfully adopts a stance within it. What results when, along with the true world, the apparent world too is abolished?

The "true world," the supersensuous, and the apparent world, the sensuous, together make out what stands opposed to pure nothingness; they constitute beings as a whole. When both are abolished everything collapses into the vacuous nothing. That cannot be what Nietzsche means. For he desires to overcome nihilism in all its forms. When we recall that, and how, Nietzsche wishes to ground art upon embodying life by means of his physiological aesthetics, we note that this implies an affirmation of the sensuous world, not its abolition. However, according to the express wording of the final division of the history of Platonism, "the apparent world is abolished." Certainly. But the sensuous world is the "apparent world" only according to the interpretation of Platonism. With the abolition of Platonism the way first opens for the affirmation of the sensuous, and along with it, the nonsensuous world of the spirit as well. It suffices to recall the following statement from *The Will to Power,* no. 820:

> For myself and for all those who live—are *permitted* to live—without the anxieties of a puritanical conscience, I wish an ever greater spiritualization and augmentation of the senses. Yes, we ought to be grateful to our senses for their subtlety, fullness, and force; and we ought to offer them in return the very best of spirit we possess.

What is needed is neither abolition of the sensuous nor abolition of the nonsensuous. On the contrary, what must be cast aside is the misinterpretation, the deprecation, of the sensuous, as well as the extravagant elevation of the supersensuous. A path must be cleared for a new interpretation of the sensuous on the basis of a new hierarchy of the sensuous and nonsensuous. The new hierarchy does not simply wish to reverse matters within the old structural order, now reverencing the sensuous and scorning the nonsensuous. It does not wish to put what was at the very bottom on the very top. A new hierarchy and new valuation mean that the ordering *structure* must be changed. To that extent, overturning Platonism must become a twisting free of it. How far the latter extends with Nietzsche, how far it can go, to what extent it comes to an overcoming of Platonism and to what extent not—those are necessary critical questions. But they should be posed only when we have reflected in accordance with the thought that Nietzsche most intrinsically willed—beyond everything captious, ambiguous, and deficient which we might very easily ascribe to him here.

25. The New Interpretation of Sensuousness and the Raging Discordance between Art and Truth

We are now asking what new interpretation and ordering of the sensuous and nonsensuous results from the overturning of Platonism. To what extent is "the sensuous" the genuine "reality"? What transformation accompanies the inversion? What metamorphosis underlies it? We must ask the question in this last form, because it is not the case that things are inverted first, and then on the basis of the new position gained by the inversion the question is posed, "What is the result?" Rather, the overturning derives the force and direction of its motion from the new inquiry and its fundamental experience, in which true being, what is real, "reality," is to be defined afresh.

We are not unprepared for these questions, provided we have traversed the path of the entire lecture course, which from the outset has aimed in their direction.

We unfolded all our questions concerning art for the explicit and exclusive purpose of bringing the new reality, above all else, into sharp focus. In particular, the presentation of Nietzsche's "physiological aesthetics" was elaborated in such a way that we now only need to grasp in a more fundamental manner what was said there. We do that in order to pursue his interpretation of the sensuous in its principal direction, which means, to see how he achieves a stand for his thought after both the true and the apparent worlds of Platonism have been abolished.

Nietzsche recognizes rapture to be the basic actuality of art. In contrast to Wagner, he understands the feeling of increment of force, plenitude, and the reciprocal enhancement of all capacities, as a being beyond oneself, hence a coming to oneself in the supreme lucidity of Being—not a visionless tumult. But in Nietzsche's view that implies at the same time the emergence of the abyss of "life," of life's essential contradictions, not as moral evil or as something to be negated, but as what is to be affirmed. The "physiological," the sensuous-corporeal, in itself possesses this beyond-itself. The inner constitution of the sensuous was clarified by emphasis on the relation of rapture to beauty, and of creation and enjoyment to form. What is proper to form is the constant, order, overview, boundary, and law. The sensuous in itself is directed toward overview and order, toward what can be mastered and firmly fixed. What makes itself known here with regard to the essence of the "sensuous" we now need grasp only in its principal relations, in order to see how for Nietzsche the sensuous constitutes reality proper.

What lives is exposed to other forces, but in such a way that, striving against them, it deals with them according to their form and rhythm, in order to estimate them in relation to possible incorporation or elimination. According to this angle of vision, everything that is encountered is interpreted in terms of the living creature's capacity for life. The angle of vision, and the realm it opens to view, themselves draw the borderlines around what it is that creatures can or cannot encounter. For example, a lizard hears the slightest rustling in the grass but it does not hear a pistol shot fired quite close by. Accordingly, the creature develops a kind of interpretation of its surroundings and thereby of all occurrence, not incidentally, but as the fundamental process of life itself: "The *perspectival* [is] the basic condition of all life" (VII, 4).

With a view to the basic constitution of living things Nietzsche says (XIII, 63), "The essential aspect of organic beings is a *new* manifold, which is itself an occurrence." The living creature possesses the character of a perspectival preview which circumscribes a "line of horizon" about him, within whose scope something can come forward into appearance for him at all. Now, in the "organic" there is a multiplicity of drives and forces, each of which has its perspective. The manifold of perspectives distinguishes the organic from the inorganic. Yet even the latter has its perspective; it is just that in the inorganic, in attraction and repulsion, the "power relations" are clearly fixed (XIII, 62). The mechanistic representation of "inanimate" nature is only a hypothesis for purposes of calculation; it overlooks the fact that here too relations of forces and concatenations of perspectives hold sway. Every point of force per se is perspectival. As a result it becomes manifest "that there is no inorganic world" (XIII, 81). Everything "real" is alive, is "perspectival" in itself, and asserts itself in its perspective against others. On that basis we can understand Nietzsche's note from the years 1886–87 (XIII, 227–28):

> Fundamental question: whether the *perspectival* is proper to the *being,* and is not only a form of observation, a relation between different beings? Do the various forces stand in relation, so that the relation is tied to a perceptual optics? That would be possible if *all Being were essentially something which perceives.*

We would not have to go far to find proof to show that this conception of beings is precisely that of Leibniz, except that Nietzsche eliminates the latter's theological metaphysics, i.e., his Platonism. All being is in itself perspectival-perceptual, and that means, in the sense now delineated, "sensuous."

The sensuous is no longer the "apparent," no longer the penumbra; it alone is what is real, hence "true." And what becomes of semblance? Semblance itself is proper to the essence of the real. We can readily see that in the perspectival character of the actual. The following statement provides an opening onto the matter of semblance within the perspectivally constructed actual: "With the organic world begin *indeterminateness* and *semblance*" (XIII, 288; cf. also 229). In the unity of an organic being there is a multiplicity of drives and capacities (each of which possesses its perspective) which struggle against one another. In such a multiplicity the univocity of the particular perspective in which the actual in any given case stands is lost. The equivocal character of what shows itself in several perspectives is granted, along with the indeterminate, which now appears one way, then another, which first proffers this appearance, then that one. But such appearance becomes semblance in the sense of mere appearance only when what becomes manifest in one perspective petrifies and is taken to be the sole definitive appearance, to the disregard of the other perspectives that crowd round in turn.

In that way, palpable things, "objects," emerge for creatures in what they encounter; things that are constant, with enduring qualities, by which the creature can get its bearings. The entire range of what is fixed and constant is, according to the ancient Platonic conception, the region of "Being," the "true." Such Being, viewed perspectivally, is but the one-sided, entrenched appearance, which is taken to be solely definitive. It thus becomes mere appearance; Being, the true, is mere appearance, error.

> *Error* begins in the organic world. "Things," "substances," properties, act-"ivities" [*Tätig"keiten"*]—one should not read all that into the inorganic world! They are the specific errors by virtue of which organisms live (XIII, 69).

In the organic world, the world of embodying life, where man too resides, "error" begins. That should not be taken as meaning that creatures, in distinction to members of the inorganic realm, can go astray. It means that those beings which in the definitive perspectival horizon of a creature appear to constitute its firmly established, existent world, in their Being are but appearance, mere appearance. Man's logic serves to make what he encounters identical, constant, ascertainable. Being, the true, which logic "firmly locates" (petrifies), is but semblance; a semblance, an apparentness, that is essentially necessary to the creature as such, which is to say, a semblance that pertains to his survival, his establishment of self amidst ceaseless change. Because the real is perspectival in itself, apparentness as such is proper to reality. Truth, i.e., true being, i.e., what is constant and fixed, because it is the petrifying of any single given perspective, is always only an apparentness that has come to prevail, which is to say, it is always error. For that reason Nietzsche says (WM, 493), "*Truth is the kind of error* without which a certain kind of living being could not live. The value for *life* ultimately decides."

Truth, that is, the true as the constant, is a kind of semblance that is justified as a necessary condition of the assertion of life. But upon deeper meditation it becomes clear that all appearance and all apparentness are possible only if something comes to the fore and shows itself at all. What in advance enables such appearing is the perspectival itself. That is what genuinely radiates, bringing something to show itself. When Nietzsche uses the word semblance [*Schein*] it is usually ambiguous. He knows it, too. "There are fateful words which appear to express an insight but which in truth *hinder* it; among them belongs the word 'semblance,' 'appearance' " (XIII, 50). Nietzsche does not become master of the fate entrenched in that word, which is to say, in the matter. He says (*ibid.*), " 'Semblance' as I understand it is the actual and sole reality of things." That should be understood to mean not that reality is something apparent, but that being-real is in itself perspectival, a bringing forward into appearance, a letting radiate; that it is in itself a shining. Reality is radiance.

Hence I do not posit "semblance" in opposition to "reality," but on the contrary take semblance to be the reality which resists transformation into an imaginative "world of truth." A particular name for that reality would be "will to power," designated of course intrinsically and not on the basis of its ungraspable, fluid, Protean nature (XIII, 50; from the year 1886, at the latest).

Reality, Being, is *Schein* in the sense of perspectival letting-shine. But proper to that reality at the same time is the multiplicity of perspectives, and thus the possibility of illusion and of its being made fast, which means the possibility of truth as a kind of *Schein* in the sense of "mere" appearance. If truth is taken to be semblance, that is, as mere appearance and error, the implication is that truth is the fixed semblance which is necessarily inherent in perspectival shining—it is illusion. Nietzsche often identifies such illusion with "the lie": "One who tells the truth ends by realizing that he always lies" (XII, 293).

Indeed Nietzsche at times defines perspectival shining as *Schein* in the sense of illusion and deception, contrasting illusion and deception to truth, which, as "Being," is also at bottom error.

We have already seen that creation, as forming and shaping, as well as the aesthetic pleasures related to such shaping, are grounded in the essence of life. Hence art too, and precisely it, must cohere most intimately with perspectival shining and letting shine. Art in the proper sense is art in the grand style, desirous of bringing waxing life itself to power. It is not an immobilizing but a liberating for expansion, a clarifying to the point of transfiguration, and this in two senses: first, stationing a thing in the clarity of Being; second, establishing such clarity as the heightening of life itself.

Life is in itself perspectival. It waxes and flourishes with the height and heightening of the world which is brought forward perspectivally to appearance, with the enhancement of the shining, that is, of what brings a thing to scintillate in such a way that life is transfigured. "Art and nothing but art!" (WM, 853, section II). Art induces reality, which is in itself a shining, to shine most profoundly and supremely in scintillating transfiguration. If "metaphysical" means nothing else than the essence of reality, and if reality consists in shining, we then understand the statement with which the section on art in *The Will to Power* closes (WM, 853): " ... 'art as the proper task of life, art as its *metaphysical* activity . . . .' " Art is the most genuine and profound will to semblance, namely, to the scintillation of what transfigures, in which the supreme lawfulness of Dasein becomes visible. In contrast, truth is any given fixed apparition that allows life to rest firmly on a particular perspective and to preserve itself. As such fixation, "truth" is an immobilizing of life, and hence its inhibition and dissolution. "We have *art* so that we *do not perish from the truth*" (WM, 822). It is *"not possible . . . to live with the truth,"* if life is always enhancement of life; the "will to truth," i.e., to fixed apparition, is "already a symptom of degeneration" (XIV, 368). Now it becomes clear what the fifth and concluding proposition concerning art avers: *art is worth more than truth.*

Both art and truth are modes of perspectival shining. But the value of the real is measured according to how it satisfies the essence of reality, how it accomplishes the shining and enhances reality. *Art, as transfiguration, is more enhancing to life than truth, as fixation of an apparition.*

Now too we perceive to what extent the relation of art and truth must be a discordance for Nietzsche and for his philosophy, as inverted Platonism. Discordance is present only where the elements which sever the unity of their belonging-together diverge from one another by virtue of that very unity. The unity of their belonging-together is granted by the *one* reality, perspectival shining. To it belong both apparition and scintillating appearance as transfiguration. In order for the real (the living creature) to *be* real, it must on the one hand ensconce itself within a particular horizon, thus perduring in the illusion of truth. But in order for the real to *remain* real, it must on the other hand simultaneously transfigure itself by going beyond itself, surpassing itself in the scintillation of what is created in art—and that means it has to advance against the truth. While truth and art are proper to the essence of reality with equal originality, they must diverge from one another and go counter to one another.

But because in Nietzsche's view semblance, as perspectival, also possesses the character of the nonactual, of illusion and deception, he must say, "The will to *semblance,* to illusion, to deception, to Becoming and change is deeper, more 'metaphysical' [that is to say, corresponding more to the essence of Being] than the will to *truth,* to actuality, to Being" (XIV, 369). This is expressed even more decisively in *The Will to Power,* no. 853, section I, where semblance is equated with "lie": "*We need the lie* in order to achieve victory over this reality, this 'truth,' which is to say, in order to *live* . . . . That the lie is necessary for life is itself part and parcel of the frightful and questionable character of existence."

Art and truth are equally necessary for reality. As equally necessary they stand in severance. But their relationship first arouses dread when we consider that creation, i.e., the metaphysical activity of art, receives yet another essential impulse the moment we descry the most tremendous event—the death of the God of morality. In Nietzsche's view, existence can now be endured only in creation. Conducting reality to the power of its rule and of its supreme possibilities alone guarantees Being. But creation, as art, is will to semblance; it stands in severance from truth.

Art as will to semblance is the supreme configuration of will to power. But the latter, as the basic character of beings, as the essence of reality, is in itself that Being which wills itself by willing to be Becoming. In that way Nietzsche in will to power attempts to think the original unity of the ancient opposition of Being and Becoming. Being, as permanence, is to let Becoming *be* a Becoming. The origin of the thought of "eternal recurrence" is thereby indicated.

In the year 1886, in the middle of the period when he labored on the planned major work, Nietzsche's first treatise, *The Birth of Tragedy from the Spirit of Music* (1872), appeared in a new edition. It bore the altered title *The Birth of Tragedy, or Greek Civilization and Pessimism; New Edition, with an Attempt at Self-criticism* (see I, 1–14). The task which that book had first ventured to undertake remained the same for Nietzsche.

He pinpoints the task in a passage that is often quoted but just as often misinterpreted. The correct interpretation devolves from the entirety of this lecture course. Rightly grasped, the passage can serve as a rubric that characterizes the course's starting point and the direction of its inquiry. Nietzsche writes (I, 4):

> ... Nevertheless, I do not wish to suppress entirely how unpleasant it now seems to me, how alien it stands before me now, after sixteen years—before an eye which has grown older, a hundred times more fastidious, but by no means colder, an eye which would not be any the less prepared to undertake the very task that audacious book ventured for the first time: *to see science under the optics of the artist, but art under the optics of life.* ...

Half a century has elapsed for Europe since these words were penned. During the decades in question the passage has been misread again and again, precisely by those people who exerted themselves to resist the increasing uprooting and devastation of science. From Nietzsche's words they gathered the following: the sciences may no longer be conducted in an arid, humdrum manner, they may no longer

"gather dust," far removed from "life"; they have to be shaped "artistically," so that they are attractive, pleasing, and in good taste—all that,
because the artistically shaped sciences must be related to "life," remain in proximity to "life," and be readily useful for "life."

Above all, the generation that studied at the German universities
between 1909 and 1914 heard the passage interpreted in this way. Even
in the form of the misinterpretation it was a help to us. But there was
no one about who could have provided the correct reading of it. That
would have required re-asking the grounding question of Occidental
philosophy, questioning in the direction of Being by way of actual
inquiry.

To explain our understanding of the phrase cited, *"to see science
under the optics of the artist, but art under the optics of life,"* we must
refer to four points, all of which, after what we have discussed, will by
now be familiar to us.

First, "science" here means knowing as such, the relation to truth.

Second, the twofold reference to the "optics" of the artist and of life
indicates that the "perspectival character" of Being becomes essential.

Third, the equation of art and the artist directly expresses the fact
that art is to be conceived in terms of the artist, creation, and the grand
style.

Fourth, "life" here means neither mere animal and vegetable Being
nor that readily comprehensible and compulsive busyness of everyday
existence; rather, "life" is the term for Being in its new interpretation,
according to which it is a Becoming. "Life" is neither "biologically"
nor "practically" intended; it is meant metaphysically. The equation of
Being and life is not some sort of unjustified expansion of the biological, although it often seems that way, but a transformed interpretation
of the biological on the basis of Being, grasped in a superior way—this,
of course, not fully mastered, in the timeworn schema of "Being and
Becoming."

Nietzsche's phrase suggests that on the basis of the essence of Being
art must be grasped as the fundamental occurrence of beings, as the
properly creative. But art conceived in that way defines the arena in
which we can estimate how it is with "truth," and in what relation art
and truth stand. The phrase does not suggest that artistic matters be

jumbled with the "conduct of science," much less that knowledge be subjected to aesthetic rehabilitation. Nor does it mean that art has to follow on the heels of life and be of service to it; for it is art, the grand style, which is to legislate the Being of beings in the first place.

The phrase demands knowledge of the event of nihilism. In Nietzsche's view such knowledge at the same time embraces the will to overcome nihilism, indeed by means of original grounding and questioning.

To see science "under the optics of the artist" means to estimate it according to its creative force, neither according to its immediate utility nor in terms of some vacuous "eternal significance."

But creation itself is to be estimated according to the originality with which it penetrates to Being, neither as the mere achievement of an individual nor for the entertainment of the many. Being able to estimate, to esteem, that is, to act in accordance with the standard of Being, is itself creation of the highest order. For it is preparation of readiness for the gods; it is the Yes to Being. "Overman" is the man who grounds Being anew—in the rigor of knowledge and in the grand style of creation.

APPENDIX, ANALYSIS, AND GLOSSARY

Appendix

A manuscript page from the lecture course *Nietzsche: Der Wille zur Macht als Kunst*, Winter Semester 1936–37

It was Heidegger's practice to write out his lectures on unlined sheets measuring approximately 21 by 34 centimeters, the width of the page exceeding the length. (These dimensions would be somewhat larger than those of a "legal pad" turned on its side.) The left half of each manuscript sheet is covered recto with a dense, minuscule script, constituting the main body of the lecture. The right half is reserved for major emendations. It is characteristic of Heidegger's manner of composition that this half is almost as densely covered as the first. Heidegger's script is the so-called *Sütterlinschrift,* devised by Ludwig Sütterlin (1865–1917), quite common in the southern German states. It is said to be a "strongly rounded" script but to the English and American penman it still seems preeminently Gothic, vertical and angular. To the exasperated Innocent Abroad it seems a partner in that general conspiracy of Continental scripts other than the "Latin" to make each letter look like every other letter.

The manuscript page reproduced following p. 223 is the one mentioned in the Editor's Preface, Archive number A 33/14. It begins with the words *der Grundirrtum Schopenhauers,* found in the Neske edition at NI, 50, line 25, and ends with the words *nichts zu tun,* found at the close of section 7, NI, 53, line 24. Hence this single page of holograph constitutes three entire pages of the printed German text. (Of course I should note that Neske's page is rather generously spaced.) The

English translation of the German text taken from this manuscript page is found on pp. 40–43 above.

The right half of the manuscript page contains five major emendations to the text and one addition to an emendation. These changes are not substitutions for something in the body of the lecture; they are expansions and elaborations of what is found there. (The addition to the emendation is a text from Nietzsche's *The Gay Science* in support of Heidegger's argument.) Precisely when these emendations were made is impossible to tell, but the handwriting suggests that they are roughly contemporaneous with the main body of the text, added in all probability before the lecture was delivered. Only in rare cases (the revised clause and the bracketed phrase discussed below) is there any evidence that changes on the holograph page may have been made substantially later—for example at the time of the publication of *Nietzsche* in 1961.

The Neske edition reproduces the lecture notes of A 33/14 word for word up to the phrase *gesetzte will* at NI, 51, line 7. At that point, the insertion of the first emendation is indicated. It is a lengthy addition, amounting to fifteen printed lines. Here the Neske edition varies in some respects from the holograph. A comparison of the two passages may be instructive:

Neske edition	*Holograph*
Der Wille bringt jeweils von sich her eine durchgängige Bestimmtheit in sein Wollen. Jemand, der nicht weiß, was er will, will gar nicht und kann überhaupt nicht wollen; ein Wollen im allgemeinen gibt es nicht; "denn der Wille ist, als Affekt des Befehls, das entscheidende Abzeichen der Selbstherrlichkeit und Kraft" ("Die fröhliche Wissenschaft," 5. Buch, 1886; V, 282). Dagegen kann das Streben unbestimmt sein, sowohl hinsichtlich dessen, was eigentlich angestrebt ist, als auch mit Bezug auf das	❬ Der Wille bringt so seinem Wesen nach in sich selbst heraus immer eine Bestimmtheit im Ganzen; jemand der nicht weiß, was er will, will gar nicht u. kann übhpt. nicht wollen; ein Wollen im Allgemeinen gibt es; wohl dagegen kann das Streben [*word crossed out*] unbedingt sein—sowohl hinsichtlich dessen, was eigentlich angestrebt ist—als auch mit Bezug auf das Strebende selbst. [*At this point a mark to the left of the emendation indicates that the passage from* The Gay Science *is to be inserted—but its*

Strebende selbst. Im Streben und Drängen sind wir in ein Hinzu . . . mit hineingenommen und wissen selbst nicht, was im Spiel ist. Im bloßen Streben nach etwas sind wir nicht eigentlich vor uns selbst gebracht, und deshalb ist hier auch keine Möglichkeit, über uns hinaus zu streben, sondern wir streben bloß und gehen in solchem Streben mit Entschlossenheit zu sich—ist immer: über sich hinaus wollen.

precise location is not indicated.] Im Streben u. Drängen sind wir in ein Hin zu-etwas mit hineingenommen —u. wissen selbst nicht was [*word crossed out*] im Spiel ist. Im blossen Streben nach etwas—sind wir nicht eigentlich vor uns selbst gebracht u. deshalb ist hier auch keine Möglichkeit—über uns hinaus zu [*word crossed out*] streben—sondern wir streben bloß [-en *crossed out*] u. gehen in solchem Streben auf [?]. Entschlossenheit zu sich ist immer über sich hinaus wollen.

The changes introduced in the Neske edition are of five sorts. First, a more variegated punctuation replaces the series of semicolons and dashes. Second, the number of stressed words (italics, reproducing underlinings) is greatly reduced. Third, obvious oversights (such as the omission of the word *nicht* after the phrase *ein Wollen im allgemeinen gibt es*) are corrected, abbreviated words written out, and crossed-out words and letters deleted. Fourth, a precise location for the quotation from *The Gay Science* is found. Fifth, and most important, several phrases are entirely recast. Thus *Hin zu-etwas* (underlined) becomes Hinzu . . . (not italicized), and the entire opening clause is revised. The holograph version of the latter would read, in translation, "Thus will, according to its essence, in itself always brings out a determinateness in the totality." The Neske lines say, "In each case will itself furnishes a thoroughgoing determinateness to its willing." When this change occurred is impossible to determine; it may well have come at the time of publication. (The *Abschrift* or typewritten copy here follows the holograph.)

At the end of this long emendation the problem mentioned in the Preface arises. The last word runs up against the edge of the page and could as easily be *mit* as *auf*. (The practice of adding a diacritical mark over the non-umlauted *u,* which often makes it resemble a dotted *i,* complicates the situation here.) The meaning of the sentence depends to a great extent upon the separable prefix: it is according to the *sense* of the holograph page that I read it as *auf*. What is quite clear is that the main body of the text continues with a new sentence: *Entschlossenheit zu sich ist immer....* The words *Wille dagegen* are inserted in the *Abschrift* in order to emphasize the distinction between "will" and "striving." Although the origin, date, and status of the *Abschrift* are unknown, I have retained them in my own reading. Finally, I have added *als* in order to make the apposition of "will" and "resolute openness" clear.

The Neske edition prints the remainder of A 33/14 with only a few alterations, all but one of them minor ones. Two further major emendations from the right half of the page are incorporated into the main body of the text without any disturbing consequences (NI, 51, line 30 to NI, 52, line 2; and NI, 52, lines 22–29). The published text of NI, 52, lines 20–21 alters the holograph rendering only slightly. Then comes the second important change. Three lines in the holograph which are set off by brackets, lines which would have appeared at NI, 53, line 18, are omitted. When Heidegger added the brackets or "bracketed out" the passage is, again, not clear. The lines read:

> Man ist glücklich beim Irrationalismus—jenem Sumpf, in dem alle Denkfaulen und Denkmüden einträchtlich sich treffen, aber dabei meistens noch allzu "rational" reden und schreiben.

In translation:

> People are delighted with irrationalism—that swamp where all those who are too lazy or too weary to think convene harmoniously; but for the most part they still talk and write all too "rationally."

Heidegger often bracketed out such sardonic remarks when a lecture manuscript was on its way to becoming a book, apparently because he considered such off-the-cuff remarks more obtrusive in print than in speech. (Cf. for example the following remarks published in Walter Biemel's edition of the lecture course *Logik: Aristoteles,* volume 21 of the Heidegger *Gesamtausgabe,* Frankfurt/Main, 1976: on fraudulent logic courses, p. 12; on Heinrich Rickert's gigantomachia, p. 91; on two kinds of Hegelian confusion, pp. 260 and 267; and on the hocus-pocus of spiritualism and subjectivism, p. 292. These are remarks which we are delighted to read but which Heidegger himself, had he edited the text, might have deleted.)

Finally, on the right half of the holograph page a general reference to WM 84 and 95 appears. These two aphorisms in *The Will to Power* juxtapose the Nietzschean sense of will as mastery to the Schopenhauerian sense of will as desire. The reference's identifying mark does not appear anywhere in the text or in the other emendations, so that the reference has nowhere to go; in the Neske edition it is omitted.

By way of conclusion I may note that the Neske edition is generally closer to the holograph than is the sole extant *Abschrift.* The text we possess—notwithstanding the one major difficulty cited—seems remarkably faithful to Heidegger's handwritten lecture notes, assuming that the relation of A 33/14 to the relevant pages of the Neske edition is typical. Whether or not that is so the editor of volume 43 of the *Gesamtausgabe* will have to determine.*

---

*In the third edition of Heidegger's *Nietzsche* (without date, but available since the mid-1970s) the Neske Verlag altered the passage discussed above by adding a period to NI, 51, line 22, between the words *mit* and *Entschlossenheit.* (Cf. p. 227 of this volume, line 10 in the first column.) The passage would thus read: "For that reason it is not possible for us to strive beyond ourselves; rather, we merely strive, and go along with such striving. Resolute openness to oneself—is always: willing out beyond oneself." The addition of the period is a significant improvement in the text, but I still prefer the full reading suggested in this Appendix and employed on p. 41 of the translation.

The third edition does not correct the erroneous duplication of the word *nicht* at NI, 189, line 5 from the bottom.

I am grateful to Ursula Willaredt of Freiburg, whose painstaking checking of the page proofs uncovered this change in the third Neske edition of *Nietzsche.*

Analysis

By DAVID FARRELL KRELL

> No judgment renders an account of the world, but art can teach us to
> reiterate it, just as the world reiterates itself in the course of eternal
> returns.... To say "yes" to the world, to reiterate it, is at the same
> time to recreate the world and oneself; it is to become the great artist,
> the creator.
>
> A. CAMUS, *Man in Rebellion*, 1951

Early in 1961 Brigitte Neske designed a set of handsome book jackets
for one of the major events in her husband's publishing career. Along
the spine of the volumes two names appeared, black and white on a
salmon background, neither name capitalized: heidegger nietzsche.
Both were well known. The latter was famous for having been, as he
said, "born posthumously." And that apparently helped to give rise to
the confusion: when the volumes first appeared in Germany no one was
sure whether they were heidegger's books on nietzsche or nietzsche's
books on heidegger.

Readers of this and the other English volumes may find themselves
recalling this little joke more than once and for more than one reason.

Aus-einander-setzung, "a setting apart from one another," is the
word Heidegger chooses in his Foreword to these volumes to characterize his encounter with Nietzsche. That is also the word by which he
translates *polemos* in Heraclitus B53 and B80. Is Heidegger then at war
with Nietzsche? Are his lectures and essays on Nietzsche polemics? In
the first part of his lecture course "What Calls for Thinking?" Heidegger cautions his listeners that all polemic "fails from the outset to

assume the attitude of thinking."[1] In Heidegger's view *polemos* is a name for the lighting or clearing of Being in which beings become present to one another and so can be distinguished from one another. Heraclitus speaks of *ton polemon xynon,* a setting apart from one another that serves essentially to bring together, a contest that unites. In these volumes the English word "confrontation" tries to capture the paradoxical sense of Heidegger's *Aus-einander-setzung* with Nietzsche's philosophy. Before we say anything about Heidegger's "interpretation" of Nietzsche we should pause to consider the *koinōnia* or community of both thinkers. For at the time Heidegger planned a series of lectures on Nietzsche he identified the task of his own philosophy as the effort "to bring Nietzsche's accomplishment to a full unfolding."[2] The magnitude of that accomplishment, however, was not immediately discernible. Heidegger's first attempt to delineate Nietzsche's accomplishment and to circumscribe his confrontation with Nietzsche traces the profile of will to power as art.

I. THE STRUCTURE AND MOVEMENT OF THE LECTURE COURSE

The published text of Heidegger's 1936–37 lecture course, "Nietzsche: Will to Power as Art," consists of twenty-five unnumbered sections.[3] Although no more comprehensive parts or divisions appear, the course unfolds in three stages. Sections 1–10 introduce the theme of Nietzsche as metaphysician and examine the nature of "will," "power," and "will to power" in his thought. Sections 12–18 pursue the significance of art in Nietzsche's thinking. Sections 20–25 compare his conception of art to that in Platonism—the philosophy which Nietzsche sought to overturn—and in Plato's dialogues. But if the first

---

[1]Martin Heidegger, *Was heisst Denken?* (Tübingen: M. Niemeyer, 1954), p. 49. Cf. the English translation, *What Is Called Thinking?,* tr. Fred D. Wieck and J. Glenn Gray (New York: Harper & Row, 1968), p. 13; cf. also Martin Heidegger, *Basic Writings,* ed. D. F. Krell (New York: Harper & Row, 1977), p. 354.

[2]Martin Heidegger, *Einführung in die Metaphysik* (Tübingen: M. Niemeyer, 1953), p. 28. Cf. the English translation, *An Introduction to Metaphysics,* tr. Ralph Manheim (Garden City, N.Y.: Anchor-Doubleday, 1961), p. 30.

[3]The sections have been numbered in the present edition to facilitate reference.

two stages, "will to power" and "art," cover the ground staked out in the title *Wille zur Macht als Kunst,* why the third stage at all? Why especially the preoccupation with Plato's own texts? What is the significance of the fact that in the Foreword Heidegger designates "Plato's Doctrine of Truth" and "On the Essence of Truth" as the first milestones along the route traversed in his lectures and essays on Nietzsche?

Perhaps we have already taken a first step toward answering these questions when we notice that the analysis of the course's three stages leaves two sections out of account, section 11, "The Grounding Question and the Guiding Question of Philosophy," and section 19, "The Raging Discordance between Truth and Art." These two sections are not mere *entr'actes* preceding and succeeding the central discussion of art; they are in fact, altering the image, the hinges upon which the panels of the triptych turn. Heidegger's lecture course on will to power as art is joined and articulated by a question that is presupposed in all the guiding and grounding of philosophy since Plato, that of the essence of truth. By advancing through a discussion of Nietzsche's metaphysics of will to power to his celebration of art in the grand style, a celebration conducted within the dreadfully raging discordance of art and truth, Heidegger tries to pinpoint Nietzsche's uncertain location on the historical path of metaphysics. That is the only way he can estimate his own position, the only way he can discern the task of his own thinking. But if the "last 'name' in the history of Being as metaphysics is not Kant and not Hegel, but Nietzsche,"[4] the first "name" is Plato. And if Nietzsche's situation at the end of philosophy is ambiguous, so is that of Plato at the beginning. Plato dare not be confounded with Platonism; Nietzsche dare not be confounded with anyone else. Heidegger designs the structure and initiates the movement of his lecture course in such a way as to let the irreducible richness of both thinkers come to light.

---

[4]Eckhard Heftrich, "Nietzsche im Denken Heideggers," *Durchblicke* (Frankfurt/ Main: V. Klostermann, 1970), p. 349. Cf. H.-G. Gadamer, *Wahrheit und Methode* (Tübingen: Mohr und Siebeck, 1960), p. 243.

The structure and movement of the course may become more palpable if we recall the task undertaken in each section, reducing it to bare essentials and ignoring for the moment the amplitude of each section. Only when we arrive at the jointures or hinges (sections 11 and 19) will the summary become more detailed.

Heidegger begins (section 1) by asserting that "will to power" defines the basic character of beings in Nietzsche's philosophy. That philosophy therefore proceeds in the orbit of the guiding question of Occidental philosophy, "What is a being (*das Seiende*)?" Yet Nietzsche "gathers and completes" such questioning: to encounter Nietzsche is to confront Western philosophy as a whole—and therefore to prepare "a feast of thought." Nietzsche's philosophy proper, his fundamental position, is in Heidegger's view ascertainable only on the basis of notes sketched during the 1880s for a major work. That work was never written. The collection of notes entitled *The Will to Power* may not be identified as Nietzsche's *Hauptwerk,* but must be read critically. After examining a number of plans for the *magnum opus* drafted during the years 1882–88 (section 3), Heidegger argues for the unity of the three dominant themes, will to power, eternal recurrence of the same, and revaluation of all values (section 4). For Nietzsche all Being is a Becoming, Becoming a willing, willing a will to power (section 2). Will to power is not simply Becoming, however, but is an expression for the *Being* of Becoming, the "closest approximation" to Being (WM, 617). As such it is eternal recurrence of the same and the testing stone of revaluation. Thus the thought of eternal recurrence advances beyond the guiding question of philosophy, *"Was ist das Seiende?"* toward its grounding question, *"Was ist das Sein?"* Both questions must be raised when we try to define Nietzsche's basic metaphysical position or *Grundstellung* (section 5).

After discussing the structural plan employed by the editors of *The Will to Power,* Heidegger situates his own inquiry in the third book, "Principle of a New Valuation," at its fourth and culminating division, "Will to Power as Art." Why Heidegger begins here is not obvious. Nor does it become clear in the sections immediately following (6–10), which recount the meaning of Being as "will" in metaphysics prior to

Nietzsche and in Nietzsche's own thought. Heidegger wrestles with the notions of "will" and "power," which must be thought in a unified way and which cannot readily be identified with traditional accounts of affect, passion, and feeling. Nor does it help to trace Nietzsche's doctrine of will back to German Idealism or even to contrast it to Idealism. The sole positive result of these five sections is recognition of the nature of will to power as *enhancement* or *heightening,* a moving out beyond oneself, and as the original *opening* onto beings. But what that means Nietzsche alone can tell us.

Section 11, "The Grounding Question and the Guiding Question of Philosophy," the first "hinge" of the course, initiates the interpretation of "Will to Power as Art" by asserting once more that the designated starting point is essential for the interpretation of will to power as a whole. In order to defend that assertion Heidegger tries to sharpen the "basic philosophical intention" of his interpretation. He reiterates that the guiding question of philosophy is "What is a being?" That question inquires into the grounds of beings but seeks such grounds solely among other beings on the path of epistemology. But the grounding question, "What is Being?," which would inquire into the meaning of grounds as such and into its own historical grounds as a question, is not posed in the history of philosophy up to and including Nietzsche. Both questions, the penultimate question of philosophy, and the ultimate question which Heidegger reserves for himself, are couched in the words "What is . . . ?" The "is" of both questions seeks an *ouverture* upon beings as a whole by which we might determine what they *in truth, in essence,* are. Both questions provoke thought on the matter of truth as unconcealment, *alētheia;* they are preliminaries to the question of the "essence of truth" and the "truth of essence." Nietzsche's understanding of beings as a whole, of what *is,* is enunciated in the phrase "will to power." But if the question of the essence of truth is already implied in the guiding question of philosophy, then we must ascertain the point where "will to power" and "truth" converge in Nietzsche's philosophy. They do so, astonishingly, not in knowledge (*Erkenntnis*) but in art (*Kunst*). The way Nietzsche completes and gathers philosophy hitherto has to do with that odd conjunction "truth and art" for which no *tertium comparationis* seems possible.

Heidegger now (section 12) begins to sketch out the central panel of the triptych. He turns to a passage in *The Will to Power* (WM, 797) that identifies the "artist phenomenon" as the most perspicuous form of will to power. Grasped in terms of the artist and expanded to the point where it becomes the basic occurrence of all beings, art is proclaimed the most potent stimulant to life, hence the distinctive countermovement to nihilism. As the mightiest *stimulans* to life, art is *worth more* than truth. Heidegger now tries to insert this notion of art into the context of the history of aesthetics (section 13) with special reference to the problem of form-content. Nietzsche's attempt to develop a "physiology of art," which seems to militate against his celebration of art as the countermovement to nihilism, focuses on the phenomenon of artistic *Rausch* (section 14). After an analysis of Kant's doctrine of the beautiful (section 15), Heidegger defines rapture as the force that engenders form and as the fundamental condition for the enhancement of life (section 16). Form constitutes the actuality of art in the "grand style" (section 17), where the apparent contradiction between physiological investigation and artistic celebration dissolves: Nietzsche's physiology is neither biologism nor positivism, however much it may appear to be. Even aesthetics it carries to an extreme which is no longer "aesthetics" in the traditional sense. At this point (section 18) Heidegger returns to the outset of his inquiry into Nietzsche's view of art and tries to provide a foundation for the five theses on art. Things go well until the third thesis: art in the expanded sense constitutes the "basic occurrence" (*Grundgeschehen*) of beings as such. A host of questions advances. What *are* beings as such in truth? Why is truth traditionally viewed as supersensuous? Why does Nietzsche insist that art is worth more than truth? What does it mean to say that art is "more in being" (*seiender*) than are other beings? What *is* the "sensuous world" of art? These questions evoke another which "runs ahead" of both the guiding and grounding questions of philosophy and which therefore may be considered the "foremost" question: truth as unconcealment, *alētheia,* the question broached in section 11.

Heidegger analyzes Nietzsche's anticipation of that question in section 19, "The Raging Discordance between Truth and Art," the second "hinge" of the course. Nietzsche stands "in holy dread" before the discordance. Why? To answer that we must inquire into the history of the *Grundwort* or fundamental word "truth." The decisive development in that history, argues Heidegger, is that "truth" comes to possess a dual character quite similar to that of Being. Truth can mean a truth, "truths" of various kinds, such as historical judgments, mathematical equations, or logical propositions. Yet each of these can be called a truth only if it participates in a single essence, traditionally designated as "the universal," always valid, hence "immutable and eternal, transcending time." According to Heidegger, Nietzsche's response to the question of truth holds to the route which deviates from the essential one:

> It is of decisive importance to know that Nietzsche does not pose the question of truth proper, the question concerning the essence of the true and the truth of essence, and with it the question of the ineluctable possibility of its essential transformation. Nor does he ever stake out the domain of the question.

But if that is so, how can Nietzsche's philosophy gather and complete all philosophy hitherto? According to the tradition, "the true" is what is *known* to be: truth is knowledge. We recall that this is not the answer for Nietzsche, whose notes on *Erkenntnis* in the first part of Book III Heidegger deliberately bypasses in order to find in those on *Kunst* the essential source of the philosophy of will to power. The implication is that, although Nietzsche does not formulate the question of the essence of truth, he removes "the true" from the realm of knowledge to the domain of art. Heidegger does not at this point draw out the consequences of such a removal, but initiates the final stage of the inquiry.

In order to elaborate the meaning of "the true" as an object of knowledge, Heidegger inquires into the doctrines of Platonism and positivism (section 20). For the former, the standard for knowledge is the supersensuous *idea;* for the latter, it is the sensible *positum.* Each doctrine understands itself as a way of attaining certain knowledge of beings, acquiring truths; the second is merely the inversion of the first. If Nietzsche describes his own philosophy as "inverted Platonism," is it then nothing other than positivism? Nietzsche's *manner* of overturning, inspired by insight into the fundamental *Ereignis* of Western history (i.e., nihilism) and by recognition of art as the essential countermovement, distinguishes his thought from positivism. Nietzsche's philosophy is not merely upside-down Platonism.

Heidegger now (sections 21–23) turns to a number of Platonic texts where the supersensuous character of *truth* and the duplicitous nature of *art* become manifest. Art haunts the sensuous realm, the region of nonbeing, which nonetheless is permeated by beauty: because it shares in beauty, art is a way of letting beings appear. However fleeting its epiphanies may be, art is reminiscent of stable Being, the eternal, constant, permanent *ideai.* The upshot is that if there is a discordance between truth and art in Platonism it must be a felicitous one; by some sort of covert maneuver Platonism must efface the discordance as such. When Nietzsche overturns Platonism, removing "the true" from knowledge to art, he exposes the maneuver and lets the discord rage (section 24). Such exposure arouses dread. For it eradicates the horizon which during the long fable of Occidental thought has segregated the true from the apparent world. Although Nietzsche treads the inessential path of "the true" and does not pose the question of the essence of truth, he pursues that path to the very end (section 25): "the true," "truth" in the traditional metaphysical sense, is fixation of an apparition; it clings to a perspective that is essential to life in a way that is ultimately destructive of life. Art, on the contrary, is transfiguration of appearances, the celebration of all perspectives, enhancing and heightening life. Nietzsche's philosophy rescues the sensuous world. In so doing it compels a question that Nietzsche himself cannot formulate: since all appearance and all apparentness are possible "only if something comes to the fore and shows itself at all," how may the thinker and artist address himself to the *self-showing* as such?

I have ignored the amplitude of each section in Heidegger's lecture course for much more than a moment. But certain questions have forced their way to the surface. Why art, in the question of truth? Why Nietzsche, in the question of art?

II. CONTEXTS

In the final hour of the lecture course Heidegger alludes to that generation—his own—which studied at German universities between 1909 and 1914. He complains that during those years Nietzsche's "perspectival optics" of creative art and life implied little more than an aesthetic "touch-up" of traditional academic disciplines and that Nietzsche's significance in and for the history of philosophy remained unrecognized.

Long before he was taken seriously as a thinker, Nietzsche achieved fame as an essayist and acerbic critic of culture. For the prewar generation in all German-speaking countries Nietzsche reigned supreme as the definitive prose stylist and as a first-rate lyric poet. He was a literary "phenomenon" whose work and fate caused his name continually to be linked with that of Hölderlin. It was the time when Georg Trakl could recite a number of verses to the aspiring poets of Salzburg's "Minerva Club" and after his confreres began to disparage the poems, believing they were his, could rise and sneer "That was Nietzsche!" and storm out of the place, abandoning them to their public confessions of incompetence.

Writing in 1930 of the "transformation" taking place in Nietzsche interpretation, Friedrich Würzbach looked back to the earliest responses to Nietzsche as a philosopher.[5] He described them as the plaints of wounded souls whose "holiest sentiments" Nietzsche had ravaged and who were now exercising vengeance. A second wave of books and articles endeavored to show that what Nietzsche had to say was already quite familiar and hence harmless; when that did not work a third wave advanced, stressing Nietzsche's utterly novel and peculiar

---

[5]Friedrich Würzbach, "Die Wandlung der Deutung Nietzsches," *Blätter für deutsche Philosophie,* IV, 2 (Berlin, 1930), 202–11.

character, as if to say that he was but a flaw on the fringes of culture which left the fabric of things intact.

It is not until the publication in 1918 of Ernst Bertram's *Nietzsche: An Essay in Mythology* that Würzbach sees a decisive transformation in Nietzsche interpretation.[6] For at least a decade afterward no book on Nietzsche could ignore Bertram's alternately fascinating and infuriating but always dazzling essay. Bertram's Nietzsche is a legendary "personality" whose individuality transcends the customary confinements of a single human life to ascend "through all the signs of the zodiac" and become a "fixed star" in the memory of man. Such legends rise of themselves in spite of all that scientific demythologizing can do, assuming for each succeeding generation a special meaning, representing a particular "mask of the god." Nietzsche, whose legend has only begun, is a mask of Dionysus crucified. He embodies "the incurability of his century." Nietzsche is torn in two; his *mythos* is "duality."

The style of Bertram's essay seems a German counterpart to the prose of Yeats' middle period. It is the "extravagant style" which the poet, according to Robartes, "had learnt from Pater." Bertram's fascination with myth and legend also is reminiscent of Yeats' *A Vision*. (Both Bertram's *Versuch einer Mythologie* and Yeats' "The Phases of the Moon" appeared in 1918.) Yeats' poem contains the following lines, spoken by Robartes but expressing Ernst Bertram's principal theme:

> . . . Eleven pass, and then
> Athene takes Achilles by the hair,
> Hector is in the dust, Nietzsche is born,
> Because the hero's crescent is the twelfth.
> And yet, twice born, twice buried, grow he must,
> Before the full moon, helpless as a worm.[7]

---

[6]Ernst Bertram, *Nietzsche: Versuch einer Mythologie* (Berlin: Georg Bondi, 1918). For the quotations in the text see pp. 7–10, 12, and 361–62.

[7]William Butler Yeats, "The Phases of the Moon," *The Collected Poems of W. B. Yeats,* Definitive Edition (New York: Macmillan, 1956), p. 161. See also William Butler Yeats, *A Vision* (New York: Collier, 1966), p. 60; note the references to Nietzsche on pp. 126 ff. and 299. Cf. Bertram, p. 10

Unlike Yeats, however, Bertram dispenses with much of Nietzsche's thought. He derides eternal recurrence—which in Heidegger's view is Nietzsche's central thought—as a "fake revelation," the "deceptively aping, lunatic *mysterium* of the later Nietzsche."

Würzbach voices the complaint of all those who struggled to free themselves from Bertram's bewitchment: however convincing his insertion of Nietzsche into the tradition of Luther, Novalis, and Hölderlin, of Eleusis and Patmos may be, it manacles Nietzsche to a moribund tradition and lets him sink with it. Bertram's extravagant style therefore seems an elaborate *Grabrede* or obsequy, soothing, mystifying, mesmerizing, in a word, Wagnerian. Ernst Gundolf and Kurt Hildebrandt reject Bertram's "supratemporal" approach to Nietzsche.[8] They are writing (in 1922) at a time of "dire need" in Germany and see in Nietzsche not the stuff of myths but "the judge of our times" and "guide to our future." For Nietzsche is the legislator of new values. His "office" is juridical. "His basic question was not 'What is?'" writes Gundolf, in opposition to what Heidegger will later assert, "but the far more compelling question, 'What is to be done?'" Yet for Kurt Hildebrandt, as for all members of the Stefan George circle, Nietzsche is ultimately a legend of the Bertramesque sort. He is a hero who wills to supply a "norm" to replace the dilapidated structures of Platonic ideality but whose role as opponent consumes him. He would be *Vollender,* apotheosis, and is but *Vorläufer,* precursor. Rejecting the Platonic *idea,* perhaps "out of envy toward Plato," Nietzsche does not achieve the heights to which Platonic eros alone could have conducted him; he remains foreign to the *Phaedrus* and is banned from the *Symposium.* Liberator he may be; creator he is not. "He was not Hölderlin, who was able to mold a new world in poetry, but the hero who hurled himself upon a despicable age and so became its victim."[9] Neither is he Stefan George. "What Nietzsche frantically craved to be

---

[8]Ernst Gundolf and Kurt Hildebrandt, *Nietzsche als Richter unsrer Zeit* (Breslau: F. Hirt, 1922). For the quotations in the text, unless otherwise noted, see pp. 4, 89, 96, and 103.

[9]Ibid., p. 92.

George *is.*"[10] Still, whatever the outcome of his contest with Plato and Socrates,[11] and of his battle against the nineteenth century, which became a battle against Wagner,[12] Nietzsche remains the "judge of our times" in search of values which will halt the degeneration of man and the decline of the state.

The outcome of preoccupations with Nietzsche as "judge" is of course hardly a fortunate one. Stefan George and his circle dream of a grandiose *politeia,* "a new 'Reich,' " as one writer puts it, created along the guidelines of "the *Dionysian Deutsch*"; they foresee the development of a supreme race combining elements of Greek and Nordic civilization, flourishing on German soil.[13] That same writer recognizes in Alfred Baeumler's *Nietzsche: Philosopher and Politician* a giant stride in the right direction.[14]

To summarize: Nietzsche first gained notoriety as a literary phenomenon; his writings were exemplary for the generation that came to maturity during the Great War; by the end of that conflict Nietzsche was a legend, a Cassandra whose prophecy was fulfilled in Europe's ruin. Interest in Nietzsche as a philosopher remained overshadowed by interest in his prophecy and personal fate. Symptomatic

---

[10]Ibid., p. 102.

[11]Kurt Hildebrandt, *Nietzsches Wettkampf mit Sokrates und Plato* (Dresden: Sibyllenverlag, 1922).

[12]Kurt Hildebrandt, *Wagner und Nietzsche: Ihr Kampf gegen das neunzehnte Jahrhundert* (Breslau, 1924). Heidegger refers to the work in section 13 of *The Will to Power as Art.*

[13]Cf. Theodor Steinbüchel, "Die Philosophie Friedrich Nietzsches, ihre geistesgeschichtliche Situation, ihr Sinn und ihre Wirkung," *Zeitschrift für deutsche Geistesgeschichte,* III (Salzburg, 1937), 280–81.

[14]Alfred Baeumler, *Nietzsche der Philosoph und Politiker* (Leipzig: P. Reclam, 1931). This is of course the work that Heidegger criticizes in section 4, above. Heidegger's opposition to the Nietzsche interpretation of Baeumler, professor of philosophy and a leading ideologue in Berlin from 1933 to 1945, I will discuss in the Analysis of *Nietzsche IV: Nihilism.* Baeumler's arguments concerning the Nietzschean *Nachlass,* which appear to have influenced Heidegger, I will take up in the Analysis of *Nietzsche III: Will to Power as Knowledge and as Metaphysics.* Baeumler's thesis on the contradiction between will to power and eternal recurrence I will consider in the Analysis of *Nietzsche II: The Eternal Recurrence of the Same.*

of that interest was the fascination exerted by his medical history, especially his insanity, and reflected in the studies by P. J. Möbius (1902), Kurt Hildebrandt (1926), Erich Podach (1930), and Karl Jaspers (1936). Only as a critic of culture, as the philosopher of *cultural* revaluation, was Nietzsche's voice heard.

But a second strain of interest in Nietzsche develops alongside that of *Kulturphilosophie,* mirrored in the title "Nietzsche and the philosophy of 'life.' "[15] Here Nietzsche is acclaimed as the passionate advocate of life and opponent of the "paralyzed, soulless formulas" of the contemporary "transcendental" philosophy. Nietzsche struggles to find a new scale of values, not in some schema imposed upon life by a transcendent world, but in life itself. He must define the *quality* of life that is desirable, yet must select criteria that are *immanent* in life. His physiology, rooted in a metaphysics of will to power, even though it fails to remain absolutely immanent in life, influences a large number of philosophers of vitalism and organism, such as Eduard von Hartmann, Henri Bergson, Hans Driesch, and Erich Becher. If Baeumler is the noxious blossom of the first strain, however, then Ludwig Klages' philosophy of "orgiastics" is the exotic bloom of *Lebensphilosophie.*[16] Klages exalts life with even wilder abandon than Zarathustra, recognizing in all forms of *Geist* (including the will) an enemy of man's embodied life or "soul." Nietzsche's "psychological achievement," according to Klages' influential book, is to demarcate the "battleground" between the "ascetic priests" of Yahweh and the "orgiasts" of Dionysus.[17] His psychological *faux pas* is that the doctrine of will remains ensnared in the machinations of those priests. Klages' final judgment is that Nietzsche's best consists of "fragments of a philosophy of orgiastics" and that everything else in his thought "is

---

[15]Cf. Theodor Litt, "Nietzsche und die Philosophie des 'Lebens,' " *Handbuch der Philosophie,* eds. A. Baeumler and M. Schröter (Munich and Berlin: R. Oldenbourg, 1931), Abteilung III D, pp. 167–72.

[16]See especially Klages' three-volume work entitled *Der Geist als Widersacher der Seele* (1929–1932), available in Ludwig Klages, *Sämtliche Werke* (Bonn: Bouvier, 1964 ff.).

[17]Ludwig Klages, *Die psychologischen Errungenschaften Nietzsches* (1926), p. 210. Cited by Theodor Steinbüchel, pp. 275–76.

worthless."[18] If Heidegger goes to great lengths to rescue Apollo, and Nietzsche too, by organizing his central discussion of art about the theme of *form* in the grand style, he does so against the din of the Dionysian *Klage* (= lament) whose bells and timbrels owe more to Bayreuth than to Thebes.

Finally, there is a nascent third strain of Nietzsche appreciation already stirring when Heidegger begins his lecture series on that philosopher, an "existentialist" appreciation. The publication of Karl Jaspers' *Reason and Existence* in 1935 and *Nietzsche: Introduction to an Understanding of His Philosophizing* in 1936 marks its advent.[19] Jaspers' work resists rapid depiction. Yet its main thrust may be felt in the third book, "Nietzsche's Mode of Thought in the Totality of Its Existence." Jaspers measures Nietzsche's significance neither in terms of biography nor on the basis of doxography; neither the life nor the doctrines alone constitute the *Ereignis* which for subsequent thinkers Nietzsche indisputably is. It is Nietzsche's dedication to the task of thought throughout the whole of his existence that elevates him to enormous heights—that dedication, plus his passion to communicate and his skill in devising masks for his passion. Ultimately it is the courage he displays in posing to *Existenz* the question of the meaning of the whole: *warum? wozu?* why? to what end? By asking about the worth of the whole Nietzsche executes a radical break with the past, past morality, past philosophy, past humanity. No one can surpass the radicality of that break. Nietzsche, writes Jaspers, "thought it through to its ultimate consequences; it is scarcely possible to take a step farther along that route." Yet what drives Nietzsche to that protracted and painful rupture with the past is something powerfully affirmative, the "yes" to life, overman, and eternal recurrence; it is in the formulation

---

[18]Ibid., p. 168. Cited by Steinbüchel, p. 276.

[19]Theodor Steinbüchel's mammoth article provides a "Christian existentialist" view of Nietzsche's "situation" in 1936–37. Karl Jaspers' *Nietzsche: Einführung in das Verständnis seines Philosophierens* (Berlin: W. de Gruyter, 1936) serves as Steinbüchel's principal source, but his article refers to much of the literature. Especially valuable in the present context is part six of Steinbüchel's essay, "Current Interpretations of Existence under the Influence of Nietzsche," pp. 270–81. For the quotations in the text see Jaspers' *Nietzsche,* pp. 393–94.

of the positive side of Nietzsche's philosophy that Jaspers foresees a successful career for subsequent philosophy. Thus he lauds Nietzsche's critique of morality as that which *"cleared the path* for the philosophy of existence." Although Nietzsche denies transcendence with every fiber of his existence, Jaspers concludes that the fury of his denial testifies willy-nilly to the embrace of the encompassing.

Of course, Jaspers is not the only philosopher of *Existenz.* Steinbüchel mentions Jaspers only after he has discussed the writer he takes to be the chief representative of the new philosophy—Martin Heidegger.[20] The works by Heidegger which Steinbüchel was able to refer to, whether explicitly or implicitly, are *Being and Time, What is Metaphysics?, On the Essence of Ground,* and *Kant and the Problem of Metaphysics.* What Heidegger was teaching in Freiburg as Steinbüchel composed his article Steinbüchel could not know. Hence what is fascinating about his remarks is that they betray what one might well have expected from a lecture course by Heidegger on Nietzsche. The gap between expectation and reality is considerable.

According to Steinbüchel, Heidegger's philosophy understands man, and Being itself, to be essentially finite; it is Nietzsche who has pointed to human finitude in an unforgettable way. That Heidegger radically extrudes man's "transcendent being toward God" is therefore due to Nietzsche. Nevertheless, Heidegger promulgates "a concealed ethics" according to which man must resolutely assume the burden of his own being. Steinbüchel sees here the "Nietzschean imperative" that man become who he most properly is, scorning the "last man" who remains steeped in "everydayness." Yet Heidegger's secret ethics, his "yes" to the Self, does not preserve Nietzsche's "tremendous faith in life." Nietzsche transfigures Dionysian insight into dithyramb, while Heidegger, in the face of the "thrownness" and "fallenness" of Dasein, can only muster a "reticent resignation."

Whatever value Steinbüchel's remarks on Nietzsche's role in Heidegger's thought may have, what remains striking is the variance between his and Heidegger's own accounts of that role. The former

---

[20]Cf. T. Steinbüchel, pp. 271–73.

mentions neither art nor truth; Nietzsche's importance for the history of metaphysics does not become conspicuous there; and that the *telos* of Heidegger's inquiry into Nietzsche should be Platonism and Plato seems on the basis of Steinbüchel's account altogether out of the question.

Yet it is only fair to say that even forty years later the context of Heidegger's inquiry into Nietzsche is not readily discernible. His investigation has little or nothing to do with Nietzsche as *littérateur,* iconoclast, legend, legislator, judge, inmate, orgiast, or existentialist. My analysis must therefore turn to Heidegger's own writings which are contemporary with or prior to the Nietzsche lectures, in search of a more relevant context.

Heidegger first studied Nietzsche during his student years in Freiburg between 1909 and 1914. He discovered the expanded 1906 edition of notes from the *Nachlass* selected and arranged by Heinrich Köselitz (pseud. Peter Gast) and Frau Elisabeth Förster-Nietzsche and given the title *Der Wille zur Macht.* That book, indispensable because of the quality of Nietzsche's unpublished notes, unreliable because of editorial procedures and unscrupulous manipulations by Nietzsche's sister, eventually occupied a central place in Heidegger's developing comprehension of Western metaphysics as the history of Being. Although he would refer to the whole range of Nietzsche's published writings during his lectures and essays two decades later, *Der Wille zur Macht* is the text he was to assign his students and the source of his principal topics: will to power as art and knowledge (from Book Three, sections I and IV), the eternal recurrence of the same (Book Four, section III), and nihilism (Book One).

That volume's influence on Heidegger is visible already in his "early writings," not as an explicit theme for investigation but as an incentive to philosophical research in general. In his *venia legendi* lecture of 1915, "The Concept of Time in Historiography," Heidegger alludes to philosophy's proper "will to power."[21] He means the urgent need for

---

[21]Martin Heidegger, *Frühe Schriften* (Frankfurt/Main: V. Klostermann, 1972), p. 357.

philosophy to advance beyond theory of knowledge to inquiry into the goal and purpose of philosophy as such, in other words, the need to advance in the direction of metaphysics. In the habilitation thesis which precedes the *venia legendi* lecture Heidegger wrestles with the problem of the historical (as opposed to the systematic) approach to philosophy.[22] Here too Nietzsche's influence is unmistakable. Philosophy possesses a value for culture and exhibits a historical situation, as Dilthey saw; it also puts forward the claim of validity, as Husserl and the Neo-Kantians argued. But Heidegger stresses a third factor, namely, philosophy's "function as a *value for life.*" Philosophy itself exists "in tension with the living personality" of the philosopher, "drawing its content and value out of the depths and the abundance of life in that personality." In this connection Heidegger refers to Nietzsche's formulation "the drive to philosophize," citing that philosopher's "relentlessly austere manner of thought," a manner enlivened, however, by a gift for "flexible and apt depiction."

That Heidegger's own drive to philosophize receives much of its impulse from Nietzsche is not immediately obvious to the reader of *Being and Time* (1927). During the intervening Marburg years Nietzsche was set aside in favor of Aristotle, Husserl, Kant, Aquinas, and Plato. Perhaps Heidegger now wished to distance himself from the Nietzsche adopted by *Lebensphilosophie* and philosophies of culture and value. His rejection of the category "life" for his own analyses of Dasein is clearly visible already in 1919–21, the years of his confrontation with Karl Jaspers' *Psychology of Weltanschauungen.*[23] And although Nietzsche's shadow flits across the pages of the published Marburg lectures, Heidegger's vehement rejection of the value-

---

[22]Ibid., pp. 137–38.

[23]See Martin Heidegger, "Anmerkungen zu Karl Jaspers' *Psychologie der Weltanschauungen,*" *Karl Jaspers in der Diskussion,* ed. Hans Saner (Munich: R. Piper, 1973), pp. 70–100, esp. pp. 78–79. (The essay now appears as the first chapter of *Wegmarken* in the new *Gesamtausgabe* edition, Frankfurt/Main, 1977.) See also D. F. Krell, *Intimations of Mortality: Time, Truth, and Finitude in Heidegger's Thinking of Being* (University Park, PA: Pennsylvania State University Press, 1986), chapter one, "From Existence to Fundamental Ontology."

philosophy of Wilhelm Windelband and Heinrich Rickert undoubtedly delayed his public confrontation with the philosopher who
demanded the revaluation of all values.[24]

In *Being and Time* itself only three references to Nietzsche's
thought appear, only one of them an essential reference, so that it
seems perverse to argue that Nietzsche lies concealed "on every printed
page of *Sein und Zeit.*"[25] Yet we ought to postpone discussion of
Nietzsche's role in awakening the question of *Being and Time* until
Heidegger's own Nietzsche lectures provide the proper occasion for
it.[26] By way of anticipation I may cite one introductory remark by
Heidegger in "The Word of Nietzsche: 'God is Dead' ": "The following commentary, with regard to its intention and according to its scope,
keeps to that one experience on the basis of which *Being and Time* was
thought."[27] If that one experience is the oblivion of Being, which
implies forgottenness of the nothing in which Dasein is suspended, we
may ask whether in *Being and Time* Heidegger tries to complete
Nietzsche's task by bringing the question of the death of God
home—inquiring into the death of Dasein and the demise of
metaphysical *logos,* both inquiries being essential prerequisites for the
remembrance of Being.

If Nietzsche's role in the question of *Being and Time* is not obvious,
neither is the role played there by art. References in Heidegger's major
work to works of art are rare, although we recall the extended reference

---

[24]See for example volume 21 of the *Gesamtausgabe* (Frankfurt/Main, 1976), which
reprints Heidegger's course on "logic" delivered in 1925–26. By Nietzsche's "shadow"
I mean such analyses as that of the development of psychology (p. 36) or that of the
protective vanity of philosophers (p. 97). Heidegger's contempt for *Wertphilosophie*
emerges throughout the course, but see esp. pp. 82–83 and 91–92.

[25]I argued this way, correctly (as I believe) but perhaps unconvincingly, in my dissertation "Nietzsche and the Task of Thinking: Martin Heidegger's Reading of Nietzsche"
(Duquesne University, 1971), but perhaps more convincingly in chapters six and eight
of my *Intimations of Mortality.* The three references to Nietzsche in *Being and Time*
appear (in Neimeyer's twelfth edition, 1972) on. p. 264, lines 15–16, p. 272 n. 1, and, the
essential reference, to Nietzsche's "On the Usefulness and Disadvantages of History for
Life," p. 396, lines 16 ff.

[26]See for example NII, 194–95 and 260.

[27]Martin Heidegger, *Holzwege* (Frankfurt/Main: V. Klostermann, 1950), p. 195.

to Hyginus' fable of *Cura* in section 42. But for the most part literature and art appear as occasions where "they" come and go talking of Michelangelo. If enjoying works of art as "they" do is symptomatic of everydayness, we might well ask how art is to be properly encountered. Yet the fact remains that art is little discussed. The distance covered between the years 1927 and 1937 in Heidegger's career of thought is enormous: Steinbüchel's expectations are evidence enough of that.

From his earliest student days Heidegger had displayed an interest in literature and art: the novels of Dostoevsky and Adalbert Stifter, the poetry of Hölderlin, Rilke, and Trakl (whose poems Heidegger read when they were first published prior to the war), and the Expressionist movement in painting and poetry. Such interest at that time did not and could not irradiate the sober, somber halls of *Wissenschaft*. But in the 1930s literature and art came to occupy the very center of Heidegger's project, for they became central to the question of truth as disclosure and unconcealment. A glance at Heidegger's lecture schedule during the decade of the 1930s suggests something of this development.

Schelling, for whose system art is of supreme importance, is taught many times, as are Hegel's *Phenomenology* and Kant's third critique. (Kant's importance for Heidegger in this respect, ignored in the literature because of the overweening significance of Heidegger's publications on the first critique, we may gauge from his stalwart defense of Kant in section 15 of *The Will to Power as Art*.) Plato, the artist of dialogue, dominates all those courses where the essence of truth is the focus. It is unfortunate that we know nothing of Heidegger's 1935–36 colloquium with Kurt Bauch on "overcoming aesthetics in the question of art." We might hazard a guess that the "six basic developments in the history of aesthetics" (section 13, above) mirror the outcome of that colloquium. It is also unfortunate that we do not know what transpires in Heidegger's seminar on "selected fragments from Schiller's philosophical writings on art," which runs parallel to these Nietzsche lectures. Perhaps the references to Schiller (pp. 108 and 113) provide clues. But of all these lectures and seminars surely the most instructive would be the 1934–35 lectures on Hölderlin's Hymns,

"The Rhine" and "Germania." From the single lecture "Hölderlin and the Essence of Poetry" (1936) we derive some "indirect light," as Heidegger says in his Foreword to the *Nietzsche* volumes, on the parallel rise of Nietzsche and of art in his thought on *alētheia*.

Perhaps further light will be shed if we consider three other works stemming from the same period. "The Anaximander Fragment" (composed in 1946 but drawing on a course taught during the summer semester of 1932), "Plato's Doctrine of Truth" (published in 1943 but based on courses held from 1930 on, especially that of the winter semester of 1931–32), and "The Origin of the Work of Art" (published in 1950 but composed in 1935–36 and revised while the first Nietzsche course was in session). But in examining these four essays I cease the work of background and try to limn the figures of the matter itself.

III. QUESTIONS

Why art, in the question of truth?
Why Nietzsche, in the question of art?

On the occasion of the publication of the fourth, expanded edition of *Erläuterungen zu Hölderlins Dichtung* (1971) Heidegger remarked that those commentaries sprang from *einer Notwendigkeit des Denkens,* "a necessity of thought."[28] But the phrase is ambiguous. I take it to mean that Heidegger's thought turns to Hölderlin out of need, *Not-wendig,* in much the same way as Nietzsche's thought of eternal recurrence is "a cry out of need," *Aufschrei aus einer Not* (NI, 310). If Hölderlin's times are destitute, the epoch of Nietzsche and Heidegger is desperate. While Hölderlin can aver, "Indeed, the gods live," Nietzsche must conclude, "God is dead." The latter refrain dominates Heidegger's lectures and essays on Nietzsche; the phrase appears in his *Rektoratsrede* as a signal of urgency; it is the key to

---

[28]Martin Heidegger, *Erläuterungen zu Hölderlins Dichtung* (Frankfurt/Main: V. Klostermann, 1971), p. 7. Cf. Beda Allemann, *Hölderlin und Heidegger* (Zurich: Atlantis, 1956), parts II–IV.

Nietzsche's precarious position at the end of metaphysics and to Heidegger's before the task of his thinking.[29]

Two remarks in Heidegger's Hölderlin essay are particularly revealing with respect to Heidegger's turn to that poet. First, Heidegger insists that the being and essence of things, hence the naming of the gods, can never be derived from things that lie at hand. They must be "freely created."[30] As the motto for his lecture course on will to power as art Heidegger chooses a phrase from *The Antichrist:* "Well-nigh two thousand years and not a single new god!" Is it then a matter of concocting novel divinities? Or of lighting a lantern in broad daylight to search out old familiar ones? A second remark from the Hölderlin essay silences these overhasty questions and redirects the inquiry. Man possesses language in order to say who he is and to give testimony. About what is he to testify? "His belonging to the earth."[31] All creation, *poiēsis,* testifies to man's dwelling on the earth, remaining in Zarathustran fashion "true to the earth." Yet it is an earth cut loose from her sun and deprived of her horizon and a dwelling that hovers in holy dread before the raging discordance of art and truth.

Heidegger's "turn out of need" to the poetry of Hölderlin should not, however, be reduced to an incident of biography. It is not merely a necessity in Heidegger's intellectual life but a turning in the history of the question of Being. Heidegger speaks of that turning in many essays composed during the 1930s and 1940s. Of special consequence here are "The Anaximander Fragment" and "Plato's Doctrine of Truth." To the situation of the former essay Heidegger gives the name "eschatology of Being." By that he means the outermost point in the history of the Occident or evening-land from which he descries the dawn. (Whether it is the dawn of Anaximander's epoch or that of a new age is impossible to tell: Heidegger can only attempt to "ponder the

---

[29]Otto Pöggeler writes, "Ever since 1929–30, when Nietzsche became a matter of 'decision' for Heidegger, his new starting point for thinking the truth of Being was dominated by the all-determining presupposition that God is 'dead.'" Otto Pöggeler, *Philosophie und Politik bei Heidegger* (Freiburg and Munich: Karl Alber, 1972), p. 25.

[30]Martin Heidegger, *Erläuterungen,* p. 41.

[31]Ibid., p. 36.

former dawn through what is imminent."[32]) The name that recurs in the opening pages of the Anaximander essay, designating the *eschaton* of the history of Being, is "Nietzsche."[33] Even if we reduce matters to biography there is no obvious reason why the name "Nietzsche" and no other must appear here. Indeed the reason is highly complex. Heidegger attempts to uncover it during his protracted lecture series on Nietzsche.

A further hint of Nietzsche's significance as a figure of dusk and dawn, *Abendland* and *Morgenröte,* and as our point of entry into the issue of Western history as a whole, emerges from the essay on "Plato's doctrine of Truth." Here too Heidegger speaks of a turning and a need.[34] But it is not merely a turning or a need apropos of Heidegger himself. It is rather "a turning in the determination of the essence of truth" and a need for "not only beings but Being" to become "worthy of question." Much later in his career Heidegger comes to doubt the validity of the thesis expounded in his Plato essay, to wit, that a transformation in the essence of truth from *unconcealment* to *correctness* occurs as such in Plato; yet his early inquiry into Plato's doctrine of truth as portrayed in the Allegory of the Cave remains a highly thought-provoking effort.[35] It is an effort to confront the

---

[32]Martin Heidegger, *Holzwege,* p. 302. Cf. the English translation, *Early Greek Thinking,* tr. D. F. Krell and F. A. Capuzzi (New York: Harper & Row, 1975), p. 18.

[33]See *Early Greek Thinking,* pp. 13–14, 17, and 22–23. See also my remarks in the Introduction to the volume, pp. 9–10.

[34]See the first and last pages of the essay in Martin Heidegger, *Wegmarken* (Frankfurt/Main: V. Klostermann, 1967). pp. 109 and 144.

[35]In "The End of Philosophy and the Task of Thinking" Heidegger explicitly rejects the thesis of his earlier essay on Plato. (See Martin Heidegger, *Zur Sache des Denkens* [Tübingen: M. Niemeyer, 1969], p. 78.) The assertion that in Plato we find an "essential transformation of truth" from unconcealment to correctness is "untenable." Heidegger apparently accedes to the arguments of Paul Friedländer and others that in Greek literature and philosophy *alēthes* always modifies verbs of speech. Although *alētheia* may indeed derive from *lēthō* (*lanthanō*) and the alpha-privative, the sense of "unconcealment" seems to have evanesced even before Homer sang. Hence there is no essential transformation of truth from unconcealment to correctness; at least, none that can be located in Plato. There is instead an essential continuity in the history of "truth," a tendency to regard the true as correctness of assertion or correspondence of statement and fact, without asking about the domain in which words and things so wondrously converge.

consequences of Plato's conjunction of *alētheia,* interpreted as *orthotēs* or correctness of viewing, and *paideia,* education in the broadest possible sense. Essential to the allegory are the transformations or rites of passage undergone by the prisoners of the cave on their way to and from the Ideas, their liberation, conversion, ascent and descent, and the attendant bedazzlements, adjustments, and insights. Heidegger emphasizes that liberation is not simply an unshackling: the liberated prisoner does not run amok but confronts fire and sun, growing accustomed to "fixing his view upon the fixed boundaries of things affixed in their forms."[36] Those rites of passage, and the correctness of viewing that underlies them, determine the history of Being as truth from Aristotle to Neo-Kantian philosophies of value. Heidegger mentions three junctures of that history in which the correspondence of assertion and state of affairs progressively obscures the sense of truth as unconcealment. Thomas Aquinas locates truth "in the human or divine intellect"; Descartes adds his peculiar emphasis, asserting that "truth can be nowhere but in the mind"; and Nietzsche, "in the epoch of the incipient consummation of the modern age," intensifies to the explosion point the assertion concerning truth's place.[37] Heidegger now cites *The Will to Power* number 493, discussed often in the Nietzsche lectures (see section 25, above): "*Truth is the kind of error* without which a certain kind of living being could not live. The value for *life* ultimately decides." Nietzsche's interpretation of truth comprises "the last reflection of the uttermost consequences of that transformation of truth from the unconcealment of beings to correctness of viewing," a transformation which devolves from the interpretation of Being as *idea.* Nietzsche's "intensification" accordingly manifests both continuity and radical departure. To identify truth as error is to persist in the paideiogogical project of correctness; yet it also displays the vacuity of that project. Similarly, to attempt a revaluation of all values is to persist in pursuit of *to agathon,* it is to be "the most unbridled Platonist in the history of Occidental metaphysics"; yet to adopt the

---

[36]Martin Heidegger, *Wegmarken,* p. 128.
[37]Ibid., pp. 138–39.

standard of "life" itself for the revaluation is to grasp *to agathon* in a
way that is "less prejudicial" than the way taken by other philosophies
of value.[38] The vacuity of Plato's educative project, and Nietzsche's
"less prejudicial" understanding of the Good, are expressions of a crisis
in the meaning of Being. Nietzsche's fundamental experience of the
death of God implies the collapse of the ontotheological interpretation
of Being, for which God was the cause of beings, the failure of
metaphysics' envisionment of the divine *ideai*, and the evanescence of
that domain of beings once thought to be most in being. It implies the
disappearance of all that once was "viewed in a nonsenuous glance . . .
beyond the grasp of the body's instruments."[39]

Heidegger had long recognized that doubts surrounding the very
meaning of "body" and "soul," "matter" and "spirit," "sensuous" and
"supersensuous," "psychical" and "ideal" concealed in themselves the
collapse of the meaning of Being.[40] In Nietzsche he found the keenest
eyewitness to that collapse. Nietzsche's efforts to "rescue" the
sensuous world, to reinterpret its reality outside the Platonic context,
and to celebrate art as the fitting means of rescue exhibited most
dramatically the critical pass—or impasse—to which the history of
Being since Plato had come. "Art, and nothing but art!" Nietzsche had
said. Perhaps that was the direction in which the question of the
meaning of Being would have to go.

The last of Heidegger's three lectures on "The Origin of the Work
of Art," delivered at Frankfurt on December 4, 1936, bears the title
"Truth and Art."[41] After reading the text of his contemporaneous

---

[38]Ibid., p. 133.

[39]Ibid., p. 141.

[40]See for example his remarks during the summer semester of 1927, in Martin Heidegger, *Die Grundprobleme der Phänomenologie* (Frankfurt/Main: V. Klostermann, 1975), pp. 30–31. See also his discussion of truth, Being, and Time during the winter semester of 1925–26 (cited in note 24, above), esp. §§ 4, 8, and 9. Traces of such doubt appear even in the *Habilitationsschrift* of 1915–16 and the doctoral dissertation of 1914: cf. M. Heidegger, *Frühe Schriften*, pp. 348, 35, and 117–120. The key text of course is *Being and Time:* see esp. chap. 3.

[41]Published as Martin Heidegger, *Der Ursprung des Kunstwerkes* (Stuttgart: P. Reclam, 1960). See pp. 63 ff.

course on will to power as art we immediately want to add the words "... in raging discordance." But in "The Origin of the Work of Art" it is not a question of discordance *between* truth and art; Heidegger uncovers discord or strife *at the heart of both* truth and art. For they share in the creative struggle for Being, presence, in the arena of disclosure and concealment.[42]

Heidegger begins the final hour of his lectures on the origin of the artwork by citing "art itself" as the origin of both work and artist. Art is not a mere general concept under which objets d'art and artists are subsumed. It is the origin of the essential provenance of a work, which is neither a mere thing nor a piece of equipment but a place where truth occurs. Such occurrence Heidegger conceives as the instigation of strife between a historical world and the sustaining earth. Such strife is gathered in the work, which possesses a peculiar autochthony and calm, and which leads a life of its own. Only at the very end of his lecture cycle does Heidegger mention the obvious fact of the work's created-ness, its creation by an artist. That suggests the major difference be-tween the Nietzschean and Heideggerian approaches to art, a difference which the Nietzsche lectures explore thoroughly. Heidegger offers no physiology of the artist. He presents no account which could be rooted in subjectivistic metaphysics. Nietzsche's defenders—at least the unliberated ones—might complain that by remaining an observer of the artwork Heidegger regresses to "feminine aesthetics." Heidegger could only rejoin that his lectures try to leave aesthetics of both stereo-typed sexes behind—and that in so doing they merely elaborate Nietzsche's understanding of art in the grand style, where the artist himself becomes a work of art and where the distinction between subject and object, active and passive, blurs. But what is entailed in the abandonment of aesthetics? Why must inquiry into art undergo radical change?

In his Frankfurt lectures Heidegger tries to distinguish between the kinds of production appropriate to handicraft and to art. His procedure

---

[42]See D. F. Krell, "Art and Truth in Raging Discord: Heidegger and Nietzsche on the Will to Power," *boundary 2,* IV, 2 (Winter 1976), 379–92.

and insight are those exhibited in the Nietzsche lectures: the *technitēs* or craftsman brings beings forth into presence and so reveals them, his labors being a kind of *alētheuein,* bringing an entity to stand in the openness of its Being. Such openness quickly narrows when the thing produced is absorbed in sheer serviceability or usefulness as a piece of equipment. In the artwork, however, the fate of openness is different. Here openness itself achieves what Heidegger calls *Ständigkeit.* Recalling that for Platonism the Being of beings is interpreted as "permanence," which is one way to translate *Ständigkeit,* we must ask whether Heidegger's interpretation of art is not only female but also metaphysical: if art brings a being to stand and lends it constancy, then is not Heidegger merely affirming the "transcendent value" of art, as aesthetics has always done? And if Nietzsche exposes Platonic "permanence" as the "permanentizing" of perspectival life, as an instinct that preserves life but at some critical point petrifies it, so that an appeal to *Ständigkeit* is ultimately fixation on an apparition, there would be reason to ask whether in his lectures on the origin of the artwork Heidegger has at all learned from Nietzsche.

He has. For the "stand" to which the truth of beings comes in the work of art is by no means to be understood as permanence or constancy.

> Only in the following way does truth happen: it installs itself within the strife and the free space which truth itself opens up. Because truth is the reciprocal relation [*das Gegenwendige*] of lighting and concealing, what we are here calling installation [*Einrichtung*] is proper to it. But truth does not exist ahead of time in itself somewhere among the stars, only subsequently to be brought down among beings, which are somewhere else. . . . Lighting of openness and installation in the open region belong together. They are one and the same essential unfolding of truth's occurrence [*Geschehen*]. Such occurrence is in manifold ways historical [*geschichtlich*].[43]

Why art, in the question of truth? Truth happens in the work of art. Both truth and art are historical; they stand in time. The work of

---

[43]Martin Heidegger, *Der Ursprung,* p. 68.

art brings forth a being "that never was before and never will come to be afterwards."[44] Its "stand" is not only no guarantee against a fall, it marks the inception of the fall. Hence the need for preservation—which itself lapses into art appreciation and the art trade. If there is something that "stands" in a more perdurant sense it is the Heraclitean and Empedoclean strife, the Anaximandrian usage, which itself becomes present only through the being that rises and falls, emerges, lingers awhile, and disappears, in that way alone announcing what *is*. Thus the "workliness" of the work of art is not supratemporal *Wirklichkeit* but the "*becoming and happening of truth.*"[45] Never renounced, always affirmed is the relation of workliness to the nothing, that is, to a source beyond all beings but achieved only in a being. To dwell in nearness to the source is to be mindful of the double shadow that each thing, in becoming, casts before and behind itself.

Why Nietzsche, in the question of art? When we speak of the rise of art in Heidegger's thought, citing Nietzsche, Hölderlin, Schelling, Schiller, and others as the instigators of such a rise, we must be careful not to subordinate one thinker or poet to another, transforming contexts into causes and questions into answers. We simply cannot say who or what comes first, whether Nietzsche's decisive importance for Heidegger—and the decisive importance of art for Nietzsche—induce Heidegger to turn to Hölderlin and to the art of Greece or of Van Gogh, or whether the lyre of Hölderlin or Trakl or Sophocles sets the tone for Heidegger's turn to Nietzsche. All of these themes reinforce and refine one another long before Heidegger speaks of them publicly. All betray the central tendency of Heidegger's thought on art: the painting, poem, statue, or symphony is not a decorative piece with an assignable cultural value but the major way in which truth, the unhiddenness of beings, transpires. Such truth is not normative but disclosive; not eternal but radically historical; not transcendent but immanent in the things wrought; not sheer light but chiaroscuro. Disclosure, historicity, immanence, and the play of light and shadow

---

[44]Ibid., p. 69.
[45]Ibid., p. 81.

occur upon a new horizon that forms and dissolves and forms again where the epoch of metaphysics wanes and no other epoch is visible. Nietzsche—the *matter of thought* for which that name stands—is a giant on the horizon. His stature, always as incalculable as the horizon itself, remains monumental for the particular reason that his philosophy, more than that of anyone since Plato, is itself a work of art.

Heidegger therefore began his lecture series on Nietzsche by tracing the profile of will to power as art. His next step was to examine the work that displays the effulgence of Nietzsche's own art, *Also sprach Zarathustra*. During the summer semester of 1937 he lectured on that book's fundamental teaching, the eternal recurrence of the same, thereby attaining the summit of his own lecture series.

Glossary

Translation should not and cannot be one-to-one substitution. If it is done that way it may be *wortwörtlich* but can never be *wortgetreu;* although literal, it will not be faithful.

The following list of words gives the options most often taken in the translation of this volume. But the only way readers can be certain about the original of any given rendering is to check the German text.

abscission	*die Zerrissenheit*
absence	*die Abwesenheit*
abyss	*der Abgrund*
actual	*wirklich*
advent, arrival	*die Ankunft*
affect	*der Affekt*
apparent world, world of appearances	*die scheinbare Welt*
apparition	*der Anschein*
at hand	*vorhanden*
attunement	*die Gestimmtheit*
basic experience	*die Grunderfahrung*
basic occurrence	*das Grundgeschehen*
basically	*im Grunde*
the beautiful	*das Schöne*
beauty	*die Schönheit*
Being	*das Sein*
being(s)	*das Seiende*
being(s) as a whole	*das Seiende im Ganzen*

care	*die Sorge,* hē epimeleia
cohere	*zusammengehören*
conception	*die Auffassung*
concordance	*der Einklang*
configuration	*die Gestalt*
confrontation	*die Aus-einander-setzung*
continuance	*die Beständigung*
copying	*das Nachmachen,* mimēsis
countermovement	*die Gegenbewegung*
to create	*schaffen*
creative	*schöpferisch*
to define	*bestimmen*
definitive	*massgebend*
delight	*das Wohlgefallen*
destiny	*das Geschick*
to determine	*bestimmen*
development	*die Entwicklung, die Tatsache*
discordance	*der Zwiespalt*
disinterestedness	*die Interesselosigkeit*
dread	*das Entsetzen*
duration	*der Bestand*
to be embodied	*leiben*
embodying life	*das leibende Leben*
emergence	*das Aufgehen,* physis
enhancement	*die Steigerung*
enigmatic	*rätselhaft*
envisionment	*das Sichtige*
essence	*das Wesen*
essential determination	*die Wesensbestimmung*
to esteem	*schätzen*
to estimate	*abschätzen*
eternal recurrence of the same	*die ewige Wiederkehr des Gleichen*
eternal return	*die ewige Wiederkunft*
event	*das Ereignis*

eventuality	*das Vorkommnis*
to excel	*sich überhöhen*
explicit	*ausdrücklich*
expression	*der Ausdruck*
expressly	*eigens*
feeling	*das Gefühl*
felicitous	*beglückend*
fixation	*die Festmachung*
fleeting appearances	*der Anschein*
force	*die Kraft*
form	*die Form*
frame	*das Gestell*
frenzy	*der Rausch*
fullness	*die Fülle*
fundament	*der Grund*
fundamental position	*die Grundstellung*
genuine	*echt, eigentlich*
the grand style	*der grosse Stil*
to grasp	*fassen, begreifen*
ground(s)	*der Grund*
grounding question	*die Grundfrage*
guiding question	*die Leitfrage*
to heed	*achten, beachten*
hierarchy	*die Rangordnung*
historicity	*die Geschichtlichkeit*
illusion	*der Anschein*
imitation	*das Nachahmen,* mimēsis
immutability	*die Unveränderlichkeit*
inversion	*die Umdrehung*
jointure	*der Fug*
know-how, knowledge	*das Wissen,* technē

law	*das Gesetz*
lawfulness	*die Gesetzlichkeit*
to let-lie-before	*vor-liegen-lassen*
to light up	*aufleuchten*
lighting	*die Lichtung*
to linger	*verweilen*
lived experience	*das Erlebnis*
lucid	*durchsichtig*
main *or* major work,	
magnum opus	*das Hauptwerk*
manifold validity	*die Vielgültigkeit*
to manufacture	*anfertigen*
matter (of thought)	*die Sache (des Denkens)*
meditation	*die Besinnung*
metamorphosis	*die Verwandlung*
mood	*die Stimmung*
nondistortion	*die Unverstelltheit,* alētheia
oblivion	*die Vergessenheit*
openness, openedness	*die Offenheit, die Offenbarkeit*
opening up	*die Offenbarung, Eröffnung*
original	*ursprünglich*
outer, outward appearance	*das Aussehen,* eidos
overturning	*die Umdrehung*
particular, individual	*einzeln*
passion	*die Leidenschaft*
perdurance	*die Dauer*
permanence	*die Beständigkeit*
perspicuous	*durchsichtig*
plenitude	*die Fülle*
poetize, write creatively	*dichten*
presence	*die Anwesenheit*
presencing,	
becoming present	*das Anwesen*

what is present	*das Anwesende*
presentative	*vorstellend*
prevail	*herrschen, walten*
to pro-duce	*her-stellen*
proper	*eigentlich*
to be proper to	*gehören*
psychical	*seelisch*
radiance	*der Schein*
the most radiant	*das Hervorscheinendste, to ekphanestaton*
rapture	*der Rausch*
reality	*die Realität*
realm	*der Bereich*
to reign	*walten*
representation	*die Vorstellung*
resolute openness	*die Entschlossenheit*
to revere	*verehren*
reversal	*das Umkehren*
rule	*die Regel, das Gesetz*
to rule	*walten*
the same	*das Selbe*
to scintillate	*aufscheinen, aufleuchten*
to seem	*scheinen*
self-assertion	*die Selbstbehauptung*
semblance	*der Schein*
the sensuous	*das Sinnliche*
severance	*die Entzweiung*
state	*der Zustand*
statement	*der Satz*
strength	*die Kraft*
the supersensuous	*das Übersinnliche*
to surpass	*sich überholen*
sway	*das Walten*
to transfigure	*verklären*
transformation	*der Wandel*

transparent	*durchsichtig*
the true	*das Wahre*
truth	*die Wahrheit*
ultimately	*im Grunde*
unconcealment	*die Unverborgenheit*
unconstrained favoring	*die freie Gunst*
the unsaid	*das Ungesagte*
valuation	*die Wertsetzung*
valuative thinking	*das Wertdenken*
the view upon Being	*der Seinsblick*
to will, want	*wollen*
will to power	*der Wille zur Macht*

MARTIN HEIDEGGER

Nietzsche

Volume II:
The Eternal Recurrence of the Same

Translated from the German, with Notes and an Analysis, by

DAVID FARRELL KRELL

Contents

Editor's Preface

This second volume of Martin Heidegger's *Nietzsche* contains Heidegger's second lecture course on Nietzsche, presented at the University of Freiburg-im-Breisgau during the summer semester of 1937. Heidegger's handwritten notes for the course bear the title *Nietzsches metaphysische Grundstellung im abendländischen Denken* ("Nietzsche's Fundamental Metaphysical Position in Western Thought"). The 1961 Neske edition of the *Nietzsche* courses (referred to throughout as NI, NII, with page number; here see NI, 255–472) alters the title in order to show the principal theme of the course: *Die ewige Wiederkehr des Gleichen* ("The Eternal Recurrence of the Same"). The two titles express Heidegger's thesis that the thought of eternal return of the same constitutes Nietzsche's fundamental metaphysical position in Western thought. *

Appended to the 1937 lecture course as Part Two of the present volume is Heidegger's public lecture *Wer ist Nietzsches Zarathustra?* ("Who Is Nietzsche's Zarathustra?"). This public lecture, delivered on May 8, 1953, to the Bremen Club and published in *Vorträge und Aufsätze* (Pfullingen: G. Neske, 1954), pages 101–26, is thematically related to Heidegger's 1951–52 lecture course at Freiburg, *Was heisst Denken?*†

---

* Volume 44 of the *Martin Heidegger Gesamtausgabe* (published in 1986) is entitled *Nietzsches metaphysische Grundstellung im abendländischen Denken: Die Lehre von der ewigen Wiederkehr des Gleichen*. This is also the title that appears in Richardson's list of courses. See William J. Richarson, *Heidegger: Through Phenomenology to Thought* (The Hague: M. Nijhoff, 1963), p. 669.

† Published under that title in 1954 by Max Niemeyer Verlag, Tübingen. See the English translation by Fred. D. Wieck and J. Glenn Gray, *What Is Called Thinking?* (New York: Harper & Row, 1968), pp. 48 ff. I am grateful to have had the opportunity to check my own translation of "Who is Nietzsche's Zarathustra?" against that of Bernd

Neither of Heidegger's texts contains footnotes, and I have resisted the temptation to reduce any of the bibliographical remarks—for example, those on the Nietzschean *Nachlass* or literary remains—to that status. Thus all notes in the present book are my own.

I have corrected a number of typographical errors and oversights in the Neske edition without drawing attention to them. Only in the most serious cases did I consult the original manuscript.

A Glossary appears at the end of the volume for readers who wish to see how I have generally rendered some of Heidegger's key words. Yet, because English possesses and employs a far more extensive vocabulary than German does, students should always check the German text whenever their interpretation hinges on a particular passage or turn of phrase. As always, I am grateful for readers' corrections or suggestions for improvement.

I have translated afresh all passages from Nietzsche's works in Heidegger's text. I am fortunate to have been able to compare my own renderings from *Also sprach Zarathustra* to those of the late Walter Kaufmann in *The Portable Nietzsche* (New York: Viking Press, 1954), pages 103–439. Heidegger himself refers to the *Grossoktavausgabe* of Nietzsche's works (Leipzig, 1905 ff.) throughout, cited in the present book by volume and page number, e.g.: (XII, 51). My own references to that edition are indicated by the letters GOA. Heidegger's references to *Der Wille zur Macht* (second, expanded edition, 1906) appear by aphorism—not page—number, e.g.: (WM, 1057). Sections 11 and 12 of the 1937 lecture course indicate that Heidegger was not wholly dependent on WM and GOA for his references to Nietzsche's posthumously published notes: he obviously had some access to the manuscripts themselves. The Analysis at the end of the present volume (especially section II, "Contexts") discusses Heidegger's work on the Nietzschean *Nachlass.* I have tried to compare Heidegger's criticisms of the GOA ordering of the notes with the information provided by the *Kritische Gesamtausgabe* of Nietzsche's works, edited by the late Giorgio Colli and by Mazzino Montinari (Berlin: W. de Gruyter, 1967–

Magnus in *The Review of Metaphysics,* vol. XX (1967), 411–31, reprinted in David B. Allison, ed., *The New Nietzsche: Contemporary Styles of Interpretation* (New York: Delta Books, 1977), pp. 64–79.

79), now available in a fifteen-volume paperback *Studienausgabe* (Deutscher Taschenbuch Verlag, 1980). I have cited the latter throughout as CM and have listed the *full* manuscript designation with the fragment number in square brackets, e.g.: (CM, M XVII 16 [4]). Not a euphonious appellation, W. C. Fields would complain, but this long designation is the only one that readers of both editions of CM and of the earlier critical editions can use. Finally, I must warn readers that not every reference has been checked; a truly critical edition would have taken years to prepare. Scholars who wish to focus on a particular Nietzschean fragment in Heidegger's text would therefore do well to search for it in CM. If they do take the trouble to search for only one or two such fragments, they will readily forgive me for not having searched out them all.

Part One

THE ETERNAL RECURRENCE OF THE SAME

Nietzsche's thought must first be brought before us if our confrontation with it is to bear fruit; our lecture course will take as its guiding thought the following words of that thinker:

> Everything in the hero's sphere turns to tragedy; everything in the demi-god's sphere turns to satyr-play; and everything in God's sphere turns to . . . to what? "world" perhaps?
>
> *Beyond Good and Evil,* number 150; from the year 1886.

1. The Doctrine of Eternal Return as the Fundamental Thought of Nietzsche's Metaphysics

Nietzsche's fundamental metaphysical position is captured in his doctrine of *the eternal return of the same.* In *Ecce Homo* (XV, 65) Nietzsche himself calls it the doctrine "of the unconditioned and infinitely reiterated circulation of all things." The doctrine contains an assertion concerning beings as a whole. Its arid and oppressive quality leaps immediately to our eyes. We therefore reject it as soon as we hear it. We close ourselves off from it all the more when we learn that nobody can "prove" it in the way we generally like to have our "proofs" demonstrated. No wonder commentators have felt it to be an obstacle and have tried all sorts of maneuvers to get round it, only grudgingly making their peace with it. Either they strike it from Nietzsche's philosophy altogether or, compelled by the fact that it obtrudes there and seeing no way out, they list it as a component part of that philosophy. In the latter case they explain the doctrine as an impossible eccentricity of Nietzsche's, something that can count only as a personal confession of faith and does not pertain to the system of Nietzsche's philosophy proper. Or else they shrug it off as something quite evident—a treatment that is as arbitrary and superficial as eliminating the doctrine altogether, inasmuch as the teaching itself remains in essence exceedingly strange. It is highly questionable whether one can brush aside its strangeness in the way Ernst Bertram does in his widely read book on Nietzsche, when he calls the teaching of the eternal return of the same "this deceptively aping, lunatic *mysterium* of the later Nietzsche."*

In opposition to all the disparate kinds of confusion and perplexity vis-à-vis Nietzsche's doctrine of return, we must say at the outset, and initially purely in the form of an assertion, that the doctrine of the eternal return of the same is the fundamental doctrine in Nietzsche's philosophy. Bereft of this teaching as its ground, Nietzsche's philosophy is like a tree without roots. Yet we learn what a root is only when we pursue the question as to how the trunk stands upon its roots; in other words, when we ask in what and in what way the root itself is rooted. But if the doctrine of return is sundered and removed to one side as a "theory," is observed as a compilation of assertions, then the resulting product is like a deracinated root, torn from the soil and chopped from the trunk, so that it is no longer a root that roots, no longer a doctrine that serves as the fundamental teaching, but merely an eccentricity. Nietzsche's doctrine of the eternal return of the same remains closed to us, and we attain no vantage-point on Nietzsche's philosophy as a whole and no view of its core, as long as we fail to *question* within a space of inquiry that grants to this philosophy the possibility of its unfolding before us—or rather, *within* us—all its abysses, all its recesses.

The doctrine of the eternal return of the same contains an assertion concerning beings as a whole. It thus aligns itself with corresponding doctrines that have been quite common for a long time and that have helped to shape in essential ways our Western history—and not merely the history of philosophy. Consider for example Plato's teaching, that beings have their essence in the "Ideas," according to which they must be estimated: whatever *is* measures itself on what *ought* to be. Or, to take another example, consider the doctrine that has permeated Western thought through the Bible and through the teachings of the Christian churches, the doctrine that a personal Spirit, as Creator, has brought forth all beings. The Platonic and the Christian doctrines concerning beings as a whole have in the course of Western history been smelted and alloyed in all sorts of combinations and thus have under-

* See Ernst Bertram, *Nietzsche: Versuch einer Mythologie* (Berlin: Georg Bondi, 1918), p. 12. The reference is discussed in the Analysis to Volume I in this series, pp. 239–40.

gone sundry transformations. Both doctrines assume preeminence, each considered alone and both taken together in their various mixtures, because two thousand years' worth of tradition have made them habitual for our ways of representing things. Such habituation remains definitive even when we are far from thinking about Plato's original philosophy, and also when the Christian faith has expired, leaving in its place notions that are utterly conformable to reason, notions of an "almighty" ruler of the universe and a "providence."

Nietzsche's doctrine of eternal return of the same is not merely one doctrine among others that concern beings; it springs from the soil of the most stringent confrontation with Platonic-Christian modes of thought—from their impact on, and deterioration in, modern times. Nietzsche posits these modes of thought as the fundamental earmark of Western thinking as such and of the entire history of Western thought.

If we ponder all this, even if only cursorily, we understand more clearly what we still have to do if we are to *question* in the direction of Nietzsche's fundamental metaphysical position within Western thought. But our first task is a preliminary report on the genesis of the doctrine of return in Nietzsche's thought, a designation of the *domain* of thought from which the teaching springs, and a description of the "configuration" that the teaching proffers. We then ought to inquire into the extent to which a fundamental metaphysical position is bound up with the doctrine, our purpose being to make out what comprises the essence of such a position. Only on that basis can we try to explicate the essential import of the doctrine in such a way that it becomes clear how the major components of Nietzsche's entire philosophy have in that doctrine their ground and their very domain. Finally, in view of Nietzsche's fundamental metaphysical position as the last position Western thought has achieved, we must ask whether and in what way the proper question of philosophy is asked or remains unposed there; and if that question is in fact not posed, then we must ask why this is so.

The procedure our lecture course will adopt may therefore be clarified with the help of four major divisions, characterized briefly in the following four points:

A. The preliminary presentation of the doctrine of the eternal return of the same in terms of its genesis, its configurations, and its
domain.

B. The essence of a fundamental metaphysical position. The possibility of such positions heretofore, throughout the history of Western
philosophy.

C. The interpretation of the doctrine of return as the *last* fundamental "metaphysical" position in Western thought.

D. The end of Western philosophy, and its *other* commencement. *

After what we have said, we no longer require elaborate assurances
that we can succeed in really grasping Nietzsche's fundamental metaphysical position only after we have worked through the fourth stage.
Whatever must remain obscure in the first stage of our presentation of
the doctrine emerges into the daylight of the fully developed question
only at this fourth stage. There the rank and the necessity alike of
philosophy are justified by philosophy itself.

---

* Heidegger added the following sentence in 1961, placing it in square brackets in the
Neske edition:

The discussion of "C' forms the conclusion of the lecture course "Will to Power as
Knowledge" [see Volume III of the English edition]; the discussion of "D" is at-
tempted under the title "Nihilism as Determined by the History of Being" [see
Volume IV of the English edition, pp. 197–250].

Hence the present volume includes discussions of only "A" and "B," and predominantly
"A," on the genesis, configurations, and domain of "eternal recurrence." Note that the
"conclusion" to "Will to Power as Knowledge," which Heidegger here cites as the place
where "C" is discussed, is not the essay that concludes all three lecture courses, "The
Eternal Return of the Same and Will to Power," but the single concluding section of the
1939 course entitled "The Essence of Will to Power; the Permanentizing of Becoming
into Presence." For further discussion of Points "A" and "B," see the Analysis of this
volume, pp. 241–53.

2. The Genesis of the Doctrine of Return

Nietzsche has bequeathed us his own account of the genesis of the thought of eternal return of the same. The reason nearest at hand for this fact is that Nietzsche attributed exceptional significance to the doctrine. The deeper reason is to be sought in Nietzsche's habit—exercised since his youth—of having an explicit and dogged self-reflection accompany his labors in thought. We might be tempted to make light of the way Nietzsche speaks of himself in his writings, thinking that an exaggerated tendency to self-observation and self-exhibition underlay his work. If we add to that the happenstance that Nietzsche's life ended in insanity, then we can readily close the case: the proclivity to take his own person so seriously we may consider the herald of his later madness. The extent to which this view is mistaken will have become obvious by the time our lecture course has come to a close. Even his final autobiographical work, *Ecce Homo: How One Becomes What One Is*, written in the autumn of 1888, on the very eve of his collapse, a work that does not appear to be lacking in extreme self-inflation, may not be judged in terms of the insanity that follows it. That book too must attain its significance from the context in which all of Nietzsche's autobiographical observations belong; that is to say, from the *task* of his thought and the historical moment of that task. If Nietzsche always and again meditates on himself, it is nonetheless the very opposite of a vain self-mirroring. It is in fact Nietzsche's perpetually renewed readiness for the sacrifice that his task demanded of him; it is a necessity that Nietzsche had sensed ever since the days of his wakeful youth. How else can we account for the fact that on September 18, 1863, as a nineteen-year-old secondary school pupil, Nietzsche writes a sketch of his life that contains sentences like these: "As a plant I was born close to God's green acres,* as a human being in a pastor's house." The conclusion of this text, tracing the path of his life up to that moment, reads as follows:

> And so the human being outgrows everything that once surrounded him. He does not need to break the fetters; unexpectedly, when a god beckons, they fall away. And where is the ring that ultimately encircles him? Is it the world? Is it God?†

This autobiographical sketch was first discovered in 1936 among the papers that were in the possession of Nietzsche's sister. Upon my recommendation the Nietzsche Archive published it in a special edition. My intention in making the recommendation was to provide contemporary and future German nineteen-year-olds with some essential food for thought.

Nietzsche's retrospective and circumspective glances at his life are never anything else than prospective glances into his task. For him that task alone is reality proper. Within it all relationships hang suspended —those he has to himself, to the friends who are closest to him, and to those strangers he would win over. This fact accounts for Nietzsche's remarkable habit of writing drafts of his letters directly into his manuscripts. He does that, not because he wants to economize on paper, but because his letters pertain to his oeuvres. Letters too are meditations. But only the magnitude of the task and the fortitude in fulfilling it give Nietzsche the right to such concentration on the solitary self. Better said, they make such concentration imperative. Nietzsche's reports concerning himself may therefore never be read as though they were someone's diary entries; they dare not be scanned solely in order to satisfy our idle curiosity. No matter how often appearances may suggest the contrary, these reports were the most difficult things for him, inasmuch as they pertain to the utter uniqueness of his mission, a mission that was his and his alone. Part of that mission consisted in telling his own story, a telling that makes palpable the fact that in a time of

---

* *Gottesacker:* literally, the cemetery.

† Heidegger cites the first edition of this text, *My Life: Autobiographical Sketches of the Young Nietzsche* (Frankfurt am Main, 1936). See Friedrich Nietzsche, *Werke in drei Bänden* (Munich: Carl Hanser, 1956), III, 107–10.

decline, a time when all is counterfeit and pointless activity, *thinking in the grand style* is genuine *action,* indeed, action in its most powerful —though most *silent*—form. Here the actual distinction between "mere theory" and useful "praxis" makes no sense. But Nietzsche also knew that it is the exceptional quality of the creator not to need others in order to be liberated from his own petty ego. "When was a great man ever his own devotee, his own disciple? He had already set himself aside when he went over to the side of greatness!" (XII, 346; from the years 1882–84). But this does not preclude—it in fact requires—that the genuine thinker stand firm on the granite within him, the bedrock of his essential thought. "Are you one who *as a thinker* is faithful to his principle, not after the manner of a quibbler, but like a soldier faithful to his command?" (XIII, 39; cf. 38). Such remarks ought to prevent our misinterpreting Nietzsche's reports about himself —that is to say, about the task within him—either as moody brooding or as the sheer flaunting of his own ego.

The biographical sketch we mentioned earlier, that of the nineteen-year-old Nietzsche, concludes with the following questions: "And where is the ring that ultimately encircles him [the human being]? Is it the world? Is it God?" Nietzsche answers the question concerning the ring that encircles and embraces beings as a whole some two decades later—with his doctrine of the eternal return of the same. In the final episode of Part Three of *Thus Spoke Zarathustra,* "The Seven Seals (or The Yea-and-Amen Song)," from the year 1884, Nietzsche writes: "Oh, how could I not be ardent for eternity and for the hymeneal ring of rings, the ring of return?" In one of the earliest plans for the presentation of the doctrine of return, marked "Sils-Maria, August 26, 1881" (XII, 427), we read: "*Fourth book:* dithyrambic, all-embracing: '*Annulus aeternitatis.*' The desire to experience it all once again, an eternity of times." Answering the question posed earlier—as to whether this ring be the world or God, or neither of the two, or both together in their original unity—proves to be the same as explicating the doctrine of the eternal return of the same.

Our first task is to hear Nietzsche's report concerning the genesis of the thought of eternal return of the same. We find that report in the book mentioned earlier, *Ecce Homo: How One Becomes What One*

Is, written in 1888 but first published in 1908 (now in volume XV of the *Grossoktav* edition). The third division of that text bears the title "Why I Write Such Good Books." Here Nietzsche describes in chronological order each of his published writings. The section on *Thus Spoke Zarathustra: A Book for Everyone and No One* begins as follows (XV, 85):

> I shall now relate the history of *Zarathustra.* The basic conception of the work, *the thought of eternal return,* the highest formula of affirmation that can ever be achieved, originates in the month of August in the year 1881. It is jotted on a page signed with the phrase "6,000 feet beyond humanity and time." On the day I wrote it I had gone walking in the woods by the lake of Silvaplana. By a mightily towering pyramidal boulder not far from Surlei I stopped. The thought came to me then.

The thought of eternal return came to Nietzsche in the landscape of the Oberengadin, which Nietzsche visited for the first time during that summer of 1881. The landscape of the Engadin seemed to him one of life's greatest gifts; from that point on it became one of his principal places of work. (Whoever is unfamiliar with this landscape will find it portrayed in the opening pages of Conrad Ferdinand Meyer's *Jürg Jenatsch.*)* The thought of eternal return was not discovered in or

---

* Conrad Ferdinand Meyer published *Jürg Jenatsch: A Tale of County Bünden* in 1874, about six years before Nietzsche's first visit to Sils-Maria. The countryside near the Julier Pass, the locale of Meyer's novel, lies a mere five kilometers from Lake Silvaplana, some ten kilometers from Sils-Maria. At the risk of transforming the Heidegger/Nietzsche encounter into a bucolic travelogue, I translate the opening paragraphs of Meyer's tale:

The midday sun shone above the bare heights of the Julier Pass and its ring of mountain cliffs in the county of Bünden. The stone walls were baking and shimmering under the stinging, vertical rays. Every now and then, when a mighty stormcloud rolled out of the distance and drifted overhead, the mountain walls seemed to move, approach one another threateningly and uncannily, oppressing the landscape. The sparse patches of snow and the tongues of glaciers suspended between the mountain crags first glared, then receded into frosty green obscurity. A humid silence covered all, broken only by the vague sound of a lark flitting among the smooth boulders. From time to time the sharp whistle of a woodchuck pierced the wilderness.

Between the soaring peaks of the pass, to the right and left of the donkey path, stood two truncated columns of rock that must have been defying time there for thousands of years. Storms had hollowed out the top of one of the columns like a basin. There

calculated from other doctrines. It simply came. But like all great thoughts it came only because, surreptitiously, its way had been paved by long labors and great travail. What Nietzsche here calls a "thought" is—grasped in a provisional way—a projection upon beings as a whole, with a view to the question of *how* being is what it is. Such a projection opens up beings in a way that alters their countenance and importance. Truly *to think* an essential thought of this sort means to enter into the novel lucidity opened up by the thought; it means to see all things in its light and to find oneself totally ready and willing to face all the decisions implicated in the thought. Of course, we are inclined to take such thoughts as "mere" thoughts, as something unreal and ineffectual. In truth, this thought of eternal return of the same has a shattering impact on all Being. The span of the thinker's vision no longer ends at the horizon of his "personal experiences." Something other than he himself looms there, abiding beneath, above, and beyond him, something that no longer pertains to him, the thinker, but to which he can only devote himself. This characteristic of the event is not contradicted by the fact that the thinker at first and for a long time preserves the insight as totally his own, inasmuch as he must become the site of its development. That is the reason why Nietzsche initially says so little concerning his insight into the "eternal return of the same." Even to his few intimates he speaks only by way of indirection. Thus on August 14, 1881, he writes from Sils-Maria to his friend and assistant Peter Gast:

> Now, my dear and good friend! The August sun is over us, the year is in retreat, and it grows quieter and more peaceful in the mountains and woods. Thoughts loom on my horizon the like of which I've never seen—I'll allow nothing to be uttered of them and will preserve myself in imperturbable tranquility. I shall have to live a *few* years longer!

At that time Nietzsche planned to lapse into silence for the following ten years, in order to make himself ready for the development of the thought of return. True, he broke this planned silence several times

---

rainwater had gathered. A bird hopped about its edge and sipped at the clear, lustral water.

Suddenly, out of the distance resounded the barking of a dog, reiterated, mocked by an echo. . . .

the next year and in subsequent years; nevertheless, in his writings he spoke of his fundamental thought either in very brief straightforward references or only circuitously, in cryptic passwords and parables. Several years later, in 1886, he characterized the attitude that encouraged his silence concerning the most essential things in these words: "One no longer loves his insight sufficiently when he communicates it" (*Beyond Good and Evil,* number 160).

At the moment when "the thought of eternal return" came over him, the metamorphosis which his fundamental mood had been undergoing for some time now reached its final stage. Nietzsche's readiness for a metamorphosis is betrayed in the very title of a book published a bit earlier in the year 1881, *The Dawn.* That book bears as its motto an epigram from the Indian Rigveda: "There are so many dawns that have not yet begun to break." The final fortification of that transformed fundamental mood, in which Nietzsche now for the first time stood firm in order to confront his fate, is announced in the title of the book that appeared the following year, 1882: *The Gay Science* (*"La gaya scienza"*). After an introductory "Prelude," the text is divided into four books. In the second edition (1887) a fifth book and an appendix were added, along with a new preface. At the conclusion of the first edition of *The Gay Science* Nietzsche for the first time spoke publicly of his thought of eternal return. And so it seems that hardly a year had passed when Nietzsche not only broke his proposed silence but also neglected to love his insight so well that he dare not communicate it. Yet his communication of it is quite strange. It is merely appended to the conclusion of *The Gay Science* as an afterthought. The thought of return is not presented there as a doctrine. It is tacked on as an eccentric notion, as though the idea had just struck Nietzsche, as though he were playing with thoughts that were merely possible. The communication is not a genuine sharing with others; it is rather a veiling. That is also true of Nietzsche's next utterance concerning the thought of return, which comes three years later in the third part of *Thus Spoke Zarathustra* (1884). Here Nietzsche does speak directly of the eternal return of the same, and in greater detail, but he does so in the poetic form of a speech placed in the mouth of a poetically fashioned figure, namely, Zarathustra (VI, 223 ff.). Furthermore, the third and final communication by Nietzsche of his most essential thought is kept quite short and is merely posed in the form of a question. It appears in *Beyond Good and Evil,* published in 1886.

When we survey this series of three utterances it seems to offer precious little for a thought that is to be the fundamental thought of an entire philosophy. Such "precious little" in the communication amounts in effect to silence. And yet it is fitting silence. Whoever grows entirely taciturn betrays his silence, but the one who speaks sparely in veiled communication grows silent in such a way that genuine silence prevails.

If our knowledge were limited to what Nietzsche himself published, we could never learn what Nietzsche knew perfectly well, what he carefully prepared and continually thought through, yet withheld. Only an investigation of the posthumously published notes in Nietzsche's own hand will provide a clearer picture. These preliminary sketches of the doctrine of eternal return have in the meantime been published; they are scattered throughout volumes XII–XVI, the *Nachlass* volumes, of the *Grossoktavausgabe.**

But in order for us to penetrate successfully the fundamental thought of Nietzsche's philosophy proper, it is very important that at the outset we distinguish between what Nietzsche himself communicated and what he withheld. Such a distinguishing between direct, presumably merely foreground communication and what seems to be an inscrutable taciturnity is—in philosophical utterances generally, and especially in those by Nietzsche—absolutely indispensable. At the same time, we dare not judge the matter pejoratively, as though what Nietzsche communicated were less significant than what he suppressed.

Philosophical communications are altogether different from scholarly publications. We have to make the distinction between these two perfectly clear, because we are all too inclined to measure philosophical communications against the standard of publications in the

---

* A detailed critical account of these GOA volumes is hardly possible here. But see section II of the Analysis for a discussion of Nietzsche's unpublished sketches of eternal recurrence.

learned disciplines. In the course of the nineteenth century these disciplines began to operate like industries. The point was to get the product that had been manufactured out onto the market as quickly as possible, so that it could be of use to others, but also so that the others could not pinch our discoveries or duplicate our own work. This has especially become the case in the natural sciences, where large-scale, expensive series of experiments have to be conducted. It is therefore altogether appropriate that we at long last have research facilities where we can gain a complete overview of the dissertations and reports on experimental results that have already clarified this or that question in this or that direction. To mention a negative example, for purposes of illustration: it has now come to light that the Russians are today conducting costly experiments in the field of physiology that were brought to successful completion fifteen years ago in America and Germany, experiments of which the Russians are totally unaware because of their boycott against foreign science.

The destiny of today's science too will be determined in conformity with the general trend in the history of man on our earth for the past hundred and fifty years, the trend, that is to say, toward industrial and technological organization. The significance of the word *Wissenschaft* will therefore develop in the particular direction that corresponds to the French concept of *la science,* whereby what is meant are the mathematical, technical disciplines. Today the major branches of industry and our military Chiefs of Staff have a great deal more "savvy" concerning "scientific" exigencies than do the "universities"; they also have at their disposal the larger share of ways and means, the better resources, because they are indeed closer to what is "actual."

What we call *Geisteswissenschaft** will not regress, however, to the status of what were formerly called the "fine arts." It will be transmogrified into a pedagogical tool for inculcating a "political worldview." Only the blind and the hopelessly romantic among us can still believe that the erstwhile structure and divisions of the sciences

---

* I.e., the so-called "human" or "historical" or "cultural" sciences, such as economy, law, art, and religion. The word was introduced by the German translator of John Stuart Mill, who sought to render with its help Mill's "moral science." The major theoretician of *Geisteswissenschaft* is of course Wilhelm Dilthey (*Introduction to Geisteswissenschaft,* 1883; *The Construction of the Historical World in the Geisteswissenschaften,* 1910).

and of scientific endeavor generally during the decade 1890–1900 can be preserved forever with all the congenial facades. Nor will the technical style of modern science, prefigured in its very beginnings, be altered if we choose new goals for such technology. That style will only be firmly embedded and absolutely validated by such new choices. Without the technology of the huge laboratories, without the technology of vast libraries and archives, and without the technology of a perfected machinery for publication, fruitful scientific work and the impact such work must have are alike inconceivable today. Every attempt to diminish or to hamper this state of affairs is nothing short of reactionary.

In contrast to "science," the state of affairs in philosophy is altogether different. When we say "philosophy" here, we mean only the creative work of the great thinkers. In the very way it is communicated such work arrives in its own time, knows its own laws. The haste to "get it out" and the anxiety about "being too late" do not apply here, if only because it belongs to the essence of every genuine philosophy that its contemporaries invariably misunderstand it. It is also the case that the philosopher must cease to be a contemporary to himself. The more essential and revolutionary a philosophical doctrine is, the more it needs to educate those men and women, those generations, who are to adopt it. Thus, for example, it still requires a great deal of effort for us today to grasp Kant's philosophy in its essential import and to liberate it from the misinterpretations of its contemporaries and advocates.

As for Nietzsche, he does not want to instill perfect comprehension by means of the few, cryptic things he says about his doctrine of eternal return. Rather, he wants to pave the way for a transformation of that fundamental attunement by which alone his doctrine can be comprehensible and effective. What he hopes for his contemporaries is that they become fathers and forefathers of those who surely must come. (See *Thus Spoke Zarathustra,* Part II, "On the Blessed Isles.").*

---

* Here Zarathustra calls himself a chilling north wind that tumbles ripe figs to the ground; those sweet fruits are his doctrines. He continues:

Once we said "God!" when we scanned distant seas. But now I have taught you to say "Overman!"

God is a conjecture; but don't let your conjectures go farther than your will to create.

For all these reasons we will first bring before us those communications ventured by Nietzsche himself; we will have to restrict ourselves to an altogether provisional commentary on them. After that we shall survey the materials that Nietzsche withheld.

Could you *create* a god? Then tell me no tales of gods! But you could well create the overman.

Perhaps not you yourselves, my brothers! But you could recreate yourselves into fathers and forefathers of the overman, and may this be your best creating!

3. Nietzsche's First Communication of the Doctrine of Return

Because the context and the mode of presentation are essential to a philosophical communication, our further efforts at understanding the thought of eternal return must be shaped by the fact that Nietzsche speaks of it *for the first time* in the year 1882 at the conclusion of his book *The Gay Science.* In the later, second edition, the one usually used today, passage number 341 constitutes the conclusion of Book IV.* Passage number 341, the penultimate one of this text (V, 265 f.), contains the thought of return. What is said there pertains to "the gay science" as such, and runs as follows:

> *The greatest burden.*—What would happen if one day or night a demon were to steal upon you in your loneliest loneliness and say to you, "You will have to live this life—as you are living it now and have lived it in the past—once again and countless times more; and there will be nothing new to it, but every pain and every pleasure, every thought and sigh, and everything unutterably petty or grand in your life will have to come back to you, all in the same sequence and order—even this spider, and that moonlight between the trees, even this moment and I myself. The eternal hourglass of

---

* Actually, of course, the first edition of *The Gay Science* closes not with number 341 but with number 342, *Incipit tragoedia.* But Heidegger wants to suggest that the latter actually belongs to *Thus Spoke Zarathustra;* that the fourth book of *The Gay Science,* "Sanctus Januarius," is the proper culmination of that work; and that number 341, "*Das grösste Schwergewicht,*" is the proper culmination of Book IV. (It is worth noting that Giorgio Colli, the senior partner in the team that prepared the new historical-critical edition of Nietzsche's works, also considers Book IV of *The Gay Science* to have achieved "the expressive high-point of a magic harmony," while Book V suffers from a certain stridency. See Friedrich Nietzsche, *Sämtliche Werke: Kritische Studienausgabe in 15 Bänden,* ed. Giorgio Colli and Mazzino Montinari [Munich/Berlin: DTV and Walter de Gruyter, 1980], III, 663.)

existence turning over and over—and you with it, speck of dust!" Would you not cast yourself down, gnash your teeth, and curse the demon who said these things? Or have you ever experienced a tremendous moment when you would reply to him, "You are a god; never have I heard anything more godly!" If that thought ever came to prevail in you, it would transform you, such as you are, and perhaps it would mangle you. The question posed to each thing you do, "Do you will this once more and countless times more?" would weigh upon your actions as the greatest burden! Or how beneficent would you have to become toward yourself and toward life to *demand nothing more* than this eternal sanction and seal?—

So this is the sort of thing Nietzsche regales us with toward the close of *The Gay Science!* A frightful prospect of a terrifying collective condition for beings in general. What is left of gaiety now? Do we not rather confront the onset of dread? Obviously. We need only cast a glance at the title of the passage that immediately follows and that concludes Book Four, passage number 342, which is entitled "*Incipit tragoedia.*" The tragedy begins. How can such knowledge still be called "gay science"? A demonic inspiration, yes, but not science; a terrifying condition, yes, but not "gay"! Yet here it is not a matter of our gratuitous remarks concerning the title *The Gay Science.* All that matters is what Nietzsche is thinking about.

What does *gay science* mean? Here *science* is not a collective noun for the sciences as we find them today, with all their paraphernalia, in the shape they assumed during the course of the last century. *Science* means *the stance adopted, and the will directed, toward essential knowing.* Of course, we cannot get around the fact that a certain amount of acquired knowledge is proper to every knowing, and in Nietzsche's time that meant especially knowledge attained by the natural sciences. But such acquired knowledge does not constitute the essence of genuine knowing. The latter lies in the basic relation— prevailing at any given time—of man to beings, and consequently also in the mode of truth and in the decisiveness we attain through this basic relation. Here the word *Wissenschaft* [science] resounds like *Leidenschaft* [passion], namely, the passion of a well-grounded mastery over the things that *confront* us and over our own way of *responding to* what confronts us, positing all these things in magnificent and essential goals.

Gay science? The gaiety mentioned here is not that of the inane "gay blade." It is not the superficiality of fleeting enjoyment, the "fun" one might have, for example, even in undisturbed engrossment in scientific questions. What Nietzsche means is the cheerfulness that comes of a certain superiority, a cheerfulness that is not dashed by even the hardest and most terrifying matters. In the realm of knowing, cheerfulness is not dashed by the most questionable matters, but is rather invigorated by them, inasmuch as cheerfulness affirms the necessity of these most questionable things.

Only a *gay science* understood in this way can embrace a knowing that fathoms the terrifying character of the thought of eternal return—hence, a knowing that fathoms the thought in its essential import. Now we are better prepared to grasp the reason why Nietzsche communicates this demonic thought only at the conclusion of *The Gay Science:* what is referred to here at the conclusion is—in terms of the matter—not the end but the beginning of the "gay science," its commencement and its end alike. The matter in question is the eternal return of the same, which the "gay science" must come to know, first and last, if it is to be proper knowing. "Gay science" is for Nietzsche nothing other than the name for that "philosophy" which in its fundamental doctrine teaches the eternal return of the same.

Two matters are of equal importance for our understanding of this doctrine: first, the fact that Nietzsche first communicates it at the conclusion of *The Gay Science;* and second, the way in which Nietzsche at the outset characterizes the *thought* of return. The appropriate passage is number 341, entitled "The greatest burden." The thought as *burden!* What do we think of when we say the word "burden"?* A burden hinders vacillation, renders calm and steadfast, draws all forces to itself, gathers them and gives them definition. A burden also exerts a downward pull, compelling us constantly to hold ourselves erect; but

---

* The German word *das Schwergewicht* nowadays means "heavyweight" and is restricted to athletics. But it carries connotations of *chief importance* or *principal emphasis,* and I have chosen the word "burden" in order to capture these connotations. Both Nietzsche and Heidegger appear to hear in the word the related term *der Schwerpunkt,* "center of gravity," and both are aware of the ambiguity attached to matters of "great weight," which may stabilize us or wear us down, but which will most certainly deflect us from our former trajectory.

it also embodies the danger that we will fall down, and stay down. In this way the burden is an obstacle that demands constant "hurdling," constant surmounting. However, a burden creates no new forces, while it does alter the direction of their motion, thus creating for whatever force is available new laws of motion.

Yet how can a "thought" be a burden, that is to say, something that becomes determinative as rendering steadfast, gathering, drawing and restraining, or as altering directions? And what is this thought to determine? Who is to be afflicted with this burden, in whom is it to be installed? Who is to bear it to great heights, in order not to remain below? Nietzsche provides the answer toward the close of the passage. As the question "Do you will this once more and countless times more?" the thought would everywhere and at all times weigh upon our *actions*. By "actions" Nietzsche does not mean merely practical activities or ethical deeds; rather, he means the totality of man's relations to beings and to himself. The thought of eternal return is to be a burden —that is, is to be determinative—for our envelopment within beings as a whole.

Yet now we would really have to insist: How can a thought possess determinative force? "Thoughts"! Such fleeting things are to be a center of gravity? On the contrary, is not what is determinative for man precisely what crowds around him, his circumstances—for instance, his foodstuffs? Recall Feuerbach's famous dictum, "Man is what he eats." And, along with nourishment, locale? Recall the teachings of the classical English and French sociologists concerning the *milieu*— meaning both the general atmosphere and the social order. But by no stretch of the imagination "thoughts"! To all this Nietzsche would reply that it is precisely a matter of thoughts, since these determine man even more than those other things; they alone determine him with respect to these very foodstuffs, to this locality, to this atmosphere and social order. In "thought" the decision is made as to whether men and women will adopt and maintain precisely these circumstances or whether they will elect others; whether they will interpret the chosen circumstances in this way or that way; whether under this or that set of conditions they can cope with such circumstances. That such decisions often collapse into thoughtlessness does not testify *against* the dominion of thought but *for* it. Taken by itself, the *milieu* explains nothing; there is no *milieu* in itself. In this regard Nietzsche writes (WM, 70; from the years 1885–86): "*Against* the doctrine of influence from the *milieu* and from extrinsic causes: the inner force is infinitely *superior.*" The most *intrinsic* of "inner forces" are thoughts. And if the thought of eternal return of the same thinks some by no means fortuitous thought, by no means either this, that, or the other; if it instead thinks being as whole, as it is; and if this thought is actually thought, that is, if as a *question* it installs us amid beings and thereby places us at a distance from them; if this thought of eternal return is "the thought of thoughts," as Nietzsche at one point calls it (XII, 64); then should it not be perfectly capable of being a "burden" to every human being, and not simply one burden among others but "*the greatest burden*"?

Yet why the burden? What is man? Is he the creature that needs a burden, the creature that always afflicts himself with burdens, and has to do so? What sort of treacherous necessity is here in play? A burden can also drag down, can humiliate a man. And when he is all the way down the burden becomes superfluous, so that now, suddenly bereft of all burdens, he can no longer descry what he once was in his ascendancy, no longer notice that he is now as low as he can go. Instead, he takes himself to be the median and the measure, whereas these are but expressions of his mediocrity.

Was it only a pointless happenstance, was there nothing behind it, when the thought of this burden came to Nietzsche? Or did it come because all prior burdens had abandoned men and gone up in smoke? The experience of the necessity of a new "greatest burden," and the experience that all things have lost their weight, belong together:

> The time is coming when we will have to *pay* for our having been *Christians* for two thousand years: we are losing the *burden* that allowed us to live. For some time we will not know whether we are coming or going. (WM, 30; written in 1888)

This statement, still obscure to us, should for the present merely indicate that Nietzsche's thought of the new "greatest burden" is rooted in the context of two millennia of history. That is the reason for the way in which the thought is introduced in its first communication: "What would happen *if* one day. . . ." The thought is introduced as a question and a possibility. Indeed, the thought is not directly proffered by Nietzsche himself. How should a contemporary man—one who does not know whether he is coming or going, and Nietzsche must account himself such a one—how should such a man come upon this thought all by himself? Rather, what we hear is: "What would happen *if . . .* a *demon* were to steal upon you in your loneliest loneliness. . . ." Neither does the thought come *from* any arbitrary human being, nor does it come *to* any arbitrary human being in his or her most arbitrary everydayness, that is to say, in the midst of all the hubbub that enables us to forget ourselves. The thought comes in a human being's "loneliest loneliness." Where and when is that? Is it where and when a human being simply goes into retreat, withdraws to the periphery, and busies himself with his "ego"? No, more likely then and there where a human being is altogether himself, standing in the most essential relationships of his historical existence in the midst of beings as a whole.

This "loneliest loneliness" subsists prior to and beyond every distinguishing of I from Thou, of I/Thou from the "We," and of the individual from the community. In such loneliest loneliness there is no trace of individuation as isolation. It is rather a matter of that kind of individuation which we must grasp as *authentic appropriation,* in which the human self comes into its own.* The self, authenticity, is not the "ego"; it is that Da-sein in which the relation of I to Thou, I to "We,"

---

* "Authentic appropriation" translates Heidegger's word *Vereigentlichung.* The novel term refers us back to the theme of "authenticity" in *Being and Time,* especially sections 25–27, on the problem of the selfhood of Dasein, and section 53, "Existential Projection of an Authentic Being toward Death." Central to the latter is the notion of the death of Dasein as the "ownmost" or "most proper" (*eigenste*) possibility of existence, a possibility that Dasein must freely face and in this sense "appropriate." Precisely at this point in *Sein und Zeit* (p. 264) Heidegger cites Zarathustra's words about the danger of our becoming "too old for our victories." In Heidegger's subsequent view, thinking the thought of eternal recurrence is one decisive way to confront the danger and to rejuvenate the task of "authentic appropriation." See Martin Heidegger, *Sein und Zeit,* 12th ed. (Tübingen: M. Niemeyer, 1972), pp. 263–64. Finally, compare "authentic appropriation" to what Heidegger in section 24, below, calls "being-a-self."

and "We" to "Ye" is grounded; it is that on the sole basis of which these relationships can first be brought under control—must be brought under control if they are to be a force. In being a self, certain things are decided: the weight that things and human beings will have, the scale on which they will be weighed, and the one who will do the weighing. Imagine what would happen if in such loneliest loneliness a demon were to steal upon you and confront you with the eternal return of the same: "The eternal hourglass of existence turning over and over—and you with it, speck of dust!"

Nietzsche does not say what would in fact happen. He continues to *question* instead, and he uncovers two alternatives. Would you curse the demon, or would you perceive in him a god? Would you be mangled by the thought, or would you ask nothing more than that it be true? Would you be dragged into the abyss by the greatest burden, or would you yourself become its even greater counterweight?

The way Nietzsche here patterns the first communication of the thought of the "greatest burden" makes it clear that this "thought of thoughts" is at the same time "the most burdensome thought" (XVI, 414). It is the most burdensome thought in several respects. It is most burdensome, for example, with respect to that which is to be thought in it, namely, being as a whole. The latter commands the heaviest weight and so is more burdensome in the sense of weightiest. But it is also the hardest to bear with respect to the thinking itself, and thus is the most difficult thought. Our thinking must penetrate in thought the innermost abundance of beings, must probe in thought the uttermost limits of being as a whole, and must at the same time proceed in thought through the human being's loneliest loneliness.

By virtue of such distinctions we are trying to clarify Nietzsche's thought. Clarification is always necessarily interpretation. For in it we employ corresponding yet different concepts and words. Let us therefore insert at this point some remarks on Nietzsche's and our own use of language.

Nietzsche does not invoke "being as a whole." We use this phrase in order to designate basically everything that is not simply nothing: nature (animate and inanimate), history (what it brings about, the personages who fill it, and those who propel it), God, the gods, and demigods. When we speak of things that are in being, we are also referring to what comes to be, what originates and passes away. For it already *is* no longer the nothing, or not yet the nothing. When we allude to things that are in being, we are also referring to appearance, illusion, deception, and falsehood. If such things were not in being they could not delude us and make us err. All these things too are named in the phrase "being as a whole." Even its limit, nonbeing pure and simple, the nothing, pertains to being as a whole, inasmuch as without being as a whole there would be no nothing. Yet at the same time the phrase "being as a whole" means beings precisely as what we are *asking* about, what is worthy of question. The phrase leaves open the questions as to *what* being *as such* is and *in what way* it is. To that extent the expression is no more than a collective noun. But it "collects" in such a way as to gather beings together; and it gathers them with a view to the question of the gathering that is proper to being itself. The phrase "being as a whole" thus designates the most questionable matter and is hence the word most worthy of question.

As for Nietzsche, he is secure in his use of language here, but he is not unequivocal. When he means to refer to all reality or to the universe he says "the world" [*die Welt*] or "existence" [*das Dasein*]. This usage derives from Kant. Whenever Nietzsche poses the question as to whether existence has meaning, whether a meaning can be defined for existence at all, his use of the word "existence" roughly parallels what we mean by "being as a whole"—though with some reservations. "Existence" has for Nietzsche the same breadth of meaning as "world"; he also uses the word "life" to say the same thing. By "life" Nietzsche does not mean merely human life and human existence. We, on the other hand, use "life" only to designate beings that are vegetable or animal; we thereby differentiate human being from these other kinds, human being meaning something more and something other than mere "life." For us the word *Dasein* definitively names something that is by no means coterminous with human being, and something thoroughly distinct from what Nietzsche and the tradition prior to him understand by "existence." What we designate with the word *Dasein* does not arise in the history of philosophy hitherto. This difference in usage does not rest on some gratuitous obstinacy on our part. Behind it stand essential historical exigencies. But these differences in language are not to be mastered by artificial scrutiny and detection. Waxing in confrontation with the matter itself, we must become capable of the capable word. (On Nietzsche's conception of *Dasein*, see, for example, *The Gay Science*, Book IV, number 341; Book V, numbers 357, 373, and 374.)*

---

* In *The Gay Science*, number 341, Nietzsche speaks of "the eternal hourglass of existence," equating such *Dasein* with "this life," the *Leben* toward which one would have to become beneficent. Section 357, one of Nietzsche's most detailed statements on the German philosophical tradition (especially Leibniz, Kant, and Hegel), cites Schopenhauer's lucubrations on the "value" or "meaning" of "existence" and Hegel's "grandiose attempt" to convince us of "the divinity of existence." In passage number 373 Nietzsche doubts whether the paragons of scientific optimism such as Herbert Spencer are capable of espying "genuinely *great* problems and question-marks," that is to say, questions pertaining to *Dasein*. Here, as in the earlier passages, Nietzsche equates *Dasein* with *Welt*, identifying optimism as a particularly naive *Welt-Interpretation*. The latter is capable of seeing only the "most superficial and most extrinsic elements of existence." Section 374 "Our new 'infinite',," also refers to the conceptual triad *Dasein*, *Welt*, *Leben*. In reproducing it I have placed these words in capitals:

How far the perspectival character of existence extends, or even whether EXISTENCE has any other character than that; whether it is not the case that an EXISTENCE without interpretation, without "sense," amounts precisely to "nonsense"; whether, on the other hand, all EXISTENCE is not essentially an *interpreting* EXISTENCE;—it is fitting that these things cannot be descried by even the most diligent, painfully scrupulous analysis and self-examination of the intellect. . . . It is futile curiosity to want to know . . . , for example, whether some creature exists that can experience time as running backwards, or alternately forward and back (at which point another segmentation of LIFE . . . would be at hand). But I think that we today at least are far removed from such ridiculous vainglory. . . . The WORLD has rather once again become "infinite" to us, inasmuch as we cannot reject the possibility that it *encompasses infinite interpretations*. . . .

4. *"Incipit tragoedia"*

The thought of eternal return of the same, as the greatest burden, is also the thought that is hardest to bear. What happens when we actually think the thought? Nietzsche provides the answer in the title of the section that follows immediately upon his first communication of the most burdensome thought, and that forms the proper conclusion to *The Gay Science* (1st edition, 1882; number 342): *"Incipit tragoedia."* The tragedy begins. Which tragedy? The tragedy of beings as such. But what does Nietzsche understand by "tragedy"? Tragedy sings the tragic. We have to realize that Nietzsche defines the tragic purely in terms of the *beginning* of tragedy as he understands it. When the thought of eternal return is thought, the tragic as such becomes the fundamental trait of beings. Viewed historically, this marks the beginning of the "tragic age for Europe" (WM, 37; cf. XVI, 448). What begins to happen here transpires in utter stillness; it remains concealed for a long time and to most men; nothing of this history goes into the history books. "It is the stillest words that bring on the storm. Thoughts that approach on doves' feet govern the world" (*Thus Spoke Zarathustra*, conclusion to Part II). "What does it matter that we more cautious and reserved ones do not for the nonce abandon the venerable belief that it is only the great thought that lends greatness to any deed or thing" (*Beyond Good and Evil*, number 241). And finally: "The world revolves, not about the discoverers of new forms of hullaballoo, but about the discoverers of new values. It revolves *inaudibly*" (*Thus Spoke Zarathustra*, Part Two, "Of Great Events").

Only the few, the rare, only those who have ears for such inaudible revolutions will perceive the *"Incipit tragoedia."* Yet how does Nietzsche understand the essence of the tragic and of tragedy? We know that Nietzsche's first treatise, published in 1872, was devoted to the question of "the birth of tragedy." Experience of the tragic and meditation on its origin and essence pertain to the very basis of Nietzschean thought. Nietzsche's concept of the tragic grew steadily clearer in step with the inner transformation and clarification of his thinking. From the very outset he opposed the interpretation of Aristotle, according to which the tragic is said to accomplish *katharsis,* the moral cleansing and elevation that are attained when fear and pity are aroused. "I have repeatedly put my finger on the egregious misconception of Aristotle, who believed he had found the tragic emotions in two depressive affects, namely, terror and pity" (WM, 851; from the year 1888). The tragic has absolutely no original relation to the moral. "Whoever enjoys tragedy *morally* still has a few rungs to climb" (XII, 177; from 1881–82). The tragic belongs to the "aesthetic" domain. To clarify this we would have to provide an account of Nietzsche's conception of art. Art is "*the* metaphysical activity" of "life"; it defines the way in which beings as a whole are, insofar as they are. The supreme art is the tragic; hence the tragic is proper to the metaphysical essence of beings.

The aspect of terror does pertain to the tragic as such, but not as what arouses fear, in the sense that the tragic would actually allow one to circumvent terror by fleeing toward "resignation," by yearning for nothingness. On the contrary, the terrifying is what is affirmed; indeed, affirmed in its unalterable affiliation with the beautiful. Tragedy prevails where the terrifying is affirmed as the opposite that is intrinsically proper to the beautiful. Greatness and great heights subsist together with the depths and with what is terrifying; the more originally the one is willed, the more surely the other will be attained. "Frightfulness is proper to greatness: let us not be deceived" (WM, 1028). Affirmation of the convergence of these opposites is tragic insight, the tragic attitude; it is what Nietzsche also calls the "heroic." "*What makes someone heroic?*" asks Nietzsche in *The Gay Science* (number 268); and he replies, "Going out to meet one's supreme suffering and supreme hope alike." The word "alike" is decisive here: not playing off one against the other, still less averting his glance from both, but becoming master over his misfortune and good fortune as well, in that way preventing his ostensible victory from making a fool of him.*

---

* On mastery of one's misfortune and good fortune, or unhappiness and happiness, see Volume I of this series, p. 159. On the entire question of beauty and the terrible or terrifying, see sections 16–17 of that lecture course.

"The *heroic* spirits are those who in the midst of tragic horror say to themselves, "Yes": they are hard enough to feel suffering as *pleasure*" (WM, 852). The tragic spirit incorporates contradictions and uncertainties (XVI, 391; cf. XV, 65; XVI, 377; and XIV, 365 f.). The tragic holds sway only where the "spirit" rules, so much so that it is only in the realm of knowledge and of knowers that the supremely tragic can occur. "The supremely tragic motifs have remained untouched up to now: the poets have no knowledge based on experience of the hundred tragedies of knowers" (XII, 246; from 1881–82). Beings themselves imply torture, destruction, and the "no" as proper to them. In *Ecce Homo,* at the place where he describes the gestation of the thought of eternal return of the same, Nietzsche calls that thought "the highest formula of affirmation that can ever be achieved" (XV, 85). Why is the thought of return supreme affirmation? Because it affirms the uttermost "no," annihilation and suffering, as proper to beings. Thus it is precisely with this thought that the tragic spirit first comes into being, originally and integrally. "*Incipit tragoedia,*" Nietzsche says. But he adds, "INCIPIT ZARATHUSTRA" (*Twilight of the Idols,* VIII, 83).

Zarathustra is the initial and proper thinker of the thought of thoughts. *To be* the initial and proper thinker of the thought of eternal return of the same *is the essence of Zarathustra.* The thought of eternal return of the same is so much the hardest to bear that no prior, mediocre human being can think it; he dare not even register a claim to think it; and that holds for Nietzsche himself. In order to let the most burdensome thought—that is, the tragedy—begin, Nietzsche must therefore first create poetically the thinker of that thought. This happens in the work that begins to *come to be* one year following *The Gay Science,* that is to say, from 1883 on. For Nietzsche's report on the gestation of the thought of eternal return of the same also says that the thought constitutes "the fundamental conception of the work."* Nevertheless, the concluding section of *The Gay Science* itself, bearing the title "*Incipit tragoedia,*" runs as follows:

---

* The "work" in question is, of course, *Thus Spoke Zarathustra.*

Incipit tragoedia.—When Zarathustra was thirty years old he left Lake Urmi and his homeland and went into the mountains. There he communed with his spirit and his solitude and for ten years did not weary of them. But at last something in his heart turned—and one morning he rose with the dawn, confronted the sun, and addressed it in this way: "You magnificent star! What would become of your felicity if you did not have those you illumine? For ten years you've been coming up here to my cave: you would have tired of your light and that path had it not been for me, my eagle, and my serpent. But every morning we waited for you, relieved you of your excess, and blessed you for it. Behold, I am glutted with my wisdom, like the bee that has gathered too much honey. I need hands that reach out, I want to give, to dispense, until the wise among men are happy again in their folly and the poor in their splendor. For that I must descend to the depths, as you do in the evening when you slip behind the sea and bring light to the very underworld, you superabundant star! Like you, I must *go down,* as men call it, and it is men I want to go down to. So bless me, then, tranquil eye that can look without envy upon a happiness that is all-too-great! Bless the cup that wants to overflow until the waters stream from it golden, bearing to all parts reflections of your delight! Behold, this cup wants to become empty again, and Zarathustra wants to become man again."—Thus began Zarathustra's downgoing.

The conclusion of *The Gay Science* constitutes the unaltered beginning of the first part of *Thus Spoke Zarathustra,* published the following year; the sole change is that the name of the lake, "Urmi," is dropped and is replaced by the phrase "the lake of his homeland." When Zarathustra's tragedy begins, so does his downgoing. The downgoing itself has a history. It is the history proper; it is not merely an end. Here Nietzsche shapes his work by drawing upon his profound knowledge of great Greek tragedy. For Greek tragedy is not the "psychological" matter of preparing a "tragic conflict," of "tying the knots," and such. Rather, everything that one usually takes as constituting "the tragedy" has already occurred at the moment tragedy as such begins. The "only thing" that happens in tragedy is the downgoing. The "only thing," we say, quite ineptly, for only now does the proper matter begin. Without the "spirit" and the "thought," all deeds are but —nothing.

5. The Second Communication of the Doctrine of Return

The book *Thus Spoke Zarathustra,* considered as a whole, constitutes the *second* communication of the doctrine of eternal return. Here Nietzsche no longer speaks of it incidentally, as though it were a mere possibility. To be sure, he does not speak of the doctrine directly and peremptorily. When Nietzsche creates poetically the figure of Zarathustra he creates the thinker, creates that other kind of humanity which, in opposition to humanity heretofore, initiates the tragedy by positing the tragic spirit in being itself. Zarathustra is the heroic thinker, and, granted the way this figure takes shape, whatever the thinker thinks must also be fashioned as tragic, that is, as the supreme "yes" to the extreme "no." And according to the statement that serves as the guiding thought of our own lecture course, everything in the hero's sphere turns to tragedy. In order to render the tragedy visible, Nietzsche must first of all create the solitary hero in whose sphere alone the tragedy will crystallize. *The ground for the figure of this hero is the thought of eternal return; this is also the case when that thought is not expressly mentioned.* For the thought of thoughts, and its teaching, require a unique teacher. In the figure of the teacher the teaching will be presented by way of a mediation.

As in the case of the first communication of the thought of return, so too in the second the *how* of the communication is initially more important than the *what.* The crucial matter is that human beings come to exist who will not be shattered by this doctrine. Prior man is unable actually to think it. He thus must be made to transcend himself, to be transformed—into the overman. When Nietzsche employs the latter word, he is by no means designating a creature that is no longer human. The "over," as an "above and beyond," is related to a particular kind of man; the determinate shape of that man first becomes visible when we have passed through him to a transformed humanity. Only then, in retrospect, can we see prior man as something preliminary; only in retrospect does prior man become visible. The man whom it behooves us to overcome is man as he is today. Man today is at the same time—reckoned from the standpoint of the humanity that overcomes him, that is, from the standpoint of the new commencement—the "last man." The last man is the man of "middling felicity." He is incomparably sly, knows just about everything, and is as busy as can be; but with him everything peters out into something harmless, mid-range, and universally bland. In the sphere of the last man each thing gets a little bit smaller every day. Even what he takes to be great is actually petty; and it is diminishing all the time.

The overman is not a fairy-tale character; he is the one who recognizes the last man as such and who overcomes him. Over-man is the one who ascends above the "last" man and thereby earmarks him as last, as the man of bygone days. In order therefore to make this opposition palpably clear at the outset, Nietzsche has the teacher of eternal return of the same refer in his first speech—in the Prologue to the first part of *Thus Spoke Zarathustra,* section 5—to the one who must be "most contemptible" to him, namely, the "Last Man."

> "Now I shall speak to them of what is most contemptible, and that is the *Last Man.*"
>
> And Zarathustra spoke thus to the people:
>
> "The time has come for man to stake out his goal. The time has come for man to sow the seed of his supreme hope.
>
> "His soil is still rich enough for that. But one day this soil will be poor and tame, and no tall tree will be able to flourish in it.
>
> "Woe! The time is coming when man will no longer shoot the arrow of his longing beyond man, and the string of his bow will have forgotten how to whir!
>
> "I say unto you: one must still have chaos in him to be able to give birth to a dancing star. I say unto you: you still have chaos in you.
>
> "Woe! The time is coming when man will give birth to no more stars.

Woe! The time of the most contemptible man is coming, the one who can no longer feel contempt for himself.

"Behold, I show you the *Last Man*."

To this passage we ought to compare the section entitled "On the Attenuating Virtue" in Part III of *Thus Spoke Zarathustra*. The last man is mentioned at the conclusion of subsection 2:

"We have placed our stools in the *middle*"—that is what your smirk tells me—"equidistant from dying warriors and pleasure-loving sows."

But this is *mediocrity,* even though it be called moderation.

However, the fact that the last man is cited as the most contemptible man at the outset of the work, the fact that Zarathustra gives vent to his feeling of nausea at the very beginning, has in terms of the work as a whole a *still more profound* sense. Zarathustra is here merely at the beginning of his path, upon which he is to become the one who he is. He himself must first of all learn; among other things he must learn how to feel contempt. As long as contempt derives from nausea in the face of what is despised it is not yet supreme contempt. Such contempt based on nausea is itself contemptible. "Out of love alone should my contempt and my admonishing bird soar in me, and not out of the swamp!" (Part III, "On Passing By"). "O my soul, I taught you the contempt that does not come gnawing like a worm; I taught you the great, the loving contempt that loves most where it most feels contempt" (Part III, "On the Great Longing").

When Nietzsche creates poetically the figure of Zarathustra he projects the space of that "loneliest loneliness" cited at the end of *The Gay Science,* the loneliness that induces the thought of thoughts. Nietzsche does so in such a way that Zarathustra resolves to follow the direction which in *The Gay Science* is mentioned as merely one possibility among others, namely, that of "becoming beneficent toward life," that is, affirming life in its extreme anguish and in its most rollicking joy.

The communication of the thought most difficult to bear, the greatest burden, first of all requires the poetic creation of the figure who will think this thought and teach it. But in such creation the doctrine itself cannot be wholly disregarded. It is in fact portrayed in the third part of

Thus Spoke Zarathustra, which was composed in 1883–84. Neverthe-less, whenever the doctrine is directly introduced, it is invoked in a poetic manner—in similes that portray the sense and the truth of the doctrine in images, that is to say, in the realm of the sensuous, so that these images are sensuous-sensible. When Nietzsche pursues the sen-suous presentation of the thought of eternal return in *Thus Spoke Zarathustra* he is following—among other essential motivations—a thought that he had jotted down during this same period (1882–84): "The more abstract the truth that one wishes to teach is, the more one must begin by seducing the *senses* to it" (XII, 335).

However, we would be misinterpreting *Zarathustra* were we to ex-trapolate the doctrine of eternal return from the work, even in the form of figures of speech, as its "theory." For the most intrinsic task of this work is the limning of the teacher himself and, through him, the teaching. At the same time, of course, it remains the case that the figure of the teacher can be comprehended only on the basis of the teaching, of what comes to light in its truth, and of the way in which the teaching—concerning as it does beings as a whole—defines the Being of beings. The implication is that our interpretation of *Thus Spoke Zarathustra* as a work can proceed only on the basis of Nietz-sche's metaphysics in its entirety.

After the publication of *Thus Spoke Zarathustra* Nietzsche had oc-casion to rue the fact that he had risked the surrender of his most intimate and loftiest experiences. With the passage of time he learned to endure this anguish as well, knowing that the publication was a necessity and that miscomprehension is part and parcel of all such communication. Nietzsche once pinpointed this insight in the follow-ing note: "The necessary *concealment* of the wise man: his awareness that he is unconditionally *not* to be understood; his Machiavellian strategy; his icy rejection of the present" (XIII, 37; from the year 1884).

What is difficult to grasp about this work is not only its "content," if it has such, but also its very character as a work. Of course, we are quick to propose a ready-made explanation: here philosophical thoughts are presented poetically. Yet what we are now to call *thinking* and *poetizing* dare not consist of the usual notions, inasmuch as the work defines both of these anew, or rather, simply announces them.

And when we say that this work constitutes the center of Nietzsche's philosophy, it remains nonetheless true that the work stands outside the center, is "eccentric" to it. Finally, when we emphasize the fact that this work is the highest peak attained by Nietzsche's thinking, we forget—or, more precisely, we are unapprised of the fact—that precisely *after* the book *Thus Spoke Zarathustra*, during the years 1884 to 1889, Nietzsche's thinking continued to take essential steps that brought him to new transformations of his thought.

Nietzsche provided the work entitled *Thus Spoke Zarathustra* with a subtitle: "A Book for Everyone and No One." What the book says is directed to all, to everyone. Yet no one ever truly has the right, as he is, to read the book, if he does not ahead of time and in the process of his reading undergo a metamorphosis. That means that the book is for no one of us as we happen to be at the moment. A book for everyone and no one, and consequently a book that can never, dare never, be "read" complacently.

All this must be said in order for us to acknowledge how very extrinsic, how full of reservations, our own way of proceeding will remain. For our provisional characterization of the second communication of the doctrine of return will indicate only quite briefly those "figures of speech," which, more directly than the other utterances, treat of the thought of eternal return.

6. "On the Vision and the Riddle"

The eternal return of the same is discussed quite clearly and explicitly as the fundamental teaching in the section entitled "On Redemption," toward the end of Part II of *Thus Spoke Zarathustra,* written in the fall of 1883. But discussion of the doctrine flourishes principally in two sections of Part III of that work, composed in January 1884.

The first of these two sections bears the title, "On the Vision and the Riddle."* It is not a matter of just any vision or just any riddle about something or other. It is a matter of that particular riddle with which Zarathustra comes face to face, *the* riddle in which being as a whole lies concealed as "the vision of the loneliest one," the riddle that becomes visible only "in our loneliest loneliness." But why a "riddle"? What the riddle conceals and contains becomes open to view whenever it is surmised. Yet surmise is essentially different from calculation. The latter discloses step by step, along the guideline of some "thread" given beforehand, something unknown from what is known. But in surmise we take a leap, without guidelines, without the rungs of any ladder which anyone can clamber up anytime. To grasp the riddle is to leap, especially when the riddle involves being as a whole. Here there is no particular being or assortment of beings from which the whole could ever be disclosed. To make surmises on this riddle we must venture a journey into the open region of what in general is concealed, into that untraveled and uncharted region which is the unconcealment (*alētheia*) of what is most concealed. We must venture a journey into truth. Such riddling ventures the truth of being as a whole.† For Nietzsche knows that he occupies an exceptional

---

* The second of the two, "The Convalescent," is treated in section 8, below.

† *Dieses Raten ist ein Wagen der Wahrheit des Seienden im Ganzen.* On the word

place in the history of philosophy. During the period of *The Dawn,* about 1881, he jots down the following note (XI, 159):

> What is novel about the position we take toward philosophy is a conviction that no prior age shared: *that we do not possess the truth.* All earlier men "possessed the truth," even the skeptics.

Corresponding to this is a later utterance which also characterizes Nietzsche's own thinking within the confines of the position he takes. In the plans for *Thus Spoke Zarathustra* (XII, 410) Nietzsche remarks, "We are conducting an experiment with truth. Perhaps mankind will perish as a result! Splendid!"

Nevertheless, we would misunderstand the riddle and our riddling on it abysmally if we were to believe that our task is to hit upon a solution that would dissolve all that is questionable. Riddling on this riddle should rather bring us to experience the fact that *as* a riddle it cannot be brushed aside.

> Profound aversion to reposing once and for all in any sort of totalized view of the world. The magic of the opposite kind of thinking: not letting oneself be deprived of the stimulation in all that is enigmatic (WM, 470; from the years 1885–86).

And in *The Gay Science* (Book V, number 375, written 1887) Nietzsche speaks of the "addiction to knowledge, which will not let the questionmark behind all things go at a bargain price."

Thus we must take these words "riddle" and "riddling" in their essential importance and scope if we are to understand why Nietzsche grants Zarathustra himself the sobriquet "riddler" (Part III, "On Old and New Tablets," section 3). What sort of visage, then, does the riddle which Zarathustra tells have? Again we must pay heed to the way he tells it, to the *where* and *when* and *to whom,* if we are to estimate the *what* aright. Zarathustra tells the riddle aboard ship, un-

---

Wagen, related to way, weight, risk, hazard, venture and adventure, see Heidegger, "Wozu Dichter?" in *Holzwege* (Frankfurt am Main: V. Klostermann, 1950), pp. 255 ff., esp. pp. 259 and 275. See the English translation by Albert Hofstadter in Heidegger, *Poetry, Language, Thought* (New York: Harper & Row, 1971), pp. 99 ff., esp. pp. 103–04 and 139–40. Heidegger's use of the word in his Nietzsche course antedates that in the Rilke lecture by almost a decade.

derway on a voyage to open, "unexplored" seas. And to whom does he tell it? Not to the other passengers but to the crew alone: "To you, bold searchers and researchers, and those that ever took to ship with cunning sails on terrifying seas. . . ." In the same vein we hear now one of the "Songs of the Outlaw Prince," appended to the second edition of *The Gay Science* in 1887:

> *Toward New Seas**
> I *will* go there, and will confide
> In myself and in my steady grip.
> Open lies the sea; into the tide
> Plunges my Genuese ship.
>
> All shines new before the mast!
> Space and time sleep at midday.
> Only *your* eye—unutterably vast
> Gazes on me, O infinity!

And when does Zarathustra tell the crew the riddle? Not the moment he comes on board, because he keeps silent for two days. That is to say, he speaks only after they have gained open sea and only after he himself has in the meantime tested the seamen to learn whether they are the right listeners.

And what does Zarathustra relate? He tells of his ascent upon a mountain path at twilight. He stresses the atmosphere of twilight when he remarks, "Not only one sun had gone down for me." In his narrative of the ascent two regions of essential imagery converge—and, in fact, Nietzsche's transposition of thought into sensuous imagery always haunts these two realms: the sea, and mountain heights.

---

* The German text reads:

> *Nach neuen Meeren*
> Dorthin—*will* ich; und ich traue
> Mir fortan und meinem Griff.
> Offen liegt das Meer, in's Blaue
> Treibt mein Genueser Schiff.
>
> Alles glänzt mir neu und neuer,
> Mittag schläft auf Raum und Zeit—:
> Nur *dein* Auge—ungeheuer
> Blickt mich's an, Unendlichkeit!

While ascending, Zarathustra must constantly overcome the "spirit of gravity." The spirit of gravity pulls downward without cease, and yet for the one who climbs, the one who carries his "archenemy" into the heights with him, that spirit is no more than a dwarf.

But as he climbs the depths themselves increase and the abyss first becomes an abyss—not because the climber plunges into it, but precisely because he is ascending. Depths belong to heights; the former wax with the latter. For that reason the following lines appear by way of anticipation in the first section of Part III, which conjoins the two realms of imagery, "mountain" and "sea":

> "Whence come the highest mountains?" I once asked. Then I learned that they come out of the sea.
> The testimony is inscribed in their stone, and in the walls of their summits. From unfathomable depths the highest must rise to its height.

In any ascent there are always way-stations where one may estimate the way up and the way down against one another. The spirit of the ascending heights and the spirit of the downward-wending path meet face to face while on the way. Zarathustra the climber *versus* the dwarf, the one who drags down. Thus, when climbing, it comes to a question for decision: "Dwarf! It is either You or me!" The way the issue is posed here, it seems as though the dwarf (named first and with the "You" capitalized) is to win supremacy. Soon, however, at the beginning of the second section of "On the Vision and the Riddle," matters are reversed:

> "Stop, dwarf!" said I. "It is I or you! But I am the stronger of us two: you do not know my abysmal thought. *That* you could not bear!"

Inasmuch as Zarathustra thinks the abyss, the thought of thoughts, inasmuch as he takes the depths seriously, he rises to the heights and surpasses the dwarf.

> Then something happened that made me lighter: the dwarf, being curious, sprang from my shoulder. He squatted on a rock in front of me. But at the very place we stopped there was a gateway.

Zarathustra now describes the gateway. With the description of the image of the gateway Zarathustra brings the riddle to vision.

In the gateway two long avenues meet. The one leads forward, the other leads back. They run counter to one another; they affront one another. Each extends infinitely into its eternity. Above the gateway appears the inscription "Moment."*

The gateway "Moment," with its avenues stretching infinitely onward and counter to one another, is the image of time running forward and backward into eternity. Time itself is viewed from the "moment," from the "now." Both ways find their point of departure here, one extending into the not-yet-now of the future, the other leading back into the no-longer-now of the past. To the extent that the most abysmal thought is to be made accessible to the vision of the dwarf squatting at Zarathustra's side, made accessible by means of this sighting of the gateway, and to the extent that for the dwarf's vision time and eternity are obviously to be transposed into sense-images, the passage as a whole suggests that the thought of the eternal recurrence of the same will now be conflated with the realm of time and eternity. But this vision, the envisaged gateway, is a sighting of the riddle itself, not of its solution. When the "image" becomes visible and is described, the riddle draws into sight for the first time. The riddle is what our riddling must aim at.

Riddling commences by questioning. Zarathustra therefore immediately directs some questions to the dwarf concerning the gateway and its avenues. The first question involves the avenues—which one, we are not told. Indeed, what Zarathustra now asks is equally pertinent to both. If anyone were to strike out on one of these avenues, and continue on and on, what would happen? "Do you believe, dwarf, that these ways contradict one another eternally?"—that is to say, do the paths run away from one another eternally, are they contrary to one another?

" 'Everything straight deceives,' murmured the dwarf contemptuous-

---

* "Moment" unfortunately fails to capture the *dramatically* temporal nature of the German *Augenblick,* literally, the glance or flash of an eye. The drama in question has everything to do with what Heidegger in *Being and Time* calls "ecstatic temporality," especially in its connection with the analysis of *death.* (See, for example, section 68a, on the "authentic present.") The gateway "Glance of an Eye" remains throughout Heidegger's lecture course the most compelling image of eternal return.

ly. 'All truth is curved; time itself is a circle.' " The dwarf resolves the difficulty—indeed, as we are expressly told, in a "contemptuous" murmur. The difficulty is not one which the dwarf would take pains with; for him it is scarcely worth even talking about. For if both ways extend to eternity, they wind up at the same place; they meet there, they link up and form one uninterrupted highway. What to us looks like two straight avenues taking off in opposite directions is in truth that segment of an enormous circle which is visible to us here and now, while the circle itself perpetually revolves back upon itself. The straight is semblance. In truth, the way the avenues take is circular; that is to say, truth itself—being as it proceeds in truth—is curved. Time's circling in itself, and hence the ever-recurring same for all beings in time, is the *way in which* being as a whole is. It *is* in the way of eternal recurrence. That is how the dwarf guesses the riddle.

But Zarathustra's narrative takes a curious turn. " 'You spirit of gravity,' I cried wrathfully, 'don't make things too easy for yourself! Or I'll leave you squatting where you are right now, lamefoot!—and I was the one who carried you high!' " Instead of rejoicing in the fact that the dwarf has thought his thought, Zarathustra speaks "wrathfully." So the dwarf has not really grasped the riddle; he has made the solution too easy. Accordingly, the thought of eternal recurrence of the same is not yet thought when one merely imagines "everything turning in a circle." In his book on Nietzsche, Ernst Bertram characterizes the doctrine of eternal return as a "deceptively aping, lunatic *mysterium.*"[*] He appends a saying of Goethe's by way of remonstrance, obviously because he views it as a superior insight which puts to shame the thought of eternal return. Goethe's saying runs, "The more one knows and the more one comprehends, the more one realizes that everything turns in a circle." That is precisely the thought of circling as the dwarf thinks it, the dwarf who, in Zarathustra's words, makes things too easy—inasmuch as he absolutely refuses to think Nietzsche's stupendous thought.

The thinker abandons anyone who thinks Nietzsche's keenest thought dwarfishly, leaves the lamefoot squatting where he squats.

---

[*] See page 6, above, for the reference.

Zarathustra lets the dwarf sit, even though he has carried him "high," transposed him to a height where he *would* see if only he *could,* and where he *could* see if he were not forever—a dwarf.

Zarathustra immediately directs a second question to the dwarf. This question refers not to the avenues but to the gateway itself, "the Moment." " 'Behold,' I went on, 'behold this Moment!' " The entire vision is to be pondered once again on the basis of the "Moment" and in relation to it. " 'From this gateway Moment a long avenue runs eternally *rearward:* behind us lies an eternity.' " All the finite things that can hasten along that avenue and that need only a finite span in order to run their course, all these finite things must therefore have already run through this eternity, must have already come along this avenue. Nietzsche summarizes an essential thought concerning his doctrine so succinctly here, in the form of a question, that it is hardly comprehensible on its own, especially since the requisite presuppositions, although mentioned, do not really become visible. Those presuppositions are: first, the infinity of time in the directions of future and past; second, the actuality of time, which is not a "subjective" Form of Intuition; third, the finitude of things and of their courses. On the basis of these presuppositions, everything that can in any way be must, as a being, already have been. For in an infinite time the course of a finite world is necessarily already completed. If, therefore, " 'everything has already been there, what do you make of this Moment, dwarf? Must not this gateway too already have been there?' " And if all things are knotted tight, so that the moment pulls them along behind, must not the moment also pull itself along behind? And if the moment also moves down the lane ahead, must not all things strike out along the avenue once again? The patient spider, the moonlight (cf. *The Gay Science,* number 341), I and you in the gateway—" 'must we not recur eternally?' " It seems as though Zarathustra's second question repeats exactly what was contained in the dwarf's answer to the first question: Everything moves in a circle. It seems so. Yet the dwarf fails to reply to the second question. The very question is posed in such a superior fashion that Zarathustra can no longer expect an answer from the dwarf. The superiority consists in the fact that certain conditions of understanding have been brought into play, conditions the dwarf cannot satisfy—because he is a dwarf. These new conditions derive from the realization that the second question is based on the "Moment." But such questioning requires that one adopt a stance of his own within the "Moment" itself, that is, in time and its temporality.

When that requirement appears, the dwarf vanishes. Indeed, he vanishes on account of an event that in itself is sinister and foreboding. Zarathustra relates: "I saw a young shepherd, writhing, choking in spasms, his face distorted: a thick black snake hung out of his mouth." The snake had bitten fast there. Zarathustra pulls at the snake, in vain. "Then the cry rose out of me, 'Bite! You must bite! Bite off the head! Bite!' "

The event and the image are difficult for us to think. But they are most intimately bound up with the effort to think the thought that is hardest to bear. Right now we will pay attention to only one aspect: after Zarathustra has posed the second question there is no place left for the dwarf, who no longer belongs in the realm of this question because he cannot bear to hear it. Questioning, riddling, and thinking, as they approach ever nearer the import of the riddle, themselves become more riddlesome, loom ever more gigantic, towering over the one who is doing the questioning. Not everyone has a right to every question. Rather than expect a response from the dwarf, and rather than provide a polished reply couched in propositions, Zarathustra continues the narrative: "Thus I spoke, and ever more softly: for I feared my own thoughts and hinterthoughts." The thought that is hardest to bear grows terrifying. Behind what one might imagine as a turning in lazy circles, it descries something altogether different. It thinks the thought in a way dwarfs never think it.

7. Zarathustra's Animals

At this point we will interrupt our interpretation of the episode "On the Vision and the Riddle." We will consider the episode again in another context later in the course. After we have portrayed the essence of nihilism as the domain of the thought of eternal return we shall be better prepared to understand what is now to transpire in that episode. We will not consider the remaining episodes of Part III, but only extrapolate some details of the fourth-to-last section, "The Convalescent."*

Zarathustra has in the meantime returned from his sea voyage to the solitude of the mountains—to his cave and to his animals. His animals are the eagle and the serpent. These two are *his* animals; they belong to him in his solitude. And when Zarathustra's loneliness speaks, it is his animals who are speaking. Nietzsche writes at one point (it was in September of 1888 in Sils-Maria, at the conclusion of a preface—no longer extant—to *Twilight of the Idols* in which Nietzsche casts a retrospective glance at *Thus Spoke Zarathustra* and *Beyond Good and Evil*): "*His love of animals*—men have always recognized the solitary by means of this trait" (XIV, 417). However, Zarathustra's animals are not chosen arbitrarily: their essence is an image of Zarathustra's proper essence, that is to say, an image of his task—which is to be the teacher of eternal return. These animals of his, eagle and serpent, therefore do not enter on the stage at some fortuitous point. Zarathustra first espies

---

* "The Convalescent" is discussed in section 8, below. Heidegger returns to his interpretation of "The Vision and the Riddle" in section 24, "Moment and Eternal Recurrence," after having raised the question of that thought's *domain*, namely, the overcoming of nihilism, in sections 21–23. Heidegger's remarks here are most important for our understanding the structure and movement of the lecture course as a whole. For further discussion, see section I of the Analysis at the end of this volume.

them at glowing midday, that part of the day which throughout the work *Thus Spoke Zarathustra* unleashes an essential image-generating force.

When Zarathustra speaks to his heart at glowing midday he hears the piercing cry of a bird. He looks inquiringly into the sky. "And behold! An eagle soared through the air in vast circles, and a serpent hung suspended from him, not as his prey but as though she were his friend: for she had coiled about his neck" (Prologue, section 10). This magnificient emblem scintillates for all who have eyes to see! The more essentially we comprehend the work *Thus Spoke Zarathustra*, the more univocal yet inexhuastible the emblem becomes.

The eagle soars in vast circles high in the air. The circling is an image of eternal return. Yet it is a circling that simultaneously rises skyward and holds itself there in the heights.

The serpent hangs suspended from the eagle, coiled about his throat. Again, the coils of the serpent, wound in rings about the eagle's throat, are symbolic of the ring of eternal return. Moreover, the serpent winds itself about the one who wends his way in great circles in the sky—a singular and essential, yet for us still obscure, tangle of coils. Through it the graphic force of the imagery gradually displays its wealth. The serpent, not as prey pinned in the eagle's talons and so suppressed, but winding itself freely about the throat as the eagle's intimate companion, winding about him and soaring upward with him in circles! Into this sensuous imagery of the eternal return of the same —circling in a ring, and coiling in a circle—we must integrate what it is the animals themselves are.

The eagle is the proudest animal. Pride is the fully developed resolution of one who maintains himself at the level of his own essential rank, a rank to which his task appoints him. Pride is the assurance of one who no longer confuses himself with anyone else. Pride is poised above, is defined by heights and elevation; yet it is essentially different from arrogance and superciliousness. The latter remain in need of a relationship with what is beneath them; they have to set themselves in relief against it and thus they remain necessarily dependent on it. For they possess nothing that would inherently enable them to imagine themselves in elevation. They can be uplifted only because they remain defined by what is beneath them; they can ascend only to something that *is* not elevated but which they fancy to be so. Pride is different.

The eagle is the proudest animal. He lives always in the heights, and for them. Even when he plunges into the depths, these are depths among mountain heights, crevasses, not plains where all is flattened out and equalized.

The serpent is the most discerning animal. Discernment suggests the mastery of actual knowledge concerning the sundry ways in which knowing announces itself, holds itself in reserve, asserts itself and yet remains flexible, avoiding its own pitfalls. Proper to such discernment are the power to metamorphose and to disguise oneself—a power that cannot be reduced to vulgar falsehood—and the mastery of masks. Discernment does not betray itself. It haunts the background while playing in the foreground; it wields power over the play of Being and semblance.

Zarathustra's two animals are the proudest and most discerning of animals. They belong together and they are out on a search. That is to say, they seek someone of their own kind, one who matches their standards, someone who can hold out with them in loneliness. They seek to learn whether Zarathustra is still living, living as one who is prepared to go under. That should be enough to let us know that the eagle and serpent are not pets; we do not take them home with us and proceed to domesticate them. They are alien to all that is domestic and usual, all that is "familiar" in the petty sense of the word. These two animals define for the first time the loneliest loneliness, and it is something different from what the usual view takes it to be. In the usual view, solitude is what liberates us, frees us from all things. Solitude, according to this view, is what happens after you post the "Do Not Disturb" sign. Yet in our loneliest loneliness the most hair-raising and hazardous things are loosed upon us and on our task, and these cannot be deflected onto other things or other people. They must penetrate us through and through, not that we might be rid of them once and for all, but that in authentic knowing and supreme discernment we may become aware that such things remain relevant. To know precisely *that* is the knowing that is hardest to bear. All too easily such knowing flies off, or creeps away, into evasions and excuses—into sheer folly.

We must think this magnificent conception of loneliness in order to grasp both the role played by these two sensuous images—the two animals of Zarathustra the solitary—and the figure of Zarathustra himself. We dare not falsify all this by romanticizing it. To hold out in loneliest loneliness does not mean to keep these two animals as company or as a pleasant pastime; it means to possess the force that will enable one to remain true to oneself in their proximity and to prevent them from fleeing. Hence at the conclusion of the Prologue to *Thus Spoke Zarathustra* we find the words:

> "Thus I bid my pride always to accompany my discernment. And if my discernment should one day leave me—alas, she loves to fly off!—then let my pride fly with my folly!"
> Thus began Zarathustra's downgoing.

A curious downgoing, which commences by exposing itself to the supreme possibilites of Becoming and Being. These cohere in the essence of will to power; that is to say, they are *one*.

What we set out to do here was to indicate briefly what the figures of Zarathustra's two animals, eagle and serpent, symbolize: first, in their circling and coiling—the circle and ring of eternal return; second, in their essential character as pride and discernment, respectively, these constituting the basic stance of the teacher of eternal return and his mode of knowledge; third, as the animals of his loneliness, being supreme exactions on Zarathustra himself. Zarathustra's animals are all the more implacable inasmuch as we hear them—not expressing certain propositions or rules or admonitions—but saying from out of their essential natures what is essential, and saying it with growing lucidity through the palpable presence of sensuous imagery. Sense-images speak only to those who possess the constructive energy to give them shape, so that they make sense. As soon as the poetic force—that is, the higher constructive energy—wanes, the emblems turn mute. They petrify, become sheer "facade" and "ornament."

8. "The Convalescent"

The reference to Zarathustra's animals has left us not totally unprepared to grasp the episode that, along with "On the Vision and the Riddle," considered earlier, treats the eternal return in a more direct fashion. This episode, the fourth-to-last of Part III, entitled "The Convalescent," remains in mysterious correspondence to that earlier one. In "The Convalescent" Zarathustra's animals speak to him about what they themselves symbolize: they speak of eternal return. They speak to Zarathustra, hovering about him, and remain present to his solitude until a particular moment when they leave him alone, cautiously stealing away. Their standing by him suggests that they are curious about him and are ever on the search for him; they want to know whether he is becoming the one he is, whether in his Becoming he finds his Being. But Zarathustra's Becoming commences with his downgoing. The downgoing itself comes to its end in Zarathustra's convalescence. Everything here is indicative of the most profound strife. Only when we grasp the various facets of the strife will we near the thought that is hardest to bear.

We shall place special emphasis on the characterization of the doctrine of eternal return, as befits the preliminary elucidations we are now engaged in. Yet we must continue to keep to the style of the present work; we must grasp everything that happens, in the way that it happens, in terms of that work itself. We must also understand the teaching, as taught, in connection with the questions as to *who* Zarathustra is, *how* the teacher of that teaching is, and *in what way* the teaching defines the teacher. That is to say, precisely where the teaching is most purely expressed in doctrines, the teacher, the one who teaches and speaks, dare not be forgotten.

How do matters stand with Zarathustra at the beginning of the section entitled "The Convalescent"? What is happening here? Zarathustra has returned once again to his cave, home from his sea voyage. One morning soon after his arrival he leaps from his bed and cries out like a madman, gesturing frantically, "as though someone were still lying in his bed and refused to get up." Zarathustra rages in a frightful voice in order to wake this other and to make sure that he will remain awake in the future. This other is his most abysmal thought, which, although it lies with him, still remains a stranger to Zarathustra; the other is his own ultimate recess, which Zarathustra has not yet conducted to his supreme height and to the most fully wakeful of lives. The thought lies *beside* him in bed, has not yet become one with him, is not yet incorporated in him and hence is not yet something truly thought. So saying, we indicate what is now to happen: the full import and the whole might of the thought that is hardest to bear must now rise and reveal itself. Zarathustra roars at it, calls it a "sluggish worm." We easily discern the meaning of the image: the sluggish worm, lying as a stranger on the floor, is the counterimage to the ringed serpent who "wrings" his way to the heights, soaring there in vast circles, vigilant in friendship. When the invocation of the most abysmal thought begins, Zarathustra's animals grow fearful; they do not flee in consternation, however, but come nearer, while all the other animals about them scatter. Eagle and serpent alone remain. It is a matter of bringing to the light of wakeful day, in purest solitude, what the animals symbolize.

Zarathustra invokes his ultimate recesses and so conducts himself to himself. He becomes what he is and confesses himself to be the one who he is: "the advocate of life, the advocate of suffering, the advocate of the circle." Living, suffering, and circling are not three distinct matters. They belong together and form one: being as a whole, to which suffering, the abyss, belongs and which *is* inasmuch as, circling, it recurs. These three manifest their mutual affinity when they are gathered in the light of day, that is, when they are thought in their unity by Zarathustra's supreme "Yes." In that supreme moment, when the thought is comprehended and is truly thought, Zarathustra cries, "Hail me!" Yet his "Hail me!" is at the same time a "Woe is me!"—for his is the victory that overcomes even itself as its greatest danger, the victory that grasps itself as downgoing.

Scarcely is it accomplished, when Zarathustra collapses. After he regains his senses he takes to his bed for seven days and seven nights. "But his animals did not abandon him, neither by day nor by night." Even so, Zarathustra remains in his solitude. The eagle, the proudest animal, flies off alone to fetch all sorts of nourishment. That means to say that Zarathustra does not lose himself, that he continues to nourish his pride and to secure the certainty of his rank, even though he must lie prostrate, even though his discernment does not bother about him now, so that he cannot even tell himself what he knows. Among other things, the eagle brings him "yellow and red berries," and we recall the earlier reference to "deep yellow and fiery red" (cf. Part III, "On the Spirit of Gravity"). *Taken together,* these two colors conform to what Zarathustra wants to have in sight: the color of deepest falsehood, error, and semblance, and the color of supreme passion, of incandescent creation.

When interpreting the two colors we have to keep in mind the fact that for will to power "error" constitutes the necessary essence of *truth* and that it is therefore not at all to be valued negatively. "Deep yellow" may also be interpreted as the gold of the "golden flash of the serpent *vita"* (WM, 577), which is "the serpent of eternity" (XII, 426). For the second interpretation "deep yellow" is the color of the eternal recurrence of the same, "fiery red" the color of will to power. For the first interpretation the two colors display the essential structure of will to power itself, inasmuch as truth as that which fixates and art as creation constitute the conditions of the possibility of will to power. In both cases the mutual affinity of the two colors points toward the essential unity of the Being of beings as thought by Nietzsche.

But after seven days "the animals felt that the time had come to talk with him." Zarathustra is now strong enough actually to think and to express himself about his most difficult thought, his ultimate recess. For what the eagle and serpent (the loneliest loneliness) wish to talk about—the only thing they *can* talk about—is the thought of eternal return. In the dialogue between Zarathustra and his animals the thought of thoughts is now brought to language. It is not presented as a "theory"; only in conversation does it prove itself. For here the speakers themselves must venture forth into what is spoken: conversation alone brings to light the extent to which the speakers can or cannot advance, and the extent to which their conversation is only empty talk.

The two animals open the conversation. They inform Zarathustra that the world outside is like a garden that awaits him. They sense somehow that a new insight has come to him, an insight concerning the world as a whole. It must therefore be a pleasure to proceed to this newly constituted world, since all things are bathed in the light of the new insight and want to be integrated into the new dispensation. Insofar as they are so illuminated and integrated, things corroborate the insight in a profound way; they heal the one who up to now has been a seeker, they cure him of the disease of inquiry. That is what the animals mean when they say to Zarathustra, "All things yearn for you. . . . All things want to be doctors to you!" And Zarathustra? He listens to the animals' talk, indeed gladly, although he knows that they are only jabbering. But after such solitude the world *is* like a garden, even when it is invoked by mere empty talk, in the sheer play of words and phrases. He knows that a cheerful loveliness and gentle humor settle over the terrifying thing that being genuinely *is;* that being can conceal itself behind semblances in what is talked about. In truth, of course, the world is no garden, and for Zarathustra it dare not be one, especially if by "garden" we mean an enchanting haven for the flight from being. Nietzsche's conception of the world does not provide the thinker with a sedate residence in which he can putter about unperturbed, like the philosopher of old, Epicurus, in his "garden." The world is not a cosmos present at hand in itself. The animals' allusion to the garden has the sense of rejecting any sedate residence; at the same time, indirectly, it has the task of referring us to the concept of world in the tragic insight. Here we must ponder an important note by Nietzsche (XII, 368, from 1882–84):

> Solitude *for a time* necessary, in order that the creature be totally permeated —cured and hard. New form of community, asserting itself in a warlike manner. Otherwise the spirit grows soft. No "gardens" and no sheer "evasion in the face of the masses." War (but without gunpowder!) between different thoughts! and their armies!

The animals talk to Zarathustra about his new insight in seductive words that tempt him to sheer intoxication. Yet Zarathustra knows that in truth these words and tones are "rainbows and sham bridges connecting what is eternally distinct." Where things most reminiscent of other things are named in the conversation, when it sounds as though the *same* is being said, then and there comes the loveliest lie: "For the smallest gap is the hardest to bridge."

What is Zarathustra thinking about? Nothing else than the sole matter under discussion, the world, being as a whole. But what response did the dwarf give to this riddle? The dwarf said that the avenues of the gateway, running counter to one another, meet in the infinite; everything turns in a circle and is a circle. And what did Zarathustra call himself when he thought his most difficult thought out of his ultimate recess, a thought he did not take lightly, as the dwarf did? He called himself the "advocate of the circle." Hence the two of them, the dwarf and Zarathustra, say the same thing. Between them lies only "the smallest gap": in each case it is an other who speaks the same words. Otherwise that same word, "circle," is but a sham bridge between things that are eternally distinct. Thus one man's circle is not another man's circle. What now comes to light is that whenever the Being of beings as a whole is to be uttered the semblance of unanimity is greatest and correct understanding—which is decisive and determinative of rank—most difficult.

It is easy for anyone and everyone to say, "A being is," and "A being becomes." Everyone thinks that anybody can understand that. Meanwhile, talking this way, "man dances above and beyond all things." Man, drifting along as he usually does, oblivious to the true dimensions and proper stages of genuine thinking, needs that kind of dance, that kind of jabbering, and Zarathustra takes joy in it. Yet he also knows that it is an illusion, that this garden is not the world, that "the world is deep, and deeper than the day has thought" (Part III, "Before Sunrise").

Thus Zarathustra does not allow the animals' talk to seduce him away from what he has known now for seven days and nights. He can find nothing reassuring in the fact that everyone confidently asserts—as though it were evident—that "everything turns in a circle," thereby to all appearances agreeing with him in their empty talk. But the animals reply, "To those who think as we do, all things themselves dance." We do not dance above and beyond the things, they seem to say, but see the things' own dance and sway: you can trust us. And now they tell how the world looks under the new sun of eternal recurrence:

> Everything goes, everything comes back; eternally rolls the wheel of Being. Everything dies, everything blooms again; eternally runs the year of Being.
>
> Everything sunders, everything is joined anew; eternally the identical House of Being is built. Everything departs, everything greets again; eternally true to itself is the Ring of Being.
>
> In every instant Being begins; around every Here the sphere of There rolls. The center is everywhere. Curved is the path of eternity.

Thus talk Zarathustra's animals. And why shouldn't they, they who *are* only insofar as they soar in vast circles and form rings? Could eternal return of the same be portrayed in more elegant words and more striking images than those employed here? How different this speech seems from the contemptuous grumblings of the dwarf! Nevertheless, the speeches of the dwarf and the animals betray a fatal resemblance. The dwarf says "All truth," that is to say, what is truly in being, in its passage and passing, "is curved." The animals say, "Curved is the path of eternity." Perhaps the animals' talk is only more effervescent, more buoyant and playful than—yet at bottom identical with—the talk of the dwarf, to whom Zarathustra objects that he makes things too easy for himself. Indeed, even the speech of his very own animals, who present his teaching to him in the fairest formulas, cannot deceive Zarathustra: " 'Oh, you rascally jesters and barrel organs,' answered Zarathusra, smiling again, 'how well you know what had to be fulfilled in seven days—' ." Yet their knowing is not knowledge. If Zarathustra calls it that he is only being ironic and is really suggesting that they know nothing. They are barrel organs: they turn his words concerning the eternal return of the same, words obtained only after the hardest struggle, into a mere ditty; they crank it out, knowing what is essential about it as little as the dwarf does. For the dwarf vanishes when things take a serious turn and all becomes foreboding, when the shepherd has to bite off the head of the black snake. The dwarf experiences nothing of the fact that really to know the ring of rings means precisely this: to overcome from the outset and perpetually what is dark and horrid in the teaching as it is expressed, namely, the fact that if everything recurs all decision and every effort and will to make things better is a matter of indifference; that if everything turns in a circle nothing is worth the trouble; so that the result of the teaching is disgust and ultimately the negation of life. In spite of their marvelous talk about the Ring of Being, Zarathustra's animals too seem to dance over and beyond what is essential. His animals too seem to want to treat the matter as men do. Like the dwarf they run away. Or they too act as mere spectators, telling what results if everything revolves. They perch before beings and "have a look at" their eternal displacement, then describe it in the most resplendent images. They are not aware of what is going on there, not aware of what must be thought in the true thinking of being as a whole, namely, that such thinking is a cry of distress, arising from a calamity.

And even if the anguished cry is heard, what is it that usually happens? When the great man cries the little man hastens to the scene and takes pity. But everything that smacks of pity keeps to the periphery, stands on the sidelines. The little man's gregariousness accomplishes only one thing: his petty consolations diminish and falsify the suffering, delay and obstruct the true insight. Pity has not an inkling of the extent to which suffering and outrage crawl down the throat and choke a man until he has to cry out, nor does it know the extent to which this is "necessary to attain the best" in man. Precisely the knowledge that chokes us is what must be known if being as a whole is to be thought.

This marks the essential and altogether unbridgeable difference between the usual kinds of spectation and cognition, on the one hand, and proper knowing, on the other. And it suggests what the dwarf failed to see when he misinterpreted eternal recurrence and turned it into a mere ditty, into empty talk. It should be apparent by now that nothing is said here about the content of the doctrine beyond what is said in the animals' ditty, that Zarathustra does not contrapose any other presentation to theirs, and that in the course of the conversation we are told *always and only by indirection* how the teaching is—or is not—to be understood. Nevertheless, the "how" does provide an essential directive for our understanding of the "what."

It is our job to pursue that directive more keenly and to ask: What is it that turns the doctrine into a ditty? The latter concedes that things do depart, die, and disintegrate; it also accepts everything destructive, negative, adverse, and outrageous. Yet at bottom these things are conceived of as eventually passing away in the world's circuitry, so that other things will come and everything shall take a turn for the better. Hence all is bound for perpetual compensation. Such compensation in fact makes everything indifferent: striving is flattened out into mere alternation. One now possesses a handy formula for the whole and abstains from all decision.

Looking back to the earlier episode, we may now ask: In what way does the dwarf make the interpretation of the imagery, that is, of the gateway and the two avenues, too easy for himself? Zarathustra indicates the answer when he goes on to command, "Look at the gateway itself—the Moment!" What does that directive mean? The dwarf merely looks at the two paths extending to infinity, and he thinks about them merely in the following way: If both paths run on to infinity ("eternity"), then that is where they meet; and since the circle closes by itself in infinity—far removed from me—all that recurs, in sheer alternation within this system of compensations, does so as a sequence, as a sort of parade passing through the gateway. The dwarf understands nothing of what Zarathustra means when he says—bewilderingly enough—that the two paths "affront one another" in the gateway. But how is that possible, when each thing moves along behind its predecessor, as is manifest with time itself? For in time the not-yet-now becomes the now, and forthwith becomes a no-longer-now, this as a perpetual and-so-on. The two avenues, future and past, do not collide at all, but pursue one another.

And yet a collision does occur here. To be sure, it occurs only to one who does not remain a spectator but who *is himself* the Moment, performing actions directed toward the future and at the same time accepting and affirming the past, by no means letting it drop. Whoever stands in the Moment is turned in two ways: for him past and future *run up against* one another. Whoever stands in the Moment lets what runs counter to itself come to collision, though not to a standstill, by cultivating and sustaining the strife between what is assigned him as a task and what has been given him as his endowment.* To see the Moment means to stand in it. But the dwarf keeps to the outside, perches on the periphery.

What does all this say about the right way to think the thought of eternal recurrence? It says something essential: That which is to come is precisely a matter for decision, since the ring is not closed in some remote infinity but possesses its unbroken closure in the Moment, as the center of the striving; what recurs—if it is to recur—is decided by the Moment and by the force with which the Moment can cope with whatever in it is repelled by such striving. That is what is peculiar to, and hardest to bear in, the doctrine of eternal return—to wit, that eternity *is* in the Moment, that the Moment is not the fleeting "now," not an instant of time whizzing by a spectator, but the collision of future and past. Here the Moment comes to itself. It determines how everything recurs. Now, the most difficult matter is the most tremendous matter to be grasped, and the tremendous remains a sealed door to little men. Yet the little men too *are;* as beings they too recur forever. They cannot be put out of action; they pertain to that side of things that is dark and repulsive. If being as a whole is to be thought, the little men too wait upon their "Yes." That realization makes Zarathustra shudder.

And now that his most abysmal thought has been thought in the direction of that abyss, Zarathustra's animals "do not let him talk anymore." For when Zarathustra recognizes that the recurrence of the little man too is necessary; when he grapples with that "Yes" spoken to

---

* *Indem er den Widerstreit des Aufgegebenen und Mitgegebenen entfaltet und aushält. Aufgegebenen* could of course also have to do with surrender, but I am conjecturing that Heidegger here wants to juxtapose the task (cf. *Aufgabe*) that we project into and as the future to the endowment (cf. *Mitgabe, Mitgift*) of skills we bring to the task from our past. For here there often seems to be a disparity, a striving, and strife. Cf. the similar phrasing in Heidegger's *Der Ursprung des Kunstwerkes* (Stuttgart: P. Reclam, 1960), p. 89 (top), ably rendered by Albert Hofstadter in Martin Heidegger, *Poetry, Language, Thought,* p. 77 (middle). And see sections 24 and 26, below.

everything that over the years wearied and sickened him, to everything he wanted to repulse; when he conquers his illness with that "Yes" and so becomes a convalescent; then his animals begin to speak again. Once more they repeat their message: the world is a garden. Again they call for Zarathustra to come out. But now they say more. They do not simply tell him to come out so that he can see and experience how all things are yearning for him. They call to him that he should learn from the songbirds how to sing: "For singing does a convalescent good." The temptation to take the thought of return merely as something obvious, to take it therefore at bottom as either contemptible mumbling or fascinating chatter, is overcome.

By now the dialogue between the animals and Zarathustra is moving upon a ground that has been transformed by the conversation itself. The animals are now speaking to a Zarathustra who has come to grips with his illness and overcome his disgust with the little man by achieving the insight that such adversity is necessary.

Now Zarathustra agrees with his animals. With their injunction to sing, the animals are telling him of that consolation he invented for himself during those seven days. Once again, however, he warns against turning the injunction to sing into a call for tunes on the same old lyre. What is being thought here? This, that the thought most difficult to bear, as the convalescent's conquering thought, must first of all be *sung;* that such singing, which is to say, the poetizing of *Thus Spoke Zarathustra,* must itself become the convalescence; but also that such singing must be *singular,* that it dare not become a popular tune. Zarathustra therefore calls himself a poet as well as one who guesses riddles. Poet and riddler, but not in the sense that he is a poet and something else in addition, namely, one who solves riddles. Both these roles are thought in an original unity, thought therefore ultimately as some third thing. Hence poetry, if it is to fulfill its task, can never be a matter for barrel organs and ready-made lyres. The lyre, viewed now as an instrument for the new singing and saying, has still to be created. The animals know that—after all, they are *his* animals. In the words they utter they gradually come closer to Zarathustra, the more so as Zarathustra comes closer to himself and to his task: "First fashion for yourself a proper lyre, a new lyre!" "For your animals know well, O

Zarathustra, who you are and must become: behold, *you are the teacher of the eternal return*—that is now *your* destiny!"

Yet if Zarathustra is the first to have to teach that teaching, must he not, as the teacher, know it ahead of time, prior to anyone else; and must he not know it differently than those who are merely learning it? Indeed, he must know that by virtue of the teaching itself, and in conformity with it, "the great destiny" is also to be his greatest danger and disease. Only when the teacher comprehends himself *in terms of the teaching* as inevitably a victim, as one who must go down because he goes over in transition, only when the one going under gives himself his blessing as such a one, does he reach his end and goal. "Thus [that is, in this way] *ends* Zarathustra's downgoing," say the animals.

"Downgoing" here means two things: first, transition as departure; second, descent as acknowledgment of the abyss. This dual characterization of downgoing must at the same time be grasped in its temporality, in terms of "eternity," correctly understood. The downgoing itself, thought with a view to eternity, is the Moment; yet not as the fleeting "now," not as mere passing. Downgoing is indeed the briefest thing, hence the most transient, but is at the same time what is most accomplished: in it the most luminous brightness of being as a whole scintillates, as the Moment in which the whole of recurrence becomes comprehensible. The apposite imagery here is the coiling serpent, the living ring. In the image of the serpent the connection between eternity and the Moment is established for Nietzsche in its unity: the living ring of the serpent, that is to say, eternal recurrence, and—the Moment. In one of his late sketches (WM, 577; from the year 1887) Nietzsche contrasts his concept of eternity with the extrinsic sense of that notion as the "eternally unchanging": "As opposed to the *value* of the eternally unchanging (note Spinoza's naiveté, and Descartes' as well), the value of the briefest and most transient, the seductive flash of gold on the belly of the serpent *vita.*" In the end, Zarathustra hears which eternity it is that his animals are proclaiming to him, the eternity of the Moment that embraces everything in itself at once: the downgoing.

When Zarathustra heard these words of his animals' "he lay still" and communed with his soul. But the serpent and the eagle, finding him thus, so silent, honored the vast stillness about him and cautiously stole away.

In what way is Zarathustra now silent? He is silent inasmuch as he is communing with his soul alone, because he has found what defines him, has become the one who he is. He has also overcome outrage and repugnance by learning that the abyss belongs to the heights. To overcome outrage is not to put it out of action but to acknowledge its necessity. As long as outrage is merely repudiated in disgust, as long as our contempt is determined merely by nausea, that contempt remains dependent upon the contemptible. Only when contempt stems from love of the task, being transformed in such a way that, undergirded by an affirmation of the necessity of outrage, suffering, and destruction, it can pass by in silence; only when the silence of such loving passing-by previals; only then does the vast stillness extend and the sphere expand about the one who in this way has become himself. Only now that the vast stillness pervades Zarathustra's spirit has he found his loneliest loneliness, a solitude that has nothing more to do with a merely peripheral existence. And the animals of his solitude honor the stillness, that is to say, they perfect the solitude in its proper essence in that now they too "cautiously steal away." The eagle's pride and serpent's discernment are now essential qualities of Zarathustra.

Zarathustra himself has become a hero, inasmuch as he has incorporated the thought of eternal return in its full import as the weightiest of thoughts. Now he is a knower. He knows that the greatest and smallest cohere and recur, so that even the greatest teaching, the ring of rings, itself must become a ditty for barrel organs, the latter always accompanying its true proclamation. Now he is one who goes out to meet at the same time his supreme suffering and supreme hope. We have already heard Nietzsche's answer to the question, *"What makes someone heroic?"* (V, 204), that is, what is it that makes a hero a hero? The response: "Going out to meet one's supreme suffering and supreme hope alike." But thanks to the motto of our own lecture course we also know that "everything in the hero's sphere turns to tragedy."

"Once I had created the overman, I draped the great veil of Becoming about him and let the midday sun stand over him" (XII, 362). The veil of Becoming is recurrence, as the truth concerning being as a whole, and the midday sun is the Moment of the shortest shadow and the most luminous brightness, the image of eternity. When *"the greatest burden"* is assimilated to Dasein, *"Incipit tragoedia."* The two final sections of *The Gay Science,* which communicate the doctrine of return for the first time, employ the two italicized phrases as their titles. The intrinsic connection between these two concluding sections becomes clear on the basis of *that* work which is designed to create poetically the figure who is to think the eternal return of the same.

With Zarathustra *"the tragic age"* commences (WM, 37). Tragic knowing realizes that "life itself," being as a whole, conditions "pain," "destruction," and all agony; and that none of these things constitutes an "objection to this life" (WM, 1052). The customary notion of "the tragic," even when it is more exalted than usual, sees in this realization nothing more than guilt and decline, cessation and despair. Nietzsche's conception of the tragic and of tragedy is different; it is essentially more profound. The tragic in Nietzsche's sense *counteracts* "resignation" (WM, 1029), if we may say that the tragic still finds it necessary to be "counter" to anything. The tragic in Nietzsche's sense has nothing to do with sheer self-destructive pessimism, which casts a pall over all things; it has just as little to do with blind optimism, which is lost in the vertigo of its vacuous desires. The tragic in Nietzsche's sense falls outside this opposition, inasmuch as in its willing and in its knowing it adopts a stance toward being as a whole, and inasmuch as the basic law of being as a whole consists in struggle.

By means of our renewed reference to the connection between these two passages, passages that constitute the first communication of the thought of eternal return of the same, we have also clarified the inner relationship between the first communication (in *The Gay Science*) and the second (in *Thus Spoke Zarathustra*). We arrive at a juncture where we will have to reflect awhile on our procedure up to now. Such considerations will quite likely remain fruitless—unless several steps in the procedure have actually been executed by now.

We have presented two of Nietzsche's communications concerning his fundamental thought. Our interpretation of that thought has been animated by several different points of view. In the first communication it was a matter of referring to the tragic insight and the fundamentally tragic character of beings in general. In the second communication it was above all the reference to the "Moment" that prevailed, that is to say, the kind of posture in which and on the basis of which the eternal recurrence of the same is to be thought, the way in which this thinking itself is to be. By means of both references the following has become clear: the matter into which we are here inquiring, being as a whole, can never be represented as some thing at hand concerning which someone might make this or that observation. To be transposed to being as a whole is to submit to certain inalienable conditions.

To elaborate such issues until they converge in the essential contexts —we will of necessity do more and more of this as our presentation of Nietzsche's doctrine of eternal return proceeds. And we will do so in such a way that the sundry issues converge on a particular center. This is what we must ponder if we are to prevent the presentation from being misunderstood as a pointless exhibition of Nietzsche's views and opinions. If we think forward unabatedly to further contexts, then we will begin to perceive the basic traits of what will later be recognized as Nietzsche's fundamental metaphysical position.

9. The Third Communication of the Doctrine of Return

People usually take Nietzsche's *Thus Spoke Zarathustra* to be the very summit of his creative work. The writings that appeared after 1884 are taken as mere commentaries and reiterations, or as desperate attempts to realize in a direct fashion what *Zarathustra* merely intimated. We hear it said that after *Zarathustra* Nietzsche could not see his way further. Such a judgment may always safely be taken as a sign that not thinkers but their know-it-all interpreters cannot see their way further. With hopeless ineptitude the interpreters conceal their predicament behind an inflated pedantry. We leave aside the question as to whether after *Zarathustra* Nietzsche could not go farther or whether indeed he could—not because the question must remain undecided but because it is not a question one poses with regard to a thinker. For to the extent that he perdures in his thinking and inquiring the thinker is always already "farther" than he himself knows or can know. In any case the designations "farther" and "not farther" are unsuited to the matter in question; they pertain to the realm of "science" and "technology," where progress is a prerequisite and where alone "farther" and "not farther" can be reckoned. In philosophy there is no "progress," hence no regress, either. Here, as in art, the only question is whether or not it is itself. We shall now merely register the fact that the *third* communication of the thought of eternal return of the same is found in *Beyond Good and Evil*. This book, which appeared two years after the third part of *Thus Spoke Zarathustra*, also yields the motto we have chosen for our own lecture course. *Beyond Good and Evil* has as its subtitle "Prelude to A Philosophy of the Future." Curious subtitle for a philosophy that is not supposed to know whether it can see its way further!

In order for us to understand the third communication too it is decisively important that we state where and in what context it stands. The passage belongs to the third major division of *Beyond Good and Evil,* embracing numbers 45 to 62, entitled "The Quintessence of Religion." The state of affairs is growing ever more riddlesome, because Zarathustra constantly calls himself the "god-less" in his speeches and with waxing vigor announces there that "God is dead." At the very commencement of his wanderings Zarathustra encounters in the forest an old man, with whom he begins to converse. Afterwards, however, "when Zarathustra was alone he spoke thus to his heart: 'Could such a thing be possible! This old saint in his forest has as yet heard nothing of this, that *God is dead!*'" (Prologue, section 2, conclusion).

What should someone who, like Zarathustra, lives and judges on the basis of such knowledge—what should Nietzsche himself—have to adduce concerning "the quintessence of religion"? Whatever it is, we want to hear it right away, and without circumlocutions. In section 56 of the third major division, "The Quintessence of Religion," we hear the following:

Whoever as a result of some enigmatic craving has, as I have, long endeavored to think pessimism down to its depths and to redeem it from the half-Christian, half-German narrowness and simplicity in which pessimism has most recently been presented in this century, namely, in the form of Schopenhauerian philosophy; whoever has with an Asiatic and Hyperasiatic eye gazed into and down upon the most world-denying of all possible modes of thought—gazed beyond good and evil and no longer, like Buddha and Schopenhauer, under the spell and delusion of morality—; such a one has perhaps, without explicitly willing it, opened his eyes to the opposite ideal: to the ideal of the boldest, most vital, and most world-affirming human being who has not only made his peace and learned to get along with whatever was and is but who wills to have it again *precisely as it was and is* into all eternity, calling insatiably *da capo* not only to himself but to the entire play and spectacle, and not only to a spectacle but at bottom to Him who has need of precisely this spectacle—who makes it necessary because he forever has need of himself—and makes himself necessary.—How's that? Would this not be—*circulus vitiosus deus?**

Although we cannot discuss the matter more closely here, it is important to note that the entire passage is constructed as a single sentence, in such a way that its articulated divisions reflect linguistically the structure of an essential thought. Such passages enable us to imagine the sort of work that would have come into being had Nietzsche been able to complete his *magnum opus.* At first we are struck by the "content" of the section we have read. We cannot believe our eyes and ears: *"circulus vitiosus deus?" Circulus* means the circle and the ring, hence eternal recurrence, indeed as *vitiosus; vitium* means defect, malady, something destructive; *circulus vitiosus* is the ring that also necessarily brings recurrently this *vitium.* Is it *deus?* Is it the god himself, the one to whom Nietzsche at the end of his way still *calls*—is it Dionysos? And in the sphere of this god—the world? The eternal return of the same: the collective character of being as a whole?

The question raised in this same treatise (section 150) is: " . . . and everything in God's sphere turns to . . . to what? 'world' perhaps?" Are world and God thereby the same? Such a doctrine, interpreted as plain fare, is called "pantheism." Is Nietzsche here teaching a pan-theism? What does the text say? " . . . Would this not be *circulus vitiosus deus?"* Here a question is posed. If it were pantheism, we would first of all still have to ask what *pan*—the universe, the whole—and what *theos*—God—here mean. At all events, here we have *a question!* So,

---

* *Circulus vitiosus deus:* the adjective "vicious" here links "circle" and "god," forming a particularly rich speculative propostion—one that can and must be traversed forward and back via its gateway. If *est* is understood at the end, the proposition becomes "God is the vicious circle" and "The vicious circle is god." Nietzsche may well be alluding to two aspects of the tradition: first, in medieval logic and rhetoric, *circulus vitiosus* is a "circular argument"; second, in the Latin of the Humanists, *circulus vitiosus* assumes its modern sense of an unbreakable chain of pernicious causes and effects. The latter, in German, is a *Teufelskreis,* "a devil's circle." Nietzsche may therefore be linking—in his vicious circle beyond good and evil—*diabolus* and *deus.* The word *deus* is especially troublesome for the translator of German: because all nouns are capitalized in that language it is difficult to know whether Nietzsche and Heidegger in any given passage are referring to "God" or "the god." Presumably, both thinkers are enjoying the ambiguity in which monotheism and pantheism, Christianity and Paganism, Dionysos and "the Crucified" exchange masks freely.

then, God is not dead? Yes and no! Yes, he is dead. But which God? The God of "morality," the Christian God is dead—the "Father" in whom we seek sanctuary, the "Personality" with whom we negotiate and bare our hearts, the "Judge" with whom we adjudicate, the "Paymaster" from whom we receive our virtues' reward, that God with whom we "do business." Yet where is the mother who will take pay for loving her child?* The God who is viewed in terms of morality, this God alone is meant when Nietzsche says "God is dead." He died because human beings murdered him. They murdered him when they reckoned his divine grandeur in terms of their petty needs for recompense, when they cut him down to their own size. That God fell from power because he was a "blunder" of human beings who negate themselves and negate life (VIII, 62). In one of the preliminary sketches for *Zarathustra* Nietzsche writes: "God suffocated from theology; and morals from morality" (XII, 329). Well, then, God and gods can die? In a preliminary study to *The Birth of Tragedy* sketched circa 1870, quite early in his career, Nietzsche notes: "I believe in the ancient Germanic dictum, 'All gods must die.' "

Thus Nietzsche's atheism is something altogether his own. Nietzsche must be liberated from the dubious society of those supercilious atheists who deny God when they fail to find him in their reagent glass, those who replace the renounced God with their "God" of "Progress." We dare not confuse Nietzsche with such "god-less" ones, who cannot really even be "god-less" because they have never struggled to find a god, and never can. Yet if Nietzsche is no atheist in the usual sense, we dare not falsify him as a "sentimental," "romantic," halfway-Christian "God seeker." We dare not turn the word and concept *atheism* into a term of thrust and counterthrust in Christianity's duel, as though whatever did not conform to the Christian God were *ipso facto* "at bottom" atheism. The Christian God can all the less be for Nietzsche the standard of godlessness if God himself, in the designated sense, is "dead." Zarathustra calls himself and knows himself to be the god-less one. As the god-less one he experiences the uttermost

---

* Heidegger's phrase echoes that of Nietzsche in *Thus Spoke Zarathustra*, Part II, "On the Virtuous": "You love your virtue, as a mother loves her child. Yet who ever heard of a mother wanting to be paid for her love?"

need, and thereby the innermost necessity, to create what is most needed. For that reason the one who is god-less in the way we have indicated confronts a question which we might formulate succinctly as follows: What would remain for human beings to create—how could they be human at all, that is to say, how could they become who they are—if gods were always available and merely at hand? If there were gods as simply as there are stones and trees and water? Is it not the case that the god must first of all be created? Do we not require supreme force to be able to create something out beyond ourselves? And prior to that, must not man himself, the last man, the contemptible man, be re-created to that end? Does not man require a burden so that he will not take his god too lightly?

The thought of thoughts derives from these considerations its definition as the greatest burden. Thus is Zarathustra the god-less overcome! To be sure. But has Nietzsche thereby come "farther," or has he slipped back onto the path of Christianity, which laid its very foundations by claiming the sole existent God all for itself? No, neither farther ahead nor farther back. For Zarathustra *begins* by *going under.* Zarathustra's commencement is his downgoing. Another essence for Zarathustra Nietzsche never for a moment entertained. Only the lame, only those who have wearied of their Christianity, look to Nietzsche's statements for quick and easy confirmation of their own specious atheism. But the eternal recurrence of the same is the thought that is hardest to bear. Its thinker must be a hero in knowing and willing, one who dare not and cannot explain away the world and the creation of a world with some gratuitous formula. "Everything in the hero's sphere turns to tragedy." Only in passage through tragedy does the question concerning the god arise, the god in whose sphere—and *this too* only as a "perhaps"—everything turns to world.

The nineteen-year-old Nietzsche, as we have already heard, asks at the end of his autobiographical portrait, "And where is the ring that ultimately encircles him [the human being]? Is it the world? Is it God?" What is now the reply to this early question? The reply is yet another question: *"Circulus vitiosus deus?"* Yet the ring has now been defined as the eternal return of the same; the *circulus* is simultaneously *vitiosus,* the terrifying; this terrifying ring surrounds beings, determines them as a whole, defines them as the world. The ring and its eternity can be grasped solely in terms of the Moment. Accordingly, the god who is sought in the experience of the ring of fright will remain a matter of inquiry solely from within the Moment. Then, the god is only a question? Indeed, "only" a question; that is, he is the one who is asked for, the one who is called. It remains to be considered whether the god possesses more divinity in the question concerning him or in the situation where we are sure of him and are able, as it were, to brush him aside or fetch him forward, as our needs dictate. The god is "only" a question. How do matters stand with this "only"? It is not merely the god who is a question—eternal recurrence too, the *circulus vitiosus* itself, is also "only" a question.

All three communications of the thought of thoughts are *questions* that vary in configuration and in stage of development. Even if we are far from penetrating their context and content, even if we are but barely aware of these things, the fact that the communications share the interrogative form is compelling. To be sure, we can clarify the state of affairs at first only with the help of determinations that are more negative than positive. The communication is no "doctrine" and no "disquisition" in the sense of a theoretical scholarly or scientific presentation. It is not some bit of "lore" asseverated by a learned person. Nor is it a philosophical treatise of the sort we have inherited from Leibniz or Kant; just as little is it a philosophical and conceptual structure modeled on those erected by Fichte, Schelling, and Hegel. If therefore Nietzsche's communication does not seem to conform either to the framework of a scientific doctrine or to familiar philosophical discussions as they had been conducted up to Nietzsche's time, or even to the form exhibited by a purely poetic configuration, only one possibility appears to remain: it can only be a "personal act of faith," perhaps no more than an "illusory figment of the imagination." Or does the remaining possibility consist in our having to *ask* what this thought, in itself and on its own, *is* in terms of its configuration? In the face of Nietzsche's labors in thought there can no longer be any doubt about whether we are permitted to force the thought summarily into our customary and common rubrics, or whether, on the contrary, such thinking must induce *us* to jettison our common notions, induce *us* to meditate.

With this meditation we have encroached on the question of the *configuration of the thought* of eternal recurrence of the same. The encroachment is intentional. It means to suggest that Nietzsche's own mode of communication must remain definitive whenever we delineate the thought's configuration. Such a caution is all the more necessary since in relation to the question of configuration a cursory glance at Nietzsche's suppressed notes might easily lead us astray. We shall now try to gain insight into what Nietzsche thought about the eternal recurrence of the same but did not himself make public. Our examination can catch a glimpse of what is essential only if it does not remain mere reportage, only if it is interpretation. On the one hand, the interpretation must be instigated by a prior glimpse of the essential questions posed by the thought of eternal recurrence of the same; on the other hand, the interpretation must allow itself to be guided by meticulous deference toward what Nietzsche himself said.

10. The Thought of Return in the Suppressed Notes

From the moment Nietzsche's "thought of thoughts" came to him in August, 1881, everything he meditated on and committed to writing concerning that thought but shared with no one was destined to be labeled as his "literary remains." If the thought of eternal recurrence of the same is Nietzsche's principal thought, then it will have been present to him during the entire subsequent period of his creative life, from 1881 to January, 1889. That this is the case is shown by the later publication of the literary remains which originated during the years mentioned. They are to be found in volumes XII through XVI of the *Grossoktav* edition. But *if* the thought of eternal recurrence of the same, the thought of thoughts, necessarily determines all of Nietzsche's thinking from the very beginning, then his reflections on this thought and the sketches containing those reflections will vary according to the particular domain, direction, and stage of development in which Nietzsche's philosophical labors happened to be advancing. That means that these so-called "literary remains" are not always the same. Nietzsche's "posthumously published notes" do not comprise an arbitrary bunch of confused and scattered observations that by chance never made it to the printer's. The sketches differ not only in terms of content but also in their form—or lack of form. They arose out of constantly changing moods, sometimes were caught fleetingly among a melee of intentions and points of view; sometimes they were elaborated fully, sometimes ventured only by way of tentative and faltering experiment; and sometimes, quick as lightning, they arrived in one fell swoop. If the thought of eternal recurrence of the same is the thought of thoughts, then it will be least explicitly portrayed or even named wherever in its essentiality it is to have the greatest impact. If for a certain stretch of time nothing or nothing explicit appears to be said about this thought in Nietzsche's notes, that by no means indicates that it has in the meantime become unimportant or even has been abandoned. We must ponder all these things if we wish to understand Nietzsche's "posthumously published notes" and think them through philosophically, instead of merely piecing together a "theory" out of some remarks we have managed to pick up here and there.

What we are here demanding—and what we will be able to achieve only in a provisional sort of way—is all the more imperative since in the publication of the literary remains heretofore the "material" as a whole has inevitably been arranged in a particular order. Furthermore, the individual fragments on the doctrine of return, which stem from different years and from disparate manuscripts and contexts, have been thoughtlessly strung together in a numerated series. However, anyone who is even slightly aware of the difficulties entailed in finding an appropriate form of publication for Nietzsche's literary remains—especially those from the later years, that is, from 1881 onward—will not inveigh against Nietzsche's initial and subsequent editors because of the procedure they elected to follow. Whatever flaws the prior editions reveal, it remains the decisive achievement of the first editors that they made Nietzsche's private handwritten papers accessible by transcribing them into a *readable* text. Only *they* could have done it—above all, Peter Gast, who after many years of collaborating with Nietzsche in the preparation of those manuscripts that were sent on to the printer was perfectly familiar with Nietzsche's handwriting and all the transformations it underwent. Otherwise a great deal in the scarcely legible manuscripts, and often the most important things, would have remained sealed to us today.

We shall now attempt a provisional characterization of the stock of sketches that deal explicitly with the doctrine of return, considering them in their chronological sequence. Nietzsche's own threefold communication of the thought of eternal return in *The Gay Science, Thus Spoke Zarathustra,* and *Beyond Good and Evil* will mark off the periods for us. It seems plausible that Nietzsche's notes from the period when the thought first struck him (August, 1881 and immediately afterward) will assume special significance. Volume XII of the *Grossoktav* edition contains unpublished materials from the years 1881–82 and from the period 1882–86 (the *Zarathustra* period). The remarks concerning the doctrine of return from the years 1881–82 are explicitly designated as such in volume XII, pages 51–69; the remarks from the *Zarathustra* period are for the most part in volume XII, pages 369–71.* The editors avoided an overhasty interpretation by refraining from ordering this stock of observations under other rubrics (metaphysics, epistemology, ethics) and by presenting them in a separate section. Yet the first notes we know of on the doctrine of eternal return, Nietzsche's earliest and most important sketches subsequent to his experience near that boulder at Surlei, are not to be found in the text proper of volume XII. They are appended to that volume in the editors' "Concluding Report" (see the second, revised edition, third printing, pages 425–28). Some of these passages appear scattered throughout the first edition of volume XII, for example, on pages 5, 3, 4, 128, and 6; some of them do not appear at all. The fact that now in the second, revised edition the most important texts are presented in the "Concluding Report" betrays the total bewilderment of the editors. We shall have to begin with those passages that limp along behind in the appendix of the present edition—passages that are all too easily overlooked.

In addition, we must free ourselves straightaway of a prejudicial view. The editors say (XII, 425): "Right from the start two different intentions run parallel to each other; the one aims at a theoretical presentation of the doctrine, the other at a poetical treatment of it." Now, to be sure, we too have spoken of a "poetic" presentation of the doctrine of eternal return in *Zarathustra*. Yet we avoided distinguishing it from a "theoretical" presentation, not because the passages cited from *The Gay Science* and *Beyond Good and Evil* are not theoretical presentations, but because here the word and concept *theoretical* do

---

* For the notes from 1881–82 see now CM V/2; for the notes from the *Zarathustra* period (1882–86) see CM VII/1–3. The *Kritische Studienausgabe* contains these notes in volumes 9 and 10–11, respectively. On the "philological question" generally, see Mazzino Montinari's Foreword to volume 14 of the *Kritische Studienausgabe*, pp. 7–17; and section II of the Analysis at the end of this volume.

not say anything, especially not when one follows the lead of the editors and of those who portray Nietzsche's "doctrine" by equating *theoretical* with "treatment in prose." The distinction "theoretical-poetical" results from muddled thinking. Even if we were to let it obtain in general, such a distinction would in any case be out of place here. In Nietzsche's thinking of his fundamental thought the "poetical" is every bit as much "theoretical," and the "theoretical" is inherently "poetical." All philosophical thinking—and precisely the most rigorous and prosaic—is in itself poetic. It nonetheless never springs from the art of poetry. A work of poetry, a work like Hölderlin's hymns, can for its part be thoughtful in the highest degree. It is nonetheless never philosophy. Nietzsche's *Thus Spoke Zarathustra* is poetic in the highest degree, and yet it is not a work of art, but "philosophy." Because all actual, that is, all great philosophy is inherently thoughtful-poetic, the distinction between "theoretical" and "poetical" cannot be applied to philosophical texts.

11. The Four Notes Dated August 1881

We turn now to four notes on the doctrine of eternal return from August, 1881. These notes are at the same time sketches for a work, and that fact alone betrays the scope that Nietzsche assigned to the thought of eternal return of the same. In terms of time, the notes were drafted a year prior to Nietzsche's first communication of the thought in *The Gay Science;* they offer a preview of Nietzsche's whole way of treating the doctrine of return in later years. The notes also serve to corroborate Nietzsche's own words concerning *Thus Spoke Zarathustra* in *Ecce Homo,* according to which the thought of return is "the fundamental conception of the work." The first sketch reads as follows (XII, 425)*:

The Return of the Same.

Plan.

1. Incorporation of the fundamental errors.
2. Incorporation of the passions.
3. Incorporation of knowledge and of the knowledge that can renounce. (Passion of insight.)
4. The Innocent. The individual as experiment. The amelioration of life, degradation, ennervation—transition.
5. The new *burden: the eternal return of the same.* Infinite importance of our knowing, erring, our habits, ways of life, for everything to come.

What will we do with the *remnants* of our lives—we who have spent the greater part of them in the most essential uncertainty? We shall *teach the*

---

* See CM, 11 [141]. The first four points of this first sketch appear in GOA in italics, while CM has them in Roman type. I have followed CM throughout in this respect. Entry 11 [141] includes a long commentary on the fourth point, projecting a "philosophy of indifference" and identifying the "innocent" as one who is capable of "child's play."

teaching—that is the most potent means of *incorporating* it in ourselves. Our kind of beatitude, as teacher of the greatest teaching.

> Early August, 1881, in Sils-Maria, 6,000 feet above sea level and much higher above all human things!

The very fact that Nietzsche expressly records the time and occasion of the note speaks for the extraordinary nature of its content and its intent. The doctrine is grasped in terms of the teaching of it and in terms of the teacher.

The title of the "plan" points directly to the sense of the whole. And yet eternal return is mentioned only when we arrive at number five; furthermore, nothing at all is said there about its content, not even by way of vague outline. Instead, the plan's key word is "incorporation."* The doctrine is called "the greatest teaching" and "the new burden." Then comes the sudden question: "What will we do with the *remnants* of our lives?" Here, then, it is a matter of decision—and of incision—in our lives, a matter of cutting away what has prevailed hitherto, what has by now run its course, from what still "remains." Obviously, the cut is made by the thought of return, which transforms everything. However, what comes before this incision and what follows it are not divided into two separate quantities. What has gone before is not rejected. Four other points precede number five, and the fourth concludes with a reference to "transition." However novel it may be, the doctrine of eternal return does not drop out of the blue, but is yoked to a "transition." Where we initially expect an explication of the doctrine's essential import, and above all an account of its various aspects and an explanation of it, all we get here, one might say, is something about the doctrine's impact on mankind, and prior to that on the teacher himself and alone. All we get is something about the

---

* The term *Einverleibung*, which also may be rendered as "ingestion," reflects Nietzsche's preoccupation in the summer of 1881 with the natural sciences and especially the science of physiology. He had been studying Wilhelm Roux, *The Struggle of Parts in the Organism: A Contribution to the Perfection of the Doctrine of Mechanistic Teleology* (Leipzig, 1881), so that these earliest notes on eternal recurrence appear in the often bizarre context of *l'homme machine*. The term also appears twice in 11 [134] and once in 11 [182], notes which W. Müller-Lauter has traced to Roux. See Müller-Lauter, "Wilhelm Roux's Influence on Friedrich Nietzsche," *Nietzsche-Studien*, VII (1978), 189–223.

"incorporation" of new knowledge and the teaching of such knowledge as a new kind of beatitude. We know from *Thus Spoke Zarathustra* how essential the question of the "incorporation" of the thought is; we know that Zarathustra first becomes a convalescent after he has incorporated the weightiest elements of the thought. If we pursue the meaning of this word we arrive at the notion of "eating," of devouring and digesting. Whatever is incorporated makes the body—and our embodiment—steadfast and secure. It is also something we have finished with and which determines us in the future. It is the juice that feeds our energies. To incorporate the thought here means to think the thought in such a way that right from the start it becomes our fundamental stance toward beings as a whole, pervading every single thought as such and from the outset. Only when the thought has become the basic posture of our thinking as a whole has it been appropriated—and taken into the body—as its essence demands.

The definitive meditation on the project entitled "the return of the same" advances directly to "incorporation." The peculiar nature of this first plan remains important. We have no "schema" into which we might pigeonhole this "project" and so make it familiar to us; we must be on the lookout for the project itself, for whatever pertains to it, for its own schema. If this were the plan for a projected book, then the book would have been something altogether its own, not only with regard to its content but also in the way it would have "appeared" as a book and then "had an impact" or "made no impact." Whatever is taught there, whatever is thought in the thought, recedes before the *way* it is taught and thought. The plan sketched here is nothing other than the germ of the plan for the coming work, *Thus Spoke Zarathustra,* hence not a sketch toward a "theoretical," prosaic elaboration of the thought of return. Even this much enables us to see how vacuous the distinction discussed earlier is.

The second plan that is relevant here is as "prosaic" as it is "poetical." It bears no title and does not pertain to the project that is presented first in the *Grossoktav* edition. Among Nietzsche's notes it does not stand together with the first plan, but is presented as fragment number 129 in volume XII.* It reads:

---

* Heidegger presents the second note in two phases, first the opening paragraph, then the four points of the plan itself, listed below. See CM, 11 [144].

It would be a dreadful thing if we were still to believe in *sin:* but no matter what we do, if we repeat it countless times it is *innocent.* If the thought of the eternal return of all things does not overwhelm you, that is no one's fault; and it is not to its credit if it does do so. —We judge our predecessors more gently than they themselves judged: we regret the errors they incorporated, not their wickedness.

The passage enlightens us as to why in point four of the first project "the innocent" is mentioned. With the death of the moral God, the sinners and the guilty parties vanish from being as a whole, and the necessity of being—as it is—assumes its prerogative.

The second plan proceeds now to reverse the sequence of the principal thoughts, inasmuch as it begins with the thought of return. It runs (XII, 426):

1. *The mightiest insight.*
2. Opinions and errors transform mankind and grant it its drives, or: *the incorporated errors.*
3. *Necessity and innocence.*
4. *The play of life.*

This plan also provides directives in some other respects: "necessity" does not refer to any arbitrary kind of necessity but to that of being as a whole. "The play of life" reminds us immediately of a fragment of Heraclitus, the thinker to whom Nietzsche *believed* he was most closely akin, that is to say, fragment 52: *Aiōn pais esti paidzōn, pesseuōn; paidos hē basilēiē.* "The aeon is a child at play, playing at draughts; dominion is the child's" (that is to say, dominion over being as a whole).

The suggestion is that innocence pervades being as a whole. The whole is *aiōn,* a word that can scarcely be translated in an adequate way. It means the whole of the world, but also time, and, related by time to our "life," it means the course of life itself. We are accustomed to defining the meaning of *aiōn* thus: "Aeon" suggests the "time" of the "cosmos," that is, of nature, which operates in the time which physics measures. One distinguishes time in this sense from the time we "live through." Yet what is named in *aiōn* resists such a distinction. At the same time, we are thinking of *kosmos* too cursorily when we represent it cosmologically.

Nietzsche's use of the word *life* is ambiguous. It designates being as a whole and also the way in which we are "caught up in the melee" of the whole. The talk of "play" is correspondingly equivocal. *

The intimations in the direction of Heraclitus are not fortuitous, especially since Nietzsche in his notes of this period often touches on another thought which one customarily—and Nietzsche too follows custom here—designates as Heraclitus' principal thought: *panta rhei* ["everything flows"]. But this is a statement which for all we know does not even stem from Heraclitus. Far from characterizing his thought, it distorts his thought beyond recognition.

The second plan for the thought of eternal return which we have adduced here does not think primarily about the "impact" of the doctrine on mankind or on the transformation of human "existence" within being as a whole. Rather, it thinks about being as a whole itself. Here it is more a question of catching a glimpse of the "metaphysical" character of the doctrine of return, whereas in the prior plan the doctrine's "existentiell"† sense preponderated—if we may employ these designations that are still common today. Or does the distinction between "metaphysical" and "existentiell," if it is a clear and viable distinction at all, have as little to do with Nietzsche's philosophy as that other one which tried to distinguish between its theoretical-prosaic and its poetical character? We will be able to decide this question only later.

The plan projected next seems to assume yet another shape.‡ Of it the editors assert that it is "the sketch for the poetical idea" of the doctrine of return:

Midday and Eternity
Pointers Toward a New Life

Zarathustra, born on Lake Urmi, left his home during his thirtieth year, went to the province of Aria, and in the ten years of his mountain solitude composed the *Zend-Avesta*.

---

* Heidegger here adds a parenthetical reference to Nietzsche's poem "To Goethe," the first of the "Songs of the Outlaw Prince," published as an appendix to the second edition of *The Gay Science* in 1887. He also draws attention to NII, 380f., where that poem is presented and discussed. See Volume IV, *Nihilism*, pp. 235–37.

† On *existentiell*, as opposed to *existenzial*, see Martin Heidegger, *Basic Writings* (New York: Harper & Row, 1977), p. 55 n.

‡ See CM, 11 [195–96].

> Once again the sun of insight stands at midday: and coiled in its light lies the serpent of eternity—it is *your* time, ye brothers of noon!

The key word in this plan is *midday*. "Midday and Eternity": both are concepts and names for time—provided we are aware of the fact that we think eternity too solely in terms of time. Now that the thought of eternal return is thought, it *is* "midday and eternity" at one and the same time; we could also say that it is the Moment. Nietzsche's project chooses the highest determinations of time as the title of a work that is to treat of being as a whole and of the new life within such being. The way being as a whole is thought is also indicated by the imagery: the serpent, the most discerning animal, "the serpent of eternity," lies coiled in the midday sunlight of insight. A magnificent image—and it is not meant to be "poetical"! It is poetized, but only because it is *thought,* and thought most deeply. And it is thought *thus,* because the project in which being as a whole is to be grasped and elevated to knowledge here ventures farthest—not into the vacuous, tenebrous space of idle "speculation," but into the domain at the midpoint of humanity's path. Concerning the time of midday, when the sun stands at its zenith and things cast no shadow, the following is said at the conclusion of Part One of *Thus Spoke Zarathustra:*

> And that is the great midday when man stands at the midpoint of his path between beast and overman, when he celebrates his way to evening as his supreme hope: for it is the way to a new morning.
>
> There and then the one who goes under will bless himself for being one who goes over in transition; and the sun of his insight will stand for him at midday.
>
> *"All gods are dead: now we will that the overman live"*—at some great midday, let this be our ultimate will!—
>
> Thus spoke Zarathustra.

When Zarathustra here says, *"All gods are dead,"* what he means is that contemporary man, the Last Man, is no longer strong enough for any one of the gods, especially since these can never simply be inherited from tradition. A tradition takes shape as a power of Dasein only where it is sustained by the *creative* will, and only as long as it is so sustained.

Midday is a luminous midpoint in the history of humanity, a moment of transition in the cheering light of eternity, when the sky is deep and fore-noon and after-noon, past and future, confront one another and thus come to decision. Indeed, the subtitle of the plan "Midday and Eternity" reads "Pointers toward a New Life." We might expect directives on how to achieve practical wisdom in our lives; but if we do so we will surely be deceived. For the "new life" meant here is a new way of standing in the midst of beings as a whole; it is a new kind of truth and thereby a metamorphosis of beings.

That we must understand the "new life" in this fashion is shown by a fourth projected plan which also stems from August, 1881.* It bears the title, "On the 'Projection of a New Way to Live,'" and is divided into four books. Here we will list only the characteristic titles of the four books:

I. On the Dehumanization of Nature.
II. On the Incorporation of Experiences.
III. On the Ultimate Happiness of the Lonely One.
IV. *Annulus aeternitatis.*

Books I and IV embrace II and III, which are to treat of humanity. Book I is to execute the dehumanization of nature. This implies that all the anthropomorphisms projected into being as a whole, such as guilt, purpose, intention, and providence, are to be expunged from nature, in order that man himself may be restored to nature (as *homo natura*). Such being as a whole is defined in Book IV as the "ring of eternity."

What is striking about these four projected plans, all of them drawn up in a little less than a month, and what we can now grasp only in an approximate way, is the wealth of prospects offered by a few essential regions of inquiry, to which Nietzsche appeals again and again. This wealth of prospects constantly compels Nietzsche to introduce new sides of the question into the scope of his project. All this allows us to speculate that with the first unfolding of the thought of eternal return of the same—as with all great thoughts—everything essential was there already at daybreak, so to speak, although not yet in a developed form.

---

* See CM, 11 [197], dated Sils-Maria, August 26, 1881. Heidegger presents only the titles of the four books, omitting what one might call Nietzsche's "stage directions" or stylistic intentions for each book.

Wherever Nietzsche attempts an elaboration, he operates at first with the already available means, derived from the prior interpretation of beings. If there is something like catastrophe in the creative work of great thinkers, then it consists not in being stymied and in failing to go farther, but precisely in advancing farther—that is to say, in their letting themselves be determined by the initial impact of their thought, an impact that always deflects them. Such going "farther" is always fatal, for it prevents one from abiding by the source of one's own commencement. The history of Western philosophy will have to be assimilated in times to come with the help of this way of looking at things. The result could be some very remarkable and very instructive insights.

Yet if everything is there for Nietzsche in the summer of 1881, so far as his thought of thoughts is concerned, will the subsequent years bring anything new? That is a question that curiosity-seekers might pose. The principal quality of the curious is reflected in the fact that whatever they are curious about ultimately and even from the outset means absolutely nothing to them. All curiosity thrives on this essential indifference. But the curious among us will be disappointed. Nietzsche ultimately produces nothing "new." He gets bogged down—or so it seems—and wearies of his greatest thought. Or is the reverse the case? Did Nietzsche remain so faithful to his thought that he had to suffer shipwreck as a result of it—quite apart from what medical science is able to determine concerning his insanity?

We ask a different sort of question—not whether anything new eventuates, but whether and in what way the very first, the "old" matters are developed and assimilated. And perhaps the most important thing in all this is not what we subsequently find as explicit observations and sketches of the doctrine of return but the new clarity that radiates in Nietzsche's questioning as a whole and brings his thinking to new plateaus. Although some commentators have tried recently to convince us that Nietzsche's doctrine of return was later dislodged and swept aside by his doctrine of will to power, we would reply by demonstrating that the doctrine of will to power springs from nowhere else than eternal return, carrying the mark of its origin always with it, as the stream its source.

12. Summary Presentation of the Thought: Being as a Whole as Life and Force; the World as Chaos

The four plans succeed in casting light on the three communications published by Nietzsche himself. Not only that. In them we catch sight of certain landmarks that will help us find our way through the entire stock of notes we are about to refer to.

The first group (XII, 51–69) derives from the period immediately subsequent to August, 1881, up to the publication of *The Gay Science* a year later. The editors have divided the lot into two sections, the first (51–63) entitled *"Presentation and Grounding of the Doctrine,"* the second (63–69) entitled *"Impact of the Doctrine on Humanity."* This division of the notes is based on criteria that do *not* stem from Nietzsche himself.* By means of this procedure of supplying titles, a procedure that ostensibly shuns every form of manipulation, the doctrine of return is stamped in advance as a "theory," which in addition is said to have "practical effects." Such a division of the stock of notes does not allow what is essential in the doctrine of return to assert itself, even in the form of a question. What is essential is the fact that it is neither a "theory" nor a piece of practical wisdom for our lives. The apparently harmless and well-nigh obvious division of the materials has contributed principally to the miscomprehension of the doctrine of return. The misinterpretation of the thought of return as a

---

* However, to be fair, one should note that the editors were doubtless following the "plan" taken up as aphorism number 1057 in *The Will to Power*. The four-point plan from winter 1883–84 (CM, Mp XVII 16 [4]) employs such turns of phrase as "presentation of the doctrine," "its *theoretical* presuppositions," and "presumable consequences."

"theory" with practical consequences seemed all the more plausible inasmuch as Nietzsche's notes, which are said to provide a "presentation and grounding," speak the language of the natural sciences. Indeed, Nietzsche reverts to the scientific writings of his era in physics, chemistry, and biology; and in letters written during these years he speaks of plans to study mathematics and the natural sciences at one of the major universities. All this demonstrates quite clearly that Nietzsche himself also pursued a "scientific side" to the doctrine of return. At all events, the appearances speak for that fact. The question, of course, is whether appearances, even when they are conjured by Nietzsche himself, dare serve as a standard of measure for interpreting the thought of thoughts in his philosophy. Such a question becomes unavoidable the moment we have grasped Nietzsche's philosophy and our confrontation with it—this is to say, with all of Western philosophy—as a matter for this century and the century to come.

So far as the division of fragments is concerned, we shall in our provisional characterization deliberately follow the lead of the available edition, even though that division is dubious. Perhaps in this way we will most readily perceive that in these fragments it is not a question of "natural science" that is being treated. The context of the particular fragments is by no means immediately evident. Above all, we must be aware of the fact that the sequence of notes numbered 90 through 132, as we encounter them in the available edition, is nowhere to be found as such in Nietzsche; these fragments, which the edition strings together, are to be found in the manuscript bearing the catalogue number M III 1, but in altogether disparate places. For example, number 92 appears on page 40 of the manuscript, number 95 on page 124, number 96 on page 41; number 105 appears on page 130, number 106 on pages 130 and 128, number 109 on page 37; number 116 appears on page 33, while number 122 is on page 140. Thus even in the sequential ordering of the fragments the editors—surely without intending to do so—have misled us.

We shall try to avoid being misled. Nevertheless, Nietzsche's manuscript offers no secure guidelines. Such a guideline can be found only in an understanding of the collective content of the whole. We shall try to set in relief the principal thought contained in the fragments that are pieced together here. What is most important in this regard is that we make clear *what* Nietzsche generally has in view and the *way* it stands in view. We could perform such a task with thoroughness only if we analyzed meticulously every single fragment. This lecture course is not the place for such a task. However, in order to be able to follow Nietzsche's lead, to move in the direction he is headed, in order to have present to our minds that principal, intrinsic node of questions on the basis of which Nietzsche speaks in these individual fragments, we elect to go the way of a summary presentation. This way too is exposed to the charge of arbitrariness. For *we* are the ones who are outlining it, and the question remains: From what sort of preview does our projected outline originate, how comprehensive is the inquiry from which that outline arises? The essential import of our summary presentation may be articulated in ten points; we shall also have to make clear the way in which they cohere.

1. *What stands in view?* We reply: *The world in its collective character.* What all pertains to that? The whole of inanimate and animate existence, whereby "animate" encompasses not only plants and animals but human beings as well. Inanimate and animate things are not juxtaposed as two separate regions. Nor are they laminated one on top of the other. Rather, they are represented as interwoven in one vast nexus of Becoming. Is the unity of that nexus "living" or "lifeless"? Nietzsche writes (XII, number 112): "Our whole world is the *ashes* of countless *living* creatures: and even if the animate seems so miniscule in comparison to the whole, it is nonetheless the case that *everything* has already been transposed into life—and so it goes." Apparently opposed to this is a thought expressed in *The Gay Science* (number 109): "Let us guard against saying that death is the opposite of life; the living creature is simply a kind of dead creature, and a very rare kind." In these passages lies the suggestion that in terms of quantity the living creature is something slight, in terms of its occurrence something rare, when we cast a glance toward the whole. Yet this rare and slight something remains forever the firebrand that yields an enormous quantity of ashes. Accordingly, one would have to say that what is dead constitutes a kind of living existence, and not at all the reverse. At the same time, however, the reverse also holds, inasmuch as what is dead comes from

the animate and in its preponderance continues to condition the animate. Thus the animate is only a kind of metamorphosis and creative force of life, and death is an intermediate state. To be sure, such an interpretation does not capture perfectly Nietzsche's thought during this period. Furthermore, a contradiction obtains between these two thoughts, which we can formulate as follows: What is dead is the ashes of countless living creatures; *and* life is merely a kind of death. In the first case, the living determines the provenance of the dead; in the second, the dead determines the manner of life of the living. The dead takes preeminence in the second, whereas in the first it becomes subordinate to the living.*

Perhaps two different views of the dead are in play here. If that is the case, then the very possibility of contradiction becomes superfluous. If the dead is taken with a view to its knowability, and if knowing is conceived as a firm grasp on what is permanent, identifiable, and unequivocal, then the dead assumes preeminence as an object of knowledge, whereas the animate, being equivocal and ambiguous, is only a kind—and a subordinate kind—of the dead. If, on the contrary, the dead itself is thought in terms of its provenance, then it is but the ashes of what is alive. The fact that the living remains subordinate to the dead in quantitative terms and in terms of preponderance does not refute the fact that it is the origin of the dead, especially since it is proper to the essence of what is higher that it remain rare, less common. From all this we discern one decisive point: by setting the lifeless in relief against the living, along the guidelines of any single aspect, we do not do justice to the state of affairs—the world is more enigmatic than our calculating intellect would like to admit. (On the preeminence of the dead, cf. XII, number 495 and ff., especially number 497).†

---

* A reminder that "the dead," *das Tote*, is not to be read as a plural, in the sense of Gogol's *Dead Souls*. The nominalized neuter singular adjective refers to the whole of inanimate nature, to the "billiard ball universe" of classical mechanics. Hence the connection with knowledge *(Erkenntnis)*, to which Heidegger draws attention in what follows.

† GOA, XII, numbers 495 ff. stress the *anorganic* basis of human life. The fragment to which Heidegger draws special attention, number 497, begins: "Fundamentally false evaluation in the world of *sensation* with regard to what is *dead*. Because that is what *we*

2. What is the *pervasive character* of the world? The answer is: *"force."* What is force? Nobody would presume to say straightforwardly and with an air of finality what "force" is. Just this one point can and must be made here at the start: Nietzsche does not—and cannot—conceive of "force" in the way that physics does. Physics, whether mechanistic or dynamic in style, thinks the concept of force always and everywhere as a quantitative specification within an equation; physics as such, in the way it takes up nature into its representational framework, can never think force as force. Given its frame of reference, physics always deals with sheer relations of force with a view to the magnitude of their spatio-temporal appearance. The moment physics conducts nature into the domain of the "experiment," it co-posits in advance the calculative, technical relation (in the broader sense) between sheer magnitudes of force and effects of force, and with calculation it co-posits rationality. A physics that is to be technically useful and yet would also like to be irrational is nonsense. What Nietzsche designates and means by the term "force" is not what physics means by it. If one wished to call Nietzsche's interpretation of beings "dynamic," inasmuch as the Greek word for force is *dynamis,* one would of course also have to say what that Greek word means; in any case, it does not mean the "dynamic" as opposed to the "static," a distinction that stems from a mode of thought which at bottom remains mechanistic. It is not fortuitous that "dynamics" and "statics" are names of two physical-technical domains of thought. *

---

are! We *belong* to it!" Inasmuch as the world of sensation is one of pain, superficiality, and falsehood, the "dead" world promises a veritable feast to the intellect. The note concludes:

> Let us see through this comedy [of sensation], so that we can *enjoy* it. Let us *not* conceive of the return to what lacks sensation as a regression! We shall become altogether *true;* we will perfect ourselves! *Death* is to be *reinterpreted!* Thus we *reconcile* ourselves to the real, that is, the dead world.

In CM see M III 1 [70].

* This paragraph reflects Heidegger's early interest in physics and mathematics—an interest that perdured up to the time of the Nietzsche lectures. For example, in his 1935–36 lecture course Heidegger devoted considerable time to the notion of force in Newtonian physics. See Martin Heidegger, *Die Frage nach dem Ding* (Tübingen: M. Niemeyer, 1962), esp. pp. 66–69; English translation in Martin Heidegger, *Basic Writings,* pp. 262–66. In his inaugural lecture of 1915 at the University of Freiburg, "The

Whoever transposes the representational modes of "dynamics" and "statics" to being as a whole only introduces measureless confusion into thought. Because Nietzsche was everywhere sure of the fundamental aims of his intellectual life—however much his utterances and formulations inevitably remained impacted in contemporary entanglements—our thinking requires a kind of rigor that far surpasses the precision of the mathematical and natural sciences, not only in degree but in essence, whenever it tries to follow Nietzsche's thought. What Nietzsche calls "force" becomes clear to him in later years as "will to power."

3. *Is force limited or boundless? It is limited.* Why? Nietzsche ascertains the reason in the very essence of force; it is the essence of force to be finite. Presupposing that force is "infinitely *waxing*" (XII, number 93), on what should it "feed"? Because force is always expended, without thereby dwindling to nothing, it must be nourished by some sort of surplus. What might the source of such a surplus be? "We insist that the world as force dare not be thought of as being unbounded—we forbid ourselves the notion of an infinite force as incompatible with the very concept 'force' " (XII, number 94). Does Nietzsche then simply decree his conception of the essential finitude of force as such? He also calls this proposition a "belief" (ibid.; cf. WM, 1065). On what is "belief" in the essential finitude of force founded? Nietzsche says that infinitude is "incompatible with the very concept 'force'." This means that "force" is in essence something determinate, something firmly defined in itself; hence it is necessarily and inherently limited. "Anything *ill*-defined about force, anything undulating, is *altogether un-thinkable for us*" (XII, number 104). This implies that the asserted essential finitude of force is not some sort of blind "belief" in the sense of a groundless supposition. It is rather a taking-for-true on the basis of the truth of knowledge concerning the correct concept of force, that is

---

Concept of Time in Historiography," Heidegger treated questions of "dynamics" in modern physics. See Martin Heidegger, *Frühe Schriften* (Frankfurt am Main: V. Klostermann, 1972), pp. 360–63. Finally, for corroboration of Heidegger's identification of *Rationalität* with calculation *(Rechnen)* in post-Galilean physics, see Thomas Hobbes, *Leviathan*, I, 4–5, which equates *ratiocinatio* with accounting and defines "Reason" as "nothing but reckoning."

to say, on the basis of its thinkability. Yet Nietzsche neither says nor asks what kind of thinking it is that thinks the essential concept; nor does he say or ask whether and in what way thought and thinkability may serve as the court of jurisdiction for the essence of beings. But perhaps he does not need to ask such a thing, seeing that all philosophy prior to him never asked such things, either. Of course, this is more an excuse than a justification. Yet at present it is a matter of setting our sights on Nietzsche's thought.

4. What results as an intrinsic consequence of the essential finitude of force? Because force, which is essentially finite, is the essence of the world, *the totality of the world itself remains finite,* indeed in the sense of a firm confinement within boundaries, a confinement that derives from being as such. The finitude of the world does not consist in colliding against something else which the world is not and which would function as an obstacle to it. Finitude emerges from the world itself. Cosmic force suffers no diminution or augmentation. "The amount of universal force is *determinate,* nothing 'infinite': let us guard against such extravagant interpretations of the concept" (XII, number 90).

5. Does not the finitude of being as a whole imply a limitation of its durability and duration? The lack of diminution and accretion in universal force signifies not a "standstill" (XII, number 100) but a perpetual "Becoming." There is no equilibrium of force. "Had an equilibrium of force been achieved at any time, it would have lasted up to now: hence it never entered on the scene" (XII, number 103). We must grasp "Becoming" here quite generally in the sense of transformation or—still more cautiously—change. In this sense passing away is also a becoming. "Becoming" here does not suggest genesis, much less development and progress.

6. From the finitude of the world we necessarily conclude to its surveyability. In reality, however, being as a whole is not surveyable; hence it is "infinite." How does Nietzsche define the relationship of essential finitude with such infinitude? We must pay special heed to Nietzsche's response to this question, since he often speaks of the "infinite" world when he is expressing his thoughts in less rigorous fashion, thus appearing to reject his fundamental assertion concerning the es-

sential finitude of the world. Precisely because the world is perpetual Becoming, and because as a totality of force it is nonetheless inherently finite, it produces "infinite" effects. The infinitude of effects and appearances does not controvert the essential finitude of beings. "Infinite" here means as much as "endless" in the sense of "immeasurable," that is to say, virtually innumerable. "The number of positions, alterations, combinations and concatenations of this force [is], to be sure, quite enormous and in practical terms *'immeasurable,'* but in any case it is still determinate and not infinite" (XII, number 90). When therefore Nietzsche elsewhere (XII, number 97) rejects the possibility of an "innumerable quantity of states," thus asserting their countability, what he means is that the determinate cosmic force "has only a 'number' of possible properties" (XII, number 92). The impossibility of such an innumerable quantity is by no means incompatible with its actual uncountability in practice.

7. Where is this cosmic force as finite world? In what space? Is it in space at all? What is space? The supposition of an "infinite space" is according to Nietzsche "false" (XII, number 97). Space is bounded and as bounded is merely a "subjective form," in the same way as is the notion of "matter": "Space first emerged by virtue of the supposition of an *empty space.* There is no such thing. All is force" (XII, number 98). Space is therefore an imaginary, imaginative bit of imagery, formed by force and the relations of force *themselves.* Which forces and relations of force it is that instigate the formation of space, that is to say, the self-formation of a representation of space, and *how* they do so, Nietzsche does not say. The assertion that space "first emerged by virtue of the supposition of an *empty space"* sounds dubious, inasmuch as space is already represented in the notion of "empty space," so that the former cannot suitably be said to originate from the latter. Nevertheless, with this remark Nietzsche is on the trail of an essential nexus, one that he never thought through, however, and never mastered. That is the fundamental phenomenon of the *void,* which of course does not necessarily have to do merely with space, or with time either, insofar as time is thought in accord with the traditional concept. In contrast, the essence of Being could include the *void.* We simply hint at the matter here, in order to show that in spite of its

initial apparent lack of sense Nietzsche's remark on the genesis of space may make sense, presupposing that space is engendered by the essence of world. *

8. How is all this bound up with time, which is usually designated together with space? In contrast to the imaginary character of space, *time* is *actual*. It is also—in contrast to the bounded character of space —unbounded, infinite. "But, of course, the time in which the universe exercises its force is infinite; that is, force is eternally the same and eternally active" (XII, number 90). In note number 103 Nietzsche speaks of "the course of infinite time." We are already familiar with the image employed in note 114, "the eternal hourglass of existence."† About the time this note on eternal return was written, Nietzsche says pointedly, "To the actual course of things an *actual* time must also correspond" (XII, number 59). Such actual, infinite time Nietzsche grasps as *eternity*. Viewed as a whole, Nietzsche's meditations on space and time are quite meager. The few thoughts concerning time that inch beyond traditional notions are desultory—the most reliable proof of the fact that the question concerning time, as a means of unfolding the guiding question of metaphysics, and the guiding question itself in its more profound origin remained closed to him. In the earlier, immensely important essay, "On Truth and Lie in an Extra-Moral Sense" (summer 1873), Nietzsche, still perfectly in tune with Schopenhauer, writes that we "produce" representations of space and time "in us and out of us with the necessity of a spider spinning its web" (X, 202). Time too is represented subjectively and is even defined "as a property of space" (WM, 862).

9. We must now conjoin in thought all these designations of the world which we have merely listed—force, finitude, perpetual Becoming, the innumerability of appearances, the bounded character of

---

* *Die Entstehung des Raumes . . . gesetzt, dass der Raum aus dem Wesen von Welt ent-steht.* In modern German *entstehen* means "to become, originate." But from the Middle Ages through the epoch of Goethe and Schiller the word meant literally the negation of "to stand," hence, "to withdraw, be missing." Heidegger here apparently wishes to think the origins of empty space in terms reminiscent of *Ent-fernung*, "un-distancing," that is to say, nearing or approaching, as analyzed in *Being and Time*, section 23.

† See *The Gay Science*, number 341, discussed in section 3, above.

space, and the infinity of time—and refer them back to the major determination by which Nietzsche defines the "collective character of the world." With that major determination we will attain solid footing for our concluding interpretation of the world, to be established in the tenth and final section of our present discussion. Here we will refer to a statement by Nietzsche found in the important and roughly contemporaneous passage numbered 109 in *The Gay Science:* "The collective character of the world is, on the contrary, to all eternity—chaos."

The fundamental representation of being as a whole as chaos, a notion that guided Nietzsche even before the doctrine of return took shape, has dual significance. In the first place, it aims to capture the guiding representation of perpetual Becoming in the sense of the customary notion of *panta rhei,* the eternal flux of all things, which Nietzsche too, along with the tradition in general, falsely took to be a kind of notion such as Heraclitus might have had. We do better to call the notion pseudo-Heraclitean. In the second place, the guiding representation *chaos* is to allow matters to stand with perpetual Becoming, not deriving it as a "many" out of "one," whether the "one" be represented as creator or demiurge, as spirit or prime matter. *Chaos* is accordingly a name for that representation of being as a whole which posits being as a manifold of necessitous Becoming, and in such a way that "unity" and "form" are excluded *ab initio.* The exclusion often seems to be the major determination of the representation of chaos, insofar as the exclusion is to be applied to everything that in any way tends to introduce anthropomorphisms into the world totality.

Although Nietzsche distinguishes his concept of chaos from the notion of a fortuitous and arbitrary jumble, a sort of universal cosmic porridge, he nonetheless fails to liberate himself from the transmitted sense of chaos as something that lacks order and lawfulness. Here the guiding experience, along with a number of essential guiding concepts, are already in eclipse. Chaos, *khaos, khainō* means "to yawn"; it signifies something that opens wide or gapes. We conceive of *khaos* in most intimate connection with an original interpretation of the essence of *alētheia* as the self-opening abyss (cf. Hesiod, *Theogony*).* For

---

* Hesiod, born at the beginning of the eighth century, B.C. in Boeotia, traces in his *Theogony* the genealogy of the Greek gods and titans. Line 116 of his poem begins:

Nietzsche the representation of the totality of the world as "chaos" is to engineer a defense against the "humanization" of being as a whole. Humanization includes both the moral explanation of the world as the result of a creator's resolve and the technical explanation pertaining to it which appeals to the actions of some grand craftsman (the demiurge). But humanization also extends to every imposition of order, articulation, beauty, and wisdom on the "world." These are all results of the "human aesthetic habit." It is also a humanization when we ascribe "reason" to beings and aver that the world proceeds rationally, as Hegel does in a statement which, to be sure, says a great deal more than what common sense is able to glean from it: *"Whatever is rational, is real; and whatever is real, is rational."* (From the Preface to Hegel's *Foundations of the Philosophy of Right.* *) Yet even when we posit irrationality as the principle of the cosmos, that too is a humanization. Equally unacceptable is the notion that a drive to self-preservation inheres in being: "To attribute a feeling of self-preservation to Being [meant is being as a whole] is madness! Ascribing the 'strife of pleasure and revulsion' to atoms!" (XII, number 101). Also the notion that beings proceed according to "laws" is a moralistic-juridical mode of thought, and hence is equally anthropomorphic. Nor are there in beings any "goals" or "purposes" or "intentions"; and if there are no purposes, then purposelessness and "accident" as well are excluded.

Ē toi men protista Khaos genet', "And in the very beginning Chaos came to be." The gap of Chaos is usually interpreted as resulting from the separation of earth and sky—even though both Gaia and Ouranos are explicitly said to emerge *after* Chaos came to be. The confusion is intensified by Hesiod's use of the verb to *become*, rather than any form of *to be*. For Hesiod, differentiation seems to come to be prior to all and sundry beings; its very *genesis* suggests that differentiation is prior. Yet such priority is given no name. For a presentation of the basic sources, see G. S. Kirk and J. E. Raven, *The Presocratic Philosophers: A Critical History with a Selection of Texts* (Cambridge, England: Cambridge University Press, 1966), pp. 24–37. I know of no detailed discussion of Hesiod in Heidegger's works, but suggest that *khaos* might be interpreted along the lines of the Timaean *khōra*, the "receptacle" of "space," namely, as the open region in which all beings can first appear and be in being, in *Einführung in die Metaphysik* (Tübingen: M. Niemeyer, 1953), pp. 50–51. See Martin Heidegger, *An Introduction to Metaphysics*, tr. Ralph Manheim (New York: Doubleday Anchor, 1961), pp. 53–54.

* See G. W. F. Hegel, *Werke in zwanzig Bänden*, Theorie-Werkausgabe (Frankfurt am Main: Suhrkamp, 1970), *7*, 24.

Let us guard against believing that the universe displays a tendency to achieve certain *forms,* that it wants to become more beautiful, more perfect, more complex! All of that is humanization! Anarchy, deformity, form—these concepts are irrelevant. For mechanics, nothing is imperfect. (XII, 111)

Finally, the notion of the collective character of the world as an "organism" is out of the question, not only because it is a special case that dare not be taken to represent the whole, and not only because human notions about what an organism is are modeled on human beings themselves, but above all because an organism always necessarily requires something other than itself, something outside itself, for sustenance and nourishment. Yet what could subsist outside the world as a whole, understood as "organism"? "The supposition that the universe is an organism is belied by the *essence of the organic"* (XII, number 93; *The Gay Science,* number 109).

How essential it is for Nietzsche to bar these humanizations from his projection of being as a whole, and how absolutely determinative the guiding notion of the world as chaos remains for him, is betrayed most clearly by the phrase that recurs again and again even when he is discussing the doctrine of return: "let us guard against," that is to say, let us shield ourselves from the tendency to project any fortuitous notion about ourselves, any human capacity, onto beings. Indeed, the crucial passage from *The Gay Science* which contains the statement concerning the collective character of the world as chaos (number 109) bears the explicit title "Let us be on guard!" Inasmuch as these humanizations for the most part simultaneously involve notions in which a cosmic ground—in the sense of a moral Creator-God—is represented, the humanization proceeds in tandem with a deification. Accordingly, the notions that suggest some sort of wisdom in the world's process, some sort of "providence" in real events, are but *"shades"* which the Christian interpretation of the world leaves behind to haunt beings and our grasp of them, when actual faith has vanished. To turn matters around, then, the dehumanizing of beings—keeping that which rises of itself, *physis, natura,* "nature" clear of human admixtures of every kind—amounts to a de-deification of beings. With a view to this interconnection, passage 109 of *The Gay Science* thus concludes:

When will all these shades of God cease to darken our paths? When will we have a nature that is altogether undeified! When will we human beings be allowed to begin to *naturalize* ourselves by means of the pure, newly discovered, newly redeemed nature?

To be sure, elsewhere we read: "To 'humanize' the world, that is to say, to feel ourselves increasingly as masters in it—" (WM, 614; cf. WM, 616). Yet we would lapse into terrible error if we were to label Nietzsche's guiding representation of the world as chaos with cheap slogans like "naturalism" and "materialism," especially if we were to think that such labels explained his notion once and for all. "Matter" (that is, tracing everything back to some elemental "stuff") is as much an error as "the god of the Eleatics" (that is, tracing it back to something immaterial).* The most fundamental point to be made about Nietzsche's notion of chaos is the following: only a thinking that is utterly lacking in stamina will deduce a will to godlessness from the will to a de-deification of beings. On the contrary, truly metaphysical thinking, at the outermost point of de-deification, allowing itself no subterfuge and eschewing all mystification, will uncover that path on which alone gods will be encountered—if they are to be encountered ever again in the history of mankind.

Meanwhile we want to heed the fact that at the time when the thought of eternal return of the same arises Nietzsche is striving most decisively in his thought to dehumanize and de-deify being as a whole. His striving is not a mere echo, as one might suppose, of an ostensible "positivistic period" now in abeyance. It has its own, more profound origin. Only in this way is it possible for Nietzsche to be driven directly from such striving to its apparently incongruous opposite, when in his doctrine of will to power he demands the supreme humanization of beings.

In Nietzsche's usage, the word *chaos* indicates a defensive notion in consequence of which nothing can be asserted of being as a whole. Thus the world as a whole becomes something we fundamentally can-

---

* *The Gay Science,* number 109, explicitly refers to "matter" and "the god of the Eleatics." Nietzsche is surely alluding to the famous "Battle of Giants," the *gigantomachia* described in Plato's *Sophist,* 242c–243a and 246a–c.

not address, something ineffable—an *arrēton.* * What Nietzsche is practicing here with regard to the world totality is a kind of "negative theology," which tries to grasp the Absolute as purely as possible by holding at a distance all "relative" determinations, that is, all those that relate to human beings. Except that Nietzsche's determination of the world as a whole is a negative theology without the Christian God.

Such a defensive procedure represents the very opposite of despair concerning the possibility of knowledge, the very opposite of an unmitigated predilection for denial and destruction. The procedure therefore becomes a salient feature in every instance of great thought, appearing again and again under different guises; nor can it be directly refuted, so long as it perseveres in its style and refrains from leaping over the barriers it has established for itself.

How do matters stand in the present case?

We have elaborated a series of determinations concerning the world totality in Nietzsche's view, reducing them to eight points. All eight are brought home in the principal determination contained in point nine: "The collective character of the world . . . into all eternity is chaos." Must we now take this statement to mean that it is properly incumbent on us to revoke the earlier determinations and to utter no more than "chaos"? Or are all those determinations implied in the concept of chaos, so that they are preserved within this concept and its application to the world totality as the sole determination of that world? Or, on the contrary, do not the determinations and relations pertaining to the essence of chaos (force, finitude, endlessness, Becoming, space, time), as humanizations, also scuttle the concept of chaos? In that case we dare not propose any determinations at all; all we can say is *nothing.* Or is "the nothing" perhaps the most human of all humanizations? Our inquiry must push on to these extremes if it is to catch sight of the uniqueness of the present task, the task of determining being as a whole.

At this juncture we must remember that Nietzsche not only defines

---

* *Arrēton,* the negation of *rhēton,* is found in Homer, Hesiod, and throughout the Classical Age. It means what is unspoken, inexpressible, unutterable, shameful, not to be divulged. *Ta arrēta* are irrational numbers or surds.

the world totality as chaos but also ascribes to chaos itself a thorough-going *trait*—and that is "necessity." In section 109 of *The Gay Science* Nietzsche says explicitly: "The collective character of the world is . . . chaos, not in the sense that it lacks necessity, but in the sense that it lacks order." The coming to be of the bounded world, which is without beginning or end (and here that means that it is eternal), is of course without "order" in the sense of an intentional arrangement—intended by someone somewhere. All the same, such Becoming is not without necessity. We know that since antiquity in the Western intellectual tradition *necessity* designates a particular trait of beings; and that necessity, as a fundamental trait of beings, has received the most variegated interpretations: *Moira, fatum,* destiny, predestination, dialectical process. *

10. With the statement *Cosmic chaos is in itself necessity* we reach the conclusion of our series. The series was to characterize provisionally the fundamental trait of the Being of that world totality to which the eternal return of the same might be attributed.

What do we achieve when we synthesize the nine (or ten) points? What we wanted to do was to bring some intrinsic order to Nietzsche's disparate sketches and demonstrations concerning the doctrine of return. Yet none of the points even mentions the thought of return, much less the various demonstrations that Nietzsche elaborated for this doctrine. Nevertheless, we have supplied ourselves with an order by which we can approach the entire question, so that we can now pursue the matter of proofs for the doctrine of return, and hence the matter of the doctrine itself. To what extent is this the case?

For one thing, we have circumscribed the field in which the thought of return belongs and which the thought as such concerns: we have surveyed this field of being as a whole and determined it as the interlacing unity of the animate and the lifeless. For another, we have

---

* On *Moira* as "fateful allotment" in Parmenides' thought, see Martin Heidegger, *Vorträge und Aufsätze* (Pfullingen: G. Neske, 1954), pp. 231–56; *Early Greek Thinking,* tr. D. F. Krell and F. A. Capuzzi (New York: Harper & Row, 1975), pp. 79–101; especially sections VI–VII. One of the rare places where Heidegger discusses dialectical thought is "Grundsätze des Denkens," in the *Jahrbuch für Psychologie und Psychotherapie,* VI (1958), 33–41.

shown how in its foundations being as a whole—as the unity of animate and inanimate—is structured and articulated: it is constituted by the character of force and the finitude of the whole (at one with infinity) that is implied in the character of force—which is to say, the immeasurability of the "phenomenal effects." Now—and we can proceed with the following only on the basis of what we have already worked out—we must show how being as a whole, which is deployed in its field and in its constitution in the manner we have indicated, is *susceptible* of the eternal return of the same; we must show how eternal return may be ascribed to being as a whole, *demonstrated* of it. At all events, this is the only possible arrangement by which we can proceed in an orderly fashion through the entire labyrinth of Nietzsche's thoughts, mastering that labyrinth as we proceed—presupposing, of course, that we wish to proceed in the way that is prescribed by the inner lawfulness of the guiding question of philosophy, the question of being as such.

13. Suspicions Concerning the "Humanization" of Beings

Yet our entire consideration of Nietzsche's doctrine of return—and what is more, that doctrine itself—stand under the shadow of a suspicion. The suspicion, which in some sense is Nietzsche's own, might make all further efforts to understand the doctrine and the evidence for it futile. The suspicion is that a humanizing tendency nestles in the thought of eternal return of the same itself, and eminently so. Thus the eternal return would be a thought that provokes more than any other the issuance of Nietzsche's own persistent warning: "Let us be on guard!"

From the outset of our presentation we have often enough emphasized that *if* a thought related to beings as a whole must *at the same time* be related to the human being who is thinking it—indeed, must be thought in terms of the human being preeminently and entirely—then this holds true for the thought of eternal return. It was introduced under the designation "the greatest burden." The essential relation of this thought to the human being who is thinking it; the essential involvement of the thinker in the thought and what it thinks; that is to say, the "humanization" of the thought and of beings as a whole as represented in it—all this is made manifest by the fact that the eternity of recurrence, hence the time of recurrence, and thus recurrence itself, can be grasped solely in terms of the "Moment."

We define the "Moment" as that in which future and past "affront one another," in which future and past are decisively accomplished and consummated by man himself, inasmuch as man occupies the site of their collision and *is* himself that collision. The temporality of the time of *that* eternity which Nietzsche requires us to think in the eternal return of the same is the temporality in which humanity stands; preeminently humanity and, so far as we know, humanity alone. Human beings, resolutely open to what is to come and preserving what has been, sustain and give shape to what is present. The thought of eternal return of the same, spawned by such temporality and grounded in it, is therefore a "human" thought in a distinctive sense—the supreme sense. For that reason the thought of eternal return is vulnerable to the suspicion that with it a correspondingly vast humanization of beings as a whole transpires—in other words, the very thing Nietzsche wishes to avoid with every means at his disposal and along every route open to him.

How do matters stand with the suspicion concerning the humanization of beings implied in the thought of return? Clearly, we can answer the question only if we are capable of penetrating the thought itself in all its ramifications, only if we are capable of thinking it fully. Nevertheless, at the present juncture of our considerations, where proofs for the thought and the thought itself in its demonstrability and truth are to be grasped, it is first of all necessary that we formulate very carefully the suspicion concerning the thought's humanizing tendency, a suspicion that threatens to render all our labors superfluous.

Every conception of the being and especially of beings as a whole, merely by the fact that it is a *conception,* is related *by* human beings *to* human beings. The relation derives from man. Every interpretation of such a conception discriminates among the ways man proceeds with his conception of the being and adopts a stance toward it. Interpretation is thereby a projection of human representations and modes of representation onto the being. Simply to address the being, to name it in the word, is to equip it with human paraphernalia, to seize it in human nets, if indeed it is true that the word and language in the broadest sense distinguish human being. Hence every representation of beings as a whole, every interpretation of the world, is inevitably anthropomorphic.

Such reflections are so lucid that whoever has engaged in them, no matter how cursorily, is compelled to see that for all their representations, intuitions, and definitions of beings human beings are cornered in the blind alley of their own humanity. We can make it perfectly clear to every Simple Simon that all human representation comes out of this or that corner of the alley, whether it involves a notion of the world stemming from a single paramount and decisive thinker or a residue of notions gradually gaining in clarity for sundry groups, eras, peoples, and families of nations. Hegel shed light on the state of affairs in a striking reference to an aspect of our linguistic usage which gives occasion for a particular play on words, one that is not at all superficial or forced. *

All our representations and intuitions are such that in them we *mean* something, some being. Yet every time I mean or opine something I at the same time inevitably transform what is meant into something that is *mine.* Every such meaning, ostensibly related solely to the object itself, amounts to an act of appropriation and incorporation by and into the human ego of what is meant. *To mean* is in itself simultaneously to represent something and to make the represented something *my own.* But even when it is not the individualized "I" that means, when the standards prevailing in the thought of any individual human being presumably do not come to dominere, the danger of subjectivism is only apparently overcome. The humanization of beings as a whole is not slighter here but more massive, not only in scope but above all in kind, inasmuch as no one has the slightest inkling concerning such humanization. This gives rise to the initially inexpugnable illusion that no humanization is in play. But if humanization pertains to world interpretation ineluctably, then every attempt to dehumanize humanization is without prospect of success. The attempt to dehumanize is itself an attempt undertaken by human beings; hence it ultimately remains humanization, raised to a higher power.

These reflections, especially for someone who encounters them or

---

* The following reference to Hegel's use of *meinen,* "to mean," as a playful way to indicate the way in which sheer "opinion" *(die Meinung)* is something purely "mine" *(mein),* in contrast to the genuine universality *(das Allgemeine)* embraced by the language of concepts, may be traced through the early sections of Hegel's *Phenomenology of Spirit,* from "Sensuous Certainty" to "Certainty and Truth of Reason." See G. W. F. Hegel, *Phänomenologie des Geistes,* ed. Johannes Hoffmeister (Hamburg: F. Meiner, 1952), pp. 82–83, 185, 220–21, and 234–36. The same play occupies a special place in Hegel's mature "system." See the "Remark" to section 20 of the *Enzyklopädie der philosophischen Wissenschaften,* 3d edition, 1830, ed. Friedhelm Nicolin and Otto Pöggeler (Hamburg: F. Meiner, 1969), pp. 54–56, where the root *mein* unites what in English we must isolate as "opinion," "meaning" or "intention," "mine," and "universal."

similar trains of thought for the first time, are staggeringly convincing. Provided a person does not immediately circumvent them and save him or herself by fleeing into the "praxis" of "life," such reflections generally relegate one to a position where only two alternatives arise: either one doubts and despairs of every possibility of learning the truth and takes it all as a sheer play of representations, or one decides *via* a confession of faith for *one* world interpretation—following the maxim that *one* is better than *none,* even if it is merely one among others. Perhaps with a bit of luck the one we choose can prove its viability in terms of its success, its utility, and the range of its propagation.

The essential postures we may adopt toward a humanization that is held to be ineradicable in itself may therefore be reduced to two: either we make our peace with it and operate now in the apparent superiority of the Universal Doubter who cannot be hoodwinked and who desires only to be left alone, or we struggle to reach the point where we forget humanization and presume that it has thereby been brushed aside, in this way achieving our tranquillity. The result in either case is that wherever suspicions concerning immitigable humanization arise we find ourselves stuck on the superficies, however easily such reflections on humanization delude themselves into thinking that they are supremely profound and, above all, "critical." What a revelation it was for the mass of people who were unfamiliar with actual thinking and its rich history when two decades ago, in 1917, Oswald Spengler announced that he was the first to discover that every age and every civilization has its own world view! Yet it was all nothing more than a very deft and clever popularization of thoughts and questions on which others long before him had ruminated far more profoundly. Nietzsche was the most recent of these. Yet no one by any means mastered these thoughts and questions, and they remain unmastered up to the present hour. The reason is as simple as it is momentous and difficult to think through.

With all these *pros* and *cons* with respect to humanization, one believes one knows ahead of time what human beings are, the human beings who are responsible for this palpable humanization. One forgets to pose the question that would have to be answered first of all if the suspicions concerning humanization are to be viable or if refutation of those suspicions is to make any sense. To talk of humanization before one has decided—that is to say, before one has asked—who man is, is idle talk indeed. It remains idle talk even when for the sake of its demonstrations it musters all of world history and mankind's most ancient civilizations—things which no one is able to corroborate anyway. Hence, in order to avoid superficial and specious discussion of those suspicions concerning humanization, whether affirming or rejecting them, we must first of all take up the question "Who is man?" A number of adroit writers have wasted no time replying to the question, without the question itself becoming any clearer. But for them the question is no more than an interrogatory blurb on a book jacket. The question is not really asked—the authors have long been in secure possession of their dogmatic replies. There is nothing to be said against that. It is merely that one should not give the impression that one is *questioning*. For the question "Who is man?" is not as harmless as it may seem, and it is not a matter to be settled overnight. If the capacities for questioning are to survive in Dasein, this question is to be Europe's task for the future, for this century and the century to come. It can find its answer only in the exemplary and authoritative way in which particular nations, in competition with others, shape their history.

Yet who else poses and answers the question of who man is, if not man himself? That is surely the case. But does it also follow that the definition of the essence of the human being is simply a humanization by human creatures? That may well be. In fact, it is necessarily a humanization, in the sense that the essential definition of human beings is executed by human beings. Nevertheless, the question remains as to whether the essential definition of human being humanizes or dehumanizes it. It is possible that the execution of the definition of human being always and everywhere remains an affair of human beings and that to that extent it is human; but it may be that the definition itself, its truth, elevates human being beyond itself and thereby *de*humanizes it, in that way ascribing even to the *human* execution of the essential definition of man a different essence. The question of who man is must first be experienced as a much-needed question. For that to happen, the need of this question concerning human being must burst on the scene with full force and under every guise. We do not do justice to the necessity of this question if we fail to examine what it is that makes the question possible first of all. Whence, and on what basis, is the essence of human being to be defined?

The essence of man may be defined—as we have long been accustomed to mean and opine according to the rules of various games—by describing him in the way one dissects and describes a frog or a rabbit. As if it had already been determined that by means of biological procedures one can come to know what a living creature is. It is rather the case that the science of biology presupposes and takes for granted in its initial steps what "life" is to mean for it. Of course, one turns his back on the opinion thus taken for granted. One shies from turning to confront it, not only because he is so busy with his frogs and other animals, but also because he experiences anxiety concerning his own opinion. It might well be that the science as such would suddenly collapse if one looked over one's shoulder, only to discover that presuppositions are very much *worthy of question*. This is the case in all the sciences—without exception. Is it not liberating for all these sciences when they are told nowadays that due to historic political exigencies the nation and the state need results—solid, useful results! "Fine," reply the sciences, "but you know we need our peace and quiet." Everyone cooperates sympathetically, and the sciences are happy in their unruffled state; they can proceed in utter ignorance of philosophical-metaphysical questions, as they have for the past fifty years. The "sciences" today experience this liberation in the only way they can. Nowadays as never before they feel perfectly assured of their necessity, taking such assurance—erroneously—as a confirmation of their very essence.

If it even occurred to anyone these days to suggest that science could assert itself essentially only if it retrieved its essence by means of an original *questioning,* such a one would be confessing himself a fool or a subverter of "science as such."* To ask about ultimate grounds is to

---

* Heidegger is of course referring to his inaugural lecture at Freiburg in 1929 and—presumably—to the outraged reply by Rudolf Carnap in 1931, "Overcoming Metaphysics through Logical Analysis of Language," which appears in an English translation in A. J. Ayer, ed., *Logical Positivism* (New York: Free Press, 1959), pp. 60–81. See especially section 5 for an account of Heidegger's syntactical errors and perversities. It is intriguing to work through the "schema" of section 5, on "the nothing," to learn the extent to which Carnap and Heidegger *agree*. An equally interesting response to Heidegger—Wittgenstein's, as recorded by Friedrich Waismann on December 30, 1929—never

promulgate a kind of inner flagellation, a process for which the heady word *nihilism* stands at our beck and call. But that ghost has been laid to rest; all is peace and quiet; the students, we now hear, are willing to go back to work! And so the universal Babbittry of the spirit may begin anew. "Science" has no inkling of the fact that its claim to be of direct practical consequence does not simply obliterate philosophical meditation; it is much more the case that at the instant of science's supreme practical relevance the supreme necessity arises for *meditation* on matters that can never be gauged according to direct practicability and utility. These matters nevertheless instill a supreme unrest in Dasein, unrest not as distraction and confusion but as awakening and vigilance—as opposed to the tranquillity of that philosophic somnolence which is nihilism proper. Yet if comfort be our standard of measure, it is doubtless easier to shut our eyes and evade the gravity of these questions, even if our sole excuse is that we have no time for such things.

An odd era for humankind, this, the age in which we have been adrift for decades, a time that no longer has time for the question of who man is. By means of scientific descriptions of extant or past forms of humanity, whether these descriptions are biological or historical or both taken together in a mélange of "anthropologies," a mixture that has become popular during recent decades, we can never come to know who man is. Such knowledge is also barred to faith, which must from the start regard all "knowledge" as "heathen" and as folly. Such knowledge thrives only on the basis of an original stance of inquiry. The question of who man is must take its departure from that point which even the most desultory view of things can identify as the point of inception for the humanization of all beings, namely, man's mere addressing and naming of beings, that is to say, *language*. It may be that man does not at all humanize beings by virtue of language; on the contrary, perhaps man has up to now thoroughly mistaken and misinterpreted the essence of language itself, and with it his own Being and its essential provenance. But when we pose the question of the essence of language we are already asking about being as a whole, provided

---

reached the public. It is now printed, with a revealing commentary, in Michael Murray, ed., *Heidegger and Modern Philosophy* (New Haven: Yale University Press, 1978), pp. 80–83.

language is not an agglomeration of words used to designate sundry familiar things but *the original resonance of the truth of a world.*

The question of who man is must in its very formulation include in its approach man in and with his relations to beings as a whole; it must include in its inquiry the question of being as a whole. But we have just now heard that being as a whole can only be interpreted by human beings in the first place—and now man himself is to be interpreted in terms of being as a whole. Everything here is spinning in a circle. Of that there can be no doubt. The question is whether and in what way we can succeed in taking this circle seriously, instead of continually closing our eyes in the face of it.

The world interpretation that devolves upon the thought of eternal return of the same shows that a relation to man announces itself in the essence of eternity as midday and moment. Here that very circle plays a role, requiring that man be thought on the basis of world, and world on the basis of man. To all appearances that would suggest that the thought of eternal return of the same bears traces of the uttermost humanization; the thought nevertheless is and wants to be the very opposite. Furthermore, this circle would explain the fact that as a consequence of the will to dehumanize world interpretation Nietzsche is compelled to will supreme humanization, hence the fact that each demands rather than excludes the other.

The upshot would be that Nietzsche's doctrine of eternal return is not to be measured by gratuitous standards, but only on the basis of its own law. It would demand that we meditate in advance on the kind of evidentiary claim and evidentiary force that are germane to the Nietzschean proofs for the doctrine of eternal return.

But we can drop the subjunctives. For what we have suggested is indeed the case.

Suspicions concerning humanization, no matter how palpably near they are and no matter how readily everyone can clumsily wield them, remain superfluous and groundless as long as they have not put themselves in question—by asking the question of who man is. That question cannot even be posed, much less answered, without the question of what being as a whole is. *However, the latter question embraces a more original question, one which neither Nietzsche nor philosophy prior to him unfolded or was able to unfold.*

14. Nietzsche's Proof of the Doctrine of Return

With the thought of eternal return of the same Nietzsche is moving in the realm of the question as to what being as a whole is. Now that we have staked out the field of Nietzsche's sense of being as a whole and described its constitution, we would do well to pursue the proofs by which Nietzsche attributes to being as a whole the determination of eternal return of the same. (In the course of such a pursuit we must set aside those suspicions concerning humanization—which, in the meantime, have become dubious indeed.) Obviously, everything depends on the evidentiary force of these proofs. To be sure, evidentiary *force.* All evidentiary force remains impotent so long as we fail to grasp the mode and the essence of the proofs in question. Yet these things, along with the respective possibility and necessity of proof, are defined by the kind of truth that is in question. A proof can be fully conclusive, without formal logical errors of any kind, and still prove nothing and remain irrelevant, simply because its point of attack misses the precise nexus of truth and alters nothing within that nexus. For example, a proof for the existence of God can be constructed by means of the most rigorous formal logic and yet prove nothing, since a god who must permit his existence to be proved in the first place is ultimately a very ungodly god. The best such proofs of existence can yield is blasphemy. Or, to take another example, one can try—and this has happened over and over again—to prove experimentally, through experience, the fundamental principle of causality. Such a proof is more deleterious than any attempt to deny the validity of that principle on philosophical or sophistical grounds; more ruinous, because it jumbles all thought and inquiry from the ground up, inasmuch as a fundamental principle in its very essence cannot be empirically proved. Always and everywhere the empiricist concludes, wrongly, that the fundamental principle cannot be proved at all. He takes his proofs and his truth to be the sole possible ones. Everything that is inaccessible to him he proclaims to be superstition, something that "simply cannot be dealt with." As if what is most magnificent, most profound, were something "we" can never "deal with" unless we deal with it by thinking empirically and thus by shutting ourselves off from it irrevocably. There are many different kinds of proofs.

With regard to Nietzsche's "proofs" for his doctrine of return, prior interpretations and presentations have been especially anxious to make Nietzsche's prediction come true: "Everyone talks about me—but nobody thinks of me." No one compels himself to think through Nietzsche's thoughts. Of course, such thinking through is confronted by a bedeviling peculiarity: it never succeeds if the thinker fails to think beyond—though not away from—the thought he is to be thinking about. Only if it thinks beyond does thinking through possess the freedom of movement that it needs if it is to avoid getting tangled up in itself.

In the case at hand, namely, the Nietzschean proofs for the eternal return of the same, it was especially gratifying to bid a quick adieu to thought—without losing face thereby. It was said that with these proofs Nietzsche had gotten sidetracked in physics which, number one, he did not understand thoroughly enough and, number two, does not belong in philosophy anyway. We perspicacious fellows know full well that you cannot prove philosophical doctrines with assertions and arguments from the natural sciences. But, it is said, we are inclined to— yes, we really must—forgive Nietzsche his aberration in the direction of natural science. After all, he too went through his positivist phase, at the end of the 1870s and in the early 1880s, a period when anyone who wanted to have any influence at all spoke up for a "scientific world view," much in the manner of Haeckel and his crew. In those decades "liberalism" was rampant; it spawned the very idea of "world view." Every "world view" in itself and *as such* is liberal! So let us say that this escapade of Nietzsche's into the natural sciences remains an historical eccentricity and let it go at that.

It seems clear that we could hardly expect persons sporting such an attitude to think through Nietzsche's thought of thoughts.

Recently, however, some attempts have been made to think through the proofs for this thought. Because of the reference to an essential connection between "Being" and "Time," some have paused to wonder, asking themselves: If Nietzsche's doctrine of eternal return of the same has to do with the universe, being as a whole, which one could roughly call "Being"; and if eternity and recurrence, as transgressions of past and future, are somehow related to "Time"; then perhaps there is something to Nietzsche's doctrine of the eternal return of the same, and maybe we had better not shrug off his proofs as effulgences of a project that was doomed to fail. And so the proofs are taken in earnest. Commentators show—by way of mathematical exertions, no less—that his proofs are not so bad, not counting a couple of "mistakes." Indeed, Nietzsche anticipated several lines of thought in contemporary physics —and what could be more important for a real contemporary man than his science! This apparently more material and more affirmative stance with respect to Nietzsche's "proofs" is, however, every bit as dubious as its opposite; it is immaterial, inasmuch as it does not and cannot confront "the matter" that comes into question here. For both the rejection and the acceptance of these proofs hold fast to the common identical presupposition that here it is a matter of proofs after the manner of the "natural sciences." This preconception is the genuine error. It precludes all understanding from the outset because it makes all correct questioning impossible.

It remains essential that we attain sufficient clarity concerning the foundations, the approach, the direction, and the region of Nietzsche's thought. Furthermore, we must recognize that even when we have achieved these things we will have performed only the most pressing preliminary work. It could be that the form in which Nietzsche applies and presents his proofs is only a foreground, and that this foreground can deceive us about the properly "metaphysical" train of his thought. In addition, we must confront the extrinsic circumstance that Nietzsche's notes are not structured in such a way as to be consistent and conclusive. And yet the principal thoughts are clear, recurring again and again in later years, long after Nietzsche had left his "positivistic" phase—the one that ostensibly caused him to get sidetracked among the natural sciences—behind. We shall limit ourselves now to indicating the principal steps on this path of thought.

The eternal return of the same is to prove to be the fundamental determination of the world totality. If we for our part are to anticipate the kind of fundamental determination of being as a whole we are confronting here, by naming it more precisely and by setting it in relief against other such determinations, then we may say that eternal return of the same is to prove to be *the way in which* being as a whole *is*. That can succeed only if we show that the *way* in which being as a whole is necessarily results from what we have called the constitution of the world totality. The latter becomes manifest to us in the determinations listed earlier. Hence we will refer back to them in order to test whether and in what way these determinations in their proper context indicate the necessity of the eternal return of the same.

The general character of force yields the finitude (closure) of the world and of its becoming. According to such finitude of becoming, the advance and progress of cosmic occurrence into infinity is impossible. Thus the world's becoming must turn back on itself.

Yet the world's becoming runs backward and forward in endless (infinite) time, as real time. The finite becoming which runs its course in such infinite time must long ago have achieved a kind of homeostasis—a state of balance and calm—if such were ever possible for it, inasmuch as the possibilities of being, finite according to number and kind, must of necessity be exhausted in infinite time—must already have been exhausted. Because no such homeostasis or equilibrium prevails, it is clear that it never was attained, and here that means that it never can come to prevail. The world's becoming, as finite, turning back on itself, is therefore a *permanent* becoming, that is to say, *eternal* becoming. Since such cosmic becoming, as finite becoming in an infinite time, takes place continuously, not ceasing whenever its finite possibilities are exhausted, it must already have repeated itself, indeed an infinite number of times. And as permanent becoming it will continue to repeat itself in the future. Because the world totality is finite in the configurations of its becoming, although immeasurable in practical terms, the possibilities of transformation in its collective character are also finite, however much they appear to us to be infinite, because unsurveyable and hence ever novel. And because the nexus of effects among the particular processes of becoming—finite in number—is a closed nexus, every process of becoming must retroactively draw the entire past in its wake; or, since it works its effects always ahead, it must propel all things forward. This implies that every process of becoming must reproduce itself; it and all the others recur as the same. The eternal return of the totality of world becoming must be a recurrence of the same.

The return of the same would be impossible only if it could be avoided in some way. This would presuppose that the world totality renounced the recurrence of the same, and this in turn would imply a forward-reaching intention to that end and a corresponding positing of the goal, namely, the positing of the ultimate goal of somehow avoiding the unavoidable. For, on the basis of the finitude and permanence of becoming in infinite time, recurrence of the same is indeed unavoidable. Yet to presuppose the positing of such a *goal* runs *counter* to the fundamental constitution of the world totality as necessitous chaos. All that remains to be said is what we have already shown to be necessary: the character of the world totality, its character as Becoming— and here that also means its character as Being—when defined as the eternal chaos of necessity, is eternal return of the same.

15. The Ostensibly Scientific Procedure of Proof. Philosophy and Science

If we look back over the train of thought we have pursued and ask how the principle of eternal return of the same may be proved, the evidentiary procedure involved seems to be something like the following: From statements concerning the constitution of the world totality we must necessarily conclude to the principle of eternal return of the same. Without entering immediately into the question as to what kind of "conclusion" this deduction arrives at, we can reach a decision that remains significant for all our further reflections, albeit only by way of a clarification of the most general kind.

We must ask whether this evidentiary procedure pertains at all to the "natural sciences," whatever we may make of its suitability and its "merits." What is "scientific" about it? The answer is: nothing at all.

What is being discussed in the deduction itself and in the series of determinations of the cosmic order which precedes it? Force, finitude, endlessness, sameness, recurrence, becoming, space, time, chaos, and necessity. None of these has anything to do with "natural science." If one wished to draw the natural sciences into consideration here at all, all he could say would be that the sciences do presuppose determinations such as becoming, space, time, sameness, and recurrence—in fact, must of necessity presuppose them as elements that remain eternally barred from their realm of inquiry and their manner of demonstration.

True, the sciences must make use of a particular notion of force, motion, space, and time; but they can never say what force, motion, space, and time are; they cannot *ask* what such things are as long as they remain sciences and avoid trespassing into the realm of philosophy. The fact that every science as such, being the specific science it is, gains no access to its fundamental concepts and to what those concepts grasp, goes hand in hand with the fact that no science can assert something about itself with the help of its own scientific resources. What mathematics is can never be determined mathematically; what philology is can never be discussed philologically; what biology is can never be uttered biologically. To ask what a science is, is *to ask a question* that is no longer a *scientific* question. The moment he or she poses a question with regard to science in general, and that always means a question concerning specific possible sciences, the inquirer steps into a new realm, a realm with evidentiary claims and forms of proof quite different from those that are customary in the sciences. *This is the realm of philosophy.* It is not affixed to the sciences or piled on top of them. It lies hidden in the innermost domain of science, so much so that it would be true to say that mere science is only scientific —that is to say, partaking of genuine knowledge, above and beyond being a repertory of certain techniques—to the extent that it is philosophical. From this we can gather the alarming proportions of nonsense and absurdity in all ostensible efforts to renew the "sciences" and simultaneously abolish philosophy.

What does it mean to say that a science is "philosophical"? It does not mean that it explicitly "borrows" from a particular "philosophy," or appeals to it for support, or alludes to it, or shares its terminology and employs its concepts. It does not at all mean that "philosophy" as such—that is to say, philosophy as a developed discipline or as an autonomous piece of work—should or could be the clearly visible superstructure for science. The grounds of science must rather be what philosophy alone sets in relief and founds, namely, the cognizable truth of beings as such. Hence, to say that a science is philosophical means that it knowingly and questioningly reverts to being as such and as a whole, and inquires into the truth of beings; such science *sets itself in motion* within the fundamental positions we take toward beings, and allows these positions to have an impact on scientific work. The standard by which such impact may be measured by no means lies in the number, frequency, or visibility of philosophical concepts and terms that occur in a scientific treatise; the standard lies in the assuredness, clarity, and originality of the questioning itself—in the durability of the will *to think*. Such a will does not swoon over the results of science, does not rest content in them. It always grasps results as nothing more than means to an end, as a route to further work.

A science may therefore become philosophical in either of two ways. First, it may approximate to the thinking that is proper to a philosophy, when at some point the *realm* of such thinking (and not merely its statements and formulas) places a direct claim on scientific inquiry and induces it to alter meticulously the very horizons of its customary operations. Second, a science may become philosophical as a result of the intrinsic inquisitiveness of the science itself. A science may get caught up in the original attractive power of knowledge by thinking back to its own origins, in such a way that these origins themselves determine every step in the operations of that science.

For these reasons a profound sense of mutual agreement is possible between philosophical thought and scientific research, without their having to act on one another in any explicit way, without each having to penetrate the other's sphere of inquiry and assign it its tasks. In spite of the enormous distance that separates thinker and researcher in their realms and modes of work, there is every likelihood that they will enter into an inherent and mutually fructifying relationship, a way of *being* with one another that is far more efficacious than the much-acclaimed but extrinsic "cooperation" of a group allied with a view to some specific purpose.

The strongest creative impulses can thrive only on the basis of such mutual agreement, which spans a luminous bridge across vast distances. Here the freedom, alterity, and uniqueness of each can come into expansive play, occasioning a properly fruitful exchange.

On the other hand, it is an old lesson based on incontrovertible experience that academically organized community efforts, arranged and outfitted for some more or less specific purpose, and "cooperative labors" among the sciences springing from utilitarian motives petrify sooner or later. They grow hollow and vacuous, precisely because of the excessive proximity, the familiarity, and the "routine" shared by the co-workers.

If therefore the natural and the human sciences, already wholly subservient to technology, are exposed to such unusual stress and such undisguised exploitation—and in our current predicament they are inevitably so exposed—we can prevent the disconcerting situation from becoming truly catastrophic only if the greatest counterweights are brought to bear on the innermost core of the sciences. And this can occur only if the sciences become thoroughly philosophical.

Precisely because chemistry and physics have become necessary to such a vast extent, philosophy is far from superfluous; it is even more necessary—"needful" in a quite profound sense—than, for example, chemistry itself. The latter, left to itself, is soon exhausted. It makes no difference whether it takes a decade or a century before the process of such potential atrophy becomes visible to the casual observer: so far as the essence of such atrophy is concerned *we must fend it off wherever it emerges.*

Nietzsche did not stray into the natural sciences. Rather, the natural science that was contemporary to him drifted dubiously into a dubious philosophy. The evidentiary procedure for the doctrine of return is therefore in no case subject to the jurisdiction of natural science, even if the "facts" of natural science should run counter to the outcome of that procedure. What are the "facts" of natural science and of all science, if not particular appearances interpreted according to explicit, tacit, or utterly unknown metaphysical principles, principles that reflect a doctrine concerning beings as a whole?

In order to hold at bay the scientific misconception of Nietzsche's train of thought it is not even necessary to refer to the straightforward state of affairs represented in Nietzsche's reflections—namely, the fact that he never limits those reflections to the region of knowledge attained by physics or the other natural sciences. On the contrary, he is concerned with the totality of beings: "Everything has returned: Sirius and the spider and your thoughts during this past hour and this very thought of yours, that everything recurs" (XII, 62). Since when are "thoughts" and "hours" objects of physics or biology?

16. The Character of "Proof" for the Doctrine of Return

As yet our reflections have decided nothing about evidentiary procedure in the form of a deductive process and about the train of Nietzsche's thought as a "proof." With the sole intention of clarifying Nietzsche's thought we shall now ask the following questions. Is Nietzsche's train of thought a *proof* at all in the usual sense? Is it a *deduction* based on a series of propositions? Are propositions concerning the veritable essence of the world posited here as major premises for a conclusion? Is the proposition of eternal recurrence deduced from such premises?

At first glimpse, this seems to be the case. We ourselves initiated the evidentiary procedure precisely in this way. We concluded from statements concerning the constitution of beings as a whole to the mode of Being of these beings; we deduced the necessity of eternal return of the same for being as a whole. Yet what gives us the right without further ado to draw conclusions concerning the import and the mode of a philosophical train of thought from the form in which we ourselves have presented it, especially when specific historical circumstances condition our presentation? The reply might be ventured: To all appearances, anything that is written and discussed consists of propositions and sequences of propositions, and these are the same whether they appear in scientific or philosophical treatises. Their "content" may differ, perhaps, but their "logic," which is what counts, is identical. Or is the very "logic" of philosophy altogether different? Must it not be totally different, and not merely because philosophical thought relates to a content that is in some respect distinguishable from the objects of the sciences? For example, the sciences deal with atomic fission, genetic inheritance, price calculation, Frederick the Great, or the criminal code; and they debate over differential equations and Sophocles' *Antigone*. Correspondingly, philosophy deals with things like eternal recurrence. Different things, different logic. If that were the way matters stood, philosophy would merely be one science among others. However, each science deals with only *one* particular domain of beings, which it always considers under *one* particular aspect; philosophy thinks beings as a whole, under the aspect that includes every other aspect, necessarily and from the outset. The "logic" of philosophy is thus not simply "something else again," but is totally different. To achieve philosophical thinking we need to adopt a wholly different stance toward thought. Above all, we need a special kind of readiness to think. No matter how much attention we pay to formal logic in the presentation of a particular evidentiary procedure, and no matter how much our procedure seems identical with the customary ones, when we think that way we are always thinking formally and extrinsically.

Let us find our way back to the question concerning the character of Nietzsche's train of thought in his "proofs" for the doctrine of return, and let us repeat the question: Is the principle of eternal return disclosed by way of a deduction from prior propositions asserted of the nature of the world? Or does not the very essence of the world first become palpable *as* an eternal chaos of necessity by means of the determination of the world totality as one that recurs in the same? If that is how matters stand, then the ostensible proof is not at all a proof that could have its force in the cogency and conclusiveness of its deductive steps. What proffered itself as a proof in our own presentation is nothing more than the revelation of positings that are co-posited— indeed necessarily co-posited—in the projection of being as a whole onto Being as eternally recurrent in the same. But then this proof is simply an articulation of the cohesion of the projection itself and what it immediately co-posits. In short, what we have here is the *unfolding* of a projection, by no means its computation and its grounding.

If our interpretation now brings us to the heart's core of Nietzsche's thought—as a metaphysical thought—then all the rest becomes highly questionable. To posit the nature of the world in terms of the fundamental character of eternal return of the same is hence purely arbitrary if the world totality does not really disclose such a basic character—if such a character is merely attributed to it, foisted onto it. Furthermore, such positing is the utter extremity of the very thing Nietzsche wished to avoid, namely, the humanizing of beings. Did not the provenance of the thought of eternal return come to show itself in the experience of the moment as the most poignantly human of attitudes toward time? The upshot is that Nietzsche not only applies one human experience to beings as a whole but also does so in contradiction to himself, inasmuch as he is the one who wants to abjure humanization. Seen in terms of the whole, Nietzsche's own procedure remains unclear in the most decisive respect—and that does not seem auspicious for a philosopher, especially one as demanding as Nietzsche. Are we to suppose that Nietzsche does not know he is "reading into things"?

He knows it, only too well. He knows it better—that is to say, more painfully and honestly—than any previous thinker ever knew it. During the very years he is trying to think the essence of the world in the direction of eternal return of the same, Nietzsche achieves waxing clarity concerning the fact that human beings always think within the confinements of their little "corner" of the world, their tiny angle of space-time. In the second edition of *The Gay Science,* published in 1887, Nietzsche writes (number 374): "We cannot see around our own corner." Here man is grasped and is designated as a veritable Little Jack Horner. Thus we find a clear expression of the fact that everything that is accessible in any way is encompassed within a particular range of vision determined by a particular corner, a clear expression and acknowledgment of the fact that the humanization of all things is unavoidable in every single step that thought takes. Hence the interpretation of the world's nature as a necessitous chaos is also impossible in the intended sense—namely, in the sense that it would strip away all humanization. Or it must be conceded merely as a prospect and a perspective that peep from their own little corner. However we decide, it remains the case that the intention to put out of action all humanizing tendencies in our thoughts on the world's essence cannot endure side by side with acknowledgment of mankind's Little-Jack-Horner essence. If this particular intention is held to be practicable, then man would have to get a grip on the world's essence from a location outside of every corner; he would have to occupy something like a standpoint of standpointlessness.

And in point of fact we still have scholars today who busy themselves with philosophy and who consider freedom-from-every-standpoint not to be a standpoint, as though such freedom did not depend upon those very standpoints. These curious attempts to flee from one's own shadow we may leave to themselves, since discussion of them yields no tangible results. Yet we must heed one thing: this standpoint of freedom-from-standpoints is of the opinion that it has overcome the one-sidedness and bias of prior philosophy, which always was, and is, defined by its standpoints. However, the standpoint of standpointlessness represents no overcoming. In truth it is the extreme consequence, affirmation, and final stage of that opinion concerning philosophy which locates all philosophy extrinsically in standpoints that are ultimately right in front of us, standpoints whose one-sidedness we can try to bring into equilibrium. We do not alleviate the ostensible damage and danger which we fear in the fact that philosophy is located in a particular place—such location being the essential and indispensable legacy of every philosophy—by denying and repudiating the fact; we alleviate the danger only by thinking through and grasping the indigenous character of philosophy in terms of its original essence and its necessity, that is to say, by posing anew the question concerning the essence of truth and the essence of human Dasein, and by elaborating a radically new response to that question.

Either the excision of every kind of humanization is held to be possible, and there has to be something like a standpoint that is free from all standpoints; or human beings are acknowledged as the cornered creatures they are, and we must deny the possibility of any non-humanizing conception of the world totality. How does Nietzsche decide in this either/or? It could hardly have remained concealed from his view, since *he* is the one who at least helped to develop it. Nietzsche decides for both—for the will to dehumanize being as a whole and also for the will to take seriously the human being as a creature of corners. Nietzsche decides for the convergence of both wills. He demands the supreme humanization of beings and the extreme naturalization of human beings, both at once. Only those who press forward to what Nietzsche's thinking wills of itself can have some inkling of his philosophy. Yet if that is how matters stand it will surely be decisive now to know which corner it is from which the human being sees—and whence that corner is defined in its place. At the same time, the breadth of the horizon that is drawn about the possible dehumanizing of beings as a whole will also be decisive. Finally, whether and in what way the view upon being as a whole definitively serves to locate that corner in which human beings necessarily come to stand—this above all else will be decisive.

Even though Nietzsche did not elevate these ramifications to clearly expressed, conceptual knowledge, he nonetheless—as we shall soon discover—advanced a stretch of the way through them, thanks to the innermost will of his thinking. From the very outset we have seen that in the presentation of his fundamental thought what is to be thought—both the world totality and the thinking of the thinker—cannot be detached from one another. Now we comprehend more clearly what this inseparability refers to and what it suggests: it is the necessary relationship of man—a being who is located in the midst of beings as a whole—to that very whole. We are thinking of this fundamental relation in the decisive disposition of human beings in general when we say that the Being of human being—and, as far as we know, of human being *alone*—is grounded in Dasein: the *Da* is the sole possible site for the necessary location of its Being at any given time. From this essential connection we also derive the insight that humanization becomes proportionately less destructive of truth as human beings relate themselves more originally to the location of their essential corner, that is to say, as they recognize and ground Da-sein as such. Yet the essentiality of the corner is defined by the originality and the breadth in which being as a whole is experienced and grasped—with a view to its sole decisive aspect, that of Being.

Our reflections make it clear that in thinking the most burdensome thought *what* is thought cannot be detached from the *way in which* it is thought. The *what* is itself defined by the *how,* and, reciprocally, the *how* by the *what.* From this fact alone we can gather how muddle-headed it is to conceive of evidences for the thought of return after the manner of physical or mathematical proofs. What *proof* means in this case, what it *can* mean, must be determined purely and simply on the basis of this utterly unique thought of thoughts.

Because of the essential inseparability of the *how* of thinking from the *what* of the to-be-thought, another important decision in yet another respect has been reached. The distinction between a "theoretical" doctrinal content of the thought and its "practical" effects is impossible from the very start. This thought can be neither "theoretically" thought nor "practically" applied. Not theoretically thought, inasmuch as thinking the thought demands that man, not only as practically acting but generally as being, be caught up in the process of thought, defining himself and his corner in terms of what is to be thought—simultaneously, and not subsequently. As long as such definition remains unachieved, the thought stagnates, remains unthinkable and unthought; and no amount of mental acuity will help to take even the smallest step forward. Yet a "practical" application of the thought is impossible also, inasmuch as it has always already become superfluous the moment the thought has actually been thought.

17. The Thought of Return as a Belief

We shall now proceed with our account of Nietzsche's unpublished notes, retaining the form the first editors of these posthumous materials gave them, and advancing to the second part of their arrangement, entitled, "Impact of the Doctrine on Humanity." In doing so, it is our purpose to show that in the fragments these editors have selected something else is at stake besides an "impact" on humanity. Even when Nietzsche aims at something of that kind we must elucidate his thought in terms of *his own* basic notions and not by means of the rough and ready notions that distinguish—apparently quite plausibly—between a doctrine's "presentation" and its "impact." The dubious nature of the point from which the editors attempted their division may be seen in the fact that the fragments numbered 113 and 114 in Division One could as readily—and perhaps with greater justice—be placed in Division Two, concerning the "impact." It is not without reason that the editors placed them at the very end of Division One, "The Presentation and Grounding of the Doctrine." In what follows we shall emphasize the major aspects, those that essentially clarify what it is that Nietzsche is saying. But such emphasis is far from providing an adequate interpretation.

Under numbers 115 through 132 a series of fragments have been collated in which the "content" of the thought of return seems to recede. Yet what comes to the fore instead is not so much the "impact" of the thought as the precise character of the thought itself. That character consists in its essential relationship to what is being thought. To *think* the thought is not to drive a vehicle through it. A vehicle remains something outside or alongside the place we reach in our thought. When we bicycle over to the hills we call "the Kaiserstuhl" our "bicycle" itself has ultimately nothing to do with "the Kaiserstuhl." Such indifference as that between "bicycle" and "Kaiserstuhl" does not obtain between the thinking of the thought of return and what is actually thought and experienced there.

The most important characterization of the thought of eternal return of the same which we encounter in these notes is its characterization as a *"belief."*

The thought and belief is a burden which, in comparison with all other weights, oppresses you far more than they do (number 117).

Future history: *this* thought will prevail more and more, and those who do not believe in it must, according to their own nature, finally *die off!* (number 121).

This doctrine is mild against those who do not believe in it; it has no hellfire, no threats. Whoever does not believe has a *fleeting life* in his consciousness (number 128).

The fact that Nietzsche called his thought a *belief* probably also led to the customary view that the doctrine of return must have been a personal confession of religious faith on Nietzsche's part. As such it would remain without significance for the "objective" import of his philosophy and thus could be struck from the record. That was especially called for because this thought was discomfiting to think anyway; it did not fit into any of the current pigeonholes of the usual concepts. Such a view—which corrupts every possible understanding of Nietzsche's philosophy proper—received some further support from the fact that in his notes Nietzsche occasionally spoke of "religion." Note 124 reads: "This thought contains more than all religions, which disdained this life as fleeting and taught us to search for some unspecified *other* life." Here the thought is indisputably brought into relation with the import of particular religions, namely, those that denigrate life on earth and posit a life "beyond" as definitive. Thus one might be tempted to say that the thought of eternal return of the same epitomizes Nietzsche's purely "earthly" religion, and hence is religious, not philosophical.

"Let us guard against teaching such a doctrine as though it were a religion that suddenly appeared," reads note 130. That note continues: "The most powerful thoughts need many millennia—*long, long* must the thought be small and weak!" Here, obviously, a religious character is not ascribed to the doctrine of return. Only "sudden" religions are mentioned at all, and even those by way of rejection. And as though to eliminate all doubts in this regard the final sentence of the concluding fragment, number 132, reads: "It [the thought of return] is to be the religion of the freest, most cheerful and sublime souls—a lovely stretch of mountain meadow between glistening ice and an unclouded sky!" This sentence, which seems to snatch the thought of return from philosophy and to turn it over to religion, and which therefore threatens to dash at a single stroke the effort we are making here, in fact achieves the very opposite. For it says that we dare not accommodate the thought and its teaching among the various religious sects or customary forms of religiosity. Rather, the thought itself defines the essence of religion anew on its own terms. The thought itself is to say what kind of religion shall exist for what kind of human being in the future. The thought itself is to define the relationship to God—and to define God himself.

Granted, one might counter that it is in any case a matter of religion —the thought is designated as a belief—and not philosophy. Yet what does "philosophy" mean here? We dare not adopt any arbitrary concept of philosophy or any customary concept of religion as standards. Here too we must define the essence of Nietzsche's philosophy in terms of *its own* thinking, in terms of *its own* thoughts. Ultimately, the thinking of that thought is such that Nietzsche may characterize it as a belief—not only may, but really must. In this respect it is incumbent on us now to do what all agree is reasonable but which no one does, namely, to examine precisely how Nietzsche conceives of the essence of such belief. Belief here surely does not mean the acceptance of articles of faith as revealed in Scripture and proclaimed by a Church. Nor does belief mean (in Nietzsche's case) an individual's trust in the justificatory grace of the Christian God.

What does belief mean in accordance with its formal concept, a concept which in its sundry configurations is still undefined? Nietzsche designates the essence of belief in the following words (WM, 15; from the year 1887): "What is a *belief?* How does it originate? Every belief is a *taking to be true."* From these words we derive one thing alone, but the most important thing: to believe means to take what is represented as true, and thus it also means to hold fast to the true and hold firm in the true. In belief there lies not only a relation to what is believed but above all to the believer himself. Taking to be true is holding firm in the true, hence holding in a dual sense: having a hold on something *and* preserving the stance one has. Such holding receives its determination from whatever it is that is posited as the true. In this regard it remains essential how we grasp the truth of the true, and on the basis of our concept of truth, what sort of relationship results between what is true and our holding fast to it. If holding firm in the truth is a mode of human life, then we can decide something about the essence of belief, and about Nietzsche's concept of belief in particular, only after we have attained clarity concerning his conception of truth as such—along with the relation of truth to "life," that is, in Nietzsche's sense, to being as a whole. Without an adequate conception of Nietzsche's notion of belief we will hardly dare to risk a judgment concerning what the word "religion" means when Nietzsche calls his most difficult thought "the religion of the freest, most cheerful and sublime souls." Neither the "freedom" nor the "cheerfulness" nor the "sublimity" involved here can be understood according to our gratuitous, humdrum representations.

However, it is unfortunately necessary at this particular juncture that we forego detailed consideration of Nietzsche's concept of "truth," as of his conception of holding firm in the "truth" and holding fast to the true. That is to say, we will not be able to elaborate on Nietzsche's concept of belief or even his conception of the relationship between "religion" and "philosophy." Nevertheless, in order that in the present context our interpretation may take its bearings from some landmark in Nietzsche's own terrain, let us appeal for assistance to a series of maxims that stem from the period of *Thus Spoke Zarathustra,* 1882–84.

We are conceiving of belief, in the sense of a taking to be true, as a holding firm in the true. Such holding firm and the stance it implies will be more genuinely successful the more originally they are determined by the stance, and the less exclusively they are defined purely by

the hold they have on things; that is to say, they will be more genuinely successful if they are essentially able to revert back to themselves and
not lean on things, not depend on them for support. Yet in this particular matter Nietzsche issues a warning to all who would be "self-
reliant." His admonition first says what it means to stand on one's own
and thus attain a stance: "You self-reliant ones—you must learn how
to stand on your own, else you'll be a pushover" (XII, 250, number
67).* Whenever a stance is nothing more than a *mere* consequence of
the hold attributed to it, whenever the hold *undergirds* it, it is no real
stance at all. The latter *holds* only if and as long as it is able to stand
on its own two feet; in the former case, the stance that relies on some
particular hold collapses as soon as the support is withdrawn.

"'I no longer believe in anything'—that is the correct way for a
creative human being to think" (number 68). What does it mean to say
"I no longer believe in anything"? Usually such an asseveration is
testimony to "absolute skepticism" and "nihilism," doubt and despair
of all knowledge, all order, and hence a sign of flight in the face of all
decision and commitment; normally it is an expression of dissolution,
where nothing holds and nothing is worth the trouble. Yet in the
present instance unbelief and unwillingness to take-for-true mean
something else. They mean refusal to embrace without further ado
whatever is pregiven; refusal to rest content and delude oneself with
merely ostensible decisions; refusal to shut one's eyes to one's own
complacency.

What is the true, according to Nietzsche's conception of it? It is
whatever in the perpetual flux and alteration of Becoming is *fixated,*
whatever it is human beings have to get a firm grip on, whatever they

---

* *"Ihr Selbstständigen—ihr müsst euch selber stellen lernen oder ihr fallt um."* It is by
no means clear what Nietzsche's admonition amounts to: *sich stellen* means to turn
oneself in, to volunteer, to muster, and even (though the context makes this unlikely) to
deceive, to fake; *umfallen* literally means to fall over, but it is a colloquialism for changing one's mind at every whim. Nietzsche may be advising those who seek self-reliance to
muster enough confidence to assert themselves and to fight—or to surrender—or to fake
it—whatever it takes not to be a "pushover." Heidegger clearly understands Nietzsche's
remonstrance to mean that if self-reliant persons are those who lean on no one and no
thing for support then they must learn to achieve a truly independent stance—without
holding on.

will to get a firm grip on. The true is what is firm. It is that about which human beings draw a boundary, as if to say "Off limits!" to all inquiry, all disturbance, all probing. In that way human beings introduce a sense of permanence into their own lives—even if it is simply the permanence of what they are used to, what they can dominate, what serves as a protection against all discomfiture and grants the consolation of tranquillity.

To believe in Nietzsche's sense is thus to fixate the ever-changing throng of beings we encounter in the specific guiding representations of whatever is permanent and ordered. To believe, furthermore, is to entrench oneself in this fixating relationship in the very terms of what is fixated. In accordance with this conception of belief, which is absolutely essential in all of Nietzsche's thought (belief as self-entrenchment in fixation), the phrase "I no longer believe in anything" suggests the very opposite of doubt and paralysis in the face of decision and action. It means the following: "I will not have life come to a standstill at *one* possibility, *one* configuration; I will allow and grant life its inalienable right to become, and I shall do this by prefiguring and projecting new and higher possibilities for it, creatively conducting life out beyond itself." The creator is thus necessarily a nonbeliever, granted the designated sense of belief as bringing to a standstill. The creator is at the same time a destroyer with respect to everything congealed or petrified. But he is such only because ahead of time and above all else he communicates to life a new possibility as its higher law. This is what the next maxim (number 69; XII, 250) says: "All creation is communication. The knower, the creator, the lover are *one.*"

Creation as communication—it is important to listen here in the right way. Every creating is a sharing with others. This implies that creation in itself grounds new possibilities of Being—erects them, or, as Hölderlin says, founds them. Creation allots a new Being to prior beings, communicates it to them. Creation as such, and not only in its utilization, is a gift-giving. Genuine creation does not need to ask, does not even possess the inner possibility of inquiring, whether and how it might best be practicable and serviceable. Only where every trace of creative force and creative standards are lacking; only where merely mimetic machinery grinds into action; only where nothing can be shared in some creative process, inasmuch as the very creativity is missing; only there do we find some *purpose* proclaimed and acclaimed—retrospectively, if need be, but more auspiciously by way of anticipation—which provides the rationale for a whole line of products.

To create is to share—the most genuine service we can think of, because the most reticent. Genuine creation is thus utterly remote from the danger of becoming its own purpose; it does not even need to defend itself against such a misunderstanding. Only the sheer semblance of creativity needs to be constantly and vociferously reassured that it does not exist for its own sake but performs a service.

However, creation can appear in yet another guise, no less corrupting than the one just mentioned. The sovereign sufficiency that belongs essentially to creation, which does not need to posit an extraneous purpose, can assume the appearance of mere purposeless whimsy, of *l'art pour l'art*. Yet this is as far removed from genuine creation, or sharing-with, as the semblance cited above. The outcome of all this is simply the fact that creation itself and what is created are always extremely difficult to recognize and to unravel. And it is good that this is so. For it is their best protection, the guarantee that they will be preserved as something that can never be lost.

From that period on in which Nietzsche's great thought comes to him he recites again and again in various turns of phrase the trinity of knowing, creating, and loving. Love he comprehends as gift-giving and in terms of the giver; often he calls it by these very names. Instead of "knowers" he also likes to speak of "teachers." If we follow Nietzsche's lead and substitute "the philosopher" for "the knower," "the artist" for "the creator," and "the saint" for "the lover," then the phrase we introduced a moment ago tells us that the philosopher, artist, and saint are *one*. However, it is not Nietzsche's purpose here to concoct an amalgam that would consist of all the things these words *used* to mean. On the contrary, he is seeking the figure of a human being who exists simultaneously in the transformed unity of that threefold metamorphosis—the knower, the creator, the giver. This human being of the future is the proper ruler, the one who has become master of the last man, indeed in such a way that the last man disappears. His disappearance indicates that the ruler is no longer defined in opposition to the last man—which is what always happens as long as future humanity, spawned by what has gone before, has to grasp itself as over-man, that is to say, as a transition. The ruler, that is, the designated unity of knower, creator, and lover, is in his own proper grounds altogether an other. Yet in order that the new form of humanity come to be and provide a standard, the figures of the knower, creator, and giver must themselves be prepared by way of a novel metamorphosis and unification. Nietzsche at one point expresses the matter in the following way: "The giver, the creator, the teacher—these are preludes to the *ruler.*" (See the supplements to *Thus Spoke Zarathustra* from the years 1882–86; XII, 363.)

In the fresh light cast by this new perspective on the matter we have to understand maxims like the following one, which, bearing the number 70, follows directly upon number 69 in the series we have been considering (XII, 250): "'Religious man,' 'fool,' 'genius,' 'criminal,' 'tyrant'—these are imperfect names and mere details, as approximations to something ineffable." If Nietzsche includes the notion of the "religious man" among the others in this sequence, we have to be quite careful. We have to think matters over quite precisely before we earmark the thought of return as a "religious" thought, in effect ostracizing it from Nietzsche's "body of knowledge," his "doctrine." Any reflective person, following the lead of our necessarily limited and scarcely elucidated comments, will already have realized how ridiculous such a procedure makes itself look. Precisely the thinking of the most difficult thought becomes supreme knowledge, it is in itself a creating; its creating is a communicating, gift-giving, and loving; and it thereby appears in the fundamental figure of the "saint" and the "religious." Yet Nietzsche does not designate this thinking of the most difficult thought as believing because it is holy and religious, that is, thanks to its character as creative love; he calls it a believing because *as a thinking* of beings as a whole it fixates beings themselves in a projection of Being. The thought's character as belief does not in the first place spring from its religious character; rather, the aspect of belief springs from its character as a thinking, inasmuch as thinking, representing relationships and constellations, always erects and intends something that is permanent.

The thinking of the most difficult thought is a believing. It holds firm in the true. Truth for Nietzsche always means the true, and the true signifies in Nietzsche's view being—that which is fixated as permanent. This occurs in such a way that the living creature secures its subsistence in and through the circle of what is fixated. As fixation, belief is the securing of permanence.

The *thought* of eternal return of the same *fixates* by determining *how* the world essentially *is*—as the necessitous chaos of perpetual Becoming. The thinking of this thought holds firm in being as a whole *in such a way* that for it the eternal return of the same serves as the Being that determines all beings. Such a truth can never of course be directly proven to particular human beings by way of particular pieces of evidence; it can never be demonstrated in its actuality by way of certain facts, inasmuch as it involves being as a whole. We come to being as a whole always and only by means of a leap that executes our very projection of it, assisting and accomplishing that projection in its process. We never come to being as a whole by moving tentatively and haltingly through a sequence of particular facts and constellations of facts aligned in terms of cause-effect relations. Consequently, what is thought in this thought is never given as some particular, actual thing at hand; it is always proffered as a possibility.

But then does not the thought lose all its weight? When Nietzsche concedes that his thought is merely a possibility, does he not forfeit the right to be taken seriously—surrender the claim that his thought is to be taken seriously? By no means. For the concession actually expresses the fact that to hold firm in this thought is essentially to co-constitute its being true; the fact that the hold itself is defined by the stance, and not vice-versa. Nietzsche provides a helpful point of reference when he says in note 119 (XII, 65):

> Even the *thought of a possibility* can shake us and transform us; it is not merely sensations or particular expectations that can do that! Note how effective the *possibility* of eternal damnation was!

On the basis of this remark we also recognize the fact that it was no accident that Nietzsche chose the particular form he did for the first communication of his thought in *The Gay Science*, the form of the demon who interrogates us by opening up a possibility: "What would happen if . . . ?* The interrogative mode of thinking corresponds to the heart's core of what is being thought here. The possibility in question—which indeed has to be interrogated thoroughly—is mightier as a possibility than anything actual or factual. One possible thing generates other possibilities, inherently and necessarily bringing them to the fore along with itself. What is possible in a given thought transposes us to a number of possibilities: we may think it in this or that way, assume a stance within it in this or that fashion. To think through a possibility truly—that is to say, with all its consequences—means to decide something for ourselves, even if the decision calls for nothing more than a retreat from and exclusion of the possibility.

In accord with the entire history of Western humanity hitherto, and in accord with the interpretation of beings that sustains that history, we are all too accustomed to thinking purely and simply in terms of actualities, to interpreting in terms of the actual (as presence, *ousia*). For this reason we are still unprepared, we feel awkward and inadequate, when it comes to thinking *possibility*, a kind of thinking that is always creative. Hence, to the extent that the thought of return involves our adopting this or that stance within the whole of beings, a range of possibilities of decision and scission opens up for human existence in general. † Nietzsche says that the thought contains "the possibility of defining and ordering anew individual human beings in their affects" (number 118). In order to elicit the full content of this statement we have to know that according to Nietzsche it is affects and drives that define the given perspectives within which human beings perceive the world. Such perspectives determine the corner for that Little Jack Horner called "man."

In the light of the thought of return a decision has to be reached as to who has or does not have the energy and the attunement required to

---

* See section 3, above: "Nietzsche's First Communication of the Doctrine of Return." On the power of the *possible*, cf. *Being and Time*, sections 31 and 53; see also the "Letter on Humanism," *Basic Writings*, p. 196.

† "Decision and scission" renders Heidegger's phrase *Entscheidung und Scheidung*. His coupling of these two words emphasizes the root of *decision*, meaning to cut off, sever, separate. Decision does not mean a subject's making up his or her mind; it means the realization that one has reached a point of radical change. *Entscheidung* suggests the crossing of a kind of watershed, *Wasserscheide*.

hold firm in the truth. Those who do not "believe" in it are the "fleeting ones." By that Nietzsche means two things. First of all, the fleeting ones are fleeing ones, in flight before magnificent, expansive prospects, which presuppose an ability to wait. The fleeting ones want their happiness right there where they can latch onto it; and they want the time to be able to enjoy it. These people who flee are fleeting in yet another sense: they themselves are without stability, are transient creatures; they leave nothing behind; they found nothing, ground nothing. The others, those who are not fleeting, are "the human beings with eternal souls and eternal Becoming and pains that tell of the future." We might also say that they are the human beings who bear within themselves a great deal of time and who live to the full the times they have—a matter that is quite independent of actual longevity. Or, to turn it around the other way: it is precisely the fleeting human being who is least fit to serve as the human being of proper transition, though appearances seem to suggest the opposite, insmuch as "transition" implies evanescence. The fleeting ones, who do not and cannot think the thought, "must, according to their own nature, finally *die off!*" "Only those who hold their existence to be capable of eternal repetition will *remain:* and with *such* people a condition is *possible* to which no utopian has ever attained!" (number 121). "Whoever does not believe has a *fleeting* life in his consciousness" (number 128).

The thought does not "work its effects" in that it leaves behind particular consequences for later times. Rather, when it is thought, when the one who is thinking it stands firm in this truth of beings as a whole, when thinkers who are of such a nature *are,* then beings as a whole also undergo metamorphosis. "From the very moment this thought exists, all colors change their hue and a new *history* begins" (number 120; cf. number 114*).

The most difficult thought is here grasped as the thought that inaugurates a new history. It is not merely that another series of happenstances unfolds; what is different is the *kind* of happening, acting, and creating. Color, the very look of things, their *eidos,* presencing,

---

* GOA, XII, number 114 is cited in section 18, pp. 138–39, below. In CM see M III 1 [148].

Being—this is what changes. "Deep yellow" and "incandescent red" begin to radiate.

However, must not a question finally claim its rights at this juncture, a question that causes the very essence of this thought, whole and entire, to dissolve into thin air? If everything is necessary—the world as a chaos of necessity—and if everything recurs as it once was, then all thinking and planning become superfluous, indeed are impossible from the outset; we must take everything as it comes; and all is indifferent. Instead of providing us with a burden, the thought deprives us of the ballast and the steadying weight of decision and action, divests us of every sense of planning and willing. It harnesses us to the self-propelling, necessitous course of an eternal cycle, opening up all avenues at once to lawlessness and sheer contingency. It ends by causing us to founder in sheer inaction—we let it all slide. And, for good measure, such a thought would not be a *"new"* burden at all, but an ancient one. For it was the history of antiquity that allowed itself to get bogged down in fatalism.

18. The Thought of Return— and Freedom

When we pause to think about these things we come up against a *question*. We would mistake what is most difficult in this exceedingly difficult thought were we to take it too lightly, that is, were we to encounter it in a merely formal dialectical way. Instead of conducting us to supreme and ultimate decisions, the thought appears to let us submerge in vacuous indifference. Yet precisely this trait—the fact that the semblance of its utter opposite dwells right alongside the proper truth of the thought—indicates that here it is a question of thinking a genuine philosophical thought. If we reflect on the question for a moment, if we make even the slightest effort to recollect it, this will suffice to reveal the profile of an earlier, truly ancient question. The difficulty that has only now emerged seems to refer us back to that earlier dilemma, which runs as follows: All being, taken as a whole and as a plenitude of details in any of its given sequences, is forged in the iron ring of the eternal recurrence of the identical collective state; whatever enters on the scene now or in the future is but a recurrence, unalterably predetermined and necessary. But then in this ring what are action, planning, resolve—in short, *"freedom"*—supposed to be? In the ring of necessity freedom is as superfluous as it is impossible. But that is a rebuff to the essence of man; here the very possibility of his essence is denied. If we wish that essence to prevail nevertheless, it is wholly obscure how it may do so.

Obviously, the thought of eternal recurrence of the same guides us back to the question of the relationship between freedom and necessity. The upshot is that this thought cannot be, as Nietzsche claims, the thought of thoughts. For if the thought of return pertains to the domain of the question of freedom and necessity, something fundamental has already been decided about its possible truth. Someone will surely point out that the question of a possible accord between necessity and freedom belongs among those unavoidable yet insoluble questions which set in motion a ceaseless dispute as soon as they intimate what it is they would like to put into question.*

Indeed, from the moment we learn about Nietzsche's doctrine of return such reflections force themselves upon us. We will be all the more inclined to such reflections since we are familiar with the young Nietzsche's school essays, "Fate and History" and "Free Will and Fate," written during the Easter holidays in 1862 (see the *Historical-Critical Collected Edition,* volume II, pages 54–63).† If at the same time we think of the nearly contemporary autobiographical composition by Nietzsche which we cited earlier, and of the fact that this early thought of his was later to become the essential center of his thinking,

---

* Heidegger's use of the word "dispute" *(Widerstreit)* echoes Kant's throughout the "Antinomies" of the *Critique of Pure Reason.* Heidegger's reference is of course to the third Antinomy (see KrV, A 444 / B 472) and to Kant's entire project of a *Critique of Practical Reason.*

† These two "school" essays, written when Nietzsche was eighteen years old, both of them exhibiting the influence of Emerson, are more intriguing than Heidegger's remarks here suggest. "Free Will and Fate" rejects the spirit of Christian "submission to the will of God" and exalts instead a "strong will." The longer essay, "Fate and History: Thoughts," bemoans throughout the prejudices that condition a youth's view of the world and make "a freer standpoint" all but impossible. The young Nietzsche designates *history* and *natural science* as two havens for his storm-tossed speculations on human fate. Having invoked the long history of human evolution and development, Nietzsche asks, "Does this eternal Becoming never come to an end?" History itself he pictures as an enormous clock: when the clock strikes twelve its hands "begin their course all over again—a new period commences for the world." Finally, against the determining forces of *fatum,* Nietzsche deploys the following:

> Yet if it were possible for a strong will to overturn the world's entire past, we would join the ranks of self-sufficient gods, and world history would be no more to us than a dreamlike enchantment of the self. The curtain falls, and man finds himself again, like a child playing with worlds, a child who wakes at daybreak and with a laugh wipes from his brow all frightful dreams.

See *Friedrich Nietzsche Werke und Briefe* (München: C. H. Beck, 1934), II *(Jugendschriften),* 54–63. These essays unfortunately do not appear in the Schlechta and CM editions.

then we seem to be on the right track from Nietzsche's own point of view when we subordinate the doctrine of return to the question of freedom and necessity. Nevertheless, such a procedure overlooks what is most essential. Let us try to make this point sufficiently clear, so that our first efforts to get acquainted with Nietzsche's "doctrine" will manage to keep at bay all inadequate approaches.

What we must pay special attention to will be clarified with the help of Nietzsche's own notes, for example, the following (XII, number 116): "My doctrine says that the task is to live in such a way that you have to *wish* to live again—you will do so *in any case!*" The appended phrase, "you will do so *in any case*" appears to obviate the necessity of assigning the task, "live in such a way. . . ." Why wish, why propose, when you have to take everything as it comes "in any case"? Yet if we read the statement in this way we are not gleaning its true import; we are not entering into its matter, not hearing what it says. The statement speaks to everyone, addressing him or her as "you" in the familiar form. It speaks to us as we are; we ourselves are the ones intended. The intention of the thought thus refers us to our own respective Dasein. Whatever is or is to be will be decided in and by Dasein, inasmuch as only those aspects of Becoming that were once a part of my life are destined to come again.

But then do we know what once was? No! Can we ever know such things? We know nothing of an earlier life. Everything we are now living we experience for the first time, although now and again in the midst of our ordinary experiences that strange and obscure experience crops up which says: What you are now experiencing, precisely in the form it is now taking, you have experienced once before. We know nothing of an earlier "life" when we think back. But can we *only* think back? No, we can also think ahead—and that is thinking proper. In such thinking we are capable in a certain way of knowing with certainty what once was. Strange—are we to experience something that lies behind us by thinking forward? Yes, we are. Then what is it that already was; what will come again when it recurs? The answer to that question is: whatever will be in the next moment. If you allow your existence to drift in timorousness and ignorance, with all the consequences these things have, then they will come again, and they will be that which already was. And if on the contrary you shape something supreme out of the next moment, as out of every moment, and if you note well and retain the consequences, then this moment will come again and will have been what already was: "Eternity suits it." But the matter will be decided solely in your *moments*. It will be decided on the basis of what you yourself hold concerning beings, and what sort of stance you adopt in their midst. It will be decided on the basis of what you will of yourself, what you are *able* to will of yourself.

Against all this one might say: Merely to represent to oneself that he or she is a progression of processes and is, as it were, forged as a link in a chain of circumstances that enter on the scene time after time in an endlessly circling monotony—merely to imagine such a thing is to be absent from onself, and is not to be the being that inherently belongs within the whole of beings. To represent a human being in this way means to fail altogether to take him into account as a self; it is like someone who undertakes to count the number of people who are present but forgets to count himself. To represent humanity that way means to calculate extrinsically, as though one could slip stealthily outside and remain aloof from it all. When we calculate in such fashion we no longer ponder the fact that as temporal beings who are delivered over to ourselves we are also delivered over to the future in our willing; we no longer ponder the fact that the temporality of human being alone determines the way in which the human being stands in the ring of beings. Here too, as in so many other essential respects, Nietzsche has not explicated his teaching and has left many things obscure. Yet certain hints appear over and over again, making it clear that Nietzsche knew and experienced a great deal more about this thought than he either sketched out or fully portrayed. We may safely judge how vehemently Nietzsche spurned extrinsic, fatalistic calculation of the import and the consequences of the thought of return, so that such calculation cannot at all be definitive for him, on the basis of note number 122 (XII, 66):

> You think you will have a long pause before you are reborn—do not deceive yourselves! Between the last moment of consciousness and the first glimmer of the new life "no time" goes by at all. It passes as quickly as a flash of

lightning, even if living creatures measure it in terms of billions of years and even then fail to measure it adequately. Timelessness and succession go hand-in-hand with one another as soon as the intellect is gone.

Here the dual possibility for our envisaging things comes more clearly to the fore: we can estimate and decide about our relationship with beings as a whole from out of ourselves, in terms of the time each of us experiences; or we can remove ourselves from this time of our temporality—covertly relying on such time, however—and settle accounts with the whole by means of an infinite calculation. In the two cases the time interval between each of the recurrences is measured according to totally different standards. Seen in terms of our own experienced temporality, no time at all passes between the end of one lifetime and the beginning of another, even though the duration cannot be grasped "objectively" even in billions of years (see Aristotle, *Physics*, Book IV, chapters 10–14). * Yet what are billions of years when measured against eternity; that is to say, at the same time, measured against the standard of the moment of decision? What Nietzsche here says about the

---

* It is difficult to know what to make of this reference to the entire "treatise on time" in Aristotle's *Physics*, Book Delta, 10–14, unless Heidegger wishes to reiterate Aristotle's importance for his own conception of Dasein as temporality. Two passages in Aristotle's treatise, which Heidegger may have had in mind when making the present reference, are the following. First, the opening of chapter 11:

> But neither does time exist without change [metabolē]. For when the state of our own minds does not change at all, or we have not noticed its changing, we do not realize that time has elapsed any more than those who are fabled to sleep among the heroes in Sardinia do when they are awakened. . . . So, just as, if the "now" were not different but one and the same, there would not have been time, so too when its difference escapes our notice the interval [metaxy] does not seem to be time.

And second, a passage from chapter 14 (223a 21 ff.), which Heidegger regards as essential to Aristotle's definition of time as the number of motion:

> Whether if soul [psychē] did not exist [mē ousa] time would exist or not, is a question that may fairly be asked; for if there cannot be someone to count there cannot be anything that can be counted. . . . But if nothing but soul, or in soul reason [nous], is qualified to count, there would not be time unless there were soul. . . .

Heidegger's most complete discussion of Aristotle in this respect, a discussion which may be viewed as an elaboration of the final sections of *Being and Time*, appears as section 19, "Time and Temporality," in Heidegger, *Die Grundprobleme der Phänomenologie* (Frankfurt am Main: V. Klostermann, 1975), pp. 327–62, esp. pp. 335 and 360–61.

timelessness of the "time in between" seems to contradict what is observed in another note from the same period (number 114):

> Man! Your entire life will be turned over and over again like an hourglass; again and again it will run out—one vast minute of time in between, until all the conditions that went into your becoming converge again in the world's circulation.

One vast minute of time in between—well, then, some time does transpire in the "in-between time," indeed "one vast minute"! Yet what Nietzsche says here does not contradict the preceding; it embraces both ways of viewing the situation in one. Over against the billions of years that are calculated objectively, one minute of time amounts to no time at all; and "one vast minute" is meant to indicate simultaneously that all the conditions for becoming again, for recurrence, are gathering meanwhile—"all the conditions from which you took your becoming." Here, to be sure, the decisive condition is not mentioned: the *decisive* condition is you *yourself,* that is to say, the manner in which you achieve your self by becoming your own master, and this by seeing to it that when you engage your will essentially you take yourself up into that will and so attain freedom. We are free only when we become free, and we become free only by virtue of our wills. That is what we read in the second section of the second part of *Thus Spoke Zarathustra,* written in 1883, "On the Blessed Isles": "To will is liberating: that is the true teaching concerning will and freedom—thus Zarathustra teaches it to you."

We know that Zarathustra is the teacher of eternal return, and that he is this alone. Thus the question of freedom, and hence of necessity too and of the relation between these two, is posed anew by the teaching of the eternal return of the same. For that reason we go astray when we reverse matters and try to cram the doctrine of return into some long-ossified schema of the question of freedom. And this is what we in fact do—insofar as the traditional metaphysical question of freedom is conceived of as a question of "causality," while causality itself, in terms of its essential definition, stems from the notion of being as "actuality."

We must admit that Nietzsche never pursued these interconnections. Yet so much is clear: the doctrine of return should never be contorted in such a way that it fits into the readily available "antinomy" of freedom and necessity. At the same time, this reminds us once again of our sole task—to think this most difficult thought as it demands to be thought, on its own terms, leaving aside all supports and makeshifts.

Let us round off our survey of Nietzsche's notes on the doctrine of return from the period when the thought of thoughts first dawned on him (1882) with an observation by Nietzsche that guides us back to his very first plans for that thought, especially the third of these plans, entitled *"Midday and Eternity."* The note to which we have already referred (number 114) closes with the following thought:

> And in every ring of human existence in general there is always an hour when the mightiest thought emerges, first to one, then to many, and finally to all: the thought of the eternal return of all things. It is, each time, the hour of midday for humanity.

What does Nietzsche want to say here? For one thing, this thought integrates the thought of return itself as propriative event into the circle of beings as a whole, which it creates afresh. The reference to "human existence" here means, not the emergence on the scene of individual beings, but the fundamental fact *that* a being like *human being* in general comes to *be* within the whole of beings. At the same time, the thought tacitly suggests as one of its presuppositions that the thought of thoughts is not always the propriative event in human existence; that event itself has its time, its hour, which is "the hour of *midday* for humanity."*

We know what Nietzsche means by this word *midday:* the moment of the shortest shadow, when fore-noon and after-noon, past and future, meet in one. Their meeting-place is the moment of supreme

---

* Heidegger's references to *Ereignis,* the propriative event, remind us that the lecture on eternal recurrence comes precisely at the time Heidegger was writing his *Contributions to Philosophy: On 'Ereignis,'* 1936–38. In the first course on Nietzsche, "Will to Power as Art," he invoked *Ereignis* as the event of *nihilism* (see Volume I of this series, p. 156 n.; see also Volume IV, p. 5.) Here the propriative event involves the thought of eternal recurrence itself, which Nietzsche proffered as the most effective *counter* to nihilism. The matter is pursued in section 23, below.

unity for all temporal things in utterly magnificent transfiguration, the moment when they are bathed in the most brilliant light. It is the moment of eternity. The hour of midday is the hour when human existence is each time transfigured to its supreme height and its most potent will. In the word *midday* a point of time is determined for the propriative event of the thought of eternal return within the eternal return of the same. No timepiece measures this point, here meant as that point in being as a whole when time itself *is* as the temporality of the moment. The most intrinsic yet most covert relation of the eternal return of the same (as the basic character of beings as a whole) to time now begins to glimmer. Every effort to grasp this teaching depends on our observing the relation that comes to light and on our being able to explicate that relation.

19. Retrospect on the Notes from the Period of *The Gay Science*, 1881–82

If we now survey the great wealth of material found in the earliest suppressed notes on the doctrine of eternal return, and if we compare all of it with what Nietzsche in the following year proceeds to communicate, then it becomes clear that the *published material represents a disproportionately small amount of what Nietzsche already thought and already knew.* Yet this remains a purely extraneous finding. Something else is more important, namely, the fact that the two passages which embody Nietzsche's first communication of the thought, at the conclusion of the first edition of *The Gay Science*, numbers 341 and 342, *"The Greatest Burden"* and *"Incipit Tragoedia,"* essentially conjoin the two fundamental directions taken by the thought in Nietzsche's very first projected plans: they exhibit the thought of return as one that participates in altering the configuration of being as a whole itself; and they exhibit the thought of return as one which—in order to be a thought, in order actually to be thought—calls for its own thinker and teacher.

In retrospect we may say, and in fact say quite readily, that at the time *The Gay Science* first appeared with these concluding passages, in the year 1882, it was indeed impossible for anyone to understand what Nietzsche knew full well, impossible to understand what he wanted. And in all fairness Nietzsche could not have expected and insisted that he be understood straightaway, especially since such understanding is always a two-edged sword.

Understanding burgeons only when those who understand essentially find themselves growing in the direction of the new thought, only when they question in the direction of those new questions out of the autochthony of their own need, in this way alone taking up those novel questions anew, and thus transfiguring themselves to a greater clarity. Yet in the education of those who are reaching out in order to understand, their own lack of understanding, their noncomprehension of the thought that has been thought prior to them, may well be a formative obstacle, perhaps even a necessary one. We know little about these processes. Those who understand fundamentally, from the ground up, that is, those who think the thought itself creatively again, are never the contemporaries of the first thinkers of the thought. Nor are they the ones who are in a hurry to take up the nascent thought as something "modern," since these are truly vagrant, begging meals wherever they can find anything à la mode. Those who properly understand are always the ones who come a long way on their own ground, from their own territory, the ones who bring much with them in order that they may transform much. That is what Nietzsche is ruminating in a note which stems from the period we are dealing with, 1881–82 (see XII, 18 f., number 35), but which belongs to the second division of notes on the doctrine of eternal return—if the schema of the original editors is to serve at all as our standard:

> A novel doctrine encounters its best representatives last. These are natures that have long been self-assured and assuring, so that their earlier thoughts exhibit the tangled growth and *impenetrability* of a fertile primeval forest. The weaker, more vacuous, sicklier, and needier types are those who first contract the new infection—the first disciples prove nothing *against* a doctrine. I believe the first Christians were the most disgusting people, with all their "virtues."

Because Nietzsche's concluding thought in *The Gay Science* could not be understood as Nietzsche meant it to be understood, namely, as the thought that would inaugurate his new philosophy, it was inevitable that the following communication too, in *Thus Spoke Zarathustra*, remained uncomprehended as a whole—all the more so since its form could only have alienated readers, ultimately distracting them from a rigorous thinking of the most difficult thought rather than guiding them toward it. And yet the poetic creation of the thinker of eternal return was for Nietzsche himself the matter that was "deepest" and was thus most essential for him: it took shape in and as the history of the coming to be—and that means the downgoing—of the hero who thinks the thought.

Let us now examine the suppressed materials from the *Zarathustra* period, basing our search on the understanding of Nietzsche's second communication of the thought of return in the way we have indicated —the communication *via* Zarathustra in the book *Thus Spoke Zarathustra*. Our search will reveal that the ratio of unpublished notes to what Nietzsche himself communicated is precisely the inverse of what it was in the period of *The Gay Science* and that book's immediate background.

20. Notes from the *Zarathustra* Period, 1883–84

The notes in question are to be found in volume XII of the *Grossoktav* edition, pages 369–71, under numbers 719 to 731. A number of scattered observations that allude to the thought of return only indirectly might also be drawn into consideration here, along with the quite extensive "materials"—maxims, plans, and references—from the preliminary sketches to *Thus Spoke Zarathustra*.

What the editors have collected under the specific title "The Eternal Return" is small in scope but significant in import. When we compare these few fragments—most of them consisting of a single statement or question—with those of the preceding period, the first thing that strikes us is the absence of "proofs" derived from the natural sciences. Commentators are wont to conclude that Nietzsche himself must in the meantime have given up on such proofs. Yet we find these ostensibly scientific statements also in notes composed some time later. What we must guard against is our own tendency to extract the import of these statements as though they were formulas of physics. If they never were pieces of scientific evidence in the first place, it cannot be a matter of Nietzsche's surrendering erstwhile proofs.

How are we to interpret the following statement? "Life itself created the thought that is hardest for it to bear; life wants to leap beyond its highest barrier!" (number 720). Here it is not a matter of the doctrine's "ethical impact" or "subjective significance." The thought pertains to "life" itself. "Life" in this case means the will to power. Being itself, as something that becomes, is creative and destructive; as creative it projects the prospects of its transfiguring possibilities ahead of itself.

Supreme creation is creation of the highest barrier, which is to say, the barrier that embodies the most stubborn resistance to creation itself, thereby catapulting creation magnificently into farther reaches of life-enhancement. The thought of eternal return is the hardest thought for life to think, precisely because life can most easily go astray on account of it, straying from itself as truly creative and allowing everything to submerge in sheer apathy and indifference. In the statement we are considering, eternal recurrence is seen to spring from the essence of "life" itself; hence it is removed at the outset from all fortuitous whimsy and all "personal confessions of faith." From the present vantage-point we can also see how the doctrine of eternal return of the same, as a doctrine of perpetual Becoming, relates to the ancient doctrine of the external flux of all things—a view that is usually called "Heraclitean."

Commentators are accustomed to equating Nietzsche's doctrine of the eternal return of the same with the teachings of Heraclitus. Appealing to Nietzsche's own utterances in this respect, they designate Nietzsche's philosophy a kind of "Heracliteanism." Now, it is indisputable that Nietzsche sensed a certain kinship between his own and Heraclitus' teachings—as *he* saw them, he along with his contemporaries. Especially about the year 1881, immediately prior to the birth of the thought of return, he often spoke of "the eternal flux of all things" (cf. XII, 30; number 57). He even called the doctrine "of the flux of things" the "ultimate truth" (number 89), that is, the truth that can no longer be incorporated. This suggests that the doctrine of the eternal flow of all things, in the sense of thoroughgoing impermanence, can no longer be held to be true; human beings cannot hold firm in it as something true because they would thereby surrender themselves to ceaseless change, inconstancy, and total obliteration, and because everything firm, everything true, would have become quite impossible.

In fact, Nietzsche had imbibed of this basic position vis-à-vis being as a whole, as eternal flow, directly before the thought of eternal return of the same came to him. Yet if as we have seen this thought is the genuine belief, the essential way of holding firm in the true, as what is fixated, then the thought of eternal return of the same freezes the eternal flow; the ultimate truth is now to be incorporated (see the first plans from the year 1881).* From our present vantage-point we can see why these first plans speak so emphatically of "incorporation." As opposed to that, it is now a matter of overcoming the doctrine of the eternal flux of things and its essentially destructive character. Once the doctrine of return emerges, Nietzsche's "Heracliteanism" is a very peculiar affair indeed. The note stemming from Nietzsche's *Zarathustra* period which we shall now cite (number 723) is crystal clear about this: "I teach you redemption from the eternal flux: the river flows ever back into itself, and you are ever stepping into the same river, as the selfsame ones."

Nietzsche's utterance is a conscious reply to a thought in Greek philosophy that was associated with Heraclitus—that is to say, with a particular interpretation of his doctrine. According to that thought, we can never step into the identical river, on account of its perpetual and ineluctable onward flow.† Nietzsche designates his doctrine—in

---

* In the plan dated August 26, 1881 (in CM see M III 1 [197]), Nietzsche entitles the second book of his projected work on eternal recurrence "On the Incorporation of Experiences." Incorporation, *Einverleibung*, must be understood initially in biological —not legal—terms, as *ingestion;* it later assumes a more social, cultural sense. Among the many passages on incorporation (e.g., M III 1 [164, 273, 314]) are the two following. Fragment number 162 begins:

In order for there to be some degree of consciousness in the world, an unreal world of error must come to be: creatures that believe in the perdurance of individuals, etc. Only after an imaginary counterworld, in contradiction to absolute flux, had originated could something *be recognized on the basis of it*—indeed, we can ultimately get insight into the fundamental error on which all else rests (because opposites can be *thought*)—yet the error cannot be extirpated without annihilating life: the ultimate truth of the flux of things does not sustain incorporation; our organs (for *living*) are oriented to error. Thus in the man of wisdom there originates the *contradiction of life* and of his ultimate decisions; his *drive* to knowledge has as its presuppositions the belief in error and the life in such belief.

And at the center of fragment number 262 we find:

Whatever corresponds to the necessary life-conditions of the time and the group will establish itself as "truth": in the long run humanity's *sum of opinions* will be *incorporated,* the opinions that were most useful to them, that is, granted them the possibility of the longest duration. The most essential of these opinions on which the duration of humanity rests are those that it incorporated long ago, for example, belief in sameness, number, space, etc. The struggle will *not* turn about *these things*—it can only be an *expansion* of these erroneous *foundations* of our animal existence.

† See, in the Diels-Kranz numeration, B 49a, 91, and 12. See also Jean Brun, *Héraclite* (Paris: Seghers, 1965), p. 136 n. 24; and G. S. Kirk and J. E. Raven, *The Presocratic Philosophers,* pp. 196–99.

opposition to the ancient one—as "redemption from the eternal flux." That does not mean brushing aside Becoming, or petrifying it; it means liberation from the irreducible, ceaseless "forever the same." Becoming is retained as Becoming. Yet permanence—that is, when understood in Greek fashion, Being—is injected into *Becoming.*

Being as a whole is still a flux, a flowing in the sense of a becoming. However, *recurrence* of the same is so essential to this becoming that it is such recurrence that primarily defines the character of Becoming. For Nietzsche a particular notion of what is called an "infinite process" is coined on this basis. *"An infinite process cannot* be thought of in any other way than as *periodic"* (number 727). In the infinitude of actual time, the only possible kind of occurrence for a finite world that is now still "becoming" is recurrence—the cycle. The sundry episodes that constitute it are not to be imagined as being lined up in some extrinsic way and then joined end to end, since this would result in a vacuous circulation; rather, every episode, each in its own way, is a resonance of the whole and a harmonious entry into the whole. "Didn't you know? In each of your actions the history of everything that has happened is repeated in condensed form" (number 726). While at first blush the doctrine of return introduces an immense, paralyzing indifference into all beings and into human behavior, in truth the thought of thoughts grants supreme lucidity and decisiveness to beings at every moment.

The haunting vision that the thought of return might enervate all being disturbed Nietzsche so profoundly that he was forced to consider quite carefully the consequences of his doctrine: "Fear in the face of the doctrine's consequences: perhaps the best natures perish on account of it? The worst adopt it?" (number 729). The worst adopt it, assert themselves in it, and establish on the basis of it the fact that beings have fallen prey to general indifference and gratuitousness. This as the consequence of a doctrine that in truth wishes to supply the center of gravity and to propel human beings beyond all mediocrity. Yet because this haunting vision cannot be dispelled, because it comes to the fore and oppresses us rudely and relentlessly, it dominates for a time the way we take the doctrine to be true:

At first the common riffraff will smile upon the doctrine of return, all who are cold and without much inner need. The most vulgar impulse to life will be the first to grant assent. *A great truth wins to itself the highest human beings last: this is what anything true must suffer* (number 730; cf. number 35).*

When we survey the few fragments of the *Zarathustra* period that explicitly meditate on the doctrine of return we realize that these are, in terms of import, quite significant; a few vigorous statements and a number of lucidly posed questions say everything that is essential. While Nietzsche's thoughtful and poetically creative work on this most difficult of thoughts drives him to excesses, a kind of pendulum effect intervenes, ensuring that his unrelenting efforts will find the midpoint. Above the turbulence of inquiry and demand prevails the cheerful calm of a victor who is long accustomed to suffering. Nietzsche achieves such calm and tranquillity also with respect to the question of the possible impact of the doctrine (XII, 398; from the year 1883):

The most magnificent thought works its effects most slowly and belatedly! Its most immediate impact is as a substitute for the belief in immortality: does it augment good will toward life? Perhaps it is not true:—may others wrestle with it!

One might be tempted to conclude from this last remark that Nietzsche himself doubted the truth of the thought and did not take it seriously, that he was only toying with it as a possibility. Such a conclusion would be a sign of superficial thinking. Of course Nietzsche doubted this thought, as he doubted every essential thought: this pertains to the style of his thinking. Yet from that we *dare not* conclude that he failed to take the thought itself seriously. What we must rather conclude is that he took the thought altogether seriously, subjecting it to interrogation again and again, testing it, in that way learning to think on his own two feet, as it were, and conducting himself to knowledge—namely, knowledge of the fact that what is essentially to be thought here is the matter of *possibility*. Every time Nietzsche writes "perhaps it is not true" he is designating with sufficient clarity

---

* GOA, XII, number 35 was cited earlier, in section 19, p. 142, above. In CM see M III 1 [147].

the character of such possibility. Nietzsche knows only thoughts that have to be wrestled with. It is another question altogether whether he is the victor and master over the thought, or whether it still remains for others to grapple with it.

21. Notes from the Period of "The Will to Power," 1884–88

In the years that immediately followed *Thus Spoke Zarathustra*, 1884 to 1886, we find plans for additions to that book and for an altogether different configuration of it. Here too the thought of return everywhere assumes center-stage in Nietzsche's thinking. The guiding notion for the new configuration is the thought of the "magnificent midday" as the "decisive time" (XII, number 419; from the year 1886).

It is important that we take into account the existence of these plans from the time *circa* 1886. In line with the general insecurity and the vacillation of Nietzsche interpretation heretofore as regards the doctrine of return, an erroneous view has recently been propagated, to the effect that Nietzsche allowed the thought of return—which ostensibly was only a personal confession of faith anyway—to recede from his thinking the moment he began to plan and prepare his philosophic *magnum opus*. It is indeed the case that as soon as he had concluded *Zarathustra* in 1884 Nietzsche became absorbed in plans for a work that was to present his philosophy as a whole in a systematic way. Labors on this work occupied Nietzsche (with interruptions) from 1884 to the end of his creative life, that is, till the end of 1888.

After everything we have heard up to now concerning Nietzsche's "thought of thoughts," with which he had been grappling ever since the year 1881, it would surely be astonishing if the plan for this major philosophical work were *not* sustained and *not* pervaded by the thought of eternal return. At all events, the earlier reference to the plan of 1886 makes one thing perfectly clear; even at *this* time the thought of eternal return constitutes the fulcrum of Nietzsche's thinking. How could he have prepared his major philosophical work during this period *without* the thought, or after having surrendered it? What more striking proof could we demand than the third communication by Nietzsche, in *Beyond Good and Evil* (number 56; from the year 1886), which demonstrates that the thought of return was not only not surrendered and not cast aside—as though it had been a mere personal confession of faith—but enhanced in a new excursion to the very limits and supreme heights of its thinkability? Was not this new attempt, which was contemporaneous with Nietzsche's most vigorous labors on his *magnum opus*, to be in the most intrinsic way at one with and at the heart's core of his projected work? Even if we had no more than the previously cited testimony for the existence of the thought of eternal return in 1886, it would be enough to unmask the erroneous view of the thought's imputed retreat. Yet how do matters stand with regard to the things Nietzsche thought and jotted down in the period 1884–88 but did not elect to communicate?

The stock of unpublished materials from these years is quite extensive and is to be found in volumes XIII to XVI in the *Grossoktav* edition. Yet we immediately have to add that the materials appear here in a way that beguiles and thoroughly misleads all interpretation of Nietzsche's philosophy during this decisive period—granted that we are speaking of an *interpretation,* that is, a confrontation *in the light of the grounding question of Western thinking.** The principal reason for the misleading nature of the arrangement of these notes lies in a happenstance that is always taken far too casually.

Ever since Nietzsche's death at the turn of the century, the editors of Nietzsche's literary remains have launched a series of attempts to collate these notes for a *magnum opus,* a work that Nietzsche himself was planning during his final creative period. In a rough and ready sort of way they tried to base their work on plans that stemmed from Nietzsche's own hand. For a time—yet, *nota bene,* only for a time, namely, the years 1886–87—Nietzsche planned to entitle his main work *The Will to Power.* Under this title Nietzsche's major work was in fact explicitly announced in the treatise that appeared in 1887, *Toward a*

---

* On the "grounding question," see the first volume in this series, section 11, pp. 67–68, and sections 25–26, below.

Genealogy of Morals, where a reference to it appeared in extra heavy type (VII, 480, number 27). The book jacket of the *Genealogy* also announced the forthcoming work. Yet Nietzsche never released that work. Not only that. He never composed it as a work—in the way that Nietzsche was wont to compose his works. Nor is it a book that was abandoned in the course of its composition and left incomplete. Rather, all we have are particular fragments.

Even this designation is deceptive, however, inasmuch as we cannot make out anything like jointures or direct references to other pertinent fragments by which the gaps among the fragments might be closed. The reason we cannot descry such jointures is the fact that we do not possess an articulation of the whole composition by which the individual notes might find their fitting place.

Ever since the editors of the literary remains took matters into their own hands and published a work called *Der Wille zur Macht* we have had a book falsely ascribed to Nietzsche; and not just any book but a *magnum opus,* to wit, that same *The Will to Power.* In truth, it is no more than an arbitrary selection of Nietzsche's notes from the years 1884 to 1888, years in which the thought of will to power only occasionally advanced into the foreground. And even for those times when it assumed preeminence it remains for us to ask why and in what way the thought of will to power thrust its way to the fore. Yet our conception of Nietzsche's philosophy during this period is predetermined from the outset by this arbitrary selection—which does, it is true, seek a foothold in Nietzsche's very sketchy plans. Nietzsche's philosophy proper is now for all commentators, quite unwittingly, a "philosophy of will to power." The editors of the book *The Will to Power,* who worked more meticulously than the subsequent commentators who have used the book, obviously could not have failed to see that in Nietzsche's notes the doctrine of eternal return also plays a role; they accordingly took up those notes into their own collation of Nietzsche's posthumously published materials, indeed along the guidelines of a plan that derives from Nietzsche himself.

What are we to make of the fact that there is now a "posthumous work" by Nietzsche with the title *The Will to Power?* Over against the factual existence of the book we must align the following incontrovertible facts: first, in spite of the fact that he announced the book, Nietzsche himself never wrote it; second, in subsequent years Nietzsche even abandoned the plan that bears this major title; and third, the last-mentioned fact is not without relation to the first-mentioned.

The upshot is that the book *The Will to Power* cannot be definitive for a comprehensive and thoroughgoing evaluation of Nietzsche's unpublished thoughts between the years 1884 and 1888. His plan for a *magnum opus* is not equivalent to the plan of *The Will to Power*. Rather, the plan that bears this title constitutes but one transitional phase in Nietzsche's labors on his main work. Yet to the extent that the phrase "will to power" announces the surfacing of something "new and essential" in Nietzsche's thinking, something which in terms of time emerged only *after* Nietzsche had experienced the thought of eternal return, we must ask how both "will to power" and "eternal return" relate to one another. Does the new thought make the doctrine of eternal recurrence superfluous, or can the latter be united with the former? Indeed, is it not the case that the doctrine of return not only can be united with will to power but also constitutes *its sole and proper ground?*

In accord with the presentation we are now attempting we must try to determine what the unpublished handwritten materials from the years 1884–88 tell us about the doctrine of return—without being beguiled by that "work" compiled by editors and called *The Will to Power*. Because we do not have these posthumously published materials before us in their untouched, actual state, we are constrained by the particular published form the editors have given them. Nevertheless, we can readily release ourselves from that constraint. All the essential notes appear in the book *The Will to Power* (*Grossoktav* edition, volumes XV and XVI). The "Appendix" of volume XVI (pages 413–67) also contains all the plans and sketches of plans projected by Nietzsche in the course of his exertions on behalf of his major work, exertions we cannot accurately reconstruct.*

With a view to the unpublished materials and plans of this final creative period we shall pose two questions. First, what does an exami-

---

* See the Analysis that concludes this volume, section II, "Contexts," for an appraisal of Heidegger's claims.

nation of the plans for a major work during the years 1884–88 tell us concerning Nietzsche's commitment to the thought of return? Second, what do the utterances that fall into this period say about the doctrine of return itself?

The first result of such an examination is recognition of the indisputable fact that the thought of return everywhere occupies the definitive position. Because this thought is to prevail over all, it can—indeed must—occupy various positions and exhibit sundry forms in the changing plans. Thus in a multifarious yet unified way it guides and sustains the whole in terms of its mode of presentation. A painstaking examination proves unequivocally that this is so: we do not find a trace of anything like a retreat of the grounding thought, eternal recurrence.

A more important outcome of such an examination is the following: the multifaceted positioning of the thought of return in the architectonic of Nietzsche's "philosophy of the future" gives an indication of the essence of the thought itself. Not only must the thought emerge out of the creative moment of decision in some given individual, but as a thought that pertains to life itself it must also be a *historical decision*—a *crisis*.

We shall now pursue the question concerning the extent to which the thought of return explicitly comes to the fore in the plans, and the way in which it does so. The first plan (XVI, 413) does not belong here, inasmuch as it stems from the year 1882 and pertains to the circle of thoughts contained in *The Gay Science*. Only with the second plan do the proposals and projected plans from the years 1884–85 begin. This is the period in which Nietzsche—above all, in letters— makes explicit mention of an expansion of his "philosophy," of providing a "main structure" for which *Thus Spoke Zarathustra* is to be the vestibule.* We do find signs of life for his plan for a *magnum opus,* but not a trace of a work entitled *The Will to Power.* The titles we find are *The Eternal Return,* in three different plans from the year 1884; or *Midday and Eternity: A Philosophy of Eternal Return,* also from the year 1884; finally, in that same year the subtitle becomes the main title—*Philosophy of Eternal Return.*

---

* See Volume I, section 3, esp. pp. 12–13, for a selection of these letters.

As opposed to these titles we find a plan from the year 1885 entitled *The Will to Power: Attempt at an Interpretation of All Occurrence.* The preface of that projected work is to treat "the threatening meaninglessness" and the "problem of pessimism." When we come to discuss the "domain" of the doctrine of return we shall grasp the fact that this entire plan must be viewed from the vantage-point of eternal return—even though it does not cite the thought as such.* From this plan we learn one thing: the question concerning will to power finds its proper place in the philosophy of eternal return. The latter thought attains preeminence over all; it is to be treated in the preface because it is all-pervading.

However, during the year 1884, the year in which Nietzsche presumably achieved clarity concerning will to power as the pervasive character of all beings, an important reference to the connection between eternal recurrence and will to power is made in a plan listed as number 2.† This plan culminates in a fifth point entitled "The doctrine of eternal return as *hammer* in the hand of the *most powerful* man." Wherever the thought of thoughts is indeed thought, that is to say, is incorporated, it conducts the thinker to supreme decisions in such a way that he expands beyond himself, thus attaining power over himself and willing himself. In this way such a man *is* as will to power.

In order to compose his philosophy within a planned major work, Nietzsche now carries out an analysis of all occurrence in terms of will to power. This meditation is essential, and for Nietzsche it comes to occupy the midpoint for the next several years, the midpoint that defines all beings themselves. It is far from the case that the doctrine of eternal recurrence is put out of play or reduced in significance; rather, that doctrine is enhanced to a supreme degree thanks to Nietzsche's efforts to shore up the main structure on all sides by means of a most thoroughgoing "interpretation of all occurrence." From the year 1885 stem some other notes (XVI, 415) in which Nietzsche clearly says what he understands by will to power, a matter that is now moving into the

---

* See section 23, below.
† See now CM, Z II 5a [80].

forefront of his labors: "Will to power is the ultimate fact we come down to."*

If we were to ponder these words alone, for the purpose of reflecting on what eternal return is, it would surely become apparent that here it is a matter of two very different things—of things that are different in several senses. Eternal return is not an ultimate fact; it is rather the "thought of thoughts." Will to power is not a thought; it is an "ultimate fact." The fact can neither suppress nor supplant the thought. The decisive question—one that Nietzsche himself neglected to pose—proves to be: What fundamental matter lies concealed behind the distinction between eternal return as the "most difficult thought" and will to power as "ultimate fact"? As long as we fail to inquire back into the domain where all these matters are grounded we cling to mere words and remain stuck in extrinsic calculations of Nietzsche's thinking.

Study of the plans from the years 1884 and 1885 nonetheless shows unequivocally that the philosophy which Nietzsche was planning to portray as a whole is the philosophy of eternal return. In order to give shape to that philosophy he had to supply an interpretation of all occurrence as will to power. The farther Nietzsche's thinking penetrated into the total presentation of his philosophy, the more compelling the principal task of interpreting all occurrence as will to power became. For that reason the locution *will to power* advanced to the very title of the planned *magnum opus*. Yet it is so transparently clear that the whole remains sustained and thoroughly defined by the thought of eternal return that one is almost reluctant to make explicit reference to this state of affairs.

The plan of 1886 bears the title *The Will to Power: Attempt at a Revaluation of All Values.* The subtitle suggests what the meditation on will to power properly has to achieve; namely, a revaluation of all values. By *value* Nietzsche understands whatever is a condition for life, that is, for the enhancement of life. Revaluation of all values means—for life, that is, for being as a whole—the positing of a new condition by which life is once again brought to itself, that is to say, impelled beyond itself. For only in this way does life become possible in its true

---

* See CM, W 17a [61]. Cf. Giorgio Colli's critique in the *Nachwort* to vol. 11 of the *Studienausgabe*, p. 726.

essence. Revaluation is nothing other than what the greatest burden, the thought of eternal return, is to accomplish. The subtitle, which is to exhibit the all-encompassing scope that will to power possesses, might therefore just as well have been the one we find in the year 1884: *A Philosophy of Eternal Return* (XVI, 414; number 5).

The plan that most fully corroborates the interpretation we are offering here is one from the year 1884 (XVI, 415; number 6*), entitled *Philosophy of Eternal Recurrence: An Attempt at the Revaluation of All Values.* The plan mentioned earlier, from the year 1886, proposes that the work be divided into four books. This fourfold division is retained in spite of all the other changes up to the end of 1888. We shall now take note of only the first and fourth books, which frame the whole. The question raised in Book One, *"The Danger of Dangers,"* takes aim once again at the "meaninglessness" that threatens—we could also say, at the fact that all things are losing their weight. The compelling question is whether it is possible to provide beings with a new center of gravity. The "danger of dangers" must be averted by the "thought of thoughts." Book IV bears the title *"The Hammer."* If we did not yet know what this word implies, we could gather its meaning perfectly well from plan number 2 of 1884 (XVI, 414). Here the final fragment—to which we have already referred—is called "The doctrine of eternal return as *hammer* in the hand of the *most powerful* man." In place of the title of Book IV, *"The Hammer,"* we could also allow the phrase "the doctrine of eternal return" to stand. (See the commentary to Book IV; XVI, 420).†

---

* See CM, W I 2 [259, 258].

† This plan (W I 8 [100]) is actually not "fragmented" in GOA as the critical apparatus to CM says, but is "padded" by a number of phrases gleaned from elsewhere in the notebooks. There are two "commentaries" to which Heidegger may be referring here. The one I have been able to locate in CM [131] reads as follows:

On Book Four

The *greatest* struggle: for it we need a new *weapon.*

The hammer: to conjure a frightful decision, to confront Europe with the *consequences,* whether its will to perish "is willing."

Prevention of the tendency toward mediocrity.

Better to perish!

This note was taken up into *The Will to Power* as WM, 1054.

The plans for a main work that were drafted in the following year, from 1887 until early 1888, manifest a thoroughly unified structure. This is the period when Nietzsche's thoughtful labors on behalf of the will to power reach their zenith. How does the doctrine of return fare during this period? It appears each time in the fourth and final book proposed by the plans. Last in terms of presentation, it is first in terms of the matter and the context that grounds the whole. It pervades all from beginning to end, which is why it can reveal itself in its full truth only at the end of the presentation. Its position at the end also indicates something else, to wit, the fact that the "doctrine" is not a "theory," that it is not to be pressed into service as a scientific explanation, as some sort of hypothesis on the origins of the world. Rather, the thinking of this thought transforms life in its very grounds and thereby propounds new standards of education.

With a view to the transformative character of the thought of return, as a matter of decision and excision, the very title of the fourth book is conceived in the individual plans of this period. *"Discipline and Breeding"* it is called in the plan of March 17, 1887, which the editors of Nietzsche's notes chose as the blueprint for the major work.* The next plan, from the summer of 1887, lists as the title of the fourth book *"The Overcomers and the Overcome* (A Prophecy)." In the following plan the title in question reads: *"Overcomers and What Is Overcome."*

If we read these titles strictly in terms of their literal content, we of course find nothing concerning eternal return. Nevertheless, one need not know a great deal about this thought to be reminded immediately by the titles of the fact that the thought which is hardest to bear confronts us with a question. It demands to know whether we renounce life in all its discordance—whether we try to sidestep it and are inadvertently crushed under its wheels, thus joining the ranks of those who are overcome—or whether we affirm life and become one of the overcomers. The appended remark, "A Prophecy," clearly alludes to the doctrine of return (XVI, 413; from the year 1884). Furthermore, a more detailed version of the plan of March 17, 1887, drawn up at the

---

* CM, Mp XVII 3b [64].

end of that year (XVI, 424), explicitly presents as the first title of the fourth book the phrase *"The Eternal Return.' "** The titles of the remaining two divisions are *Grand Politics* and *Prescriptions for Our Lives.* However, the most telling evidence for the undiminished importance of the doctrine of return at the center of the whole—even during the period when will to power achieves preeminence—consists in the fact that the fourth book is thought of as a victorious countermove to the first, which treats of European nihilism and its upsurgence.

Nihilism is the propriative event by which the weight in all things melts away—the fact that a center of gravity is missing. Yet the lack first becomes visible and palpable when it is brought to light in the question concerning a new center of gravity. Seen from this vantage-point, the thinking of the thought of eternal recurrence, as a questioning that perpetually calls for decision, is the fulfillment of nihilism. Such thinking brings to an end the veiling and painting over of this event, in such a way that it becomes at the same time the transition to the new determination of the greatest burden. The doctrine of eternal return is therefore the "critical point," the watershed of an epoch become weightless and searching for a new center of gravity. It is the crisis proper. Hence, in considerations surrounding plans from the period in which "will to power" is emphasized we find the following (XVI, 422): "The doctrine of *eternal return:* as fulfillment of it [i.e., nihilism], as *crisis.* "

Even the plans from the spring and summer of 1888, the final year of Nietzsche's creative life, whatever transformations they indicate, clearly exhibit the identical articulation: in each case the plan wends its way to the summit, where we find the thought of eternal return. The titles of the final parts vary in any given instance: "The Inverted Ones; Their Hammer, 'The Doctrine of Eternal Return' " (XVI, 425); "Redemption from *Uncertainty"* (426); "The *Art of Healing* for the Fu-

---

* The plan GOA calls the "third draft" of the plan of March 17, 1887, is to be found in CM at W II 4 [2] and is dated early 1888. Neither it nor the preceding plan in GOA (W II 1 [164]) can so readily be called later "drafts" of the March 17 plan. Nor is there any convincing reason for the latter's having been chosen as the basis for the volume *Der Wille zur Macht.*

ture" (426). For Nietzsche, the "art of healing," as an "art," is a value. That is to say, it is a condition posited by the will to power, indeed, a condition of "life-enhancement." The "art of healing for the future" is *the* condition that defines the center of gravity in being as a whole for times to come. In order for this condition to work its effects it is first of all necessary that a *"stronger species of human being"* be there.

In the final plans, from the fall of 1888, the title *The Will to Power* disappears, making room for what used to be the subtitle, *Revaluation of All Values*. Here the titles of Book Four read as follows: "The Redemption from Nihilism"; *"Dionysos:* Philosophy of Eternal Return"; *"Dionysos philosophos";* and again, *"Dionysos:* Philosophy of Eternal Return."*

This apparently extraneous examination of the plans aims to respond to the following question: Where in the articulated structure of Nietzsche's planned communication of his philosophy do we find the place where the thought of return is to be presented?

If this teaching is the *"crisis,"* then it must face in two opposite directions. On the one hand, the doctrine must be communicated at the point where the question concerning the center of gravity surfaces as the question of the evanescence of all prior sources of weight. On the other hand, the doctrine must be explicated at the point where the new center of gravity is itself established in beings.

The editors of Nietzsche's works from the period after *Thus Spoke Zarathustra* up to the end proved that in this respect they saw matters in the proper light. For they distributed the available fragments on the doctrine of return between two places in the volume they composed, namely, *The Will to Power:* first, in the first book, "European Nihilism," Chapter One, Part Four, "The Crisis: Nihilism and the Thought of Return," numbers 55 and 56 (XV, 181–87); and then in the fourth book, "Discipline and Breeding," as the conclusion to the entire "work": "The Eternal Return," numbers 1053 to 1067 (XVI, 393–402). To be sure, there exist a number of clear indications in Nietzsche's sketches which support such a distribution. The question of nihilism and the thought of return, treated in the first book, requires

---

* See Heidegger's delayed commentary on these titles in section 26, below.

separate discussion.* Let us now therefore refer only briefly to those materials that are taken up into Book IV. Our guideline will be the question of the extent to which the notes between 1884 and 1888 exhibit a further development of the teaching, and of the particular direction such a development takes.

When we compare the main features of these fragments with those from the period of *The Gay Science* (XII) and with the doctrinal import expressed in *Thus Spoke Zarathustra,* nothing much appears to have changed. We find the same reflections in regard to both the "proofs" for the doctrine and the doctrine's "impact." Yet when we look more carefully at these materials, having pondered the fact that the notes pertain to a period in which Nietzsche was trying to think through his philosophy as a whole and to bring it to a configuration, the picture changes altogether. The precondition for our seeing this is the refusal simply to accept the given order of the fifteen passages as they appear in their current published form. Rather, we must first of all place them in their *chronological* order. In the present edition the fragments are *jumbled higgledy-piggledy.* The first one belongs to the year 1884, the last one, which at the same time concludes the entire work, stems from the year 1885, while immediately prior to it appears one from the final year, 1888. Let us therefore establish the chronological sequence of the notes. To the year 1884 belong numbers 1053, 1056, 1059, and 1060. To the year 1885 numbers 1055, 1062, 1064, and 1067. From the period 1885–86 comes number 1054; from the period 1886–87 number 1063; from the period 1887–88 numbers 1061 and 1065. Number 1066 belongs to the year 1888. Two fragments from the period 1884 to 1888 which we cannot date precisely but which, judging from the handwriting, presumably stem from the year 1884–85 are numbers 1057 and 1058.†

---

* See section 23, below. Heidegger's 1940 lecture course on nihilism (Volume IV of this series), by and large neglects eternal return as the countermovement to nihilism. See the Analysis at the end of the present volume.

† The folder containing the sheets on which WM, 1057 and 1058 are jotted (Mp XVII 1b [4,7]) is dated by CM "Winter 1883–84," a year earlier than Heidegger's estimate. Otherwise, Heidegger's dating of the passages, following GOA, is accurate. Readers should note important textual changes in WM, 1064 (cf. CM, W I 3a [54] and WM, 1066 (cf. CM, W II 5 [188]). I have been unable to locate WM, 1061 in CM.

Because our interpretation proper of Nietzsche's fundamental thought—an interpretation that is to be a confrontation—will have to refer back to Nietzsche's final utterances, let us postpone for the present a more detailed discussion of the fragments we have just now listed. Only *one* essential circumstance should be emphasized immediately. Nietzsche speaks more clearly than before about the "presuppositions" of the doctrine of return, indeed about "theoretical" and "practical" ones. This seems strange at first. If the doctrine of eternal return is to be the fundamental doctrine, determining everything, then it cannot entertain any presuppositions as such. On the contrary, it must be the presupposition for all additional thoughts. Or does Nietzsche's manner of speaking suggest that the doctrine of return, while not surrendered, is yet to be deposed from its foundational significance and relegated to a subordinate position? We can reach a decision in this matter only if we come to know what Nietzsche means by these "presuppositions." He does not directly say what he means. But from the allusions he makes and the general tendency of his thinking we can unequivocally state that he is referring to the will to power as the pervasive constitution of all beings. The thought of return is now explicitly thought on the basis of the will to power. Hence we might now conclude that the thought of eternal return is to be traced back to will to power. Yet such a conclusion would be too hasty and altogether extrinsic.

Even if such were the case—even if will to power were the presupposition for the eternal return of the same—it would by no means follow that will to power precludes the doctrine of eternal return, that the two cannot subsist side by side. The very reverse would hold: will to power would *demand* the eternal return of the same.

Nevertheless, the outcome of our survey of the plans from this period is the realization that the doctrine of return nowhere suffers a setback. It asserts its determinative position everywhere. Accordingly the only thing we must ask is: *How do will to power, as the pervasive constitution of beings, and eternal return of the same, as the mode of Being of beings as a whole, relate to one another?* What is the significance of the fact that Nietzsche posits will to power as a "presupposition" for the eternal return of the same? How does he understand "presupposition" here? Does Nietzsche have a clear, well-grounded conception of the relation that obtains between the two? Nietzsche indeed possesses no clear insight—and certainly no conceptual insight —into the relation which we have now named but not yet pondered.

The will to power can be the "presupposition" for the eternal recurrence of the same in any of the following three ways. First, eternal return of the same can be demonstrated on the basis of will to power, the latter expressing the character of force in the world totality. Here will to power would be the *cognitive ground* of eternal recurrence of the same. Second, eternal return may be seen as being possible only if the constitution of will to power is indeed appropriate to beings as such. Here will to power would be the *material ground* of eternal recurrence of the same. Third, will to power can be the "presupposition" of eternal recurrence of the same inasmuch as the constitution of the being (its "what," *quidditas*, or *essentia)* grounds its mode of Being (the being's "how" and "that" "it is," its *existentia).* As long as the designated relationship between the *constitution* of the being and its *mode* of Being remains undetermined, the possibility also arises that the reverse is true—that the constitution of the being springs from its mode of Being.

The relationship now in question cannot be defined in terms of a relation between something that conditions and something that is conditioned, between what grounds and what is grounded. In order for the relationship to be defined we first need to discuss the essential provenance of the essence of Being.

With these questions we are already anticipating decisive steps in our interpretation and determination of the relation between eternal return of the same and will to power. Yet an apparently extrinsic circumstance betrays how much this obscure relation, which Nietzsche was unable to come to grips with, was what really lay behind the restlessness of Nietzsche's thinking during this final creative period. The fragment that concludes the "work" entitled *The Will to Power,* in its current textual arrangement, namely, number 1067, is as it now stands the revised version of an earlier note (XVI, 515). To the question "And do you also know what 'the world' is to me?" Nietzsche's earlier version replies: it is eternal return of the same, willing back whatever has been and willing forward to whatever has to be. In the second version the reply is: *"This world is will to power—and nothing besides!"**

Again we stand before the question that has confronted us many times. Do we merely want to remain entrenched in the extrinsic distinction between these two locutions and turns of phrase, *eternal return of the same* and *will to power?* Or do we by now realize that we come to grasp a philosophy only when we try to *think* what it says? At all events, the revision we have referred to shows that will to power and eternal return of the same cohere. With what right could Nietzsche otherwise substitute the one for the other? Yet what if the will to power, according to Nietzsche's most proper and intrinsic intentions, were in itself nothing else than willing back to that which was and a willing forward to everything that has to be? What if the eternal recurrence of the same—as occurrence—were nothing other than the will to power, precisely in the way Nietzsche himself understands this phrase, though not in the way some view or other of "politics" bends it to its own purpose?† If matters stood this way, then the designation of being as will to power would only be an elaboration of the original and

---

* See the commentary in CM to fragment [12] of the group of sheets bearing the archive number 38 (from June–July, 1885); in the *Studienausgabe,* vol. 14, p. 727. Nietzsche's revised reply, *"will to power—and nothing besides,"* was taken up into the book *Beyond Good and Evil* as passage number 36 and hence has become quite well known. The passage that Nietzsche excised from the earlier version, and which originally appeared at the decisive word "ring" near the end of WM, 1067, reads as follows:

a ring of good will, turning ever about itself alone, keeping to its wonted way: this world, *my* world—who is luminous enough to look at it without wishing to be blinded? Strong enough to hold his soul up to this mirror? His own mirror up to the mirror of Dionysos? His own solution to the riddle of Dionysos? And were anyone able to do this, would he not have to do more in addition? To *plight his troth* to the "ring of rings"? By taking the oath of his own *return?* By means of the ring of eternal self-blessing, self-affirmation? By means of the will to will oneself once more and yet again? The will to will back all the things that ever have been? To will forward to everything that ever has to be? Do you now know what the world is to me? And what I am willing when I will *this* world?—

† The reference is presumably to Alfred Baeumler's *Nietzsche: Philosopher and Politician.* In addition to the material in my Analyses of Volumes I and IV, see also Mazzino Montinari, "Nietzsche zwischen Alfred Bäumler und Georg Lukács," in *Basis,* vol. 9 (Frankfurt am Main: Suhrkamp, 1979), 188–207, esp. pp. 201 ff.

primary projection of being as eternal recurrence of the same. In truth, matters do stand this way.

Will to power is a "presupposition" for eternal return of the same, inasmuch as will to power alone allows us to recognize what eternal return of the same means. Because in terms of the matter itself eternal return of the same constitutes the ground and the essence of will to power, the latter can be posited as the ground and point of departure for insight into the essence of eternal return of the same.

Yet even after the essential coherence of will to power and eternal return of the same has come to light we still find ourselves at the very beginning of philosophical comprehension. Whenever being as such and as a whole takes on the sense of eternal return of the same, of will to power, and of the coherence of these two notions, in this way confronting our thinking, the question arises as to *what* is being thought here in general and *how* it is being thought.

Hence our survey of those aspects of the doctrine of return which Nietzsche communicated and those which he suppressed concludes with questions that must open a path that will lead us to what we shall call Nietzsche's fundamental metaphysical position. Such a survey of the gestation of the doctrine of return is itself carried out with a view to the way that doctrine comes to stand in the whole of his philosophy; this view, for its part, keeps unbroken watch over the whole of Nietzsche's philosophy. For that reason our presentation was repeatedly constrained to go beyond mere reportage, making further connections visible by means of questions. In that way we tacitly performed the preliminary work for a discussion of questions that now must be answered explicitly—the questions of the *configuration* and the *domain* of the doctrine of return.

22. The Configuration of the Doctrine of Return

Before we try to define the configuration of the doctrine of return we shall have to ask whether it possesses any configuration at all. If the survey we have conducted exhibits *anything* it is the multifaceted figure, or better, the figurelessness or unfinished figure cut by the doctrine. But what do we mean by the doctrine's *configuration,* and why are we inquiring into it? Our inquiry would be of only secondary importance if the doctrine's configuration were nothing more than a subsequent collation of doctrinal statements and fragments, arranged according to such fortuitous points of view as the doctrine's greatest possible impact or the likelihood of its being understood. However, we are asking about the configuration in order to advance beyond an initial survey and get a closer look at other more essential matters.

By the *configuration* of the doctrine we understand the inner structure of the truth of the doctrine itself, the structure that is prefigured in the doctrine's proper truth. The "structure of its truth" does not refer to the way in which statements are ordered into arguments, and sequences of arguments into books; it means the way in which the *openness* of being as a whole is structured into being itself, so that being first shows and articulates itself by means of such openness. Does Nietzsche's doctrine possess a configuration in this sense? The question cannot be answered immediately—especially inasmuch as a configuration understood in this way could exist even if its presentation were not finished and perfectly polished. If a determining ground is always proper to a configuration, a ground by virtue of which a truth comes to prevail on its own grounds; if therefore a configuration is possible only on the basis of a fundamental position; and if we on the path of our own interpretation are presupposing such a fundamental position for Nietzsche's thinking; then whatever it is that calls for a configuration and makes it possible will be vital to Nietzsche's philosophy.

When we look back we discern that a particular law of truth announces itself everywhere in Nietzsche's thought, at least indirectly. The announcement is heard in our realization that every attempt to characterize the doctrine by pigeonholing it into customary representations comes to grief. Whether we distinguish between its "scientific" import and its "ethical" significance; or, more generally, between its "theoretical" and "practical" sides; and even if we substitute some terms which we today prefer, although they are hardly clearer, distinguishing between the doctrine's "metaphysical" meaning and its "existentiell" appeal—in each case we take refuge in *two-sided* affairs, neither side of which is apt. And this is a sign of the intensified predicament in which we find ourselves, however reluctant we may be to admit it. What is essential and peculiar to the doctrine is not brought to light in this way; it is rather clothed in other representational modes long since grown customary and threadbare. The same is true of those somewhat novel distinctions between a "poetic" and a "prosaic" presentation of the doctrine, or of its "subjective" and "objective" aspects. We have already achieved something of considerable importance when we have noticed that in the case of this "doctrine," no matter how ill-defined or uncertain our experience of it may be, the above-mentioned efforts at interpretation are dubious—they distort our view of the doctrine. To attain this insight is the first intention of our inquiry into the configuration.

The initial consequence of our rejection of these comfortable representational arrangements will be that we must strive to attain a perspective within which the configuration or the determining grounds of the configuration's law begin to glimmer. Yet how are we to catch sight of the perspective itself? The perspective can arise only from a preview of the entirety of Nietzsche's philosophy, of the totality which impels itself to its own configuration in accord with its own law. Where do we encounter this impulse, this thrust and counterthrust? Nowhere else but in Nietzsche's efforts surrounding his "main work." The oscillation of the plans must perforce exhibit those matters that are to be maintained, rejected, or transformed; here the axes must come to light on which all the vast restlessness of Nietzsche's thinking turns.

The three axes, which run counter to one another and about which all the restlessness of Nietzsche's search for a configuration turns, are recognizable in the three rubrics that were successively chosen as the main titles of the planned work. None of these three ever managed to suppress the remaining two. The three titles are: the eternal return, the will to power, and the revaluation of all values. The articulation of these three, indeed the articulation that is prefigured in these three titles themselves, is the configuration—the configuration which we are seeking and which indeed is seeking itself. All three rubrics apply to the entirety of Nietzsche's philosophy, while none of them is perfectly apt, inasmuch as the configuration of this philosophy cannot be leashed to a single strand.

Although at the outset we are utterly unable to take up *one* single unequivocal anticipation of the articulated structure in which "eternal return," "will to power," and "revaluation of all values" would cohere as one, all of them with equal originality, we must just as certainly assume that Nietzsche himself for his part saw a number of distinct possibilities for the shaping of his work. For without this vision the sense of security which we find reflected in the fundamental stance shared by the whole range of plans would be incomprehensible.

However, these plans and arid lists of titles and fragment numbers will come to *speak* to us only when they are penetrated and pervaded by the light of a certain kind of knowledge—namely, knowledge of what it is they wish to grapple with. We do not possess such knowledge. It will take decades for it to mature. Our attempt to locate the structural law in these plans by way of a comparison of one plan with another therefore threatens to wind up being an artificial procedure that presumes to sketch the outline of Nietzsche's "system" in a purely extrinsic way. In order to approach our goal—indeed, in order to set ourselves a goal in the first place—we must select a provisional way that will also enable us to avoid the danger of mouthing hollow catchwords like so many clichés.

What we are seeking is the inner structure of a thought's truth, the thought of eternal return of the same, the fundamental thought of Nietzsche's philosophy. The truth of this thought concerns being as a whole. Yet because the thought essentially wants to be the greatest burden, because it therefore would define human being (that is to say, define us) in the midst of beings as a whole, the truth of this thought is such only when it is *our* truth.

Someone might counter that this is obvious and to be taken for granted, inasmuch as the thought of eternal return of the same involves all beings, hence ourselves as well, we who belong to being as particular cases of it—perhaps as specks of dust blown hither and thither in it. Yet this thought *is* only when those who are *thinking*— are. Accordingly, those who are thinking are more than, and something other than, mere *particular cases of what is thought.* Those who think the thought are not merely a given set of human beings who come to the fore somewhere at some time or other. The thinking of this thought has its most proper historical necessity; the thinking itself determines a historical moment. Out of this moment alone the eternity of what is thought in the thought looms large. Thus what the thought of eternal return of the same encompasses, the domain to which it reverts and which it pervades, constituting that domain for the first time, is not yet circumscribed when we aver in summary fashion that all beings are contained in it like walnuts in a sack. The thought's domain first of all needs to be staked out. *Only with a view to the domain* do we really have any hope of discerning something of the articulated whole which the truth of this thought demands for itself as its configuration.

23. The Domain of the Thought of Return: The Doctrine of Return as the Overcoming of Nihilism

We would have been thinking the thought of return quite extrinsically —in fact, we would not have been thinking it at all—if an awareness of the *domain* of that thought too had not everywhere encroached upon us. By the concept of the *domain* of the thought of eternal return we understand the unified context in terms of which this thought is defined and is itself definitive; *domain* means the unity of the regions of the thought's provenance and dominion. Our inquiry into the domain aims to grant the thought of thoughts its determinateness, inasmuch as this most general thought is easily thought all too generally, that is to say, thought in an indiscriminate manner that drifts off into generalities.

Every thought that thinks being as a whole seems to be circumscribed in its domain unequivocally and conclusively, at least as long as the *as a whole* is represented as the region that "encompasses" everything. And yet this *as a whole* is actually a locution that tends more to veil than to pose and to explicate an *essential question*. The *as a whole* in this designation "being as a whole" is always to be understood as an interrogative phrase, a questionable phrase, one worthy of the following questions: How is the *as a whole* determined; how is the determination grounded; and how are the grounds for the grounding established? Whenever it is a matter of thinking being as a whole the question of the domain becomes a burning question.

However, in Nietzsche's thought concerning being as a whole there is something else, something distinctive, which we must think as well

—not as a supplementary addition but as a preliminary characteristic that arises at the very outset to suggest the thought's possible configuration. This distinctive characteristic touches the essential core of the thought—the fundamental thought of Nietzsche's philosophy. Nietzsche's philosophy, in the intrinsic movement of its thought, is a countermovement. Yet it may well be that a countermovement is what every philosophy is, opposing every other philosophy. Nevertheless, in Nietzsche's thinking the movement of this countering has a special sense. It does not wish to reject that which is *countered* in its thought, in order to replace it with something else. Nietzsche's thinking wills to *invert*. Yet that toward which the inversion and its particular kind of countermovement aim is not some arbitrary past tendency (or even present trend) in one type of philosophy or another. It is rather the whole of Western philosophy, inasmuch as such philosophy remains the form-giving principle in the history of Western man.

The collective history of Western philosophy is interpreted as Platonism. Plato's philosophy provides the standard of measure for the way we conceive of all post-Platonic as well as pre-Platonic philosophy. That standard remains determinative inasmuch as philosophy posits specific *conditions* for the possibility of being as a whole and for man as being within this whole. Such conditions set their seal on being. That which first and last *obtains,* that which accordingly constitutes the condition of "life" as such, Nietzsche calls *value.* What properly sets the standard are the uppermost values. If therefore Nietzsche's philosophy wants to be the countermovement to the whole of prior Western philosophy in the designated sense, it must set its sights on the uppermost values posited in philosophy. But because Nietzsche's countermovement possesses the character of an inversion, when it homes in on the uppermost values it becomes a "revaluation of all values."

A countermovement of such scope and significance must of course be sufficiently *necessary.* Whatever impels it cannot rest on some gratuitous views and opinions concerning what is to be overcome. That in opposition to which the countermovement would set to work must itself be worthy of such work. Hence the most profound acknowledgment lies concealed in the countermovement that manifests such a style; the countermovement takes whatever has donned the colors of the opposition with consummate seriousness. In turn, such esteem presupposes that whatever stands in opposition has been experienced and thought through in its full power and significance; that is to say, has been suffered. The countermovement must in its necessity arise from such an original experience; and it must also remain rooted in such an experience.

Now, if the eternal return of the same is the fundamental thought of Nietzsche's philosophy proper, and if his philosophy is itself a counter-movement, then the thought of thoughts is inherently a *counter-thought*. The essence of this thought and its thinking, however, are a taking-for-true in the sense explained earlier: they are a belief. The thought of eternal return of the same is thus the counterbelief, the sustaining and guiding stance in the entire countermovement. The counterbelief itself is rooted in a particular experience involving prior philosophy and Western history in general, the experience that gener-ates the necessity of a countermovement or inversion in the sense of a revaluation.

What is this experience? What kind of need is experienced in it, as a need that makes a wending of the way necessary, a needful wending that calls for a revaluation and thereby a new valuation?* It is that propriative event in the history of Western man which Nietzsche designates by the name *nihilism*. What this word says is not something we can gather in some arbitrary way from a hodgepodge of political notions or world views. We must define it *solely* in terms of its meaning for Nietzsche. In his experience of the development of nihilism, the whole of Nietzsche's philosophy is rooted and suspended. At the same time, that philosophy strives to clarify in an initial way the experience of nihilism and to make the scope of nihilism increasingly transparent. With the unfolding of Nietzsche's philosophy we also find a deepening of Nietzsche's insight into the essence and the power of nihilism, as well as a development of the need and the necessity of its overcoming.

What we have just said also suggests that the concept of nihilism can

---

*On the "needful wending," *Not-wend-igkeit*, see the note on page 175, below.

be thought adequately only if we assimilate simultaneously the fundamental thought—the counterthought—of Nietzsche's philosophy. Hence the reverse obtains as well: the fundamental thought, to wit, the doctrine of eternal return, can be grasped solely on the basis of the experience of nihilism and knowledge of the essence of nihilism. If we are to take the measure of the full domain of this most difficult thought; if our gaze is to penetrate at one and the same time the regions of that thought's provenance and dominion; then we must also adjoin to our provisional characterization of the thought's import and the manner of its communication a characterization of nihilism.

If we turn to the word itself we may say that nihilism is an event—or a teaching—whereby it is a matter of the *nihil,* the nothing. Considered formally, the nothing is a negation of something—indeed of every kind of something. What constitutes being as a whole is *every* such something. To posit the nothing is thus to negate being as a whole. Nihilism thereby has as its explicit or tacit fundamental teaching the following: being as a whole is nothing. Yet precisely this avowal can be understood in such a way that it would be susceptible to the Nietzschean suspicion that it is not at all an expression of nihilism.

That which determines being as a whole is Being. At the beginning of his general metaphysics (in *The Science of Logic)* Hegel makes the following statement: Being and the Nothing are the same. One can also easily alter the proposition to read as follows: Being is the Nothing. Yet the Hegelian proposition is so little nihilism that it can be said to embody something of that very *"grandiose initiative"* that Nietzsche sees in German idealism (WM, 416*) which would overcome nihilism. The practice of referring broadly to "nihilism" whenever the *nothing* emerges in Hegel's text, especially when it stands in essential relation to the doctrine of Being; and furthermore the practice of speaking of nihilism in such a way as to give it a tinge of "Bolshevism," is not merely superficial thinking but unconscionable demagogy.

---

* WM, 416 (CM, W I 8 [106]) begins as follows:

The significance of German philosophy (Hegel): to constitute in thought a *pantheism* in which evil, error, and suffering are *not* felt to be arguments against divinity. This *grandiose initiative* was misused by the reigning powers (the state, etc.), as though to sanction the rationality of whoever happened to be ruling.

Above all, such trivial reductions fail to grasp or even touch on Nietzsche's thought, either in terms of its understanding of nihilism or in the kind of nihilism that is proper to it. For Nietzsche does understand his own thinking in terms of nihilism: his thinking passes through "consummate nihilism," and Nietzsche himself is "Europe's first consummate nihilist, one who in himself has lived nihilism as such to its end, who has left it *behind, beneath,* and *outside* himself" (WM, Preface, section 3). *

The domain of the thought of eternal return of the same—of that thought's provenance and dominion—will open itself to us only when we have come to recognize the propriative event of nihilism, that is, only when we ponder the fact that Nietzsche experienced and thoroughly interrogated nihilism as the fundamental development of history as such. Nietzsche experienced and interrogated nihilism to the utmost by pursuing the path of *his own* thinking. The thought of eternal return thinks being in such a way that being as a whole summons us without cease. It asks us whether we merely want to drift with the tide of things or whether we would be creators. Prior to that, it asks us whether we desire the means and the conditions by which we might again *become* creators.

Insight into nihilism remains something terrifying. Hence it is terribly difficult to think the thought that is hardest to bear and to prepare for the coming of those who will think it truly and creatively. What is most difficult at the outset is the confrontation with nihilism along with the thought of return, inasmuch as the latter itself betrays a nihilistic character in the fact that it refuses to think of an ultimate goal for beings. From one point of view, at least, this thought ascribes the "in vain," the lack of an ultimate goal, to eternity. To this extent it is an utterly crippling thought (WM, 55; from the years 1886–87):

> Let us think this thought in its most frightful form: existence as it is, without meaning and goal, yet inevitably recurring; existence with no finale to sweep it into nothingness: *eternal recurrence.*

---

* In 1961 Heidegger added the following in square brackets: "A detailed explication and discussion of the essence of nihilism is to be found in Volume II of the present publication." See Volume IV of this English-language series, entitled *Nihilism.*

That is the utterly extreme form of nihilism: the nothing ("meaningless-ness") eternally!

Yet when we think the Nietzschean thought of eternal return in this way we are doing so halfheartedly—in fact we are not thinking it at all. For we are not grasping it in its character as decision, the character of the moment. Only when this happens do we plumb the depths of the thought in its proper domain; only when this happens *is* there in Nietzsche's view such a thing as the overcoming of nihilism. As an over-coming, the thought obviously presupposes nihilism, in the sense that it takes up nihilism into its thought, thinking it through to its uttermost end. Understood in this way, the thought of return too is to be thought "nihilistically," and only so. But this now implies that the thought of return is to be thought only in conjunction with nihilism, as what is to be overcome, what is already overcome in the very will to create. Only the one whose thinking ventures forth into the uttermost need of nihil-ism will be able to think the overcoming thought, which is the needed thought—the thought that wends its way toward the need as such.*

---

* *Nur wer in die äusserste Not des Nihilismus hinausdenkt, vermag auch den über-windenden Gedanken als den not-wendenden und notwendigen zu denken.* Cf. Heidegger's brief Foreword to the fourth edition of *Erläuterungen zu Hölderlins Dichtung* (Frankfurt am Main: V. Klostermann, 1971), p. 7. The above phrase plays on the rootedness of both "overcoming" and "necessity" in a kind of *wending* or *turning* toward the need in our destitute time. See also the discussion of need and needlessness in Volume IV of this series, pp. 244–50, including the note on pp. 244–45.

24. Moment and Eternal Recurrence

What is the fundamental position in the midst of beings that results from such thinking? Earlier we heard that the serpent that coils itself in rings about the eagle's throat, thus becoming a ring that itself turns in the widening spiral of the eagle's ascent into the heights, is the image of the ring in the doctrine of eternal return. In the middle of our account of "The Vision and the Riddle," while we were recounting Zarathustra's tale told on shipboard of how he had once climbed a mountain in company with the dwarf, we broke off at a particular point with the remark that the remainder of Zarathustra's tale would become comprehensible only later. We have now arrived at that juncture at which we can take up the matters postponed earlier. At the same time we can once again think through the entire tale—the tale that thinks the thought that is hardest to bear.

We recall that Zarathustra poses two questions to the dwarf concerning the vision of the gateway. The second question the dwarf does not answer. Indeed, Zarathustra reports that his own talk concerning what is decisive in this vision of the gateway—namely, the question of the "moment"—grows softer and softer, and that he himself begins to fear his "own thoughts and hinterthoughts." He himself is not yet master of this thought—which is tantamount to saying that the victory of his thought is not yet decided, not even for Zarathustra. True, he tells the dwarf, "It is either You or me!" and he knows that he is the stronger one; still, he is not yet master of his own strength; he must test it and thus attain it for the first time, in confrontation. Whither the confrontation tends, and what domain of provenance and dominion the thought of thoughts occupies, we have in the meantime considered. With one eye on this domain we may now proceed to interpret the remainder of Zarathustra's tale.

Zarathustra is approaching his ownmost thought, fearing it more intensely with each advancing step. "Then suddenly I heard a dog nearby *howling.*" It is now a dog that comes into Zarathustra's vicinity, not an eagle with a serpent coiled about its throat; and now we hear, not the singing of songbirds, but a "howling." Now all the images turn counter to the mood of the thought of eternal return.

When the dog howls Zarathustra's thoughts "race back" to his childhood. The reference to childhood shows that we are now retreating to the earlier history of Zarathustra, the thinker of the thought of return, and also to the vast prehistory of that thought—to the genesis and emergence of nihilism. At some point in his childhood Zarathustra saw a dog, "bristling, its head raised, shivering in the stillest midnight, when even dogs believe in ghosts." The scene, with all its counter-images, is thus defined in greater detail. It is midnight, the most remote time, the hour that is farthest removed from midday—midday being the time of the most luminous, shadowless moment. "For at that instant the full moon, silent as death, rose over the house and then stood still, a round, glowing coal; stood still on the flat roof, as though trespassing on a stranger's property. . . ." Instead of the brilliant sun it is the full moon that is shining here; it too is a light, but a merely borrowed light, the most pallid reflection of actual illumination, a diaphanous ghost of light. Yet it shines enough to affright the dogs and set them baying—"since dogs believe in thieves and ghosts." At that time the child took pity on the dog that took fright at a ghost and yowled and raised a great din. In such a world compassion is most likely to be found among children—who comprehend nothing of what is happening and who are not of age with respect to being.

"And when I heard such howling once again I took pity." Zarathustra reports that even now—though he is no longer a child—he slips into the mood of pity and compassion, imagining on the basis of that mood how the world must look. Through Zarathustra's words, Nietzsche is here alluding to the time when Schopenhauer and Wagner determined his outlook on the world. Both of them taught, albeit in divergent ways, a form of pessimism—ultimately the flight into dissolution, into nothingness, into sheer suspension, into a sleep which promised itself an awakening only in order that it might go on sleeping undisturbed.

Meanwhile, Nietzsche himself had renounced all slumbering and dreaming; for he had already begun to question. The world of Schopenhauer and Wagner became questionable to him early on, earlier than even he knew, already at the time he was writing the third and fourth of his *Untimely Meditations,* "Schopenhauer as Educator" and "Richard Wagner in Bayreuth." However much in both of these writings he appeared to be an advocate of Schopenhauer's and Wagner's, and however much he wanted to be precisely that, here already we see a struggle for release, though not yet a real awakening. Nietzsche was not yet his own man, was not yet hard by *his own* thought. He first had to pass through the prehistory of that thought, and through the limbo that always leaves us so perplexed—a limbo of past experiences which we cannot truly come to terms with and of things to come which we cannot yet truly penetrate. Where exactly was Zarathustra? "Was I dreaming? Was I awakening? At one stroke I stood among wild cliffs, alone, bleak, in the bleakest moonlight." Bleakness pervades the period 1874 to 1881, the years Nietzsche once described as the period in which his life plunged to its nadir. Nevertheless, the bleakness of this lunar light was peculiarly bright, bright enough to enable him to see and to be visionary, especially when he heard the howling of a dog, having in the meantime developed an ear for that miserable specimen which is more whelp than human being and which has lost all pride, believing only in its own believing and nothing more.

And what did Zarathustra descry in this bleak lunar light? *"A man was lying there!"* The italic print lends special emphasis to what is seen: a human being lying prostrate on the ground—not erect and standing. Yet this is not enough. "And, truly, what I now saw was unlike anything I had ever seen." A man lying on the ground may be nothing unusual; and the experience that human beings do not often rouse themselves to stand, do not take a stand, that they generally lurch on with the help of crutches and supports, is a common one; and that humankind is in a wretched state is the customary jeremiad of pessimism, with all its inexhaustible twists and turns. Yet the way in which Zarathustra saw humanity at that moment was a way it had never been seen before. A human being, prostrate. But of what sort, and in what circumstances? "I saw a young shepherd, writhing, choking in spasms, his face distorted; a thick black snake hung out of his mouth." It is a young man, then, one who has barely left his childhood behind; perhaps he is the very one who heard the howling dog, namely, Zarathustra. A young shepherd, one who intends to guide and lead. He lies prostrate in the bleak light of illusion. "Had he been sleeping? A snake crawled into his mouth—and there it bit fast."

By now we are sufficiently prepared to discern in the "thick black snake" the counterimage of the serpent that winds itself about the eagle's throat, the eagle in turn soaring in the midday sky and holding effortlessly in the heights. The black snake is drear monotony, ultimately the goallessness and meaninglessness of nihilism. It is nihilism itself. Nihilism has bitten the young shepherd during his sleep and is now firmly entrenched. Only because the shepherd was not vigilant could the power of the snake assert itself, could the snake wriggle its way into the young shepherd's mouth, incorporating itself in him. When Zarathustra sees the young shepherd lying there, he does the first thing anyone would do. He pulls at the snake, tugs at it, "—in vain!"

The implication is that nihilism cannot be overcome from the outside. We do not overcome it by tearing away at it or shoving it aside—which is what we do when we replace the Christian God with yet another ideal, such as Reason, Progress, political and economic "Socialism," or mere Democracy. Try as we might to cast it aside, the black snake attaches itself ever more firmly. Zarathustra thus immediately gives up such rescue operations. "With one cry," he now relates, "it cried out of me." What is this *it?* Zarathustra replies, "All my goodness and my wickedness." Zarathustra's complete essence and his entire history precipitate in him and cry out, "Bite! You must bite!" We need not say a great deal more in order to make the meaning of the passage perfectly clear. The black snake of nihilism threatens to incorporate humanity altogether; it must be overcome by those who are themselves inflicted with it and endangered by it. All tugging—all that frantic activity from the outside, all temporary amelioration, all mere repulsion, postponement, and deferment—all this is in vain. Here nothing avails if human beings themselves do not bite into the danger, and not blindly, not just anywhere. We must bite off the *head* of the black snake, its properly definitive and leading part, which looms at the forefront.

Nihilism will be overcome only from the ground up, only if we grapple with the very head of it; only if the ideals which it posits and from which it derives fall prey to *"criticism,"* that is, to enclosure and overcoming. Yet such overcoming transpires only in the following way: everyone who is affected—and that means each of us—must bite into the matter for himself or herself; for if we leave it to another to tug at the darkling need that is our own, all will be futile.

—But the shepherd bit as my cry urged him to, bit with a good bite! He spewed out the snake's head, spat it far away, and leapt to his feet.

No longer a shepherd, no longer human, but as one transformed, il-luminated—one who *laughed!*

What sort of gaiety gives vent to such laughter? The gaiety of *the gay science.* Now, at the end of our long path, we recognize—and we recognize it as no accident but as the most intrinsic necessity—that at the conclusion of the treatise which Nietzsche entitled *The Gay Science* the thought of eternal return of the same is communicated for the first time. For this thought is the *bite* that is to overcome nihilism in its very foundation. Just as Zarathustra is no one else than the thinker of this thought, so too is the bite nothing other than the over-coming of nihilism. Thus it becomes transparently clear that the young shepherd is Zarathustra himself. In this vision Zarathustra is advancing toward himself. With the full force of his complete essence he must call out to himself, *"You must bite!"* Toward the end of the tale that Zarathustra recounts to the seamen—those searchers and re-searchers—Zarathustra poses this question to them: *"Who* is the shep-herd into whose gorge the snake crawled?" We can now reply that it is Zarathustra, the thinker of the thought of eternal return. Zarathustra's ownmost animals, his eagle and his serpent, exalt him only after he has overcome the world of the howling dog and the black snake. Zara-thustra becomes a convalescent only after he has passed through a period of illness, only after he has come to know that the black snake that chokes us pertains to knowledge as such, that the knower must also come to terms with the disgust occasioned by the contemptible human being as something that is necessary.

Now for the first time we can recognize the inner correspondence of the two passages from Part III of *Thus Spoke Zarathustra* on which we have been commenting. Now we understand why Zarathustra replies as follows to his animals, who wish to perform for Zarathustra's enjoyment the delightful ditty of the eternal return of the same in the loveliest words and tones: "The intense disgust with man—*this* choked, me, *this* had crawled into my throat, this and also what the soothsayer had said: 'It is all alike, nothing is worthwhile, knowledge chokes.' " Whoever takes the thought of eternal return to be a ditty belongs among those who flee from genuine knowledge, inasmuch as such knowledge "chokes." Thus in the episode entitled "The Convalescent," with explicit reference to the section "On the Vision and the Riddle," precisely at the point when Zarathustra begins to respond to the animals' ditty, we hear the following:

> "Oh, you rascally jesters and barrel organs, be still now!" replied Zarathustra, smiling once again. "How well you know what had to be fulfilled in seven days—and how that beast wriggled down my throat and choked me! But I bit its head off and spewed it far away from me.
>
> And you? You've made a hurdy-gurdy song out of it! Here am I, lying here, weary of this biting and spewing, still sick from my own redemption. *And you looked on all the while?*

These two distinct episodes, "On the Vision and the Riddle" and "The Convalescent," hence coalesce, both in terms of their content and their place in the work in question. We achieve a more balanced understanding of the book as a whole. Yet we must guard against the presumption that we now belong among those who really understand. Perhaps we too are mere onlookers. Perhaps we do not heed the second question Zarathustra poses straightaway to the crew. He asks not only "Who is the shepherd?" but also *"Who* is the human being into whose gorge all that is heaviest and blackest will creep?" The answer is that it is the one who thinks—in company with others—the thought of eternal return. Yet he or she is not thinking the thought in its essential domain until the black snake has penetrated the gorge and its head has been bitten off. The thought *is* only as that bite.

As soon as we understand this we realize why Zarathustra grows fearful when he thinks the thought of the moment, and why the dwarf, rather than answering, simply vanishes. The moment cannot be thought before the bite has occurred, because the bite answers the question as to what the gateway itself—the moment—is: the gateway of the moment is that decision in which prior history, the history of nihilism, is brought to confrontation and forthwith overcome.

The thought of eternal return of the same *is* only *as* this conquering thought. The overcoming must grant us passage across a gap that seems to be quite narrow. The gap opens between two things that in one way are alike, so that they appear to be the same. On the one side stands the following: "Everything is nought, indifferent, so that nothing is worthwhile—*it is all alike.*" And on the other side: "Everything recurs, it depends on each moment, everything matters—*it is all alike.*"

The smallest gap, the rainbow bridge of the phrase *it is all alike,* conceals two things that are quite distinct: "everything is indifferent" and "nothing is indifferent."

The overcoming of this smallest gap is the most difficult overcoming in the thought of eternal return of the same as the essentially overcoming thought. If one takes the thought ostensibly "for itself" in terms of its content—"Everything turns in a circle"—then it is perhaps sheer delusion. But in that case it is not Nietzsche's thought. Above all, it is not the thought "for itself," inasmuch as for itself it is precisely the overcoming thought, and this alone.

If we survey once again at a single glance our presentation of Nietzsche's thought of eternal return of the same, we cannot but be struck by the fact that our explicit discussion of the thought's *content* has receded markedly before our constant emphasis on the right *way* of approaching the thought and its conditions. The conditions may be reduced to two—and even these cohere and constitute but one.

First, thinking in terms of the moment. This implies that we transpose ourselves to the temporality of independent action and decision, glancing ahead at what is assigned us as our task and back at what is given us as our endowment.

Second, thinking the thought as the overcoming of nihilism. This implies that we transpose ourselves to the condition of need that arises with nihilism. The condition requires of us that we meditate on the endowment and decide about the task. Our needy condition itself is nothing other than what our transposition to the moment opens up to us.

Yet what accounts for the fact that with this thought it is precisely thinking, and the conditions of thinking, that are emphasized so essentially? What else could it be but the thought's "content," what it gives us to think? Accordingly, the content does not really go into abeyance, as it seemed to; rather, it comes to the fore in a singular way. For now the conditions of the thought-process as such thrust their way to the forefront. With the thought in question, *what* is to be thought recoils on the thinker because of the *way* it is to be thought, and so it compels the thinker. Yet it does so solely in order to draw the thinker into what is to be thought. To think eternity requires that we think the moment, that is, transpose ourselves to the moment of being-a-self.* To think the recurrence of the same is to enter into confrontation with the "it is all alike," the "it isn't worthwhile'; in short, with nihilism.

Only by way of nihilism and the moment is the eternal recurrence of the same to be thought. Yet in such thinking the thinker as such slips into the ring of eternal recurrence, indeed in such a way as to help achieve the ring, help decide it.

Whence does it arise that precisely in the fundamental thought of Nietzsche's philosophy the recoil of what is to be thought on the thinker—and the thinker's being drawn into what is thought—come so decisively to light? Is it because this kind of relation between thought and thinker is instituted in Nietzsche's philosophy alone? Or does such a relation obtain in every philosophy as such? If the latter, to what extent is this the case? With that question we arrive at the second major division of our lecture course.

---

* See chapter 4 of *Being and Time*, sections 25–27. Cf. p. 24, above.

25. The Essence of a Fundamental Metaphysical Position; The Possibility of Such Positions in the History of Western Philosophy

Whenever we think the thought of eternal recurrence of the same, what is to be thought recoils on the one who is thinking, and the thinker is drawn into the thought. The reason for this is not simply the fact that the eternal recurrence of the same is being thought, but that this particular thought thinks being as a whole. We call such a thought "metaphysical." Because the thought of return is *the* metaphysical thought in Nietzsche's case, it is characterized by the relationship of the recoil that includes and the inclusion that recoils. Of course, there must be a special reason for the fact that this relationship comes to prevail in such a conspicuous way precisely with Nietzsche, and that reason can lie only in Nietzsche's metaphysics; we can say where and how and why it lies there only if we have defined what we call *metaphysics* by means of a sufficiently clear concept. Such a concept must clarify what we mean by a "fundamental position." In the designation "fundamental metaphysical position" the word *metaphysical* is not appended in order to indicate a special case among "fundamental positions." Rather, the word *metaphysical* designates the domain that is opened up as metaphysical only by virtue of the articulation of a fundamental position. If this is so, then what does the phrase *fundamental metaphysical position* mean?

The title of this section, which indicates the task we have just outlined, bears a subtitle. The subtitle invokes the possibility of a fundamental metaphysical position in the history of Western philosophy. Here it is not so much a matter of referring to the manifold approximations to such fundamental metaphysical positions and to their historical sequence. Rather, what we must emphasize is the fact that what we are calling a *fundamental metaphysical position* pertains expressly to Western history, and to it alone, helping to determine that history in an essential way. Something like a fundamental metaphysical position was possible heretofore only in our tradition; and to the extent that such positions are attempted in the future as well, what has prevailed up to now will remain in force as something not overcome, not assimilated. Here we intend to discuss the possibility of a fundamental metaphysical position in the most fundamental sense of the phrase, and not to sketch some sort of historiographical account. In accordance with what we have said, this fundamental discussion will nonetheless be essentially historical.

Since in the present lecture course we are to portray *Nietzsche's* fundamental metaphysical position, our discussion of that concept can only be of a preparatory nature. Furthermore, a well-rounded, essential consideration of the matter is quite impossible: we lack all the prerequisites for such a consideration.

It behooves our tentative characterization of the concept *fundamental metaphysical position* to begin with the word and concept *metaphysical*. We use the word to designate matters germane to "metaphysics." The latter has for centuries referred to that range of questions in philosophy which philosophy sees as its proper task. *Metaphysics* is thus the rubric indicative of philosophy proper; it always has to do with a philosophy's fundamental thought. Even the customary meaning of the word, that is to say, the meaning that has come into general and popular use, still reflects this trait, albeit in a faint and fuzzy way. When we speak of something *metaphysical* we are pointing to reasons lying behind something else, or perhaps going out beyond that thing in some inscrutable way. We sometimes employ the word in a pejorative way, whereby those "reasons behind" a thing are taken as mere figments and, at bottom, absurdities; at other times we use the word *metaphysical* positively, taking it as referring to the impalpable and ultimate, the decisive. In either case, however, our thinking hovers in indeterminacy, insecurity, and obscurity. The word refers more to the end and limits of our thinking and inquiring than to their proper beginning and unfolding.

Yet when we refer merely to the devaluation the word *metaphysics* has suffered we are not entertaining the proper significance of that word. The word and its origins are quite strange; odder still is its history. And yet the configuration of the Western intellectual world and thereby the world in general depends to an essential extent on the power and preeminence of this word and its history. In history, words are often mightier than things and deeds. The fact that we ultimately still know very little about the power of this word *metaphysics* and its hegemony makes us realize how paltry and extrinsic our knowledge of the history of philosophy has remained, and how ill-prepared we are to enter into confrontation with that history, its fundamental positions, and the unifying and determinative forces within those positions. History of philosophy is not a matter for historiography, but a matter of philosophy. The first philosophical history of philosophy was that of Hegel. He never elaborated that history in book form, but presented it in lecture courses taught at Jena, Heidelberg, and Berlin.

Hegel's history of philosophy is the only philosophical history heretofore, and it will remain the only one until philosophy is forced to think historically—in a still more essential and original sense of that word—taking its ownmost grounding question as its point of departure. Wherever this is already occurring, in its initial stages, it still seems as if it is all nothing more than a slightly altered formulation of the earlier "historiographical" interpretation of the history of philosophy. The further illusion arises that historical observation restricts itself to what has been and does not have the courage—does not even have the capacity—to say something "new" of its own. The illusion will persist as long as there is no one who surmises—and is able to estimate the implications of—the following fact: in spite of the ascendant power of technology and of the universally technicized "mobilization" of the globe, hence in spite of a quite specific preeminence of an ensnared nature, an altogether distinct fundamental power of Being is on the rise; this power is *history*—which, however, is no longer to be represented as an object of historiography. We allude to these matters here simply because the following historical meditation on the essence of metaphysics may well seem to be nothing more than a highly abridged excerpt from some handbook or other on the history of philosophy.

Metaphysics is the name for the full range of philosophy's proper questions. If these questions are many, they are nonetheless guided by one single question. In truth, drawn as they are into that question, they are in effect but *one* question. Every question, and especially the one question of philosophy, as a question is always bathed in a light that emanates from the question itself. That is why the very inception of inquiry at the grand commencement of Western philosophy possesses some knowledge of itself. Such autochthonous knowledge of philosophic inquiry initially defines itself by circumscribing and comprehending what it is asking about. Philosophy inquires into the *archē*. We translate that word as "principle." And if we neglect to think and question rigorously and persistently, we think we know what "principle" means here. *Archē* and *archein* mean "to begin." At the same time, they mean to stand at the beginning of all; hence, to rule. Yet this reference to the designated *archē* will make sense only if we simultaneously determine that *of* which and *for* which we are seeking the *archē*. We are seeking it, not for some isolated event, not for unusual and recondite facts and relationships, but purely and simply for being. Whenever we say the word *das Seiende*, we are referring to everything that is. But when we inquire into the *archē* of being, all being—as a whole and in entirety—is placed in question. With the question concerning the *archē*, something about being as a whole has already been said. Being as a whole has now become visible for the first time *as* being and *as a whole.*

Whenever we inquire into the *archē* we experience being as a whole at the very beginning, the very rise of its presence and radiance. When the sun begins to radiate its light we speak of "sunrise"; accordingly, we conceive of the upsurgence of what is present as such as a rise. We are asking about the *archē* of being as a whole, about its rise, to the extent that this rising pervades being in terms of both what it is and how it is. Thus we are asking about a kind of dominion. We mean to acquire knowledge concerning the rise and dominion of being as a whole; such knowledge of the *archē* is therefore to know what being is insofar as it is being. Accordingly, the question of philosophy, as an inquiry into the *arché*, may be posed in the following form: What is being, insofar as it is viewed as being? *Ti to on hei on? Quid est ens qua ens?* This question, once its manner of inquiry has thus been established, may be simplified to the following formula: *Ti to on?* What is being? To ask this question, to find the answer to it once it has been posed and secured, is the primary and proper task of philosophy—it is *prōtē philosophia*. At its very commencement Western philosophy delineates philosophic inquiry in terms of the question *ti to on?* In that commencement Western philosophy comes to its essential conclusion. It is Aristotle in particular who achieves this essential clarification of philosophic inquiry in the most lucid way. Hence at the outset of one of his essential treatises *(Metaphysics,* VII, 1) Aristotle writes the following words: *Kai dē kai to palai te kai nun kai aei dzētoumenon kai aei aporoumenon, ti to on?* "And so it is asked, from ancient times to the present, and on into the future, even though the paths to this question stop short or are utterly lacking,—What is being?"

In order for us to understand—and that means to assist in asking—this apparently quite simple question, it is important from the outset to attain clarity concerning the following point, a point we will have to think about again and again: inasmuch as being is put in question with a view to the *arché*, being itself is already determined. If we ask whence and in what way being rises and, as rising, comes to presence, being itself is already defined *as* the *upsurging* and as what holds sway and *presences* in such upsurgence. The Greeks called such rising-presencing governance *physis.* The latter word means something else, something more, than our word *nature.* At all events, the following becomes clear: when the *arché* is sought, being itself is defined more closely, determined in a correspondingly far-reaching and penetrating way.

A peculiar experience arises as part and parcel of this process: in addition to beings that come to the fore on their own, there seem to be other beings that are first produced by human beings—whether such production occur in handicraft manufacture, in artistic performances, or in the ordered conduct of public affairs. Accordingly, one proceeds to make a distinction with respect to being as a whole between what is preeminently and straightforwardly *physis,* namely, *on physei,* and what is *on technēi, thesei,* and *nomōi.* *

The definitive meditation on being will always first cast its eye on being as *physis—ta physei onta*—there to perceive what being as such is. Such knowledge, related as it is to *physis,* is an *epistēmē physikē,* "physics," though not at all in the contemporary sense of that word. It is of course nonetheless true that physics today has a great deal of work to do, more than it is aware of, or can possibly be aware of. "Physics" is perspective on, and circumspection within, being as a whole; yet its view to the *archē* always sets the standard. Thus within the philosophical meditation on being (that is, on *physis)* there are studies that enter more deeply into being and its various regions, for instance, the inanimate or animate; and there can also be studies that concentrate less on the characteristic details of a given region than on the question of what being is when viewed as a whole. If we designate the first series of investigations with the word *physikē,* in the sense of *scientia physica,* then the second series is in a certain sense posterior to it; yet although it follows in the wake of the first series, the second series contains the ultimate and genuine studies. Viewed from the outside, in terms of the order, division, and sequence of the investigations and in terms of the kind of knowledge that is attained in treatises that come *post physicam,* such studies may be given the Greek designation *meta ta physika.* At the same time, what we have already indicated readily opens onto a further insight: inquiry into the *archē* asks what determines and dominates being as a whole in its governance. The question *ti to on?* inquires out beyond being as a whole, although the question always and everywhere relates precisely *back to it.* Such knowledge of the *physika* is not merely *post physicam* but *trans physicam.* Metaphysics, *meta ta physika,* is knowledge and inquiry that posit being as *physis.* Metaphysics does so in such a way that in and through the positing it inquires out beyond being, asking about being *as* being. To inquire into the *archē*—to ask the question *ti to on?*—is metaphysics. Or, to put it the other way around, metaphysics is the inquiry and the search

---

* That is to say, a distinction between beings that rise and come to presence under their own power and those that derive from the arts and crafts *(technēi),* or are set down in words *(thesei),* or are proclaimed in laws *(nomōi).*

that always remains guided by the sole question "What is being?" We therefore call this question the *guiding question* of metaphysics. *

The question "What is being?" inquires so universally and so encompassingly that all the efforts incited by it at first and for quite some time afterwards strive after this one thing—to find an answer to the question and to secure that answer. The more this question becomes the guiding question, and the longer it remains such, the less the question itself becomes an object of inquiry. Every treatment of the guiding question is and remains *preoccupied with the answer,* preoccupied with *finding* the answer. The latter has assumed sundry configurations ever since the commencement of Western philosophy with the Greeks, as philosophy pursued its circuitous route through the age of Christendom and into the age of modernity and modernity's conquest of the world, up to Nietzsche. Yet no matter how varied the configurations have been, they remain unified by the framework of the sole guiding question; once it is posed, the question seems to pose itself automatically—and hence to recede as a question. The question is not unfolded along the lines of its own articulation.

With the responses to this wholly undeveloped guiding question, certain positions adopted toward being as such and toward its *archē* arise. Being itself, as it is definitively experienced from the outset— whether as *physis* or as the creation of some Creator or as the realization of an absolute spirit—and the way being is defined in its *archē* provide the ground on which, and the respect in which, the guiding question troubles itself about the proffered answers. The questioners themselves, and all those who pattern and ground their essential knowledge and action within the realm of the prevailing response to the guiding question, have adopted a stance toward being as a whole, a stance in relation to being as such, in conformity to the guiding question—whether or not they are aware of the guiding question as such. Because the stance in question originates from the guiding question and is simultaneous with it, and because the guiding question is what is properly metaphysical in metaphysics, we call the stance that

---

* See Volume I of this series, section 11, pp. 67–68, for further discussion of the *Leitfrage.*

derives from the undeveloped guiding question *the fundamental meta-physical position.* *

The concept *fundamental metaphysical position* may be grasped in propositional form as follows: The fundamental metaphysical position expresses the way in which the one who poses the guiding question remains enmeshed in the structures of that question, which is not explicitly unfolded; thus enmeshed, the questioner comes to stand within being as a whole, adopting a stance toward it, and in that way helping to determine the location of humanity as such in the whole of beings.

All the same, the concept of a fundamental metaphysical position is not yet clear. Not only the concept but also the historically developed fundamental positions themselves are necessarily in and for themselves altogether opaque and impenetrable. That is the reason we invariably represent the fundamental metaphysical positions—for instance, those of Plato, or of medieval theology, or of Leibniz, Kant, and Hegel—so extrinsically, according to the various doctrines and propositions expressed in them. The best we can do is to say what predecessors influenced these philosophers and what standpoint they adopt in matters of ethics or in the question of the demonstrability of God's existence or with regard to the issue of the "reality of the external world." We invoke sundry "aspects," which apparently just happen to be there and which we take up as evident, totally ignorant of the fact that there can be such aspects only because a fundamental metaphysical position has been adopted here. The position in question is adopted because knowledge and thought themselves stand under the dominion of the guiding question from the very beginning. And the guiding question itself is *not developed.*

The concept of a fundamental metaphysical position and the corresponding historical positions themselves attain essential clarity and definition only when the guiding question of metaphysics and thereby metaphysics itself in its essence come to be developed. It is almost

---

* *Die metaphysische Grundstellung,* literally, "the metaphysical ground position." Readers must hear in the word *fundamental* the German word *Grund.* Heidegger always and everywhere contraposes the guiding question of metaphysics to its grounding question, *die Grundfrage.*

superfluous to say that an original, thoughtful stance adopted with regard to a particular metaphysics is possible and fruitful only if that metaphysics is itself developed in terms of its own fundamental position and only if the way in which it *responds to the guiding question* can be defined. The mutually prevailing fundamental positions must first of all be worked out in and for every genuinely philosophical confrontation.

The essence of what we are calling a *fundamental metaphysical position* develops with and in the unfolding of the guiding question of metaphysics. Such unfolding of the guiding question is not solely and not even primarily motivated by the desire to achieve a better conception of the fundamental metaphysical position as such. Rather, the determining ground of the development of the guiding question is to be sought in a renewed posing of the question, indeed, in a more original asking of that question. Yet that is not a matter we shall be able to treat here. What we are to communicate now is rather the bare result of the development of the guiding question. We shall present it in a highly compressed, well-nigh arid form, in textbook fashion, so that the inner articulation of the guiding question becomes visible—if only as a skeleton devoid of flesh and blood.

The guiding question of Western philosophy is, "What is being?" To *treat* this question as stated and posed is simply to look for an answer. To *develop* the question as it is formulated, however, is to pose the question more essentially: in asking the question one enters explicitly into those relationships that become visible when one assimilates virtually everything that comes to pass in the very asking of the question. When we treat the guiding question we are transposed forthwith to a search for an answer and to everything that has to be done on behalf of that search. Developing the guiding question is something essentially different—it is a more original form of inquiry, one which does not crave an answer. It takes the search for an answer far more seriously and rigorously than any straightforward treatment of the guiding question can—given the particular stance such treatment has adopted. An answer is no more than the final step of the very asking; and an answer that bids adieu to the inquiry annihilates itself as an answer. It can ground nothing like knowledge. It rests content with the sheer opinions it traces and in which it has ensconced itself. A question—especially a question that involves being as a whole—can be appropriately answered only if it is adequately posed in the first place. The guiding question of philosophy is adequately posed only when it is *developed.* Here the development assumes such proportions that it transforms the very question, bringing to light the guiding question as such in its utter lack of originality. For that reason we call the question "What is being?" the *guiding question,* in contrast to the more original question which sustains and directs the guiding question. The more original question we call the *grounding question.*

Whenever we present the development of the guiding question "schematically," as we are now doing, we easily awaken the suspicion that here we are merely making inquiries concerning a question. To question questioning strikes sound common sense as rather unwholesome, extravagant, perhaps even nonsensical. If it is a matter of wanting to get to beings themselves—and in the guiding question this is surely the case—then the inquiry into inquiry seems an aberration. In the end, such an attitude, asking about its asking, seems nothing short of noxious or self-lacerating; we might call it "egocentric" and "nihilistic" and all the other nasty names we so easily come by.

That the development of the guiding question appears to be merely inquiry piled on top of inquiry—this illusion persists. That an inquiry concerning inquiry ultimately looks like an aberration, a veritable walk down the garden path—this illusion too cannot be squelched. Confronting the danger that only a few or no one at all will be able to muster the courage and the energy required to think through and examine thoroughly the development of the guiding question; and in the expectation that these few might stumble against something quite different from a question that is posed merely for its own sake or a piece of sheer extravagance, we shall here undertake to sketch briefly the articulation of the developed guiding question.

The question asks *ti to on?* What is being? We shall begin to explicate the question by following the direction the inquiry itself takes, gradually unraveling all the matters we come across.

What is being? What is meant is being *as such,* neither some particular being nor a group of beings nor even all of them taken together, but something essentially more: what is meant is the whole, being taken as a whole from the outset, being taken *as* such unity. Outside of this one, this being, there is no other, unless it be the nothing. Yet the nothing is not some kind of being which is merely other. How matters stand with the nothing is not the question we are now to pursue. We only wish to keep in mind the full range of the area we are approaching when we ask the question "What is being, being as a whole, this unity that admits no other?" Let us then resolve not to forget in anything that follows what it was that rose to meet us in our first tentative step in the question concerning being, namely, the incontrovertible happenstance that we stumbled across the nothing.

Seen from the point of view of the question iself, that which the question is heading toward is the matter to be interrogated—we may call it the field of the question. Yet this field—being as a whole—is not staked out in our questioning merely so that we can take cognizance of its incalculable abundance; nor is it our intention merely to make being a familiar station on our way; rather, the question aims right from the start at being insofar as it is being. With regard to the field of interrogation, we are asking about something that is peculiar to it, something that is most its own. What name shall we give it? If we interrogate being solely with a view to the fact that it is being, interrogate being as being, then with the question as to what being is we are aiming to discover what makes being a being. We are aiming to discover the beingness of being—in Greek, the *ousia* of *on*. We are interrogating the Being of beings.

In the field of the question, in the very staking out of the field, the goal of the question is itself already established—what we are asking *for* in the matter interrogated, to wit, the Being of beings. Just as we collided against the nothing when we undertook to set the field of the question in relief, so here the staking out of the field and the establishment of the goal that is at stake condition one another reciprocally. And if we may say that the nothing looms at the border of this question, then, in accordance with the reciprocity of the field and the goal of the question, we may experience the proximity of the nothing also in the goal, that is, in the Being of beings; provided, of course, that we are actually inquiring, that our aim is true, that we are on target. To be sure, the nothing seems to be an utter nullity; it is as though we were doing it too great on honor when we call it by name. Yet this utterly common affair proves to be so uncommon that we can experience it only in unusual experiences. The meanness of the nothing consists precisely in the circumstance that it is capable of seducing us into thinking that our empty chatter—our calling the nothing an utter nullity—can really shunt the matter aside.* The nothing of being follows the Being of being as night follows day. When would we ever see and experience the day as day if there were no night! Thus the most durable and unfailing touchstone of genuineness and forcefulness of thought in a philosopher is the question as to whether or not he or she experiences in a direct and fundamental manner the nearness of the nothing in the Being of beings. Whoever fails to experience it remains forever outside the realm of philosophy, without hope of entry.

If inquiry were no more than what the superficial view often readily takes it to be; if it were simply a fleeting being-on-the-lookout for something, or a dispassionate scrutiny of an object of inquiry, or a passing hit-or-miss glance at a given goal; if inquiry were any of these things, then our unfolding of the question would already be at an end. And yet we have scarcely begun. We are seeking the Being of beings; we are trying to reach it. To that end we must approach being itself and bring it into our ken. Whatever is interrogated is questioned in a number of specific respects, never in an altogether general way, inasmuch as the latter runs counter to the very essence of questioning. And so we come to what is asked *for*. The field is examined in a dual perspective, inasmuch as it is surveyed by a preliminary view toward the goal. The being as such is viewed with respect to what it is, what it looks like, hence with respect to its intrinsic composition. We may call this the *constitution* of the being. At the same time, a being that is constituted in this or that fashion has its *way* to be—as such, being is either possible or actual or necessary. Thus the guiding question,

---

* When Heidegger refers to the nothing as "this utterly common affair" (*dieses Gemeinste*), and when he invokes the "meanness" of the nothing (*das Gemeine am Nichts*), he adds a new dimension to Hegel's play on the words *mein, meinen, Meinung,* and *Allgemeine,* discussed on p. 100, above. Being as a whole is not the universal; its common border is with the nothing. And there is something insidious in the intimacy of being and the nothing.

besides having its field and its goal, possesses above all its range of vision. Within that range it thinks beings as such according to a two-fold respect. Only in terms of both respects, as they are reciprocally related, can the Being of beings be defined.

When we first hear it, and even long afterwards, the guiding question "What is being?" sounds altogether indefinite; its universality appears to be engaged in a contest with its haziness and impalpability. All highways and byways seem to be open to its fortuitous search. A re-examination and testing of the various steps involved in the question seems to be without prospect. Certainly—as long as one leaves the question undetermined! Yet our prior explications ought to have made it clear by now that this question possesses a very definite though presumably very complex articulation, one which we have hardly fathomed and are even less able to master. Of course, we would mistake this articulation from top to bottom if we were to wield it academically and technically in the form of a merely "scientific" formulation—if, for example, we expected to be able to test the steps involved in the question as though they resembled the directly graspable, calculable result of an "experiment."

Our inquiry into the guiding question is separated from that kind of procedure by a veritable gulf. And being as a whole, itself the field of the question, can never be patched together out of isolated assortments of beings. All the same, the guiding question too in each case sustains an exceptional relationship with a particular region of beings within the field, a region that therefore assumes special importance. This fact has its grounds in the essence of inquiry itself, which, the more sweeping it is at the start, the more closely it wants to approach what it is interrogating, in order to survey it with an inquiring gaze. If it is ultimately the question concerning being that is involved here, the first thing we have to heed is the fact that being, in its constitution and its ways to be, discloses not only an articulated abundance but also a number of orders and stages which shed light on one another. Here it is by no means a matter of indifference which orders of being become definitive for the illumination of the others—whether, for instance, living beings are conceived in terms of lifeless ones, or the latter in terms of the former.

Whatever the particular case, each time the guiding question is posed *one* region of beings becomes *definitive* for our survey of being as a whole. In each case the guiding question unfolds in itself something that sets the standard. By this "setting the standard" we understand the preeminence of an exceptional region within being as a whole. The remaining beings are not actually derived from that exceptional region; yet that region provides the light that illumines them all.

26. Nietzsche's Fundamental Metaphysical Position

In the foregoing we have attempted to portray Nietzsche's fundamental thought—the eternal return of the same—in its essential import, in its domain, and in the mode of thinking that is expressly proper to the thought itself, that is, the mode demanded by the thought as such. In that way we have laid the *foundation* for our own efforts to define Nietzsche's *fundamental metaphysical position in Western philosophy.* The effort to circumscribe Nietzsche's fundamental metaphysical position indicates that we are examining his philosophy in terms of the position assigned it by the history of Western philosophy hitherto. At the same time, this means that we are expressly transposing Nietzsche's philosophy to that sole position in which it can and must unfold the forces of thought that are most proper to it, and this in the context of an inescapable confrontation with prior Western philosophy as a whole. The fact that in the course of our presentation of the doctrine of return we have actually come to recognize the region of thought that must necessarily and preeminently take precedence in every fruitful reading and appropriating of Nietzschean thought may well be an important gain; yet when viewed in terms of the essential task, namely, the characterization of Nietzsche's fundamental metaphysical position, such a gain remains merely provisional.

We shall be able to define Nietzsche's fundamental metaphysical position in its principal traits if we ponder the response he gives to the question concerning the *constitution* of being and being's *way to be.* Now, we know that Nietzsche offers two answers with regard to being as a whole: being as a whole is will to power, and being as a whole is eternal recurrence of the same. Yet philosophical interpretations of Nietzsche's philosophy have up to now been unable to grasp these two simultaneous answers *as* answers, indeed as answers that necessarily cohere, because they have not recognized the questions to which these answers pertain; that is to say, prior interpretations have not explicitly developed those questions on the basis of a thoroughgoing articulation of the guiding question. If, on the contrary, we approach the matter in terms of the developed guiding question, it becomes apparent that the word "is" in these two major statements—being as a whole is will to power, and being as a whole is eternal recurrence of the same—in each case suggests something different. To say that being as a whole "is" will to power means that being as such possesses the constitution of that which Nietzsche defines as will to power. And to say that being as a whole "is" eternal recurrence of the same means that being as a whole *is,* as being, in the manner of eternal recurrence of the same. The determination "will to power" replies to the question of being *with respect to the latter's constitution;* the determination "eternal recurrence of the same" replies to the question of being *with respect to its way to be.* Yet constitution and manner of being do cohere as determinations of the beingness of beings.

Accordingly, in Nietzsche's philosophy will to power and eternal recurrence of the same belong together. It is thus right from the start a misunderstanding—better, an outright mistake—of metaphysical proportions when commentators try to play off will to power against eternal recurrence of the same, and especially when they exclude the latter altogether from metaphysical determinations of being. In truth, the *coherence of both* must be grasped. Such coherence is itself essentially defined on the basis of the coherence of *constitution* and *way to be* as reciprocally related moments of the beingness of beings. The constitution of beings also specifies in each case their way to be—indeed, as their proper ground.

What fundamental metaphysical position does Nietzsche's philosophy assume for itself on the basis of its response to the guiding question within Western philosophy, that is to say, within metaphysics?

Nietzsche's philosophy is the end of metaphysics, inasmuch as it reverts to the very commencement of Greek thought, taking up such thought in a way that is peculiar to Nietzsche's philosophy alone. In this way Nietzsche's philosophy closes the ring that is formed by the very course of inquiry into being as such and as a whole. Yet to what extent does Nietzsche's thinking revert to the commencement? When we raise this question we must be clear about one point at the very outset: Nietzsche by no means recovers the philosophy of the commencement in its pristine form. Rather, here it is purely a matter of the reemergence of the essential fundamental positions of the commencement in a transformed configuration, in such a way that these positions interlock.

What are the decisive fundamental positions of the commencement? In other words, what sorts of answers are given to the as yet undeveloped guiding question, the question as to what being is?

The *one* answer—roughly speaking, it is the answer of Parmenides —tells us that *being is.* An odd sort of answer, no doubt, yet a very deep one, since that very response determines for the first time and for all thinkers to come, including Nietzsche, the meaning of *is* and *Being* —permanence and presence, that is, the eternal present.

The *other* answer—roughly speaking, that of Heraclitus—tells us that *being becomes.* The being is in being by virtue of its permanent becoming, its self-unfolding and eventual dissolution.

To what extent is Nietzsche's thinking the end? That is to say, how does it stretch back to both these fundamental determinations of being in such a way that they come to interlock? Precisely to the extent that Nietzsche argues that being *is* as fixated, as permanent; and that it *is* in perpetual creation and destruction. Yet being is *both* of these, not in an extrinsic way, as one beside another; rather, being is in its very ground perpetual creation (Becoming), while as creation it needs what is fixed. Creation needs what is fixed, first, in order to overcome it, and second, in order to have something that has yet to be fixated, something that enables the creative to advance beyond itself and be transfigured. The essence of being is Becoming, but what becomes is and has Being only in creative transfiguration. What is and what becomes are fused in the fundamental thought that what becomes *is* inasmuch as in creation it *becomes being* and *is becoming.* But such becoming-a-being becomes a being that comes-to-be, and does so in the perpetual transformation of what has become firmly fixed and intractable to something made firm in a liberating transfiguration.*

Nietzsche once wrote, at the time when the thought of return first loomed on his horizon, during the years 1881–82 (XII, 66, number 124): "Let us imprint the emblem of eternity on *our* life!" The phrase means: let us introduce an eternalization to ourselves as beings, and hence to beings as a whole; let us introduce the transfiguration of what becomes *as* something that becomes being; and let us do this in such a way that the eternalization arises from being itself, originating for being, standing in being.

This fundamental metaphysical demand—that is, a demand that grapples with the guiding question of metaphysics—is expressed several years later in a lengthy note entitled *"Recapitulation,"* the title suggesting that the note in just a few sentences provides a résumé of the most important aspects of Nietzsche's philosophy. (See *The Will to Power*, number 617, presumably from early 1886.)† Nietzsche's "Recapit-

---

* The text is extraordinarily difficult to unravel: *Dieses Seiendwerden aber wird zum werdenden Seienden im ständigen Werden des Festgewordenen als eines Erstarrten zum Festgemachten als der befreienden Verklärung.* The oxymorons of this highly involuted sentence dramatize the inevitable petrifaction of Becoming in a metaphysics of Being. Only as permanence of presence can Becoming come to *be.* The wording of the sentence in Heidegger's original manuscript (1937) varies only slightly from the 1961 Neske text. Yet a series of energetic lines draws the word *befreienden,* "liberating," into the sentence, as though to break up all such petrifaction. For the *liberating transfiguration* of Becoming is what Heidegger elsewhere calls the most intrinsic *will* of Nietzschean thinking.

† As the note on page 19 of Volume I of this series relates, Heidegger employs the "Recapitulation" note (WM, 617) at crucial junctures throughout his Nietzsche lectures. See, for example, NI, 466 and 656; NII, 288 and 339; and p. 228, below. Yet the title "Recapitulation" stems not from Nietzsche himself but from his assistant and later editor Heinrich Köselitz (Peter Gast). Furthermore, the sentences from this long note which Heidegger neglects to cite by no means corroborate the use he makes of it. The whole of Nietzsche's sketch (now dated between the end of 1886 and spring of 1887, as it appears in CM, Mp XVII 3b [54], reads as follows:

To *stamp* Becoming with the character of Being—that is the supreme *will to power.*

Twofold falsification, one by the senses, the other by the mind, in order to preserve a world of being, of perdurance, of equivalence, etc.

That *everything recurs* is the closest *approximation of a world of Becoming to one of Being: peak of the meditation.*

ulation" begins with the statement: "To *stamp* Becoming with the character of Being—that is the supreme *will to power*." The sense is not that one must brush aside and replace Becoming as the impermanent—for impermanence is what Becoming implies—with being as the permanent. The sense is that one must shape Becoming as being in such a way that *as becoming* it is preserved, has subsistence, in a word, *is*. Such stamping, that is, the recoining of Becoming as being, is the supreme will to power. In such recoining the will to power comes to prevail most purely in its essence.

What is this recoining, in which whatever becomes comes to be being? It is the reconfiguration of what becomes in terms of its supreme possibilities, a reconfiguration in which what becomes is transfigured and attains subsistence in its very dimensions and domains. This recoining is a creating. To create, in the sense of creation out

---

The condemnation of and dissatisfaction with whatever becomes derives from values that are attributable to being: after such a world of Being had first been invented.

The metamorphoses of being (body, God, ideas, laws of nature, formulas, etc.)

"Being" as semblance; inversion of values: semblance was that which *conferred value*—

Knowledge itself impossible within Becoming; how then is knowledge possible? As error concerning itself, as will to power, as will to deception.

Becoming as invention volition self-denial, the overcoming of oneself: not a subject but a doing, establishing; creative, not "causes and effects."

Art as the will to overcome Becoming, as "eternalization," but shortsighted, depending on perspective: repeating on a small scale, as it were, the tendency of the whole

What *all life* exhibits, to be observed as a reduced formula for the universal tendency: hence a new grip on the concept "life" as will to power

Instead of "cause and effect," the mutual struggle of things that become, often with the absorption of the opponent; the number of things in becoming not constant.

Inefficacy of the old ideals for interpreting the whole of occurrence, once one has recognized their animal origins and utility; all of them, furthermore, contradicting life.

Inefficacy of the mechanistic theory—gives the impression of *meaninglessness*.

The entire *idealism* of humanity hitherto is about to turn into *nihilism*—into belief in absolute *worth*lessness, that is to say, *sense*lessness . . .

Annihilation of ideals, the new desert; the new arts, by means of which we can endure it, we *amphibians*.

Presupposition: bravery, patience, no "turning back," no hurrying forward

N.B.: Zarathustra, always parodying prior values, on the basis of his own abundance.

beyond oneself, is most intrinsically this: to stand in the moment of decision, in which what has prevailed hitherto, our endowment, is directed toward a projected task. When it is so directed, the endowment is preserved. The "momentary" character of creation is the essence of actual, actuating eternity, which achieves its greatest breadth and keenest edge as the moment of eternity in the return of the same. The recoining of what becomes into being—will to power in its supreme configuration—is in its most profound essence something that occurs in the "glance of an eye" as eternal recurrence of the same. The will to power, as *constitution* of being, is as it is solely on the basis of the *way* to be which Nietzsche projects for being as a whole: *Will to power, in its essence and according to its inner possibility, is eternal recurrence of the same.*

The aptness of our interpretation is demonstrated unequivocally in that very fragment which bears the title "Recapitulation." After the statement we have already cited—"To *stamp* Becoming with the character of Being—that is the supreme *will to power*"—we soon read the following sentence: "That *everything recurs* is the closest *approximation of a world of Becoming to one of Being: peak of the meditation.*" It would scarcely be possible to say in a more lucid fashion, first, how and on what basis the stamping of Being on Becoming is meant to be understood, and second, that the thought of eternal return of the same, even and precisely during the period when the thought of will to power appears to attain preeminence, remains *the* thought which Nietzsche's philosophy thinks without cease.

(During our discussion of the plans for Nietzsche's *magnum opus* [see page 160, above], several students noted that whereas sketches for such plans from the final year of Nietzsche's creative life (1888) mention Dionysos in the titles of their projected fourth and final books, our lecture course up to now has said nothing about this god.

Nevertheless, we ought to pay close attention to the phrases that follow the god's name in these titles: "philosophy of eternal return," or simply "philosophos."

Such phrases suggest that *what* the words *Dionysos* and *Dionysian* mean to Nietzsche will be heard and understood only if the "eternal return of the same" is thought. In turn, that which eternally recurs as the same and in such wise *is,* that is, perpetually presences, has the ontological constitution of "will to power." The mythic name *Dionysos* will become an epithet that has been *thought through* in the sense intended by Nietzsche the thinker only when we try to think the *coherence* of "will to power" and "eternal return of the same"; and that means, only when we seek those determinations of Being which from the outset of Greek thought guide all thinking about being as such and as a whole. [Two texts which appeared several years ago treat the matters of Dionysos and the Dionysian: Walter F. Otto, *Dionysos: Myth and Cult,* 1933; and Karl Reinhardt, "Nietzsche's 'Plaint of Ariadne,' " in the journal *Die Antike,* 1935, published separately in 1936.])*

Nietzsche conjoins in one both of the fundamental determinations of being that emerge from the commencement of Western philosophy, to wit, being as becoming and being as permanence. That "one" is his most essential thought—the eternal recurrence of the same.

Yet can we designate Nietzsche's way of grappling with the commencement of Western philosophy as an *end?* Is it not rather a reawakening of the commencement? Is it not therefore itself a commencement and hence the very opposite of an end? It is nonetheless the case that Nietzsche's fundamental metaphysical position is the end of Western philosophy. For what is decisive is not *that* the fundamental determinations of the commencement are conjoined and *that* Nietzsche's

---

* The paragraphs contained within parentheses appear as an indented extract in the Neske edition as they do here. Heidegger's original manuscript from the summer of 1937 does *not* show these paragraphs. Surprisingly, there is no extant *Abschrift* or typescript of this course; nor is the typescript that went to the printer in 1961 available for inspection. As a result, the date of the passage remains uncertain. My own surmise is that Heidegger added the note not long after the semester drew to a close: the reference to students' questions and to those two works on Dionysos that had "recently" been published make it highly unlikely that the note was added as late as 1960–61. The works Heidegger refers us to are of course still available—and are still very much worth reading: Walter F. Otto, *Dionysos: Mythos und Kultus* (Frankfurt am Main: V. Klostermann, 1933); Reinhardt's "Nietzsches Klage der Ariadne" appears now in Karl Reinhardt, *Vermächtnis der Antike: Gesammelte Essays zur Philosophie und Geschichtsschreibung,* edited by Carl Becker (Göttingen: Vandenhock & Ruprecht, 1960), pp. 310–33. See note 20 of the Analysis, p. 275, for further discussion of the Reinhardt article.

thinking stretches back to the commencement; what is metaphysically essential is *the way in which* these things transpire. The question is whether Nietzsche reverts to the incipient commencement, to the commencement as a commencing. And here our answer must be: no, he does not.

Neither Nietzsche nor any thinker prior to him—even and especially not that one who before Nietzsche first thought the *history* of philosophy in a philosophical way, namely, Hegel—revert to the incipient commencement. Rather, they invariably apprehend the commencement in the sole light of a philosophy in decline from it, a philosophy that arrests the commencement—to wit, the philosophy of Plato. Here we cannot demonstrate this matter in any detail. Nietzsche himself quite early characterizes his philosophy as inverted Platonism; yet the inversion does not eliminate the fundamentally Platonic position. Rather, precisely because it seems to eliminate the Platonic position, Nietzsche's inversion represents the entrenchment of that position.

What remains essential, however, is the following: when Nietzsche's metaphysical thinking reverts to the commencement, the circle closes. Yet inasmuch as it is the already terminated commencement and not the incipient one that prevails there, the circle itself grows inflexible, loses whatever of the commencement it once had. When the circle closes in *this* way it no longer releases any possibilities for essential inquiry into the guiding question. Metaphysics—treatment of the guiding question—is at an end. That seems a bootless, comfortless insight, a conclusion which like a dying tone signals ultimate cessation. Yet such is not the case.

Because Nietzsche's fundamental metaphysical position is the end of metaphysics in the designated sense, it performs the grandest and most profound gathering—that is, accomplishment—of all the essential fundamental positions in Western philosophy since Plato and in the light of Platonism. It does so from within a fundamental position that is determined by Platonism and yet which is itself creative. However, this fundamental position remains an actual, actuating fundamental metaphysical position only if it in turn is developed in all its essential forces and regions of dominion in the direction of its *counterposition*. For a thinking that looks beyond it, Nietzsche's philosophy, which is inherently a turning against what lies behind it, must itself come to be a foward-looking counterposition. Yet since Nietzsche's fundamental position in Western metaphysics constitutes the end of that metaphysics, it can be the counterposition for our other commencement only if the latter adopts a *questioning* stance vis-à-vis the initial commencement —as one which in its proper originality is only now commencing. After everything we have said, the questioning intended here can only be the unfolding of a more original inquiry. Such questioning must be the unfolding of the prior, all-determining, and commanding question of philosophy, the guiding question, "What is being?" *out of* itself and *out beyond* itself.

Nietzsche himself once chose a phrase to designate what we are calling his fundamental metaphysical position, a phrase that is often cited and is readily taken as a way to characterize his philosophy: *amor fati,* love of necessity. (See the Epilogue to *Nietzsche contra Wagner;* VIII, 206).* Yet the phrase expresses Nietzsche's fundamental

---

* The text Heidegger refers us to begins as follows:

I have often asked myself if I am not more profoundly indebted to the most difficult years of my life than to any of the others. What my innermost nature instructs me is that all necessity—viewed from the heights, in terms of an economy on a *grand* scale—is also what is inherently useful: one should not merely put up with it, one should *love* it. . . . *Amor fati:* that is my innermost nature.

Nietzsche repeats the formula twice in *Ecce Homo* (II, 10 and III, "Der Fall Wagner," 4), the first time as the ultimate explanation of his "discernment":

My formula for greatness in a human being is *amor fati:* that one does not will to have anything different, neither forward nor backward nor into all eternity. Not merely to bear necessity, though much less to cloak it—all Idealism is mendacity in the face of necessity—but to *love* it. . . .

Nietzsche had first cited the formula six years earlier, at the outset of Book IV of *The Gay Science,* as the very essence of affirmation: "I want to learn better how to see the necessity in things as what is beautiful—in that way I shall become one of those who make things beautiful. *Amor fati:* let this be my love from now on!" And he had written to Franz Overbeck, also in 1882, that he was possessed of "a fatalistic 'trust in God' " which he preferred to call *amor fati;* and he boasted, "I would stick my head down a lion's throat, not to mention. . . ."

The fullest statement concerning *amor fati,* however, appears as WM, 1041 (CM, W II 7a [32], from spring-summer, 1888). Although the note as a whole merits reprinting, and rereading, the following extract contains the essential lines. Nietzsche explains that

metaphysical position only when we understand the two words *amor* and *fatum*—and, above all, their conjunction—in terms of *Nietzsche's* ownmost thinking, only when we avoid mixing our fortuitous and familiar notions into it.

Amor—love—is to be understood as *will*, the will that wants whatever it loves to be what it is in its essence. The supreme will of this kind, the most expansive and decisive will, is the will as transfiguration. Such a will erects and exposes what it wills in its essence to the supreme possibilities of its Being.

Fatum—necessity—is to be understood, not as a fatality that is inscrutable, implacable, and overwhelming, but as that turning of need which unveils itself in the awestruck moment as an eternity, an eternity pregnant with the Becoming of being as a whole: *circulus vitiosus deus.*

Amor fati is the transfiguring will to belong to what is most in being among beings. A *fatum* is unpropitious, disruptive, and devastating to the one who merely stands there and lets it whelm him. That *fatum* is sublime and is supreme desire, however, to one who appreciates and grasps the fact that he belongs to his fate insofar as he is a creator, that is, one who is ever resolute. His knowing this is nothing else than the knowledge which of necessity resonates in his love.

The thinker inquires into being as a whole and as such; into the world as such. Thus with his very first step he always thinks out beyond the world, and so at the same time back to it. He thinks in the direction of that *sphere* within which a world becomes world. Wherever that sphere is not incessantly called by name, called aloud, wherever it is held silently in the most interior questioning, it is thought most purely and profoundly. For what is held in silence is genuinely preserved; as preserved it is most intimate and actual. What to common sense looks like "atheism," and has to look like it, is at bottom the very

---

his "experimental philosophy" aims to advance beyond nihilism to the very opposite of nihilism—

> to a *Dionysian* yes-saying to the world as it is, without reduction, exception, or selection; it wants eternal circulation—the same things, the same logic and dislogic of implication. Supreme state to which a philosopher may attain: taking a stand in Dionysian fashion on behalf of existence. My formula for this is *amor fati.*

opposite. In the same way, wherever the matters of death and the nothing are treated, Being and Being alone is thought most deeply— whereas those who ostensibly occupy themselves solely with "reality" flounder in nothingness.

Supremely thoughtful utterance does not consist simply in growing taciturn when it is a matter of saying what is properly to be said; it consists in saying the matter in such a way that it is named in nonsaying. The utterance of thinking is a telling silence.* Such utterance corresponds to the most profound essence of language, which has its origin in silence. As one in touch with telling silence, the thinker, in a way peculiar to him, rises to the rank of a poet; yet he remains eternally distinct from the poet, just as the poet in turn remains eternally distinct from the thinker.

> Everything in the hero's sphere turns to tragedy; everything in the demi-god's sphere turns to satyr-play; and everything in God's sphere turns to . . . to what? "world" perhaps?

---

* *Erschweigen*, an active or telling silence, is what Heidegger elsewhere discusses under the rubric of *sigetics* (from the Greek *sigaō*, to keep silent). For him it is the proper "logic" of a thinking that inquires into the other commencement.

Part Two

WHO IS NIETZSCHE'S ZARATHUSTRA?

Our question, it would seem, can be easily answered. For we find the response in one of Nietzsche's own works, in sentences that are clearly formulated and even set in italic type. The sentences occur in that work by Nietzsche which expressly delineates the figure of Zarathustra. The book, composed of four parts, was written during the years 1883 to 1885, and bears the title *Thus Spoke Zarathustra*.

Nietzsche provided the book with a subtitle to set it on its way. The subtitle reads: *A Book for Everyone and No One.* "For Everyone," of course, does not mean for anybody at all, anyone you please. "For Everyone" means for every human being as a human being, for every given individual insofar as he becomes for himself in his essence a matter worthy of thought. "And No One" means for none of those curiosity mongers who wash in with the tide and imbibe freely of particular passages and striking aphorisms in the book, and who then stagger blindly about, quoting its language—partly lyrical, partly shrill, sometimes tranquil, other times stormy, often elevated, occasionally trite. They do this instead of setting out on the way of thinking that is here searching for its word.

Thus Spoke Zarathustra: A Book for Everyone and No One. How uncannily true the work's subtitle has proven to be in the seventy years that have passed since the book first appeared—but true precisely in the reverse sense! It became a book for everybody, and to this hour no thinker has arisen who is equal to the book's fundamental thought and who can take the measure of the book's provenance in its full scope. Who is Zarathustra? If we read the work's title attentively we may find a clue: *Thus Spoke Zarathustra.* Zarathustra speaks. He is a speaker. Of what sort? Is he an orator, or maybe a preacher? No. Zarathustra the speaker is an advocate *[ein Fürsprecher*].* In this name we

---

* *Ein Fürsprecher,* literally, is one who speaks *before* a group of people *for* some particular purpose. In what follows, Heidegger discusses the related words *für* ("for") and *vor* ("fore," "in front of"). The English word "advocate" (from *ad-vocare:* to call, invite, convene) offers a kind of parallel. For a full discussion of the German words see Hermann Paul, *Deutsches Wörterbuch,* 6th ed. (Tübingen: M. Niemeyer, 1966), pp. 758–62.

encounter a very old word in the German language, one that has multiple meanings. *For* actually means *before*. In the Alemannic dialect, the word *Fürtuch* is still the common word for "apron."* The *Fürsprech* speaks "forth" and is the spokesman. Yet at the same time *für* means "on behalf of" and "by way of justification." Finally, an advocate is one who interprets and explains what he is talking about and what he is advocating.

Zarathustra is an advocate in this threefold sense. But what does he speak forth? On whose behalf does he speak? What does he try to interpret? Is Zarathustra merely some sort of advocate for some arbitrary cause, or is he *the* advocate for the one thing that always and above all else speaks to human beings?

Toward the end of the third part of *Thus Spoke Zarathustra* appears a section with the heading "The Convalescent." That is Zarathustra. But what does "convalescent," *der Genesende,* mean? *Genesen* is the same word as the Greek *neomai, nostos,* meaning to head for home. "Nostalgia" is the yearning to go home, homesickness. "The Convalescent" is one who is getting ready to turn homeward, that is, to turn toward what defines him. The convalescent is under way to himself, so that he can say of himself who he is. In the episode mentioned the convalescent says, "I, Zarathustra, the advocate of life, the advocate of suffering, the advocate of the circle. . . ."

Zarathustra speaks on behalf of life, suffering, and the circle, and that is what he speaks forth. These three, "life, suffering, circle," belong together and are the selfsame. If we were able to think this threefold matter correctly as one and the same, we would be in a position to surmise whose advocate Zarathustra is and who it is that Zarathustra himself, as this advocate, would like to be. To be sure, we could now intervene in a heavy-handed way and explain, with indisputable correctness, that in Nietzsche's language "life" means will to power as the fundamental trait of all beings, and not merely human beings. Nietzsche himself says what "suffering" means in the following words (VI, 469): "Everything that suffers wills to live. . . ." "Everything" here

---

* For *Fürtuch* (literally, "fore-cloth") Bernd Magnus has found a felicitous English parallel: the pinafore!

means all things that are by way of will to power, a way that is described in the following words (XVI, 151): "The configurative forces collide." "Circle" is the sign of the ring that wrings its way back to itself and in that way always achieves recurrence of the same.

Accordingly, Zarathustra introduces himself as an advocate of the proposition that all being is will to power, a will that suffers in its creating and colliding, and that wills itself precisely in this way in eternal recurrence of the same.

With the above assertion we have brought the essence of Zarathustra to definition—as we say at school. We can write the definition down, commit it to memory, and bring it forward whenever the occasion calls for it. We can even corroborate what we bring forward by referring specifically to those sentences in Nietzsche's works which, set in italic type, tell us who Zarathustra is.

In the above-mentioned episode, "The Convalescent," we read (314): *"You* [Zarathustra] *are the teacher of eternal return. . . !"* And in the Prologue to the entire work (section 3) stands the following: *"I* [Zarathustra] *teach you the overman."*

According to these statements, Zarathustra the advocate is a "teacher." To all appearances, he teaches two things: the eternal return of the same and the overman. However, it is not immediately apparent whether and in what way the things he teaches belong together. Yet even if the connection were to be clarified it would remain questionable whether we are hearing the advocate, whether we are learning from this teacher. Without such hearing and learning we shall never rightly come to know who Zarathustra is. Thus it is not enough to string together sentences from which we can gather what the advocate and teacher says about himself. We must pay attention to the *way* he says it, on what occasions, and with what intent. Zarathustra does not utter the decisive phrase "You are the teacher of eternal return!" by himself to himself. His animals tell him this. They are mentioned at the very beginning of the work's Prologue and more explicitly at its conclusion. In section 10 we read:

When the sun stood at midday he [Zarathustra] looked inquiringly into the sky—for above him he heard the piercing cry of a bird. And behold! An eagle soared through the air in vast circles, and a serpent hung suspended from him, not as his prey, but as though she were his friend: for she had coiled about his neck.

In this mysterious embrace about the throat—in the eagle's circling and the serpent's coiling—we can already sense the way circle and ring tacitly wind about one another. Thus the ring scintillates, the ring that is called *anulus aeternitatis:* the signet ring and year of eternity. When we gaze on the two animals we see where they themselves, circling and coiling about one another, belong. For of themselves they never concoct circle and ring; rather, they enter into circle and ring, there to find their essence. When we gaze on the two animals we perceive the things that matter to Zarathustra, who looks inquiringly into the sky. Thus the text continues:

> "These are my animals!" said Zarathustra, and his heart was filled with joy.
> "The proudest animal under the sun and the most discerning animal under the sun—they have gone out on a search.
> "They want to learn whether Zarathustra is still alive. Verily, am I still alive?"

Zarathustra's question receives its proper weight only if we understand the undefined word *life* in the sense of *will to power*. Zarathustra asks whether his will corresponds to the will which, as will to power, pervades the whole of being.

The animals seek to learn Zarathustra's essence. He asks himself whether he is still—that is, whether he is already—the one who he properly is. In a note to *Thus Spoke Zarathustra* from Nietzsche's literary remains (XIV, 279) the following appears: " 'Do I have time to *wait* for my animals? If they are *my* animals they will know how to find me.' Zarathustra's silence."

Thus at the place cited, "The Convalescent," Zarathustra's animals say the following to him—and although not all the words are italicized, we dare not overlook any of them. The animals say: "For your animals know well, O Zarathustra, who you are and must become: behold, *you are the teacher of eternal return*—that is now *your* destiny!" Thus it comes to light: Zarathustra must first *become* who he is. Zarathustra shrinks back in dismay before such becoming. Dismay permeates the entire work that portrays him. Dismay determines the style, the hesitant and constantly arrested course of the work as a whole. Dismay extinguishes all of Zarathustra's self-assurance and presumptuousness at the very outset of his way. Whoever has failed and continues to fail to apprehend from the start the dismay that haunts all of Zarathustra's speeches—which often sound presumptuous, often seem little more than frenzied extravaganzas—will never be able to discover who Zarathustra is.

If Zarathustra must first of all become the teacher of eternal return, then he cannot commence with this doctrine straightaway. For this reason another phrase stands at the beginning of his way: *"I teach you the overman."*

To be sure, we must try to extirpate right here and now all the false and confusing overtones of the word *Übermensch* that arise in our customary view of things. With the name *overman* Nietzsche is by no means designating a merely superdimensional human being of the kind that has prevailed hitherto. Nor is he referring to a species of man that will cast off all that is humane, making naked willfulness its law and titanic rage its rule. Rather, the overman—taking the word quite literally—is that human being who goes beyond prior humanity solely in order to conduct such humanity for the first time to its essence, an essence that is still unattained, and to place humanity firmly within that essence. A note from the posthumously published writings surrounding *Zarathustra* says (XIV, 271): "Zarathustra does not want to *lose* anything of mankind's past; he wants to pour everything into the mold."

Yet whence arises the urgent cry for the overman? Why does prior humanity no longer suffice? Because Nietzsche recognizes the historic moment in which man takes it on himself to assume dominion over the earth as a whole. Nietzsche is the first thinker to pose the decisive question concerning the phase of world history that is emerging only now, the first to think the question through in its metaphysical implications. The question asks: Is man, in his essence as man heretofore, prepared to assume dominion over the earth? If not, what must happen with prior humanity in order that it may "subjugate" the earth and thus fulfill the prophecy of an old testament? Must not prior man be conducted beyond himself, *over* his prior self, in order to meet this challenge? If so, then the "over-man," correctly thought, cannot be the product of an unbridled and degenerate fantasy that is plunging headlong into the void. We can just as little uncover the nature of overman historically by virtue of an analysis of the modern age. We dare not seek the essential figure of overman in those personalities who, as major functionaries of a shallow, misguided will to power, are swept to the pinnacles of that will's sundry organizational forms. Of course, one thing ought to be clear to us immediately: this thinking that pursues the figure of a teacher who teaches the over-man involves us, involves Europe, involves the earth as a whole—not merely today, but especially tomorrow. That is so, no matter whether we affirm or reject this thinking, whether we neglect it or ape it in false tones. Every essential thinking cuts across all discipleship and opposition alike without being touched.

Hence it behooves us first of all to learn how to learn from the teacher, even if that only means to ask out beyond him. In that way alone will we one day experience who Zarathustra is. Or else we will never experience it.

To be sure, we must still ponder whether this asking out beyond Nietzsche's thinking can be a continuation of his thought, or whether it must become a step back.

And before that, we must ponder whether this "step back" merely refers to a historically ascertainable past which one might choose to revive (for example, the world of Goethe), or whether the word *back* indicates something that *has been*. For the commencement of what has been still awaits a commemorative thinking, in order that it might become a beginning, a beginning to which the dawn grants upsurgence.*

Yet we shall now restrict ourselves to the effort to learn a few provisional things about Zarathustra. The appropriate way to proceed would be to follow the first steps taken by this teacher—the teacher that Zarathustra is. He teaches by showing. He previews the essence of overman and brings that essence to visible configuration. Zarathustra is

---

* See "The Anaximander Fragment," in *Early Greek Thinking,* pp. 16–18.

merely the teacher, not the over-man himself. In turn, Nietzsche is not Zarathustra, but the questioner who seeks to create in thought Zarathustra's essence.

The overman proceeds beyond prior and contemporary humanity; thus he is a transition, a bridge. In order for us learners to be able to follow the teacher who teaches the overman, we must—keeping now to the imagery—get onto the bridge. We are thinking the crucial aspects of the transition when we heed these three things:

First, that from which the one who is in transition departs.

Second, the transition itself.

Third, that toward which the one in transition is heading.

Especially the last-mentioned aspect we must have in view; above all, the one who is in transition must have it in view; and before him, the teacher who is to show it to him must have it in view. If a preview of the "whither" is missing, the one in transition remains rudderless, and the place from which he must release himself remains undetermined. And yet the place to which the one in transition is called first shows itself in the full light of day only when he has gone over to it. For the one in transition—and particularly for the one who, as the teacher, is to point the way of transition, particularly for Zarathustra himself—the "whither" remains always at a far remove. The remoteness persists. Inasmuch as it persists, it remains in a kind of proximity, a proximity that preserves what is remote as remote by commemorating it and turning its thoughts toward it. Commemorative nearness to the remote is what our language calls "longing," *die Sehnsucht*. We wrongly associate the word *Sucht* with *suchen*, "to seek" and "to be driven." But the old word *Sucht* (as in *Gelbsucht*, "jaundice," and *Schwindsucht*, "consumption") means illness, suffering, pain.

Longing is the agony of the nearness of what lies afar.

Whither the one in transition goes, there his longing is at home. The one in transition, and even the one who points out the way to him, the teacher, is (as we have already heard) on the way home to the essence that is most proper to him. He is the convalescent. Immediately following the episode called "The Convalescent," in the third part of *Thus Spoke Zarathustra,* is the episode entitled "On the Great Longing." With this episode, the third-to-last of Part III, the work

Thus Spoke Zarathustra as a whole attains its summit. In a note from the posthumously published materials (XIV, 285) Nietzsche observes, "A *divine* suffering is the content of Zarathustra III."

In the section "On the Great Longing" Zarathustra speaks to his soul. According to Plato's teaching—a teaching that became definitive for Western metaphysics—the essence of thinking resides in the soul's solitary conversation with itself. The essence of thinking is *logos, hon autē pros hautēn hē psychē diexerchetai peri hōn an skopēi,* the telling self-gathering which the soul itself undergoes on its way to itself, within the scope of whatever it is looking at *(Theaetetus,* 189e; cf. *The Sophist,* 263e). *

In converse with his soul Zarathustra thinks his "most abysmal thought" ("The Convalescent," section one; cf. Part III, "On the Vision and the Riddle," section 2). Zarathustra begins the episode "On the Great Longing" with the words: "O my soul, I taught you to say 'Today' like 'One day' and 'Formerly,' I taught you to dance your round-dance beyond every Here and There and Yonder." The three words "Today," "One day," and "Formerly" are capitalized and placed in quotation marks. They designate the fundamental features of time. The way Zarathustra expresses them points toward the matter Zarathustra himself must henceforth tell himself in the very ground of his essence. And what is that? That "One day" and "Formerly," future and past, are like "Today." And also that today is like what is past and what is to come. All three phases of time merge in a single identity, as the same in one single present, a perpetual "now." Metaphysics calls the constant now "eternity." Nietzsche too thinks the three phases of time in terms of eternity as the constant now. Yet for him the constancy consists not in stasis but in a recurrence of the same. When Zara-

---

* Schleiermacher translates the *Theaetetus'* definition of *dianoia,* "thinking," as follows: "A speech which the soul goes through by itself concerning whatever it wants to investigate." And Cornford translates it: "As a discourse that the mind carries on with itself about any subject it is considering." The passage from *The Sophist* reads as follows:

Oukoun dianoia men kai logos tauton. Plēn ho men entos tēs psychēs pros hautēn dialogos aneu phōnēs gignomenos tout'auto hēmin epōnomasthē, dianoia?

Then, thought and speech are the same, except that the inner conversation of the soul with itself, which proceeds altogether without sound, is called thinking?

Theaetetus replies on behalf of Western intellectuality as a whole: "Certainly."

thustra teaches his soul to say those words he is the teacher of eternal return of the same. Such return is the inexhaustible abundance of a life that is both joyous and agonizing. Such a life is the destination toward which "the great longing" leads the teacher of eternal return of the same. Thus in the same episode "the great longing" is also called "the longing of superabundance."

The "great longing" thrives for the most part on that from which it draws its only consolation, that is to say, its confidence in the future. In place of the older word "consolation," *Trost* (related to *trauen*, "to trust," "to betroth," and to *zutrauen*, "to believe oneself capable"), the word "hope" has entered our language. "The great longing" attunes and defines Zarathustra, who in his "greatest hope" is inspired by such longing.

Yet what induces Zarathustra to such hope, and what entitles him to it?

What bridge must he take in order to go over to the overman? What bridge enables him to depart from humanity hitherto, so that he can be released from it?

It derives from the peculiar structure of the work *Thus Spoke Zarathustra,* a work that is to make manifest the transition of the one who goes over, that the answer to the question we have just posed appears in the second part of the work, the preparatory part. Here, in the episode "On the Tarantulas," Nietzsche has Zarathustra say: "For *that man be redeemed from revenge*—that is for me the bridge to the highest hope and a rainbow after long storms."

How strange, how alien these words must seem to the customary view of Nietzsche's philosophy that we have furnished for ourselves. Is not Nietzsche supposed to be the one who goads our will to power, incites us to a politics of violence and war, and sets the "blond beast" on his rampage?

The words "that man be redeemed from revenge" are even italicized in the text. Nietzsche's thought thinks in the direction of redemption from the spirit of revenge. His thinking would minister to a spirit which, as freedom from vengefulness, goes before all mere fraternizing —but also before all vestiges of the sheer will to punish. It would minister to a spirit that abides before all efforts to secure peace and before all conduct of war, a spirit quite apart from that which wills to establish and secure *pax,* peace, by pacts. The space in which such freedom from revenge moves is equidistant from pacifism, political violence, and calculating neutrality. In the same way, it lies outside feeble neglect of things and avoidance of sacrifice, outside blind intervention and the will to action at any price.

Nietzsche's reputation as a "free spirit" arises from the spirit of freedom from revenge.

"That man be redeemed from revenge." If we pay heed even in the slightest way to this spirit of freedom in Nietzsche's thinking, as its principal trait, then the prior image of Nietzsche—which is still in circulation—will surely disintegrate.

"For *that man be redeemed from revenge*—that is for me the bridge to the highest hope," says Nietzsche. He thereby says at the same time, in a language that prepares yet conceals the way, whither his "great longing" aims.

Yet what does Nietzsche understand here by "revenge"? In what, according to Nietzsche, does redemption from revenge consist?

We shall be content if we can shed some light on these two questions. Such light would perhaps enable us to descry the bridge that is to lead such thinking from prior humanity to the overman. The destination toward which the one in transition is heading will only come to the fore in the transition itself. Perhaps then it will dawn on us why Zarathustra, the advocate of life, suffering, and the circle, is the teacher who simultaneously teaches the eternal return of the same *and* the overman.

But then why is it that something so decisive depends on redemption from revenge? Where is the spirit of revenge at home? Nietzsche replies to our question in the third-to-last episode of the second part of *Thus Spoke Zarathustra,* which bears the heading "On Redemption." Here the following words appear: *"The spirit of revenge:* my friends, up to now that was man's best reflection; and wherever there was suffering, there also had to be punishment."

This statement without reservation attributes revenge to the whole of humanity's reflection hitherto. The reflection spoken of here is not some fortuitous kind of thinking; it is rather that thinking in which man's relation to what is, to being, is fastened and hangs suspended. Insofar as man comports himself toward beings, he represents them with regard to the fact that they are, with regard to what they are and how they are, how they might be and how they ought to be—in short, he represents beings with regard to their Being. Such representing is thinking.

According to Nietzsche's statement, such representation has heretofore been determined by the spirit of revenge. Meanwhile human beings take their relationship with what is, a relationship that is determined in this fashion, to be the best possible sort of relationship.

In whatever way man may represent beings as such, he does so with a view to Being. By means of this view he advances always beyond beings—out beyond them and over to Being. The Greeks said this in the word *meta*. Thus man's every relation to beings as such is inherently metaphysical. If Nietzsche understands revenge as the spirit that defines and sets the tone for man's relationship with Being, then he is from the outset thinking revenge metaphysically.

Here revenge is not merely a theme for morality, and redemption from revenge is not a task for moral education. Just as little are revenge and vengefulness objects of psychology. Nietzsche sees the essence and scope of revenge metaphysically. Yet what does revenge in general mean?

If at first we keep to the meaning of the word, although at the same time trying not to be myopic, we may be able to find a clue in it. Revenge, taking revenge, wreaking, *urgere:* these words mean to push, drive, herd, pursue, and persecute. In what sense is revenge persecution?* Revenge does not merely try to hunt something down, seize, and take possession of it. Nor does it only seek to slay what it persecutes. Vengeful persecution defies in advance that on which it avenges itself. It defies its object by degrading it, in order to feel superior to what has been thus degraded; in this way it restores its own self-esteem, the only estimation that seems to count for it. For one who seeks vengeance is galled by the feeling that he has been thwarted and injured. During the years Nietzsche was composing his work *Thus*

* The clue may reside in the fact that the word here translated as "persecution," *Nachstellen,* is a morphological pendant to the word *Vorstellen,* "representation."

Spoke Zarathustra he jotted down the following observation: "I advise all martyrs to consider whether it wasn't vengeance that drove them to such extremes" (see the third *Grossoktav* edition, XII, 298).

What is revenge? We can now provisionally say that revenge is persecution that defies and degrades. And such persecution is supposed to have sustained and permeated all prior reflection, all representation of beings? If the designated metaphysical scope may in fact be attributed to the spirit of revenge, that scope must somehow become visible in terms of the very constitution of metaphysics. In order to discern it, if only in rough outline, let us now turn to the essential coinage of the Being of beings in modern metaphysics. The essential coinage of Being comes to language in classic form in several sentences formulated by Schelling in his *Philosophical Investigations into the Essence of Human Freedom and the Objects Pertaining Thereto* (1809). The three sentences read:

—In the final and highest instance there is no other Being than willing. Willing is primal Being, and to it [willing] alone all the predicates of the same [primal Being] apply: absence of conditions; eternity; independence from time; self-affirmation. All philosophy strives solely in order to find this supreme expression.*

Schelling asserts that the predicates which metaphysical thought since antiquity has attributed to Being find their ultimate, supreme, and thus consummate configuration in willing. However, the will of the willing meant here is not a faculty of the human soul. Here the word *willing* names the Being of beings as a whole. Such Being is will. That sounds foreign to us—and so it is, as long as the sustaining thoughts of Western metaphysics remain alien to us. They will remain alien as long as we do not think these thoughts, but merely go on reporting them. For example, one may ascertain Leibniz's utterances concerning the Being of beings with absolute historical precision— without in the least thinking about what he was thinking when he defined the Being of beings in terms of the monad, as the unity of *perceptio* and *appetitus,* representation and striving, that is, will. What

---

* Heidegger cites *F. W. J. Schellings philosophische Schriften* (Landshut, 1809), I, 419. In the standard edition of Schelling's *Sämtliche Werke* (1860), VII, 350.

Leibniz was thinking comes to language in Kant and Fichte as "the rational will"; Hegel and Schelling, each in his own way, reflect on this *Vernunftwille.* Schopenhauer is referring to the selfsame thing when he gives his major work the title *The World* [not man] *as Will and Representation.* Nietzsche is thinking the selfsame thing when he acknowledges the primal Being of beings as will to power.

That everywhere on all sides the Being of beings appears consistently as will does not derive from views on being which a few philosophers furnished for themselves. No amount of erudition will ever uncover what it means that Being appears as will. What it means can only be asked in thinking; as what is to be thought, it can only be celebrated as worth asking about; as something we are mindful of, it can only be kept in mind.

In modern metaphysics, there for the first time expressly and explicitly, the Being of beings appears as will. Man is man insofar as he comports himself to beings by way of thought. In this way he is held in Being. Man's thinking must also correspond in its essence to that toward which it comports itself, to wit, the Being of beings as will.

Now, Nietzsche tells us that prior thinking has been determined by the spirit of revenge. Precisely how is Nietzsche thinking the essence of revenge, assuming that he is thinking it metaphysically?

In the second part of *Thus Spoke Zarathustra,* in the episode we have already mentioned, "On Redemption," Nietzsche has Zarathustra say: "This, yes, this alone is revenge itself: the will's ill will toward time and its 'It was.' "

That an essential definition of revenge emphasizes revulsion and defiance, and thus points to revenge as ill will, corresponds to our characterization of it as a peculiar sort of persecution. Yet Nietzsche does not merely say that revenge is revulsion. The same could be said of hatred. Nietzsche says that revenge is the will's ill will. But *will* signifies the Being of beings as a whole, and not simply human willing. By virtue of the characterization of revenge as "the will's ill will," the defiant persecution of revenge persists primarily in relationship to the Being of beings. It becomes apparent that this is the case when we heed what it is on which revenge's ill will turns: revenge is "the will's ill will against time and its 'It was.' "

When we read this essential definition of revenge for the first time—
and also for a second and a third time—the emphatic application of
revenge to *time* seems to us surprising, incomprehensible, ultimately
gratuitous. It has to strike us this way, as long as we think no further
about what the word *time* here means.

Nietzsche says that revenge is "the will's ill will toward time. . . ."
This does not say, toward something temporal. Nor does it say, toward
a particular characteristic of time. It simply says, "Ill will toward
time. . . ."

To be sure, these words now follow: ". . . toward time and its 'It
was.'" But this suggests that revenge is ill will toward the "It was" of
time. We may insist, quite rightly, that not only the "it was" but also
the "it will be" and the "it is now" also pertain just as essentially to
time. For time is defined not only by the past but also by future and
present. If therefore Nietzsche stresses the "It was" of time, his characterization of the essence of revenge obviously refers, not to time *as
such,* but to time in one particular respect. Yet how do matters stand
with time "as such"? They stand in this way: time goes. And it goes by
passing. Whatever of time is to come never comes to stay, but only to
go. Where to? Into passing. When a man dies we say he has passed
away. The temporal is held to be that which passes away.

Nietzsche defines revenge as "the will's ill will toward time and its 'It
was.'" The supplement to the definition does not mean to put into
relief one isolated characteristic of time while stubbornly ignoring the
other two; rather, it designates the fundamental trait of time in its
proper and entire unfolding as time. With the conjunction *and* in the
phrase "time and its 'It was,'" Nietzsche is not proceeding to append
one special characteristic of time. Here the *and* means as much as
"and that means." Revenge is the will's ill will toward time and that
means toward passing away, transiency. Transiency is that against
which the will can take no further steps, that against which its willing
constantly collides. Time and its "It was" is the obstacle that the will
cannot budge. Time, as passing away, is repulsive; the will suffers on
account of it. Suffering in this way, the will itself becomes chronically
ill over such passing away; the illness then wills its own passing, and in

so doing wills that everything in the world be worthy of passing away. Ill will toward time degrades all that passes away. The earthly—Earth and all that pertains to her—is that which properly ought not to be and which ultimately does not really possess true Being. Plato himself called it *mē on,* nonbeing.*

According to Schelling's statements, which simply express the guiding representations of all metaphysics, the prime predicates of Being are "independence from time," "eternity."

Yet the most profound ill will toward time does not consist in the mere disparagement of the earthly. For Nietzsche the most deepseated revenge consists in that reflection which posits supratemporal ideality as absolute. Measured against it, the temporal must perforce degrade itself to nonbeing proper.

Yet how should humanity assume dominion over the earth, how can it take the earth as earth into its protection, so long as it degrades the earthly, so long as the spirit of revenge determines its reflection? If it is a matter of rescuing the earth as earth, then the spirit of revenge will have to vanish beforehand. Thus for Zarathustra redemption from revenge is the bridge to the highest hope.

But in what does redemption from ill will toward transiency consist? Does it consist in a liberation from the will in general—perhaps in the senses suggested by Schopenhauer and in Buddhism? Inasmuch as the Being of beings is will, according to the doctrine of modern metaphysics, redemption from the will would amount to redemption from Being, hence to a collapse into vacuous nothingness. For Nietzsche redemption from revenge is redemption from the repulsive, from defiance and degradation in the will, but by no means the dissolution of

---

* Heidegger's remarks recall the decisive words of Mephistopheles in Goethe's *Faust,* Part One (lines 1338–40): *" . . . denn alles, was entsteht, / Ist wert, dass es zugrunde geht."* "For everything that comes to be is worthy of its own demise." Yet because Heidegger here speaks of *Vergehen, Vergängliches,* his phrasing has a diabolical way of embracing the concluding words of Part Two (the very words Nietzsche parodied in the first of his *Songs of the Outlaw Prince),* words that try to reduce "all that passes away" to a mere image of eternity. Thus Mephisto and the *chorus mysticus,* the good and evil of metaphysics and morals, join voices to chant revenge, to denigrate time and its "It was."

all willing. Redemption releases the ill will from its "no" and frees it for a "yes." What does the "yes" affirm? Precisely what the ill will of a vengeful spirit renounced: time, transiency.

The "yes" to time is the will that transiency perdure, that it not be disparaged as nothing worth. Yet how can passing away perdure? Only in this way: as passing away it must not only continuously go, but must also always come. Only in this way: passing away and transiency must recur in their coming as the same. And such recurrence itself is perdurant only if it is eternal. According to the doctrine of metaphysics, the predicate "eternity" belongs to the Being of beings.

Redemption from revenge is transition from ill will toward time to the will that represents being in the eternal recurrence of the same. Here the will becomes the advocate of the circle.

To put it another way: Only when the Being of beings represents itself to man as eternal recurrence of the same can man cross over the bridge and, redeemed from the spirit of revenge, be the one in transition, the overman.

Zarathustra is the teacher who teaches the overman. But he teaches this doctrine only because he is the teacher of eternal recurrence of the same. This thought, eternal recurrence of the same, is first in rank. It is the "most abysmal" thought. For that reason the teacher comes out with it last, and always hesitantly.

Who is Nietzsche's Zarathustra? He is the teacher whose doctrine would liberate prior reflection from the spirit of revenge to the "yes" spoken to eternal recurrence of the same.

As the teacher of eternal recurrence, Zarathustra teaches the overman. According to an unpublished note (XIV, 276), a refrain accompanies the latter doctrine: "Refrain: 'Love alone will make it right'—(the creative love that forgets itself in its works)."

As the teacher of eternal recurrence and overman, Zarathustra does not teach two different things. What he teaches coheres in itself, since one demands the other as its response. Such correspondence—in the way it essentially unfolds and the way it withdraws—is precisely what the figure of Zarathustra conceals in itself, conceals yet at the same time displays, thus allowing the correspondence to provoke our thought.

Yet the teacher knows that what he is teaching remains a vision and a riddle. He perseveres in such reflective knowledge.

We today, because of the peculiar ascendancy of the modern sciences, are caught up in the strange misconception that knowledge can be attained from science and that thinking is subject to the jurisdiction of science. Yet whatever unique thing a thinker is able to say can be neither proved nor refuted logically or empirically. Nor is it a matter of faith. We can only envisage it questioningly, thoughtfully. What we envisage thereby always appears as *worthy* of question.

To catch a glimpse of the vision and the riddle which the figure Zarathustra manifests, and to retain that glimpse, let us once again cast our eyes on the spectacle of Zarathustra's animals. They appear to him at the outset of his journeyings:

> . . . He looked inquiringly into the sky—for above him he heard the piercing cry of a bird. And behold! An eagle soared through the air in vast circles, and a serpent hung suspended from him, not as his prey, but as though she were his friend: for she had coiled about his neck.
> "These are my animals!" said Zarathustra, and his heart was filled with joy.

A passage we cited earlier—yet purposely only in part—from the first section of "The Convalescent" reads: "I, Zarathustra, the advocate of life, the advocate of suffering, the advocate of the circle—I summon you, my most abysmal thought!" In the second section of the episode "On the Vision and the Riddle," in Part III, Zarathustra describes the thought of eternal recurrence of the same in identical words. There, in his confrontation with the dwarf, Zarathustra tries for the first time to think that riddlesome thing which he sees as meriting his longing. The eternal recurrence of the same does remain a vision for Zarathustra; but it is also a riddle. It can be neither proved nor refuted logically or empirically. At bottom, this holds for every essential thought of every thinker: something envisaged, but a riddle—worthy of question.

Who is Nietzsche's Zarathustra? We can now reply in the following formula: Zarathustra is the teacher of eternal return of the same and the teacher of overman. But now we can see more clearly—perhaps also beyond our own formula—that Zarathustra is not a teacher who

instructs us concerning two sundry items. Zarathustra teaches the overman because he is the teacher of eternal return of the same. Yet the
reverse is also true: Zarathustra teaches eternal return of the same because he is the teacher of overman. These doctrines are conjoined in
a circle. In its circling, the teaching corresponds to that which is—to
the circle which as eternal recurrence of the same makes out the Being
of beings, that is, what is permanent in Becoming.

The teaching, and our thinking of it, will achieve such circling
whenever they cross over the bridge called "Redemption from the
Spirit of Revenge." In this way prior thinking is to be overcome.

From the period immediately following the completion of the work
Thus Spoke Zarathustra, the year 1885, comes a note that has been
taken up as number 617 in the book that was pieced together from
Nietzsche's literary remains and published under the title *The Will to
Power.* The note bears the underscored title *"Recapitulation."** Here
Nietzsche with extraordinary perspicuity condenses the principal
matter of his thinking into just a few sentences. A parenthetical remark
appended to the text makes explicit mention of Zarathustra.
Nietzsche's "Recapitulation" begins with the statement: "To *stamp*
Becoming with the character of Being—that is the supreme *will to
power.*"

The supreme will to power, that is, what is most vital in all life,
comes to pass when transiency is represented as perpetual Becoming in
the eternal recurrence of the same, in this way being made stable and
permanent. Such representing is a thinking which, as Nietzsche emphatically notes, *stamps* the character of Being on beings. Such thinking takes Becoming, to which perpetual collision and suffering belong,
into its protection and custody.

Does such thinking overcome prior reflection, overcome the spirit of
revenge? Or does there not lie concealed in this very *stamping*—which
takes all Becoming into the protection of eternal recurrence of the
same—a form of ill will *against* sheer transiency and thereby a highly
spiritualized spirit of revenge?

We no sooner pose this question than the illusion arises that we are

---

* See the explanatory note on pp. 201–02, above.

trying to discredit Nietzsche, to impute something as most proper to him which is precisely what he wants to overcome. It is as though we cherished the view that by such imputation we were refuting the thought of this thinker.

The officious will to refute never even approaches a thinker's path. Refutation belongs among those petty intellectual entertainments which the public needs for its amusement. Moreover, Nietzsche himself long ago anticipated the answer to our question. The text that immediately precedes *Thus Spoke Zarathustra* in Nietzsche's corpus appeared in 1882 under the title *The Gay Science*. In its penultimate section (number 341), under the heading "The Greatest Burden," Nietzsche first delineated his "most abysmal thought." Following it is the final section (342), which was adopted verbatim as the opening of the Prologue to *Thus Spoke Zarathustra*. In the posthumously published materials (XIV, 404 ff.) we find sketches for a foreword to *The Gay Science*. There we read the following:

> A spirit fortified by wars and victories, which has developed a need for conquest, adventure, hazard, pain; become accustomed to the crispness of the upper air, to long wintry walks, to ice and mountain crags in every sense; a kind of sublime malice and extreme exuberance of revenge—for there is *revenge* in it, revenge on life itself, when one who suffers greatly *takes life under his protection.*

What is left for us to say, if not this: Zarathustra's doctrine does not bring redemption from revenge? We do say it. Yet we say it by no means as a misconceived refutation of Nietzsche's philosophy. We do not even utter it as an objection against Nietzsche's thinking. But we say it in order to turn our attention to the fact that—and the extent to which—Nietzsche's thought too is animated by the spirit of prior reflection. Whether the spirit of prior thinking is at all captured in its definitive essence when it is interpreted as the spirit of revenge—this question we leave open. At all events, prior thinking is metaphysics, and Nietzsche's thinking presumably brings it to fulfillment.

Thus something in Nietzsche's thinking comes to the fore which this thinking itself was no longer able to think. Such remaining behind what it has thought designates the creativity of a thinking. And where a thinking brings metaphysics to completion it points in an exceptional way to things unthought, cogently and confusedly at once. Yet where are the eyes to see this?

Metaphysical thinking rests on the distinction between what truly is and what, measured against this, constitutes all that is not truly in being. However, what is decisive for the *essence* of metaphysics is by no means the fact that the designated distinction is formulated as the opposition of the suprasensuous to the sensuous realm, but the fact that this distinction—in the sense of a yawning gulf between the realms —remains primary and all-sustaining. The distinction persists even when the Platonic hierarchy of suprasensuous and sensuous is inverted and the sensuous realm is experienced more essentially and more thoroughly—in the direction Nietzsche indicates with the name *Dionysos*. For the superabundance for which Zarathustra's "great long-ing" yearns is the inexhaustible permanence of Becoming, which the will to power in the eternal recurrence of the same wills itself to be.

Nietzsche brought what is essentially metaphysical in his thinking to the extremity of ill will in the final lines of his final book, *Ecce Homo: How One Becomes What One Is*. Nietzsche composed the text in October of 1888. It was first published in a limited edition twenty years later; in 1911 it was taken up into the fifteenth volume of the *Grossok-tav* edition. The final lines of *Ecce Homo* read: "Have I been under-stood?—*Dionysos versus the Crucified. . . .*"

Who is Nietzsche's Zarathustra? He is the advocate of Dionysos. That means that Zarathustra is the teacher who in and for his doctrine of overman teaches the eternal return of the same.

Does the preceding statement provide the answer to our query? No. Nor does it provide the answer after we have pursued all the references that might elucidate the statement, hoping in that way to follow Zara-thustra—if only in that first step across the bridge. The statement, which looks like an answer, nonetheless wants us to take note, wants to make us more alert, as it conducts us back to the question that serves as our title.

Who is Nietzsche's Zarathustra? The question now asks who this teacher is. Who is this figure which, at the stage of metaphysics' com-pletion, appears within metaphysics? Nowhere else in the history of

Western metaphysics has the essential figure been expressly created in this way for its respective thinker—or, to put it more appropriately and literally, nowhere else has that figure been so tellingly *thought*. Nowhere else—unless at the beginning of Western thought, in Parmenides, though there only in veiled outlines.

Essential to the figure of Zarathustra remains the fact that the teacher teaches something twofold which coheres in itself: eternal return and overman. Zarathustra is himself in a certain way this coherence. That said, he too remains a riddle, one we have scarcely envisaged.

"Eternal return of the same" is the name for the Being of beings. "Overman" is the name for the human essence that corresponds to such Being.

On what basis do Being and the essence of human being belong together? How do they cohere, if Being is no fabrication of human beings and humanity no mere special case among beings?

Can the coherence of Being and the essence of human being be discussed at all, as long as our thinking remains mired in the previous conception of man? According to it, man is *animal rationale,* the rational animal. Is it a coincidence, or a bit of lyrical ornamentation, that the two animals, eagle and serpent, accompany Zarathustra; that *they* tell him who he must become, in order to be the one he is? In the figure of the two animals the union of pride and discernment is to come to the fore for those who think. Yet we have to know what Nietzsche thinks concerning these two traits. Among the notes sketched during the period when *Thus Spoke Zarathustra* was composed we read: "It seems to me that *modesty* and *pride* belong to one another quite closely. . . . What they have in common is the cool, unflinching look of appraisal" (XIV, 99). And elsewhere in these notes (101):

> People talk so stupidly about *pride*—and Christianity even tried to make us feel *sinful* about it! The point is that whoever *demands great things of himself, and achieves those things,* must feel quite remote from those who do not. Such *distance* will be interpreted by these others as a "putting on airs"; but he knows it [distance] only as continuous toil, war, victory, by day and by night. The others have no inkling of all this!

The eagle: the proudest animal; the serpent: the most discerning animal. And both conjoined in the circle in which they hover, in the ring that embraces their essence; and circle and ring once again interfused.

The riddle of who Zarathustra is, as teacher of eternal return *and* overman, is envisaged by us in the spectacle of the two animals. In this spectacle we can grasp more directly and more readily what our presentation tried to exhibit as the matter most worthy of question, namely, the relation of Being to that living being, man.

> And behold! An eagle soared through the air in vast circles, and a serpent hung suspended from him, not as his prey, but as though she were his friend: for she had coiled about his neck.
>
> "These are my animals!" said Zarathustra, and his heart was filled with joy.

✻   ✻   ✻

A NOTE ON THE ETERNAL RECURRENCE OF THE SAME

Nietzsche himself knew that his "most abysmal thought" remains a riddle. All the less reason for us to imagine that we can solve the riddle. The obscurity of this last thought of Western metaphysics dare not tempt us to circumvent it by some sort of subterfuge.

At bottom there are only two such routes of escape.

Either one avers that this thought of Nietzsche's is a kind of "mysticism" that our thinking should not bother to confront.

Or one avers that this thought is as old as the hills, that it boils down to the long-familiar cyclical notion of cosmic occurrence. Which notion can be found for the first time in Western philosophy in Heraclitus.

This second piece of information, like all information of that sort, tells us absolutely nothing. What good is it if someone determines with respect to a particular thought that it can be found, for example, "already" in Leibniz or even "already" in Plato? What good are such references when they leave what Leibniz and Plato were thinking in the same obscurity as the thought they claim to be clarifying with the help of these historical allusions?

As for the first subterfuge, according to which Nietzsche's thought of eternal recurrence of the same is a mystic phantasmagoria, a look at the present age might well teach us a different lesson—presupposing of course that thinking is called upon to bring to light the *essence* of modern technology.

What else is the essence of the modern power-driven machine than *one* offshoot of the eternal recurrence of the same? But the essence of such machines is neither something machine-like nor anything mechanical. Just as little can Nietzsche's thought of eternal recurrence of the same be interpreted in a mechanical sense.

That Nietzsche interpreted and experienced his most abysmal thought in terms of the Dionysian only speaks for the fact that he still thought it metaphysically, and had to think it solely in this way. Yet it says nothing against the fact that this most abysmal thought conceals something unthought, something which at the same time remains a sealed door to metaphysical thinking.

(See the lecture course "What Calls for Thinking?" taught during the winter semester of 1951–52 and published in book form by Max Niemeyer, Tübingen, in 1954.*)

---

*Translated by Fred D. Wieck and J. Glenn Gray as *What Is Called Thinking?* in 1968 for the Harper & Row Heidegger Series.

ANALYSIS AND GLOSSARY

Analysis

By DAVID FARRELL KRELL

Heidegger is so insistent about our heeding the kinds of *music* eternal recurrence makes—whether it is a thought plucked on skillfully fashioned lyres or cranked out of barrel organs—that we may be justified in listening now to a brief selection of its orchestrations. I shall pass over in silence a large number of the thought's earlier echoes, such as those pious ones we find in Goethe, and cite a few of the more daring anticipations and recapitulations of Nietzsche's most thoughtful burden.

Early in 1902, seven years before the first English translation of *Also sprach Zarathustra* appeared and six years before H. L. Mencken began to exalt Nietzsche to the English-speaking world, a young American novelist on the threshold of a lifelong conversion to socialism sported briefly yet passionately the banner of overman:

> I sat in silence. "Do I gather from your words," I asked, "that immortality is not one of the privileges of this race?"
> He smiled again. "The spiritual life," he said, "does not begin until the thought of immortality is flung away. . . ."
> "This people," I asked—"what do they know about God?"
> "They know no more than men do," was the answer, "except that they know they know nothing. They know that the veil is not lifted. It is not that for which they seek—life is their task, and life only; to behold its endless fruition; to dwell in the beauty of it, to wield power of it; to toil at its whirling loom, to build up palaces of music from it. . . ."
>
> UPTON SINCLAIR, *The Overman*

Yet Upton Sinclair was not the first American writer to respond to the raptures of Nietzschean thought. Another managed it when Nietzsche himself was only six years old. Herman Melville places poor Queequeg in his coffin, then observes:

> How he wasted and wasted away in those few long-lingering days, till there seemed but little left of him but his frame and tattooing. But as all else in him thinned, and his cheek-bones grew sharper, his eyes, nevertheless, seemed growing fuller and fuller; they became of a strange softness of lustre; and mildly but deeply looked out at you there from his sickness, a wondrous testimony to that immortal health in him which could not die, or be weakened. And like circles on the water, which, as they grow fainter, expand; so his eyes seemed rounding and rounding, like the rings of Eternity. An awe that cannot be named would steal over you as you sat by the side of this waning savage, and saw as strange things in his face, as any beheld who were bystanders when Zoroaster died.

> HERMAN MELVILLE, *Moby-Dick,* chapter CX

Queequeg survives the illness, of course, and uses his coffin as a sea-chest. After the catastrophe Ishmael will use it as a writing table. Ishmael's account will unite the two principal sources of Zarathustran imagery—mountain summits and the sea—the heights and depths visited by Zarathustra's eagle:

> There is a wisdom that is woe; but there is a woe that is madness. And there is a Catskill eagle in some souls that can alike dive down into the blackest gorges, and soar out of them again and become invisible in the sunny spaces. And even if he for ever flies within the gorge, that gorge is in the mountains; so that even in his lowest swoop the mountain eagle is still higher than other birds upon the plain, even though they soar.

> *Moby-Dick,* chapter XCVI

A more recent attestation to the thought of eternal recurrence involves the demise and return of a "distinguished phenomenologist," and hence expresses the more scientific side of Nietzsche's fundamental thought:

> Would the departed never nowhere nohow reappear?
> Ever he would wander, selfcompelled, to the extreme limit of his cometary orbit, beyond the fixed stars and variable suns and telescopic planets, astronomical waifs and strays, to the extreme boundary of space, passing from land to land, among peoples, amid events. Somewhere imperceptibly

he would hear and somehow reluctantly, suncompelled, obey the summons of recall. Whence, disappearing from the constellation of the Northern Crown he would somehow reappear reborn above delta in the constellation of Cassiopeia and after incalculable eons of peregrination return an estranged avenger, a wreaker of justice on malefactors, a dark crusader, a sleeper awakened, with financial resources (by supposition) surpassing those of Rothschild or of the silver king.

What would render such return irrational?

An unsatisfactory equation between an exodus and return in time through reversible space and an exodus and return in space through irreversible time.

JAMES JOYCE, *Ulysses, "Ithaca"*

Finally, the following poem by Rainer Maria Rilke expresses the more playful side of the thought that is hardest to bear, indeed as though spinning to a hurdy-gurdy tune:

The Carrousel
Jardin du Luxembourg

With a roof and the roof's vast shadow
turns awhile the whole assembly
of pinto ponies fresh from the country
which, long delaying, finally goes down.
True, some are hitched to wagons,
Though mien and mane are fierce;
an angry snarling lion goes with them
and now and then a snow white elephant.

Even a buck is there, as in a wood,
except he wears a saddle, and astride,
a little girl in blue, strapped tight.

And a boy palely rides the lion
and grips with a warm hand,
while the lion bares its teeth, loops its tongue.

And now and then a snow white elephant.

And on the ponies they glide by,
girls, too, aglow, this leap of ponies
almost outgrown; as they plunge
they look up, gaze absently, this way—

And now and then a snow white elephant.

On and on it whirls, that it might end;
circles and spins and knows no goal.
A red, a green, a gray sailing by,
a tiny profile, just begun—.
And, turned this way, sometimes a smile,
beaming, blinding, lavished utterly
on this breathless sightless play. . . .

from Neue Gedichte, 1907

In 1936 Heidegger began his series of lecture courses on Nietzsche's philosophy with an inquiry into will to power as art, now published as Volume I of this series. The axial question of that inquiry proved to be the discordant relation in Nietzsche's thought between art and truth. The latter was no longer to be associated primarily with knowledge *(Erkenntnis)* but with the grand style of artistic creativity. What role "the rigor of knowledge" might play in Nietzsche's philosophy became the object of Heidegger's 1939 course on will to power as knowledge, published in Volume III of this series. The centrality of "the grand style of creation" was clear from the start, however: art and the artist's devotion to eternal recurrence were to serve as the countermovement to nihilism, the theme of Heidegger's fourth and final lecture course on Nietzsche, delivered in 1940 and now appearing in Volume IV of this series. Thus the thought of eternal return of the same, which Heidegger interpreted during the summer semester of 1937, serves as a point of convergence or departure for virtually all of Heidegger's lectures on Nietzsche's philosophy.

Yet the significance of that thought extends beyond the scope of the lecture courses themselves. Whereas the *essays* of the 1940s tend to constrict the thought of eternal return in a schematic, quasi-scholastic interpretation—will to power as the *essentia* of beings, eternal recurrence as their *existentia*—the 1937 lecture course remains sensitive to the multiplicity of perspectives and the full range of registers in eternal recurrence, a thought that encroaches on the fundamental experience of *Being and Time* and on the experience of *thinking* in Heidegger's later work. Hence it is to the 1937 lecture course that Heidegger's renewed preoccupations with Nietzsche in the early 1950s repair. For all these reasons, "The Eternal Recurrence of the Same" may be called the summit of Heidegger's lecture series, or, paraphrasing Nietzsche, the peak of Heidegger's meditation.

I. THE STRUCTURE AND MOVEMENT OF THE 1937 LECTURE COURSE AND THE 1953 PUBLIC LECTURE

In the first section of the lecture course Heidegger sketches the four major divisions he intends his course to have. The first is to be a "preliminary presentation" of the doctrine of eternal return in terms of its *genesis,* its sundry *configurations,* and its unique *domain.* The second major division is to define the essence of a "fundamental metaphysical position" and to delineate various such positions in prior metaphysics. The third is to interpret Nietzsche's as the *last* possible position. Finally, the fourth is to thematize the end of Western philosophy as such and the inauguration of a new, "other" commencement.

A remark that Heidegger makes at the end of section 24 suggests that only two of the original plan's four divisions saw the light of day. As was quite often the case, Heidegger had planned more than he could deliver. No more than the first division received full treatment; time permitted only a brief sally into the second. A *fin du semestre* Coda on the themes of Nietzschean *amor fati* and Heideggerian "telling silence" brought the course to its precipitous close.

The first major division of the course (sections 1–24) focuses on Nietzsche's *communication* of the eternal recurrence of the same; the second interprets that doctrine as a *fundamental metaphysical position.* Each object commands its own methodology, the first division requiring a close reading of Nietzsche's texts, the second a daring yet more distant effort to locate Nietzsche in the history of Western philosophy as a whole. The juxtaposition of these two strategies—close contact and vast distance, detail and perspective, thrust and feint, reading and writing—lends the lecture course its particular tension. Nevertheless, the entire drama develops but one theme. The *first* sentence of the *first* section of the *first* division reads: "Nietzsche's fundamental metaphysical position is captured in his doctrine of *the eternal return of the same.*"

The first major division presents Nietzsche's own communications of eternal return. Yet a curious rift threatens its very structure. In the middle of his account of "On the Vision and the Riddle" (in section 6) Heidegger stops abruptly. The occasion for the caesura is that curious shift of scene in the vision—from the gateway "Moment" to the stricken shepherd. Heidegger does not recommence his account of the latter until section 24. In other words, sections 7 to 23, the bulk of the course as such, constitute a kind of parenthesis in Heidegger's analysis of the second (and principal) communication of eternal recurrence. The larger part of that parenthesis deals with Nietzsche's unpublished notes on eternal return. However, no matter how vital Heidegger believes such notes to be, he carefully inserts his entire discussion of them into that communication of Nietzsche's entitled *Thus Spoke Zarathustra.* In fact, he begins to discuss the notes only after he has moved forward unobtrusively to the themes of Zarathustra's solitude, his animals, and his convalescence (sections 7 and 8). He even advances to Nietzsche's *third* communication of eternal return, in *Beyond Good and Evil.* In retrospect, this unobtrusive move forward to "The Convalescent," seeking as it does to define the thought that is hardest to bear in terms of Nietzsche's own communication of it, is the most communicative gesture of the entire lecture course.

Heidegger begins (section 1) by affirming eternal recurrence as the fundamental thought of Nietzsche's philosophy. As a thought that reaches out toward being as a whole, eternal return of the same stands in vigorous opposition to the fundamental metaphysical positions represented by Platonism and by the Christian tradition as a whole. Nietzsche's fundamental thought has its immediate genesis (section 2) in the landscape of the Oberengadin, which Nietzsche first saw in 1881; yet echoes of it can be found in an early autobiographical sketch and in the late work *Ecce Homo.* Heidegger ventures into these autobiographical texts, not in order to reduce eternal return to a mere confession of faith on Nietzsche's part, but to establish as the fundamental task of Nietzsche's life the thinking of eternal recurrence of the

same. Nietzsche communicates the thought only reluctantly, crypti-
cally, and leaves most of his notes concerning it unpublished. His first
communication of it (section 3), in *The Gay Science,* portrays eternal
recurrence as "the greatest burden," that is, a thought that both inquires into being as a whole and testifies to the thinker's "loneliest
loneliness." The affirmation of existence—of our lives as we have lived
them—and of the ceaseless reiteration of the same is tied to what Heidegger calls the "authentic appropriation" of our existence as a "self."
Perhaps for that reason the thought of return (section 4) is said to be
the hardest to bear of all thoughts, the tragic thought *par excellence.*
To think it is to join Zarathustra in the fateful and fatal adventure of
downgoing *(Untergang)* and transition *(Übergang).* The "eternity" of
eternal return provides nothing resembling sanctuary from time, death,
or decision.

The second communication of the thought (section 5) occurs in and
as *Thus Spoke Zarathustra.* Nietzsche creates the figure of Zarathustra
for the express purpose of communicating his thought of thoughts.
The thought itself appears in that work in "figures of speech," metaphors, images, simulacra of all kinds; the *how* of the communication is
at least as important as the *what.* The book *Thus Spoke Zarathustra,*
written for everyone and no one, is for those who are learning to be
beneficent to life. Yet the difficulties of reading—plus Heidegger's
reservations concerning his own procedure—make all complacency
impossible. The crucial section of the book proves to be "On the Vision and the Riddle," which Heidegger proceeds to discuss (section 6).
After a mammoth interruption (sections 7 to 23), he takes up the
thread of the riddle in section 24, the culminating section of the first
major division of his course.

In section 6 Heidegger suggests that the riddle has to do with the
"loneliest loneliness" of the thinker who thinks the truth—that is, the
openness and unconcealment, *alētheia*—of being as a whole. He recounts Zarathustra's tale of his encounter with the spirit of gravity, the
dwarf, at the gateway *Augenblick,* "Glance of an Eye," or "Moment."
The eternity that each avenue at the gateway traverses—one forward,
the other rearward—is for the dwarf a matter of contempt. Thus a

common interpretation of eternal recurrence (as the cyclical nature of sacred time and the perfect ring of truth) is placed in the mouth of the dwarf who takes things too easily. For the thought itself, suggesting that "in an infinite time the course of a finite world is necessarily already completed," threatens to cripple all action in the present. When Zarathustra poses his *second* question to the dwarf, whether "I and you in the gateway" must not have recurred countless times, the dwarf not only fails to reply but vanishes altogether. The spirit of gravity cannot adopt a stance of its own in the Moment and so must disappear, leaving riddlers to pose a number of questions concerning the gateway and its avenues—questions such as (1) the infinity of past and future time, (2) the reality or actuality of time as something more than a mere form of intuition, and (3) the finite existence of beings in time. These are among the questions that propel Heidegger to Nietzsche's unpublished notes.

However, before he takes up the suppressed notes Heidegger turns his attention to the animals that accompany Zarathustra up to a certain point in his convalescence (sections 7–8) and to the third communication of eternal return as *circulus vitiosus deus* (section 9). These sections constitute no mere interlude in Heidegger's account. In "The Convalescent" (section 8), which we must now recall more closely, Heidegger in fact appears to reach the core of Nietzsche's second communication of eternal return.

Zarathustra's animals, his proud eagle and discerning serpent, are the companions and enforcers of his solitude. Their conjunction, a vortex of coils and rings, yields the most compelling emblem of recurrence. The animals speak to Zarathustra of eternal return during the latter's convalescence, which is the culmination of his downgoing. Their master must recuperate from the encounter with his own most abysmal thought, his own ultimate recess, which he has not yet truly incorporated. The circle of recurrence proves to be the circle of life and suffering; however much the eagle of its emblem soars, the circle itself tends to *Untergang*. Under the weight of his most abysmal thought, Zarathustra collapses. Seven days and nights he lies prostrate, feeding on the red and yellow berries his pride has fetched, berries of semblance and passionate creativity, the colors of will to power as eternal recurrence. The animals now try to seduce Zarathustra back into the world, as though it were a garden of delights rather than the theater of tragedy. The thought of eternal return—seduction *and* sobriety, intoxication *and* lucidity, contemptuous grumbling *and* rhapsodic song, satyr-play *and* tragedy, the conjunction in each case bridging the smallest gap—must now become Zarathustra's thought. Yet the suspicion obtrudes that Zarathustra's animals are humming the dwarf's own ditty. How can the difference between the thought's two modes of reception be preserved? What decides whether there is any difference at all? Not for nothing is the thought of return both the hardest to bear and the most difficult: to think being as a whole as eternal displacement of the goal is to utter "a cry of distress and calamity," and not to whistle a happy tune.

What turns the doctrine into a ditty? The assurance that all is bound for Emersonian compensation—though, to be fair, Emerson too, as Nietzsche well knew, had recurrent doubts—implies that we may dispense with all decision. Thus the dwarf makes light of the thought of return. He refuses to abandon his perch on the periphery and to enter the gateway itself. He declines to stand in the Moment. Viewed from the sidelines, the two avenues diverge as if to meet indifferently in some distant eternity. Yet when a self stands in the gateway where past and future "affront one another" and "collide," existence ceases to be a spectator sport. In the "flash of an eye" the thinker must look both fore and aft, "turned in two ways," and must study the internecine strife of time. "Whoever stands in the Moment lets what runs counter to itself come to collision, though not to a standstill, by cultivating and sustaining the strife between what is assigned him as a task and what has been given him as his endowment." It is the effrontery of time that in it we collide against mortality and strive with it, closing in the glance of an eye and not in some remote infinity. Nevertheless, the strife of time dare not provoke our revulsion or antagonism; it is not effrontery after all but an affronting, or better, a confronting. To stand in the Moment—to *be* the Moment—is to decide how everything recurs. Certain matters are of course already decided. The eternal return of the Last Man, the little man, for example. As though he had as much right to the gateway as one's self. Zarathustra's heroism rests in his having gone to meet his supreme suffering—the eternal recurrence of the Last Man—as well as his supreme hope—the inception of overman. At this juncture Heidegger reminds us of the motto inscribed over his own lecture course, as over a gateway: "Everything in the hero's sphere turns to tragedy. . . ." With Zarathustra the tragic era begins. Tragic insight has nothing to do with either pessimism or optimism, "inasmuch as in its willing and in its knowing it adopts a stance toward being as a whole, and inasmuch as the basic law of being as a whole consists in struggle." In such struggle the teacher of eternal return must come to understand himself as transition and demise, *Übergang* and *Untergang*. "In the end, Zarathustra hears which eternity it is that his animals are proclaiming to him, the eternity of the Moment that embraces everything in itself at once: the downgoing."

Thus the entire discussion of Nietzsche's first two communications of eternal return, in *The Gay Science* and *Thus Spoke Zarathustra,* respectively, comes to a head in section 8, "The Convalescent." The first communication stresses the essentially tragic nature of beings in general, the second the tragic insight gained in the glance of the eye— eternity as the Moment. These communications converge, according to Heidegger, in the *matter of thinking,* namely, thinking eternal recurrence in the essential context of the question of *being as a whole,* in pursuit of Nietzsche's *fundamental metaphysical position.* The third communication of eternal return (section 9) takes us one step closer to that position.

The third communication proceeds from "Zarathustra the godless" to "the quintessence of religion." The latter is the *circulus vitiosus deus,* the "ring" of recurrence that conjoins divinity and " 'world' perhaps?" Because the Christian God of morality is utterly dead, the *question* of world, of being as a whole, becomes compelling. The question itself necessitates the creation of gods and the re-creation of humanity. Reason enough to call it the greatest burden! The *circulus vitiosus* itself exhibits the trajectory of downgoing, the descensional movement of tragic inquiry.

Heidegger's reading of the posthumously published notes on eternal recurrence (sections 10–21) is preceded by a warning "that Nietzsche's own mode of communication" in his published writings must set the standard. Heidegger recognizes that his own procedure is duplex and even duplicitous: his interpretation must be guided by a prior sense of the *questions* at stake in eternal recurrence—lest it be a mere rehash; and yet that interpretation must be undertaken in a spirit of "meticulous deference" to Nietzsche's own texts. Heidegger divides the suppressed notes (section 10) into three principal groups: (1) those stemming from the initial discovery of the thought of return in 1881–82; (2) those from the period of *Thus Spoke Zarathustra*, 1883–84; and (3) those pertaining to plans for a major work, roughly, 1884–88. He criticizes the lack of order in the first group as presented in the *Grossoktav* edition and the editors' division of the notes into "theoretical" and "poetical" groups. Principal themes in the first group are those of "incorporation," foreshadowing the lesson of Zarathustra's convalescence, and of "teaching" and "decision," the latter to have an impact on being as a whole now that mankind has reached its "midday." Heidegger attempts a summary presentation (section 12) of Nietzsche's doctrine as contained in the first group of notes: eternal return applies to the world in its collective character, or to being as a whole, whether animate or inanimate; that character shows itself as force, limited force, the world totality thus proving to be finite; although "infinite" in the sense of "immeasurable," the world totality exists as exertions of limited force in bounded space and unlimited time ("eternity"). Force, finitude, perpetual Becoming, immeasurability, bounded space, and infinite time are all predicates of *chaos*. Yet the crucial issue turns out to be, not this or that cosmological speculation on chaos, but Nietzsche's "negative ontology," as it were, in which one must be on guard against every humanization and deification of being as a whole. For Nietzsche the world as such is an *arrēton*. The "necessitous" character of cosmic chaos is to guide us toward the notion of eternal return. But how? It is precisely in the thought of return that the circle or ring of humanity and being as a whole is joined (section 13). Thus it is a matter neither of pseudo-scientific skepticism nor of religious faith, but of *questioning* being as a whole. Such questioning bears a special relation to *language*. Yet neither Nietzsche nor philosophy prior to him raises that question adequately.

Whatever his notebooks might suggest, Nietzsche does not try to "prove" eternal return "scientifically" (sections 14–16). The finitude of Becoming and the necessary recurrence of the same in infinite time remain staples of Nietzsche's thought; yet Nietzsche himself is keenly aware of the dilemma in which his passion to eliminate anthropomorphisms places him with regard to all such staples. When he opts for *both* dehumanization *and* maximal humanization in will to power, he compels but does not elaborate the question of Da-sein. The thought of return cannot be designated as a "belief" (section 17), unless we are willing and able to reinterpret the meaning of religion and of all taking-for-true. The latter is not only an expression of Nietzsche's passion to dehumanize, however; Heidegger stresses the sense of creative knowing, giving, and loving—the sense of thoughtful *possibility*. The thought of return therefore involves the problem of freedom and necessity (section 18), not as an antinomy of reason, but as an invitation to rethink the temporality of the moment as a matter of and for *decision*. Such decision, Heidegger says, is a taking up of one's self into the willing act. Yet precisely *how* this is to occur Nietzsche never managed to communicate. Heidegger suggests that while such taking up is an authentic appropriation of self it is also the *propriative event* for historical mankind as a whole. As *Ereignis*, eternal recurrence of the same displays the covert, essential relationship of *time* to *being as a whole*. Yet it is a time, we might add, which for Heidegger hovers somewhere between the *ecstatic temporality* of individualized Dasein and the *essentially historical unfolding* of Being. The latter, in 1937, is still beguiled by the hollow rhetoric of "peoples" and "nations" in "competition with one another."

The posthumously published notes from 1881–82 (section 19) already stress the fact that the thought of return refers to being as a whole *and* to the need for a thinker and teacher to execute its thinking. The notes from the *Zarathustra* period (section 20) demonstrate that the thought of return is most resistant to incorporation, unless it be conceived as *redemption* from the flux of Becoming. Such redemption does not freeze the flow of Becoming, but, in the moment of decision, prevents Becoming from being reduced to endless repetition. All depends on how the possibility of recurrence is thought through. "Nietzsche knows only thoughts that have to be wrestled with." Finally, the unpublished materials from 1884 to 1888 (section 21) indicate the way in which eternal recurrence dominates Nietzsche's philosophy of will to power. Eternal return is the culminating thought for will to power, both as an interpretation of all occurrence and as a revaluation of all values. Eternal return is the essential counterthrust to nihilism. Heidegger's principal question directed to the notes taken up into *The Will to Power,* is as follows: *"How do will to power, as the pervasive constitution of beings, and the eternal return of the same, as the mode of Being of beings as a whole, relate to one another?"* The relationship cannot be expressed in terms of conditions or presuppositions.

> Yet what if the will to power, according to Nietzsche's most proper and intrinsic intentions, were in itself nothing else than a willing back to that which was and a willing forward to everything that has to be? What if eternal recurrence of the same—as occurrence—were nothing other than the will to power, precisely in the way Nietzsche himself understands this phrase. . . ? If matters stood this way, then the designation of being as will to power would only be an elaboration of the original and primary projection of being as eternal recurrence of the same. In truth, matters do stand this way.

Thus it is not so much that Nietzsche's thinking of will to power and eternal return must be reduced to the metaphysical categories of *essentia* and *existentia.* It is rather that the mysterious *coherence* of these two notions impels the question "as to *what* is being thought here in general and *how* it is being thought." The conjunction of the *what* and *how* Heidegger formulates as Nietzsche's *fundamental metaphysical position.*

In order to bring the first major division of his course to its *question,* Heidegger inquires into the "configuration" of the doctrine of return (section 22) and its "domain" (section 23). By configuration, *Gestalt,* Heidegger means the inner structure of the doctrine's truth, that is, the *openness* of being that shows itself in it. His strategy is to study the three axes in Nietzsche's plans for a *magnum opus,* to wit, eternal return, will to power, and revaluation of all values. Yet Heidegger is aware that merely to juggle these titles is an extrinsic procedure that may never catch sight of the "inner structure" of Nietzsche's philosophy. Because the thought of return involves the thinker and his historical moment, the question of its domain, *Bereich,* assumes preeminence. The thought's domain is staked out by nihilism, the event in which being as a whole comes to nothing. Nietzsche's thought is a countermovement to nihilism, eternal recurrence its counterthought. Eternal recurrence shares in the essence of nihilism inasmuch as it commits the goallessness of being to eternity—"the nothing ('meaninglessness') eternally!"—and yet its creative impulse, "in its character as decision, the character of the moment," shows that eternal return is "the thought that wends its way toward the need as such." Hence Heidegger's return to the crucial matter of the *Augenblick,* the moment of eternal recurrence, in section 24.

Section 24 is to bring the first major division of Heidegger's course to a close. Heidegger returns to that point in Zarathustra's account of "The Vision and the Riddle" where a baying hound announces a striking change of scene. The change is to indicate what is decisive in the image of the gateway "Moment" or "Glance of an Eye." The dog's howling sends Zarathustra racing back to his childhood—the period in Nietzsche's life which Heidegger associates with Schopenhauerian pessimism and Wagnerian delirium. Yet the vision of the young shepherd and his black snake is a matter of nihilism, not pessimism. Nihilism must be overcome from the inside, bitten off at the head; that bite alone introduces man to golden laughter and the gay science. It now becomes clear why Heidegger moved forward (in section 8) to "The Convalescent," inasmuch as it is here that we learn the identity of the young shepherd—it is Zarathustra himself, seeking to recover from the poison of his contempt for man. It also becomes clear why Zarathustra cannot be fooled by eternal recurrence as a hurdy-gurdy song. To think return is to bite decisively into the repulsive snake of nihilism; it is to choose between the two ways to say "It is all alike," the two ways to define man's fundamental position within being as a whole.

Eternal return thus has its proper content, not in the trite assertion "Everything turns in a circle," but in a dual *movement* by which the thought recoils on the thinker and the thinker is drawn into the thought. That dual movement occurs when eternal recurrence is thought, first, in terms of the moment, "the temporality of independent action and decision," and second, in terms of nihilism, the "condition of need" that defines both the task and the endowment bequeathed to contemporary man. Heidegger stresses the first, "the moment of being-a-self," in an explicit reference back to the analysis of Dasein in *Being and Time*. Yet the "moment" is now a far more "epochal" gateway than it was in 1927: the focus falls equally on the propriative event of nihilism. The recoil of eternal recurrence on Martin Heidegger is felt in the insistent question of the relation between thought and thinker—the question of what calls on us to think. In the present case, that is how the thinker "slips into the ring of eternal recurrence, indeed in such a way as to help achieve the ring, help decide it."

The fragmentary "second major division" of Heidegger's course inquires into the essence and possibility of "fundamental metaphysical positions" in Western philosophy (section 25), as well as into the specific matter of Nietzsche's fundamental metaphysical position (section 26). Its ironic thesis is that in Western philosophy the metaphysical *Grundstellung* is such that the *Grundfrage* never gets asked: the guiding question "What is being?" is not explicated *as* such. Heidegger's question with regard to Nietzsche is why the relationship of thought and thinker, "the recoil that includes and the inclusion that recoils," becomes so conspicuous with him; presumably, that question is not unrelated to Heidegger's own unrelenting efforts to unfold and develop the guiding question of metaphysics. Philosophy inquires into the *archē*, the rise and dominion of being as a whole; it takes the beings of *physis* or "nature" as definitive, although the role of man among the various regions of beings vies with nature for preeminence; it seeks an *answer* to the question of what being is. The one thing it does not do is unfold the guiding question itself, pose the historical *grounding* question. The latter confronts something which again may not be totally unrelated to Nietzsche, namely, the nothing that surrounds and insidiously pervades the field of being as a whole.

> Thus the most durable and unfailing touchstone of genuineness and forcefulness of thought in a philosopher is the question as to whether or not he or she experiences in a direct and fundamental manner the nearness of the nothing in the Being of beings. Whoever fails to experience it remains forever outside the realm of philosophy, without hope of entry.

Finally, Heidegger's effort to unfold the guiding question by way of the grounding question notes that each time the guiding question is raised one region of beings rises to set the definitive standard for being as a whole; and this may have something to do with the theme of "humanization" discussed so penetratingly in section 13.

The original title of Heidegger's lecture course as listed in the university catalogue was "Nietzsche's Fundamental Metaphysical Position in Western Thinking: the Doctrine of Eternal Recurrence of the Same." Perhaps the principal difficulty the course encounters is that whereas Nietzsche's position is identified as the end, accomplishment, or fulfillment of metaphysics, the doctrine of return is seen (at least partly) as a response to the *traditional, undeveloped* guiding question of metaphysics. Heidegger begins by aligning Nietzsche's two replies to that question—will to power and eternal return—with the traditional distinction between the constitution of being *(essentia)* and its way to be *(existentia)*. He asserts the coherence of these two answers. Yet before proceeding to demonstrate that coherence Heidegger further defines Nietzsche's position at the end of metaphysics. It is the end, Heidegger suggests, because it reaches back to the pseudo-Parmenidean and pseudo-Heraclitean responses to the guiding question, insisting that being both *becomes* and *is*. Thus Nietzsche interlocks these responses in such a way that they yield no further food for thought. However, because these responses are in effect derivative Platonistic interpretations of early Greek thinking, the commencement of Western thought remains curiously untouched by the Nietzschean closure. The interlocking takes place when Nietzsche delineates being as both perpetual creation (hence Becoming) and ineluctable fixation (hence Being as permanence of presence). Creative transfiguration too, and not merely metaphysico-moral thought, require the stability that fixation alone grants. The entire question of Nietzsche's fundamental metaphysical position therefore rests on the further question of what it means that we wish to "imprint the emblem of eternity on *our* life!" A "recoining" and creative transfiguration of Becoming are to occur. In such reconfiguration Becoming would attain subsistence *(Bestand)*, subsistence of course being the principal metaphysical designation of

Being as permanence *(Beständigkeit)*. However, Heidegger does not push the interpretation in this obvious direction; he insists on creation as transcendence and surpassment, confrontation in the moment of decision. He nonetheless fails to elaborate a positive interpretation of the mythic figure of Dionysos as a way of avoiding any Platonistic (mis)interpretation of creation. Instead, he insists that the Nietzschean inversion of the Platonic hierarchy represents the virtual entrenchment of Platonism. Entrenchment *versus* end: such is the ambivalence that characterizes Heidegger's reading of Nietzsche from start to finish.

At the end of his lecture course Heidegger tries to limn three intricate subjects with as many strokes of the pen, peremptory, suggestive, incomplete. First, he juxtaposes Nietzsche's ostensible position with his own Janus-headed *counterposition* vis-à-vis the commencement, the latter referring both to the beginnings of Western thought and the inauguration of "another" kind of thinking. Second, he discusses briefly the phrase *amor fati* in terms of both will to power and eternal return as expressions of resolute creativity in thought. Third, he offers a glimpse into his major philosophical work of the 1930s, *Contributions to Philosophy,* when he invokes "telling silence" and the theme of language generally in his "other" commencement. The motto from *Beyond Good and Evil* on tragedy, satyr-play, and world recurs as an epigram of both commencement and close.

More than fifteen years separate the public lecture "Who Is Nietzsche's Zarathustra?" from the lecture course on eternal recurrence. Yet the consistency of theme is remarkable. Not that the Heidegger/Nietzsche confrontation experienced no ups and downs. In the early 1940s Heidegger's waxing anxiety concerning the will-to-will that then seemed on the rampage drew Nietzsche into its somber sphere. In 1939, while lecturing on "Will to Power as Knowledge," Heidegger was jotting a number of notes on "Nietzsche's Metaphysics" that were devastatingly critical and even polemical: he called Nietzsche's metaphysics the most extreme form of alienation from Greek civilization, a turgid expression of planetary technology, a pan-European rather than a truly "German" style of thinking. Not only did Nietzsche lack conceptual rigor, even his enthusiasm for artistic creation boiled down to a fascination with technical achievement: the greatest *stimulans* to life was ultimately no more than an object of calculative thought, a prescription for "genius." And so on.

The patient, measured reading of "Who Is Nietzsche's Zarathustra?" is thus a bit of a surprise. It seems as though in the early 1950s Heidegger executed a sympathetic *return* to Nietzsche—not primarily as the metaphysician of will to power and technician of artistic frenzy but as the *thinker* of eternal recurrence. The lecture "Who Is Nietzsche's Zarathustra?" springs from the 1951–52 lecture course at Freiburg entitled "What Calls for Thinking?" There Heidegger calls Nietzsche, not the last metaphysician, but the last *thinker* of the Western world.[1] Here too Heidegger stresses the *difficulty* of Nietzsche's thought in *Thus Spoke Zarathustra:* no matter how intoxicating its language may be, the book's "fundamental thought" and "provenance" remain sobering challenges. In "What Calls for Thinking?" Heidegger advises his students to equip themselves for these challenges by studying Aristotle for ten or fifteen years! In "Who Is Nietzsche's Zarathustra?" (as in the second part of "What Calls for Thinking?") Heidegger conjoins the names of Nietzsche and Parmenides.

Zarathustra is the advocate of life, suffering, and the circle. He teaches the doctrines of eternal recurrence and overman. The *circle* of life and suffering and the *coherence* of will to power, eternal return, and overman take center stage in Heidegger's reflections. At the beginning and end of his lecture stands the emblem of Zarathustra's animals, the sign of both Nietzsche's and Heidegger's longing. Eagle and serpent are totems of Zarathustra, the thinker of eternal return, and talismans for Heidegger, who thinks the relationship of Being and human being. The teaching of eternal recurrence is nothing whimsical: *dismay* marks Zarathustra's very style, consternation in the face of his most abysmal thought. Nor is the doctrine of overman an expression of boldness and presumption. "Over-man" Heidegger defines as "that hu-

---

[1] Martin Heidegger, *Was heisst Denken?* (Tübingen: M. Niemeyer, 1954), p. 61. English translation by Fred D. Wieck and J. Glenn Gray, *What Is Called Thinking?* (New York: Harper & Row, 1968), p. 46.

man being who goes beyond prior humanity solely in order to conduct such humanity for the first time to its essence." Overman is Nietzsche's answer to the question of whether man is prepared to assume dominion over the earth. Heidegger's own reflection has less to do with achieving dominion than with *rescuing* the earth; yet he puts this difference in abeyance and focuses on Zarathustra as the teacher of eternal return. That teaching points the way of transition to the overman, although the destination itself remains remote. If *dismay* is the first of Zarathustra's characteristics, then the second is *longing*. The episode "On the Great Longing" begins with Zarathustra's invocation of "Today," "One day," and "Formerly" as aspects of the perpetual *now* of eternity. True, Nietzsche's is an eternity of recurrence rather than a *nunc stans;* yet the tendency of Heidegger's argument here is to reduce the doctrine of return to familiar metaphysical structures.

A second thrust of inquiry now intervenes and proves to be less familiar. Once again the theme of time occupies the spotlight, when Heidegger asks about the bridge to overman. That bridge is called "Redemption from the Spirit of Revenge," and revenge is defined as man's ill will toward time and its "It was." Nietzsche diagnoses such revenge at the heart of all the tradition held most sacrosanct, including its "best reflection." His understanding of revenge is thus metaphysical, in the sense that he understands it as having determined man's relation to all being. If in modern metaphysics man's best reflection is representation *(Vorstellen),* the shadow of representation is persecution *(Nachstellen).* In the defiant projection of beings in modern metaphysics and science, in its aggressive disparagement of transiency, Heidegger discerns something that more than resembles revenge. He will later shrink from the full consequences of his own discovery and endeavor to "leave the question open"; yet these pages on revenge, which the earlier lecture course needed but did not find, retain their own force.

The introduction of Schelling's identification of primal Being as willing has a double edge in Heidegger's text. One edge cuts Nietzsche, the philosopher of will; the other cuts metaphysics, the tradition of ill will. It remains to be seen whether Heidegger himself escapes unscathed. The forceful analysis of revenge now deepens into an inquiry into time. Most surprising perhaps is the fact that now the "It was" of time all but swallows the two remaining ecstases or phases of time. Whereas in *Being and Time* and the writings surrounding it the priority of the future is emphasized again and again as the origin of transcendence, projection, and existentiality, it is now the passing away of time that marks time's essential unfolding: time, *and that means,* its "It was." From Plato's disparagement of *mē on* to Schelling's embrace of "eternity" and "independence from time" the ill will toward time and transiency vents its subtle spleen. Yet Heidegger emphasizes not the deprecation of the sensuous realm as such but the sheer distinction between being and a supratemporal ideality, the *chōrismos* or gap that runs through metaphysics from its inception to its end.

What may grant redemption from the revulsion against time? Nietzsche does not embrace the Schopenhauerian solution—dissolution of the will as such. He wills instead that transiency perdure. Such perdurance can obtain only as eternal recurrence of the same. Heidegger is quick to remind us that in traditional metaphysics "eternity" is predicated of primal Being. At this point he once again invokes the essential coherence of eternal return and overman. Eternal return appears to assume preeminence—as the thought that would liberate reflection from revenge and so lead to the overman. Once again Heidegger invokes the spectacle of Zarathustra's animals, the emblem of interfused circles, as indicative of the essential affinity of Nietzsche's two principal doctrines and as mimetic of the very Being of beings, eternal recurrence. And once again the "Recapitulation" note (WM, 617) assumes its central place in Heidegger's interpretation. On the basis of that note Heidegger *attributes to Nietzsche himself* the supreme will to power, that is, the will to stamp Being (as perdurance, stability, fixity, permanence of presence) on Becoming. Overlooking the second sentence in that note, which begins, "Twofold falsification. . . ," Heidegger asks whether eternal recurrence itself may not be reduced to such coinage, whether it therefore does not conceal in itself an even more highly spiritualized spirit of revenge than that contained in prior reflection. He adduces a note from the *Nachlass* which attributes an "extreme exuberance of revenge" to Nietzsche's own will to be life's advocate. And so the case seems to be closed.[2]

The lecture "Who Is Nietzsche's Zarathustra?" reaches its climax in Heidegger's avowal that Zarathustra's doctrine of eternal return fails to achieve redemption from revenge. His avowal is not meant as a refutation or critique of the Nietzschean philosophy but as a query—an inquiry into the extent to which "Nietzsche's thought too is animated

---

[2] It may be worthwhile noting that Heidegger's reduction of eternal return to a "stamping" of Being on Becoming, overlooking as it does the reservations in WM, 617 ("twofold falsification"; "closest approximation"), brings his interpretation discomfitingly close to that of Alfred Baeumler. In Chapter Seven of *Nietzsche: Philosopher and Politician* (Leipzig: P. Reclam, 1931), pp. 79 ff., Baeumler writes:

> At its highpoint the philosophy of will to power and eternal *Becoming* shifts to the concept of *Being*. Being *is*. . . . The problem of the transition from Becoming to Being greatly preoccupied Nietzsche. The doctrine of eternal return belongs among the most famous elements of his philosophy. Objectively considered, this doctrine is nothing else than an attempt to cancel the image of eternal Becoming and to substitute for it an image of eternal Being. . . .

Baeumler proceeds to cite WM, 617 precisely in the way Heidegger will later cite it, that is, omitting the second sentence *("Zwiefache Fälschung . . .")* and indeed the bulk of the note. The result is that eternal recurrence ceases to be the *"closest approximation"* of a world of Becoming to one of Being, and is reduced to a metaphysical conception pure and simple—hence a conception that could hardly redeem prior reflection from the spirit of revenge. The notion of eternal recurrence, says Baeumler, threatens to "cancel the system" by imposing Parmenidean Being on Heraclitean flux. His formulation here too foreshadows Heidegger's own. Yet for Baeumler eternal return is "without importance" when viewed from the standpoint of Nietzsche's system. Whereas will to power is a "formula for occurrence in general" and thus has "objective sense," eternal recurrence of the same—arising as it does during a time when Nietzsche was "still underway to the system of will to power," a time when he was still "transported by the pipes of the Dionysian Pied Piper" and "led down the garden path" (85)—is no more than a "subjective," "personal," and "religious" *Erlebnis* (80–81). From the outset of his lecture series on Nietzsche, Heidegger is determined to resist Baeumler's repudiation of eternal recurrence. Nevertheless, his own reading of WM, 617 brings him perilously close to the point where Baeumler's exclusion of eternal return seems the only option.

Yet a footnote to this footnote is called for, lest the introduction of Baeumler's reading of WM, 617 imply something like guilt by association. For Baeumler and Heidegger are by no means alone in reading the note this way: the late Giorgio Colli, principal editor of the new *Kritische Gesamtausgabe* of Nietzsche's works, surely one who harbored no sympathy for Alfred Baeumler, also cites the note in Baeumlerian fashion, designating it "a specifically metaphysical confession, a declaration on behalf of 'Being'!" (See the *Studienausgabe*, CM, *13*, 655.)

by the spirit of prior reflection." Finally, Heidegger withdraws or re-treats from Nietzschean suspicion, he leaves "open" the question of revenge in prior thinking; at the same time he imputes to Nietzsche a mere inversion of the Platonic hierarchy, the inversion itself retaining the metaphysical distinction between true being and nonbeing. (The imputation, both here and in the 1937 lecture course, is all the more surprising inasmuch as in his *first* lecture course on Nietzsche Heidegger had shown that when the true world "finally becomes a fable" the very horizon for the Platonic hierarchy evanesces.) Here once again the theme of Dionysos is not taken up positively but is equated with a still metaphysical conception of the sensuous. The upshot is that Zarathustra the teacher remains a figure that appears *within* metaphysics at metaphysics' *completion.* Heidegger abandons the riddle of Zarathustra for the latter's enigmatic emblem, descrying in the encirclements of eagle and serpent a presentiment of "the relation of Being to that living being, man."

Surely the most curious part of Heidegger's text is its addendum on eternal recurrence of the same. Eternal return, the "last thought of Western metaphysics," remains a riddle which we dare not try to escape. The first possible subterfuge, which declares that the thought is sheer mysticism, by now needs no further discussion—and, indeed, Heidegger's introduction of the Adamsian dynamo as an exemplar of eternal recurrence is nothing if not an embarrassment. More intriguing is the way in which criticism of the second possible subterfuge—attribution of the thought of eternal recurrence to earlier figures in the tradition such as Heraclitus, Plato, or Leibniz—recoils on Heidegger's own text. If one were to recall Heidegger's use of Schelling with regard to will, one might wonder whether Heidegger's "Note" does not blunt the edge that he would turn against Nietzsche. Similarly, the final words of the "Note," while they do reduce the meaning of *Dionysos* to metaphysics, concede that Nietzsche's most abysmal and abyssal thought "conceals something unthought, something which at the same time remains a sealed door to metaphysical thinking."

As this outsized résumé draws to a close, we shall have to find our way to some *questions.* Herewith a first attempt. Heidegger's inquiry into revenge, the will's ill will toward time and transiency, marks an important advance over the 1937 lecture course. In section 12 of that course Heidegger complained that Nietzsche's notes on time—fragmentary and all too traditional in import—revealed the fact that Nietzsche had attained no insight into the role of *time* in the development of the guiding question of metaphysics. Why did the Nietzschean theme of revenge elude him then? Why even in 1953 does he pursue Nietzsche's analysis closely and convincingly, then abandon it in order to leave the matter "open"? Does this eluding, along with the apparent neglect of the emblem of Dionysos, reflect something of Heidegger's perennial fascination with Nietzsche as a thinker—even after he had apparently located Nietzsche securely within metaphysics, in order to proceed unencumbered toward his own "other" commencement?

II. CONTEXTS

The structure and movement of Heidegger's 1937 lecture course, especially its first major division, indicates that Heidegger felt obliged to divide his attention between Nietzsche's published and unpublished writings on eternal return. In no other lecture course does Heidegger pay such scrupulous attention to Nietzsche's communication of his thought in the figures, images, emblems, and tropes of Nietzsche's texts; and nowhere else does Heidegger devote so much time and energy to a thoughtful reconstruction of the Nietzschean *Nachlass*. Here we find the fitting context for matters touching philology in Heidegger's reading of Nietzsche.

In 1935 Heidegger had asked his students whether what they were hearing in his courses was "a mere product of the violent and onesided Heideggerian method of exegesis, which has already become proverbial."[3] In the meantime it has become a commonplace in criticism of Heidegger's Nietzsche interpretation that there is more to Nietzsche than meets Heidegger's eye; much of that criticism has placed the blame on Heidegger's evaluation and treatment of the posthumously published notes.

---

[3] Martin Heidegger, *Einführung in die Metaphysik* (Tübingen: M. Niemeyer, 1953), p. 134; English translation by Ralph Manheim, *An Introduction to Metaphysics* (Garden City: Anchor-Doubleday, 1961), p. 147.

A more finely differentiated criticism is called for. In the confined space of these "contexts" I would like to examine at least three aspects of the problem: first, Heidegger's treatment of the early notes on eternal recurrence from the years 1881–82; second, his treatment of Nietzsche's plans for a *magnum opus* during the years 1884 to 1888, plans dominated during the middle years by the title *Der Wille zur Macht,* with special reference to the position of eternal return in those plans; and third, the nature of Heidegger's own research at the Nietzsche-Archive in Weimar in the late 1930s and early 1940s and the extent of his familiarity with the holograph materials. Discussion of these three aspects may contribute to a more balanced critique and appreciation of that truly proverbial Heideggerian method of exegesis.

Nietzsche's earliest notes on eternal recurrence of the same appear in the notebook labeled M III 1 in the Nietzsche-Archive.[4] This notebook embraces a great variety of themes—although such variety is typical of almost all the notebooks—from the mild aroma of tea and the stimulus of coffee to the depredations of Occidental moralities. The sheer variety tempts one to adopt the minimalist strategy of Jacques Derrida, who suggests that all of Nietzsche's notes are as resistant to interpretation as one we find in the subsequent notebook (N V 7 [62]): " 'I forgot my umbrella.' "[5] However playful Derrida's minimalism may be—inasmuch as his own willingness to *interpret* Nietzsche's texts quite seriously is visible throughout *Spurs*—it serves as a warning to all who trespass on the *Nachlass.* Particular fragments leap out at the reader (different ones to different readers) and there is no way to take a high, abstract view of these materials. Walter Kaufmann phrased it well years ago: " . . . we look into a vast studio, full of sketches, drafts, abandoned attempts, and unfinished dreams. And in the end we should be less tempted than ever to mistake a random quotation for an ultimate position."[6]

---

[4] In CM this notebook is found at V/2, 339–474; in the *Studienausgabe,* which I will be citing throughout the Analysis, at *9,* 441–575.

[5] See Jacques Derrida, *Éperons* (Paris: Garnier Flammarion, 1978), pp. 103 ff. Readers will be relieved to know that the missing umbrella has been found and returned to the pages of *Research in Phenomenology,* XIII (1983), 175–82.

[6] See Friedrich Nietzsche, *The Will to Power,* ed. Walter Kaufmann (New York: Vintage Books, 1968), p. 557.

That said, I do want to compare my own reading of M III 1 to Heidegger's. In my view the following three points may safely be made concerning the contents of this notebook. First, notes on a variety of problems in the natural sciences obtrude, reflecting Nietzsche's study of a number of "popularizing" works on mechanics, chemistry, and physiology.[7] The notes on eternal recurrence are thus embedded in preoccupations with the notion of *Kraft,* physical, cosmic, and organic force or energy. Second, many of the notes contained in M III 1 are early drafts of passages in *The Gay Science.* For example, a number of the words whispered by that demon who steals upon us in our loneliest loneliness appear scattered throughout the notebook in slightly different form. Whereas the demon of *The Gay Science* speculates in what way the thought of eternal return would transform you "if that thought came to prevail in you" *(Wenn jener Gedanke über dich Gewalt bekäme),* the earlier note [143] betrays a more naturalistic flavor: "If you incorporate the thought of thoughts into yourself. . . ." *(Wenn du dir den Gedanken der Gedanken einverleibst. . .).* And third, the notes (especially the outlines and plans) concerning eternal return do seem to possess the special significance in M III 1 that Heidegger ascribes to them. Whatever unity the notebook manifests derives from the thought of recurrence. There is in fact a great deal of material on "the world's circulation" that Heidegger does not cite in support of his interpretation. Yet these same notes also betray a more tentative and "experimental" character than the material Heidegger presents. Specifically, Nietzsche is undecided about whether or not a finite source of cosmic energy can in an infinite time produce situations that are precisely the same: the return of the "same" is not confidently proclaimed here as a doctrine but debated back and forth as a possibility. The greater number of notes support the "conclusion" that recurrence of the same is plausible, but a considerable range of

---

[7] Among these works are: (1) J. R. Mayer, *Thermal Mechanics,* 1874; (2) the first volume of J. G. Vogt, *Force: a Realist-Monistic View of the World,* 1878, which treats "the energy of contraction, the single ultimate mechanical-causal form by which the world substrate works its effects"; (3) Wilhelm Roux, *The Struggle of Parts in the Organism,* 1881, which represents "the doctrine of mechanistic teleology", and (4) a translation of Herbert Spencer's *Ethics* published in 1879.

notes cast doubt on the entire matter.[8] Perhaps the principal flaw in Heidegger's presentation of these notes and plans from late summer, 1881, is that it pays insufficient heed to the tensions and misgivings that pervade the thought of recurrence. The principal virtue of his presentation is its avoidance of the selection of notes taken up into *The Will to Power* and its detailed criticisms of the *Grossoktavausgabe* treatment of M III 1.

Turning now to the second area of inquiry, we may ask whether Heidegger's treatment of the plans from the period 1884–88 (the so-called "Will to Power" period) is adequate. Since Heidegger depended on the GOA for the *Nachlass* texts—in spite of whatever direct access he may have had in the 1930s to the manuscripts themselves—this question implies a further one: How satisfactory is the GOA selection of those plans? Finally, what is the relationship between the thought of eternal recurrence and the hypothesis of will to power during these years? Does eternal return retain its early supremacy as Nietzsche's thought of thoughts up to the end?

In an effort to reply to these questions I have catalogued some 140 plans and titles projected by Nietzsche for his major philosophical work between 1884 and 1889. I should emphasize that I deliberately overlooked several series of plans, namely, those that seemed mere reiterations or only slight modifications of immediately preceding ones. Merely to list the catalogue numbers of these notes would fill a page of text, so that in what follows I will refer to but a small selection of the relevant materials.

Our first response to these questions must be that Heidegger does follow the GOA in streamlining the astonishing variety and complexity of Nietzsche's plans for a *magnum opus*. For instance, in the year 1884 alone we find plans and titles (most of them foreshadowing themes taken up into *Beyond Good and Evil*) such as the following: *Philosophy of the Future, Wisdom and Love of Wisdom, The Way to*

---

[8] Among the many notes that affirm the plausibility of a repetition of the "same," see numbers 152, 232, 245, 269, and 305; doubts are forcefully expressed however in fragments such as 202, 254, 292, 293, 311, 313, and 321. It is also noteworthy that one of the earliest references to the notion of *will to power* in Nietzsche's thought occurs in the second-to-last note of this same notebook: number 346.

Wisdom, To the Wind "Mistral", The New Hierarchy, To the Higher Men, The New Enlightenment, The Good European, and *Knowledge and Conscience.* Nevertheless, Heidegger is correct when he asserts that the thought of eternal return dominates the plans and titles early in this period, during the years 1884–85. A representative example is the following plan (W I 1 [6]; cf. [323]) from the spring of 1884:

The Eternal Return

A Prophecy

First Major Division

"It Is Time!"

Second Major Division

The Magnificent Midday

Third Major Division

The Oathtakers

The thought of eternal recurrence appears to suffer eclipse in the course of the year 1885, especially as the notion of will to power, "the ultimate fact we come down to" (W I 7a [61]), assumes preeminence. Yet in a list of his "Collected Works" drawn up in late summer of 1885 (W I 5 [1]) Nietzsche cites after *Thus Spoke Zarathustra* a projected work with the following title: *Midday and Eternity: A Seer's Legacy.* In the plans for the volume to be entitled *The Will to Power* the thought of return at first seems to retreat, only to emerge once again as the very culmination of that project. Among plans from late 1885 through 1886 (W I 8 [70–75]) we find both will to power and eternal recurrence at first subordinated to the themes of *Beyond Good and Evil,* but then eternal return and "Midday and Eternity" reappear as main titles. Eternal return is often the fourth and culminating division of such plans, so that, as Heidegger suggests, will to power indeed appears to be in service to Nietzsche's "most burdensome thought." In a plan from the summer of 1886 [100] the thought of eternal return seems to have receded before the issues of nihilism, revaluation, legislation, and "the hammer,"all of which (except perhaps the last) Heidegger would consider manifestations of value thinking, *Wertdenken.* Yet later in the same notebook we find a plan [129] for a separate volume with "eternal return" as its title:

The Eternal Return
Zarathustran Dances and Processions
First Part: God's Wake
by
Friedrich Nietzsche

1. God's Wake
2. At Magnificent Midday
3. "Where Is the Hand for this Hammer?"
4. We Oathtakers

In a plan sketched presumably in 1887 (N VII 3 [75]) "eternal return" is again to be the fourth and culminating division of a book with the title *The Will to Power: Attempt at a Revaluation of All Values.* Early in 1888 we find the same phrase in a jumbled list of rubrics. Yet Nietzsche's own numeration of that list suggests that "eternal return," along with "grand politics," will be the work's apotheosis. In the course of the year 1888 references to eternal return dwindle, although we do find "Midday and Eternity" and "The Magnificent Midday" still cited. Eternal return is cited near the end of a plan from spring or summer of 1888 (W II 7a [71–72]), while a detailed plan for *The Will to Power* [86] drops it. A plan to which Nietzsche attached much importance (Mp XVII 5 and Mp XVI 4b [17]), dated Sils-Maria, the last Sunday of August 1888, has the following as its projected fourth and final division:

Fourth Book: The Magnificent Midday
First Chapter: The Principle of Life's "Hierarchy."
Second Chapter: The Two Ways.
Third Chapter: The Eternal Return.

Even after Nietzsche had altered the main title of his planned work to *The Revaluation of All Values* in late summer or fall of 1888, eternal return retained its place as the summit of Nietzsche's thought. In the series of folders and notebooks listed under the archive number *19* we find a plan cited by Heidegger (19 [8]), dated September 1888, which lists as the title of Book Four *"Dionysos:* Philosophy of Eternal Return." A similar plan appears in notebook W II 8b [14] from this same period. Only in the final autobiographical plans related to *Ecce*

Homo does the thought of eternal recurrence completely disappear—
and only after the notion of will to power has gone into eclipse.

The game of hide-and-seek that I am now playing with the title
"eternal return" should not distract us however from the decisive point:
everything we can gather from Nietzsche's plans between 1884 and
1889 corroborates Heidegger's assertion that eternal return is the abiding, crucial thought for Nietzsche, and that will to power, as "ultimate
fact," has less staying power, less *thinking* power, than eternal recurrence of the same. Even when the locution *eternal return* disappears
behind the rubrics of "yes-saying," "Dionysos," or "midday and eternity," the issue expressed in these turns of phrase carries us back to the
experience of the thought "What would happen if . . .?"

But now to the third and final aspect of the philological context. In
more than one place in the *Nietzsche* volumes (see, for example, NI,
233 and 260) Heidegger indicates that he was familiar with the notebooks preserved as Nietzsche's literary remains in the Nietzsche-
Archive at Weimar.[9] From 1935 to 1941 Heidegger served as a
member of the commission organized in the early 1930s, "The Society
of the Friends of the Nietzsche-Archive," in order to prepare a
historical-critical edition of Nietzsche's *oeuvres*. The principal editors
were Carl August Emge, Hans Joachim Mette, and Karl Schlechta,
although it was another of the "Friends," Walter F. Otto, who urged
Heidegger to participate. On December 5, 1934, Otto had reported as
follows to the commission:

A task that is as extraordinarily difficult as it is necessary awaits the editors of
the posthumous materials from the final years. What is demanded of them
is nothing less than that they present the notes on the theme of "will to
power" for the first time without arbitrary editorial intrusions; they must
present such notes precisely as they are found in the handwritten notebooks.
The latter, scarcely legible, must be collated afresh.[10]

Whether or not Heidegger was present when Otto read his report, it
is certain that he came to share the view held by him and by Mette,

[9] The following information concerning Heidegger's connection with the Nietzsche-
Archive in Weimar derives primarily from private communications with Professor Otto
Pöggeler of the Hegel-Archive at Bochum. Professor Pöggeler worked closely with Heideg-
ger during the preparation of the *Nietzsche* volumes for publication in 1961.

[10] Quoted by Mazzino Montinari in his Foreward to Volume 14 of the *Studienausgabe*, p. 12.

the view that the notebooks would have to be retranscribed. Heidegger's own efforts in section 21 of the 1937 lecture course to establish the chronology of the notes on eternal recurrence that were taken up into the Gast-Förster edition of *The Will to Power* is evidence enough of his sympathy with the commission. Between 1935 and 1941 Heidegger apparently traveled often to Weimar, where the notebooks that had gone into the making of *The Will to Power* occupied his attention. He presumably worked through a number of them and familiarized himself with the entire stock of unpublished notes and aphorisms. It is reported that he even presented a plan to the Friends for the publication of the *Nachlass*. Precisely how extensively Heidegger was able to examine the holograph materials of the Nietzschean *Nachlass* during these Weimar junkets is impossible to say. Yet a certain amount of internal evidence in the lecture course allows us to speculate on the matter. In section 12 Heidegger evaluates the GOA editors' handling of manuscript M III 1; his detailed criticisms betray a first-hand familiarity with the holograph. Yet later in his lecture course (for example, in section 21) he uses the GOA uncritically even when similar sorts of criticisms are called for. (An exception is Heidegger's treatment of WM, 1057 and 1058.) Heidegger does not refer to the later manuscripts and notebooks from 1884 to 1889 by their catalogue number but solely by the GOA designation. The implication is that Heidegger's detailed work at Weimar never really advanced beyond the *Zarathustra* period to the more bedeviling problem of that nonbook *Der Wille zur Macht.* I have not been able to ascertain the precise nature of Heidegger's plan for the publication of Nietzsche's literary remains. We may surmise that he opposed the prevailing view that a complicated scholarly apparatus with variant readings would be necessary for the new collation: we are familiar with his resistance to the passion for "completeness" and the tendency to construct a "biographical" framework into which Nietzsche's every utterance would be fitted.[11] Nevertheless,

---

[11] See Volume I of this series, pp. 9–10. Yet Heidegger's general criticisms of the proposed *Historisch-kritische Gesamtausgabe* do not tell us enough about his precise role in the commission. Printed protocols of the commission's meetings are extant, according to Otto Pöggeler, and stored in a Bonn archive. They await some enterprising Sherlock Holmes of a doctoral candidate.

Heidegger's treatment of the notes on eternal return in *The Will to Power* indicates that he accepted the fundamental principles of the Friends' edition: only if the notes were ordered chronologically, and only if an attempt were made to align those notes with the various stages of Nietzsche's plans for a major work, would readers of the Nietzschean *Nachlass* be adequately served.

Heidegger resigned from the commission in 1941 when the Propaganda Ministry—apprised of Nietzsche's derision of all anti-Semitism —claimed the right of *Imprimatur* for the edition. Indeed, the project as a whole soon foundered: after 1942 no further volumes were produced. Heidegger nonetheless remained interested in the editing of Nietzsche's works in later years. When the controversial edition by Karl Schlechta appeared in 1956 Heidegger was chagrined. However much he had discouraged an unwieldy apparatus for the historical-critical edition of the *Nachlass,* Heidegger found Schlechta's assemblage of "Notes from the 1880s" chaotic. He complained that his own work and that of the commission as a whole had "gone to the dogs."

It is important to emphasize this second side—surely the less well-known side—of Heidegger's relationship to philological matters. His opposition to the paraphernalia of scholarly editions did not imply indifference to the matter of providing an adequate textual base. Nor did his active participation in the work of the Friends suggest anything like disdain for collective editorial efforts. Contrary to what Heidegger's critics have often led us to believe, Heidegger's practice in matters of Nietzsche scholarship and of philology in general was remarkably meticulous. One might well contrast Heidegger's care with the far more casual method of Karl Jaspers or of many another commentator who has dealt with Nietzsche in this century. Heidegger's diligence in such matters is no surprise to his students and to those who knew his cautious, painstaking ways; yet the myth of the Olympian Heidegger who scorned philology and worked his will on whatever text he treated still enjoys a robust life. Alas, the myth will not in any way be diminished by the current edition of Martin Heidegger's own *Nachlass.*

By way of conclusion, one is compelled to appreciate *and* to criticize Heidegger's use of the "suppressed notes" and plans for a Nietzschean *magnum opus.* Given the nature of the materials in the *Grossoktav* edition that were available to him, and granted that his own work on Nietzsche's manuscripts at Weimar was perforce limited—even in the 1950s philologists at the Nietzsche-Archive were astonished at the amount of material that had not yet even been collated—Heidegger's presentation of Nietzsche's unpublished notes is far more balanced, heedful, and perceptive than his critics have charged. Yet the clarity, range, and power of Nietzsche's own published versions of eternal recurrence, in passages from *The Gay Science, Thus Spoke Zarathustra,* and *Beyond Good and Evil* which Heidegger himself sets before his listeners and readers, argue against any tendency to regard the suppressed notes as the essential source for the thought.

The very worst thing that could happen however is that the *thinking* of eternal recurrence, a thinking in which Nietzsche and Heidegger share, should get lost in the barren reaches of the philological debate. As important as it is to attain a more highly differentiated critical view of Heidegger's approach to the Nietzschean text, we dare not let such efforts blind us to the larger questions that loom in the thought of return and in Heidegger's thinking of it. Eternal recurrence is not the most burdensome thought simply because its textual base is disputable. It is not the tragic thought merely because it offers innumerable knots for the scholar's unraveling. It is not the scintillating and provocative thought of thoughts solely because of its "hides and hints and misses in prints."

III. QUESTIONS

Why does Nietzsche's analysis of the revenge against time elude Heidegger's 1937 lecture course? Why in both 1937 and 1953 does Heidegger neglect to pursue the mythic figure of Dionysos? Do the oversight and the refusal tell us anything about Heidegger's ambivalent relation to Nietzsche as the last metaphysician *and* last thinker of the West? Finally, what does Heidegger's positive interpretation of the moment of eternity as *Übergang* and *Untergang* portend with regard to both his earlier attempt to raise the question of Being on the horizon of time and his later attempt at "another" commencement—the adventure of *Ereignis?*

To these questions one might want to subtend a thesis that would have only heuristic value, a thesis to be planted as a suspicion that may flourish for a time and then go to seed. One of Heidegger's most efficacious strategies when interpreting the "unthought" of a thinker—the cases of Kant and Hegel immediately come to mind—is to assert that the thinker in question saw precisely what Heidegger sees in the thinker's text but that he *shrank back* before the abyss of his own insight, leaving what he saw unthought. That strategy allows Heidegger to say that Kant surmised yet did not really know what the transcendental imagination would do to his Critical project, or that Hegel himself experienced yet did not bring to words the groundlessness of all experience as *Erfahrung.* My thesis, or suspicion, or strategem, asserts that in his interpretation of Nietzsche as a metaphysician Heidegger shrinks from the consequences of his own interpretation of eternal recurrence of the same. Why? Because that thought proves to be too close to unresolved dilemmas in both *Being and Time* (1927) and the *Contributions to Philosophy: On "Ereignis"* (1936–38). We recall that according to Heidegger's interpretation eternal return must be thought (1) in terms of the moment, that is, "the temporality of independent action and decision"; and (2) in terms of the "condition of need" that defines our own "task and endowment." These two ways of thinking Nietzsche's fundamental thought thus correspond to Heidegger's own thought concerning (1) the "authentic appropriation" required of Dasein as being-a-self and (2) the "propriative event" of nihilism in Western history as a whole. Could it be that in both areas Nietzsche's thinking is too close to Heidegger's own, not in the sense that Heidegger foists his own thoughts onto Nietzsche, but that Nietzsche somehow displaces and even undercuts the essential matters of Heideggerian thought? Could it also be the case that Heidegger finds his own critique of modern metaphysical representation—as an aggressive setting upon objects—anticipated and even radicalized in Nietzsche's analysis of revenge?

Yet one would have to modify the thesis, temper the suspicion, and refine the strategy right from the start: in 1951–52, with his lecture course "What Calls for Thinking?" Heidegger returns to Nietzsche's thought with undiminished energy and dedication. "In the face of

Nietzsche's thinking," he says, "all formulas and labels fail in a special sense and fall silent."[12] In these lectures Heidegger remains true to his own dictum: "If we want to go to encounter a thinker's thought, we must magnify what is already magnificent in that thought."[13] Symptomatic of the caution he exercises here—as in the first major division of the 1937 course—is the fact that in the tenth lecture of *What Calls for Thinking?* Heidegger declines to speculate on the success or failure of Nietzschean redemption from the spirit of revenge. Although in other respects "Who Is Nietzsche's Zarathustra?" serves as a faithful résumé of the 1951–52 lectures, the emphasis on thinking and thoughtfulness in those earlier lectures seems to restrain the interpretation in this one respect. Heidegger does not relegate Nietzsche to a metaphysical tradition which he—Heidegger, and not Nietzsche —would have decisively overcome; he does not insist that Nietzsche's thought is animated by the spirit of prior reflection. In transition to Part Two of the course, on Parmenides, Heidegger instead insists on the "darkness" surrounding the thought of recurrence, its difficulty, and hence its exemplary character for the question "What is called—and what calls us to—thinking?"

A further modification of my thesis is called for—so that one must begin to wonder whether theses are worth the trouble. Redemption from revenge, that is, the "success" or "failure" of the Zarathustran venture, is by no means a settled question. We dare not begin by asserting that Heidegger is merely mistaken when in "Who Is Nietzsche's Zarathustra?" he charges Nietzsche with such failure. In fact, we might well commence our questioning by elaborating a somewhat more "genealogical" account of Nietzsche's failure to secure redemption from revenge. In this way we would support the conclusion of Heidegger's lecture and yet at the same time introduce the disruptive figure of Dionysos into its argument. Why is that introduction necessary? According to Eugen Fink, Heidegger's disregard of Dionysos constitutes the most serious oversight in Heidegger's entire reading of Nietzsche. Fink's remarks on Dionysian play in Nietzsche's thought will thus guide us toward the central matter of these "questions": I will

---

[12] Heidegger, *Was heisst Denken?*, p. 21; English translation, p. 51.
[13] Heidegger, *Was heisst Denken?*, p. 72; English translation, p. 77.

argue that the Nietzschean "moment of eternity," thought in Heideggerian fashion as *Übergang* and *Untergang*, goes to the heart of the analysis of ecstatic temporality in *Being and Time* and also to the core of what Heidegger calls *Ereignis*. Both issues are extremely difficult to think through, and we will have to be content here with mere hints. Finally, extending the Heidegger/Nietzsche confrontation to more recent areas of discussion, I will try to see whether Pierre Klossowski and Jacques Derrida shed light on the subversive encroachment of Nietzsche on Heidegger—Klossowski with respect to the question of being-a-self in the thinking of eternal recurrence, and Derrida with respect to *Ereignis*. The thesis will then dissolve, the suspicion burst, and the strategy forget itself in a concluding question on the nature of the satyric.

In "Who Is Nietzsche's Zarathustra?" Heidegger expresses doubts as to whether Nietzsche's thought of eternal recurrence of the same can achieve redemption from the spirit of revenge. These doubts arise from Heidegger's own highly dubious reduction of eternal return to that will to power which stamps Being on Becoming and so proves to be incorrigibly metaphysical. Yet we may invoke such doubts in another way, a way that is closer to Nietzsche's own genealogical critique of metaphysics and morals, by introducing a theme we might call "the decadence of redemption." In *Twilight of the Idols* Nietzsche writes that when he renounces the Christian God—"previously the greatest *objection* to existence"—he denies all answerability in God. He then concludes: "Only *thereby* do we redeem the world" (CM, *6*, 97). Yet what makes Nietzschean redemption of the world essentially different from the self-immolation of the Crucified? In his analysis of the "Redeemer-type" in *The Antichrist* (*6*, 199 ff.) Nietzsche isolates two typical "physiological realities" of that type:

[1] *Instinctive hatred of reality:* consequence of an extreme capacity for suffering and an extreme irritability, which no longer wants to be "touched" in any way, because it feels every contact too deeply.

[2] *Instinctive exclusion of all disinclination and animosity,* all limits and distances in feeling: . . . unbearable *aversion* to every resistance or compulsion to resist. . . . Love as the sole *ultimate* possibility of life.

The Redeemer-type is a decadent *par excellence,* one who has exchanged his dinner jacket for a hairshirt. The very "cry for 'redemption,'" Nietzsche elsewhere concedes, arises from the introverted cruelty that is spawned by ascetic ideals (CM, 5, 390). The will to transfigure the world betrays *ressentiment* against it. How then can a transition from the spirit of revenge avoid the decadence of redemption? How should yes-saying or the tragic pathos avoid the passion of the Redeemer-type? How may thinking find its way to Dionysos? Do we achieve tragic pathos in the "metaphysical comfort" of one who witnesses tragedy and affirms against Silenus that "in spite of the flux of appearances life is indestructibly powerful and pleasurable" (CM, 1, 56)? In his 1886 "Attempt at a Self-Critique" Nietzsche reaffirms that in the artistry of Greek tragedy "the world is at every moment the *achieved* redemption of God" (1, 17). Yet is our access to Greek tragedy invariably one that speaks the vocabulary of redemption? Do we know any way to Dionysos that does not leave us stranded on the Golgotha of the Crucified? Heidegger refers us to Otto and Reinhardt but does not himself undertake to seek the way.

Dionysos, twice born, twice buried, and his mother Semele, "bride of thunder," who casts her shadow across the life and deeds of the god—how do we reach them? However Socratized Euripides may be, in *The Bacchae* he acknowledges the contradictions of the search:

> Dithyrambus, come!
> Enter my male womb. (11. 526–27)[14]

In the action of Euripides' play the god of contradictions prepares to move against Pentheus the King, who prefers human wisdom to divine madness. Conscientious, capable, resolute, this reasonable young man will not risk foolishness, would restore order. Dionysos invokes the god he himself is:

> Punish this man. But first distract his wits;
> bewilder him with madness. (1. 850)

---

[14] I use the translation by William Arrowsmith throughout, in the University of Chicago *Complete Greek Tragedies* edited by David Grene and Richmond Lattimore (Chicago: University of Chicago Press, 1959).

"Distract his wits" is a way of translating a word we might also render by its cognate as follows: cause this man to stand outside himself, make him *ecstatic,* make him *existential.*

For us latecomers the ecstatic experience of Dionysos is perhaps best captured in the phenomenon of "inspiration," in this case Nietzsche's own inspiration while composing *Thus Spoke Zarathustra.* In *Ecce Homo* (CM, *6,* 335 ff.) Nietzsche recounts how Zarathustra "swept over" him during this period of "great healthfulness" in his life. Spurning the frigid pieties of the soul, Nietzsche affirms that in artistic inspiration "the *body* is inspired." However, Nietzsche's "great healthfulness" does not lie like a dog in the sun; it strides headlong toward its fateful adventure and *"initiates* the tragedy." (Recall Heidegger's remarks on the "commencement" of tragedy in section 4 of the 1937 course: the inception of tragedy is itself the downgoing.) Merely to recount the ecstasy in which the metaphors and similes of *Thus Spoke Zarathustra* arrived is nonetheless to exchange the grand style of dithyramb for a far more pallid kind of language: Nietzsche says of his book that "it is *yes-saying* unto justification, unto redemption even of everything past" (*6,* 348). Yes-saying unto *redemption*—unto the *decadence* of redemption. Thus the thought that ought to be hardest to bear occasionally dwindles to a paltry consolation:

A certain emperor always kept in mind the transiency of all things, in order not to take them too much to heart and to remain tranquil in their midst. To me, on the contrary, everything seems much too valuable to be allowed to be so fleeting: I seek an eternity for everything. Ought one to pour the most costly unguents and wines into the sea? My consolation is that everything that was is eternal: the sea spews it forth again.[15]

The decadence of redemption: every attempt to communicate the Dionysian affirmation of eternal recurrence brings us full-circle to the Redeemer-type, excluding all "limits and distances in feeling," all "resistance or compulsion to resist." Gilles Deleuze is right when he in-

---

[15] WM, 1065; CM, W II 3 [94]; composed sometime between November 1887 and March 1888. See also Krell, "Descensional Reflection," in *Philosophy and Archaic Experience: Essays in Honor of Edward G. Ballard,* ed. John Sallis (Pittsburgh: Duquesne University Press, 1982), p. 8.

sists that we do not know what a thinking that is utterly stripped of *ressentiment* (and so redeemed from the spirit of redemption) would be like: eternal recurrence is the "other side" of will to power, an affirmative thinking that remains beyond our powers.[16] Clearly, eternal recurrence, under the sign of Dionysos, must be "another" kind of thinking. However much we may try to drag it back to the decadence of redemption or the closure of metaphysics, such thinking, an ungraspable Maenad, eludes our pursuit.

In the 1937 lecture course Heidegger refuses to entertain the figure of Dionysos, even after his students come to life (for the first and last time) and insist that he do so. He reduces the Dionysian to the sensuous realm of a Platonism that has been inverted but is still intact. Fifteen years later he avers that the name *Dionysos* is an unfailing sign of the metaphysical nature of Nietzsche's thinking. In neither case does Heidegger elaborate Nietzsche's "new interpretation of the sensuous," the theme that closed his lecture course on will to power as art.[17] Does Nietzsche's "inversion" of the Platonic hierarchy in fact leave the meaning of sensuousness unchanged? Or, to take another example, does the meaning of sensuousness remain unaltered when Walt Whitman eschews the Gifts of the Holy Ghost and instead intones his litanies to the body?

> Head, neck, hair, ears, drop and tympan of the ears,
> Eyes, eye-fringes, iris of the eye, eyebrows,
>   and the waking or sleeping of the lids. . . .[18]

Or when in the *Phaedo* Plato has Socrates define the sensuous as "contamination" and then gather up Phaedo's curls in his hand, do we with our hasty appeal to "Socratic irony" know precisely what is going on? Is Nietzsche's (or Whitman's or, for that matter, Plato's) a mere "coarsening" of the Platonic position? Or does Heidegger's reluctance to think the body and the realm of sensuousness as a whole indicate the single greatest lacuna in his preoccupations with "neutral" Dasein

---

[16] Gilles Deleuze, *Nietzsche et la philosophie* (Paris: Presses Universitaires de France, 1962), pp. 40–41; 197 ff.

[17] See Volume I of this series, pp. 211–20; see also MHG *55*, 18–19, and *39*, 189ff.

[18] Whitman, "I Sing the Body Electric," section 9, 1. 133, from *Children of Adam* (1855).

and "reticent" Being? "Would there not be in Heidegger," asks Michel Haar, "a recoil of the Platonistic sort in the face of 'the madness of the body'?"[19] A recoil of the *Platonistic* sort—precisely at the point where Heidegger calls *Nietzsche's* fundamental metaphysical position the *entrenchment* of Platonism! If the 1936–37 lectures on will to power as art overlook woman, those on eternal recurrence neglect Dionysos; the two omissions (Molly Bloom would call them *frequent* omissions) are perhaps not unrelated.[20]

Nor is Heidegger's neglect of Dionysos irrelevant to his own effort to conjoin eternal recurrence and will to power in Nietzsche's thought. Fink is right to insist that these two doctrines converge solely in the figure of Dionysos. Recalling that revised fragment (WM, 1067) whose two versions interlock the ring of recurrence and will to power—"and nothing besides!"—Fink reminds us that the Dionysian world of creation and destruction remains the site of the unification. Furthermore, no matter how firmly Nietzsche may be "imprisoned" in the traditional metaphysical categories and oppositions (Being and Becoming, truth

---

[19] Michel Haar, "Heidegger et le Surhomme," in *Revue de l'enseignement philosophique*, vol. 30, no. 3 (February–March 1980), 7.

[20] On the neglect of woman in "Will to Power as Art," see Jacques Derrida, *Éperons*, pp. 59–76. What at first seems an odd conglomeration of themes in *Spurs*—interpretation, style, and woman—actually rests on a rich tradition of Nietzsche scholarship. Karl Reinhardt's suggestive piece, "Nietzsche's 'Plaint of Ariadne' " (see the source cited on p. 204 n., above) is a case in point; and Heidegger's neglect of Dionysos and woman becomes all the more baffling when we read Reinhardt as he suggests we do. Reinhardt's point of departure is a careful comparison of the "Plaint of Ariadne" (in *Dionysos-Dithyramben*, 1888; CM, *6*, 398–401) with its original version, namely, the complaint of "The Magician" (in Part IV of *Thus Spoke Zarathustra*, 1885; CM, *4*, 313–17). Initially the wail of a doddering God-seeker, half martyr, half charlatan, the plaint now rises from the labyrinth of Ariadne. The change of sex is astonishing, as is the new sympathy Nietzsche feels for the god-seeker. Reinhardt suggests that this fascination with *Dionysos philosophos*, nascent in the final pages of *Beyond Good and Evil* (especially section 295), implies nothing less than an abandonment of overman and even of Zarathustra-the-godless. It betrays a surrender to the seductive, aberrant, satyric god of desire, who wears the mask of woman. Nietzsche's surrender ultimately fails, according to Reinhardt: "The language refuses to speak" (331). And for *us* to unravel the meaning of the mystery "would require that we elaborate the whole intricate Ariadnic problem of the mask that looks on itself as a mask, of the text that interprets itself as interpretation, of the thread we pursue outward to our own hand—in short, that we elaborate the entire problem in the later Nietzsche of the *circulus vitiosus deus*" (330).

and semblance, and so on), and no matter how deeply rooted in Platonism Nietzsche's value thinking may be, his reflection on the Dionysian "play of the world" makes him the inaugurator of a new kind of thinking—"the stormy petrel of a new experience of Being."[21] Nietzsche's counterposing of Dionysos and the Crucified is thus not simply an extreme counterwill to the Christian tradition. Dionysos too is a suffering god. Nevertheless, his passion rises on the swell of desire; he is lord of death and rebirth, but not of ascension beyond the earth. *His* is the trajectory of transition and downgoing so brilliantly portrayed in the 1937 lecture course; *his* is the passing by, *Vorbeigang,* which Heidegger's *Contributions to Philosophy* envisages as the very essence of divinity in our time.

Dionysian "world play" finds its avatars in the child, the artist, and the poet. Play itself, according to Fink, is nothing less than the "ecstatic openness" of human beings to the "ruling world."[22] "Man at play, standing open ecstatively for the figureless-configuring god who is at play," and caught up in what Fink calls the "play-time" of the world, thus gestures toward both areas of Heidegger's interpretation of eternal return. Man at play "most deeply wills to turn toward the need"; he is *not-wendig* in the sense that he finds himself in the propriative event of nihilism. Likewise, man at play stands without reserve in the *Augenblick.* Fink uses the word "rapture," *Entrückung,* to capture the sense of Dionysian joy; yet this is the crucial word in Heidegger's own analysis of ecstative temporality in *Being and Time.*[23] Thus it seems that the figure of Dionysos ought to prevail in both the earlier and later Heideggerian projects, instead of being relegated to "metaphysics."

Let me turn now to the earlier project, the matter of "rapture," in

---

[21] Eugen Fink, *Nietzsches Philosophie* (Stuttgart: W. Kohlhammer, 1960), p. 179. For this and the following see all of Chapter Five, "Nietzsche's Relation to Metaphysics as Imprisonment and Liberation," pp. 179–89.

[22] Fink, pp. 88–89, for this and the following. See also the whole of Eugen Fink, *Spiel als Weltsymbol* (Stuttgart: W. Kohlhammer, 1960).

[23] Martin Heidegger, *Sein und Zeit,* 12th ed. (Tübingen: M. Niemeyer, 1972), section 68a. Cited in the text as SZ, with page number. See Krell, *Intimations of Mortality: Time, Truth, and Finitude in Heidegger's Thinking of Being,* chapter three, "The Raptures of Ontology and the Finitude of Time."

the Marburg lectures surrounding *Being and Time*. The issue is highly complicated—suffice it to say that here Heidegger is seeking to understand the precise relationship between time and being in Western philosophy. Although he knows in a general way that time has always been the standard upon which beings have been classified and evaluated, Heidegger is searching for the very *unfolding* of time in original human experiences. In *Being and Time* he describes human temporality as "the *ekstatikon* as such" (SZ, 329). The Greek work *ekstasis* means *displacement*. Precisely because Heidegger's "ecstatic" analysis of time is so radical it threatens to displace every atomic notion of self and to make incomprehensible all *appropriation* of self, authentic or otherwise, in the ontology of Dasein. The *Entrückung* of finite temporality, without a stable horizon in either future, past, or present, threatens to undermine the very *Da* of Dasein. Rapture is well-nigh rupture. Hence Heidegger's Marburg lecture courses immediately prior and posterior to *Being and Time* remain obsessed with the problem of an *a priori* horizon of temporality, a problem that Heidegger's shift to interrogations of the history of Being does not resolve. It may well be that this shift in Heidegger's thinking, which the *Nietzsche* volumes are supposed in some way to reflect, arises not so much from a failure of the ecstative analysis of temporality in *Being and Time* as from the embarrassment of its smashing success.

Yet what does any of this have to do with Nietzsche's thought of thoughts? An initial connection is established when we observe that the two temporal ecstases that dominate Heidegger's search for a unified horizon of time, namely, future and present, are precisely those that Heidegger rejects in "Who Is Nietzsche's Zarathustra?" as being of secondary importance for time's essential unfolding. The *Zeitwesen* as such is "time and its 'It was.'" To stand in the moment of time is not to stand—in the sense of a *nunc stans*—at all. The crucial words in Heidegger's interpretation of the gateway are *Untergang*, downgoing, and *Übergang*, transition. The latter word is precisely the one that Heidegger appeals to in his final Marburg lectures in order to translate the Greek *nun* and Latin *nunc*, the "now" of time in its character as ceaseless movement or *metabolē*. Although Heidegger himself never alludes to the affinity between *Übergang* as the Aristotelian metabolism of time itself and *Übergang* as the Nietzschean eternity of the moment, we may ask whether it is in fact this affinity, and not the interlocking of pseudo-Parmenidean and pseudo-Heraclitean positions, that constitutes Nietzsche's definitive encounter with the commencement of philosophy. It would then be Nietzsche who thinks the tragic, Dionysian metabolism of original time and who therefore anticipates the fundamental insight of Heidegger's own inquiry into time and being. Yet the versions of *Übergang* do not stop even there. When in 1928 Heidegger searches for a way to delineate the destiny of his own fundamental ontology, once again he can find no better word than *metabolē, Übergang,* transition as such. Confrontation with its own transition and demise makes of fundamental ontology not merely a "meta-ontology" but what I have called "frontal" ontology.[24]

The way in which Dionysian *Entrückung* or rapture characterizes each phase of time and hence subverts every attempt to uncover a unified and stable horizon for time finds a parallel in Pierre Klossowski's interpretation of eternal return.[25] Heidegger interprets the eternity of the moment as *decision,* understanding decision as the authentic appropriation of being-a-self. Yet if the self that thinks eternal return is a ceaseless going-over and going-under, how lucid can it be to itself? Can anything like an "appropriation" occur in its thinking?

Klossowski emphasizes the "ecstatic character" of Nietzsche's experience of eternal recurrence. The dilemma such an experience confronts us with is that it seems as if the thought can never have occurred to us before; the one who experiences eternal return appears to attain an insight that was hitherto closed to him or her. A forgetting and remembering, and *anamnesis,* thus appear to be "the very source and indispensable condition" of the thought of recurrence. Riddling at the riddle of how one can stand in the moment of recurrence *each moment anew,* Klossowski suggests that the ecstatic thinking of return

---

[24] See Krell, *Intimations of Mortality,* chapter two, "Fundamental Ontology, Meta-Ontology, Frontal Ontology," esp. pp. 44–46.

[25] Pierre Klossowski, *Nietzsche et le cercle vicieux* (Paris: Mercure de France, 1969). I shall cite the second, corrected edition of 1978 in the text merely by page number in parentheses. See the passages in English translation in *The New Nietzsche,* ed. David B. Allison (New York: Delta Books, 1977), pp. 107–20.

must transform—if not abolish—the very identity of the thinker. " . . .
I learn that I was *other* than I am now for having forgotten this truth,
and thus I have become another by learning it. . . . The accent must
be placed on the loss of a given identity" (93). Not even the act of
willing can salvage the ruined self: to will myself again implies that in
all willing "nothing ever gets constituted in a *single sense,* once and for
all" (101). To will the eternal recurrence of the same is to don the
masks of "a multitude of gods," the masks of Dionysos fragmented,
"under the sign of the *divine vicious circle*" (102). Klossowski concludes as follows (107):

> Re-willing is pure adherence to the vicious circle. To re-will *the entire series
> one more time*—to re-will every experience, all one's acts, but this time not
> as *mine:* it is precisely this *possessiveness* that no longer has any meaning,
> nor does it represent a goal. Meaning and goal are liquidated by the circle—
> whence the silence of Zarathustra, the interruption of his message. Unless
> this interruption is a burst of laughter that bears all its own bitterness.

Does the "possessiveness" that is so suspect in Heidegger's conception of the authentic appropriation of being-a-self, that is to say, in his
thinking of eternal recurrence as decision, disappear when we proceed
to his thought of the propriative event? If eternal return subverts *Vereigentlichung* does it leave *Ereignis* untouched?

In his early essays, especially "The Ends of Man," Derrida has tried
to show that Heidegger's metaphorics of *proximity* (of man, the being
that questions, to Being; of the voice, and the call of conscience, to
existence; of that very *propriety* by which man belongs to, is proper to,
hears and heeds Being) endeavors to close up the distance that human
ek-sistence is heir to. His question is: "Is not that which is being displaced today this security of the near . . . ?"[26] In his most recent work
on Nietzsche and Heidegger, commencing with *Spurs,* Derrida has
pursued the question of distance and proximity in novel directions.
Although he is fully aware of Heidegger's meticulous deference with
regard to Nietzsche's texts, Derrida questions the attempt to plumb the

---

[26] Jacques Derrida, "Les fins de l'homme," in *Marges de la philosophie* (Paris: Édi-
tions de Minuit, 1972), p. 161. Translated by Alan Bass (Chicago: University of Chicago
Press, 1982), p. 133.

depths of Nietzsche's "ownmost *(eigensten)* thoughtful will." It is precisely in the 1937 lecture course on eternal recurrence of the same that Heidegger emphasizes his effort to reach what *most properly belongs* to Nietzsche's *own* thought. And it is precisely here, we might add, that the distance between Heidegger and Nietzsche reopens and allows for a new constellation. Derrida suggests that each time Heidegger invokes words like "own," "authentic," "appropriation," "assimilation," "propriation," and "propriative event" *(eigen, eigentlich, eigen, aneignen, ereignen, Eregnis)* a kind of "dehiscence" occurs. Whereas a covert valorization of the *proprius* + *prope* —possession and propinquity—runs as an unbroken thread through Heidegger's thought, and whereas the very process of propriation inscribes the history and truth of Being as metaphysics, the structure of the "ownmost" everywhere proves to be *abyssal,* that is, radically without grounds. All thought of proximity and propriation invariably passes into something that is radically "other."[27]

Is not the abyss of Zarathustra's most abysmal thought, in which the very identity of this figure-in-transition is held in continual suspense, somehow related to the abyss or *Ab-Grund* of Heidegger's later thinking? Would not Zarathustran downgoing epitomize such thinking of the abyss? Is not Heidegger's insistence that *Ereignis* be thought not only as the granting of time and being but also as *withdrawal, reticence, withholding*—in short, as *finitude*—a kind of ek-sistence in the gateway *Augenblick?*[28]

Derrida describes his own venture in *Spurs* as a "runway" for rereading Heidegger's *Nietzsche.* He wishes to "fly" with this book, or to "flee" and abscond with it, beyond the hermeneutic circle of appropriative interpretation. His flight would be, not on the wings and rings and coils of eagle and snake, but on dove's feet. To mix the metaphor. Such a reading would pose another question to Heidegger's questions to Nietzsche: Does not the sphere of satyr-play alone, for all its appar-

---

[27] See *Éperons,* pp. 94–96.

[28] On the finitude of *Ereignis,* see the conclusion to the Protocol of the Todtnauberg Seminar on "Zeit und Sein," in Martin Heidegger, *Zur Sache des Denkens* (Tübingen: M. Niemeyer, 1969), p. 58. English translation by Joan Stambaugh in *On Time and Being* (New York: Harper & Row, 1972), p. 54.

ent buffoonery, effectively interlock the sphere of tragedy and the sphere of the world . . . perhaps?

Heidegger says that to think being as a whole as eternal displacement of the goal is to utter a "cry of distress and calamity." Nietzsche at times agrees, at other times replies:

> Calamity! is rancor's cry;
> The jester calls it Play!

Glossary

abysmal, abyssal	*abgründlich*
accomplishment	*die Vollendung*
actual	*wirklich*
to address	*ansprechen*
advent	*die Ankunft*
advocate	*der Fürsprecher*
to affront	*sich vor den Kopf stossen*
agony, anguish	*der Schmerz*
animate	*lebendig*
anthropomorphizing	*die Vermenschlichung*
appearance	*die Erscheinung, der Schein*
articulation	*das Gefüge*
aspect	*der Gesichtspunkt*
to assimilate	*aneignen*
at hand	*vorhanden*
authentic appropriation	*die Vereigentlichung*
beatitude	*die Seligkeit*
Becoming	*das Werden*
Being	*das Sein*
being(s)	*das Seiende*
a being	*(ein) Seiendes*
being(s) as a whole	*das Seiende im Ganzen*
beingness	*die Seiendheit*
bounded	*begrenzt*
to bring under control	*bewältigen*
burden	*das Schwergewicht*
burdensome	*schwer*

to calculate	*rechnen (be-, er-)*
capable	*gewachsen*
center	*die Mitte*
center of gravity	*das Schwergewicht*
claim	*der Anspruch*
clarification	*die Verdeutlichung*
coherence, cohesion	*die Zusammengehörigkeit*
coinage	*die Prägung*
collective	*Gesamt-*
commemorative thought	*das Andenken*
commencement	*der Anfang*
communication	*die Mitteilung*
community	*die Gemeinschaft*
completion	*die Vollendung*
computation	*die Errechnung*
concealing	*die Verbergung*
concealment	*die Verborgenheit*
conception	*die Auffassung, der Begriff*
configuration	*die Gestalt*
to confront	*begegnen, sich*
	auseinandersetzen
confrontation	*die Auseinandersetzung*
constantly	*stets*
contemptible	*verächtlich*
correspondence	*die Entsprechung*
counter-	*Gegen-*
to create poetically	*dichten*
creation	*das Schaffen*
creative	*schöpferisch*
cycle	*der Umlauf*
the dead	*das Tote*
deception	*der Trug*
de-deification	*die Entgöttlichung*
deduction	*die Schlussfolgerung*
deed	*das Tun*

to define	*bestimmen*
definitive, authoritative	*massgebend*
dehumanization	*die Entmenschung*
deification	*die Vergöttlichung*
destiny	*das Schicksal, das Geschick*
to determine	*bestimmen*
difficult	*schwierig*
discerning	*klug*
dismay	*der Schrecken*
domain	*der Bereich*
dominance, dominion	*die Herrschaft*
downgoing	*der Untergang*
durability	*die Dauerfähigkeit*
duration	*die Dauer*
eidos	*das Aussehen*
emblem	*das Sinnbild*
embodiment	*das Leiben*
to encounter in thought	*entgegendenken*
endowment	*das Mitgegebene*
energy	*die Kraft*
enhancement	*die Steigerung*
envelopment	*das Mitteninnestehen*
essence	*das Wesen*
essential definition, determination	*die Wesensbestimmung*
essential unfolding	*das Wesen* (verbal)
to esteem	*schätzen*
to estimate	*abschätzen, einschätzen*
eternal recurrence of the same	*die ewige Wiederkehr des Gleichen*
eternal return	*die ewige Wiederkunft*
(propriative) event	*das Ereignis*
evidentiary	*Beweis-*
exigencies	*die Notwendigkeiten*
explicit(ly)	*ausdrücklich*

to express	*ausdrücken*
expressly	*eigens*
finite	*endlich*
finitude	*die Endlichkeit*
fixation	*die Festmachung*
force	*die Kraft*
to found	*stiften*
fright	*die Furcht, die Furchtbarkeit*
fulfillment	*die Vollendung*
fundamental	*Grund-*
fundamental metaphysical position	*die metaphysische Grundstellung*
to gather	*versammeln*
genesis, gestation	*die Entstehung*
genuine	*echt, eigentlich*
gift-giving	*das Verschenken*
going over	*das Übergehen*
going under	*das Untergehen, der Untergang*
to grapple with	*bewältigen*
to grasp	*begreifen, fassen*
to ground	*begründen*
ground(s)	*der Grund*
grounding question	*die Grundfrage*
to guess	*erraten*
guiding question	*die Leitfrage*
to heed	*achten, beachten*
hierarchy	*die Rangordnung*
to hold fast to	*sich halten an*
to hold firm in	*sich halten in*
ill will	*der Widerwille*
illusion	*der Anschein*
image	*das Bild, das Sinnbild*

impact	*die Wirkung*
inalienable	*ureigen, innerst*
incipient	*anfänglich*
incorporation	*die Einverleibung*
individuation	*die Vereinzelung*
inherently	*in sich*
insight	*die Erkenntnis, der Einblick*
interpretation	*die Auslegung, die Deutung*
isolation	*die Absonderung*
to know	*wissen*
knowledge	*das Wissen, die Erkenntnis*
last	*letzt*
literary remains	*der Nachlass*
to live through	*erleben*
the living	*das Lebende*
locale	*die Ortschaft*
loneliness	*die Einsamkeit*
main, major work; *magnum opus*	*das Hauptwerk*
mastery	*das Herrsein, die Herrschaft*
matter (of thought)	*die Sache (des Denkens)*
to matter	*angehen, anliegen*
measure	*das Mass*
to mediate	*vermitteln*
to meditate	*besinnen*
metamorphosis	*die Verwandlung*
midday	*der Mittag*
midpoint, fulcrum	*die Mitte*
Moment	*der Augenblick*
mood	*die Stimmung*
mystery	*das Geheimnis*
need	*die Not*

to need	*bedürfen, benötigen*
to negate	*verneinen*
notes	*die Aufzeichnungen*
the nothing	*das Nichts*
vacuous nothingness	*das leere Nichts*
nothing worth	*das Nichtige*
nullity	*die Nichtigkeit*
occur essentially	*wesen*
on hand	*zuhanden*
open (region)	*das Offene*
openness	*die Offenheit*
origin	*der Ursprung*
overcoming	*die Überwindung*
overman	*der Übermensch*
passing away	*das Vergehen*
permanence	*die Beständigkeit*
to persecute	*nachstellen*
pertinent	*zugehörig*
pervasive	*durchgängig*
plan	*der Entwurf*
poetic	*dichterisch*
poetical	*poetisch*
to ponder	*bedenken*
to portray	*darstellen*
posthumously published notes	*der Nachlass*
presence	*die Anwesenheit*
presencing	*das Anwesen*
what is present	*das Anwesende*
the present (temporal)	*die Gegenwart, das Gegenwärtige*
to present	*darstellen*
to preserve	*bewahren*
presumption	*die Anmassung*
to prevail	*herrschen, walten*

project(ion)	*der Entwurf*
proof	*der Beweis*
proper	*eigentlich*
to be proper to	*gehören*
proposal	*der Entwurf, der Vorschlag*
propriative event	*das Ereignis*
proposition	*der Satz*
provenance	*die Herkunft*
proximity	*die Nähe*
questionable	*fragwürdig*
questioning, inquiry	*das Fragen*
radiance	*das Aufleuchten, das Scheinen*
real	*wirklich*
realm	*der Bereich*
to recognize	*erkennen*
to recoin	*umprägen*
reconfiguration	*das Hineingestalten*
redemption	*die Erlösung*
remote, far remove	*die Ferne*
to represent	*vorstellen*
resolutely open	*ent-schlossen*
resoluteness, decisiveness	*die Entschiedenheit*
resonance	*das Aufklingen*
to respond	*entgegnen, entsprechen*
revenge	*die Rache*
to riddle	*raten*
riddle	*das Rätsel*
rise	*der Aufgang*
to secure	*sichern*
securing of permanence	*die Bestandsicherung*
the self-same	*das Selbe*
semblance	*der Schein*

sense	*der Sinn*
sense-image	*das Sinnbild*
sensuous	*sinnlich*
to share with	*mit-teilen*
sketches	*die Aufzeichnungen*
solitude	*die Einsamkeit*
spectacle	*der Anblick*
stability	*der Bestand*
stance	*die Haltung*
statement	*der Satz*
strength	*die Kraft*
subsistence	*der Bestand*
subterfuge	*die Ausflucht*
suprasensuous	*übersinnlich*
to surmise	*erraten, ahnen*
surveyability	*die Übersehbarkeit*
suspicions	*Bedenken*
to take for true	*Für-wahr-halten*
task	*die Aufgabe, das Aufgegebene*
telling silence	*das Erschweigen*
the terrifying	*das Furchtbare*
transfiguration	*die Verklärung*
transformation	*der Wandel*
transiency	*das Vergängliche*
transition	*der Übergang*
the true	*das Wahre*
truth	*die Wahrheit*, alētheia
ultimately	*im Grunde, letztlich*
unconcealment	*die Unverborgenheit*
to unfold, develop	*entfalten*
to unriddle	*erraten*
upsurgence	*das Aufgehen, das Anheben, physis*
utterance	*das Sagen*

vacuous	*leer*
valuation	*die Wertsetzung*
value thinking	*das Wertdenken*
to venture	*wagen*
visage, vision	*das Gesicht*
the void	*die Leere*
weighty	*gewichtig*
to wend	*wenden* (cf. *not-wendig*)
to will, want	*wollen*
will to power	*der Wille zur Macht*
withdrawal	*der Entzug*
worthy of question	*frag-würdig*